Quantum Buddhism:
Dancing in Emptiness - Reality Revealed at the Interface of Quantum Physics & Buddhist Philosophy

Graham Smetham

Shunyata Press

Shunyata Press

Brighton, Sussex, England

www.shunyatapress.com

ISBN 987-1-4452-9430-8

Contents

Preface & Acknowledgements

Two days ago I sat down to write this preface and this is what I wrote then:

As I sit down to write this preface I have on my table a book just published, and delivered to me this morning, called *The Heart of the Universe*. A core perspective of this short work by the Buddhist scholar Mu Soeng is the interconnection between modern quantum physics and Buddhist philosophy:

> In the paradigm of quantum physics there is ceaseless change at the core of the universe; in the paradigm of Mahayana wisdom too there is ceaseless change at the core of consciousness and the universe.[1]

Mu Soeng also writes that:

> In experiments subatomic particles showed the same paradoxical nature as light, manifesting as either particles or waves depending on how the experiment was set up. Quantum physicists, confronting the mysteries of the universe, were left with language that evokes Zen Koans: the sound of a quark, the shape of a resonance, the nature of strangeness![2]

And by some kind of strange resonance, in the week that I finally put the final touches to a research project that has been the central focus of my life for the last ten years, I came across another recently published work, *From Eternity to Here*, by Sean Carroll, who is described in the front inside flap of the dust jacket as one of the 'leading theoretical physicists of his generation,' which confidently asserts that the mysteries of quantum mechanics should not be taken to:

> ...offer an excuse to believe whatever you want. In particular, quantum mechanics doesn't mean you can change reality by thinking about it, or that modern physics has rediscovered ancient Buddhist wisdom.[3]

And in the amplificatory footnote to this stern admonishment Carroll writes:

> This is not to say that the ancient Buddhists were not wise, but their wisdom was not based upon the failure of classical determination at atomic scales, nor did they anticipate modern physics in any meaningful way, other than the inevitable random similarities of word choice when talking about grand cosmic concepts.[4]

So at the beginning of 2010 we have two books published by experts in their field, the first being that of Buddhist philosophy and the second quantum and relativistic physics, which come to diametrically opposed conclusions regarding the significance of the frequently noted apparent parallels and connections between Buddhist philosophy and quantum physics. Is there any way of adjudicating the issue?

Today, two days later, I walked into the bookshop where I frequently have an afternoon coffee and found a friend of mine perusing yet another salient publication: *Decoding Reality* by Vlatko Vedral. Vedral is Professor of Quantum Information Theory at the Universities of Oxford and Singapore so his credentials should be certainly up to caliber of Carroll's, and according to Vedral's understanding of quantum theory:

Quantum physics is indeed very much in agreement with Buddhistic emptiness.[5]

Emptiness, or *shunyata,* is the Buddhist concept of a fundamental non-substantial 'empty' ground of potentiality which gives rise to the multitudinous productions within dualistic experience through the operation of a primordial activity of cognition. And this is the kind of vision of the process of reality which Vedral considers is necessitated by the evidence of quantum theory:

> The Universe starts empty but potentially with a huge amount of information. The first key event is the first act of symmetry breaking...[6]

It is a very encouraging that a physicist of Professor Vedral's stature articulates as his quantum conclusion one of the core perspectives of my book. Vedral's conclusions also clearly lend support to Mu Soeng's perspective. So why is Carroll so sure that quantum theory has absolutely nothing to do with Buddhist insights? Carroll's brazen certainty seems rather incongruous in the face of Vedral's equally authoritative opinion!

The reasons offered by Carroll for rejection of the connections perceived by Mu Soeng (of course Carroll could not have known about Mu Soeng's book when he made his claim, it just happens to be coincidental that both works came into my purview as I was wrapping up my own research project), as well as quite a few others, are, firstly, the fact, or rather what Carroll assumes as a fact, that Buddhist philosophers did not have a 'classical' atomic theory which failed in the first place, and secondly, Carroll's dubious belief that when anyone contemplates the mysteries of the universe and begins to talk 'about grand cosmic concepts' there is an inevitability that 'random similarities of word choice' with modern physics will occur.

However, contrary to Carroll's ill informed observation, Buddhist philosophy two thousand years ago did have an atomistic perspective upon the ultimate nature of reality: the *Sarvastivada* analysis of the process of reality; this is pointed out in Mu Soeng work. I would feel quite confident in placing a bet that Carroll actually knows nothing of the astonishingly prescient analyses of the functioning of reality contained in the Yogachara-Chittamatra and Madhyamaka schools of Mahayana Buddhist philosophy.

Yet at the same time it must be said that the Sarvastivada view of the atomic nature of reality did not fail for the same reasons as the 'classical' atomic theory of modern physics failed. The Buddhist philosophers who rejected the Sarvastivada view of reality did not conduct experimental investigations into the innermost structure of external materiality by firing tiny quantum particles (alpha particles) at gold sheets (as Rutherford did), or conducting mind-bendingly precise split-beam experiments (as many modern quantum physicists have done), or building hugely expensive Large Hadron Colliders.

What they did was use rigorous philosophical reasoning and they also employed dramatic meditation techniques in order to explore the nature of the reality of their own minds. They did this because of their complete confidence in their knowledge that the ultimate nature of the process of reality was of the nature of Mind, not Matter. This fundamental knowledge has now, contrary to Carroll's somewhat arrogant Western 'scientific' smug disbelief, been validated by modern quantum physics (although many physicists are simply not willing to accept the clear implications of their own investigations).

According to Carroll, and others of this culturally egocentric point of view, any statement which *appears* to be saying something similar, or even perhaps the same, as something asserted by modern physics cannot actually be saying the same thing; it must be due to some kind of random grasping after 'grand cosmic words' on the part of less sophisticated minds. I had a very similar response, much to my dismay, from a physicist I have great respect for and was communicating with regarding my research. With reference to the issue of the relationship between 'classical' and quantum manifestations of reality, a quantum conundrum which I consider to be thoroughly elucidated by the Buddhist Madhyamaka metaphysical presentation of the 'two truths,' Professor Henry Stapp emailed me:

> How *thorough* can it have been on elucidating this issue before it possessed the details of classical physics (f=ma…) … or quantum physics. Because of the lack of available-to-human-beings words and concepts, any description back then must be vague and mystical…a mere groping…[7]

In this observation Professor Stapp makes the assumption that the empirical data, together with its theoretical interpretations, gained by science since the seventeenth century, including the quantum era, is required to come to the philosophical conclusion that the world described by 'classical' science is actually an 'illusion.' (Buddhist terminology uses the term 'illusion-like' to indicate that what Buddhist philosophy refers to as the 'conventional' realm, which corresponds to the 'classical' world of physics, does not exist 'as it appears to'). Worse still, there seems to be an impli-cation that the philosophical and conceptual abilities of these Buddhist think-ers are not up to the task, being far too 'vague and mystical.'

According to Stapp, then, the 'mystical' philosophy of Buddhist philoso-phers could not be anything other that a 'mere groping', and according to Carroll they would only be capable of coming up with 'inevitable random similarities of word choice.' The problem with such a remarkably patronis-ing attitude, however, is that it is clearly refuted by the precision, detail and extent of the parallels and interconnections demonstrated within this current work.

The following comes from the eleventh century 'Book of Kadam':

> Now I shall cast to the winds concepts of solid objects with mass[8].

And:

> This world of deceptive conventions is a lie; ...
> Since these manifestations without existence are devoid of core ...
> All things are but mere appearances ...
> Even should the entire world surround me
> And argue against me, claiming that phenomena are real,
> I ... would find them the greater laughingstock.[9]

Here the Buddhist pundit Dromtonpa vigorously proclaims that external, independent, self-powered, 'real,' by which he means independent of mind, solid and inherently massive objects do not *ultimately* exist in the way that they appear to. In other words the eleventh century Buddhist thinkers had figured out that the very impressive and imposing illusion of a completely independent 'material' reality, an apparently external to consciousness structure of 'matter' which has its own internal 'solid' 'mass' was 'devoid of core' and devoid of independent internal mass.

This completely counter-intuitive, and from the perspective of everyday experience clearly insane, claim has now been completely vindicated by modern physics. As Nobel Prize winner Professor Frank Wilczek writes in his wonderful book *The Lightness of Being*:

> Matter is not what it appears to be. ... The mass of ordinary matter is the embodied energy of more basic building blocks, themselves lacking mass.[10]

And in his essay for the recent collection of cutting edge quantum physics essays *Science and Ultimate Reality* Professor Anton Zeilinger refers to the pre-quantum viewpoint as involving 'the obviously wrong notion of a reality independent of us.'[11] The physicist that this collection of essays was in celebration of, Professor John Wheeler, who was an inspiration for some of the most significant physicists of the twentieth century, stated that the evidence of quantum physics indicates that the Universe is 'self-synthesized' through the perceptual activities of the 'observer participants of all times and all places,'[12] a view which clearly sits well with the core Mahayana Buddhist psycho-metaphysical claim that the material environment is a collective construction created by the collective karma, or intentional actions, of all sentient beings inhabiting the Universe.

Once the astonishing detail and precision of the interconnections between modern physics, especially quantum physics, and the extraordinary insights of Buddhist philosophy, are appreciated, the claim that nothing other than vague random word similarities are at work seems nothing other than short-sighted and ill-informed prejudice.

Whilst there are some significant works dealing with the specific area of quantum physics and Buddhism – the works of B. Alan Wallace and Victor Mansfield are significant in this arena, there is to my knowledge, and I have spent ten years investigating the terrain, nothing as detailed, rigorous and comprehensive as this current work. My intention was to leave no doubt that, by fully comprehending the Quantum Mind-Only metaphysical perspective which derives from the interface of quantum physics and Buddhist philosophy; it is possible to also fully comprehend the nature and functioning of the process of reality.

When I began this project there were very few works dealing with the subject of quantum physics and Buddhism, although there was significant interest in quantum theory and various 'mystical' worldviews, an interest which generated a great deal of animosity in hardened scientific-materialist enclaves. This interest and research in the 'mystical' dimensions of quantum theory, a viewpoint which has vociferous opponents, has been dubbed 'quantum mysticism.' The first chapter of this book briefly overviews this area. The significant works devoted to science and Buddhism in particular were those by B. Alan Wallace (*Choosing Reality*) and Matthieu Ricard and Trinh Xuan Thuan (*The Quantum and the Lotus*). During the research and writing of this book, however, interest and publications in this arena have increased significantly.

When I registered the domain name www.quantumbuddhism.com a google search on the term 'quantum Buddhism' would not have produced a great many significant hits. Shortly after registration of this domain and the setting up of my site, however, the number of sites purporting to deal in some way with this topic seemed to increase dramatically. Very few of these sites, however, seem to offer any new deep insights which would really justify the appellation *quantum Buddhism.*

It was always my intention to firstly offer new, detailed and profound insights and elucidations in the research into parallels, interconnections and mutually reinforcing perspectives of quantum physics and Buddhist philosophy, and secondly, to do so with a manner of exposition approaching the philosophical beauty of the Madhyamaka, the central philosophy of Mahayana Buddhism, as T.R.V. Murti calls it.

I have done my best, with the help of my indefatigable friend and editor Erik Scothron who has on occasion resorted to wrathful means to make me rewrite sections which weariness would otherwise have had me leave not fully fashioned. How successful I have been in approaching the philosophical beauty of the Madhyamaka (in chapters such as *Quantum Emptiness* for instance), of course, I can only let the reader judge.

I am confident, however, that this work does contain profound and significant insights which go beyond those already researched and proposed elsewhere. Some of the insights unique to this work are (the chapters within which the insights are dealt with are indicated):

- How quantum physics shows that 'emptiness' (*shunyata*), conceived of as 'hovering between existence and non-existence' is essential for the functioning of reality. (*Why the Quantum?*)

- An explanation of the structural homomorphism between the Mind-Only three-natures analysis of the process of reality and the 'collapse of the wavefunction'. (*Illusion or Reality?*)

- A thorough analysis of the ontological implications of the phenomenon of superposition, as exemplified in split beam experiments, which shows the identity of the state of superposition with the Madhyamaka existential tetralemma of extremes – neither existent, nor non-existent, nor both nor neither. (*Quantum Emptiness*).

- How the Buddhist Yogachara account of the functioning of reality, combined with the quantum insights of David Bohm, John Wheeler, Henry Stapp, Wojciech Zurek (quantum Darwinism) and others provides an account of the origin of the probabilities within wavefunctions. (*Quantum Karma*)

- How the Quantum Mind-Only account of the functioning of reality explains how the 'many-worlds' of the mental continuums of all sentient beings are 'unfolded' from the 'implicate' ground consciousness (*alayavijnana*) of the quantum universal wavefunction and then subsequently new potentialities for future life experiences are 'enfolded' to be activated in the future lifetimes of the countless mental continuums of sentient beings within the universal process of reality. (*Many Worlds of Illusion*).

- How a Quantum Mind-Only analysis of the structure of the Schrödinger wave equation can elucidate the process of quantum evolution within the evo-devo (evolutionary-development) Universe. (*Many Worlds of Illusion*)

- A Quantum Mind-Only account, based on the Extended Everett Concept of Michael Mensky together with the work of Stapp, of the scope and process of 'free will.' (*Choosing Reality*)

- How the 'collapse' of the wavefunction indicates that the process of reality is actually a process of Universal Self-Perception. The ground of the Universe is an infinite pool of potentiality and awareness, or empty-cognizance, which must create the infinite illusions within the dualistic experiential realm because of its fundamental nature of awareness. This gives rise to the two 'illusions' of 'selfhood' – the personal 'self' and the imputation of a 'self' in phenomena. (*Self-Perceiving Universe*)

- How the Jonang Other-Emptiness teachings are replete with indications that the Buddhist philosophers were aware that the nature of 'unobserved' reality should be conceived of as a 'matrix' of potentiality in the same way that Max Planck asserted that 'Mind is the Matrix of Matter'. (*Quantum Luminous Heart of the Empty Wave of Reality*)

- Buddhas do not collapse wavefunctions! (*Quantum Luminous Heart of the Empty Wave of Reality*)

The above sketches of some of the significant insights in this book are not exhaustive, but should give a flavor of what is to come for the reader willing to make a little effort, for it must be said that this is not an easy, intellectually sanitised work. But then, if you want to know how and why the Universe functions it would surely make sense that some kind of effort would be required!

As previously mentioned I owe a great debt of gratitude to fellow quantum-minded Buddhist philosopher Erik Scothron. Erik and I met when I was in the initial stages of my research and had written several prototype chapters. Erik, having grasped my perspective and intentions in conversations, patiently read them and came back with suggestions for improving readability, and subsequently was vital in developing the book through various stages with many insightful suggestions as to how to improve readability and content. He has been my companion and front-line editor throughout the arduous process of trying to make a difficult, extraordinary and important topic - the fact that reality is nothing like we ordinarily take it to be and, furthermore, the Buddhist philosophers knew the *metaphysical* details of the quantum 'illusion-like' nature of reality at least two thousand years ago – understandable and approachable, whilst not 'dumbing-down' the content to the extent that detail and precision is lost.

I am also grateful for the encouragement that Professor Henry Stapp offered when I initially contacted him and he read chapters *Quantum Karma* and *Many Worlds of Illusion*. However, although he initially said that I did 'a great service to humanity in showing the parallels' between the two areas of thought, when he later discovered the extent of my claims regarding the achievements of Buddhist philosophers he then vehemently disagreed, as I have already indicated.

The Tibetan translator and Buddhist teacher Karl Brunnhölzl, author of the wonderful *The Center of the Sunlit Sky*: *Madhyamaka in the Kagyü Tradition* (2004), also contributed to my work by reading, and approving, the chapters which use his translations and introductions: *Luminous Heart: The*

Third Karmapa on Consciousness, Wisdom and Buddha Nature (2009) and *In Praise of Dharmadhatu* (2007).

The controversial biologist Rupert Sheldrake read sections of chapters dealing with quantum evolution in connection with his ideas of morphogenesis and was also encouraging. Also Ajhan Amaro read a chapter and made useful comments.

Finally I must thank my friends and associates who have provided help, succor, encouragement and intellectual inspiration along the way: my Dharma friends Daniel Davide (assistant editor), Gavin Lee and David Glendining of the Forest Sangha Group, Deborah Woolf and Phil Tucker of the Anahata Health Clinic in Brighton, transhumanist philosopher Dave Pierce for many intriguing discussions over coffee, Tony Hobbs who supplied a place of refuge in his internet café for a while when the going was tough, Steve Howard who helped in lean times and Chris MacLachlan who proved to be an invigorating intellectual sparing partner. Finally I would like to thank from the depths of my heart-mind all the amazing practitioners and teachers of the Dharma, the truth concerning the nature of reality and the correct way to conduct oneself within its grip. Within this category I must mention the Ajahn Sumedho, who lit up the room within which the religious studies group met at Sussex University with his great-hearted wisdom and mirth twenty-five years ago, and the inspirational presence and practice of the monks and nuns of Chithurst monastery.

Note concerning quotes: I wrote these chapters, sometimes initially as essays, over ten years in various versions. Because of this various quotes were used in different combinations. As the book took on its final shape it became clear that some quotes are repeated across chapters as they are contrasted with other quotes. Because the juxtaposition of quotes is an essential part of the elucidation of the terrain I have left the repetition in. I beg the reader's indulgence in my reluctance to prune away the repetition.

Note concerning the phase 'collapse of the wavefunction': This term is used extensively as indicating whatever 'happens' 'physically' – using this term to indicate the ultimate nature of the process of reality (which is not a matter of 'matter') – in correspondence to the physically implied movement from quantum multiple potentiality to an experienced actuality.

Website: www.quantumbuddhism.com

Facebook forum:

http://www.facebook.com/group.php?gid=185195343194

Quantum Buddhism?

Nothing exposes the perplexity at the heart of physics more starkly than certain preposterous claims a few outspoken physicists are making concerning how the world really works. If we take these claims at face value, the stories physicists tell resemble the tales of mystics and madmen.[13]

- Nick Herbert

… physicists are not the only people who view the world this way. They are only the newest members of a sizable group; most Hindus and Buddhists also hold similar views.[14]

- Gary Zukav

To a Mahayana Buddhist exposed to Nagarjuna's thought, there is an unmistakable resonance between the notion of emptiness and the new physics. If on the quantum level, matter is revealed to be less solid and definable than it appears, then it seems to me that science is coming closer to the Buddhist contemplative insights of emptiness and interdependence.[15]

- Dalai Lama

The doctrine that the world is made up of objects whose existence is independent of human consciousness turns out to be in conflict with quantum mechanics and with facts established by experiment. [16]

- Bernard d'Espagnat

For a parallel to the lesson of atomic theory regarding the limited applicability of such customary idealisations we must in fact turn … even to that kind of epistemological problems with which already thinkers like Buddha and Lao Tzu have been confronted, when trying to harmonize our position as spectators and actors in the great drama of existence.[17]

- Niels Bohr

The fact that quantum physics is mysterious has been regularly endorsed by a good few physicists in recent years. The subject of the physical and philosophical implications of the theories of modern physics, quantum physics in particular, has captured the imagination of a considerable audience and the popular science sections of major bookstores are replete with expositions expounding the marvels and perplexities of quantum theory, many written by quantum physicists eager to boggle the minds of their readers. Quantum entities are said to be waves and particles at the same time, they do not exist fully until they are observed, they can be in two places at the same time, and they can hover between existence and non-existence. These are a few of the bizarre properties that appear to lie at the heart of the quantum realm.

In just about all of these current expositions you can find somewhere an observation similar to Nick Herbert's indication that the ideas of quantum physics conjure up a scenario worthy of 'tales of mystics and madmen'. Some physicists who rely on the theory for their work do not feel comfortable with it. The quantum gravity theorist Lee Smolin, for instance, says of the Uncertainty Principle, which states that it is not possible to know a quantum particle's precise position and momentum at the same time, that:

> ...the mind rebels: it is hard to work one's way through to the logical consequences of a principle like the uncertainty principle when one's first response is simply to disbelieve it. I myself do not really believe it, and I do not think that I am the only physicist who feels this way. But I persist in using it because it is a necessary part of the only theory I know that explains the main observed facts about atoms, molecules and elementary particles.[18]

Another physicist, Jim Al-Khalili, tells his readers that: 'You are not meant to be comfortable with the conclusions of quantum physics'.[19] Sir Roger Penrose, who was knighted for his contributions to modern physics, suggests that quantum theory is a 'strange and, in many ways, philosophically unsatisfying view of a world.'[20] In fact Penrose continuously reiterates that he finds quantum theory completely unsatisfying, despite its remarkable precision:

> Taken at its face value, the theory seems to lead to a philosophical standpoint that many (including myself) find deeply unsatisfying. At best, and taking its descriptions at their most literal, it provides us with a very strange view of the world indeed. At worst, and taking literally the proclamations of some of its most famous protagonists, it provides us with no view of the world at all.[21]

Penrose is so dissatisfied with quantum theory that he vigorously maintains that it must be incomplete and is apparently still anticipating a new revolution in physics; in the September 2009 issue of Discover magazine he suggested that 'the human brain—and the universe itself—must function according to some theory we haven't yet discovered'.[22]

The view that quantum theory must be incomplete was shared by Einstein, who played a vital role in the development of the theory but famously rebelled against the probabilistic nature of the theory with the observation that 'God does not play dice'. Einstein engaged in an intense dialogue with Niels Bohr, another of the founders of the theory, to try and convince him that quantum theory was incomplete.

Bohr was one of the proponents of the Copenhagen interpretation of the theory; a rather ambiguous interpretation of the quantum evidence that implies that the entities and attributes of quantum theory can not be considered to be really 'real' in their own right; instead they should be treated as convenient conceptual devices that enable physicists to describe the outcomes of their experiments. Science writer Jim Baggott describes the Copenhagen view:

> Although we may speak of electron spin, velocity, orbital angular momentum, and so on, these are properties we have assigned to an electron for convenience-each property becomes 'real' only when the electron interacts with an instrument specifically designed to reveal that property.[23]

So at the early stages of the development of quantum theory the nature of reality was thrown into question, for at the quantum level it seems that apparently fundamental aspects of reality did not completely own their own natures so to speak. Instead it seems that what quantum entities seem to *be* depends on how they are looked at!

Einstein, however, could not accept a view which threw away the notion of a really existing external reality, a reality that could be uncovered and described by the 'physical' concepts of science. Einstein lost the debate and there is still no complete consensus concerning the nature of the 'really real' reality that lies beyond the mathematical theory.

Quantum physics attributes the fundamental description of unobserved reality to a mathematical realm of potential existence; for each possibility within the realm of potentiality the mathematical 'formulism', or description, assigns a probability that it will come into existence when the system in question is 'measured'. The mathematical description of potential existence is called a 'wavefunction', but as the physicist and popular science writer Michio Kaku indicates, 'no one knows what is doing the waving.'[24] Gary Zukav concurred with this evaluation, in his popular book *The Dancing Wu Li Masters* he pondered:

> Is it possible for a physicist to predict something, calculate equations which describe it, and still not know what he is talking about?[25]

As we shall quickly see the answer seems to be yes!

Quantum physicist Nick Herbert, in his book *Quantum Reality*, gives one of his chapters the title 'Physicists Losing Their Grip'. At the head of the chapter he quotes two other physicists, Bryce DeWitt and Neill Graham:

> No development of modern science has had more profound impact on human thinking than the advent of quantum theory. Wrenched out of centuries-old thought patterns, physicists of a century ago found themselves compelled to embrace a new metaphysics. The distress which this reorientation caused continues to the present day. Basically physicists have suffered a severe loss: their hold on reality.[26]

Herbert concurs and he calls the fact that physicists have lost their grip 'one of the best-kept secrets of science'[27]. The physicists Bruce Rosenblum and Fred Kuttner, in their important book *Quantum Enigma: Physics encounters consciousness*, have made a similar observation regarding the far reaching implications of quantum theory:

> ...we suspect that something beyond ordinary physics awaits discovery. Not all physicists would agree. Many would like to dismiss the enigma, our 'skeleton in the closet'[28]

This quantum 'skeleton in the closet', which consists of the fact that physics seems to have 'encountered consciousness', has caused much consternation and dispute within the physics community, many physicists seem desperate to find any other interpretation for the evidence.

Lee Smolin tells us that:

> I have worked on projects in quantum gravity where everything went smoothly until the collaborators discovered one day over dinner that we had radically different understandings of the meaning of quantum theory. Everything went smoothly again after we had calmed down and realised that how we thought about the theory had no effect on the calculations we were doing.[29]

He adds the following observation for emphasis:

> It is true that there is only one mathematical formulism of quantum theory. So physicists have no problem in going ahead and using the theory even though they do not agree about what it means.[30]

And this lack of consensus concerning the nature of reality at the quantum level is by no means a recent state of affairs in the history of quantum theory:

> The founders of quantum theory, such as Einstein, Bohr, Heisenberg and Schrödinger did not agree ...There is now no more agreement about what quantum theory really means...[31]

This is an astonishing situation. The founding 'fathers' of quantum theory were in disagreement concerning the implications of the mathematical calculations that they were using and this uncertainty about the meaning and implications for our understanding of the material world echoes down to the present day. All the gadgets of the modern world, radios, televisions, cd-players, computers, scanners, printers, iPods, the list is endless, all depend on our knowledge of the *functioning* of the quantum realm and yet the founding fathers of quantum physics, and their descendents, were, and still are, completely in the dark as to what *really* is going on beyond the probabilistic predictive mathematics; they certainly do not know what 'exists' at the quantum level. Quantum physicists are still not in agreement about what it all means.

In a recent book *Quantum Paradoxes* (2005) quantum physicists Yakir Aharanov and Daniel Rohrlich refer to a remark made by the charismatic physicist Richard Feynman that once Einstein's theory of relativity was made public it was not long until many people understood it; in contrast Feynman suggested that nobody understood quantum physics:

> …you get down a blind alley from which nobody escapes. Nobody knows how it can be like that.[32]

Feynman made this observation in 1965; Aharanov and Rohrlich are writing 40 years later and, according to them, very little has changed in the intervening years. They refer to a Woody Allen joke in which someone goes to a psychiatrist to complain that his brother thought himself to be a chicken. The psychiatrist suggests that the man should commit his brother to an insane asylum; the man replies 'Are you crazy we need the eggs!' Aharanov and Rohrlich observe that:

> Quantum Mechanics is crazy – but we need the eggs!'[33]

When the ideas of quantum physics are viewed from the perspective of our ingrained familiarity with the way that the everyday world *appears* to function, quantum concepts appear to be completely insane; but they work! So, as Jim Baggott in his book *beyond measure* says, quantum physics always leads back to philosophy.[34] This is because after a century of controversy concerning the implications of the theory there is still a great deal of perplexity, and even controversy, within the physics community concerning the ontological status of quantum phenomena.

Quantum physics today is in the most extraordinary situation. To describe the current state of affairs starkly, but correctly, the truth seems to be that there is not a physicist alive who knows what quantum physics is, ultimately, a science of. Words and concepts such as 'physical reality', 'matter', and so on are routinely used, but when it comes to trying to find out exactly what these refer to in substantial terms the task is frustrating. No-one knows. As the maverick physicist David Bohm pointed out:

[Physicists] do use the ideas of fields and particles and so on, but when you press them they must agree that they have no image whatsoever what these things are and they have no content other than the results of what they can calculate with their equations. [35]

This depiction might seem to be a little extreme so it is probably wise to look at what a few more physicists have to say on the matter. The celebrated mathematical physicist Roger Penrose tells the following story:

I cannot resist quoting a remark that was made to me by Professor Bob Wald, of the University of Chicago, at a dinner party some years ago: If you really believe in quantum physics, then you can't take it seriously. [36]

Heisenberg, one of the founding fathers and the inventor of quantum matrix mechanics, also lamented after dinner:

Can nature possibly be as absurd as it seems to us in these atomic experiments? [37]

Aephraim M. Steinberg, writing in 2004, points out that:

For all of our apparent understanding of quantum mechanics, our ability to calculate remarkable things using this theory, and the regularity with which experiment has borne out these predictions, at the turn of the twenty first century it seems as if there are as many puzzles on the road to a true *understanding* of quantum theory as there were at the start previous century. [38]

The level of dissent between physicists themselves can be startling. For instance one no-nonsense determinedly materialist physicist, Victor Stenger, confidently asserts that:

The most economical conclusion to be drawn from the complete library of scientific data is that we are material beings composed of atoms and molecules, ordered by the largely-chance processes of self-organisation and evolution to become capable of the complex behavior associated with the notions of life and mind. The data provide us with no reason to postulate undetectable vital or spiritual, transcendent forces. Matter is sufficient to explain everything discovered thus far by the most powerful scientific instruments. [39]

The picture of reality that quite unmistakably underlies this depiction is that of a definitely existing independent world of material particles, 'atoms and molecules'. This world is quite evidently supposed to be a really existing structure of materiality which clubs together, so to speak, to produce the 'complex behavior' of 'life and mind'. The picture is quite clear; it is the naturalistic picture of the material world which generally underlies the everyday life of most people. Stenger is adamant that 'matter is sufficient to explain everything' so presumably he must know what 'matter' is.

Most physicists today, however, are much less confident about the matter of matter. In fact the hugely expensive CERN Large Hadron Collider has been commissioned in large part to search for the Higg's boson, a quantum entity which it is thought creates the appearance of 'mass', a physical phenomenon which is responsible for the weightiness of matter. At the moment the origin of a good deal the mass of the Universe is a mystery; Noble prize winning physicist Frank Wilczek, for instance, says that:

> Mass, a seemingly irreducible property of matter, and a byword for its resistance to change and sluggishness, turns out to a harmonious interplay of symmetry, uncertainty, and energy. Using these concepts, and the algorithms they suggest, pure computation outputs the numerical values of the masses of particles we observe. Still, as I've already mentioned, our understanding of the origin of mass is by no means complete. We have achieved a beautiful and profound understanding of the origin of *most* of the mass of ordinary matter, but not of *all* of it.[40]

It is quite clear from this observation that mass is in no way an ontologically primary and irreducible aspect of reality. The bit of it for which an explanation is not missing turns out to be a result of 'interplay of symmetry, uncertainty, and energy.' And not all physicists agree with Wilczek about his belief that *most* of the mass of the Universe is accounted for. In a recent article on the Large Hadron Collider Bill Bryson, after discussing the issue with physicists working on the project, wrote that:

> ...the proton is a hundred times more massive than the three quarks that make it. Where does all the mass come from? We have no idea.[41]

And this does not take into account the mysterious 'dark matter,' which apparently makes up a much greater part of the Universe, the nature of which physicists are truly in the dark about.

However, this fact does not stop some 'philosophers' embracing an uncompromising, not to say pugilistic, materialist stance. Foremost amongst these 'thinkers' is Daniel Dennett:

> The prevailing wisdom, variously expressed and argued for, is *materialism*: there is only one sort of stuff, namely *matter* – the physical stuff of physics, chemistry and physiology – and the mind is somehow nothing but a physical phenomenon. In short the mind is the brain.[42]

The extent to which Dennett's assertion can be taken seriously, however, is suggested by the fact that, although he refers to 'matter' as 'the 'physical stuff of physics,' if one turns to the index of the book that this quote is taken from, *Consciousness Explained*, there is no entry for 'quantum physics' or any phenomenon of the quantum realm, and yet today quantum physics *is* physics.

Dennett is clearly aware of the contrary views of a good few highly respected physicists concerning this matter; in one of his other works, for instance, he quotes award winning physicist Freeman Dyson:

> ...the architecture of the Universe is consistent with hypothesis that the mind plays an essential role in its functioning.[43]

However, in the face of the rapidly growing evidence that the 'classical', or pre-quantum, concept of matter is an illusion, there is a remarkably aggressive backlash on the part of a significant and vociferous section of the Western intellectual and academic community who stubbornly plant their feet upon what they think is ultimately solid material ground and pronounce that it is not 'matter' that is the 'illusion', on the contrary they cry, it is 'consciousness' that is the illusion. According to Dennett for instance:

> An impersonal, unreflective, robotic, mindless little scrap of molecular machinery is the ultimate basis of all the agency, and hence meaning, and hence consciousness, in the universe.[44]

So here we find a dramatic intellectual confrontation regarding the ultimate nature of reality; and this confrontation is of ultimate and crucial significance, because, as we shall see in great detail, what we think about the world, what we perceive within reality, affects and conditions reality at a very deep, quantum level. If we think that reality is meaningless, it will become for us, and maybe in reality, meaningless; and if we think it meaningful then, well perhaps it is worth handing over to Professor Henry Stapp, one of the few current physicists who worked with some of the founding fathers of quantum theory:

> ...each such choice is *intrinsically meaningful*: each quantum choice injects meaning ...[45]

And:

> ...the quantum universe tends to create meaning: the quantum law of evolution continuously creates a vast ensemble of forms that can act as carriers of meaning...[46]

In other words 'meaning', and therefore consciousness, is an *intrinsic* aspect or quality of reality, not an adventitious accident.

Today we are in the midst of a crucial intellectual show down at the very metaphysical limits of our conception of reality. Dennett, and those of his persuasion, think that tiny scraps of 'mindless matter' club together to miraculously produce 'all the agency, and hence meaning, and hence consciousness, in the universe.' Stapp and a great many significant quantum physicists, on the other hand, taking into consideration the evidence of quantum physics, consider that it is the functioning of consciousness which 'injects meaning' into the universe; and this process produces the subjective experiences of what appears to be an independent material reality. The quantum viewpoint that is now emerging is that it is consciousness which is the ontological ground of reality; in some fashion consciousness creates the 'stuff' of the material world.

The ubiquity with which significant quantum physicists support this kind of view is impressive. Here's John Wheeler, considered to be one of the twentieth century's great physicists:

> Directly opposite to the concept of universe as machine built on law is the vision of *a world self-synthesized.* On this view, the notes struck out on a piano by the observer participants of all times and all places, bits though they are in and by themselves, constitute the great wide world of space and time and things.[47]

Here's Edward Teller, the physicist in large part responsible for the development of the hydrogen bomb:

> In order to understand atomic structure, we must accept the idea that the future is uncertain. It is uncertain to the extent that the future is created in every part of the world by every atom and every living being.[48]

Here's Martin Rees, Cambridge University professor and Astronomer Royal:

> In the beginning there were only probabilities. The universe could only come into existence if someone observed it. … The universe exists because we are aware of it.[49]

No wonder Dennett doesn't like to take physics seriously when it comes to ultimate explanations of reality; it seems that a lot of highly regarded physicists disagree with him!

Henry Stapp completely disagrees with Dennett and Stenger's anachronistic materialist ontology:

> We live in an *idealike* world, not a matterlike world.' The material aspects are exhausted in certain mathematical properties, and these mathematical features can be understood just as well (and in fact better) as characteristics of an evolving idealike structure. There is, in fact, in the quantum universe no natural place for matter. This conclusion, curiously, is the exact reverse of the circum-

stances that in the classical physical universe there was no natural place for mind.[50]

And there are quite a few other significant physicists who side with Stapp's evaluation of the ultimate nature of the world as being more mind-like than matter-like.

However there is significant discord regarding such matters in the physics community and, despite the avalanche of quantum evidence to the contrary, within the general intellectual climate of Western academia materialism seems to be the viewpoint that matters and carries the most weight, so to speak.

How can it be that practitioners of the same intellectual and experimental discipline are either at a loss or committed to absolutely antithetical opinions concerning the inner nature of the very heart of the subject they are investigating? This is a conundrum which we should really take seriously. If we are to accept that our knowledge of what constitutes reality should be mediated by the experts who study the area of knowledge we are concerned with, then surely we should expect that there is at least a modicum of agreement. If the experts cannot come to any kind of consensus on the issue of the nature of reality then the only possible conclusion is that the modern world, for all its spectacular advances in the 'material' manipulation of the world, has no idea whatsoever what reality is, or isn't.

And the crucial issue that has provoked, and still provokes, controversy is the implication that consciousness is in some way implicated at the quantum level. This implication came as an enormous shock to physicists in the early part of the twentieth century. Up until that point it was thought that science was purely concerned with the nature of an external 'material' world; a world that had been assumed to exist independently of consciousness. Indeed the primary view of consciousness within mainstream Western thinking generally was that it was a production of the material world; although how this trick was achieved no-one had a clue.

In quantum experiments, however, it turned out that the way reality presented itself depended on conscious decisions made by the experimenters. The most widely known instance of this is the experiments which demonstrate the famous wave-particle duality of matter. When an experiment is performed in one way reality seems to be composed of waves, when done another way it then appears to consist of particles. So the inevitable question arose as to how a supposedly material reality could be both wave and particle at the same time? And how can the intervention of a conscious decision influence the appearance of a reality which should be separate from consciousness?

Lee Smolin has indicted that the early founding fathers of quantum theory were in disagreement; however there were a significant number who came to a radical conclusion regarding the role of consciousness, or mind, in the process of reality. According to Schrödinger, for instance:

> Mind has erected the objective outside world … out of its own stuff.[51]

And Max Planck came to a similar conclusion:

> All matter originates and exists only by virtue of a force... We must assume behind this force the existence of a conscious and intelligent Mind. This Mind is the matrix of all matter.[52]

More recently, in an article in the New Scientist (23rd June 2007) Michael Brooks, commenting on quantum entanglement experiments carried out by teams led by Markus Aspelmeyer of the Austrian Academy of Sciences and Anton Zeilinger of the University of Vienna, tells us that the conclusion reached by the physicists involved is that:

> … we now have to face the possibility that there is nothing inherently real about the properties of an object that we measure. In other words measuring those properties is what brings them into existence.[53]

And Professor Vlatko Vedral, quantum researcher at the University of Leeds commented that:

> Rather than passively observing it, we in fact create reality.[54]

The headline for the article proclaims that:

> To track down a theory of everything, we might have to accept that the universe only exists when we are looking at it…[55]

This dramatic conclusion is prompted by recent extremely delicate experimental investigations of the interaction of the observations being made and the nature of the resulting experimental outcomes.

The miniscule scale of these quantum experiments is staggering. For instance it is possible to fit in the order of 100000 atoms across the width of a human hair and the scale of the quantum experiments that have been conducted, which involve the constituents of atoms, are at an order beneath this. The breathtaking scale and precision of experiments which delve beneath the sphere of atomic 'particles' into the realm of deeper quantum phenomena has been constantly refined to ever more unimaginable and mind warping tiny scales of accuracy. Physicist Robert Oerter describes the accuracy required for these investigations as that 'you would need to shoot a gun and hit a Coke can – if the can were on the moon'[56]. Richard Feynman, one of the most significant physicists of the twentieth century, compared the accuracy of quantum experiments to measuring the distance between New York and Los Angeles to the precision of the width of one human hair![57] At this miniscule level of investigation the material world vanishes almost, but not quite, into nothingness. Furthermore, as we shall see, at this vanishingly infinitesimal scale of examination the material world completely dissolves into what Buddhist philosophers call *Emptiness.*

The experiments in question indicate that the characteristics of the quantum entities being investigated are determined by the nature of the observation being made. It is this fact which has led quantum physicists to conclude that such quantum characteristics are not inherently real. This insight into the lack of 'inherent reality' or lack of 'inherent existence' is the hallmark of *Emptiness*, or *shunyata*, a concept used by Buddhist philosophers to indicate the inner nature of reality. Emptiness does not denote 'nothingness' but, rather, denotes 'dependent origination', the central concept of the Madhyamaka, the central 'Middle Way' doctrine of Mahayana Buddhism. In particular the central core of the doctrine of Emptiness is precisely that all phenomena lack 'inherent existence', which is to say that no phenomenon can be a completely independent, self-sufficient and self-enclosed entity or event; everything is interdependent with everything else in a web of inter-penetration. From another point of view Emptiness denotes a realm of pot-entiality, hovering between existence and non-existence that underlies the possibility of all phenomena.

The *Yogachara-Vijnanavada*, or Cognition-Only, and *Chittamatra*, or Mind-Only[58], Buddhist metaphysical perspectives add the further insight that consciousness is instrumental in bringing phenomena into existence:

> ..all these various appearances,
> Do not exist as sensory objects which are other than consciousness.
> Their arising is like the experience of self knowledge.
> All appearances, from indivisible particles to vast forms, are mind.[59]

When considering such a perspective, however, it is important to bear in mind that the claim is not that all the phenomena of the dualistic everyday world are endowed with fully-manifested consciousness as possessed by the higher sentient beings but that all phenomena are of the essential nature of consciousness. The actual nature and degree of the quality of awareness will depend upon the nature of the organisation and interaction of the funda-mental levels of primitive consciousness, so to speak, involved in any particular phenomenon. This is in line with quantum physicist Andrei Linde's observation:

> Is it possible that consciousness, like space-time, has its own intrinsic degrees of freedom and that neglecting these will lead to a description of the universe that is fundamentally incomplete? What if our perceptions are as real as (or maybe, in a certain sense, are even more real) than material objects?[60]

It is quite clear, then, from these brief initial considerations that there is at least a prima facie case for the possibility that there might be significant connections between aspects of Buddhist philosophy and some insights of modern physics. We shall discover in the following pages that these tip-of-the-iceberg similarities are indicative of a remarkably deep and detailed terrain.

The new quantum physical worldview is so dramatically different from that which had held sway from Newton's time until the beginning of the twentieth century that some physicists began to wonder whether the prevailing notions concerning the realms of consciousness and matter needed to be completely updated in the light of the quantum results. They now suggest that the quantum experiments show conclusively that consciousness is the primary force within reality. Others, however, have poured scorn on such ideas and as a result the physics and philosophical community seems split into two camps, between those who continue to assert that the view that consciousness is significant at the quantum level is nonsensical mysticism, and a significant, and growing, number of more adventurous and visionary minds who have seen that the conclusion that consciousness is involved is now inescapable.

The physicists and philosophers who have maintained their belief in the fundamental significance of consciousness for the understanding of the functioning of reality have done so in the face of quite aggressive criticism. The dismissive and long suffering tone of the following quote from Richard Dawkins, for instance, is quite obvious:

> Another convergence has been alleged between modern physics and Eastern philosophy. The argument goes essentially as follows. Quantum physics … is deeply mysterious and hard to understand. Eastern mystics have always been deeply mysterious and hard to understand. Therefore Eastern mystics must have been talking about quantum physics all along.[61]

The committed materialist Victor Stenger is scathing of 'quantum mystical' claims. The latest findings of physicists, he says, are increasingly difficult for non-physicists to understand:

> And this lack of understanding in the public mind is made worse by the misleading claims of persuasive lecturers and popular authors, whose interest is mainly to capitalize on trendy ideas rather than to consider scientific evidence objectively.[62]

Perhaps it might be said that there is a kind of enthusiastic lack of restraint amongst some 'new age' quantum prophets which provokes opponents such as Stenger and others within the materialist camp to exasperation. However opponents of such exuberant quantum 'mystical' indulgence exhibit an astonishing conviction as to the firmness of their ground, given its quantum lack of solidity. So much so that they appear to feel quite at liberty to adopt a condescending demeanor when admonishing proponents of what has come to be disparagingly called 'quantum-mysticism', which involves the claim that consciousness is significant within the functioning of the quantum realm. Now, however, it appears that the experimental evidence is beginning to stack up in favor of the view of the ontological primacy of consciousness, a situation which very few would have been brave enough to have predicted a few years ago.

Even now, despite the dramatic evidence to the contrary, the current mainstream worldview that remains fundamental to the basic operating guidelines of Western thought is more or less that described by the dissenting quantum physicist David Bohm as the 'mechanistic order'[63], a view which clearly derives from the basic attitude of pre-quantum physics:

> physics has become almost totally committed to the notion that the order of the universe is basically mechanistic. The most common form of this notion is that the world is assumed to be constituted of separately existent, indivisible and unchangeable 'elementary particles'', which are the fundamental 'building blocks' of the universe. [64]

The physicist Amit Goswami, another dissenter from the mainstream scientific paradigm, depicts this fundamental viewpoint as follows:

> The current worldview has it that everything is made of matter, and everything can be reduced to elementary particles of matter, the basic constituents – building blocks – of matter. And cause arises from the interactions of these basic building blocks or elementary particles; elementary particles make atoms, atoms make molecules, molecules make cells, and cells make the brain. But all the way, the ultimate cause is always the interactions between elementary particles. This is the belief – all cause moves from the elementary particles.[65]

Both Goswami and Bohm, amongst others, indicate that, although in theory this view of reality was dramatically overturned sometime during the beginning of the twentieth century with the development of quantum physics, in practice it still lingers on as an ingrained way of viewing reality.

This residual tendency to hold on to the idea that there must be an independent external reality, however, is beginning to be seriously questioned; in their recent work Rosenblum and Kuttner, for instance, clearly state that the fact of wave-particle duality implicates consciousness:

> The physical reality of an object depends on how you choose to look at it. Physics had encountered consciousness but did not yet realize it.[66]

The attribution of wave-particle duality as a fundamental characteristic of quantum phenomena was necessary because it is the only way that the behavior of 'particles' taking part in the double slit experiment can be accounted for. In this experiment when quantum particles are not directly observed by a consciousness they behave like waves, which means that they spread out over a significant volume, but when observed they turn into particles. So the fact that consciousness determines the appearance of the phenomena in these quantum experiments indicates that it must clearly be involved in some way. But this view is by no means universal despite the mounting evidence in favor of it. In fact the majority of physicists have displayed a marked distaste for indulging in speculation concerning the philosophical foundations of quantum theory, and speculations involving notions of the significance of consciousness have often been greeted with not a little derision.

Because the implications of the proposal that consciousness is entangled within the quantum level are generally considered to be outlandish, many physicists just dismiss the evidence out of prejudice. The world cannot be like this! But the greatly admired physicist John Wheeler wrote in 1978 that:

> The universe does not 'exist, out there,' independent of all acts of observation. Instead, it is in some strange sense a participatory universe.[67]

Wheeler suggests that quantum theory requires a participatory universe, which means that somehow phenomena which appear to be external and independent of the minds of sentient beings cannot be so. Buddhist philosophers have made a similar point for at least two thousand years:

> ...when we see houses and fields in dreams, we think of them as being external objects that are not created by the mind, even though they are nothing other than projections of our mind. All that we see when we are awake is also nothing other than a creation of the mind.[68]

This might, at first sight, seem far fetched, but it is not. It is indicated by quantum theory, which is why quantum physicist Wojciech H. Zurek refers to quantum theory as 'the dream stuff is made of.'[69] Quantum physics clearly shows that we are involved, or are participators, in the existence of objects, a view which clearly accords with Wheeler's perspective. Indeed Wheeler also wrote that:

> ...no phenomenon is a phenomenon until it is an observed phenomenon.[70]

And, speaking in April 2003 to the American Physical Society, he made the following remarkable; perhaps one might say 'mystical', sequence of remarks:

The Question is what is the Question?
Is it all a Magic Show?
Is Reality an Illusion?
What is the framework of the Machine?
Darwin's Puzzle: Natural Selection?
Where does Space-Time come from?
Is there any answer except that it comes from consciousness?
What is Out There?
T'is Ourselves?
Or, is IT all just a Magic Show?[71]

To Wheeler's question as to the possibility that reality might be an illusory 'Magic Show' Buddhist philosophy answers in the affirmative:

Phenomena as they appear and resound
Are neither established or real in these ways,
Since they keep changing in all possible and various manners
Just like appearances in magical illusions.[72]

And, as has been previously indicated, Mind-Only Buddhist analysis also indicates the primary involvement of consciousness.

The phenomenon which lies at the heart of the issue of the relevance of consciousness in the functioning of reality is a quantum technicality termed the 'collapse of the wavefunction'. A wavefunction is a mathematical entity which allows physicists to determine the probabilities of various quantum events occurring when an observation, or measurement, is made. The crucial point is that within the quantum mathematical formulism the wavefunction, which is all we have of 'reality' before an observation is made, does not have full 'physical' reality, if, that is, by 'reality' we mean an experienced reality. Prior to interaction with consciousness it appears that all of the possibilities latent within the wavefunction have a kind of semi-reality all at the same time. But, somehow, when consciousness interacts with the multiple potentialities contained within a wavefunction only one of them materialises, the rest appear to disappear. As Goswami pithily sums up the phenomenon of the 'collapse':

In quantum physics, objects are depicted as possibilities (a possibility wave); yet when an observer observes, the possibilities collapse into an actuality (the wave collapses into particle, for example). This is the observer effect.[73]

The actual nature of the wavefunction is one of the issues that is still a matter of contention, but it is clear that it is not a completely 'real' experienced physical entity in the usual sense. The problem is, however: what does it mean to be not completely real? As Penrose has so cogently observed:

Undoubtedly the world is strange and unfamiliar at the quantum level, but it is not unreal. How, indeed, can real objects be constructed from unreal constituents?[74]

The quantum quandary throws the concept of 'reality' into a light of deep ambiguity.

In quantum theory experienced 'physical' reality only seems to manifest from the probabilities within the wavefunction when a measurement takes place. And a measurement, of course, usually requires a conscious observer. In his 1989 book *The Emperor's New Mind* Penrose mused:

Is the presence of a conscious being necessary for a 'measurement' *actually* to take place? I think that only a small minority of quantum physicists would affirm such a view.[75]

This is an example of the remarkable reluctance on the part of physicists to accept the implications of their own theories, a reluctance that continues to this day. For instance Jim Al-Khalili, writing twenty years after Penrose, admonishes his readers:

…hardly anyone still takes seriously the notion of consciousness being a requirement for collapse of the wavefunction.[76]

This assertion, however, is not true today; there are actually quite a few significant physicists who do accept this possibility. And it is notable that in his 1994 book *Shadows of the Mind* even Penrose was forced by the evidence to concede that:

At the large end of things, the place where 'the buck stops' is provided by our *conscious perceptions*.[77]

Penrose made this observation despite the fact that also he clearly stated that he found this implication 'philosophically unsatisfying.'

It is quite true that there were, at the time, few quantum physicists who would have strongly endorsed the idea that consciousness was required for a transition of wavefunctions from potentiality to reality; but, as Rosenblum and Kuttner point out in regard to the attitude of mainstream physics since the 1950's:

In physics departments a conforming mind-set increasingly meant that an untenured faculty member might endanger a career by serious interest in the fundamentals of quantum physics. Even today it is best to explore the meaning of quantum mechanics while also working a 'day job' on a mainstream physics topic.[78]

In other words there was an overwhelming materialist prejudice within the academic world which determined what physicists felt might be acceptable speculation within their discipline.

But there were physicists who held the view of the primacy of consciousness. Most notably, of course, the first significant exposition of the possible connections between aspects of modern physics and the worldviews proposed by the 'mystical' philosophies of the East was Fritjov Capra's *The Tao of Physics* published in 1975, fifteen years before Penrose's musings on the role of consciousness within quantum theory. Capra had no doubts concerning the role of consciousness at the quantum level; the following observation clearly foreshadows Penrose's later speculations:

> At the atomic level 'objects' can only be understood in terms of the interaction between the processes of preparation and measurement. The end of this chain of processes lies always in the consciousness of the human observer.[79]

It is this implication that consciousness is significant within the quantum realm that provides one of the significant reasons for the comparison of the theory with philosophical perspectives from the East.

*The Tao of Physic*s struck a cord with an audience eager to break out of the confines of what was perceived to be a rigidity and sterility of the mechanical and lifeless confines of Western science and philosophy. The nineteen sixties and seventies were a time of intellectual expansion in all cultural areas. This was especially true amongst the young who were experiencing a new radical identity that articulated itself within philosophy and well as music and experimentation with mind altering drugs. The idea for the *Tao of Physics* actually came to Capra whilst he was under the influence of a psychedelic drug; and the book became a cult classic on university campuses, along side books such as *The Way of Zen, Tibetan Book of the Dead, The Divided Self* and *Zen and the Art of Motorcycle Maintenance* (a book which had very little to do with Zen).

The aspect of Eastern thought that Capra considered of fundamental significance is an awareness of unity and interrelationship, the experience of all phenomena as manifestations of a fundamental oneness:

> The most important characteristic of the Eastern worldview – one could almost say the essence of it – is an awareness of the unity and mutual interrelation of all things and events, the experience of all phenomena in the world as manifestations of a basic oneness. All things are seen as interdependent and inseparable parts of this cosmic whole; as different manifestations of the same ultimate reality.[80]

Capra's critics have demonstrated a deep distaste for the suggested connections; the physicist Jeremy Bernstein, for instance, certainly pulled no punches:

Thus I agree with Capra when he writes, 'Science does not need mysticism and mysticism does not need science but man needs both.' What no one needs, in my opinion, is this superficial and profoundly misleading book.[81]

Bernstein targets his main criticism at 'Capra's methodology – his use of what seems to me to be accidental similarities of language as if these were somehow evidence of deeply rooted connections.'

Capra defends against the charge of the 'accidental' nature of similarities by pointing to the consistency with which the parallels occur. Initially, he tells us, he was of the same opinion regarding the weak cogency of the parallels:

And I said that it may seem that these parallels are superficial, and, as far as I remember, I said that one could draw parallels to Marxist philosophy or to any kind of philosophy on the basis of a similarity of words.[82]

The weight of consistency with which the parallels occur, however, persuaded him otherwise. His detractors, however, remain unconvinced. This is a very important issue. When is a similarity, or even a seeming identity, of concepts and words between two apparently disparate frames of thought to be taken as indicating some deep connection? Is it just in the eye of the beholder?

Capra appealed to weight of consistency, the frequency of overlap between the two spheres, in order to claim significance for his assertion of interconnection and parallelism between the fields of modern science and Eastern philosophy. This current work concerning the fields of Buddhism and quantum theory adds to Capra's methodological criterion of density of overlap the further requirement of precise detail; and Buddhist philosophy is particularly well suited in this regard because of the precise nature of its philosophical discourse and its empirical attitude.

As an example of such precision consider the following assertion by the eleventh century Kadampa Buddhist adept Dromtonpa:

Now I shall cast to the winds concepts of solid objects with mass.
I shall burn the logs of conceptualizing thoughts into flames.[83]

In this observation Dromtonpa not only declares that the notion that the objects which appear to exist externally of sentient perception are in fact not solid as they appear and do not have inherently existent mass, he also indicates that trying to grasp the essence of reality with 'conceptualizing thoughts' is mistaken.

A great many physicists prior to 1900 and shortly thereafter thought that matter was 'solid', Planck, for instance, thought that 'matter' was continuous, and Dirac around 1918 considered atoms as being 'very hypothetical things'[84]; and before the advent of quantum physics mass was considered to be an inherent and objective property that objects had as part of their own ontological makeup. In our current quantum days, however, the origin of mass has become a mystery, although Wilczek has claimed to have derived most 'mass without mass.'[85] But either way 'mass' is known not to be an inherent feature of the 'particles' which are considered to be fundamental. And the notion of the conceptual ungraspability of the ultimate and final substance and form of reality was clearly echoed by Bohr when he spoke of the necessity for 'renunciation' of 'pictorial representation' of the quantum realm.[86]

To be sure it is difficult for many Western scientists and philosophers, habituated to the general view that it is only the Western scientific methodology which provides the road to reality, to accept that the Buddhist philosophers over a thousand years ago were fully conversant and comfortable with some of the essential features of the substantial, or lack of substantial, implications of what we know as quantum theory, i.e. the lack of independent, inherent substantiality of all phenomena, which they termed the 'illusion-like' nature of reality. But the only way to avoid such a conclusion would be to claim that Dromtonpa, in this case, meant something entirely different from what his words appear to say. But, given the sheer weight of detail presented by this book such a view would be almost perverse.

The Buddhist philosophical perspective has always had a thoroughly experiential and fundamentally empirical approach, although obviously not experimental in the manner of Western science, to the investigation of the process of reality, especially to the investigation of the phenomena of consciousness. So important is this pragmatically empirical approach within the Buddhist worldview that the current fourteenth Dalai Lama has clearly indicated his commitment to the appropriate authority of Western science:

> Suppose that something is definitely proven through scientific investigation, that a certain hypothesis is verified or a certain fact emerges as a result of scientific investigation. And suppose, furthermore, that fact is incompatible with Buddhist theory. There is no doubt that we must accept the result of scientific research.[87]

The 'non overlapping magisteria' viewpoint, the view that science and religion are spheres of investigation which cannot share a common discourse, which has been asserted by Stephen Jay Gould,[88] is not held by Buddhist thought. In fact such a notion is completely foreign to it. For Buddhist philosophers the enquiry into the ultimate nature of reality, which is essential for the practice of the path towards liberation from its deficiencies, requires knowledge of the nature of reality on all levels. When Buddhist philosophers asserted that all phenomena were 'empty' of inherent existence they meant all phenomena, including the apparently external, independent material world.

The physicist Peter Woit, author of the book *Not Even Wrong,* a critique of string theory, is clearly outraged that *The Tao of Physics*, along with a very similar book that was published shortly after – Gay Zukav's *The Dancing Wu Li Masters* and 'other books of the same genre' still grace the shelves of major bookstores and are selling very well. Such titles, according to Woit, are part of 'an embarrassing new age cult.' Surveying the literature dealing with this area it is impossible not be struck by the severe polarisation into pro-quantum mysticism and anti-quantum mysticism positions. Unfortunately most passionate proponents of the quantum mysticism worldview tend to be rather loose in the standards of evidence and philosophical rigor that they employ or require. Books like *The Tao of Physics* or *Dancing Wu Li Masters* do not need rigorous argument and detailed exposition to appeal in this quarter. This is perhaps one reason why entrenched detractors of this perspective tend to be quite exasperated, not to say contemptuous, when attempting to keep the unruly worldview under control. Capra has remarked about Bernstein's comments:

> When you read his review, you notice immediately that his reaction to my book is very emotional, and parts of the review are very aggressive.[89]

It is indeed true that the opponents of attempts to question the validity of the unquestioning materialism which has marked the general Western academic attitude up until the present, and is still prevalent, tend to display a marked aggressive attitude, often resorting to sarcastic contempt. Peter Woit, for instance, is so contemptuous of Buddhist philosopher B. Alan Wallace's book *Hidden Dimensions – The Unification of Physics and Consciousness* (2007), a book which prefigures many of the detailed investigations within this current work, that he cannot be bothered to marshal any actual reasoning to support his contempt:

> After enraging lots of philosophers, I fear that now I'll enrage lots of Buddhists, in particular by having no interest in wasting time discussing Wallace's ideas.[90]

However, the books and essays penned by Wallace, focusing on the significance of the interrelationship between the Buddhist philosophy and modern science, are actually fairly meticulously argued and cogent. It might be said that *Hidden Dimensions* does not present all the detailed argumentation to thoroughly make his case that:

> ...the measurement problem in quantum mechanics, the time problem in quantum cosmology, and the hard problem in brain science are all profoundly related.[91]

However, if the reader explores the directions indicated in his book, Wallace's contention is well supported, as is fully elucidated in this current work.

Wallace's book *Choosing Reality* (2003) still remains one of the most thoughtful and intelligent investigations into the epistemological and metaphysical interconnections between the Buddhist Madhyamaka and modern Western science. Wallace also edited the collection of essays *Buddhism and Science: Breaking New Ground* which was inspired by the interdisciplinary dialogues, organised by the Mind and Life institute, between Buddhist practitioners (including the Dalai Lama) and philosophers, physicists and cognitive scientists. The depth and rigour of the analysis found these thoughtful essays generally goes far beyond that found within the tirades targeted by critics at what we can call the 'Quantum Buddhism' perspective. It appears that those who wish to undermine the significant appraisal of the interconnections between the areas of science and Buddhism rarely take on the task of rigorously demonstrating their objections to any serious philosophical examination of the field.

A significant point which really requires consideration by proponents of such a self confidently contemptuous and dismissive attitude towards the view that 'matter has moved towards mind'[92], as Henry Stapp describes the situation, is surely that, if the viewpoint is so juvenile, so worthy of haughty contempt by the more rigorous and insightful minds of the anti-quantum-mysticism lobby, then why did the great minds of the development of quantum theory come to conclusions such as that mind creates the material world 'out of its own stuff' (Schrödinger), or 'Mind is the Matrix of all matter' (Planck), or that space-time 'comes from consciousness' (Wheeler), to cite just a few. Were these physicists imbeciles?

Here's an observation made by Robert Oppenheimer, one of the physicists bearing a great responsibility for the development of the atomic bomb:

> ... discoveries in atomic physics are not in the nature of things wholly unfamiliar, wholly unheard of or new. Even in our own culture they have a history, in Buddhist and Hindu thought a more considerable and central place. What we shall find [in modern physics] is an exemplification, an encouragement, and a refinement of old wisdom.[93]

Heisenberg also indicated his appreciation of Hindu philosophy for easing his way towards accepting paradoxical quantum formulations. According to Fritjov Capra:

> He talked a lot with Tagore about Indian philosophy. Heisenberg told me that these talks had helped him a lot with his work in physics, because they showed him that all these new ideas in quantum physics were in fact not all that crazy. He realized there was, in fact, a whole culture that subscribed to very similar ideas. Heisenberg said that this was a great help for him.[94]

Did Oppenheimer and Heisenberg suffer from the same mental deficiency that Woit seems to attribute to Fritjov Capra, Alan Wallace and others of their persuasion?

According to Penrose:

> Quantum theory was not wished upon us by theorists. It was (for the most part) with great reluctance that they found themselves driven to this strange and, in many ways, philosophically unsatisfying view of the world.[95]

This is an important point to bear in mind because it lends great weight to the discoveries of quantum theory. The remarkable features of quantum functioning were not unearthed by physicists who set out to uncover them; quite the opposite. The American experimental physicist Robert Millikan, for instance, could not accept Einstein's picture of the light photon as both wave and particle and he therefore set out on a series of difficult experiments in order to prove that Einstein was wrong. The physicist and science writer John Gribben writes concerning this:

> ... he only succeeded in proving that Einstein was right ... In the best traditions of science, it was this experimental confirmation of Einstein's hypothesis (all the more impressive since it was obtained by a skeptic trying to prove the idea wrong) that established clearly, by about 1915, that there was something in the idea of light quanta.[96]

Towards the end of his life Millikan commented on this episode:

> I spent ten years of my life testing that 1905 equation of Einstein's and contrary to all my expectations, I was compelled in 1915 to its unambiguous verification in spite of its unreasonableness.[97]

So it is not the case that a deviant group of mad scientists got together sometime at the beginning of the twentieth century and decided that they were bored with the idea of a completely 'material' world, and would therefore like to concoct a more exciting version of reality; a numinous vision within which matter was asserted to be similar to an illusion generated in some strange fashion by the operation of mind or minds. Nor did they go to bed one evening and, because of some strange *Day of the Triffids*[98] like cosmic event, wake up next morning turned into incoherent rabid mystics, somewhat akin to Franz Kafka's unfortunate protagonist in the short story *Metamorphosis*, who went to bed a human being and woke up an insect.

Quantum physics is the way it is because of the extraordinarily precise and detailed experimental evidence which clearly shows that reality is like quantum physics. In their book *Quantum Enigma*, the industrial strength quantum physicists Rosenblum and Kuttner, conclude that

...physics' encounter with consciousness, demonstrated for the small, applies to everything. And that 'everything' can include the entire Universe.[99]

The universe, then, is a quantum universe. And, as we shall see beyond scientific and philosophic doubt, from both Western and Buddhist points of view, it is a universe whose fundamental nature is consciousness. Furthermore, when the precise details of the mechanisms through which consciousness operates to create the astonishing illusion of the material world are a thoroughly illuminated, a great deal of light is thrown on fundamental issues of reality and existence, including the fundamental significance of *esoteric* religious perspectives and practices. It is a truly incredible circumstance that a precise and detailed understanding of the quantum functioning of consciousness, and therefore reality, provides a foundation for a proper appreciation of the reality and importance of the *mystical and esoteric* religious dimensions of our experience of reality.

A possible reason for the exasperation of physicists and philosophers who seem to have pledged themselves to valiantly resist the 'mystical' encroachment of consciousness into the realm of the physical lies in the exuberant claims made by a group of new age type gurus who have jumped onto the quantum band wagon with various more or less outlandish mystical claims on the basis of their interpretations of quantum mystery. The claims made for the implications of the new quantum 'spiritual' worldview seem to multiply with each new quantum–spiritual publication; and from the point of view of the materialist perspective the claims made seem outlandish. And, indeed, it might be said that *some* of the claims of *some* of the works within the terrain of 'quantum mysticism' do seem to head towards the absurd.

In 1993 the quantum physicist Amit Goswami entered the arena with his ebullient and cogently argued *The Self Aware Universe* with its spectacular claim that quantum physics proves that reality must be nothing other than consciousness; matter is an illusion generated by mind. According to Goswami all of the current problems of interpretation within quantum theory can be defused by his Idealist view that reality is a play of consciousness. As we shall see the core claims and arguments of this work are cogent and carry over seamlessly into the realm of Buddhist philosophy. However, the presentations of the quantum-mystical worldview subsequently acquired a kind of optimistic exuberance which many found distasteful.

In 1996 Fred Alan Wolf, another physicist with mystical leanings published *The Spiritual Universe: How quantum physics proves the existence of the soul*. In 2001 Goswami added yet another title to the growing list of books announcing the dawning of the age of quantum spirituality: *The Quantum Book of Life, Death, Reincarnation and Immortality*. Both authors, like others in the field, followed their respective works with a string of follow ups on similar quantum mystical topics. And recently Goswami, Wolf and others have upped the stakes in this area of controversy with their involvement with the production of the cult film *What the Bleep Do We Know*. This film is the cinematic figurehead for a movement promoting the message that anyone can transform their life once they get on the quantum bandwagon. It also appears to help if you buy lots of products from the *What the Bleep* new age internet store. It is unfortunate that the *What the Bleep* enterprise seems tailor made to cheapen and infantilize a serious and important topic. Wolf for instance gives lecture tours in the guise of Dr. Quantum; there is even a new *What the Bleep* promoted book with a cartoon of him as a kind of quantum superman.

The film has drawn considerable critical hostility because of its naïve and simplistic message that anyone can transform reality once they grasp the nature of the quantum ground within the universal consciousness; the film also seems to imply that it is possible to easily learn to manipulate the material world through conscious manipulation of the quantum ground. This apparent claim has led one critic to challenge Goswami to leap out of a 20th floor window and change material reality on the way down so that he landed unharmed[100], an easy but perhaps justified criticism which highlights the obviously deep problem which confronts anyone who wishes to claim that the material world is amenable to direct manipulation by consciousness.

The extreme advocates of the implications of quantum weirdness are spectacularly reckless in the sweeping claims that they make. Fred Alan Wolf for instance, promoting his CD *Dr Quantum Speaks: A Users Guide to your Universe*, which is part of the material offered to devotees of the *What The Bleep* enterprise, is quite brazen with his quantum optimism:

> Matter can move backward and forward in time. Objects may be in two places at once. Simply looking at an event can alter it instantaneously. Quantum physics is an astounding (and mind-boggling) field of science—but can you actually use it to change your life? The answer, teaches Dr. Quantum, is absolutely yes.

This is followed by quite blatant new age salesmanship:

> Your Mind is a Quantum Engine—Are You Ready to Fire It Up? … Prepare to Unlock Your Own Quantum Superpowers…[101]

In the face of such absurdity it is no wonder that scientists and commentators committed to a rigorous scientific paradigm lose patience. This is unfortunate because the issues concerned are of vital significance, and the truth is that the new metaphysical insights that are being, in this case carelessly, dealt with contain deep truths about the nature of reality. What is required is a detailed and rigorous investigation of the evidence. It is this need that this book attempts to address.

There are more than a few significant physicists who entertain the implication of the primacy of consciousness as being valid. Amongst those who entertain a strong emphasis, in various guises, are Andrei Linde, Eugene Wigner, Henry Stapp, Bernard D'Espagnat, Amit Goswami, David Bohm, Euan J. Squires, to name just a few. Bruce Rosenblum and Fred Kuttner, both respectable physicists who have worked in industry, have explicitly written their book *Quantum Enigma: Physics Encounters Consciousness* in order to undermine the excesses that new age mystical cults such as the *What the Bleep* brigade are currently indulging in:

> … we argue that it is a social responsibility of the physics community to openly present physics' mysterious encounter with consciousness, the quantum enigma. Only by so doing can we challenge the purveyors of pseudoscience who use the mysteries of quantum mechanics to promote their quantum nonsense.[102]

They refer to the 'confrontation with consciousness' that has been forced upon physics through its own development as 'the skeleton in the closet' which most physicists are keen to avoid confronting.

In his book *The Self Aware Universe* Amit Goswami makes the claim that all of the mysteries of quantum physics are solved when the fact that consciousness is the creator of the material world is understood; consciousness is the prime substance, not matter. This is the claim that has prompted a tirade of criticism, the main thrust of which is that the conclusions go far beyond the evidence. However, when the substance of Goswami's central claims are soberly considered his basic reasoning concerning the relationship between consciousness and matter in the light of quantum theory are actually sound. Indeed it is ironic that Rosenblum and Kuttner use the same basic arguments as Goswami to clearly demonstrate that consciousness must be implicated by quantum physics. But they take great pains to distance themselves from association with the quantum mysticism perspective; quantum physics, they say:

> hints at the existence of something beyond what we usually consider physics – beyond what we usually consider the 'physical world.' *But that's the extent of it!* Physics can certainly suggest directions for speculation. We should, however, be careful – in dealing with the mysteries of quantum mechanisms, we walk the edge of a slippery slope.[103]

And the slippery slope, Rosenblum and Kuttner rightly say, is exemplified by the *What the Bleep* film 'with its implication of a quantum connection with the channeling of a 35,000 year old Atlantis god named Ramtha and other such nonsense.'[104]

According to Rosenblum and Kuttner the correct antidote to this kind of nonsense is for the physics community to come clean about the 'skeleton in the closet' which is the inevitable intrusion of consciousness into the quantum realm. In this way, it is supposed, it will be possible to keep a lid on wild speculation; and an important feature of such a policing of inter-pretations and speculations is that it requires some way of determining when boundaries have been breached:

> A touchstone test for such misuse is the presentation of these ideas with the implication that the notions promulgated are derived from quantum physics rather than merely suggested by it.[105]

This, however, leaves significant latitude for a more circumspect and balan-ced investigation of the implications of quantum mystery. Indeed where exactly is the boundary between 'derivation' and 'suggestion'; isn't the boundary, to a large extent, a matter of subjective interpretation, or even taste?

The philosopher of science Arthur Fine suggested the notion of the natural ontological attitude (NOA) to indicate the innate tendency for the embodied psyche of human beings to impute a world of 'real' independently existing objects as existing in an external 'reality' as being the most comfortable and natural way of conceiving the experiential world. Because of this 'natural' manner of viewing things it takes less compelling evidence to accede to this way of looking at the world than it does to see it from a counter intuitive point of view, even if the counter intuitive view is more in keeping with the actual way of things.

The viewpoint of the natural ontological attitude, of course, is exactly the view of inherently existent independent things, which as we have briefly seen is repudiated by both quantum theory and Buddhist philosophy, both of which 'suggest' an interdependent and interconnected field of phenomena. However, because the appearance of the world in its NOA aspect is so overwhelmingly persuasive in its sheer immediacy to our senses, the evidence required for an explanation from the NOA point of view is generally much less stringent than for a counter intuitive account. This is perhaps one of the reasons (along with distaste for a 35,000 year old Atlantis god named Ramtha) why Rosenblum and Kuttner, for example, writing fifty years after many of the great early quantum physicists committed themselves to a primacy of consciousness ontology, are apparently so cagey on the issue of the primacy of consciousness, despite the overwhelming cogency of the evidence which they themselves present. In other words they require much greater weight of evidence before they will employ the word 'derived' over and above the term 'suggested'. But this really is a matter of subjective preference for emphasis than a rigorous logical determination.

Certainly the fact that a bunch of new-age entrepreneurs, for want of a better phrase – which is the way in which the new-age type quantum mystics are viewed by more down to earth materialist-leaning scientists and philosophers – have decided to take a leaf out of the book of the millionaire Christian tele-evangelists and do the same with the implications of quantum theory should not stop serious investigation into the 'directions for speculation' that physics 'suggests'; and, as the authors of *Quantum Enigma* state quite clearly:

> There is no way to interpret quantum theory without in some way addressing consciousness.[106]

The direction that physics is pointing us is towards consciousness as a fundamental requirement of reality.

In his recent book *Physics and Philosophy* the physicist and philosopher Bernard d'Espagnat, having reached the conclusion that physics is incapable of ever unveiling the nature of a quantum 'veiled' reality conceived of as existing separately and independently of consciousness suggests that insights into the nature of reality might very well come from other directions amongst which he cites mysticism[107]. In particular he refers to Buddhist thought which:

> ...rejects the notion of a 'ground of things' and even lays stress on the opposite notion, the one of an 'absence of foundation' or 'emptiness.'[108]

The concept of *shunyata*, usually translated as 'Emptiness', lies at the core of one of the most rigorous, precise and profound conceptual and philosophical analysis of the nature of reality ever undertaken; the central Mahayana philosophy of the Madhyamaka, or the Middle Way. And, as we shall see, this exhilarating analysis of the nature of reality can actually begin to unravel some of the interpretative conflicts and confusions within quantum philosophy.

Emptiness is both a simple and very complex concept which has many levels of meaning which unfold as its aspects are explored and understood, both intellectually and experientially. As indicated previously it is vital to understand that Emptiness does not mean nothingness. Emptiness is intimately connected with the idea of inherent existence; what phenomena are 'empty of' is 'inherent existence,' 'ultimately established existence' or 'true existence,' there are various synonyms for this notion. When the elements of the everyday world are rigorously analyzed they are found to lack a solid inner core or essence. This is because everything in the universe depends on other causes and conditions; there is nothing, therefore, anywhere to be found which exists solely because of its own independent essence:

> ...all phenomena originate from infinite interdependent causes and conditions and thus lack any intrinsic nature ...[109]

According to the view of the Madhyamaka there is a mistaken attribution of an inherent, independent own-nature built into the very process of perception. This means that the idea of objects existing in their own right is instinctively superimposed on all everyday experiences. There is, in other words, a mistake built into the very heart of perception; objects which in reality are 'empty' of inherent existence are routinely experienced as if they were inherently existent. According to Buddhist thought this mistaken mode of perception is very deep within the process of reality; it is in fact the mechanism which actually creates an illusion of a dualistic world.

It is important to be aware that this mistake, which resides within the perception of experience, is not an obvious blunder which can be put right simply. The idea that a Zen master simply needs to utter some Zen koan, such as one should not 'mistake the finger for the moon' or some such, in order for a whole new way of perception to instantaneously emerge, is overplayed; in general it requires the use of the sophisticated techniques of analysis and meditation practice techniques for developing insight. The mistaken mode of perception lies deep beneath surface levels of consciousness and because of this the Buddhist methods of practice such as the Madhyamaka have had to develop very subtle analyses in order to demonstrate the operation of Emptiness in the everyday world. The techniques of the Madhyamaka deconstruct the usual mode of perception in order to reveal a whole new dimension within reality. It is like looking at a magic eye picture, to begin with there is nothing there but suddenly a whole new 3-D image snaps into place when the eyes focus correctly.

The Buddhist doctrine of the two truths divides experiential reality into the spheres of the 'seeming' and the 'ultimate' and thus introduces a fundamental distinction within our understanding of what is real, depending the mode of perception:

> Thus two kinds of world are seen:
> The one of yogins and the one of common people.
> Here, the world of common people
> Is invalidated by the world of yogins.[110]

The 'seeming' or 'conventional' mode of perception, which corresponds to the 'classical' realm of modern physics, is the way that the world of phenomena *appears* within the experiential continuums of embodied, and unenlightened, sentient beings, who are reliant upon 'physical' sense organs and the structures of perception which interpret the incoming 'signals'. As Frank Wilczek points out:

> ...we build our world models from strange raw materials: signal-processing tools 'designed' by evolution to filter a universe swarming with information into a very few streams of incoming data. Data streams? Their more familiar names are vision, hearing, smell and so forth.[111]

For a long time it has been quite clear that the experiential field which is presented within the consciousness of any sentient being can only be a construction and interpretation based on the meeting of sense faculties and the incoming 'data streams.' As a consequence the nature of the 'data stream' itself, as it is independent of the interpretative activities of the senses, became a matter of great scientific and philosophical interest. And the most significant answer provided by science to date is that the nature of the unobserved 'stuff' of the data-streaming is 'quantum' in nature.

As we shall see, a recent understanding of this data-streaming 'stuff' of reality, which Wilczek calls the 'Grid'[112], is that it is 'epiontic' 'dream stuff', a designation which when fully appreciated can only mean that it is a kind of awareness-stuff that is capable of creating the remarkable intersubjective 'dream' of an independently existing 'material' world (*epiontic* means that the activity of perception creates ontology). Thus the Buddhist division of reality into the 'seeming' and the 'ultimate' is mirrored within modern physics by the fundamental distinction between the 'classical' realm, the everyday realm we are all familiar with, and the 'quantum' realm.

The fundamental Buddhist distinction into the seeming, or conventional, and the ultimate depends on the *mode of perception of the same fundamental reality*. The 'Magic Eye' analogy is useful in this context. Magic Eye images on first viewing seem quite two dimensional and unremarkable but when viewed in a particular manner produce a three dimensional image which is quite different from the bland two-dimensional image. There is nothing altered in the actual picture, it is the mode of perception that is changed. For 'common' people, those who have not achieved the insight of 'yogic' perception, the ordinary everyday world of materiality appears quite naturally as an independent realm which is the source of the experience of an external reality. The seeming world functions as if there were independent inherent entities and processes.

These entities within the seeming world are called by the Madhyamaka 'functioning things' precisely because they do function as if they were 'things'; but when analysed the 'thingness', or inherent existence, disappears. Seeming reality appears to the vast majority of beings to be solid and truly existent, but according to the Madhyamaka analysis it is deceptive; and the reason that the 'seeming' reality is said to be deceptive is simply that when it is analysed it is found to not exist in the way that it appears to:

> [The seeming] is not a stable reality, because it does not withstand analysis and because it does not appear as an object of the meditative equipoise of the noble ones ...[113]

The Madhyamaka practitioners were not merely philosophers; they also investigated the nature of reality through profound meditation techniques. They therefore analysed their experience of reality through both reason and also direct meditative investigation.

The Madhyamaka asserts the possibility of having a direct experience of ultimate reality which lies beyond the duality which is a feature of ordinary perception in the everyday world. Such perception, however, is achieved by very few determined practitioners who achieve extraordinary meditative abilities. The conclusions which Madhyamikas reached through reasoning were put to the test empirically, although the kind of empiricism involved is rejected, wrongly, within Western thought.

The process of the Madhyamaka conceptual deconstruction takes place in stages, each stage depending on the starting view, or configuration of consciousness, of the person concerned. Within the various schools of Mahayana views of reality there are various outlooks on the nature of the process of reality which can be considered to be conceptual frameworks of perception on a graduated path of deepening understanding. Each view presents a fixed delineation of reality for exploration:

> Also the yogins, due to differences in insight,
> Are overruled by successively superior ones.[114]

The Prasangika is the final phase of the analysis within which it is comprehended that all views fail to capture the profound ultimate nature of the process of reality.

The Madhyamaka viewpoint adopts a clear distinction between a manner of argument which dogmatically asserts conceptual formulations to be exact descriptions of a separate and completely describable reality, and a manner which considers that theoretical argument is a matter of employing conceptual tools to elucidate aspects of reality towards a greater understanding of the interconnected process of what appears to be a 'reality'. This is the process of 'cleansing the face of wisdom':

> It's just as if the sun's eclipse is taking place,
> You see reflections of its changing shapes. To say the sun and its reflection
> Touch or do not touch would indeed be absurd.
> Such things arise dependently and on the level of convention.
> Reflections are not real, but using them we smarten our appearance.
> In just the same way we should understand that arguments
> That have the power to cleanse the face of wisdom.[115]

When watching a reflection of an eclipse of the sun, in a mirror or pool of water, to speak of separate, inherently existent phenomena touching or not touching is beside the point and meaningless. In one sense the reflection is the eclipse; in another it is completely different. This is the way things are within the causal nexus of dependently originated phenomena, and the situation of a reflection of a shadow is certainly an example of an interconnected and dependently arisen situation.

In this context the reflection stands in for the conceptual systems of Madhyamaka[116] thought. The actual eclipse, of course, is the ultimate nature to be understood by applying the conceptual reflections of thought. Whilst these conceptual systems are not 'real', they are, however, part of the interconnected process of using thought in order to understand reality. Such conceptual pictures do not touch or not touch the ultimate nature because they are not separate entities which could enter into this kind of relationship to a separate ultimate reality. This highlights the fact that, for the Madhyamika philosophers, such conceptual systems are employed within a process of training the minds of practitioners to comprehend the nature of the process of reality in increasingly subtle levels of precision, but they do not *directly describe* the exact nature of the ultimate reality.

The final, dramatic, phase of the Madhyamaka movement of thought is when Emptiness is applied to itself:

> What is dependent origination
> Is explained as emptiness.
> It is a dependent designation
> And in itself the middle path.[117]

Here Emptiness is identified as a 'dependent designation'. It is because everything which seems to 'exist' is actually dependent on a web of interconnectivity that phenomena are empty. But the Madhyamaka system is subtle; Emptiness itself is a dependent designation, so Emptiness itself is empty. In other words the Madhyamaka deconstructs itself in the last phase of understanding; only a self deconstructing system can deconstruct the illusion of reality in order to reveal the true nature beyond concepts. It is important to understand however that the deconstruction will not be effective unless the configuration of consciousness is prepared through the necessary analysis and meditation. Simply reading 'existence is neither this nor that' is not going to do the trick.

What has all this to do with quantum physics? In his book *Choosing Reality* B. Alan Wallace makes the following observation concerning the possibility of discovering a final overarching Theory of Everything in terms of inherent existence:

> …there is a strong human urge to formulate grand unified theories, while rejecting evidence that does not fit. The assumption underlying this motive is that reality itself is one grand unified system that can be represented by our theories. If this assumption is unfounded, the quest for an ultimate, comprehensive supertheory is futile. In that case we must be satisfied with the more modest pursuit of developing complementary theories, each one seen as relative to the mode of questioning that produced it.[118]

Wallace calls this viewpoint the principle of 'ontological relativity'. The fundamental insight of this perspective, outlined in *Hidden Dimensions*, is that it is the nature of the process of reality to reveal itself within experience in a multitude of forms dependent upon the nature of questioning, or perceiving, which is undertaken by the sentient beings that are the perceiving agents of the process of reality. This multitudinous interdependent revelation of the potentialities of the process of reality takes place at all levels of manifestation. As we shall see it is the nature of the quantum process of reality that holds the key to a deep comprehension of the nature of this unfolding of the potentialities of existence.

In the commentary to the *Adornment of the Middle Way* the nineteenth century Tibetan scholar Ju Mipham wrote that:

> ... even though there is an infinite variety of beliefs; none of them ever gets beyond the assumption of true existence.[119]

The Madhyamaka analysis indicates that whenever the assumption that there are truly existent entities, or truly existent processes, forms the foundation of a view of the totality of reality, the resulting conceptual system will be ultimately internally inconsistent. Such internally inconsistent systems will automatically generate an alternative view which highlights the inconsistencies in the original system. Any view that begins with the assertion of the reality of inherent existence, therefore, will lead to a proliferation of alternative, equally inconsistent and unsatisfactory views.

In his book *Quantum Reality* Nick Herbert identifies eight different interpretations, or views, concerning what quantum theory really means. The eight views identified by Herbert are:

- **Copenhagen interpretation part 1** – there is no deep quantum reality, it's all a fiction. Herbert attributes this view to Niels Bohr: 'Bohr does not deny the evidence of his senses. The world around us is real enough, but it floats on a world that is not real. Everyday phenomena are themselves built not out of phenomena but out of an utterly different kind of being.'[120] Aside from the configuration of the attribution of reality, this view corresponds remarkably well with the Madhyamaka view of Emptiness as being the 'utterly different kind of being' that underpins the everyday world.
- **Copenhagen interpretation part 2** – reality is created by observation: 'What we see is undoubtedly real ... but these phenomena are not really there in the absence of observation'[121]
- **Reality is an undivided wholeness** – this is the view that David Bohm presented in his significant book *Wholeness and the Implicate Order*: 'The inseparable quantum interconnectedness of the whole universe is the fundamental reality.'[122]
- **Many worlds interpretation** – According to Herbert: 'Of all the claims of the New Physics none is more outrageous than the contention that myriads of universes are created upon the occasion of each measurement act.'[123]
- **Quantum logic** – the world is non logical or has a different logic to humans: 'the quantum revolution goes so deep that ... to cope with

the quantum facts we must scrap our very mode of reasoning, in favour of a new quantum logic.'[124]

- **Neo realism** – the world must be real, quantum physics is wrong. In other words the quantum world is just like the everyday world.
- **Consciousness creates reality**: 'only an apparatus endowed with consciousness ... is privileged to create reality.'[125]
- **The world consists of potentials and actualities** – 'The duplex world of Werner Heisenberg ... the unmeasured world is merely semireal and achieves full reality status during the act of observation...'[126]

Rosenblum and Kuttner, in their more recent work *Quantum Enigma*, give nine, briefly and simplistically described they are:

- **Copenhagen**: Quantum theory is a convenient way of speaking about reality as we experience it. The entities described are weird but as we don't see them we need not worry about this. The only reality worth bothering with is everyday reality, which we definitely know is real. This is the 'interpretation' that one of the founding fathers of quantum theory, Niels Bohr, bullied some of his colleagues into believing.
- **Extreme Copenhagen**: The viewpoint developed by Bohr's son and his colleague Ole Ulfbeck. According to this view quantum theory is a convenient fiction. In actuality atoms and their quantum components do not exist.
- **Decoherence:** The everyday world of big objects overwhelms the vulnerable tiny world of the quantum realm and forces it to behave properly.
- **Many Worlds**: At every moment in time countless numbers of new realities are springing into existence. An inhabitant of one universe at one moment in time is, unknowingly and unceremoniously, rent into countless copies, existing within a vast number of newly created 'parallel universes' in the next moment. These copies are relentlessly projected into the multitude of new 'parallel' realities constantly being created by the quantum process of the 'multiverse'.
- **Transactional**: Reality is produced by a two way quantum interaction which takes place both forwards and backwards in time.
- **Bohm**: David Bohm is usually described as a maverick physicist because of his unconventional views. In his early phase he suggested that quantum particles were guided by quantum waves. Later he suggested that reality consisted of a complex interlinking network of enfolded 'orders' of consciousness.

- **Ghirardi, Rimini and Weber**: Quantum waves are unstable and because of this every hundred million years or so a wave will turn into particle and this causes other waves to also turn into particles.
- **Ithaca:** Only quantum correlations are real.
- **Quantum Logic:** We need a new logic to describe things.

Generally speaking all of these views are considered to be mutually exclusive, they are considered to be inherently real interpretations of reality. In a later chapter, however, we shall see that, when they are divested of their claim to ultimate and inherent objective reality, most of them may be considered, to a greater or lesser extent, as different dualistic perspectives upon a common nondual empirically transcendent reality.

The Madhyamaka asserts that whenever a conceptual framework starts from a belief in inherent existence then a proliferation of views will follow. This tendency was clearly indicated by the great founder of the Madhyamaka, Nagarjuna:

> This situation seems to have provided for Nagarjuna but one instance of the inveterate tendency of the human mind, the tendency to cling, to seize. This tendency, which functions under a false imagination and not on right understanding, is the root of suffering in life and of dead-ends and conflict in understanding.[127]

In quantum physics we certainly find a proliferation of views. So it might be pertinent to ask if the issue of inherent existence has got anything to do with this situation. The answer, which is demonstrated in the following pages, is that all these views operate from the basis of a belief in a definite inherently existent reality to some degree. One of the central messages of all forms of Buddhist philosophy is, however, that the process of reality is not inherently existent!

In order to clarify the quantum situation we shall employ the deep analysis of the Madhyamaka and apply the ideas of Emptiness to the quantum situation. When we do this we find that an answer to John Wheeler's important question 'How come the quantum?', and therefore a possible answer to his further question 'How come existence?' naturally emerges. It will become clear that some of these viewpoints are, to some degree, partial disclosures of a realm which by its very nature cannot be caught within one fixed conceptual formulation. But we shall also find that some are closer to the truth than others.

Within the scope of Buddhism there are both Realist and Idealist interpretations of reality but the most significant perspective is the Madhyamaka concept of 'Emptiness' that goes beyond these extremes to articulate the nature of reality in a manner not achieved in the modern West. Emptiness can be considered to be the creative realm of indeterminacy beyond the concepts within which human thought is generally trapped. Its articulation within the philosophical vehicle of the Madhyamaka is by no means a matter of Eastern inscrutability or vagueness; it is, rather, razor sharp and crystalline in precision. The view of Emptiness develops through a spectacularly precise and breathtakingly profound analysis of the way that human conceptuality functions in relation to what is supposed to be ultimate reality. As the analysis progresses so also does the view of reality. The conceptual unveiling of illusion moves from one point of view to another through increasingly subtle phases until there is no further view to move to; which is the introduction to Emptiness.

The metaphysical-epistemological analysis called the Yogachara-Vijnanavada, or Cognition-Only, school of Buddhism also has important connections with the current revelations within quantum physics. Both indicate that consciousness is the primary constituent of the process of reality. According to the Yogachara perspective the external world, which seems to be composed of matter, is a projection by mind of seemingly externally independent and separate entities; a projection based on the web of interdependent experiential appearances. Because of our inescapable familiarity with the solidity of what appears to be an external world, the deeply rooted conception develops that there must be external entities that correspond to the repeated experience of solidity. Furthermore the more the dualistic world is perceived in this manner the more its appearance is solidified.

As we shall see this mistaken view of an external realm of independent materiality is logically demolished by Madhyamaka reasoning, leading to the conclusion that:

> Finding no perceiving subject and no thing perceived
> And understanding that the triple world is merely consciousness,
> The Bodhisattvas[128], … abide in wisdom,
> Knowing that the mind alone is ultimate reality.[129]

The actual demonstration depends, in part, upon the logical process of determining the exact manner in which the perceiver and that which is perceived can be isolated as separate entities independently of each other. The result is the realisation that neither entity actually exists independently of the other. This logical conclusion echoes Bohr's conclusion from quantum evidence that:

> Now, the quantum postulate implies that any observation of atomic phenomena will involve an interaction with the agency of observation not to be neglected. Accordingly, an independent reality in the ordinary physical sense can neither be ascribed to the phenomena nor the agencies of observation.[130]

But whereas Bohr's observation relates to the microscopic world, the Madhyamaka assertion regarding the lack of separation between perceiver and perceived applies to all levels of reality. The Madhyamaka analysis actually reveals the quantum nature of the macroscopic world; it is able, therefore, to address the important issue of the quantum split between microscopic and macroscopic.

Of particular relevance in this context is the doctrine of the two levels of reality, or the two truths. The two truths are the conventional truth of everyday reality and the ultimate truth of the indeterminate nature of reality. These two are also denoted as the seeming and the ultimate:

> The Knower of the world distinguished these two realities.
> The one is the seeming and the other the ultimate–
> There is no other third reality [131]

For ordinary beings the appearance of macroscopic reality is a 'seeming' reality that obscures the actual ultimate nature in which all phenomena are indeterminate and illusion-like. This division of reality into two levels maps directly onto the dichotomy between the quantum level and the experiential macroscopic level of the everyday world.

The profound understanding that all phenomena have no determinate core of substantial reality is repeatedly demonstrated within the Madhyamaka analysis. The seeming reality of the everyday world is taken as the ground from which the analysis begins; a thorough analysis, however, reveals repeated signs that point towards the ultimate nature:

> These phenomena are like bubbles of foam …
> Like illusions, like lightening in the sky,
> Like water-moons; like mirages. [132]

This is not to say that there is absolutely nothing; but rather there is nothing substantial to be found in the manifestation of the seeming play of appearances.

The Madhyamaka is not only capable of elucidating the way that quantum paradoxes can fit into a harmonious worldview; it also provides a much needed antidote to the rampant materialist realism that still underpins the mainstream Western scientific and philosophical perspective. The Madhyamaka analysis forces us to examine our conceptual pictures of reality at a very deep and subtle level. It asks us to answer the question of whether the various models of reality which are taken for granted without a deep analysis are coherent with some of our very basic assumptions about reality. The most fundamental question posed by the Madhyamaka is whether the elements that we postulate as comprising the 'real' world actually fulfill the requirements of what we think a 'real' thing should be. The image of a 'real' phenomenon that has always been basic to physics is exactly that of independent self sufficient 'particles' and their counterparts, the nebulous fields whose presence is detected by their effects on the relevant particles.

Both of these entities are generally considered to be inherently existent phenomena.

The notion of self-sufficient independent elements of reality has profound implications for the way we must expect the fundamental features of reality to exist. If this foundational picture of reality is correct then it should be possible to find elements of reality which are completely independent and not reliant on any other elements; and such self enclosed, independent elements cannot be caused by other elements because to be caused is to be dependent. This is crucial, to be caused is to be dependent and therefore a caused phenomenon cannot be an elementary basic self-enclosed feature of reality.

Such a view of reality has been completely shattered by quantum theory. In all experiments at the quantum level the appearance of a particle aspect or a field aspect, i.e. a wave, crucially depends upon the entire constellation of the experimental setup:

> An electron's so called attributes belong jointly to the electron
> and the measuring device.[133]

And, in the last analysis, this interdependence seems to include, to some degree, the consciousness of the experimenter or experimenters. It quite clearly follows therefore that the entities which are supposed to be fully 'real' do not fulfill the requirements that we expect from truly real aspects of reality because they do not exist independently by themselves.

This situation is precisely analyzed by the Madhyamaka in its investigation into the nature of the reality on an ultimate level. According to Madhyamaka reasoning a 'real' independent feature of reality must have an inner essence, a self power which depends on nothing else, at its core. This requirement, which is given the technical term 'inherent existence' or 'true existence' (*svabhava*), is absolutely essential if we wish to hold up the entity as it were and say 'this is real'. To assert this degree of reality must be to assert that this entity depends on nothing else, and if we are looking for an ultimate independent reality upon which we wish to construct all other experienced features of reality this stringent requirement is essential. However when all phenomena are closely examined there is nothing which exhibits the required self containment to act as an ultimate entity:

> Since there is no phenomenon
> That is not dependently originating,
> There is no phenomenon
> That is not empty.[134]

This argument from dependent origination, the fact that everything comes into manifestation in dependence on other phenomena, is called the King of Reasonings by the Madhyamaka because it is a simple, yet irrefutable, demonstration of the central assertion of the Madhyamaka; there is nothing in the entire universe, or multiverse, of reality that is not 'empty' of inherent existence; which means the kind of absolutely independent features of reality which have always been assumed by physics to be fundamental simply do not exist.

Far from being vague and inscrutable, the minds of the Yogachara, Chittamatra and Madhyamaka philosophers that feature in the following pages: Nagarjuna, Aryadeva, Kamalashila, Asanga, Shantarakshita, Shantideva, Dharmakirti, Chandrakirti, to mention a few, are some of the most brilliant and incisive tools of analytic investigation ever to turn attention onto the task of elucidating the nature of reality. The magnificent intellectual vehicle of discovery that they left to us, little known to the West outside of a small circle of Buddhist scholars, is capable of elucidating problems of the conceptual interpretation of the paradoxes of quantum physics and philosophy. In the following pages you will discover that the answers which emerge are astonishing; the Yogachara-Chittamatra and Madhyamaka perspectives offer a dramatic and dazzling perspective upon the quantum ultimate nature of reality.

Note: In this chapter 'Emptiness' has been emphasised with a capital 'E' to emphasise that it is a Buddhist technical term denoting the ultimate ground and nature of reality which is not equivalent to 'nothingness.' The point now having been made, future chapters will simply use the more natural 'emptiness.'

Bohr and Einstein discussing the nature of reality - in this picture Einstein looks smug and Bohr looks rattled. This is because Einstein thinks he has got the better of Bohr in having disproved a vital ingredient in the new quantum understanding of reality. Bohr stayed up all night to discover Einstein's mistake. Next morning at breakfast Einstein's smugness was demolished![135]

Bohr and Einstein debating the nature of reality (2).

Tibetan monks debating the nature of reality.

Interconnected
Lightness of Being

There is a wonderful net which has been hung by some cunning artificer in such a manner that it stretches out indefinitely in all directions. In accordance with the extravagant tastes of deities, the artificer has hung a single glittering jewel at the net's every node, and since the net itself is infinite in dimension, the jewels are infinite in number. There hang the jewels, glittering like stars of the first magnitude, a wonderful sight to behold. If we now arbitrarily select one of these jewels for inspection and look closely at it, we will discover that in its polished surface there are reflected all the other jewels in the net, infinite in number. Not only that, but each of the jewels reflected in this one jewel is also reflecting all the other jewels, so that the process of reflection is infinite.[136]

-Avatamsaka Sutra

There is a ghostly web of quantum connections crisscrossing the universe and coupling you and me to every last bit of matter in the most distant galaxy. We live in a telepathic universe. What this actually means physicists have not yet figured out.[137]

-Marcus Chown

Light is this background which is all one but its information content has the capacity for immense diversity. Light can carry information about the entire universe.[138]

-David Bohm

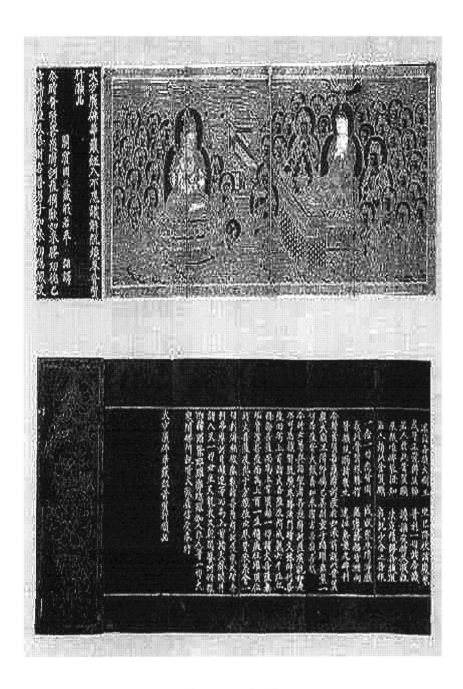

Avatamsaka Sutra

In a recent work offering simplified explanations of cutting edge theories of physics about the ultimate nature of the universe the popular mass consumption science writer Marcus Chown claims that the everyday phenomenon of partial reflection by glass, the fact that in many situations a glass window will produce a faint reflection of someone looking through it, tells us:

> ...something profound and shocking about fundamental reality. It is telling you that the Universe, at its deepest level, is founded on randomness and unpredictability, the capricious role of a dice – that, ultimately, things happen for no reason at all.[139]

We shall see in this chapter that this claim is false; in fact the phenomenon of the 'face in the window'[140] tells a very different story.

The situation in which the phenomenon of partial reflection is most apparent, of course, is night time when the room one is looking out from is lighted; in this situation the reflection of the observer looking out is generally very clear. This indicates the fact that about 5% of the light which falls upon the window from the interior lighted room is reflected back. The great twentieth century physicist Richard Feynman tells us that this physical occurrence has long been a great mystery, impenetrable to great scientists like Newton and Huygens, both of whom devoted a great deal of thought and investigation concerning the nature of light. Indeed, as we shall see, the phenomenon still remains deeply mysterious, and deeply revelatory of a surprising and remarkable fact about the nature of ultimate reality. But this deep truth does not indicate a fundamentally random nature within the ultimate functioning of the universe; in fact the truth is far from this conclusion.

Before delving into the details of the phenomena of partial reflection however, it will be useful to familiarize ourselves with the nature of light as understood by modern physics. Throughout history there have been two competing theories concerning the nature of light: the particle theory and the wave theory. This division of opinion began in early Greek thought, the 5th century BC Greek philosopher Empedocles thought that mysterious rays shone out from the eyes, whilst Lucretius was the first we know of to propose that light consisted of a stream of particles:

> The light and heat of the sun; these are composed of minute atoms which, when they are shoved off, lose no time in shooting right across the interspace of air in the direction of the shove.[141]

In the late 1600's Western thought also divided into two basic camps. Descartes, for instance suggested that space was filled with a 'plenum' which transmitted pressures created by a light source onto the eyes. Christian Huygens and Robert Hooke extended Descartes' viewpoint by proposing a fully fledged wave theory of light. Newton took the opposing view that light is corpuscular, which is to say that light consists of particles. The problem in fully deciding the issue was that there appeared to be evidence for both viewpoints, but at the time the evidence for the corpuscular view seemed more cogent. For instance light always travels in straight lines but it was known at the time that wave motion should give rise to a ripple-like spreading behavior which can be observed in water waves and the evidence for such wavelike behavior in light phenomena was not compelling at the time.

However the English physicist Thomas Young carried out an important series of experiments in the late eighteenth century which provided significant evidence for the wave theory of light. The modern version of Young's experiment is the double slit experiment which is described in the next chapter. At the beginning of the nineteenth century the investigations carried out by Augustin Jean Fresnal of the phenomenon of diffraction, which is the way in which a light beam which is interrupted by an object forms a pattern of light and dark rings on a screen, due to the same kind of interference effect (fig 2.1), provided overwhelming evidence for the wave nature of light.

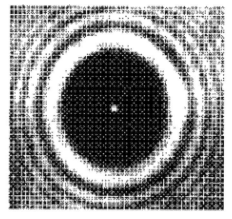

Fig 2.1

In the 1860's the work of James Clerk Maxwell established that light consisted of an interrelated twofold wave motion of electric and magnetic fields. The electric component of the wave vibrates at a right angle (90°) to the magnetic component and vice versa. When explaining how an electromagnetic wave 'propagates', or travels, through space physicists suggest that the electric disturbance drives the magnetic phase and vice versa. The electromagnetic wave is conceived of as a self-sustaining, or self-reinforcing, energetic field of radiation (fig 2.2).

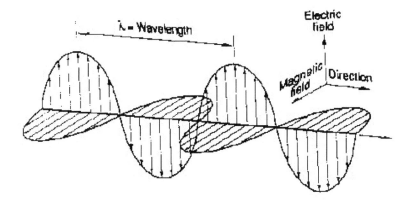

Fig 2.2

When considering fundamental aspects of electromagnetic waves, or in fact any wave, significant features such as wavelength, frequency and amplitude are defined in terms of a wave represented as vibrating in just one dimension. Fig 2.3 indicates the two fundamental defining features of any wave, its amplitude, which is the maximum extent of transverse vibration, and its wavelength, the distance between the same point on one wave and its successor wave cycle.

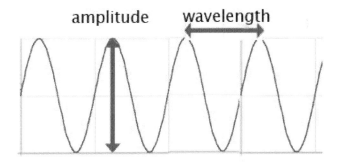

Fig 2.3

The frequency of a wave is the number of times it vibrates in one second (fig 2.4), the higher the frequency the greater the energy of the wave. The wavelength and frequency are related; shorter wavelengths have higher frequencies, in mathematical terms the frequency is the inverse of wave-length. The frequency of an electromagnetic wave ranges over a spectrum as

Frequency

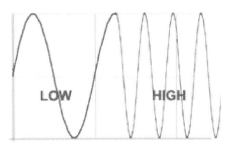

Fig 2.4

shown in fig 2.5 and the type of electromagnetic wave depends on the frequency (or wavelength). Radio waves for instance have long wavelengths and low frequency, visible light has much shorter wavelengths and higher frequencies. Below the visible spectrum there is the infra-red, microwave and radio frequencies; above the visible spectrum there are the shorter wavelengths and higher frequencies of ultra-violet, x-rays and gamma-radiation.

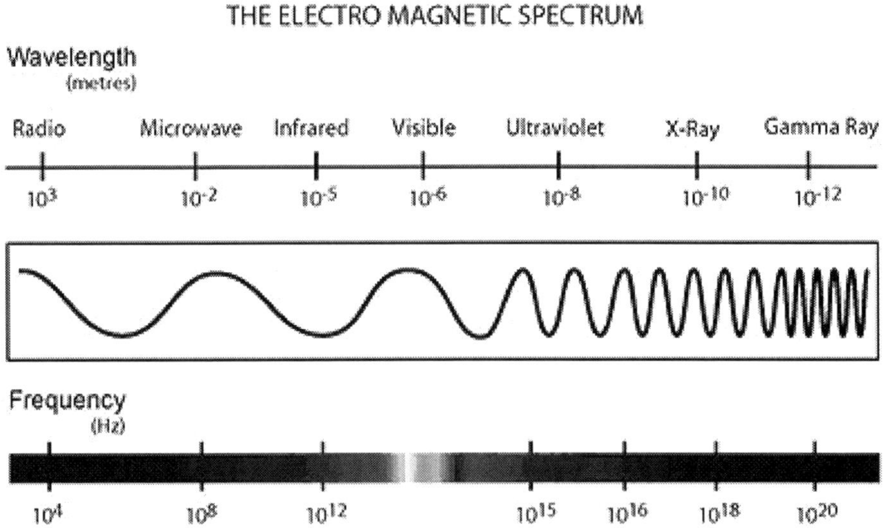

THE ELECTRO MAGNETIC SPECTRUM

Wavelength
(metres)

Radio	Microwave	Infrared	Visible	Ultraviolet	X-Ray	Gamma Ray
10^3	10^{-2}	10^{-5}	10^{-6}	10^{-8}	10^{-10}	10^{-12}

Frequency
(Hz)

| 10^4 | 10^8 | 10^{12} | | 10^{15} | 10^{16} | 10^{18} | 10^{20} |

Fig 2.5

Max Planck (1901)

According to 'classical', pre-quantum theory (roughly speaking prior to 1900) electromagnetic radiation was considered to be continuous. In 1900 Max Planck used a mathematical trick in order to solve an important outstanding problem of physics, 'black body' radiation, which overturned this view. This problem concerned the way in which light radiation was emitted from perfect absorbers of light, which are called 'black bodies' because they appear black precisely because they absorb all light frequencies. Planck's mathematical trick, which he described as 'an act of desperation', required that he made the non-classical assumption that radiation could only be emitted or absorbed in discrete units, or 'quanta', rather than continuously. With this assumption he was able to derive the correct equation for black body radiation whereas all other attempts had failed. With this achievement Planck unknowingly instigated the quantum era.

Planck, however, was quite a conservative fellow and apparently was a little nervous about upsetting the classical barrel. Einstein however, made of sterner stuff, seized Planck's discovery and used it to solve the problem of the photoelectric effect, for which he was awarded a Nobel Prize. When a beam of light is shone onto a metal plate electrons are emitted from the plate. Classical physicists were puzzled by the fact that the energy of the emitted electrons did not depend on the intensity of the incident light but depended on the frequency, the speed of vibration, of the light. This behavior was contrary to classical expectations; according to classical theory the energy of the emitted electrons should have been proportional to the amplitude (the extent of wave oscillation), which was assumed to be an indication of the amount of energy carried by the wave. Experiment, however, showed that the energy of the emitted electrons depended on the frequency of the light.

Einstein showed that the effect could be accounted for by assuming that the incident light was made up of individual wave-units, 'wave-particles' of light which were later called photons (fig 2.6). One photon would knock one electron out of the metal and the energy of the emitted electron depended on the frequency of the photon; the higher the frequency the greater the energy of the emitted electrons. The important point in this view of light is that it was now shown to be made of particles, or photons, of electromagnetic wave motion! This is an example of the famous wave-particle duality nature of the quantum world.

In 1905 Einstein suggested that a beam of light 'consists of a finite number of energy quanta, localised at points of space, which move without subdividing and are absorbed or emitted only as units.'[142] At the time, however, Einstein's proposal was greeted with little enthusiasm within the physics community, which received the idea of a light being comprised of individual units 'with disbelief and skepticism bordering on derision.'[143] The idea that light could be considered to be a particle and a wave at the same time was simply too outlandish for the classical minds of the time. Today, however, this is the image that physicists use; a ray of light is conceived of as consisting of a beam of wave-particles of electromagnetic energy called photons.

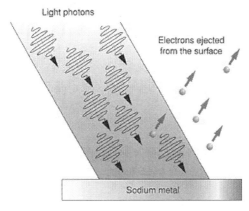

Fig 2.6

We are now ready to return to the phenomenon of partial reflection (fig 2.7). The first question that arises is clearly: what is the difference between those photons that pass through the glass and those that are reflected? How do the 5% that get reflected 'know' that they are the ones to get reflected rather than transmitted? According to the physical picture of the nature of light all photons are supposed to be the same. But suppose we make a first attempt to answer this conundrum by supposing that there are two, subtly different, types of photon involved, the first type having some kind of internal mechanism or characteristic which marks it out as one of those to be reflected whilst the second has a corresponding internal mark of being a reflected type of photon. This explanation will not do simply because if we were to let the beam made up of the 95% of transmitted photons, which should all be of the 'transmittable' type of photon, fall upon a second identical pane of glass in exactly the same way as the first pane, then 5% of those photons would be reflected, even though they should, according to our attempted explanation, be transmitted.

This kind of behavior, in which quantum entities seem to change their mode of operation according to some apparent quantum whim, seems to be a favorite trick of photons and other quantum entities. Another example involves photons encountering semi-silvered mirrors. When a beam of photons is directed at a semi-silvered mirror 50% of the incident beam will be transmitted and 50% will be reflected. If we pass the 50% transmitted beam through two further semi-silvered mirrors as shown in fig 2.8 we get the transmission/reflection configuration shown in the figure.

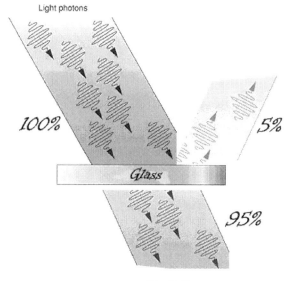

Fig 2.7

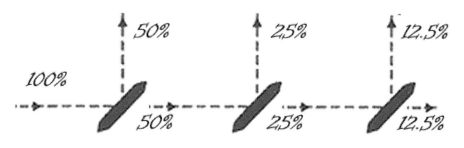

Fig 2.8

Now if we think that whether an individual photon is transmitted or reflected depends upon the intrinsic nature of the photon this is an extremely surprising situation. In order to emphasize just how surprising this quantum behavior is Jeffrey Satinover, in his book *The Quantum Brain*, gives the following analogy:

> As babies are born at a local hospital, the girls are brought through one door into a pink room, the boys through another door into a completely separate blue room. But when the babies are brought out of the pink room, or out of the blue room, through doors at the other end, they once again must be sorted into boys and girls.[144]

The point is that if the feature of being a transmittable photon or a reflectable photon were an inherent characteristic of a photon, in the same way that being a boy or girl is certainly inherent in the gender of babies (rather than switching between the two depending on which rooms the babies have been carried in and out of), then once a photon had been transmitted through the first semi-silvered mirror we would expect it to be transmitted through both of the following mirrors.

However, this is not what happens. It seems, rather, that the photons miraculously change their behavior in order to precisely fit a pattern. In the case of the partial reflections in windows the pattern is that 95% are always transmitted and 5% are reflected; and in the case of the semi-silvered mirrors 50% are always transmitted and 50% are reflected. It is this remarkable mutability of quantum entities in conformance to a precise pattern that Marcus Chown describes as indicating that 'the Universe, at its deepest level, is founded on randomness and unpredictability' and, furthermore, he concludes that:

> A photon goes through a window rather than bouncing back out of sheer bloody mindedness for no reason at all.[145]

Does this seem right? If a photon really were as 'bloody-minded' as Chown claims wouldn't it (allowing ourselves the same photonic anthropomorphism as Chown indulges in) think to itself something like: 'I'm really getting bored always getting reflected from windows 5% of the time and always getting transmitted through semi-silvered mirrors 50% of the time, I want a change from this soul destroying monotony so I think I'll change the pattern of my photonic behavior!'

But photons do not do this, they remain remarkably well behaved, despite their claimed 'bloody-mindedness,' they always conform to the same pattern in conformance to the situation they are subjected to. And yet Chown tells us that:

> The recognition of the microscopic world is controlled by irreducible random chance is probably the single most shocking discovery in the history of science.[146]

But, if photons religiously conform to the appropriate patterns of transmission and reflection for the situations they find themselves in does it really make sense to make such a dramatic and absolutist claim that the quantum realm is thoroughly, outrageously, bloody-mindedly, irreducibly and irredeemably random? What is going on here?

The quantum plot thickens when we reflect upon the remarkable phenomenon of quantum entanglement and non-locality, an aspect of quantum reality that Einstein famously referred to as 'spooky action at a distance' and concerning which Chown tells us that 'many physicists consider that this instantaneous influence the greatest mystery of quantum theory.'[147]

Crudely stated the quantum phenomenon of non-locality means that when an 'entangled' quantum entity is observed and thereby 'influenced' to adopt some particular quantum characteristic at some point in the universe, its entangled quantum partner, which may be on the other side of the universe, will instantaneously be 'influenced' to adopt a corresponding characteristic.

For example quantum particles have an attribute called 'spin' which is equally likely to be clockwise (known as 'up') or anticlockwise ('down'). But the quantum situation requires that until a measurement is made any particle is in a weird indefinite state, a 'superposition' of both spins. This is a state in which a particle is potentially in both spins at the same time but not fully in either! When two particles are in a special state called an entangled state, the spins of the two particles are inseparably linked and until a measurement is made neither particle has a definite spin, they both share spin 'up' and spin 'down' and the particles can move vast distances away from each other whilst remaining in an 'entangled' state of sharing both spin 'up' and spin 'down'. When a measurement is made to determine the spin of one of the particles, however, both particles will instantaneously adopt a definite spin. If you find that one of the particles' spin is 'up', you'll find that the other is spin 'down', and vice versa. So it is as if the two entangled particles, no matter how far they are apart, are not really separate at all, and the spin interconnection is instantaneous even if the particles are separated by huge distances. What happens in one part of the Universe can have instantaneous 'non-local' consequences in other parts, no matter how far away they might be.

In order to comprehend this quantum marvel it is necessary to have an appreciation of the quantum phenomenon called the 'collapse of the wavefunction.' This is a controversial topic because it implies a dramatic re-evaluation of our understanding of the ultimate nature of reality. Instead of conceiving of reality as consisting of an independent and self-enclosed mechanism of material bits and pieces we are forced to accept that mind or consciousness is fundamental within the functioning of the universe. But, although the precise interpretation of the quantum 'collapse' mechanism is still somewhat contentious, the manner in which the quantum realm relates to the way that reality connects to our direct experience is well understood mathematically, and it is this mathematical understanding which underpins the description of the 'collapse of the wavefunction' as it pertains to quantum non-locality.

Because of the dramatic and counter intuitive nature of the quantum mechanisms which underpin the functioning of the universe as we now understand them, terms such as 'reality' become somewhat ambiguous. This is because in quantum physics there are two degrees of 'reality' so to speak. There is the reality of reality prior to observation by a sentient being (an animate organism which has conscious awareness) and there is the way that reality becomes real within the experience of sentient beings.

First we must consider the way in which reality is 'real' before it is observed. Prior to being observed in some form or another reality consists of a mathematically described sea of potentiality for experience. At this point there is nothing which can be called a fully manifested locatable object, quantum entities are said to be 'smeared out' in a 'wavefunction' of quantum probability. For current purposes a wavefunction can be considered to be a mathematical description of the probability that a quantum entity will spring into existence at any particular point.

At the quantum level entities do not exist in the way that they appear to do at the level of our experience of the everyday world. In fact it is probably more correct to say that there are no entities at the quantum level, there are only the possibilities for the experience of entity-ness, so to speak. An actual experience of an entity occurs when an aspect of reality capable of experiencing, i.e. a subjective consciousness, meets a field of possibilities for experience. Quantum physicist Henry Stapp describes these 'objective tendencies' for experience as follows:

> The central idea in Heisenberg's picture of nature is that atoms are not 'actual' things. The physical state of an atom, or of an assembly of atoms, represents only a set of 'objective tendencies' for certain kinds of 'actual events' to occur.[148]

Heisenberg was one of the founding fathers of quantum theory and an originator of the viewpoint that objective reality consists of 'objective tendencies' for possible experience rather than a definite pre-existing external realm of materiality. From this perspective unexperienced reality is mere potentiality for experience; not actuality. Whether the meeting of subjective consciousness and the possibility for an experience results in an actual experience, or an event, for the subjective consciousness depends on whether the interaction produces a reinforcing resonance. Such a resonance constitutes an experience within the dualistic realm of apparent subjectivity and objectivity within a field of the individual awareness of a sentient being.

Each possibility for experience contained within the wavefunction can be assigned a probability. In order to get a taste of the scenario let us suppose that we have discovered a strange new particle which can only 'exist' in a special box. The term 'exist' is in inverted commas to indicate a quantum wavefunction existence, which is to say that there is a potentiality for existence but not a full experienced reality. In order to avoid having to make this distinction in future, let us use the term 'wf-exist' in future to indicate such wavefunction potentiality for existence. The strangeness of our imaginary particle lies in the fact that experiment shows that it can only be experienced in three places inside the box; it is never experienced at any other place. Millions of experiments have been done so we know that this is definitely the case. On half of the occasions it is experienced exactly in the center of the box, a quarter of all occasions it is experienced half way between the center and the left hand wall, and the remaining quarter of the occasions it is experienced half way between the center and the right hand wall.

Let us now introduce the following, quite innocuous, notation:

C represents particle experienced center;
L represents particle experienced left position;
R represents particle experienced right position;
X represents particle experienced anywhere else (which is never).

Now we use the notation P(.) to represent the probability that the particle will be found at the position indicated by the '.' inside the brackets. So we have

P(C) is the probability that the particle is experienced center;
P(L) is the probability that the particle is experienced left position;
P(R) is the probability that the particle is experienced right position;
P(X) is the probability that the particle is experienced anywhere else (which is zero).

So we end up with the particle's wavefunction:

$$P(C) = \tfrac{1}{2};$$
$$P(L) = \tfrac{1}{4};$$
$$P(R) = \tfrac{1}{4};$$
$$P(X) = 0.$$

When someone looks in the box there is a probability of ½ that it will be experienced center, ¼ experienced left, ¼ experienced right and it will never be experienced anywhere else.

The question which immediately arises, of course, is what actual state the particle is in when no one is looking in the box? The answer that quantum physics requires is that the particle is in a state of wf-existence which corresponds to what the Madhyamaka calls emptiness. For each position where it might be found we have to agree with the Buddha that, with regard to the ultimate nature of phenomena:

From certain single perspectives
[The Buddha] taught them as either 'nonexistent' or 'existent.'
From both perspectives,
He expressed them as 'neither existent nor nonexistent.'
Since they do not exist as they appear,
He talked about their 'nonexistence.'
Since they appear in such ways,
He spoke about their 'existence.'[149]

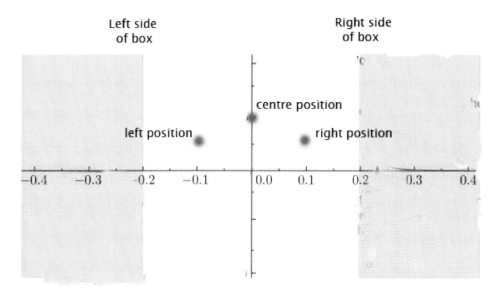

Fig 2.9

In fact in the places where the particle might be experienced it can be said to 'hover between existence and non-existence'; and it is important to be clear that it is not the case that the particle is in one of the three possible places but we do not know which; the theory of quantum mechanics clearly tells us that such a particle hovers between existence and non-existence in each of the three places. The way that quantum physicists describe this situation is to say that the particle is in a *superposition* of being in the three places. This state of superposition in the three positions would be graphically represented as shown in fig 2.9. The height above, or depth below, the central horizontal axis, which is measured by the vertical axis, indicates the probability that the 'particle' will manifest in the position shown by the horizontal axis.

To finish off this outline of the nature of the wavefunction it is necessary to point out that the above account is not quite a 'real' wavefunction because wavefunctions should be continuous, they should not have discontinuous breaks like the example of our imaginary particle of the three positions. Also the probability of existence is actually derived by squaring, or multiplying by itself, the value of the wavefunction. The above description only gives a simplified flavor of the nature of a wavefunction.

Fig 2.10 shows the wavefunction of an electron which is 'confined' inside a quantum potential 'box' or 'well'; this means that the electron, a quantum constituent of atoms, is only allowed to 'exist' within the confines of the box which is made up of quantum potential energy. The height of the probability curve represents the probability that *when an observation is made the electron magically springs into full experiential existence* at the indicated point.

In order to fully understand the wavefunction nature of reality before observations are made it is vital to comprehend that, using the term 'reality' and 'existence' with our usual expectations and connotations, quantum entities do not fully 'exist' and are not fully 'real' until they are observed. Prior to observation, or measurement, they 'hover' between existence and non-existence at every point at which they could possibly manifest. The potential electron prior to observation is existentially smeared out over all the possible points covered by the curved line. However when someone makes an observation of the quantum situation by quantumly peeking into the box the electron will spring into existence at one of the possible points and its potential existence will disappear at all other possible points.

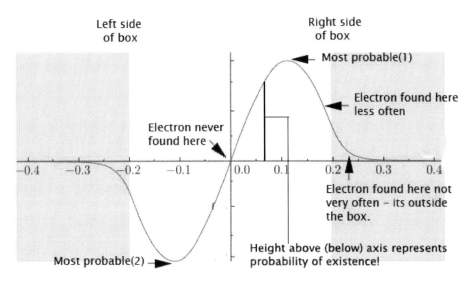

Fig 2.10

It is important to grasp the fact that the quantum situation means that the act of observation manifests the electron into full existence out of a sea of possibility; the electron does not fully exist prior to observation, it 'hovers between existence and non-existence.' But when the potential electron is 'observed' it springs into full existence at a definite position. This is called the 'collapse' of the wavefunction. Furthermore it *appears* that where the electron springs into existence is a matter of electronic 'bloody-mindedness', apart from the fact that over a period of time observations will conform to the established probability patterns.

In the case of the spin of entangled quantum particles before observation the situation is that the potential particles in question share the same wavefunction. So in a very real sense they are not separate entities, they are rather interconnected possible manifestations of existence which are encoded into a single quantum entity of potentiality. When an observation or 'measurement' is made at some point in the Universe the wavefunction of the 'entangled' particles 'collapses' and thereby manifests two particles with corresponding attributes, in this case one has spin up and the other spin 'down'. Chown, with characteristic dramatic exuberance, says of this situation:

> Quantum theory … permits the insanity of instantaneous influence at a distance.[150]

But at the same time as he, following Einstein's inclinations concerning this phenomenon, proclaims the non-locality of quantum entanglement to be 'insanity', he also, on the same page, makes a much more obvious and natural observation: 'They *know* about each other' (his italics).

The real 'insanity' in this situation is hardly the quantum operation of entangled non-locality, or partially transmitted and reflected photons; it is, rather, the employment of two radically opposed metaphors, one of which, that of a minimal quantum 'knowingness', makes perfect sense, although counter intuitive from the perspective of everyday intuitions, whilst the other, that of the attribution of 'irreducible' and 'bloody-minded' randomness to the realm of quantum functioning, is clearly ruled out by the simple fact of the consistent and precise configuration of the patterning of behavior displayed by quantum entities such as photons.

Let's return the phenomenon of partial reflection. As with all such quantum experiments it is possible set it up to investigate this phenomenon whilst sending photons towards the glass one at a time and the result, in terms of the proportions reflected and transmitted, will be the same (95% transmitted and 5% reflected). In terms of probability theory the situation is that each individual photon has a .95 chance of being transmitted and .05 chance of being reflected.

Just for the moment switch over to thinking about tossing a coin, the chance or probability of getting a head is ½ or 0.5; and according to probability theory the chance of getting two heads in sequence is (½ × ½) which is ¼ (0.25), and for getting three heads in sequence is (½ × ½ × ½) which is 1/8 (0.125) and so on. Furthermore according to probability theory the probability of getting another head having already thrown two previous heads is still ½. This is because the two previously thrown heads are considered to be irrelevant to the next throw (whatever our intuitions might be). However prior to embarking upon the sequence of throws the probability of throwing three coins without getting at least one tail somewhere in the sequence, which is the same as getting three heads, is 1/8; this means that the probability of getting at least one tail somewhere in the sequence is 1–1/8 which is 7/8ths. By similar reasoning the probability of throwing 100 coins and getting at least one tail is $1-(1/2)^{100}$ which to all intents and purposes is 1, i.e. it is close to certainty; which means of course that the probability of throwing 100 coins and getting 100 heads is virtually zero.

Now to return to the partial reflection situation; the probability of sending 100 photons towards the glass and having them all pass through is $(.95)^{100}$ which is approximately 0.006, the probability for 1000 is $(.95)^{1000}$ which is a vanishingly small number; this means that the probability of getting at least one photon reflected when we send a 1000 photons is virtually a certainty. So suppose by some quantum glitch we have sent a million photons towards the glass and they have all been transmitted through the glass, what do you think the probability of the next photon passing through is? How often do you think it is possible to throw a million coins and not get a tail?

At the quantum level the number of photons, and other quantum entities, involved is astronomical and with such vast numbers the patterns involved might as well be considered to be fixed and etched into the quantum ground. If this were not the case then the material world would not function in the coherent way that it does. So imagine your self into the position of the next photon to go after the million have already passed through the glass window (just as Einstein imagined travelling along side a photon); it will surely have a heavy duty to get reflected. But how would it know?

According to Chown photons involved in the partial reflection example must be considered to completely isolated, self-enclosed entities which have no link to any other phenomenon which could have any kind of cause and effect impact upon the situation:

> …there is no prior event from which the probability of a photon going through a window can be determined, no hidden machinery whirring beneath the skin of reality, … There is nothing deeper…[151]

And Chown is by no means alone in asserting that the patterns of reality spring magically from nowhere. Quantum physicist Anton Zeilinger for instance calls the randomness which is thought to be endemic within the quantum realm 'objective' randomness:

> It's not only that I don't know where the particle will land, but the particle itself does not know.[152]

According to this view at the quantum level there is no causal chain or underlying mechanism for the behaviour of an individual particle. It simply does something completely without reason; a complete surprise even to itself!

However, as we have seen, the patterns of behaviour over large numbers of quantum events do not exhibit this waywardness. And, furthermore, the idea that the situation of partial reflection, for instance, is a state of affairs which is completely and 'objectively' random, or a matter of 'bloody-minded' quantum pathology, is massively counter intuitive simply because if the photons produce a pattern then there surely must be something coordinating the production of the pattern. To use Chown's and Zeilinger's mode of description, the particles must in some sense 'know' where to land otherwise there could be no pattern. How can a 'bloody-minded' and 'objective' random process produce a pattern? How can a very large number of photons which have no idea where they are going, and not only behave 'objectively' randomly but also apparently exhibit a pathological desire to behave randomly, suddenly organise themselves into a precise pattern? There must be some kind of patterning process. Furthermore, the pattern produced is the same every time; it seems to be built into the behaviour of large numbers of photons.

In the case of the non-local instantaneous influence, which appears to occur when entangled 'particles' become un-entangled when their wave-function is collapsed, physicists such as David Bohm wondered whether their might be 'hidden variables', which is to say there is some kind of hidden information local to quantum particles operating outside the limits of our detection capabilities. The attempt to account for the phenomenon in this way, however, failed. The experiments with entangled particles, which have been repeated over and over again, clearly shows that the patterns which emerge from the interactions of the particles do not emerge on the basis of the particles having certain *local* attributes prior to their separation, so entangled particles are not carrying on-board information that is hidden from us. This has been proved experimentally on many occasions by the demonstration that quantum entities violate a mathematical formula called Bell's inequality[153], an issue explored in a later chapter (*What's the Matter with Matter?*).

It is intriguing that in the case of entanglement Chown adopts a completely different viewpoint than he does regarding the quantum phenomenon of partial reflection. In the case of partial reflection photons are said to be delinquently random, having nothing to do with cause and effect mechanisms, whereas in the case of entanglement:

> There is a ghostly web of quantum connections crisscrossing the universe and coupling you and me to every last bit of matter in the most distant galaxy. We live in a telepathic universe. What this actually means physicists have not yet figured out.[154]

The fact that 'physicists have not yet figured out what this actually means' actually means that they have not been able to account for this phenomenon in the kind of terms which they like or prefer; terms which do not imply that the universe might actually be in some deep sense 'self-aware' as the dissident physicist Amit Goswami suggests.[155]

A pressing issue which requires attention is why, if the two phenomena – partial reflection and non-local entanglement – both exhibit a similar appearance of involving at least a minimalist 'ghostly' interconnection or even awareness, they are interpreted so radically differently. The answer is simply that in the case of entanglement the interconnection is too obvious to be ignored, whilst in the case of transmission and reflection of photons it is possible to ignore the possibility of interconnection and awareness simply by making the assumption that the photons are separate, independent, isolated and self-contained entities.

This assumption that all phenomena are separate and cut off from all other phenomena was called by the important maverick physicist David Bohm 'the mechanistic attitude' which he described as follows:

> ...physics has become almost totally committed to the notion that the order of the universe is basically mechanistic. The most common form of this notion is that the world is assumed to consist of a set of separately existent, indivisible and unchangeable 'elementary particles, which are the fundamental 'building blocks', of the entire universe.[156]

Bohm's position is very different. He tells us that:

> ...one finds, through a study of quantum theory, that the analysis of a total system into a set of independently existing but inter-acting particles breaks down in a radically new way. One discovers, instead, both from consideration of the meaning of the mathematical equations and from results of the actual experiments, that the various particles have to be taken literally as projections of a higher-dimension reality which cannot be accounted for in terms of any force of interaction between them.[157]

In order to illustrate his view he describes the device shown in fig 2.11. We imagine a fish tank, containing a fish, with transparent sides which has two cameras aimed at it. The cameras are arranged as shown; one is aimed at the side at right angles to the side that the other is aimed at. The cameras are connected to two different displays both of which are in another room. Bohm points out that, although the images shown by the screens will be different to each other, they will also be related. For example if the fish is looking straight out of one, it will be side on in the other and if the fish turns to look straight out of the side it was previously side on to, it will obviously now appear side on in the screen that it was previously staring out of. The images on the two screens will clearly be precisely correlated, in a manner analogous to the spins of entangled particles:

What we are proposing here is that the quantum property of a non-local, non-causal relationship of distant elements may be understood through an extension of the notion described above. That is to say, we may regard each of the 'particles' constituting a system as a projection of a 'higher-dimensional' reality...[158]

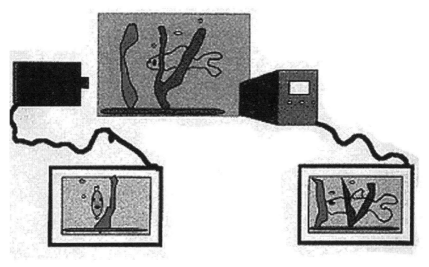

Fig 2.11

Bohm also considered that the way that all phenomena were linked together within the higher dimension, the domain of the wavefunction, which he called the 'implicate order,' was analogous to a hologram, in which the 'whole' is written into each and every part. Bohm, then, maintained that a radical new view of the way that the elements of physics were considered to relate to each other was necessary; a perspective that emphasised the 'undivided wholeness' which underpins all the manifested phenomena of the experienced universe.

The intellectual attitude that Bohm referred to as the 'mechanistic order', the view of classical physics, corresponds remarkably with what the Buddhist Madhyamaka, or Middle Way philosophy, calls 'inherent existence', or *svabhava* (*sva*='own', *bhava*='being'). In the domain of physics this fundamental view of the nature of reality manifests in the basic assumption that all the quantum entities which are attributed 'particle' status can be assumed to function as if they were inherently existent entities which are independent of each other. It was this view that Bohm, basing his conclusions on the evidence of quantum physics, considered to be no longer viable.

The Buddhist philosophical concept of inherent existence is remarkable in that, although it plays a central and crucial role in the Madhyamaka philosophical investigation and analysis of reality, it is, according to that very analysis, something which is entirely non-existent within the Universe; a phenomenon which has its own self-enclosed svabhava, or independent and substantial inner essence, is as nonexistent as 'the horns of a rabbit.'[159] Indeed the core Madhyamaka doctrine of *shunyata*, or 'emptiness', asserts that all phenomena are 'empty' of inherent existence. As the Buddhist scholar Jeffrey Hopkins says:

> Phenomena are empty of a certain mode of being called 'inherent existence', 'objective existence', or 'natural existence'. This 'inherent existence' is not a concept superimposed by philosophical systems but refers to our ordinary sense of the way that things exist...[160]

The deeply important issue at stake is that the natural view of the way phenomena exist, a view deeply embedded in the human psyche, is exactly that they do have some kind of inner core of self-enclosed independent existence which is all their own so to speak; it is this 'naturalistic' perception of the way things exist which is rejected by the Buddhist doctrine of emptiness. And it is now a view of reality which is also rejected by quantum physics.

There are several approaches through which the core concept of 'emptiness', the Buddhist view of the ultimate nature of phenomena, is presented. Perhaps one of the most approachable is that of 'dependent origination', the idea that all phenomena are interdependent and no one of them could stand independently existent without the others. A further implication of this view is also the understanding that all phenomena come into existence in dependence on all others and therefore all phenomena are interdependent and interpenetrate at a deep level of reality.

This view of the fundamentally participatory and interdependent nature of the process of reality, the ultimate nature of which is identified as being non-substantial mind, a sparkling process of an infinite play of interpenetrating and mutually resonating and reinforcing cognition, finds its most spectacular embodiment in the Flower Garland Sutra (*Avatamsaka Sutra*) which presents the *Dharmadhatu*, the ultimate expanse of phenomena, as an immense field of mutually interpenetrating holographic elements of mind in the guise of Indra's net (see opening quote).

In this image the whole universe is portrayed as an interpenetrating multidimensional net of jewels, which may be thought of as representing the infinite sparks of interconnected consciousness which underlie the appearances of the phenomena world. Jewels are set at every intersection of the net and each jewel reflects the light reflected in all the jewels around it, and each of those jewels in turn reflects the light from all the jewels around them, and this multifaceted mutually reflective process is repeated infinitely. In this way, all phenomena – events, entities and sentient beings reflect and express the radiance of the entire universe. All of totality can be seen in each of its parts. This later became incorporated into the Hua-yen doctrine which views the entire cosmos as a single nexus of conditions in which everything simultaneously depends on, and is depended on by, everything else. As Marcus Chown explains, according to quantum theory:

> Everything in the Universe is in some weird sense linked, since all particles – those out of which you are made and those which constitute the most distant galaxy – were once together in the same state in the Big Bang. The 'spooky' connectedness of particles, in violation of the cosmic speed limit, was cited by Einstein as a reason why quantum theory had to be wrong. Unfortunately for Einstein, careful experiments carried out in laboratories since the early 1980s have confirmed that particles can indeed communicate with each other instantaneously.[161]

Exactly like photons orchestrating the dance of the phenomenon of partial reflection!

Why the Quantum?

Quantum Theory appears to many as strange, unwelcome, and forced on physics as it were from outside against its will. In contrast, if the essential point could be grasped in a single phrase, we can well believe that the quantum would seem so natural that we would recognize at once that the universe could not even have come into being without it.[162]

- John A. Wheeler: physicist

Perhaps, in some sense, this is 'why' we, as sentient beings, must live in a quantum world, rather than an entirely classical one, despite all the richness, and indeed mystery, that is already present in the classical universe. Might a quantum world be *required* so that thinking perceiving creatures, such as ourselves, can be constructed from its substance?[163]

- Roger Penrose: physicist

Whatever is dependently arisen
Does not arise, does not cease,
Is not permanent, is not extinct,
Does not come, does not go
And is neither one thing nor different things.[164]

-Nagarjuna: Buddhist philosopher

Behind it all is surely an idea so simple, so beautiful, that when we grasp it - in a decade, a century, or a millennium - we will all say to each other, how could it have been otherwise?[165]

- John A. Wheeler: physicist

John Wheeler

John Wheeler, one of the great physicists of the twentieth century, indicated that the solution to the question 'Why the quantum?' might contain the solution to the question of existence itself:

> ...eventually we will have an answer to the question 'How come the quantum?' And to the companion question, 'How come existence?'[166]

According to Wheeler, then, the answer to the question concerning the quantum nature of reality might contain the answer to the question which the philosopher Heidegger considered to be the most important question for philosophy; 'why is there something rather than nothing?' The confrontation between the everyday world and the quantum world leads us to the very limits of what we can know about reality. And according to Wheeler the solution to the question regarding why the world has a quantum basis will provide an insight into the nature of existence itself. This is, indeed, an extraordinary possibility which should be sought at all cost.

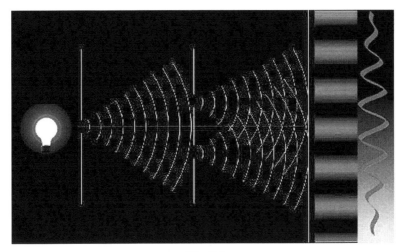

Fig 3.1

For those not acquainted with the bizarre world of quantum reality the following example, which is the modern version of the eighteenth century Thomas Young experiment referred to in the second chapter, will serve as an introduction. According to Richard Feynman this experiment is 'designed to contain all of the mystery of quantum mechanics.'[167] Jim Al-Khalili refers to the behavior displayed in this experiment as 'nature's conjuring trick'[168], a very apt rubric.

When light is shone through two narrow slits onto a screen beyond the slits (Fig 3.1) the light rays, which were originally thought to be continuous electromagnetic waves, interact with each other to produce a pattern of light and dark stripes. This happens because the light waves which meet from the different slits are either in phase, in which case they reinforce each other, or they are out of phase, in which case they cancel each other out; areas where the light waves are in phase are bright, and where they cancel dark areas are produced (fig 3.2).

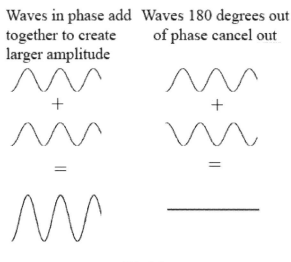

Fig 3.2

So far the situation may not seem at all outlandish. There are waves going through the top slit and waves going through the bottom slit. The waves go through one or other of the slits and interfere on the other side. But this picture is not quite correct. Light is actually made up of 'particles' of electromagnetic waves called photons; which are little pieces of electromagnetic vibration which should be indivisible. Even now there is no problem, we can think that some of the particles go through the top slit, others through the bottom, and then they interact to produce the light and dark pattern on the other side.

Now we introduce the conjuring trick; we send the particles, each one of which should be an indivisible wave-particle, through the slits one at a time. Because we are sending light particles through the apparatus one at a time it would seem reasonable to suppose that they would go through either the top slit or the bottom slit. It also seems reasonable to suppose that there will be no other wave-particles on the other side to interact with, so we would not expect to get the light and dark stripes, which should only occur because of the interaction of many waves going through top and bottom slits at the same time. There should be just two stripes, one for each slit.

This, however, does not happen. The light and dark interference pattern still remains just as it was when a lot of wave-particles were going through the slits. How can this be? What is the wave-particle doing? Although the wave-particle does have a wave aspect it is also supposed be an indivisible particle which should travel like a particle, which means it should go through just one of the slits. It should not, according to common sense, go through both slits.

Now suppose we decide to really find out what is going on; we change the experiment so that we place a detector at one of the slits to see through which slit the wave-particles travel. As soon as we do this the interference stripes disappear. It seems as if just looking at the slits to see what is happening changes the way that the wave-particles behave. It actually appears that if we do not look the wave-particle divides itself up, in a way that it should not be able to, in order to go through both slits. As soon as we look, however, it changes its behavior so that it goes through just one of the slits. It appears to 'know' when we are looking. When we look, then, we find that it is a particle. But when we do not look, it becomes something else. And this something else seems to be able to do the impossible. It divides itself up, whilst still remaining one indivisible thing, and then comes back together on the other side. Jim Al-Khalili likens this to a skier going around a tree on both sides (fig 3.3).

Fig 3.3

This not only happens with light wave-particles, it also happens with electrons, protons, atoms, and molecules, all of which have a quantum wave aspect. When there is no way of knowing which path the 'particles' take the interference pattern appears, which seems to suggest that they take both paths, even though this should be impossible because the particle aspect should be indivisible. When we know which path is taken, however, the interference pattern disappears. The remarkable implication of this evidence is that conscious interference in the experiment has a direct effect at the quantum level. As Rosenblum and Kuttner say:

> Physics had encountered consciousness but did not yet realize it.[169]

It looks as if the nature of the quantum realm is surprisingly mutable and is able to respond to the entire configuration of the experimental apparatus, including the observers and the nature of the observation.

This kind of quantum behavior is often presented as being totally incomprehensible. However, the first opening quote from John Wheeler suggests the necessity for grasping the 'essential point' concerning quantum reality which can 'be grasped in a single phrase' that reveals that the quantum world is 'so natural that we would recognize at once that the universe could not even have come into being without it'. Anton Zeilinger, a physicist who has carried out some of the most precise and subtle quantum experiments currently possible, has written in appreciation of Wheeler's work of Wheeler's:

> …realisation that the implications of quantum physics are so far-reaching that they require a completely novel approach in our view of reality and in the way we see our role in the universe. This distinguishes him from many others who in one way or another tried to save pre-quantum viewpoints, particularly the obviously wrong notion of a reality independent of us.[170]

Can we find an 'essential point' which can 'be grasped in a single phrase' which supplies 'a completely novel approach in our view of reality and in the way we see our role in the universe' which rectifies 'the obviously wrong notion of a reality independent of us' and is also 'so natural that we would recognize at once that the universe could not even have come into being without it?'

As we shall see, the concept of emptiness, or dependent co-origination, one of the core concepts of the Madhyamaka, the central philosophical foundation of Mahayana Buddhism, is certainly a good candidate. It is vital to understand at the outset that emptiness does not mean the same as nothingness. The concept of emptiness refers to the fact that the Madhyamaka analysis of the process of reality has uncovered the lack of 'inherent existence' in all phenomena; so the Madhyamaka describes all phenomena as being *empty* of inherent existence; phenomena have no inner independent essence which cuts them off from the rest of reality, and it because of this that all phenomena are responsive to all other phenomena.

The concept of emptiness is introduced in the third opening quote, from the great second century Madhyamika master Nagarjuna. It illuminates what the Madhyamaka asserted, roughly two thousand years ago, about the inner nature of reality. All phenomena are illusion-like, interdependent appearances which, contrary to the nature of their appearance, lack any independent self-substantiality:

> Since these phenomena without existence are devoid of a core …
> If those who assert true existence were indeed correct,
> How could these phenomena fit into space?
> …sever the ropes of grasping conceptions this instant;
> …illusions that project appearances but do not exist. [171]

Truly existent phenomena could not fit into space because to do so they would have to have a relationship with the phenomenon of space, in which case they would not be completely independent of all other phenomena. 'True existence' is a synonym for 'inherently existent.' Our natural manner of relating to the objects that surround us in everyday life is to believe that they are truly or inherently existent, which means they are completely self-enclosed and independent entities. It is this picture of 'things' that the Madhyamaka seeks to undermine. Although the world appears to truly exist, this picture is deceptive; when we come to grasp the significance of emptiness it will become apparent that 'true existence' is, like a 'horn of a rabbit'[172], non-existent.

An important difference between 'true existence' and the notion of a 'rabbit's horn', however, is that everyone knows that rabbits do not have horns. There is no need to construct sophisticated philosophical techniques of analysis to prove the lack of rabbit's horns in reality. 'True existence', however, is a different kettle of fish. According to the Madhyamaka the perception of true existence is virtually a universal mode of perceiving the world. It is an innate mode of perception which has been 'hard wired' into the perceptual apparatus of all unenlightened sentient beings. The natural way to apprehend the numerous objects that we interact with in everyday life is simply to treat them as if they existed from 'their own side', completely independent of our, and everyone else's, mind. We also assume that each object is self enclosed, so to speak, and cut off from all other objects. This is an innate mode of understanding the world, and it was the mode which underpinned the pre-quantum 'classical' understanding of the physical world:

> …the world is regarded as constituted of entities which are outside of each other, in the sense that they exist independently in

different regions of space (and time) and interact through forces that do not bring about any changes in their essential natures.[173]

The point is that such ultimate 'things' must be self-enclosed and independent of all other things.

The concept of emptiness actually has several levels of understanding, each succeeding level more subtle than the previous. However it may be considered as beginning from an analysis of 'thinghood.' This is an example of how the Madhyamaka gets to the heart of reality from very humble beginnings. Very few people, West or East, stop to think about the way in which they conceive reality down at a basic level, or the implications of this unexamined assumption. According to the Madhyamaka the untrained mind invariably conceives of 'things' as being ultimately unchanging, self-enclosed and independent. We may pay lip service to the obvious fact that 'things always change', but deep down the mind thinks of 'things' as things which do not change. And the point that the Madhyamaka succinctly makes is that such self enclosed and independent entities could not exist. According to the *Sagaramatinirdesha-sutra*:

> Everything arising by dependence,
> No 'thingness' does it have in any sense.
> All that is devoid of entity
> Does not arise in any way.[174]

And from the *Hastikakshya-sutra*:

> A thing that in itself is truly born
> Is utterly beyond our observation.[175]

And from the *Ratnakara-sutra*:

> All things are devoid of entity.[176]

When a 'thing' is conceived of as being inherently existent it must be unchangeable, it must have an inner core of reality which is immutable. If some thing is inherently existent its thinghood requires an inner unchanging essence which makes it what it is. The Madhyamaka has always denied the possibility of this kind of 'thing' actually existing in reality. A point of view which, when fully comprehended, has deep and remarkable ramifications.

The significance of the Madhyamaka rejection of thinghood may not be immediately obvious, and may seem irrelevant, because we are so used to thinking about 'things' relating and interacting with each other all the time. But the Madhyamaka is relentless and draws attention to the fact that it is a basic requirement of an *ultimately* real 'thing', so to speak, to be unchangeable. This is the conception of thinghood which seems inherent to the human mind; even if we let the boundaries of the conception slip and become fuzzy for everyday convenience. But during any interaction 'things' change to accommodate the interaction and therefore do not remain in their state of self enclosed thinghood. When we speak of 'things' in everyday life we are employing the term loosely for convenience. But in actuality something which changes into some 'thing' else can't be the 'thing' we thought it was because it has ceased to be that 'thing' so has lost its thinghood. Ultimate things actually must for ever maintain an unchanging self-enclosed aloofness from all other things in order to maintain their thinghood.

According to the Madhyamaka this notion of things is not a merely surface phenomenon. The idea that things exist as independent self-enclosed and self-powered entities is a very deep assumption within the minds of all sentient beings. It is like one of Kant's categories of thought, or perception, which resides deep within human psyches; because of this the notion of inherent entities creeps into all corners of human thought. It was certainly a fundamental aspect of pre-quantum physics and it still undermines a full appreciation of the full implications of quantum physics, leading to the fragmentation of views described in the first chapter.

The second opening quote, from Nagarjuna, is a pithy summing up of the implications of the view that all things are 'empty' of 'inherent existence'. To comprehend the unsettling and counter intuitive play on concepts it is vital to hold in mind that the following paradoxical analysis applies to some 'thing' which is considered as 'arising' as an inherently existing thing, which is a changeless entity that is independent of all other entities:

> Whatever is dependently arisen
> Does not arise, does not cease,

An inherently existing entity would have to be changeless and therefore, by definition, could not 'arise' simply because it cannot come into or go out of existence! Here we find the notion of dependent origination, which is the hallmark of emptiness, what is being asserted here is that if something arises dependently then it does not arise as an inherently existent entity and neither can it cease as an inherently existent entity because it has not arisen in the first place! Furthermore, inherently existent entities cannot cease by definition. Something which arises on the basis of something else cannot be given credence as being a 'real' thing because it has arisen in dependence on something else, so it is not self-powered, it depends on something else. It follows that this illusory 'thing', which means an inherently existent 'thing', that we might think has come into inherent being has not actually arisen because it's not actually there as an inherently existent entity! It cannot, inherently, cease because there is nothing inherently existent to cease.

The next line is:

> Is not permanent, is not extinct,

It cannot be permanent because it appeared to arise in the first place and because of this it cannot become extinct because there was never anything inherently existent to become extinct!

Does not come, does not go

Something which has not come into existence (as an inherently existent thing) can not come or go!

And is neither one thing nor different things.

It cannot be one inherently existent thing because it has arisen and so is not an inherently existent thing in the first place. It cannot be different things because the analysis would apply to each of those things in turn and, anyway, it has appeared as being in the guise of one thing. The Madhyamaka begins, then, with a complete demolition of the notion of ultimate 'things' and ultimate thinghood, which it denotes by the term 'inherent existence', intrinsic existence' or 'own-nature' (*svabhava*).

It might be thought that such a paradoxical deconstruction could not be of much relevance to the problems of quantum physics. However, the problems of quantum interpretation can be traced, in part, back to the disappearance of the 'things' of classical physics. As Lee Smolin says:

> Newtonian physics … gives rise to the illusion that the world is composed of objects. … But relativity and quantum theory each tell us … no, better, they scream at us, that our world is a history of processes.[177]

So the disappearance of 'objects' and 'things' from the primary conceptual armory of physics is obviously important to the quantum revolution; Jonathan Allday, in his recent book *Quantum Reality: Theory and Philosophy*, points out that quantum entanglement:

> …presents us with a philosophical challenge, one that threatens to pick away at our notion of what a 'thing' is.[178]

A deep problem that faces quantum physicists is this: although they have developed mathematical tools to describe and predict the functioning of the quantum world, they do not have ordinary concepts, so to speak, because none of our ordinary concepts apply to what seems to be going on. And, make no mistake, the difference between the way 'objects' behave at the quantum level and the everyday level is dramatically different. The constituents of the quantum realm behave in such a bizarre manner from the point of view of our ordinary reality that it seems impossible to explain how our everyday world can possibly develop out of the quantum world. As Allday says:

> The problem is that the small-scale laws describe a way of behaving that, judged by the standards of everyday experience, is utterly bizarre. It is very difficult to see how all the funny business going on at the atomic scale can lead to the regular, reliable world we spend our lives in.[179]

In the quantum world 'things', using this term very loosely, do not have definite boundaries the way that they seem to do in everyday life. They partially exist in many different states at the same time whilst waiting to be discovered in one of their possible states. And, it seems, that the only time that these nebulously existent entities at the quantum level decide to 'get real' is, like the wave-particle going through a slit, when someone looks at them.

The extraordinary nature of the quantum experimental results indicating that the attributes of reality are created by consciousness cannot be over-emphasised. In their book *Quantum Enigma* Rosenblum and Kuttner refer to the fact that at the quantum level physics has run up against the issue of the nature of consciousness as physics' 'skeleton in the closet.' Most physicists have been, and still are, uncomfortable with this conclusion because of the far reaching implications. Rosenblum and Kuttner, however, are adamant about their conclusion:

> Consciousness and the quantum enigma are not just two mysteries; they are *the* two mysteries; first, our physical demonstration of the quantum enigma, faces us with the fundamental mystery of the objective world 'out there;' the second, conscious awareness, faces us with the fundamental mystery of the subjective, mental world 'in here.' Quantum mechanics seems to connect the two.[180]

In the West the nature of consciousness is generally considered to be problematic and difficult. Within Buddhist philosophy however, the nature of consciousness is deeply understood both through direct experience and rigorous philosophical analysis; and this understanding can shed light on many of the problems of understanding how the quantum realm and consciousness interconnect. As we shall see later the Yogachara[181] perspective gives a remarkable account of the functioning of reality which may be conceived of as embracing the ground quantum field of reality which can only be of the nature of consciousness. Indeed we shall discover that it is the operation of the fundamental creative force of consciousness which is responsible for the emergence of the 'classical' world.

There is an enormous gulf between quantum entities and everyday objects, the two spheres of reality, so to speak, appear to be so different that it seems impossible that the everyday world appears from the quantum; and yet it does. The confrontation between the everyday world and the quantum world leads us to the very limits of what we can know about reality. So, if Wheeler is correct about the enormous philosophical import of understanding the nature of quantum reality, the possibility of a deep knowledge of the essence of reality lies at the boundary between the quantum realm and the everyday world. We know that the quantum realm cannot be a figment of the imagination of a group of mad scientists; we have cd-players, camcorders, mobile phones, and computers and so on. The technology of the last one hundred years depends upon our knowledge of quantum physics. We also know that there is a very different realm of our direct experience of our everyday world. And, if Wheeler is right, the solution to the question of existence is to be found in understanding the nature of the boundary between the two.

It is here that the Madhyamaka can offer significant insight. There is a very deep reason why the world must be quantum in nature; and this reason is connected to understanding the deep nature of existence. Furthermore this understanding is illuminated by an appreciation of the remarkable Madhyamaka exposition of the concept of emptiness according to which the apparent 'things' of the everyday world function as if they were real 'things' because they actually do not fully exist! They appear to exist as independent entities but in actuality in their 'ultimate' nature they hover between existence and non-existence. As the Madhyamika Bhavaviveka (1st-2nd century) indicated the character of reality is

> Neither existent, nor nonexistent
> Nor both existent and nonexistent, nor neither.
> …true reality
> …is free from these four possibilities.[182]

This assertion indicates that emptiness can be considered to be the fundamental level of reality which somehow 'hovers' between existence and nonexistence. The reader might at this point think that this must be pushing the limits of comparison between abstruse and impenetrable Buddhist mystical musings and the modern science of quantum physics to breaking point. But this is not so. The Madhyamaka analysis was meant to be, and is, a precise analysis of the inner nature of reality, and it corresponds to the discoveries of quantum theory in a remarkable fashion.

The paradox of Schrödinger's cat is a famous quantum conundrum by which Schrödinger indicated to Einstein that quantum weirdness must have everyday implications. A cat which is sealed inside a container in such a way that its life or death depends upon a probabilistic quantum event must actually hover between existence and non-existence. The following is from science writer Marcus Chown's book *The Never-Ending Days of Being Dead*, which contains entertaining elucidations of cutting edge physics:

> So, what of a water droplet that hovers half in existence and half out of existence? It goes without saying that nobody has actually seen such a schizophrenic water droplet … Where does the quantum weirdness go.[183]

Here Chown clearly indicates that the condition of hovering between existence and non-existence is precisely the nature of 'quantum weirdness'. So it is somewhat remarkable that the Madhyamaka asserts that the empty nature of reality, which is indicated by the fact that the ultimate nature of reality is a hovering between existence and non-existence, is essential for the universe to function:

> If things were not empty of inherent existence, nothing could function…It is their emptiness of inherent existence that allows everything to operate satisfactorily.[184]

In the light of this assertion that emptiness, the fundamental hovering between existence and non-existence, is essential for the manifestation of the world of experience, we might ask whether there is anything within quantum physics that corresponds to this claim. In a recent work the science writer Michio Kaku tells us that:

> The reason why molecules are stable and the universe does not disintegrate is that electrons can be in many places at the same time. ….electrons can exist in parallel states hovering between existence and non-existence.[185]

The ability of a quantum particle to be in two places at the same time, whilst still maintaining an identity as a single entity, is a feature of quantum behavior that is absolutely crucial for the functioning of reality. It is a primary feature of the quantum world that from a classical perspective should be completely impossible. However, the fact that quantum entities are fundamentally wave-like makes this magical trick, which is given the name 'delocality', inevitable.

Quantum delocality is the mechanism which accounts for alpha decay of a radioactive nucleus. The radioactive elements are those that have heavy nuclei, with many protons and neutrons; Uranium 238, for instance, has 92 protons and 146 neutrons. Such large atoms have unstable nuclei and on occasion a very stable combination of 2 protons and 2 neutrons, an alpha particle, forms internally as a single unit. If the alpha particle were completely 'localised' inside the nucleus it would not be able to escape. But the alpha particle is actually, when not observed, not a particle. It only displays its particle-like face when it is observed. In the absence of detection there is only a wavefunction of probabilities and:

> Schrödinger's equation predicts that… the alpha particle's wavefunction may be sizable at very large distances outside the nucleus. This is because wavefunctions have wave-like properties and therefore are not confined by the same rules as particles.[186]

The alpha particle, then, is able to jump the boundary which contains it within the atom.

This mechanism, which is a consequence of the fundamental wave nature of the unobserved quantum realm, is called 'quantum tunnelling'. For instance when an electron is confined inside a box it has a probability wave as shown in figure 3.4. There is a non-zero probability that the electron can be found outside the box. Because of this an electron which is supposedly trapped inside a container will sometimes 'tunnel' to the outside of the box. Because the electron is a 'smeared out' probability wave, part of this wave will actually already be on the right hand side, so sometimes an electron can 'tunnel' through the barrier (fig 3.5).

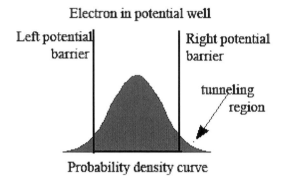

Fig 3.4

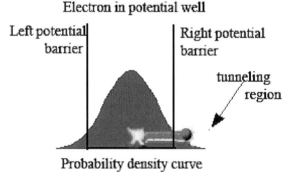

Fig 3.5

The electron does not literally tunnel through, but rather, because it has a fundamental wave nature it already has a quantum probability of being over on the right hand side, and because it has this probability of being on the other side of the barrier, it sometimes can appear on the other side of the barrier in accordance with the probability. So on a proportion of occasions, the quantum particle will jump the barrier because its wave nature makes it able to be in two places, either side of the barrier. It will sometimes magically appear to have performed an impossible feat of jumping an insurmountable obstacle. In actuality it only appears to 'tunnel' because there is a probability wavefunction which straddles the energy barrier in the middle.

This quantum marvel is a result of the fact that quantum entities are partially in many places at the same time; and this functioning underlies all the significant processes that maintain the universe and the life within it. Until quantum entities are observed they actually are not here, not there, not here and there, and not neither here or there. As Michio Kaku says it is this remarkable hovering between existence and non-existence which forms the ground for the functioning of reality.

This incredible mechanism of quantum delocation is the 'glue' which holds molecules together. The behavior of electrons is of paramount importance in the way that the atoms combine to produce the fabric of the material world. Elements are able to form molecules by combining together by sharing of electrons between atoms. An atom consists of a central nucleus comprised of protons and neutrons around which electrons are supposed to orbit in shells. The word 'supposed' is slipped in here to remind us that in actuality the atom is not inherently like this; this is a picture used for analysis.

According to Pauli's exclusion principle the number of electrons allowed in each shell is strictly determined by various parameters. An atomic energy shell cannot contain two electrons with the same parameters. The first and lowest energy shell can only contain a maximum of two electrons, one with spin up and the other with spin down. As we move to orbits further away from the nucleus the greater the number of electrons that are allowed. The chemical properties of any element are determined by the electron configuration of the outermost shell. Chemically active elements like lithium, sodium and potassium have gaps in their outer electron shells whereas inert elements, like helium and neon, have full outer shells. Because of the gaps in the outer shells atoms of the active elements are able to share electrons with other atoms, and in so doing they make molecules.

Oxygen, for instance, has two electron gaps in its outer shell and a hydrogen atom has one electron and one gap. This means that one oxygen atom can combine with two hydrogen atoms to form H_2O – water. The hydrogen electrons are shared with the oxygen atom so that the outer shell of the oxygen has a full complement of electrons. On their own hydrogen and oxygen are incomplete, so to speak, their incomplete outer shells are 'looking' to get filled in; the water molecule, on the other hand, is stable because by sharing electrons the outer shells of both the oxygen and hydrogen atoms are completed (fig 3.6, fig 3.7).

The conventional picture of bonding electrons (fig 3.7) is that they sit between the two nuclei that they bond. This picture, however, does not take into account the wave properties of quantum entities and does not really give a full account of the phenomenon. A more adequate account can be given by considering an electron's potential energy curve and its wave properties. From this point of view electrons are not so much 'particles' but are much more like clouds of 'probability fluid.' Fig 3.8 shows the configurations of

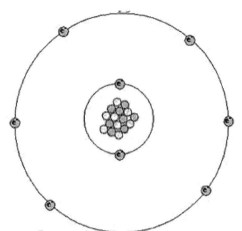

Hydrogen atom:
1 proton and 1
electron, there is
room for one more
electron in the
innermost electron
shell

Oxygen has room for two more
electrons in outer shell because the
maximum allowed number is 8

Fig 3.6

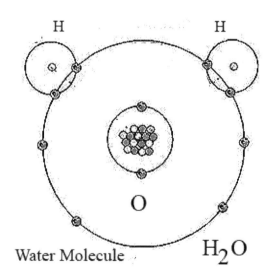

Water Molecule H_2O

Fig 3.7

this electronic probability fluid for various sets of parameters for a hydrogen atom. The actual title for these images is 'probability density plots' for the hydrogen wavefunction. It is a staggering truth about the make up of the apparently solid material world that it is actually held together precisely by such nebulous clouds of probable existence! As Nick Herbert says:

> …something seems smeared out to fill the atom, an indescribable something we call a 'probability cloud,' 'realm of positional possibilities,' 'electron wavefunction,' or 'quantum stuff,' without really being sure what we are talking about. Whatever it is, though, the whole world is made of it.[187]

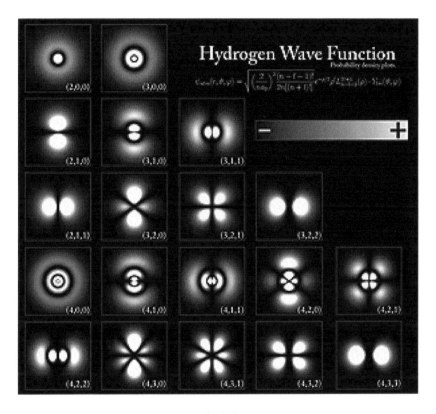

Fig 3.8

Fig 3.9 shows the electron potential/kinetic energy curve against distance from a nucleus, in this case a hydrogen nucleus, which is a single proton. The shaded region shows the range of distances and energies that an electron can have when it occupies the lowest shell in a hydrogen atom, which has just one electron. The electron can be viewed as a 'probability fluid' which occupies the shaded region[188].

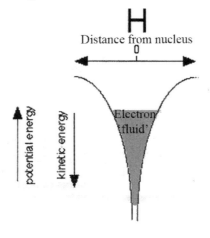

Fig 3.9

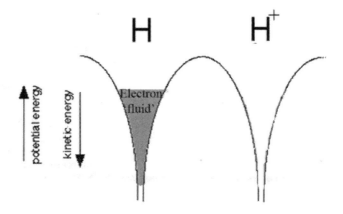

Fig 3.10

Now suppose we bring a bare hydrogen nucleus (H⁺), a single positively charged proton without an accompanying electron up to the electron probability haze which surrounds the first hydrogen atom (fig 3.10). The single proton provides a potential well which is waiting to be filled with what we can think of as electron probability fluid. But, as the diagram shows there is an energy barrier which, in the classical world, would be insurmountable. The electron probability 'fluid' however can 'tunnel' through the barrier to occupy both potential wells, although never being located in between them, whilst keeping its identity as a single electron (fig 3.11). This is how electrons, by being in two places at the same time whilst keeping a single identity, act as the glue which holds molecules, and hence the universe, together.

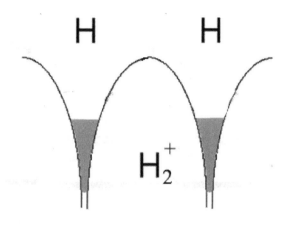

Fig 3.11

Electrons are able to perform the role of connecting atoms together because, as Kaku says, they hover between existence and non-existence. It is because they do not exist as definitely locatable entities that they are able to function as molecular glue. If they existed in the way we conceive of every-day objects to exist, which is to say inherently and determinately 'real', then there would be no way that they could perform this remarkable feat and so perform the task of molecular coupling. It is the wave-like aspect of elect-rons that is crucial for the functioning of reality.

What a remarkable state of affairs; the manifestation of the solidity of the everyday world requires an essential lack of solidity at the quantum level, a lack of solidity which bears the hallmark of neither existence or non-existence nor both nor neither; how remarkable it also is that two thousand five hundred years ago:

> The one who knows all things and all absences of things,
> The Transcendent Conqueror,
> Refuted both existence and non-existence[189]

And:

> From certain single perspectives
> [The Buddha] taught them as either 'nonexistent' or 'existent.'
> From both perspectives,

He expressed them as 'neither existent nor nonexistent.'
Since they do not exist as they appear,
He talked about their 'nonexistence.'
Since they appear in such ways,
He spoke about their 'existence.'[190]

The Madhyamaka is precise about the fact that emptiness is essential for cause and effect to function. Emptiness is the essence of cause and effect; it is the ungraspable glue that holds cause and effect together. At the quantum level phenomena balance on the edge of existence, which is to say they hover between existence and non-existence. In his book *Entanglement: The Greatest Mystery In Physics* Amir D Aczel describes the situation:

> I'm at the bank, and there are two lines in front of the teller windows. They're both equally long, and there's no one behind me. I want to be in the line which moves the fastest, but I don't know which one that will be. I stand between the two lines, or I keep jumping from one line to the other as one or the other becomes shorter. I am in 'both lines at once'[191]

It is this hovering between the two extremes, the dance of almost existing which is the dance of emptiness, which allows causality, and the universe, or multiverse, to function. This observation is not an obscure piece of oriental vagueness, it is actually completely precise. If the fundamental nature of reality were other than emptiness, the fundamental quality of reality which allows electrons to function as the 'glue' which supports the manifestation of an experienced world, then there would be no experienced world.

The Madhyamika philosophers obviously did not know the theory of quantum interactions in the form that physicists today do. They were, however, aware of 'subtle particles' which flicker in and out of 'existence' within the void from which the universe is manifested; and it is extraordinary that they performed a remarkable razor sharp analysis of the nature of causality and reality which led them to say that the universe functioned only because of its essential 'emptiness,' which is described as the ability to hover between the four 'extremes' of existence, nonexistence, not both, nor neither, but maintain a state beyond them all, until, that is they are observed.

This state of hovering between extremes of existence – neither existent, nor non-existent, nor both existent and non-existent, nor neither – but not fully occupying any is both the hallmark of the unobserved quantum realm and of emptiness. For instance Jeffrey Alan Barrett in his book *The Quantum Mechanics of Minds and Worlds* cites this paradoxical quantum config-uration of existence:

> …a neutral K meson is typically not a K^0 meson, not a $-K^0$ meson, not both and not neither.[192]

And Giancarlo Ghirardi, in his book *Sneaking a Look at God's Cards*, clearly indicates that this paradoxical logical configuration lies at the heart of the quantum situation. When describing the existential possibility configuration for a quantum chair, i.e. a chair considered as a quantum object, he writes:

> What meaning can there be in a state that makes it illegitimate to think that our chair is *either* here or in some other place? ... only potentialities exist about the location of the chair, potentialities that cannot be realized, unless we carry out a measurement of position? How can it be understood that, attached to these potentialities, is a *nonepistemic* probability that in a subsequent measurement of position the chair will be found here or there (which is equivalent to asserting that, before the measurement was carried out, the chair could be neither here nor there, nor in both places, nor in neither place)?[193]

The (in the original) italicized word 'nonepistemic' is emphasized because the situation of 'hovering' between possibilities of existence is not a matter of our lack of knowledge; it *is the ontological condition of the quantum entity.* This crucial issue will be returned to in the later chapter *Quantum Emptiness.*

For good measure it is worth noting that J. Robert Oppenheimer made a similar observation when discussing the Heisenberg Uncertainty Principle:

> If we ask, for instance, whether the position of the electron remains the same, we must say 'no;' if we ask whether the electron's position changes with time, we must say 'no;' if we ask whether the electron is at rest, we must say 'no;' if we ask whether it is in motion, we must say 'no.' The Buddha has given such answers when interrogated as to the conditions of man's self after his death; but they are not familiar answers for the tradition of seventeenth and eighteenth-century science.[194]

(The Buddha said that the self after death neither exists, nor does not exist, nor both nor neither).

The Heisenberg Uncertainty Principle, which states that it not possible to precisely measure both the position and momentum of a quantum entity, accounts for the fact that quantum entities can 'hover' between existence and nonexistence. This principle, which Ghirardi describes as 'one of the most immediate consequences of the quantum formulism,'[195] is the aspect of quantum functioning which allows the phenomena of the universe to function coherently. And, as we have seen, the Buddhist concept of emptiness, which describes the ultimate metaphysical nature at the heart of the process of reality, appears to map seamlessly onto the ontological structure of the Heisenberg Uncertainty Principle. It would appear, then, that we can answer

Wheeler's question 'Why the Quantum?' with the Madhyamika master Nagarjuna's answer:

> For those for whom emptiness is possible,
> Everything is possible,
> For those for whom emptiness is not possible,
> Nothing is possible.[196]

What's the Matter with Matter?

One might try to interpret the 'matter' occurring in this formula as the 'matter' that occurs in classical physics. But this kind of 'matter' does not exist in nature.[197]

- Henry Stapp

...variables can no longer provide us with a definite, unique and unambiguous concept of matter in the quantum domain. Only in the classical domain is such a concept an adequate approximation.[198]

- David Bohm

Quantum theory provides a superb description of physical reality on a small scale, yet it contains many mysteries. Without doubt, it is hard to come to terms with the workings of the theory, and it is particularly difficult to make sense of the kind of 'physical reality' – or lack of it – that it seems to imply for our world.[199]

- Roger Penrose

...because experiments confirm that quantum mechanics does describe fundamental physics, it presents a frontal assault on our basic beliefs as to what constitutes reality.[200]

- Brian Greene

The laws of physics were saying that matter as we know it simply can't exist. It was time for some new laws of physics.[201]

- Robert Oerter

Niels Bohr

Matter does not exist; or, to be more precise, quantum physics has clearly shown that the concept of 'matter' as understood within pre-quantum physics or 'classical' physics, the physics from Renee Descartes' time (17th century) down to the early twentieth century, does not exist. At the turn of the twentieth century the comfortable world of classical physics began to look less solid than had previously been thought and subsequently the classical notion of 'matter' can no longer be validly connected with any existent entity within the universe.

The scientific investigation of the physical world was facilitated by the epistemological framework established by Descartes in the seventeenth century. It is generally well known that he divided reality up into two fundamental 'substances': 'matter', which he defined as characterised by extension and solidity, and thinking substance (mind or consciousness), which comprised the realm of ideas that reflected the external forms of matter. According to the Cartesian worldview these two principle existents were considered to be ultimate categories of existence; any phenomenon would fall into one or other division. Descartes defined these categories as having no common qualities, they were opposite in nature, such concepts are referred to by Buddhist philosophy as being concepts of 'mutual abandonment.' Matter, which was conceived as extended and continuous, had no thought-like qualities or capacities and consciousness was immaterial, having no extension in space.

Descartes was well aware that by defining his basic categories as being completely antithetical in fundamental nature there could be no way to account for the manner in which they could interact with, or relate to, each other. This problem was hastily glossed over by assuming that God played the part of the universal coordinator between the two spheres of reality.

The Cartesian demarcation of reality into two mutually distinct aspects set the stage for the subsequent philosophical discourse concerning the nature of the relationship between the two. Such philosophical speculations, of course, invariably elevated one or the other to primacy whilst deprecating the other. Hence the development of philosophy from this point consisted of the working through of variously more subtle formulations of materialism or idealism, the former asserting the ontological primacy of matter and the latter the primacy of consciousness or mind.

Descartes also developed some of the basic mathematical tools which were vital in the scientific project, foremost being the Cartesian co-ordinate grid which formed the basis for analytical geometry and calculus. Using these conceptual tools the configurations and movements of objects could be analysed. Isaac Newton used the new epistemology and mathematical framework to stunning effect with his analysis of motion and gravity. Subsequently this kind of mathematical analysis of the purely material aspects of reality, which required precise quantitative measurement, with a corresponding disregard for the qualitative aspects of experience, became the paradigm for further scientific investigation of the material world.

Ever since the establishment of the Cartesian and Newtonian scientific paradigm the bold and relentless mapping of the mechanical lineaments of reality suggested a world that functioned according to the immutable and mechanical laws of physics. Science, then, seemed to have revealed the inner clockwork of reality and this clockwork was unswerving in its mechanistic demeanor. This mechanistic vision was inevitable, given the fundamental split made by Descartes into the realms of matter on the one hand, and mind, or consciousness on the other. As Fritjov Capra in his book *The Tao of Physics* observes:

> The 'Cartesian' division allowed scientists to treat matter as dead and completely separate from themselves, and to see the material world as a multitude of different objects assembled into a huge machine. Such a mechanistic world view was held by Isaac Newton who constructed his mechanics on its basis and made it the foundation of classical physics. From the second half of the seventeenth to the end of the nineteenth century, the mechanistic Newtonian model of the universe dominated all scientific thought.[202]

The Newtonian viewpoint was a view of a vast complexity of deterministic material interactions. The external world was conceived of as being composed of independent physical objects interacting according to definite and determinate mathematical patterns. This view was elevated to an inviolate principle, a metaphysical absolute that was considered to be completely unquestionable.

This viewpoint consisted of a fixed space-time framework within which individual self-enclosed independent bits of reality moved around and interacted with each other either through contact with each other or through the various forces which emanated from them and connected them to other entities subject to the same force. The forces known at the end of the nineteenth century were the electromagnetic and gravitational. The important point to grasp is that all the separate entities making up reality were thought of as being fundamentally separate from each other and the forces were conceived of as being external. As quantum physicist David Bohm characterised what he terms the mechanistic order:

> …the principle feature of this order is that the world is regarded as constituted of entities which are *outside of each other*, in the sense that they exist independently in different regions of space (and time) and interact through forces which do not bring about any changes in their essential natures.[203]

Our understanding of this basic viewpoint is quite clearly derived from our macroscopic, everyday reality, and to a large extent derives from our own experience of being independent entities capable of exerting various forces on aspects of the world around us.

This 'classical' viewpoint is summed up by the physicist Amit Goswami, a dissenter from the mainstream scientific paradigm, who depicts this fundamental viewpoint as follows:

> The current worldview has it that everything is made of matter, and everything can be reduced to elementary particles of matter, the basic constituents - building blocks – of matter. And cause arises from the interactions of these basic building blocks or elementary particles; elementary particles make atoms, atoms make molecules, molecules make cells, and cells make the brain. But all the way, the ultimate cause is always the interactions between elementary particles. This is the belief – all cause moves from the elementary particles.[204]

The same observation is articulated by Bohm, another physicist who became a dissenter from the mainstream view of quantum interpretation:

> physics has become almost totally committed to the notion that the order of the universe is basically mechanistic. The most common form of this notion is that the world is assumed to be constituted of separately existent, indivisible and unchangeable 'elementary particles'', which are the fundamental 'building blocks of the universe. [205]

Both Goswami and Bohm, amongst others, indicate that, although in theory this mechanistic view of reality was dramatically overturned at the beginning of the twentieth century with the dawn of quantum physics, in practice it still lingers as an ingrained way of viewing reality.

At the end of the nineteenth century the nature of 'matter,' the stuff of the world which was thought to be completely external to, and independent of consciousness, was a matter of some dissent within the physics community. The existence of atoms, tiny fundamental bits and pieces of supposedly solid units of material, was not universally accepted. Max Planck in his early career did not accept their reality; instead he considered that matter was continuous and thus infinitely divisible.

However, despite this uncertainty, in 1900 William Thompson (Lord Kelvin) 'pronounced that physics was over'[206]; in his view the only outstanding 'clouds on the horizon' were the problems of 'black body radiation' and the failure to detect the aether, the purportedly universal substance through which light was supposed to travel. It was the solution to the first of these problems that ushered in the quantum revolution that destroyed the fundamental physical worldview of the late nineteenth century.

As we have previously seen in 1900 Max Planck solved the problem of black body radiation by an 'act of desperation' and so inadvertently triggered the quantum age. The subsequent discoveries suggested that light had both a particle and wave aspect to its basic nature, a feature later characterised by Bohr as the famous wave-particle duality postulate.

The fact that matter was not continuously solid but had some kind of internal atomic structure was suggested by the discovery of alpha particles and beta particles. In 1887 the great experimental physicist J.J. Thomson showed that the mysterious rays known as 'beta' rays were actually made up of streams of particles carrying a negative electric charge. On the basis of his work Thomson proposed one of the first models of the atom, referred to as the 'plumb pudding model' (fig 4.1). This picture of the atom consisted of a ball of positive charge with smaller balls of negative charge, the electrons, embedded within the larger ball, like plums in a pudding. The hugely significant physicist Niels Bohr worked for a time at the Cavendish laboratory with Thomson but after a year Bohr moved on to work with Ernest Rutherford who proposed the model of the atom that supplanted Thomson's.

Rutherford's atomic model was based on a spectacular experiment he had performed whilst investigating the behaviour of high velocity alpha particles (composed of two protons and two neutrons). The particles were fired at thin gold foil and the scattering of the alpha particles was monitored (fig 4.2). The results were surprising. Some of the alpha particles were deflected through large angles but most passed through (fig 4.3), something that could not happen if Thomson's model had been correct. The fact that the majority had passed straight through clearly suggested that the greater part of the atom was composed of empty space. The particles that had been deflected back must have met something that had given them an appreciable kick. The conclusion that Rutherford came to was that the positively charged alpha particles had been deflected by the positive charge of a central nucleus of the gold atoms. The electrons, therefore, must be orbiting the nucleus like planets and most of the atom was empty space.

Fig 4.1

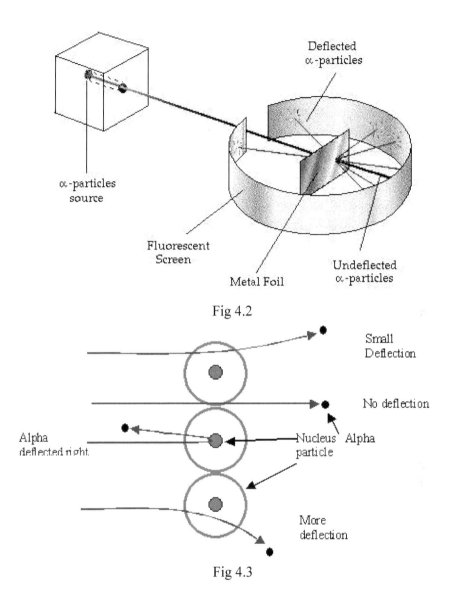

Fig 4.2

Fig 4.3

In fact atoms are more than 99.999999999 percent empty space. At the centre of an atom the nucleus contains positively charged protons and neutral neutrons, which make up the nucleus, and the negatively charged electrons orbit at a considerable distance away (fig 4.4). A rough indication of the amount of nothingness inside an atom can be comprehended by the illustration that if an atomic nucleus is represented by a football at the centre of St Paul's cathedral, the electrons would be grains of sand orbiting around in the outer stalls. Figure 4.4 therefore is schematic and its scale is incorrect – the electrons are much, much smaller than protons and neutrons (nucleons) and the distance between the nucleus and electrons much greater.

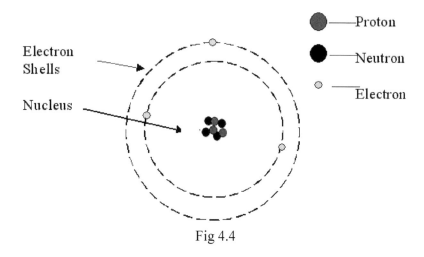

Fig 4.4

Bohr started to work out the details of how Rutherford's planetary model could be understood. From a classical point of view the model was impossible because accelerating electrons (anything orbiting in a circle is accelerating) should radiate energy and quickly (about a thousandth billionth of a second) fall into the nucleus. Bohr wondered whether quantum ideas could be applied to Rutherford's model of the atom and began to speculate in this direction. An acquaintance drew his attention to the Balmer series of spectral lines produced by radiation emissions of the hydrogen atom (fig 4.5). When the emitted radiation from an atom is analysed with spectroscopy a spectrum of the radiation is produced; the spectrum is a series of lines corresponding to the different frequencies of radiation that the atom is emitting or absorbing. Bohr realised that the discreteness of the series of lines was indicative of its quantum origin. The reason why electrons did not lose energy through continuous energy emission was that they could not emit energy continuously; electrons must emit and absorb energy in quantum packets.

On the basis of his analysis of the lines and the Balmer formula Bohr proposed a model of the atom in which electrons were restricted to discrete orbits with fixed energy levels. The different frequencies emitted by the atom were accounted for by electron transitions between higher energy level orbits and lower energy level orbits. As the diagram indicates the Balmer series is produced when electrons jump to orbit n=2 from the higher levels. Other spectral line series are produced when electrons jump down to other orbits. Bohr proposed this atomic model, which at the time worked only for the hydrogen atom, in 1913 (fig 4.6).

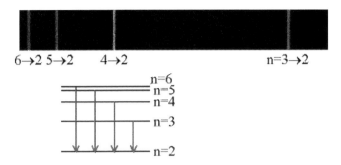

Fig 4.5

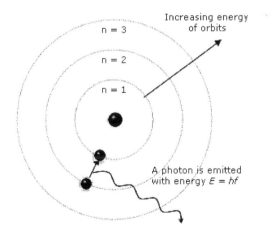

Fig 4.6

The world of physics at this time was in confusion as to what to believe regarding the new ideas that were being produced in the wake of Planck's discovery of the quantum nature of radiation and the subsequent proposal of wave-particle duality. The theories and models of quantum behaviour were a kind of hotchpotch of classical ideas with new quantum ideas patched in. Bohr's model of the atom, for instance, looks classical in essence but had to incorporate the non-classical quantum feature that electrons absorbed or emitted energy in quantum units.

Some features of Bohr's model caused consternation amongst some of his contemporaries. The transitions between energy levels, or electron 'shells,' had to be instantaneous for the model to work. This is to say that an electron would have to be in shell 4, say, at one moment and instantaneously it would leave shell 4 and appear in shell 2, for instance, without travelling the distance between shells. An aspect of the Bohr model that Einstein particularly disliked was the fact that quantum jumps between the shells were unpredictable. It was possible to give probabilities but exactly when a jump would take place was not a value that could be calculated. In other words the phenomenon of quantum jumping apparently occurs spontaneously, apparently without an immediate cause. Although a jump is caused by the difference in energy levels, the exact moment of the jump did not seem to have a cause. However, despite the fact that Bohr's model of the atom had serious conceptual problems it did begin to give an account of how electron 'orbits' were organised and how this related to the emission of radiation by atoms.

The wave-particle feature of the new quantum perspective which had developed up until the early 1920s applied only to radiation. This was conclusively demonstrated when in 1923 Arthur Compton and Peter Debye demonstrated how light quanta could be 'bounced' off electrons with a concomitant frequency change corresponding to the change in momentum of the light particles. This experiment demonstrated that light had momentum corresponding to its particle nature.

The next development went, literally, to the heart of the matter, or rather to the heart of matter. Prince Louis de Broglie suggested that if radiation, which was once thought to be exclusively wave-like, had turned out to be also particle-like, then it seemed likely that what was at the time still considered to be exclusively particle like, particles of 'matter,' should also have a wave-like nature. If this were the case then it should, De Broglie suggested, be possible to get a diffraction pattern when an electron beam is directed through a narrow aperture.

Diffraction is the phenomenon of bending of waves around the edge of an obstacle. Ordinarily light travels in straight lines through a uniform, transparent medium, but light waves that just pass the edges of an opaque body are bent, or deflected. The diagram shows the diffraction of waves through a wide slot (fig 4.7a). If the width of the slot is comparable to the wavelength, as shown in fig 4.7b, then the diffraction produces curved wave fronts as shown.

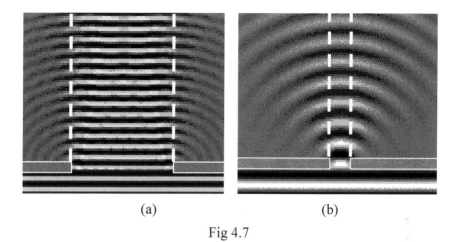

(a)   (b)

Fig 4.7

The diffraction of x-rays by crystals is used to examine the atomic and molecular structure of crystals. When electromagnetic waves are diffracted through a crystal lattice interference effects caused by the interaction of the diffracted waves causes a diffraction pattern when projected onto a light sensitive screen. Wave interference is due to the way that waves can reinforce to produce bright areas when they meet in phase, or cancel each other to produce dark areas when out of phase. If De Broglie's suggestion was correct then a diffraction pattern should be produced if electrons were also sent through such a crystal lattice. De Broglie made his suggestion in 1923. In 1925 an electron diffraction pattern was demonstrated by sending a beam through nickel crystals. Fig 4.8 shows an x-ray diffraction pattern and an electron diffraction pattern.

By using his idea that quantum sized particles also have a wave nature de Broglie was able to extend the Bohr atomic model in a remarkable manner. He visualised the fixed electron orbits as being the result of standing electron waves. A standing wave forms when there is a whole number of half-wavelengths occupying the distance into which the standing wave fits. It is the phenomenon of standing waves which underlies the mechanism by which a violin or guitar for instance, produces a note. The musician controls the length of the string with a finger and the stroking of the bow or plucking of the string creates a standing wave that fits into the length of string (see Fig4.9A).

Prince Louis De Broglie

Fig 4.8

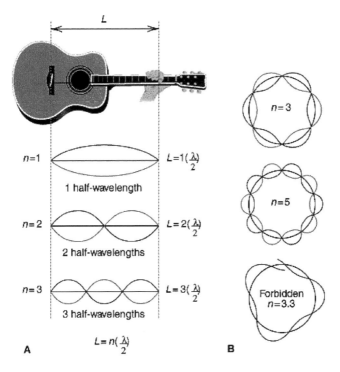

Fig 4.9

In the case of an electron standing wave the wave fits around the nucleus so that an integral number of wavelengths fit into the circumference of the orbit (see diagram). This means that when the wave motion of the electron has travelled around the circumference it meets its starting point at the same amplitude as the starting point. In Fig 4.9B the n=3 (3 wave-lengths fit around the nucleus) and n=5 orbits are allowed because they fit into the circumference without discontinuity; the n=3.3 is disallowed because the wave motion is broken, the ends do not match. The fixed positions of the orbits, then, are explained by the fact that the electrons can only occupy orbits that will contain a fixed number of wavelengths.

De Broglie's extension of the wave-particle duality into the realm of 'matter' completed the first phase of the quantum revolution. The pre-quantum, or classical, version of 'matter' was, or at least should have been, completely destroyed. The notion of 'matter' has been replaced by a scientific vision of the world as orchestrated by an astonishing complex field of quantum resonant interactions of some kind of energy which is the funda-mental 'stuff' of reality.

The basic concepts employed in classical physics were essentially derived from human experience of the macroscopic, everyday world. For instance the ideas of 'matter, 'inertia', and 'force,' concepts which are fundamental to Newton's laws, quite clearly derive their effectiveness from human physical embodiment. 'Matter' is the amount of 'stuff'; the more of this stuff an object contains the greater its 'inertia' or resistance to change of motion; the greater the inertia the greater the force that is required to bring about a change in motion. Such concepts are readily comprehended from experience of moving objects around using human muscles. Aching muscles assume that they have been dealing with something weighty and substantial existing independently in an external world.

The idea that the basic units of matter - protons, neutrons and electrons – were in fact more like waves than solid little balls is completely contrary to the classical notion of the material world. The notion of 'matter' was thrown into a kind of suspended state, but physicists still continued to use the term as if its classical connotation was still valid. In a sense they had no choice because there were no alternatives to substitute. But what is very strange is that even today, a hundred years after the beginning of the quantum era, a great many physicists still employ the term as if the classical concept had not been called into question.

For instance in his book *The Theory of Almost Everything* Robert Oerter tells us that:

> The laws of physics were saying that matter as we know it simply can't exist. It was time for some new laws of physics.[207]

But later on in the book we read:

> Is the quantum field real? True, it describes the motion of matter …[208]

And again:

> Dark matter has never been directly detected: How, then, can we know that it's not normal matter?[209]

It is quite clear that Oerter should be using the term in the same sense on the various occasions he employs it but it is not at all clear that this is the case. Oerter's book, like just about all other popular books about quantum physics, and perhaps other less introductory or popular works, allows the term 'matter' to slip and slide in a fashion which renders it virtually vacuous, as vacuous as the 'stuff' denoted by the term actually is! The term 'matter' only appears to have a conceptual force because of its everyday connotation, not because of any clarification with the realm of theoretical physics. What exactly is 'normal matter?' Quantum physics has now shown that it is not the solid, extended 'stuff' of reality imagined by Descartes and also taken for granted, despite its non-existence, by just about everyone on planet Earth.

The use of the term 'matter' in an ambiguous manner can be located in most current scientific writing, and in so doing the writers are illicitly employing a classical concept in a quantum context. The concept of 'matter' has not been explicitly given a physical quantum definition. Classical 'matter' and 'mass' is weighty and graspable, so to speak. It involves our everyday notions of substance. Quantum 'matter' or 'mass', on the other hand, has none of these attributes. At the quantum level the notion of matter is cut adrift from the comfortable solidity of everyday experience, so much so that it is a completely different concept because it is just a mathematical symbol; but the use of the term by a great many physicists generally covers over the discontinuity.

In the early days of the development of quantum theory progress was achieved by cobbling together new theories using classical concepts but giving them a new context. As Baggott says:

> As is typical in such a radical change in the approach to acquiring scientific understanding; old and often unsuitable concepts were forced into service to meet the needs of the new description.[210]

As the theory developed many of the elements of the theory began to have significances which were not easily pinned directly onto definite aspects of reality:

> ... the theory's concepts appeared to become increasingly disconnected from the reality the theory was trying to describe.[211]

Later the theory's mathematical formulation did in many ways loose contact with our notions of everyday reality. However the concept of 'matter' was never explicitly re-evaluated so its significance still seems to be located in the classical world.

When Erwin Schrödinger gave a presentation of de Broglie's ideas, a physicist in the following discussion observed that to talk about waves without a wave equation was 'childish.'[212] This lack Schrödinger promptly set out to rectify and in a few weeks he concocted a wave equation that worked. The Schrödinger equation is a differential equation which, when solved for a specific quantum situation, provides a wavefunction which describes the behaviour of that quantum situation. He presented his work at the end of January 1926.

A wavefunction for the Bohr hydrogen atom model was derived from the Schrödinger equation and it successfully predicted the fixed orbits. Subsequently the Schrödinger equation underwent modifications as new quantum complexities arose and it was extended to apply generally to the quantum realm. At about the same time another mathematical method of describing quantum behaviour was discovered. This was Heisenberg's matrix mechanics that Schrödinger demonstrated to be mathematically equivalent to the wavefunction approach although it looked very different.

Erwin Schrödinger

The success of the Schrödinger equation in providing wavefunctions that gave probabilities for quantum events presented a deep problem: what were the derived wavefunctions wavefunctions of? Schrödinger conceived of the wave aspect of quantum phenomena to be primary and he had hoped to rescue, in some manner, some of the physical reality of classical concepts through the establishment of the wavefunction. One of his views of the wavefunction was that it represented 'a vibration in an electromagnetic field.'[213] His hopes of resurrecting some form of physical reality were dashed, however, when Max Born indicated that the wavefunction was not 'real' in the sense of physical reality. Instead it represented the way that our possible *knowledge* of a physical system develops with time. From this point of view the wavefunction ceases to have a direct physical, in the sense that the term 'physical' was used in classical physics, connection with reality:

> ...no one really knows what the wavefunction actually is. Most physicists regard it as an abstract mathematical entity that can be used to extract information about nature. Others assign it to its own, very strange, independent reality.[214]

According to Born's interpretation, which is now the accepted viewpoint, the wavefunction is a probability wave. When the amplitude of the wavefunction, for a particular position and time, is squared (multiplied by itself) its value represents the probability that a particle will be located by a process of measurement at that time and in that position.

However, the wavefunction squared does not give the probabilities of where a pre-existing particle can be found. It actually gives the probabilities that, when a measurement interaction, seemingly involving human consciousness, is performed at a particular time and in a particular location, the measurement will register the presence of a particle. The particle, however, does not exist prior to the interaction:

> The object was not there before you found it there. Your happening to find it there *caused* it to be there.[215]

A wavefunction precisely predicts the time evolution of the state of a quantum system, a 'state' being the, possibly infinite, collection of possibilities contained within the wavefunction. But then, as Penrose describes:

> From time to time – whenever we consider that a 'measurement' has occurred – we must discard the quantum state that we have been laboriously evolving, and use it only to compute various probabilities that the state will 'jump' to one or another of a set of *new* possible states.[216]

And, significantly, the new states appear as classically 'physical' states whereas prior to the measurement event the wavefunction is a purely abstract mathematical construction to which a 'classical' physical reality cannot be ascribed.

If the apparently classically physical states are not continuously measured they will immediately revert to being non-physical (using the term 'physical' in a 'classical' sense) probability waves until another measurement occurs. Penrose adopted the symbols **U** and **R** to indicate the two processes. Adding the **M** to indicate a measurement the situation can be represented, scanning left to right:

M	**M**	**M**
⇓	⇓	⇓

U> U> U> U> R> U> U> U> U>R> U> U> U> U> U> R> U> U> U>

U= continuous development of wavefunction

M = measurement

R = momentary discontinuous, indeterminate transition to 'physically real' configuration.

The important point here is that, whilst each successive **U** evolves deterministically from the previous **U,** the transition from **U** to **R** is abrupt and non-deterministic. One of the probabilities contained in the **U** will be actualised but which one cannot be predicted with certainty.

Jim Al-Khalili gives an entertaining analogy for the behaviour of a wavefunction. The police are trying to keep track of a burglar recently released from prison but they do not want to physically follow him. Instead they keep a probability distribution of the likelihood of a burglary occurring at various places on the city map. When the burglar is first released the probability that he will commit a burglary a long way from the prison is zero whilst the possibility that he might burgle a house close to the prison is high. As time progresses, however, the probability distribution will spread out over the city map. After a long time the burglar could be anywhere and, barring other factors, the probability distribution will be fairly uniform over the city map. Suddenly a burglary occurs with the unmistakable modus operandi of the released burglar somewhere in the city. As far as the police are concerned the place of the burglary was non-deterministic, it only had a probability. But now the probability distribution is abruptly altered. The probability of another burglary close to the burglary just committed is high and tails off as the distance increases. Subsequently the probability distribution spreads out again.

In this analogy the burglary represents the measurement that triggers the **R** process of an actualised physical reality and the spreading out of the probability with time is the **U** process. This is, in fact, the way that wavefunctions behave; the probability distribution spreads out over space as the time since the last measurement increases:

> ...a wavefunction spreads out from the point where the electron was last seen and knowledge of the wavefunction allows us to assign probabilities to where it might show up next.[217]

Unlike the burglar, however, the electron does not exist as a definite independent entity between measurements. According to quantum theory it is literally spread out as a probability distribution. But what this means in terms of physical reality is just not known. This is why quantum physicists come to blows at the dinner table; they all have different views on the matter!

The abrupt transformation from a pure possibility to physical reality is referred to as the 'collapse of the wavefunction' or 'reduction of the state vector.' Prior to measurement the wavefunction is said to contain a 'superposition' of possibilities, which means that each possibility is contained in potential form within the wavefunction. They do not fully exist 'physically', but each possibility has a potential existence at the same time as the others. In fact the wavefunction implies that all possibilities exist in some sense, but not fully, *at the same time*. The reason for the imprecision in description is that there are no concepts in our description of familiar classical reality that describes this situation.

This unavoidable model[218] of the way that quantum probabilities materialise into actualities brings to the fore the crucial question that is at the core of the problem of the interpretation of quantum theory. What causes, or constitutes, a measurement? It is certainly difficult to comprehend how a completely non-conscious apparatus can be said to measure something but there are physicists who wish to claim such a thing. Suppose a ruler falls down beside an object with nobody looking on. Does the ruler 'measure' the object? Obviously not; but if an interested party comes along and looks to see how long the object is then clearly a measurement has been performed. This is a very crude example compared with the quantum situation; the question is, however, does the principle hold in the quantum context?

In the crude ruler example there is, obviously, no implication that the act of measurement has a direct agency in the creation of the object measured. However, the quantum situation is different because if the quantum measurement performed does require a consciousness, or consciousnesses, for its effectiveness then there is no alternative but to say that the agency of consciousness has had a creative effect at the quantum level. In this case the conclusion that consciousness determines, to some extent, the outcome is inescapable. It is vital, however, to be clear that this does not necessarily mean that a human being can determine which probability within a wavefunction is actualised by an act of intentionality. For the moment it could only be claimed that the agency of consciousness prompts one of the probabilities to actualise without consciously determining which one actualises.

The double slit experiment demonstrates the seemingly 'creative' agency of consciousness at the quantum level. The Heisenberg uncertainty principle is another conundrum related to wave-particle duality that implicates the agency of consciousness. The wavefunction that we have been considering so far has been the position wavefunction, which indicates the probabilities of where a particle will be located. There is another wavefunction, the momentum wavefunction, which contains the probabilities of the momentum of a particle (momentum = mass x velocity). The position wavefunction can be transformed into the momentum wavefunction by applying a Fourier Transform, and vice versa. A spread out position wavefunction always produces a localised momentum wavefunction, and vice versa. This means that more precisely we determine the position of a particle, the less precisely we know the momentum, and vice versa. When we consider that prior to our determination neither position nor momentum have actual physical reality it becomes clear that it is possible to actualise to a greater precision one or other of the position – momentum pair. This clearly requires a conscious decision.

It is this appearance of consciousness within the quantum realm, which was imposed by the theory against the wishes of physicists, that leads physicists to question the reality, or the completeness, of the theory. The notion that consciousness might be implicated in some manner in the creation of the actual world seems simply too outlandish. Penrose quotes with approval 'a remark that was made to (him) … at a dinner party':

> "If you really believe in quantum mechanics, then you can't take it seriously."[219]

But recent experiments are beginning to suggest that this view is simply the only way of accounting for the way reality behaves.

The wavefunction explanation is generally taken to offer some kind of explanation of quantum behaviour, but it is an explanation which completely divorces the mathematical description of the wavefunction from everyday reality. According to this view quantum particles do not exist until they are measured or observed. The unobserved quantum world consists of a spread out wavefunction which describes the probability of finding a particle when we perform a measurement. Wavefunctions, therefore, do not partake of the same solid reality that we expect from the everyday world. They describe probabilities rather than actualities. Despite this ghostly existence however, these probability waves do interact to produce an interference pattern of particles. Jim Al-Khalili describes the situation as follows:

> Before the particle hits the screen, the wavefunction is all we have to describe reality. The wavefunction is not the atom itself but only our description of how it behaves when we are not looking at it. … So provided we deal with only what the wavefunction looks like at any time and follow the rules of how to use it to predict the chance of the atom being there and having certain properties we can do business quite happily. Almost all physicists work this way. This is because they have given up hope of ever being able to figure out what is actually going on using concepts rooted in Newtonian mechanics.[220]

This amounts to saying that we can calculate how a particle arrived at a certain point, but we have no idea what a particle is!

It is very important to be clear about what is being claimed here. Schrödinger's wavefunction is often presented as a merely mathematical device which can be used to predict the probabilities of finding particles in certain places. It is tempting to think therefore that the particle is somewhere really but we just do not know where. However this is not the case, the disturbing feature about quantum physics is that whilst the wavefunction does appear to be a mathematical formulism, it must at the same time have some kind of 'physical', if this word means anything in the quantum realm, effectiveness. The only way in which the double slit experiment can be 'explained' is if the particles do in some sense change into a wave, or rather manifest their wave aspect once not being observed. In this way they are able to squeeze through both slits and thus interfere with themselves on the other side (fig 4.10).

Jim Al-Khalili remarks that he keeps "insisting that the wavefunction is not the physical entity itself but only a mathematical description of it."[221] However the nature of the 'physical entity' has to be left unsaid because, as quantum physicists clearly indicate, they have no idea what kind of 'physical' entity could possibly correspond to the kind of functioning which is found at the quantum level. Despite this situation, however, it seems impossible to avoid using some kind of 'physical' language whilst, at the same time, denying the actuality of 'physicality' at the quantum level:

> On encountering the slits, the wavefunction – being spread out – splits in two with each piece going through one of the slits. Note that I am describing here the way a mathematical entity is changing … I can never know what is really going on, or even be sure whether there is anything real going on at all. ….
> …we are not dealing with a real wave that washes up against the screen but a set of numbers…[222]

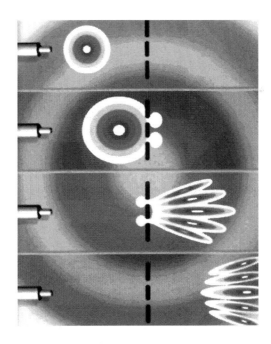

Fig 4.10 (reproduced from *Quantum: A Guide for the Perplexed*)

Although the wavefunction cannot be a 'physical entity', it is pictured as being one for the purposes of trying to give a 'feel' for what is going on. When Jim Al-Khalili tells us that he is referring to a 'mathematical entity' he is really not telling the whole truth. What he is really describing is the incoherent physical picture that was employed by physicists as a thought model to get their mathematical imaginations on the case. There can be no 'entity' passing through both slits simultaneously because entities do not do this sort of thing.

Al-Khalili does tell us that the behaviour of 'particles' in the double slit experiment, is analogous to a skier passing through a tree, with the left leg and ski going round the opposite side of the tree to the right leg and ski. However, like most quantum physicists, he does not follow up this observation by accepting the obvious implication that matter does not exist in the way that we think it does. This sort of behaviour means that 'matter' is nothing like classical physics always supposed it to be. He shies away from this conclusion and joins the large gathering of physicists sitting on the fence of bridging and embracing the ambiguity of the 'real' and the 'unreal' whilst hoping for an implausible restoration of an inherent reality:

> I feel that Einstein as right. He believed that the job of physical theories is 'to approximate as closely as possible to the truth of physical reality'. ... I would prefer to think that 'the truth is out there'.[223]

But it is simply not possible to visualise quantum behaviour appropriately using ordinary concepts; because of this Bohr said that is necessary to 'renounce' the search for a visual model of the quantum physical world.[224] This however really amounts to renouncing the quest for a full understanding of the physical world entirely.

Al-Khalili tells us that we have no right to expect such an everyday 'physical' understanding:

> ...some of the greatest physicists believe this to be a dangerous and futile pursuit, and that the worrying is best left to philosophers, who have nothing better to do with their time![225]

This cavalier attitude to the task of actually giving some kind of account of what is actually going on 'physically' seems to be the most popular. For instance in the otherwise excellent survey of the field *The New Quantum Universe* Tony Hay and Patrick Walters exemplify exactly this retreat from engaging with crucial philosophical issues which are posed by quantum weirdness. They quite openly announce that they wish to 'avoid becoming embroiled in purely philosophical mire.'[226]

However, this view is not shared by all. The discoverer of the fundamental differential equation which mathematically describes the wave equation for the quantum behaviour, Erwin Schrödinger, was desperate to reinstate some semblance of a 'classical' reality. But as the development of quantum physics gathered momentum the classical world dissolved with breathtaking rapidity. Schrödinger could not find a realistic interpretation for his mathematical brilliance:

> But what was the physical significance of Schrödinger's quantum waves? Schrödinger very much wanted to find a real physical interpretation for his quantum waves, but was eventually forced to admit defeat.[227]

In his book *Shadows of the Mind* Roger Penrose sets out to try to discover some new understanding of quantum theory that makes sense 'at all levels'.[228] And Jim Baggott in his illuminating work *beyond measure* places the philosophical implications for the nature of physical reality in the foreground:

> It is a central argument of this book that, no matter where we look, we are always led back to philosophy.[229]

And, of course, Baggott is right. Quantum physicists and philosophers have been employing delaying and avoidance tactics for eighty years but the serious philosophical problems raised by the stunning accuracy of such a staggeringly anti-materialist mathematical formulism have not disappeared. As one of the significant developers of the core quantum theory, John Bell, pointed out:

> Theoretical physicists live in a classical world, looking out into a quantum mechanical world. The latter we describe only subjectively, in terms of procedures and results in our classical domain. This subjective description is effected by means of quantum-mechanical state function Ψ, which characterize the classical conditioning of quantum-mechanical systems and permit predictions about subsequent events at the classical level. The classical world of course is described quite directly-'as it is.'[230]

The early developments were, of course, firmly located within the classical world view and it was only gradually that a new viewpoint began to emerge, as the presuppositions of the classical worldview collapsed. However after almost a hundred years of intense investigations and reflections on the part of many gifted scientists and philosophers, an accepted and definite interpretation of what quantum physics really implies for our understanding, or interpretation, of the ultimate nature of reality is still illusory precisely because Western scientist and philosophers refuse to accept the implications of the evidence. A recently published introduction to quantum theory tells us that:

> ...we do not have as tight an intellectual grasp of quantum theory as we would like to have. We can do sums, and in that sense,

explain the phenomena, but we do not really understand what is going on.[231]

This lack of understanding, however, is clearly caused by a refusal to accept the implications which are now rapidly becoming clear. Quantum entities do not intrinsically have defining characteristics in the way that 'classical' objects are assumed to do. They are ciphers which can take on various aspects in order to maintain a pattern of behaviour within an over all group. This fact is clearly spelled out in the Bell type experiments which have recently been extended by a group of physicists led by Aspelmeyer. The results of these experiments show that there is no objective independent reality.

These experiments involve the unsettling phenomenon of quantum entangled states. Particles are said to be in a state of quantum entanglement if they have been produced in a manner which produces a kind of inner connection between the two particles. For instance a photon which passes through a polarizing filter will 'randomly' collapse into a definite state of polarisation and either pass through or be reflected. Until it encounters the filter the photon does not have a definite polarisation, instead it is in a superposition of possible polarisations. Its polarisation is randomly determined the moment it reaches the filter. Brian Greene explains entanglement:

> The astounding thing is that such a photon can have a partner photon that has sped miles away in the opposite direction and yet, when confronted with the same 50-50 probability of passing through another polarised sunglass lens, will somehow do whatever the initial photon does. Even though each outcome is determined randomly and even though the photons are far apart in space, if one photon passes through so will the other.[232]

It is as if there was some kind of instantaneous communication between the entangled particles. This aspect of the quantum world is termed 'non-locality'. It demonstrates that there are, contrary to what classical physics expected, non-local, instantaneous connections and interdependencies across vast reaches of space. This was what Einstein referred to as 'spooky action at a distance'. Einstein hated the idea and spent a great deal of time trying to refute it. However, it was eventually confirmed experimentally. Greene remarks that:

> Numerous assaults on our conception of reality are emerging from modern physics … But of those that have been experimentally verified, I find none more mind-boggling than the recent realisation that our universe is not local.[233]

In order to convey the 'mind-boggling' nature of the quantum phenomenon of non-locality David Lindley, in his book *Where Does the Weirdness Go,* presents the situation in terms of a pair of gloves. Suppose someone buys a pair of gloves and then sends the left glove to someone in Hong Kong and the right to someone else in New York. This represents the 'common-sense' situation under the 'locality' view that we are familiar with from our everyday macroscopic world; the 'leftness' of the Hong Kong glove is 'local' to Hong Kong and the 'rightness' of the other glove is 'local' to New York. There can be no instantaneous interconnection between the two gloves which affects their handedness at the moment that one of the packages containing either glove is opened. But if these gloves were quantumly entangled then both gloves would be in a state of hovering between 'leftness' and 'rightness' until one of the packages containing the individual gloves was opened, at which point the gloves would magically adopt a definite 'leftness' and corresponding 'rightness.' Thus there is a non-local instantaneous interconnection between the gloves, an interconnection which defies 'common sense.'

The 'local' verses 'non-local' debate raged for a few years. Einstein argued against non-locality until his death. In 1935 Einstein, together with Boris Podolsky and Nathan Rosen wrote a paper in which they argued that, contrary to the predictions of quantum physics, particles must have definite local attributes. This paper became famous as the EPR paper and, unfortunately for Einstein and his colleagues, this paper actually formed the basis for proving the opposite. In 1964, nine years after Einstein's death and nearly 30 years after the EPR paper, the physicist John Bell concocted his crucial inequality which was used to determine the 'local' verses 'non-local' question experimentally.

The following explanation is based on the presentation of Bohm's version of the inequality by Tony Hey and Patrick Walters in their book *The New Quantum Universe*. Consider the situation of set of photons which are fired back to back in opposite directions towards polarizing filters, one to the left the other to the right. We arrange the experiment so that we know that when the polarizing filters are vertical the results of the encounter of left and right photons with their respective filters always agree, they both either pass or fail to pass. We assume the EPR hypothesis that the interconnection can only be the result of a pre-determined local configuration, and therefore the photons must start out with definite attributes which determine how the photons will behave. Another way to think of this situation is that each photon has, in some unspecified way, 'on-board' information as to how it should behave (for purposes of the discussion consider 12 photons). Suppose that they all have vertical polarisation and the filters are also vertically aligned. In this case all the photons will pass through both left and right polarizing filters (fig 4.11). We consider the numbers of disagreements $N(\Theta_1, \Theta_2)$ when one photon passes through and the other does not. In this case:

$$N(0,0) = 0$$

where $N(\Theta_1,\Theta_2)$ is the number of disagreements when the left polarizing filter is aligned at Θ_1 to the vertical and the right Θ_2;

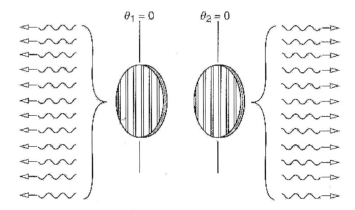

Fig 4.11

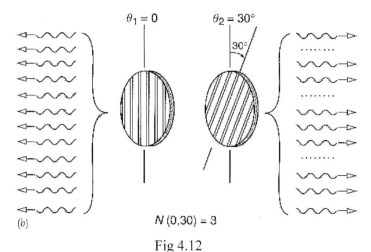

Fig 4.12

Now if we set Θ_2 to be 30 degrees to the vertical, as shown in fig 4.12, quantum theory tells us that the number of photons which will pass the right filter is given by $(\cos 30)^2$ which is ¾. So nine photons pass on the right, twelve on the left which gives 3 disagreements:

$$N(0,30) = 3$$

The same is true the other way around (fig 4.13):

$$N(-30,0) = 3$$

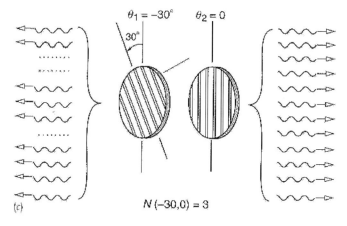

$\theta_1 = -30°$ $\theta_2 = 0$

30°

$N(-30,0) = 3$

(c)

Fig 4.13

Now consider N(-30,30), the left filter is set to -30 degrees and the right to +30 degrees. This is the point which requires careful contemplation. Three photons fail to pass on both left and right as shown in the previous situations. But because which ones actually pass is determined randomly it is possible that the three which fail to pass on the left correspond to three which pass on the right and vice-versa; in other words failures on the left will not correspond to failures on the right. This will maximise the disagreements and will give six disagreements (fig 4.14).

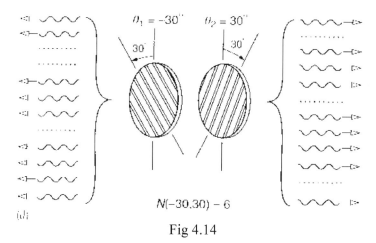

$\theta_1 = -30''$ $\theta_2 = 30''$

30   30

$N(-30,30) - 6$

(d)

Fig 4.14

On the other hand is also possible that the three failures on the left will correspond to those on the right sides in which case there will be no disagreements (fig 4.15). This means that:

$$0 \quad =< N(-30,30) <= 6$$

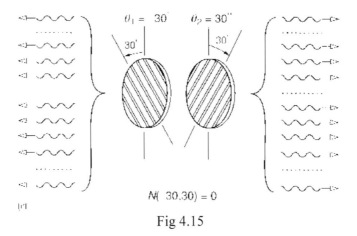

$$N(30,30) = 0$$

Fig 4.15

This means that N(-30,30) <= 6 ('<=' means less than or equal to) and as the maximum possible disagreements is given by N(-30,0) + N(0,30) = 6, we can derive a form of Bell's inequality:

$$N(-30,30) <= N(-30,0) + N(0,30)$$

This inequality must hold true if the EPR assertion of local reality, which means that the photons are locally predetermined in some way as to whether they pass or fail to pass, is correct. But, remarkably, quantum theory itself violates Bell's inequality, and if this inequality is violated experimentally then quantum non-locality is shown to be true. This is because a consistent pattern of interconnection which violates this inequality can only be the result of some kind of non-local, so called because it acts instantaneously across large distances, interconnection between what Einstein called 'elements of reality.' Einstein thought that such 'elements of reality' must be independent of each other and therefore not connected by 'spooky' non-local interconnections.

This non-local connection between entangled particles was spectacularly demonstrated by Alain Aspect and his collaborators in experiments carried out in the late 1970's and early 1980's. What these experiments, and even more precise experiments subsequently performed, show is that there is an intimate connection between entangled particles which operates instantaneously no matter how distant they may be. It seems to imply that if no measurements were to take place then the entire universe must become a complex web of quantum entanglement within which every particle would be non-locally connected to all other particles. As Penrose tells us:

> So long as these entanglements persist, one cannot, strictly speaking, consider any object in the universe as something on its own ... Why is it not necessary to consider that the universe is not just one incredibly complicated quantum entangled mess that bears no relationship to the classical-like world that we actually observe?. In

practice, it is the continual use of the procedure **R** that cuts the entanglements free …[234]

Penrose uses the symbol '**U**' to denote the underlying wavefunction that propagates through time according to the mathematics of the wavefunction, and the symbol '**R**' to refer to the outcome when a wavefunction collapses into actuality, seemingly through the agency of consciousness. One interpretation of entanglement, then, following Penrose's observation is that it is the phenomenon of consciousness which 'un-entangles' the universal predisposition to entanglement! It is also quite clear that Penrose's assertion that it would not be possible to 'consider any object in the universe as something on its own' corresponds precisely to the Buddhist assertion that all phenomena lack inherent existence.

The experiments conducted by Alain Aspect and his team examined the status of Bell's inequality as applied to two entangled particles. Subsequently astounding experiments have been conducted on three entangled particles. The experiment involves measuring vertical, horizontal, and circular polarisation of the three particles. Quantum theory predicts a 'dance' of these attributes which can in no way be possible if there are locally predetermined programs, or 'local' hidden determining features, for the particle states.

This analysis is truly beautiful although it requires effort of concentration. We have three entangled photons **A**, **B** and **C** and we have three detectors which can measure horizontal polarisation *H*, vertical polarisation *V* or left, right circular polarisation: *Cl* and *Cr*. Quantum theory predicts, and experiments have confirmed the following correlations:

1. If photon **A** is *V* then **B** and **C** must have the same circular polarisations *Cl : Cl* or *Cr : Cr*.
2. If photon **A** is *H* then **B** and **C** must have the opposite circular polarisations *Cl : Cr* or *Cr : Cl*.
3. These correlations equally apply to **B** or **C** being *V* or *H*.

We allocate values to the possibilities for analytic convenience. *Cl* and *V* are assigned the value +1 and *Cr* and *H* are assigned the value -1. This means that allowed possibilities always gives a value of +1 when the values are multiplied together. For instance if **A** is *V* then **B** and **C** must be either both *Cl* or both *Cr*. If we multiply the values we get +1 in both cases:

$$V \times Cl \times Cl = (+1) \times (+1) \times (+1) = +1$$

and

$$V \times Cr \times Cr = (+1) \times (-1) \times (-1) = +1$$

(remembering that $-1 \times -1 = +1$).

And if **A** is *H* then **B** and **C** must be take attributes *Cl* and *Cr,* or *Cr* and *Cl* . If we multiply the values we also get +1 in both cases:

$$H \times Cl \times Cr = (-1) \times (+1) \times (-1) = +1$$

and

$$H \times Cr \times Cl = (-1) \times (-1) \times (+1) = +1$$

Allowed combinations, then, should always give a combined multiplied value of +1.

If reality is 'local', which is to say that the outcomes of the various patterns that we can obtain experimentally are in some way locally pre-determined then they must also be consistent, which means that the implied patterns must hold over all possible situations without contradiction. Suppose we have the following:

$$\mathbf{A} \Rightarrow H \ (-1)$$
$$\mathbf{B} \Rightarrow Cr \ (-1)$$
$$\mathbf{C} \Rightarrow Cl \ (+1)$$

This gives -1 × -1 × +1 = 1.

If locality applies then the particles and their local hidden variables (if they exist) must make the predetermination work over all possibilities. So suppose we measure the vertical measurement of **B** and find it to be *V*. This means that **A** and **C** must be in identical circular polarisations. But **C** must be *Cl* in order to cover the previous possibility. Therefore we must have:

$$\mathbf{A} \Rightarrow Cl \ (+1)$$
$$\mathbf{B} \Rightarrow V \ (+1)$$
$$\mathbf{C} \Rightarrow Cl \ (+1)$$

This gives +1 × +1 × +1 = 1.

So far so good. Now let's suppose that photon **C** is *V*. In this case **A** and **B** must be in identical polarisations. But at this point we run into a problem; the next set of results must be consistent with the previous if we assume a predetermined local reality. But if **C** is *V* then **A** and **B** must have identical circular polarisations, but to be consistent with the previous experimental situations we can only have:

$$\mathbf{A} \Rightarrow Cl \ (+1)$$
$$\mathbf{B} \Rightarrow Cr \ (-1)$$
$$\mathbf{C} \Rightarrow V \ (+1)$$

This gives +1 × -1 × +1 = -1.

This inconsistent situation indicates that the behaviour of the quantum 'particles' involved cannot be locally predetermined. This is because a locally predetermined interaction would not give rise to such inconsistency. Therefore the assumption of a local predetermination of attributes is refuted by quantum theory and experimental investigation of that theory. As Michael Horne observes:

> Einstein's 'elements of reality' do not exist. No explanation of the beautiful dance among the three particles can be given in terms of an objectively real world. The particles simply do not do what they do because of how they are; they do what they do because of quantum magic.[235]

Einstein's assertion of independent 'elements of reality,' each with its own separate on-board bit of information, is false. It is an interconnected pattern, a pattern that contradicts the possibility of separate, independently existent elements with definite attributes, which constitutes the fundamental reality that surrounds us, and within which we have our being. The ultimate quantum question is "Where does the pattern arise from?" As we have seen it is the pattern of the dance of quantum emptiness. It seems that in some minimalist sense entangled particles 'know' what the others are doing.

All of the quantum phenomena that we have explored in this overview display a behavioural profile which is completely at odds with any kind of notion that anybody ever had concerning independently existing, objective *matter*. However, we have seen occasions when the employment of the term 'matter' actually undermines the insights of quantum theory by introducing an inappropriate 'classical' flavour into the fluid, evanescent appearance of quantum reality. We have also seen that seminal experiments clearly indicate that quantum elements have modes of interacting and modes of being which are completely at variance with classical matter. The question remains – Why do physicists still refer to 'matter' as if it were valid to conceive of matter as having classical attributes clearly negated by the discovery of the nature of quantum reality? For, as the early Buddhist contemplative-philosophers clearly knew, such an aspect of reality is an illusion, as the following assertion by the eleventh century Kadampa Buddhist adept Dromtonpa indicates:

> Now I shall cast to the winds concepts of solid objects with mass.[236]

This assertion prefigured Planck's later observation that 'There is no matter as such'[237] by eight hundred years. And it is salutary to remember that in the early phase of his scientific career Planck thought that 'matter' was the solid, continuous and independent material 'stuff' of reality, whereas at the end of his quantum investigation of the matter of the stuff of reality he came to the conclusion that:

> I regard consciousness as fundamental. I regard matter as derivative from consciousness.[238]

Quantum Emptiness

Electrons passing through this apparatus, in so far as we are able to fathom the matter, do not take route *h* and do not take route *s* and do not take both of these routes and do not take neither of these routes; and the trouble is that those four possibilities are simply all of the logical possibilities...[239]

- David Z Albert (twentieth century physicist)

Its character is neither existent, nor non-existent,
Nor both existent and non-existent, nor neither.
Centrists should know true reality
That is free from these four possibilities.[240]

- Bhavaviveka (2nd century Madhyamika)

We can now demonstrate that 'quantum moons' do not exist when unobserved. Such 'experimental metaphysics' has an extraordinary resonance with the Middle Way Buddhist principle of emptiness...[241]

- Victor Mansfield (twentieth century physicist)

The violent reaction on the recent development of modern physics can only be understood when one realises that here the foundations of physics have started moving; and that this motion has caused the feeling that the ground would be cut from science.[242]

- Werner Heisenberg (twentieth century physicist)

Werner Heisenberg

The similarity in logical structure between the first two opening quotes, which are separated by nineteen hundred years and a few continents, is evident. The first quote concerns the behaviour of electrons in a quantum split beam experiment within which they seemingly travel on one of two routes (*h* or *s*) depending upon whether they are transmitted or diverted by a beam splitter. A schematic illustration of the hypothetical experiment that Professor David Z. Albert discusses in his book *Quantum Mechanics and Experience* is shown in Fig 5.1. Electrons are fed, one at a time, into a contraption which divides them up depending on an hypothetical attribute called 'hardness'; hard electrons are diverted to the left and thus emerge out of the top opening in the diagram, soft electrons travel straight through as shown. The hard electrons ostensibly travel on route *h* whilst soft are supposed to travel along route *s*. The split beam is reunited at the 'black box' and emerge together along path *h and s*.

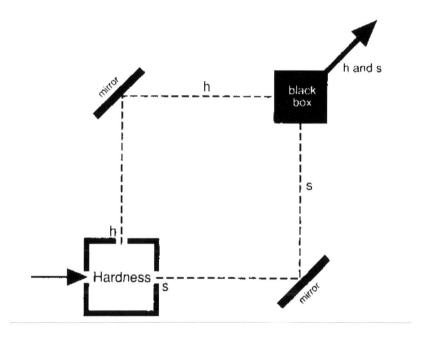

Fig 5.1

The experiment will be fully described presently; for the moment we merely need to take note of the conclusion that Albert reaches after a thorough analysis of the results. The electrons cannot be said to travel on either one of the paths, nor on both, nor on neither, a conclusion that quite clearly has severe implications for our understanding of the type of existence which is exhibited by the electrons.

The second observation was made by the 2nd - 3rd century Madhyamika philosopher Bhavaviveka who, we can be fairly certain, had no knowledge of electrons and split beam experiments. In his observation Bhavaviveka describes the innermost character of reality as being neither existent nor non-existent nor both nor neither. According to the Madhyamaka this existential paradox, the tetralemma (like a dilemma, but there are four of them) of the existential extremes, lies at the heart of reality and, remarkably, the electrons in Albert's experiment certainly seem to confirm this view.

The electron attributes that Albert uses for purposes of exposition are fictional – hardness (hard or soft) and color (black or white). The description of the experiment, however, does precisely describe the quantum behavior exemplified by actual experiments which have been performed on many occasions; the actual attribute of electrons usually employed in these experiments is electron 'spin'.[243] When experiments of this nature are performed with photons the attribute used is the photon's polarisation. The following discussion, which recapitulates Albert's exposition, follows his illustrative terminology for clarity and convenience.

The theoretical experiment requires the use of a 'hardness' box and a 'color' box. The 'hardness' box is able to split electrons up according to whether they are 'hard' or 'soft.' Hard electrons emerge from the top opening and soft along the horizontal. In a similar fashion a 'color box' sends 'black' electrons out the top opening and 'white' electrons along the horizontal.

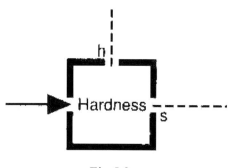

Fig 5.2

The first experiment involves three successive boxes, a color box followed by a hardness box and then another color box. The experiment is performed with a large number of electrons that are sent into the first color box one at a time. The results are surprising. The first color box sorts out electrons into black, which are ejected out of the line of fire as shown, and white, which continue on to the next box which is a hardness box; all of the electrons that enter this hardness box should be white. This hardness box should sort the incoming white electrons into hard and soft as shown, so the electrons emerging from the right hand opening of the hardness box should be white and soft. It follows that all these electrons, being all white, should pass straight through the final color box.

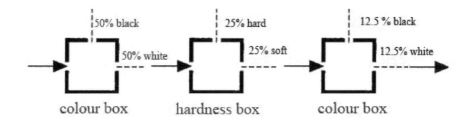

Fig 5.3

Percentages are of the original number of electrons entering the first color box.

However this is not what happens; when the experiment is performed half of the remaining white electrons (12.5% of the original number sent into the first color box) mysteriously turn into black electrons. It seems that the attributes of the electrons are not intrinsic to the electrons but, rather, the electrons adopt attributes in order to fit a pattern. In this case the pattern clearly is that in any group of electrons they behave as if 50% are white (or hard) and 50% black (or soft) no matter what has happened, in terms of determining their characteristics, in previous experimental interactions. This quantum behavior is similar to that described for photons in the previous chapter *Interconnected Lightness of Being*.

The next experiment discussed by Albert is the setup discussed at the beginning of this chapter which is shown in diagram Fig 5.1. Electrons are fed into the hardness box that sends 'hard' electrons out along route *h* and soft electrons out along route *s*. Hard and soft electrons meet at the black box which sends both out along route *h and s* without altering the hardness or softness of the electrons. Electrons are fed into the hardness box one at a time. The hardness box has the effect of randomizing the color so that white electrons emerge 50% black and 50% white and black electrons also emerge 50% black and 50% white. We check that soft electrons, when sent through the hardness box, emerge as soft electrons and hard electrons as hard and then perform some experiments.

1) Send white electrons into the hardness box. Fifty percent of these will be hard and take route *h,* and the other 50% will be soft and take

route *s*. So the result, as expected, is that 50% hard and 50% soft emerge along *h and s*.

2) Send hard electrons into the hardness box. The hardness box randomizes the color of the electrons so 50% are white and 50% black. All the electrons take route *h* and the result is, as expected, 50% white and 50% black emerge along *h and s*.

3) Send soft electrons into the hardness box and the result is, as expected, 50% white and 50% black emerge along *h and s*. Furthermore we know that these electrons have travelled along route *s*.

4) Now we send white electrons into the hardness box and measure the color at *h and s*. We expect that 50% of the electrons will be hard and so travel route *h* and 50% are soft so take route *s*. Now consider the 50% of hard electrons on route *h*. We have already done the experiment 2) which tells us that 50% of these (25% of the total) will emerge black and the remainder white. And, similarly according to experiment 3) 50% of the soft electrons (25% of the total) will be black and the remainder white. So overall we expect to get 50% white and 50% black along *h and s*. What actually happens, however, is that we get 100% white along *h and s*.

In other words the last experiment contradicts experiments two and three. The electrons are doing something unexpected, seemingly changing their behavior due to some whim, or quirk of nature.

The next stage is to introduce a sliding screen which can block electrons along one of the paths, *s* for instance.

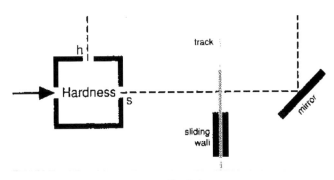

Fig 5.4

Now we have seen that when the wall is out we get 100% white along *h and s* (experiment 4), 50% of the electrons having travelled route *s* and 50% route *h*. So we would naturally expect that when we slide the wall in to block the electrons on route *s* that all of the electrons (50% of the original number) along *h and s* will still be white, having travelled along *h*. But we know that the hardness box changes the color of the electrons so that 50% are white 50% black; and what we actually get, when the sliding wall blocks off route *s*, is 50% white (25% of original number) and 50% black. Albert comments on this remarkable situation:

> Now we're in real trouble. Consider an electron which passes through our apparatus when the wall is out. Consider the possibilities as to which route that electron could have taken. Can it have taken *h*? Apparently not, because electrons which take *h* are known to have the property that their color statistics are fifty-fifty, whereas an electron passing through our device with the wall out is known to have the property of being white at *h and s*! Can it have taken *s*, then? No, for the same reasons. Can it somehow have taken *both* routes? Well, suppose that when a certain electron is in the midst of passing through this apparatus, we stop the experiment and look where it is. It turns out that half the time we find it on *h*, and half the time we find it on *s*. We never find two electrons in there, or two halves of a single split electron, one on each route, or anything like that. There isn't any sense in which the electron seems to be taking both routes. Can it have taken neither route? Certainly not. If we wall up *both* routes, nothing gets through at all.[244]

It is clear, then, that there is a fundamental malleability, or indeterminism, regarding the characteristics, or attributes, of quantum entities. As Albert says:

> It's that any electron's even *having* any definite color apparently entails that it's neither hard nor soft nor both nor neither, and that any electron's even having any definite hardness apparently entails that it's neither black nor white nor both nor neither.[245]

So, Albert says, if an electron has a definite hardness then it will be in a superposition of being white or black. And this state of being in a super-position means that it is *neither black nor white nor both nor neither*. In other words the condition of being *neither this nor that nor both nor neither* can be identified with the state of being in a superposition:

> So, it follows that a white electron can't *be* a hard one, or a soft one, or (somehow) both, or neither. To say that an electron is white must be just the same as to say that it's in a *superposition* of being hard and soft.[246]

And, furthermore and crucially, Albert is completely adamant that:

> ... it isn't *at all* a matter of our being unable to simultaneously *know* what the color and the hardness of a certain electron is (that is: it isn't a matter of *ignorance*). It's deeper than that.[247]

In other words when an electron is forced to adopt a definite hardness its color flips into a superposition of possibility, which means that there actually is no definite color. It might be said that the color 'hovers' between black and white.

This feature of being in a superposition, as we have seen, is the fundamental nature of the wavefunction, and the wavefunction is the fundamental quantum nature of unobserved reality. In the case of the electrons we are currently discussing, when they are unobserved they have the fundamental probability distribution:

P(White) = 50%; P(Black) = 50%

Or

P(Hard) = 50%; P(Soft) = 50%

Which superposition applies depends on which characteristic, hardness or color, has been determined by observation. If we arrange things so that an electron is determined as being in a definite color its hardness is thrown into a state of superposition; and if we arrange things so that an electron is determined as being in a definite hardness its color is thrown into a state of superposition. It is clear, therefore, that some form of conscious interference is required in order to alter the existential superposition configuration.

It must follow therefore that the fundamental characteristic of the electrons when not manifested to consciousness, which is the same as the fundamental nature of the wavefunction which underlies the manifestation of reality is that, as Bhavaviveka so succinctly describes it:

> Its character is neither existent, nor non-existent,
> Nor both existent and non-existent, nor neither.

The way that this tetralemma of the extremes of existence, which the Madhyamaka considers to be the hallmark of emptiness, emerges within Albert's experimental setup is that if an electron is forced into existence as having a definite color, then it is also necessarily forced into the superposed state of the tetralemma of the extremes of existence with regard to its hardness. Conversely if an electron is forced into existence as having a definite hardness then it is also necessarily forced into the superposed state of the tetralemma of the extremes of existence with regard to its color.

It might be thought that at least these electrons are only half superposed, so to speak, we can make a definite white, or black, one but we just have the problem that this process will send its characteristic of hardness into the superposed condition of hovering between extremes of existence. Or, on the other hand, we can grab a definite hard, or soft, one and send its characteristic of color into the superposed realm of the tetralemma. However, if we are speaking in terms of knowledge of the ultimate nature of the electrons, this will not do. Any ultimate knowledge of the nature of these electrons, or anything for that matter, presupposes knowledge of the way that they are within themselves, independent of experimental or observational interference. And it is quite clear that prior to any interaction with the experimental setup both characteristics, hardness and color, must be considered to be in the realm of the tetralemma of the extremes of existence; which is the same as saying that they reside in the realm of emptiness, the realm of the potentiality for dependent origination.

It is extremely important that the reader comprehends the significance of the analysis thus far. The perennial criticism of the kind of comparison which has been undertaken in this work, between quantum physics and an 'Eastern philosophy', is that it merely indicates a random coincidental similarity of language which has no serious significance. However, the precision and clarity of the mapping, or correspondence, between the two domains which has been demonstrated with regard to Albert's analysis of the implications of a fundamental quantum experiment and the Madhyamaka analysis and description of the inner nature of reality is far too conspicuous for any such critique to be seriously entertained. Furthermore, as we saw in the chapter *Why the Quantum?* [p45-], this quantum existential configuration seems to be a fundamental feature of quantum reality.

According to the Madhyamaka the tetralemma of the extremes of existence constitutes the innermost nature of the ultimate reality of all phenomena:

> Since they [phenomena] neither exist by themselves nor by any
> intrinsic character,
> Since they do not abide as their own entities,
> And since they do not exist as they are apprehended,
> He [the Buddha] presented their lack of nature.[248]

The phrase 'lack of nature' indicates a lack of inherent, autonomous, self-enclosed, independent and unchangeable characteristics.

The tetralemma of the extremes of existence describes emptiness, which is also a term denoting the nature of the fundamental ground of reality:

> If emptiness is summarised,
> Suchness, the true end,
> Signlessness, the ultimate,
> And the dharmadhatu are its synonyms.[249]

'Suchness', 'signlessness', 'lack of nature', or 'lack of intrinsic character' are all characterisations of emptiness. The *dharmadhatu* refers to the ultimate 'expanse of phenomena,' a term which in many salient respects is equivalent to the realm of the wavefunction.

The fact that the electrons which take part in Albert's experiment, and any other quantum experiment, do not have an 'intrinsic character' has certainly turned out to be correct. Furthermore they cannot 'abide as their own entities' because they alter their characteristics in dependence on the overall pattern of manifestation; this means that the characteristics that the electrons display depend on what the other electrons manifest. So these electrons, as they exist at their most fundamental level, quite dramatically exemplify the characteristics of emptiness, insofar as one of the characteristics of emptiness is to lack definite intrinsic characteristics. And this situation clearly threatens to undermine any grip on the reality of the notion of independent entities and their characteristics. As Nagarjuna said:

> A thing without a characteristic does not exist anywhere.
> If a thing without a characteristic does not exist,
> What do characteristics characterize? [250]

It might be said that the fundamental characteristic of Albert's electrons is a profound lack of definite characterisation which would mean, of course, that emptiness is a fundamental characteristic of these electrons.

The configuration of the tetralemma of the extremes of existence, which has the basic form:

> Neither existent,
> Nor non-existent,
> Nor both existent and non-existent,
> Nor neither existent nor non-existent,

is fundamental to the Madhyamaka analysis of reality. The Madhyamaka insists that this configuration, the configuration of emptiness, lies at the heart of reality, and quite obviously, the issue of exactly what is meant by 'reality' is thrown into question by such seemingly paradoxical assertions. As, indeed, does the behavior of Albert's electrons. As Penrose says:

> Undoubtedly the world is strange and unfamiliar at the quantum level, but it is not unreal. How, indeed, can real objects be constructed from unreal constituents? [251]

Here we are presented with the conundrum of which realm, quantum or the more familiar world of everyday objects, we take to be real. As Jan Westerhoff says in his recent work *Nagarjuna's Madhyamaka*:

> It is therefore quite ironic that our best candidates for ultimately real entities existing independently of human conceptualisation turn out to be objects that are so highly theory dependent and the existence of which seems to be considerably less secure than that of the medium sized dry goods with which we interact daily. [252]

And this is putting it mildly, for, as we have seen, there is a growing consensus amongst physicists that quantum 'objects' depend in some way on observing consciousnesses.

This was the deep paradox which threw the philosophical sensibilities of the early quantum physicists into stunned perplexity and the only way that they could find a way forward was to consent to a philosophical evasion. This view, which was primarily advocated by Niels Bohr, became enshrined as the Copenhagen interpretation:

> According to this interpretation, it is not meaningful to regard a quantum particle as having any intrinsic properties independent of some measuring instrument … each property only becomes 'real' when the electron interacts with an instrument specifically designed to reveal that property.[253]

This perspective clearly contains the crucial idea that quantum entities, whatever they may be, do not have intrinsic properties, or characteristics, until some form of interaction takes place. But, at the same time, it also avoids the issue of the necessity for consciousness to be involved in the interaction by referring to the interaction as being with a 'measuring instrument.' Bohr describes his view as follows:

> I have advocated the application of the word *phenomenon* exclusively to refer to the observations obtained under specified circumstances, including an account of the whole experimental arrangement.[254]

According to Bohr it is only within the context of the macroscopic arrangement of the experimental setup that the concepts employed within quantum physics can avoid being the subject of 'confusion' and 'ambiguity'. [255]

Rosenblum and Kuttner give the following insightful parody of the Copenhagen view:

> Since we supposedly never see the microworld 'directly,' we can just ignore its weirdness, and thus ignore physics' encounter with consciousness.[256]

Bohr wanted to leave the issue of the strange nature of the quantum realm in a philosophical limbo in order to avoid dealing with the severely difficult problems of understanding the deep implications for our understanding of the process of reality. Indeed the implications were so unsettling that often the early philosophical attempts to come to terms with them were very confused, a situation which was sometimes attributed to the necessity of using 'classical' concepts in an inappropriate context; a context so inappropriate that the issue of its reality would be better ignored. The following statement is attributed to Bohr:

> There is no quantum world. There is only an abstract quantum physical description. It is wrong to think that the task of physics is to find out how nature is. Physics concerns what we can say about nature.[257]

The implication is quite clear. The fact that a quantum physicist has to employ mind bending notions in order to deal with the quantum realm does not mean that the quantum realm really corresponds to those concepts. In fact, if the quantum world exists at all, it lies beyond description with ordinary everyday concepts; and in view of this notion Bohr spoke of the necessity of the 'renunciation of explanation in terms of a pictorial representation' for atomic phenomena.'[258]

However, these early philosophical attempts at comprehending the seeming division between quantum reality and our everyday reality are now wearing thin. It is now possible to actually produce images of arrangements of atoms using a scanning tunnelling microscope (fig 5.5) so the idea that we need to 'renounce' the possibility of visualizing quantum phenomena seems inappropriate. Even if we restrict Bohr's use of the term of 'visualisation' to mean an intellectual grasp of quantum behaviour this again is not necessarily correct; it only applies to an intellectual attitude which clings to the vision of 'inherent existence' as a necessary feature of reality.

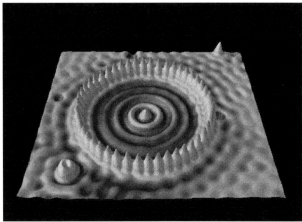

Fig 5.5

Figure 5.5 shows a ring of 48 iron atoms which were 'assembled' on to a copper surface. The undulations inside the ring of atoms show the probability density distribution for electrons within the surface. The peak at the centre is not an atom; it is the most probable electronic location. As Jim Al-Khalili says 'this is the closest physicists have got to actually seeing the quantum wavefunction'[259]. It might also be said that it is the closest that they have got to seeing the objective face of emptiness! In the face of 'visualised' data such as this it seems inappropriate to attribute complete unreality to the quantum realm.

The Copenhagen view allocates full reality to the macroscopic everyday world whilst demoting the quantum realm to a fictional mathematical convenience. But if we adopt such a view we are faced with the dilemma of accounting for the production of reality from unreality and the nature of the existence to be attributed not only to quantum phenomena, but also our everyday reality is severely compromised. Such problems are generated by a rigid and desperate attempt to cling to some kind of substantial reference points to which we can fix reality as being this or that definite entity and a refusal to see that the whole of reality is simply more or less quantum, depending upon the level of interaction:

> Everything is real and not real,
> Both real and not real,
> Neither real nor not real.
> This is the Lord Buddha's teaching.[260]

Paradoxical formulations like this are certain to incur the wrath of hardened physicists with materialist leanings. They will probably consider this to be no more than facile wordplay. The fact remains however that, as Albert's electrons indicate, this formulation is an existential configuration which conforms to the state of being in a superposition. In other words it is a quite reasonable indication of the nature of the wavefunction.

The quantum realm clearly exhibits a mode of functioning which corresponds to what the Madhyamaka terms emptiness, the indeterminate hovering between the existential extremes, until, that is an observation is made. However the large scale world, our everyday world, appears to be very different. The appearance of the ineluctable external world of materiality is relentless in its solidity and immutability; it is this fact that leads to the astonishment which it is still possible to find amongst physicists. The quantum physicist Wojciech Zurek refers to the quantum 'stuff' of reality as 'dream stuff'[261] and Erich Joos tells us the appearance of the classical world from out of the quantum realm is a 'delusion,'[262] a view which precisely corresponds to the Madhyamaka assertion that the 'seeming' reality of the 'conventional' world is 'deceptive.' So where did it come from? We shall see later that, according to quantum physicist John Wheeler, it is a collective illusion, built up over vast stretches of time by the perceptions of countless sentient beings!

Because it is a collective illusion, stabilised within the quantum 'dream stuff' over unimaginable vistas of time it has built up a momentum of stability which gives it the appearance of immutability. According to the Madhyamaka, however, its essential, ultimate, we might even say quantum nature is that the everyday 'classical' world is 'like a dream, like an illusion.'[263]

It might be wondered why this is an important thing to know about. The answer is simply that most people really do think that the everyday world they appear to inhabit as a separate entity is real in the way that it appears, and because of this the importance and significance of spiritual practice is simply not understood. Even for people who feel drawn to a spiritual practice a belief in the external world of matter undermines the mechanisms of spiritual practice. For instance a belief in the material world and the onto-logical primacy of matter clearly undermines knowledge concerning karma and future lives. When the fact that the world that appears to be an independent material world is constructed from quantum 'dream stuff' which is of the nature of mind, or consciousness, is comprehended then the significance of Buddhist doctrines such as karma and future lives becomes clear. This will become apparent in future chapters.

This is why cultivating an insight that sees everything to be like an illusion, which is in fact seeing it the way that it really is, is important for effective Mahayana Buddhist practice. And it is for this reason that the Madhyamaka has developed various incisive analyses of the process of reality which demonstrate their illusion-like nature even within the 'classical' everyday world. The Madhyamaka has developed effective ways to decon-struct this overwhelming facade in order to reveal the fact that these imp-ressive appearances are in fact not able to withstand a concerted analysis as to whether they exist in the way that they appear to exist. When the 'seeming' phenomena of the everyday world are analysed thoroughly it is discovered that their ultimate nature belongs to the quantum realm. Whilst they may not be 'identical' it is appropriate to consider the quantum realm to be the 'objective' aspect of the ultimate nature, just as 'mind' can be considered to be the 'subjective' aspect.

The Madhyamika scholar and teacher Khenpo Tsültrim Gyamtso writes concerning the illusion-like samadhi, or meditative awareness, that:

> These days, the samadhi that sees everything to be like an illusion
> is easier to practice than ever before, because modern technology
> has produced so many new examples of empty forms. Movies,
> televisions, telephones, faxes, email, the internet-all of these are
> wonderful examples of how things can appear due to the coming
> together of causes and conditions, while at the same time being
> empty of any inherent nature.[264]

However, probably the most significant illustration of the illusion-like nature of reality comes from an appreciation of quantum physics, which shows us, in dramatic fashion, that the everyday world does emerge from a realm of emptiness and floats within emptiness like a stubborn illusion.

The fundamental task of the philosophical arm of the Madhyamaka is the employment of rigorous logical analysis in order to unmask the 'seeming' and 'classical' appearance of a separately and independently existing realm of inherently existent objects and processes. The notion of 'inherent existence', or *svabhava*, is vital in this analysis for it is the appearance of inherent existence within the seeming world of externality that gives it its flavour of immutability and separateness, the concrete mode of apparent self-enclosed existence, or inherent self-identity, with which we are so thoroughly familiar. The Madhyamaka analysis, however, demonstrates that this imputed feature of inherent existence is in fact non-existent.

However, because the appearances of the conventional, seeming realm of everyday reality are so overwhelming these deconstructive analytic reasonings must be performed and meditated upon frequently:

> …we can examine with our intelligence and see that things do not really exist, but then, if we get stuck with a needle, we will have this very vivid experience of existence, and we will think, 'Well maybe there really is something there after all.' Thus, when we analyze with logical reasoning, we can gain certainty that things do not truly exist, but we still keep having experiences in which things seem to be so real, contradicting the results of our earlier analysis. This is why it is so difficult to gain certainty in emptiness.[265]

Before the advent of quantum theory the Madhyamaka deconstructive reasonings were the main method for gaining intellectual certainty concerning emptiness. Today, however, quantum physics directly shows us the objective face of emptiness.

In order to facilitate this deconstructive analysis the Madhyamaka employs the surprising and effective technique of *treating all concepts and imputations as if the entities they denoted were inherently existent and then demonstrating the impossible or absurd consequences that follow*[266]. This method is adopted because the imputation of inherent existence is precisely our innate mode of perception. This means that all objects, attributes and processes are treated as if they were completely separate, self-enclosed and independent of each other. This leads to some very difficult and counter intuitive conceptual juggling and it can easily appear that some of the reasoning is absurd. But this is only because our natural bent of mind is to ignore the absurdity of the picture of reality that results from adherence to a perception and view of the ubiquity of inherent existence within the illusion-like appearances of reality.

In order to get a feel for the type of reasoning that is at the center of the Madhyamaka deconstructive dialectic it is valuable to consider the analysis of the relationship between a chariot and its parts which is a precursor of the demonstration of the lack of inherent existence of the personal 'self'. The primary purpose of this Madhyamaka analysis is that of freeing individuals from the illusion that there is an inherently existent 'self' that somehow has control of the psychophysical complex that constitutes human individuals.

This notion, according to Buddhist thought, is deluded and leads to all kinds of suffering whereas seeing into the illusory nature of such an imputed 'self' leads to personal liberation.

The primary level[267] Buddhist analysis of reality is based on the immediacy of psychophysical embodiment, which means that the classification into *skandhas*, 'aggregates' or 'heaps'[268], takes subjective experience as its domain. This is in contrast to the Western attitude which immediately assumes the reality of an independent external world as being a primary, although unproven, fact of existence. The experiential world is divided into the five basic aggregates of form, feeling, discrimination, volitional dispositions and consciousness. 'Form' is the realm of the body and its sensations of objects; 'feeling' is the reactive attribution of pleasantness, unpleasantness or neutrality; 'discrimination' apprehends or grasps the distinguishing features of phenomena, 'volitional dispositions' are mental dispositions of perception and action, 'consciousness' is the primary function or quality of awareness that underlies all sense and mental functioning. According to the first Buddhist analysis of reality these five categories of experience exhaust the experiential field of psychophysical embodiment.

According to this analysis the experiential field of embodiment is exhausted by the five aggregates which operate in a co-ordinated manner according to the functioning of dependent origination and causality. All sentient beings, however, have an overwhelming sense of being a 'self'. This 'self' is experienced as an independent centre of operations which is experienced as being in charge of and in control of the psychophysical apparatus of embodiment. It is this central sense of an independent 'self' of a person which the first 'turning' of Buddhism targets as an illusion that needs deconstruction. The second turning of the wheel of Buddhist philosophy turned attention to the lack of selfhood, or intrinsic identity, within all the phenomena of experience, including the material world.

In order to demonstrate the lack of inherent existence of the 'self', which most human beings experience as being the centre of their activities, the Madhyamaka analysis investigates the relationship between the notion of a self, conceived of as an inherently existent centre of psychophysical embodiment, and the aggregates. Generally this analysis is not presented immediately but is preceded by the analysis of a chariot and the parts of a chariot which clearly demonstrates the reasoning that unmasks a lack of inherent existence, or emptiness. The chariot reasoning is:

> A chariot does not inherently exist because of not being its parts, not being other than its parts, not being in its parts, not being that within which its parts exist, not possessing its parts, not being the composite of its parts, and not being the shape of its parts.[269]

As previously indicated in order to appreciate the Madhyamaka perspective it is necessary to view this reasoning in terms of inherent existence. This means that the chariot and its parts must be conceived of as independent and self-sufficient entities. If the chariot is inherently existent then it must exist in its own right, which is to say independent of other phenomena, including its parts. This means that whereas on the conventional level the chariot and its parts are mixed together, so to speak, from the perspective of an ultimate analysis we must separate them out and treat the chariot as having its own individual and separate nature and then investigate the nature of the relationship with its parts.

Now we can ask is the chariot identical to its parts? This cannot be correct because the parts are many whilst the chariot is one. Furthermore the chariot can be viewed as a separate agent that conveys its parts when it moves. If the chariot were identical with its parts then conveyer and conveyed would be identical which is absurd. On the other hand the chariot cannot be different from its parts because if this were so the chariot would be one entity separate from its parts. We would then be able to put the chariot in one place, as it were, whilst placing its parts elsewhere. Again this is obviously absurd. Furthermore it is a Madhyamaka requirement that entities which are inherently 'other' than each other cannot be related to each other; relationship depends upon some basis of commonality, but things which are completely 'other' have no such basis. So if the chariot were an inherently different entity there could be no connection with its parts.

We might now ask if the chariot is in its parts or if the parts are in the chariot. For the chariot to be inherently in its parts or for the parts to be inherently in the chariot the chariot and the parts would have to be completely 'other' than each other, or separate from each other in the first place. This would be like placing an object or objects inside a box for example. The chariot is not separate from its parts, for instance, in the same way that a box is separate and independent of its contents. The same is true if the chariot were to inherently possess its parts; the two would have to be separate just like a man who possesses a cow. But the chariot does not stand separately from its parts as would be required for these configurations to be applicable.

The chariot cannot be the inherent composite of the parts because if it were the composite would have to exist as a separate entity which could be apprehended without apprehending the parts. In fact in this case the terms 'composite' and chariot are synonymous so all the above reasonings also apply. Lastly the chariot is not the shape of its parts because in this case a chariot could be said to be the shape of its parts before it is assembled which cannot be the case.

All these demonstrations of impossibility accrue from the fact that the chariot has been treated as an independent entity, which it obviously is not. The lack of inherent existence of the chariot, which is established through the analysis of its relationship with its parts, is actually quite obvious in the first place. The absurd consequences follow because of the way the situation was initially set up; treating the chariot as a separate entity from its parts necessarily leads to the paradoxical demonstrations of impossibility. However, this analysis is not primarily performed in order to prove the lack of inherent existence of the chariot, although it does do this, it is an example of how to analyse a situation in order to demonstrate a lack of inherent existence. Once it is seen that the demonstrations indicate a lack of inherent existence for the chariot they can be applied in situations in which the state of affairs is not so clear. In particular it can be applied to anything which can be said to be dependent on its parts; such as the illusion of the personal self which depends upon the skandhas, the psychophysical aggregates or constituents, of embodiment.

Once the essential point of the chariot deconstruction is appreciated the same analysis can be extended to everything because everything is composed of parts. For instance the Madhyamaka refutes the idea that there can be a partless particle, either ultimately or conventionally. Some non-Buddhist and also some non-Madhyamaka Buddhist schools of thought assert the existence of ultimate partless, or infinitesimal, particles from which the world is constructed. This viewpoint is succinctly refuted by the Madhyamaka as follows. Consider a partless particle which is, if possible, connected to six other particles which are located around the central particle in the six principle directions:

> If six particles join it simultaneously,
> This infinitesimal particle would have six parts.
> If all six together are partless,
> Then also their aggregation would be just an infinitesimal particle. [270]

If a particle is able to club together with other particles in order to produce the world of extension and experienced solidity then quite obviously it would need to connect in some way with the other particles. In other words the central particle would need to be connected to the others through its faces and this entails that any particle which can play a role in creating a world must have parts, which means that the 'partless' particles must have 'parts'! It follows that the world cannot be constructed from ultimate entities devoid of parts. If these particles were devoid of parts then the world would simply collapse because it is impossible to produce extension from an extensionless entity:

> If you insist that this is truly so
> (Though it must also face the other particles),
> How is it that earth and water
> And all other things extend – or maybe they do not? [271]

And so

> If you say that sides that face
> The different particles are different,

> How come the finest particle is one:
> A single entity devoid of parts?[272]

It is remarkable that this establishment of the necessity of effective world-creating particles to have their own parts can lead to a devastating demonstration of the lack of inherent existence, and thus the illusory nature, of the world.

If the world really is substantial then it must be constructed from an ultimate substance, or substances, and this must imply the existence of an ultimate particle or particles of some sort. If this is the case then when we repeatedly divide up particles, we are supposed arrive at a final particle which is the fundamental building block. If we find that particles are infinitely divisible into their parts then we can only stop when we reach a partless particle. But if this particle is truly partless then, as we have seen, it could not take part in the construction of the world because in order for a partless particle to connect to another partless particle it is necessary for one part of a partless particle to connect to a part of another partless particle! So particles must be infinitely divisible, each particle itself having parts. This means that each particle, like the chariot, cannot be inherently existent because, like the chariot, each particle is made up of its parts.

This lack of inherent existence cascades down through the levels of assumed particles without end demonstrating that there is simply nothing that can be found at the base which can provide a solid foundation:

> The particle, it's proved, does not exist inherently.
> And therefore it is clear that ... substance and the rest,
> The many things proposed by ours and other schools,
> Have no intrinsic being.[273]

This is called the reasoning of freedom from unity and multiplicity which is said to open the door of emptiness. If it is not possible to demonstrate an ultimately unitary particle which exists independently with no dependence upon its parts then there can be no inherent unity. If there is no unitary entity to enter into the construction of a multiplicity there can be no inherent multiplicity either.

Although this demonstration does not deny that there is an appearance of unity and multiplicity of entities at the conventional level, an ultimate analysis indicates that this appearance is, ultimately, an illusion. As Brunnhölzl describes the situation which the reasoning reveals:

> To be sure, this reasoning does not negate the mere conventionality that one thing has many parts. The point here is that neither the thing in question nor its parts really exist by themselves.[274]

This conclusion should, of course, come as no surprise to a quantum physicist. Bohm, for instance, tells us that:

> ...no coherent concept of an independently existent particle is possible, neither one in which the particle would be an extended body, nor one in which it would be a dimensionless point.[275]

Lee Smolin certainly seems to concur with the conclusion that 'things' lack inherent existence; as he says:

> Quantum physics tells us, no it screams at us, that reality is not composed of things. It is made up of processes...[276]

From the point of view of the Madhyamaka, however, this assertion merely moves the focus from inherently existent things to inherently existent processes. Indeed what do inherently real processes amount to without inherently existent things to take a 'part'?

The Madhyamaka therefore also refutes the notion of inherently real causal processes, using the 'Diamond Slivers' reasoning, which is given this appellation because like a diamond it is indestructible and is able to cut through wrong views concerning the nature of reality. This reasoning focuses on the possible modes of ultimate production for any entity, and it has the familiar logical structure of the Madhyamaka tetralemma:

> Neither from itself nor from another,
> Nor from both,
> Nor without a cause,
> Does anything whatever, anywhere arise.[277]

The refutation of production from self is aimed at a school of philosophy extant at the time which claimed that all phenomena were actually manifestations of a permanent primal cosmic substance. Therefore any entity, such as a sprout, was asserted to be produced from its own nature.

This viewpoint, however, produces some rather absurd consequences. If an entity which already exists reproduces itself, the reproduction is pointless because the entity already exists. Furthermore if self-production were an inherent feature of an entity then once it had reproduced itself it would necessarily have to do so again because self-production would be an inherent feature of the entity. This must lead to an infinite, never ending, sequence of reproductions. A seed, therefore, would never get around to producing a sprout because it would be too busy reproducing itself! Also, obviously, if the seed and its sprout, the cause and the effect, were the same and yet the one produces the other then the seed and the sprout should appear to be exactly the same which is absurd. Effects are usually apprehended when the cause has ceased, but if the effect and the cause are identical then the effect should cease as soon as the cause does. And so on.

The assertion that entities are produced from causes which are 'other' is the more usual view, a view which is derived from observation of the processes of the 'common-sense,' conventional, everyday world. The idea that this view is impossible, then, can come as quite a shock. But the reasoning is unimpeachable:

If something can arise from something other than itself,
Well then, deep darkness can arise from tongues of flame,
And anything could issue forth from anything.
For 'nonproducer,' like 'producer,' is an 'other.'[278]

It is essential to bear in mind all the time when following Madhyamaka reasoning that the entities involved must always be viewed through the lens of inherent existence. From this perspective it is not possible to have gradations of 'otherness.' Something is either an 'other' or it is not. There are no in between states; this is a consequence of the lens of inherent existence and is entailed if we consider that things are inherently existent. So if we say that production is from something 'other' than what is produced, a rice seed being 'other' to a rice plant for instance, then the producer, or the cause, and another entity which we think is a nonproducer, a barley seed for instance, must actually be equal in otherness. The barley seed and the rice seed must be considered to be equally 'other' to a rice plant. So, if both a barley seed and a rice seed are equal in otherness, both of these, or neither, must be capable of producing the rice plant. If both are capable then anything can indeed issue forth from anything. It is worth spending time becoming familiar with this reasoning because it does throw the notion of substantial causation into a new, and startling, light.

The assertion of production from both self and other is refuted by employing both of the above refutations. Finally, if things arise causelessly, then things should be produced randomly which would essentially be the same as anything arising from anything. This, however, is not observed in the world.

The diamond slivers and the partless-particle reasonings, then, deconstruct any notion that there are inherently real causal processes involving definite entities to be found in reality. This is not to say, however, that the appearance of such processes does not occur because, quite obviously, they do. But these appearances are conventional manifestations within a seeming, illusion-like reality. This completes the Madhyamaka demolition of the notion that there are definite, inherently real, entities and processes in an external, or internal, independent reality.

Illusion or Reality?

For me the biggest mystery of all lies at the heart of reality: how to explain the weird behaviour of the subatomic world. We have a very powerful theory that explains the atomic world-quantum mechanics. But the problem is no one understands what it means.[279]

-Jim Al-Khalili

Just like a reflection in a mirror,
I understand that the nature of appearances is empty.
Just like seeing some spectacle displayed in a dream,
I understand that the nature of being empty is to appear.[280]

-Tragba Gyaltsen

How something is, or what its state is, is an illusion. It may be a useful illusion for some purposes, but if we want to think fundamentally we must not loose sight of the essential fact that 'is' is an illusion.[281]

- Lee Smolin

Phenomena as they appear and resound
Are neither established nor real …
Since they keep changing in all possible and various manners
Just like appearances in magical illusions. [282]

- Asvaghosa

We must now come to terms with the fact that there is no hard evidence for this common sense reality to be gained from the entire history of human thought. There is simply nothing we can point to, hang our hats on and say *this is real.*[283]

-Jim Baggott

Everything is real and not real,
Both real and not real,
Neither real nor not real.
This is the Lord Buddha's teaching.[284]

-Nagarjuna

Wolfgang Pauli

In his book *Quantum Physics–Illusion or Reality* physicist Alastair Rae observes that the facts of quantum physics have led some people:

> To believe that it is the actual human observer's mind that is the only reality – everything else, including the whole physical universe is an illusion.[285]

The general attitude adopted by the great many physicists working today is that of a retreat into the use of the mathematical procedures of quantum physics whilst ignoring the deep philosophical problem of what actually exists at the quantum level. Such an attitude, however, indicates a deep discomfort with some of the inescapable conclusions which cannot be avoided with integrity. As the contemporary Buddhist philosopher Karl Brunnhölzl points out:

> …according to quantum physics there are no such things as matter, roads, cars, or bodies, so who or what is driving home after an exciting day at the quantum lab.[286]

Such questions, however, are sidestepped by the majority of physicists who tend to simply rely on the mathematical notion of the wavefunction to do their calculations but do not bother about metaphysical implications.

At the quantum level entities do not exist in the way that they appear to do at the level of our experience of the everyday world. In fact it is probably more correct to say that there are no entities at the quantum level, there are only the possibilities for the experience of entity-ness, so to speak. An actual experience of an entity occurs when an aspect of reality capable of experiencing, i.e. a subjective consciousness, meets a field of potentialities for experience. Henry Stapp describes these 'objective tendencies' for experience:

> The central idea in Heisenberg's picture of nature is that atoms are not 'actual' things. The physical state of an atom, or of an assembly of atoms, represents only a set of 'objective tendencies for certain kinds of 'actual events' to occur.[287]

Heisenberg was one of the founding fathers of quantum theory and an originator of the viewpoint that objective reality consists of objective tendencies for possible experience rather than a definite pre-existing external realm of materiality. From this perspective unexperienced reality is mere potentiality; not actuality. Which experience results from the meeting of subjective consciousness and the possibilities for an experience depends on the nature of the interaction. One might think that the interaction produces a kind of reinforcing resonance. Such a resonance constitutes an experience within the dualistic realm of apparent subjectivity and objectivity within a field of the individual awareness of a sentient being.

When wavefunctions are experienced to have one particular value they are said to 'collapse' into one value, all the other possibilities that were contained within the wavefunction prior to the experience disappear. So it seems that every time a subjectivity, or a consciousness, interacts with a wavefunction, the wavefunction collapses into one value and the individual consciousness in question has a corresponding experience. Immediately after the experience, however, the wavefunction begins to spread out, becoming more and more spread out over a larger area of possibility until it is 'collapsed' again; this process is schematically shown in fig 6.1. In this diagram the 'eye' represents a subjective consciousness which interacts with the objective field of the wavefunction in order to 'collapse' it into definite experiences. Between the experiences the wavefunction spreads out into an increasingly more diffuse field of possibility. This illustration, which is based on descriptions by Penrose and Jim Al Khalili[288], must not be understood as suggesting that an individual can intentionally 'collapse' a wavefunction by an intentional focusing of mind. This process, rather, seems to take place at an instinctual level beneath self-aware intentional consciousness.

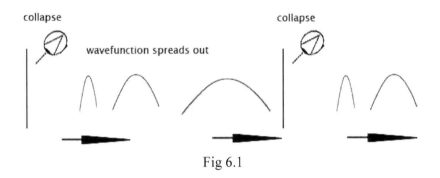

Fig 6.1

So we see that there are two levels of description for quantum physics. The first is the description of the 'propagation', or movement, of probabilities of the possibilities for experience that semi-exist, or wf-exist, in the realm of the wavefunction. The second level, or phase, occurs when an observation produces a 'collapse' into a fully experienced 'reality' of one of the possibilities.

The same quantum principle should theoretically apply to people, paths, fences, bushes and houses; according to quantum theory when they are not observed they dematerialise into wf-existence. In fact, according to some quantum physicists:

> …even an object as large as the Moon, full of atoms held together by gravity and jiggling about with the random thermal motion appropriate to its temperature, does not exist when nobody is looking at it.… The Moon doesn't simply disappear when nobody is looking at it … The probability waves spread out very slowly, from the states they were in when they were last observed; the

whole moon begins to dissolve away into a quantum ghost. But because the Moon is so big the process is very slow. It doesn't take a few nanoseconds but millions (perhaps billions) of years for the Moon to dissolve away into quantum uncertainty.[289]

For large objects, therefore, the period of time over which they would have to be unobserved in order for them to begin to dissolve in a quantum fashion, is unimaginably vast. But theoretically when unobserved even the moon's existence should begin to 'smear out' over a range of probabilities.

Despite this limitation on the perception of quantum dissolution which derives from physical and temporal scale, however, the quantum nature permeates all phenomena; but at the large scale sentient beings generally cannot perceive it; our perceptual situation masks the quantum nature of the phenomenal world. Because of our perceptual limitations, therefore, we end up with the a picture of the process of reality within which there is a realm of wf-existence which is hidden from us – the realm of the wavefunction with its multitude of possibilities for experience, and the realm of actual experienced people, paths, fences, bushes, houses and moons.

The advent of quantum theory, then, introduced a split in our physical picture of reality between, on the one hand, the everyday world of seemingly independent and inherently existent entities and the causal processes that they seemingly participate in and, on the other, the underlying quantum realm of the probabilistic wavefunction. In order for a quantum process to manifest into a full experienced reality it is necessary for a conscious observer or observers to be involved. The boundary between these two modes of reality, therefore, is provided by the apparent dependency on consciousness. Our familiar everyday reality appears to be independent of mind but, in reality, the manifestation from the quantum realm seems to depend on the mind of the observer or observers.

The quantum split in reality leads directly and insistently to the central issue of the nature of reality. As Penrose points out:

> …it makes no sense to use the term 'reality' just for objects that we can perceive … denying that the term can apply at some deeper underlying level. Undoubtedly the world is strange and unfamiliar at the quantum level, but it is not 'unreal'. How, indeed, can real objects be constructed from unreal constituents? [290]

The problems which have been raised by quantum physics lead directly to the vexed philosophical problem of the allocation of illusion and reality. This philosophical issue had found its canonical expression within the Western philosophical tradition in the conceptual confrontation between idealism, the idea that consciousness was, in some guise, the primary 'stuff' of reality and the opposing materialist viewpoint. Within the realm of quantum philosophy this dichotomy reappears as the division between the quantum level, with its implication of the primacy of consciousness, and the everyday realm of macroscopic phenomena.

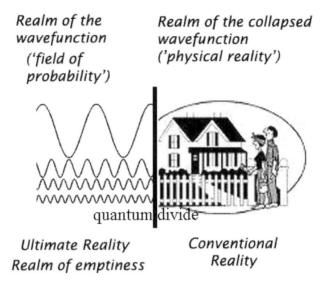

Realm of the wavefunction
('field of probability')

Realm of the collapsed wavefunction
('physical reality')

quantum divide

Ultimate Reality
Realm of emptiness

Conventional Reality

Fig 6.2

One of the most crucial philosophical issues that is posed by the most recent understanding of quantum physics focuses on how it is possible for the realm of the familiar 'classical' everyday world to 'emerge' from the quantum level. And the direction in which the evidence is pointing is extremely counter-intuitive, suggesting that we must discount our everyday experience as being an indicator of 'reality' in its 'ultimate' guise. Reality is quantum through and through and our perceptions of the macroscopic world are the result of an extraordinary process of illusion. Quantum physicist Lee Smolin certainly agrees with this analysis:

> How something is, or what it state is, is an illusion. It may be a useful illusion for some purposes, but if we want to think fundamentally we must not loose sight of the essential fact that 'is' is an illusion.[291]

Quantum physicist Erich Joos is more startling in his view of the matter, according to him the classical realm is a 'delusion.'[292]

Mainstream western scientific and philosophical thought has as yet completely failed to make any headway in the metaphysical understanding of this area of discourse. In the face of this inability to cope on the part of Western thought a consideration of what the Madhyamaka, which is sometimes translated as 'Centrism', has to offer proves extremely fertile. The quantum schism of reality is mirrored within the Madhyamaka by the doctrine of the two truths. The term 'truth' in this context indicates not a logical truth but an experiential manner of engaging with reality. Each 'truth' may be thought of as a mode of experiential engagement with reality which conditions the manner in which reality reveals itself within experience:

> In Centrism, reality is understood in an experiential or perceptual sense and not ontologically as some hard-and-fast 'real existence' in a substantial, independent, or absolute manner. Rather, this notion of real existence is precisely what Centrists keep denying.[293]

For the perspective of the Madhyamaka 'reality' is considered be what manifests within the experiential continuums of sentient beings, so in a sense there are as many realities as there are sentient beings. Such a viewpoint is generally viewed with great suspicion by Western philosophers (especially the Anglo-American variety) as leading to what is called 'relativism'. Relativism, as understood by the Western philosophical tradition is generally presented as the doctrine that there is no absolute truth at all but only relative truth, which is a truth relative to an experiential domain. This way of presenting the view of relativism, however, is at variance with the perspective of the Madhyamaka; which is that there is an 'ultimate' truth which is implicit, hidden to ordinary consciousness, but at the same time immanent within the multitude of relative truths which manifest within the mental continuums of all sentient beings.

Without the, illusion-like, existence of 'relative,' or 'conventional,' truths it would be impossible to be aware of an 'ultimate' truth:

> Without reliance on conventions,
> The ultimate cannot be taught.[294]

The Madhyamaka conceives of an ultimate reality, which is beyond words, concepts and expressions but which is hiddenly revealed within the relative experiences of sentient beings. Furthermore, within the experiences and articulations of reality within the mental continuums of the multitude of beings, some are closer to the ultimate than others; and in particular:

> Thus, two kinds of world are seen:
> The one of yogins and the one of common people.
> Here, the world of common people
> Is invalidated by the world of Yogins.[295]

The first truth, or mode of experiencing, is that of 'conventional' or 'seeming' reality. This is the everyday engagement with reality which is experienced by ordinary beings that have not undertaken and completed the deep and transformative investigation into the 'real' nature of reality. The experiences which are generated within the perspective of conventional or seeming reality, which are termed conventional 'truths', are said to be truths only for a 'concealer of suchness'.[296] 'Suchness', or *tathata*, is a Madhya-maka term for the direct experience of the ultimate nature which manifests to a `Yogin's`[297] awareness when the true nature of the seeming truths of conventional reality are penetrated and seen to be illusory. Thus practitioners who have achieved the ultimate realisation of *tathata*, the 'thusness' or 'suchness' of the process of reality, are called *tathagatas*, which literally means 'those who have gone to thusness.'[298]

Conventional 'truths', therefore, are only truths for an 'ignorant consciousness'[299] which is a consciousness which is constrained to experience phenomena through the deep and innate belief in 'inherent existence', the deeply seated notion that entities exist as they appear to, independently of consciousness. Conventional experience of reality therefore grasps phenomena as existing in their own right, with their own self-enclosed and independent self-nature, independent of the mind. For ordinary beings the appearance of macroscopic reality is a 'seeming' reality that obscures the actual ultimate nature in which all phenomena are dependent on the mind and are therefore illusion-like.

The two levels of reality as described by physics, 'quantum' and 'classical', are theoretical and 'objective' descriptions, whilst within the Madhyamaka the two truths are subjective modes of experience. Geshe Yeshe Tobden describes the two truths as follows:

> In relation to the two truths, ultimate truth is defined as what is realised explicitly by a direct, valid perceiver without dualistic appearances. Conventional truth is defined as what is realised explicitly by a direct, valid perceiver with dualistic appearances.[300]

Conventional truths, therefore, are 'realised' by most people all of the time. Ultimate truth, on the other hand, is 'realised' by a handful of 'realised' or 'enlightened' beings, usually after lifetimes[301] of effort and practice in training their minds to penetrate through levels of consciousness to a non-dualistic mode of awareness:

> At the point when expanse and awareness fuse,
> Entities, characteristics, negations, affirmations,
> And any grasping at reference points vanish on their own-
> This is resting in the actuality of the nature of phenomena
> Free from the duality of perceiver and perceived.[302]

This state of deep meditative nondual awareness is considered to be a direct realisation of the ground of reality which is given the term *dharmadhatu*, the 'expanse of dharmas':

> The basic element, which is the seed,
> Is held to be the basis of all dharmas.
> Through purification, step by step,
> The state of Buddhahood we will attain.[303]

The term *dharma* indicates any phenomenon, the *dharmadhatu*, therefore, is the basis from which all phenomena manifest and an awareness of this level is necessarily beyond duality, and is therefore unconditioned and has the quality of complete peacefulness:

> The nature of the dharmadhatu is space.
> Like this element of space, it lacks causes and conditions.
> It is without birth, aging, abiding,
> And ceasing, and thus is the unconditioned.
> It is inseparable from the Buddha qualities
> And accordingly bears their disposition.
> It lacks falsehood, deception, and harm.
> Therefore, it is primordial, natural peacefulness.[304]

The purification required to generate direct awareness of this dimension is the practice of methods of pacifying mental habits which underlie dualistic perception. These habits, amongst which the innate, mistaken, perception of inherent self-sufficient existence in all phenomena is primary, exist at a very deep level of psychophysical embodiment. They are also referred to as being 'obscurations' which obscure the correct comprehension of the nature of reality; these are divided into emotional obscurations, or afflictions, which block the possibility of 'liberation' from the cyclic process of *samsara* and cognitive obscurations which obscure the omniscient mind of nondual wisdom of buddhahood. The reason that a sentient being's mind is able to achieve this nondual awareness which lies at the heart of all phenomena is simply that all phenomena, both objective and subjective, are of the nature of mind, or consciousness[305]:

> Whatever is apprehended is like a reflection
> And arises from beginningless mind.
> So it is with consciousness that takes on the aspect of the apprehended,
> Both being like mutually related reflections.[306]

It is important to be aware of the use of terms 'mind' and 'consciousness' in this quote. The term 'mind' is used for the overall beginningless, and end-less, continuum of cognitional activity which arises from fundamental non-dual awareness, which is generally referred to as *jnana* or nondual wisdom-awareness.

The Sanskrit term for consciousness is *vijnana*, which literally denotes a cut (*vi*) in the fundamental undivided wisdom-awareness (*jnana*). The *dharmadhatu* is the matrix, totality, or limitless all-pervading space of awareness in which all phenomena arise, abide, and cease. The illusory app-earances of apprehender and apprehended, perceiver and perceived arise as reflections of each other due to inner cognitive processes, which take place on the basis of previous cognitive processes. This illusory realm of subject and object is the realm of *vijnana*, or divided awareness-wisdom, which is consciousness. It is intriguing to note that the Western term consciousness means 'knowing together (con-sciousness)', whilst the Sanskrit term *vijnana* indicates a split in a fundamental nondual awareness.

The Chittamatra, Mind-Only, school of Buddhist philosophy presents their analysis of the two truths from the perspective of their doctrine of the three natures of the mind based process of reality: the imputed or imaginary nature, the dependent or other-powered nature, and the perfect or fully established nature. According to Khenpo Ngakchung, an influential Dzogchen master of recent times:

> All the dualistic phenomena of the imputed nature and the mind and mental phenomena of the dependent nature are the deceiving phenomena of delusion, the relative truth. The essence of the dependent nature, which is the naturally luminous consciousness, and the fully established nature, which is the fact that this [i.e., the dependent nature] is empty of the dualistic projections of the imputed nature—comprising the nature of reality and wisdom—are said to be the absolute truth.[307]

As we shall see this analysis can be mapped into the functioning of the quantum wavefunction in a remarkable way.

The place to begin exploring this analysis is the 'dependent nature' which has also been called the 'other-powered' nature.[308] And the fact that the dependent nature is said to be 'naturally luminous consciousness' gives us a clue as to how the perspective of the three natures can be related to the functioning of the quantum realm. First we recall that, in their important work *Quantum Enigma,* Rosenblum and Kuttner have asserted that:

> Consciousness and the quantum enigma are not just two mysteries; they are *the* two mysteries; first, our physical demonstration of the quantum enigma, faces us with the fundamental mystery of the objective world 'out there;' the second, conscious awareness, faces us with the fundamental mystery of the subjective, mental world 'in here.' Quantum mechanics seems to connect the two.[309]

Furthermore the quantum physicist Nick Herbert has concluded that:

> every quantum system has both an 'inside' and an 'outside', and that consciousness both in humans as well as in other sentient beings is identical to the inner experience of some quantum system. A quantum system's outside behavior is described by quantum theory, it's inside experience is the subject matter of a new 'inner physics'....[310]

These conclusions quite naturally suggest that the 'inner' quality of individualised awareness that is referred to by the term 'consciousness' should be identified as the inner, qualitative, direct experiential manifestation of the functioning of the quantum realm of the wavefunction. Herbert quite clearly explains, in a completely coherent fashion that is consistent with the views of several other significant quantum physicists, how quantum physics connects the two realms of the inner and the outer and thus *demystifies* the 'mysteries' of consciousness and the 'quantum enigma.' The fundamental requirement for this demystification, however, is that we must accept the quantum evidence which clearly validates the Mind-Only assertion that:

> …all phenomena are merely mind-the all-ground consciousness manifesting as environment, objects and the physical body, as a result of residual tendencies stored within the all-ground.[311]

This leads us to the picture of the Quantum Mind-Only view of the functioning of the process of reality which is schematically shown in fig 6.3. According to the Mind-Only school of Buddhist philosophy (Yogachara-Chittamatra) the dualistic experiences of the 'seeming' world arise from a deep level of awareness called the *alaya* (all-ground) which can be thought of as a foundational experiential potentiality which has an internal function of cognition. When the cognitive function activates the potentiality of the alaya it becomes the *alayavijnana,* the all-ground consciousness, which is an increasingly divided process of awareness becoming individuated into the dualistic realms of consciousness, giving rise the mental continuums of all sentient beings. The all-ground consciousness operates by receiving impressions from all the activities of the higher levels which are 'stored' for later activation when surrounding co-operating conditions act as a resonant triggering mechanism. It is this mechanism which gives rise to 'all the dualistic phenomena of the imputed nature and the mind and mental phenomena of the dependent nature' of the relative truth or reality.

The following are the first four stanzas of the *Stanzas on the Three Natures* which were composed by the fourth century Buddhist master Vasubandhu:

> The imaginary, the other-dependent,
> And the perfect as well-
> The three natures are held to be
> The profound object to be understood by the wise.
> What appears is the other-dependent
> And the way it appears is the imaginary,
> Since it comes about being subject to conditions
> And since it exists as mere imagination.
> The fact of the invariable absence
> Of the way it appears in what appears
> Is known to be the perfect nature
> Since it is never otherwise.

What appears here? The imagination of what is nonexistent.
How does it appear? By way of having the character of duality.
What is its non-existence [within that duality]?
The very nature of nonduality in it.[312]

Here the dependent-nature is characterised as the 'other-dependent' nature, a formulation which emphasizes that the dependent nature is a field of interdependent potentiality which is devoid of inherent substantiality. Hopkins translates the Sanskrit *paratantra* as 'other-powered' nature, emphasizing that the phenomena of this nature have no intrinsic power of existence but depend on all other phenomena, which also lack any self-powered internal independent existence.

The other-dependent nature, therefore, can be conceived of as a field of potentiality into which the 'imaginary' nature is imputed as really existing phenomena (fig 6.4). The 'other', in the term 'other-dependent', refers to the 'latent tendencies', created by previous cognitive activities, which provide the potencies to be activated as experiential moments of subject-object cognition. These potencies of the latent tendencies make up the *alayavijnana*, the ground-store-consciousness that collects the potencies for future activation. This is the karmic process of *karma-vipaka*, action and effect, which is investigated in detail in the next chapter.

We can see that the dependent, or other-powered, nature can be compared to the nature of the wavefunction which is equally a field of potentiality for experience. In fact the correspondence with the following description of the nature of the quantum wavefunction by Stapp is remarkable:

> *'potentialities for future psychophysical events'*: i.e. as a representation of *objective tendencies*, created by past psychophysical events, for the occurrence of future psychophysical events.[313]

Here, then, Professor Stapp suggests that the potentialities within the wavefunction are created by previous activations of the wavefunction into experienced events exactly in the same way that the 'latent tendencies' of the other-powered field of potentiality, which are contained within the *alayavijnana*, are also built up according to the Mind-Only perspective.

The imputed nature or imaginary nature (*parikalpita*) consists of the imputed and mistaken appearances of definite, inherent and independent entities that are conceived of as existing in an external realm separate from the perceiving consciousness. According to the Mind-Only perspective the way that the entities of everyday life are imputed as existing independently and substantially is, from an ultimate point of view, mistaken. It is an imputation, or superimposition, onto or into the other-dependent nature.

It is important to understand, however, that according to the Mind-Only analysis this imputation is a deep seated, instinctual process which is built into a foundational level of the psychophysical functioning of sentient beings

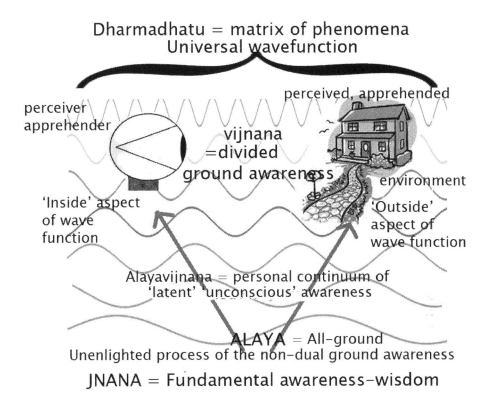

Fig 6.3

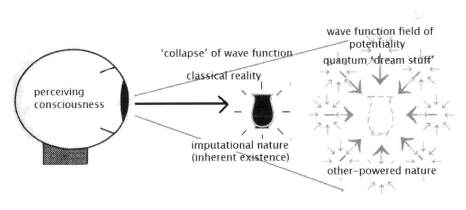

Fig 6.4

- it is not a surface level intellectual imputation, it is, rather, a fundamental psychophysical process which brings the appearance of the solidity of the material world into being. This can be related to the quantum phenomenon of the 'collapse' of the wavefunction. This is graphically and simplistically illustrated in figure 6.4. This is not meant to suggest that an individual consciousness collapses the wavefunction, intentionally or otherwise, it is the way that the process appears to function; this is elucidated in the next chapter.

The final nature, the perfect-nature, or fully-established-nature (*pariniṣpanna*) highlights the fact that the imputational-nature is an ultimately illusory imputation. Vasubandhu expresses this as:

> The fact of the invariable absence
> Of the way it appears in what appears

This is an extremely subtle and accurate description because it indicates that, whilst there is an appearance, it is the manner of the appearance which is illusory; it is the appearance of inherent independent existence which is illusory. The fully, or thoroughly-established nature, or perfect-nature, is the recognition that the imaginary, imputed nature is in fact absent from the dependent-nature. The appearance of conventional entities as independently substantial is a superimposition into the potentialities of the other-powered-nature or dependent nature:

> The non-existence of such an imaginary nature in a dependent nature is a thoroughly established nature. ... An object which is a different entity from a subject does not exist; a subject which is a different object from an object does not exist...[314]

In fact it is the very appearance of the duality of subject and object which is delusive, although it is a remarkably convincing illusion.

An example which is often used to illustrate the three natures is that of a mirage. The three natures may be likened respectively to (a) the mistaken belief that water exists in a mirage; (b) the appearance itself of the mirage, dependent on atmospheric causes and conditions; and (c) the empty nature of the mirage, inasmuch as it is completely dependent on causes and conditions, including the observer. The belief that water exists in the mirage is completely false and is similar to the imaginary, or illusory, nature. The simple appearance of the mirage relative to its causes and conditions is similar to the dependent nature. The empty character of the mirage, inasmuch as it is dependent and exists nowhere except in the mistaken mind of the observer, is similar to the thoroughly-established-nature.

This analysis can be likened to the quantum situation. The realm of the wavefunction, which includes the observing consciousness or consciousnesses, provides the interdependent ground of potentiality which constitutes the other-powered nature and, because there is a tendency within the process of reality for the inner nature of this ground to misperceive itself, a realm of imputedly independent and inherently existent phenomenon manifests within an illusory field of duality. This is the illusory domain of the non-existent imputational and imaginary nature, which is the domain of experienced duality of apprehender-apprehended, subject-object. The relationship between the conventional arena of the experienced 'material' world, which seems to emerge through the apparent collapse of the wavefunction, can clearly be likened to the superimposition of the imputational nature onto the field of other-powered potentiality.

The Quantum Mind-Only viewpoint can be compared with the 'rainbow' illustration of the quantum situation (fig 6.5) offered by physicist and philosopher Bernard d'Espagnat:

> ...a rainbow, obviously, may not be considered an object-per-se. For, indeed, if we move it moves. Two differently located persons do not see it having its bases at the same places. It is therefore manifest that it depends, in part, on us. ... But still, even though the rainbow depends on us, it does not depend exclusively on us. For it to appear it is necessary that the sun should shine and that raindrops should be there. Now similar features also characterize quantum mechanically described objects, that is, after all ... any object whatsoever. For *they* also are not 'objects-per-se.' The attributes, or 'dynamical properties,' we see them to posses depend in fact on our 'look' at them...[315]

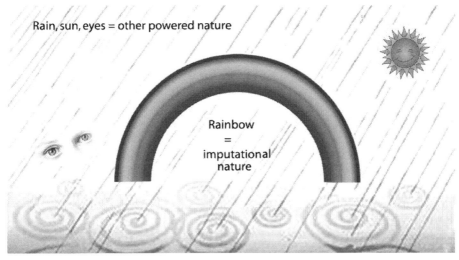

Fig 6.5

In this analogy the sun, raindrops and observer correspond to the other-powered realm of interdependent phenomena and the appearance of a seemingly external and independent rainbow corresponds to the imputational nature. The Mind-Only perspective uses the term 'imputational' to indicate not just a surface conceptual imputation but a directly experienced sensory imputation such as the rainbow example. The rainbow does not exist at all as an independent phenomenon, it is therefore 'imaginary', in fact the imputational nature is sometimes translated as the 'imaginary nature.'

An important aspect of the doctrine of the two truths, or two experiential realities, is the fact that they are not separate entities. They are different perceptual engagements with the same entity, which is the underlying process of reality. Buddhist philosopher Karl Brunnhölzl suggests the analogy of 'Magic Eye' pictures in which the same visual image has a radically different appearance depending upon the manner in which the viewer's eyes are focused. The actual Magic Eye image does not change in any way; the transformation is completely within the mode of perception of the viewer.

Applying this analogy to our experience of the seemingly solid everyday world that most of us inhabit everyday, however, is extremely difficult. The idea that the computer I am using to write this chapter, the table which supports the computer, the floor which supports the table and even my own body can be considered as being analogous to a Mind-Only illusion seems, on immediate consideration, to be preposterous. But before we come to such commonsense and 'natural' conclusions we really must consider the evidence presented to us by physics. Quantum physics is as real as it comes, and just about all of modern technology depends upon its correctness. And there is a suggestion made by physicists regarding the nature of reality which fits very closely with the Mind-Only scenario, the proposal of the holographic universe.

A holograph is a special two dimensional photographic image which is produced by splitting a beam of laser light and bouncing one of the beams off the target and then bringing the beams back together onto a photographic plate. The result is a two-dimensional photographic image which produces a three-dimensional image when a beam of light is passed through it, or bounced off of it. In the early 1990's the Dutch Nobel laureate physicist Gerald 't Hooft and his associate Leonard Susskind suggested that the universe might operate holographically. This notion was derived from the fact that the maximum amount of information contained within a region of space depends on its surface area not its volume. Brian Greene's description gives a flavor of this highly counter-intuitive and unlikely scenario:

> What we experience in the 'volume' of the universe – in the *bulk*, as physicists often call it – would be determined by what takes place on the bounding surface, much as what we see in a holographic projection is determined by information encoded on a

bounding piece of plastic. The laws of physics would act as the universe's laser, illuminating the real processes of the cosmos – processes taking place in a thin, distant surface – and generating the holographic illusions of everyday life.[316]

And you thought the ideas of the Chittamatra and Madhyamaka were mind bending!

In this presentation of the holographic universe idea is it is suggested that the 'laws of physics' act as a 'laser' to unfold the illusion of a 3-D world from the 2-D hologram in a similar manner to the way in which the Mind-Only perspective suggests that dualistic consciousness imputes solidity into the potentiality of the 'dependent nature.' However it is necessary to ask just where the 'laws of nature' come from! According to John Wheeler:

> It is preposterous to think of the laws of physics as installed by Swiss watchmaker to endure from everlasting to everlasting when we know that the universe began with a big bang. The laws must have come into being. … That means that they are derivative, not primary … Observer-participancy … gives what we call tangible reality to the universe … [317]

Which can only mean that consciousness must have had a creative role in the production of the unfolding 'laser' of the 'laws of physics.' But, given the fact that consciousness is implicated in the collapse of the wavefunction, it is far more natural to consider that consciousness itself is the primary unfolding mechanism.

It seems, however, that a great many physicists in speculative metaphysical mode today would prefer to indulge in any ill-formed wild speculation rather than take note of the clear quantum implication that consciousness is the major player in the process of reality. As a consequence the absurd nature of the speculations that do the rounds as seriously entertained 'theories' is harrowing. For instance some of our most advanced and respected physicists are speculating, or perhaps fantasising is a more appropriate word, about the Universe as a computer simulation concocted by alien beings, or even a 'fake' universe, whatever that means.

A recent editor's choice article on the online science magazine *Fqxi* (Foundational Questions Institute), entitled *Down the Rabbit Hole*, begins:

> You are not really reading this article. This article does not exist. *You* do not exist. The computer you're reading this article on doesn't exist, either. But in one way, the computer is more real than you are: It may be the nearest we will ever come to understanding the truth of our universe. Welcome to the simulation hypothesis. Here's the idea: An advanced civilisation decides to create a detailed computer simulation of another civilisation. They fill up their mock world with people, plants and animals, and they

write the rules of nature governing how the fake universe evolves.[318]

Shades of *The Matrix* of course; but the astonishing thing is that such hypotheses seem to be advanced as serious possibilities, whereas Roger Penrose's suggestion that consciousness might be a significant feature of the proposed simulation is rejected because it 'boils down to a religious proposition!'[319] At least at the end of the article the author tells us that Paul Davies seems to come to his senses when he says of the simulation hypothesis:

> A thought experiment that goes to absurd extremes ... suggests that something must be wrong with the underlying assumptions. ... lets pretend the world is real...[320]

But why pretend? Why not get to the bottom of the matter, or lack of it? The crucial issue seems to be that, from the point of view of the great majority of physicists, the notion that the immaterial metaphysical category of fundamental awareness-consciousness should turn out to be the ultimate driving force of the process of reality is simply considered to too outlandish and therefore unacceptable, anything else is better, even alien computer simulations!

The situation is little better in mainstream Western philosophy. The kind of laxity of conceptual use which is endemic within Western philosophy is beautifully illustrated by a story recounted by the 'philosopher' Ian Hacking. A friend of his was conducting an experiment which was designed to measure a fractional electric charge on subatomic entities. The experiment required changing the charge on a tiny niobium ball. Hacking asked his friend how this was done:

> 'Well at that stage,' said my friend, 'we spray it with positrons to increase the charge or with electrons to decrease the charge.' From that day forth I've been a scientific realist. *So far as I am concerned, if you can spray them then they are real.*[321]

This account is shocking because of the remarkable disregard for ontological precision; such an attitude displays a maverick lack of concern for discovering the 'reality' of the situation on the part of Hacking, who is, after all, a professional, although Western, academic philosopher specialising in the philosophy of science. From the perspective of the precision of the Madhyamaka to call Hacking's observation 'philosophical' is simply laughable as it shows no concern with really getting to the real nature of the reality of reality. Hacking is quite happy to pretend that an illusion is real for a quiet, and metaphysically simplistic, intellectual life!

The version of the holographic universe proposed by 't Hooft and Susskind was not the first. David Bohm had worked on one of the early wonders of the quantum realm – the behavior of collections of particles such as electrons in plasmas. Plasmas are formed when a large number of electrons start to behave as in they were an interconnected whole. Bohm was impressed by the way in which such large numbers of what were supposed to be disconnected quantum entities could loose their individuality when they formed a larger quantum group identity such as plasmas. Bohm shared Einstein's dissatisfaction with the prevalent views concerning quantum mechanics and they engaged in a series of intense conversational investigations into alternative viewpoints.

Bohm's primary objection to the prevailing consensus concerning quantum phenomena was its 'mechanistic' emphasis which treated quantum entities as separate and disconnected phenomena. The intellectual attitude that Bohm is describing here corresponds with what the Madhyamaka calls the belief in 'inherent existence,' which the Madhyamaka considers to be at the root of a fundamental misperception of reality.

Bohm points out that the levels of 'particle' analysis rapidly descend in scale, first atoms, then protons, electrons and neutrons and then quarks, and more recently, subsequent to the time that Bohm was writing, physicists have speculated into scales unimaginably smaller than this with the notion that everything consists of 'strings' of some kind of energy existing at a scale beyond what we could ever hope to achieve direct physical knowledge of. There seems no end to the levels of the rapidly vanishing ultimate particle, a fact which is mirrored in the Madhyamaka analysis of the 'partless particle,' and yet:

> ...there seems to be an unshakable faith among physicists that either such particles, or some other kind yet to be discovered, will eventually make possible a complete and coherent explanation of everything.[322]

Bohm wrote this in 1980, twenty nine years ago, and yet at the time of writing (2009) the same attitude seems to prevail. At the moment the scientific community and the Western media are expectantly awaiting the repair and resurrection of the Large Hadron Collider at CERN. And one of the primary hopes for the data which will be gathered from this hugely expensive apparatus is the expected discovery of the Higg's particle which is thought to be the source of the experience of mass within the universe. It rarely, if at all, crosses the minds of physicists that the source of the experience of mass might actually be consciousness.

Part of the hype surrounding the commissioning of the LHC was the possibility of the eagerly awaited theory of everything, or TOE. As Steven Hawking wrote in his much lauded, bought and apparently little read *Brief History of Time*:

> The eventual goal of science is to provide a single theory that describes the whole universe.[323]

This book, however, contains no reference of the phenomenon of consciousness. It's as if Hawking has made up his mind, as many physicists seem to do, that consciousness is not a phenomenon that is part of the 'whole universe.' It seems that it is seldom noticed that, without an explanation of consciousness, an aspect of reality which physics now shows to be significant, any such TOE won't have a leg to stand on. As Roger Penrose writes:

> ...a physical 'theory of everything' should at least contain seeds of an explanation of the phenomenon of consciousness. It seems to me that this phenomenon is such a fundamental one that it cannot be simply an accidental concomitant of the complexity of brain action...[324]

The cosmologist Andrei Linde has also queried:

> Is it possible that consciousness, like spacetime, has its own intrinsic degrees of freedom, and that neglecting these will lead to a description of the universe that is fundamentally incomplete? What if our perception is as real as (or maybe in a certain sense, are even more real than) material objects?[325]

All the evidence is now mounting up ineluctably towards the conclusion that the answer to these questions is yes. Consciousness is 'more real' than 'material objects' because it is the ontological primary aspect of the process of reality And without a deep understanding of the nature and functioning of consciousness any description of the universe is completely incomplete!

An answer that physicists like to give in order to avoid the central issue of modern physics, the 'skeleton in the closet' of physics, is that the ultimate particles that are supposed to make up reality are enumerated in the 'standard model' of the ultimate building blocks of reality, which is illustrated in fig 6.6. And it would be easy to get the impression that these particles so deftly illustrated as independently existent little balls of definite existence are the independent ultimate building units of reality. Such a picture of ultimately existent particles of 'matter', so easily, and misleadingly, presented by some physicists is, however, completely false. The particles of this physical model only appear in relation to a measurement performed by human consciousness; they are a manifestation of an interaction of consciousness and a hidden ground of potentiality which must exist at the quantum level. The Madhyamaka describes the situation:

> They are without nature, just like space,
> But since they come about due to mere dependent origination,
> They are not utterly nonexistent,
> Similar to cause and effect in dreams.[326]

This is actually a precise description of the nature of what physicists call subatomic particles, and also atomic level entities, and therefore also all phenomena. They do not have an independent 'nature' of their own because they originate due to an interaction of interdependent aspects of reality, including consciousness.

Because of this they can said to be a 'matter' of 'dependent origination'. They are not 'utterly nonexistent' because they do appear under the appropriate conditions; but neither are they fully and independently existent because without the necessary causes and conditions they do not appear. Their essential nature seems more akin to the phenomena of dreams rather than a solid independent reality. Indeed the quantum physicist Wojciech H. Zurek describes the quantum realm in the following terms:

> ...quantum states, by their very nature ... are simultaneously a description of the state, and the 'dream stuff is made of.'[327]

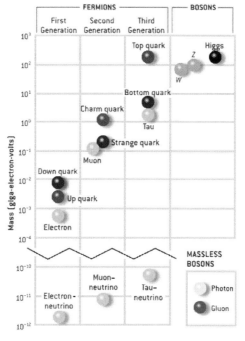

Fig 6.6

Bohm's observations of plasma behavior led him to his innovative theoretical investigations into the nature of quantum reality which emphasised the interconnected nature of the quantum realm. This aspect of quantum reality he called the 'holomovement', an idea which incorporated the phenomenon of consciousness as the ontologically primary aspect of reality. The notion of the interdependent relationship of consciousness and matter, or the appearance of matter, played an important part in Bohm's alternative quantum perspective, a perspective which met with little enthusiasm from other physicists.

One of the significant aspects of Bohm's approach was his emphasis on the idea that the manifested realms of 'matter' and 'mind' were projections of a more unified field of potentiality that he called the 'implicate order'. He conceived of the implicate order as functioning analogously to a hologram, forming an 'enfolded' order of implicit structure from which the experiential realms of objectivity and subjectivity 'unfolded'. A fundamental feature of this viewpoint is that:

> One discovers ... both from consideration of the meaning of the mathematical equations and from the results of the actual experiments, that the various particles have to be taken literally as projections of a higher dimensional reality...[328]

And one of the implications of Bohm's viewpoint is that the realms of subjectivity and objectivity must be interconnected within this higher dimensional reality. It becomes clear, then, that the Madhyamaka notion of two levels of reality, one of which lies veiled behind the dualistic realm of illusory phenomena, fits quite snugly into some of the most penetrating philosophical and scientific thinking regarding the meaning of quantum phenomena.

The fact that the ground of reality must be of the nature of consciousness[329] is indicated by Bohm in terms of what he calls the implicate order:

> ... consciousness has to be understood in terms of an order that is closer to the implicate than it is to the explicate. ... The question which is arises here, then, is that of whether or not (as was in a certain sense anticipated by Descartes) the actual 'substance' of consciousness can be understood in terms of the notion that the implicate order is also its primary and immediate actuality.[330]

A similar observation is made by Bernard d'Espagnat of the University of Paris, one of the worlds leading authorities on the conceptual foundation of quantum physics:

> ...some data are now available that tend to suggest that, far from being a mere efflorescence from neurons, thought has structures that might be, somehow, directly connect to those of 'the Real.' ... They consist of a kind of parallelism between, on the one hand, the structures of thought and, on the other hand, the structures of quantum mechanics...[331]

Like Bohm, d'Espagnat is rigorous and remorseless in his analysis of the implications of quantum physics for our understanding of the categories of 'matter' and 'consciousness' in relation to what we consider to be the nature of an ultimate reality. Our understanding of the nature of the wavefunction, which cannot but indicate something fundamental about the nature of reality as it is when not being observed, or experienced, and the manner in which subjective consciousness interacts with wavefunctions to produce the appearance of the entities of dualistic experience clearly implies that what we once thought of as 'matter' *cannot* generate consciousness. As d'Espagnat says:

> How – to repeat – could mere 'appearances to consciousness' generate consciousness?[332]

This observation by d'Espagnat echoes the following by the sixth century Madhyamika sage Chandrakirti:

> How can you say the elements, which are the object of your mind,
> Compose the latter's nature? This surely cannot be!
> …
> Dense ignorance enshrouds the world as though by massing clouds;
> Because of this phenomena are misperceived.[333]

The 'elements', by which is meant the existence of inherently and independently existent physical phenomena, the kind of ultimate bits and pieces of reality which are thought by materialist thinkers to be foundation units of reality, are in fact not other than an appearance within mind and are therefore incapable of producing the mind that they depend upon for their appearance!

It appears, therefore, that at this stage of our analysis the ultimate categories of reality are not the realms of 'matter' and 'consciousness', the delineation of our experience of the world established by Descartes. Instead of this outmoded delineation, quantum physics has replaced it with on the one hand the 'objective' realm of the wavefunction and, on the other, the experience within the continuum of individual consciousness of the 'emergence' of an illusory and seemingly 'material' world. And a vitally important point concerning this new delineation is that, whereas the connection between mind and matter has always been problematic because they have completely opposite natures, the connection between aspects of reality which share the same nature is comprehensible.

This issue regarding the nature of the connection between the two aspects is highlighted as being significant by both Bohm and Stapp. Bohm points out that the Cartesian definitions of 'matter' (extended substance) and consciousness (thinking substance) indicate that they are fundamentally distinct and mutually exclusive and because of this conceptual configuration it is not possible to coherently conceive of a plausible interconnection between them:

> Descartes clearly understood this difficulty and indeed proposed to resolve it by means of the idea that such a relationship is made possible by God …Since then, the idea that God takes care of this

requirement has generally been abandoned, but it has not been noticed that thereby the possibility of comprehending the relationship between matter and consciousness has collapsed.[334]

Chandrakirti

This problem, however, is completely resolved through the quantum discovery that 'matter' is an appearance to consciousness and therefore must also share the nature of consciousness.

The fact that the conceptual configuration of 'matter' and 'consciousness' could only resolve itself into the view of the fundamental primacy of consciousness was clearly stated by the eighth century Madhyamika scholar Shantarakshita:

Consciousness arises as the contrary
Of matter, gross, inanimate.
By nature, mind is immaterial
And it is self-aware.

…

Because this is its very nature,
Consciousness is apt for self-cognition.
But how can consciousness cognize
Those things of a nature foreign to itself?

The nature of the mind is absent from non-mental things.
How then could self-cognizing consciousness
Know other things? For you have said
The knower and the known are two different entities.[335]

These verses are addressed to a proponent of the Vaibhashika school of Buddhist philosophy, a pre-Madhyamaka school which maintained that the mind, or consciousness, was innately capable of directly, or nakedly, grasping the essence of material objects even though matter and consciousness were completely different, mutually exclusive aspects of reality. The point is made here that it is simply illogical to claim that there can be a connection between two aspects of reality which are mutually exclusive. Such concepts are described within Tibetan logic as having natures of 'mutual abandonment'.

Professor Stapp articulates this situation and describes how the new quantum understanding resolves the issue as follows:

> The mind-matter difficulty in classical mechanics stems directly from the *logical* disjunction of Descartes' two realms. In science we seek to see related phenomena in terms of a logically cohesive whole, so that the related phenomena are not simply placed together in an ad hoc way, but rather hang together from logical necessity in precisely the way that they are empirically observed to do. The logical disjunction of the Cartesian concepts of mind and matter renders any such rational understanding of their connection impossible. … Heisenberg's ontology, like that of Descartes, consists of two parts: (1) the Heisenberg state, which represents objective tendencies, and also the wavelike aspects of nature; and (2) the actual events, each of which represents a sudden change in the Heisenberg state, and also the particlelike aspects of nature. These two parts are logically connected, and they represent the two sides of the empirically observed wave-particle duality. [336]

Stapp treats the human brain-mind, and in Stapp's presentation these two aspects of embodied reality are treated as two sides of 'empirically observed wave-particle duality', as being a measuring device which determines, in a fashion as yet unknown, which of the 'objective tendencies' that are contained within the surrounding environmental, or universal, wavefunction are selected for actualised experience.

The question of exactly what mechanism actually does the selection, Stapp admits, is left open. An avenue of exploration which he indicates as being possibly fruitful, however, is that suggested by one of the early quantum physicists Wolfgang Pauli, who was impressed with the psychologist C. G. Jung's ideas concerning synchronicity and the emergence of experience from a realm of archetypes, which are preexisting modes of potential experience. Jung had conducted a lifelong investigation of the symbolic and mythological material of the world's diverse cultures and as a result he was able to demonstrate that there are recurring themes and motifs which were exemplified in different specifics. This led him to his notion of an archetype:

> There are as many archetypes as there are typical situations in life. Endless repetition has engraved these experiences into our psychic constitution, not in the form of images filled with content, but at first only as forms without content, representing merely the possibility of a certain type of perception and action. When a situation occurs that corresponds to a given archetype, that archetype becomes activated...[337]

Archetypes, therefore, can be thought of as subjective propensities to experience our experience certain ways.

In his work as psychologist Jung was primarily concerned with working with archetypes which were relevant to the integration of the psychic functioning of his patients. Generally these would be related to what Jung termed the individuation process whereby aspects of the individual psyche were helped to integrate and co-ordinate in a harmonious fashion. But Jung also extended his interest in integration to deeper religious and philosophical levels in his investigations into alchemy with its emphasis on the interpenetration of psyche and the material world which he articulated in the concept of the *Unus Mundus*, the unified 'one' world; a notion which has resonances with Bohm's idea of the implicate order.

The view of the mechanism which gives rise to the experience of the macroscopic material world that emerges from this perspective is exactly that of a kind of 'holographic' interaction of an 'objective' field of potentiality for experience, a wavefunction, with a deeply seated 'inner', subjective realm of archetypal predispositions for experience, and thereby 'collapse' the wavefunction in a pre-designated way. In this manner the experience of an external structure of apparent materiality is actually a resonance effect due to the interaction of the 'objective' wavefunction of reality and the countless individuated subjective structures of possible experience which are etched into the psyches of all sentient beings (fig 6.7).

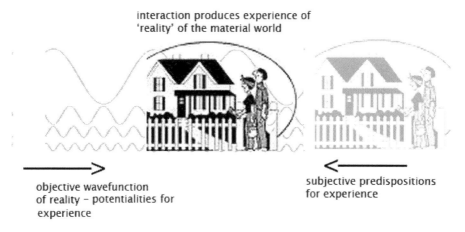

interaction produces experience of
'reality' of the material world

objective wavefunction
of reality – potentialities for
experience

subjective predispositions
for experience

Fig 6.7

A further feature of this perspective involves the interconnected nature of all events within the universe which appears to span across mind and the appearance of matter. In his autobiography *Memories, Dreams and Reflections* Jung recounts several examples of synchronous events which span the divide between the mind and matter.

As we have seen quantum physics has discovered that non-local connections exist between particles in a phenomenon called entanglement. Two or more 'particles' which interact at some point will remain in an entangled state as long as their interconnected wavefunction is not collapsed by an observation. This entangled wavefunction, encompassing both, or many, particles can spread over large distances, but if the wavefunction is collapsed in one place, by an observation, it will instantaneously collapse in the other places in which other entangled particles materialise. Furthermore the characteristics of all the materialised particles will be coordinated even though there can be no normal physical communication between the particles. It is as if all the manifested particles are interconnected through a hidden dimension.

In their explorations of the analogies between the realms of the quantum world and the world of the human psyche, Jung and Pauli were convinced that mind and matter were themselves complementary aspects of a deeper level of reality in the same way that wave and particles were complementary aspects of quantum reality. So in just the same way as the archetypes of the human mind could give structure to the inner world of the psyche it made complementary sense for an archetypal process involving 'subjective' propensities for experience to create, or impose, structure upon the multiple possibilities within the 'objective' tendencies of 'objective' wavefunctions. Pauli was so convinced of the idea that the realm of the 'physical' and that of 'mind' must be seamlessly linked at a deep level of reality that he wrote in a letter to a friend:

> When he speaks of 'reality' the layman usually means something obvious and well known, whereas it seems to me that precisely the most important and extremely difficult task of our time is to work on elaborating a new idea of reality. This is also what I mean when I always emphasize that science and religion *must* be related in some way.[338]

The sixth century Madhyamika Shantideva describes the two realities as follows:

> The seeming and the ultimate-
> These are asserted as the two realities.
> The ultimate is not the sphere of cognition.
> It is said that cognition is the seeming.[339]

According to Shantideva, then, it is the act of cognition which divides the seamless potentiality of the ultimate ground of reality into the duality of the experienced realm of the seeming. And, as we have seen, it is exactly the process of cognition which collapses the unified wavefunction of potentiality into definite outcomes. As Stapp says regarding what he calls 'the two-way quantum psycho-physical bridge':

> ...the connection between physical behaviour and human knowledge was changed from a one way bridge to a mathematically specified two-way interaction that involves *selections* made by conscious minds.[340]

The apparent collapse of the global wavefunction is caused by an interaction with the combined wavefunctions of individuated consciousnesses. This interaction, which has the nature of a resonance, produces a definite outcome from the possibilities. This constitutes the act of cognition that brings a definite experienced reality into experienced duality from a deeper sphere of possibility.

This act of cognition can be thought of as constituting the measurement that collapses the wavefunction of the ultimate sphere into the realm of manifestation. As *The Sutra of Richly Adorned* indicates:

> The ultimate is free from cognition and knowable objects.
> Measure and faculties have been relinquished.
> It is not an object of minds and consciousnesses.
> This is the object of those who are released.[341]

The last line suggests that enlightened beings have developed the capacity to move within reality without disturbing, and thereby collapsing, the global wavefunction of reality and they are therefore 'released' from the tyranny of the seeming manifestations which take place within the dualistic illusion of reality.

Those of us who remain, unfortunately, unreleased are still trapped in an extraordinary illusion of a seemingly solid and immutable dualistic material world. A pressing question, then, is just how such a dramatically convincing illusion can possibly entrap such a vast number of sentient beings. Stapp concludes his thoughts regarding Pauli's interpretation of the ideas of Jung in the context of quantum physics as follows:

> ...if the quantum and the synchronistic processes are indeed essentially the same process, then an empirical window may have been opened on the process that had been thought by quantum theorists to lie beyond the ken of empirical knowledge.[342]

And the process that Stapp is referring to here is *the creation of the illusion of the material world!*

Carl Gustav Jung

Quantum Karma

...quantum theory demands – a draconian shift in the very subject matter of physical theory, from an imagined universe consisting of causally self-sufficient mindless matter, to a universe populated by allowed possible physical actions and possible experienced feed-backs from such actions.

-Henry Stapp

From a Buddhist point a view, the karma of all sentient beings that inhabit the universe plays a role in shaping the formation of the universe.[343]

- Dalai Lama

The entire world was created through latent karmic imprints. When these imprints developed and increased, they formed the earth, the stones, and the seas. Everything was created through the development or propagation of these latent karmic potentials.[344]

- Thrangu Rinpoche

Directly opposite to the concept of universe as machine built on law is the vision of *a world self-synthesized.* On this view, the notes struck out on a piano by the observer participants of all times and all places, bits though they are in and by themselves, constitute the great wide world of space and time and things.

- John Wheeler

...quantum states, by their very nature share an epistemological and ontological role – are simultaneously a description of the state, and the 'dream stuff is made of.' One might say that they are *epiontic.* These two aspects may seem contradictory, but at least in the quantum setting, there is a union of these two functions.[345]

- Wojciech Zurek

David Bohm

David Bohm and the Dalai Lama

The idea of the concept of *karma* that is generally held in the West involves the notion of a purely moral repayment. This view is incorrect; although there is a moral dimension to the operation of the mechanism of *karma-vipaka*, universal cause and effect, in actuality karma-vipaka operates autonomously on all levels of the process of reality, including the morally neutral. Karma:

> ...is the theory of cause and effect, or action and reaction; it is a natural law, which has nothing to do with the idea of justice or reward and punishment. Every volitional action produces its effects or results.[346]

Karma actually simply means 'action', although as the above quote indicates the element of 'volition', or attachment to result, is a crucial element in the creation of an effect. The term 'karma' is now often associated with the process by which actions have subsequent consequences. This two stage process is more correctly termed karma-vipaka, actions and subsequent consequences, in this chapter, however, the term 'karma' will be often used in its loose Westernised form which covers karma-vipaka, action and effect.

The mechanism of karma lies at the center of the process of embodied existence. Sentient beings are karmic beings, the very nature of their embodied existence means that their function within the process of reality is to act and subsequently experience the results of those actions. And this view of the nature of the central role of a person within the process of reality finds a remarkably precise echo from quantum theory. As Henry Stapp describes one of his central conclusions from a lifetime of pondering the mystery of the quantum revelation:

> According to the orthodox interpretation, these interventions are probing actions *instigated by human agents who are able to 'freely' choose which one, from among the various probing actions they will perform.* ... The concept of intentional actions by agents is of central importance. Each such action is intended to produce an experiential feedback.[347]

Within the Buddhist perspective karma is the central mechanism which drives the process of the wheel of existence within the realm of the dualistic world; actions and subsequent effects make up the process of dualistic experience on all levels of reality. Remarkably this view finds a deep resonance at the level of the microscopic foundations of the process of reality within the discoveries of quantum physics.

The first opening quote indicates the fundamental mechanism of actions and results, or, employing Stapp's characterisation, actions and feedbacks, which operates at the quantum level. The process and mechanism of actions and feedback, or karma-vipaka, is the fundamental quantum process of reality. According to Stapp the evidence of quantum theory, a theory which places *actions* at the center of the ontological structure of reality:

> ...upsets the whole apple cart. It produced a seismic shift in our ideas about both the nature of reality, and the nature of our relationship to the reality that envelops and sustains us. The aspects of nature represented by the theory are converted from elements of *being* to elements of *doing*. The effect of this change is profound: it replaces the world of *material substances* by a world populated by *actions*, and by *potentialities* for the occurrence of the various possible observed feedbacks from these actions.[348]

In other words even the material world becomes a construct within experience which is generated through a karmic action-feedback mechanism.

This perspective is shared by John Wheeler:

> The universe is a self excited circuit. As it expands, cools and develops, it gives rise to observer-participancy. Observer-participancy in turn gives what we call tangible reality to the universe ... Of all the strange features of the universe, none are stranger than these: time is transcended, laws are mutable, and observer participancy matters.[349]

In fact, as we shall see, not only does observer participancy matter, it creates matter, or the appearance of matter.

We find here a deep and extraordinary interconnection between significant features of quantum theory and Buddhist metaphysics. According to the Buddhist worldview all actions performed by all unenlightened beings, including seemingly neutral perceptions, cause repercussions. Karma-vipaka, action and resultant effect, action and feedback, is the universal process of cause and effect which operates on all levels of reality, including the appearance of a material world. This means that there is a dimension of the operation of karma which is involved in the manifestation of what we perceive as an external 'material' reality:

> ...since beginningless time we have been perceiving sights, sounds, smells, tastes and bodily sensations and these perceptions have been creating imprints or latencies in the ground consciousness. Habituation of having experienced a certain visual form will create a latency for that very form. Eventually, that latency will manifest from the ground consciousness as a visual form again, but it will be perceived as external to ourselves.[350]

In this chapter we shall see that this understanding of the universal process of karma completely accords with the implications of quantum physics. In fact it is clearly implied by the functioning of the quantum realm.

Quantum physics tells us that any perception has an impact upon the quantum realm of the wavefunction, it 'collapses' the wavefunction into manifestation. Now we shall extend this view, with the help of the Buddhist Yogachara-Vijnanavada (consciousness-only) epistemological-metaphysical understanding of the process of reality. This analysis asserts that the process of reality is driven at the fundamental level by an infinitely creative primordial awareness-consciousness or cognitive-awareness, which is a viewpoint that is becoming increasingly inescapable within quantum theory. As quantum physicist Eugene Wigner said:

> When the province of physical theory was extended to encompass microscopic phenomena, through the creation of quantum mechanics, the concept of consciousness came to the fore again; it was not possible to formulate the laws of quantum mechanics without reference to consciousness.[351]

The Yogachara-Vijnanavada exposition refers to the deep level of reality which collects imprints of the actions performed by sentient beings as the ground consciousness, or *alayavijnana*, a concept that, as we shall see, clearly corresponds to Bohm's notion of an implicate order, which was his characterisation of the realm of the wavefunction. This fundamental level of the 'store-consciousness' 'collects' the 'seeds' or latencies which form the basis for future experience.

According to the picture of the fundamental structure of reality suggested by Bohm the quality of meaning which is a fundamental quality of consciousness enfolds both the objective and subjective world of experience, and it points beyond itself into what he calls an 'implicate order' which he believed was necessary for our understanding of quantum phenomena:

> If matter and consciousness could in this way be understood together, in terms of the same general notion of order, the way would be opened to comprehending their relationship on the basis of some common ground. Thus we could come to the germ of a new notion of unbroken wholeness, in which consciousness is no longer to be fundamentally separated from matter.[352]

The implicate order underlies the duality of matter and individuated consciousness. It is the ground from which they both arise as coordinated aspects of a deeper order that is usually beyond the direct reach of dualistic awareness. The realms of individuated mind and the appearance of matter mutually unfold from the implicate order into what Bohm termed the 'explicate' order. Mind and matter, subject and object, are coordinated manifestations from the deeper enfolded order of the non-local 'implicate order.'

To illustrate his idea of the relationship between the implicate order and the manifest order Bohm used the example of the following device (fig 7.1):

…two concentric glass cylinders, with a highly viscous fluid such as glycerine between them, which is arranged in such a way that the outer cylinder can be turned very slowly … A droplet of insoluble ink is placed in the fluid and the outer cylinder is turned, with the result that the droplet is drawn out into a fine thread-like form that eventually becomes invisible. When the cylinder is turned in the opposite direction the thread-like form draws back and suddenly becomes visible …[353]

The state of the apparatus when the droplet is drawn into an invisible thread is representative of the 'enfolded' implicate order. Turning the cylinder back 'unfolds' the implicate order until at a certain point the manifest 'explicate' order of the drop will become apparent. Individual drops can be enfolded by the process, each being enfolded in a closely aligned sequence so that when the cylinder is turned to unfold the enfolded drops they will manifest as if there was a single moving drop. The drop appears to be a single moving entity but this illusion is mistaken. In actuality the appearance of a single moving drop is a succession of enfolded drops which manifest sequentially from the implicate order.

Fig 7.1

This thought model of reality, prompted by the implications of quantum physics, conforms to the metaphysical proposal that there is a unified reality beyond the appearance of the seeming world which is embodied within the conventional realm of the subject-object, or mind-matter, dualism.

Bohm notes that the connection between the realms of matter and mind has always been difficult to comprehend because of the fundamental difference in the qualities that they present within our experience. However, if they do arise from a more unified level of reality then 'consciousness has to be understood in terms of an order that is closer to the implicate than it is to the explicate.'[354] In other words the deeper level has to be of the nature of consciousness. The question which naturally arises from Bohm's metaphysical model of reality is how does the implicate order, or the realm of the wavefunction become 'enfolded' with content which then unfolds at some later time? The implicate order was Bohm's metaphysical reworking of the quantum notion of the global wavefunction. As we shall see the patterning of future possibility becomes enfolded into, and unfolded from, the implicate order through a quantum karmic process.

Stapp describes the manner in which he envisages the internal operation of the global wavefunction; Bohm's implicate order, in terms of its 'objective' and 'subjective' aspects as follows:

> To describe these external events themselves in mathematical form one can introduce the idea of an *objective wavefunction* ... that represents the external world itself, and changes when the transition from 'possible' to 'actual' take place...[355]

And:

> ...this evolving quantum state would represent the 'potentialities' and 'probabilities for actual events. ... the 'primal stuff' represented by the evolving quantum state would be idealike rather than matterlike, apart from its conformity to mathematical rules.[356]

The way that the 'transition from possible to actual' takes place is by the making of 'quantum choices':

> ... choices are not fixed by quantum laws; nonetheless each choice is *intrinsically meaningful* : each quantum choice injects meaning, in the form of enduring structure into the physical universe.[357]

Such 'choices' ultimately must be acts of consciousness, although not necessarily fully individuated acts of fully conscious intentional 'free will'. The entire structure of consciousness, or vijnana (this Sanskrit term which is translated as consciousness actually translates more precisely as 'divided nondual awareness'), actually involves the operation of deep hidden levels, what is commonly referred to as the 'unconscious' in the West. The process by which consciousness, on all levels, can inject 'meaning' and 'structure' into the physical universe is to inject structure into the potentials of the 'objective wavefunction', by acts of quantum intentionality, mostly 'unconscious' in Western terminology, through which the 'objective' wavefunction 'collapses' into dualistic experience of the 'classical' world.

The idea that the appearance of the material world is actually a result of an interaction of a field of probabilistic potentialities for experience with individualised and also collective subjective aspects of reality is by not an isolated whim on the part of Bohm and Stapp:

Popper, Heisenberg, and others, have suggested a 'propensity' interpretation of quantum theory. It is based upon the idea that the actual things in nature are 'events', and that quantum theory specifies the 'objective tendencies', or 'propensities' for such events to occur. These events are identified, by Heisenberg, Wheeler, and others as the formation of 'records'.[358]

Such records are etched both into the objective wavefunction of propensities and also the subjective experiencing knots of consciousness that are enfolded into the overall wavefunction of reality.

In his important work *Wholeness and the Implicate Order* Bohm indicates that reality encompasses both the objective aspects and the subjective aspects of what is essentially an interconnected and undivided 'wholeness'; Bohm calls this totality the 'holomovement':

> ...what carries the implicate order is the *holomovement*, which is unbroken and undivided totality. In certain cases we can abstract particular aspects of the holomovement ..., but more generally, all forms of the holomovement merge and are inseparable.[359]

In an interview for Omni magazine Bohm explained:

> I propose something like this: Imagine an infinite sea of energy filling empty space, with waves moving around in there, occasionally coming together and producing an intense pulse. Let's say one particular pulse comes together and expands, creating our universe of space-time and matter. But there could well be other such pulses. To us, that pulse looks like a big bang; In a greater context, it's a little ripple. Everything emerges by unfoldment from the holomovement, then enfolds back into the implicate order. I call the enfolding process "implicating," and the unfolding "explicating." The implicate and explicate together are a flowing, undivided wholeness. Every part of the universe is related to every other part but in different degrees.[360]

Another example that Bohm gives is that of the way in which a radio or tv electromagnetic wave encodes the transmitted content within, or on top of, another frequency. The original content is 'unfolded' by tuning to the carrier frequency. Each sentient being 'unfolds' a continuum of experience from out of the holomovement which takes place within the implicate order.

For Bohm the process of reality is the unfolding of an experienced world from the potentialities within the holomovement; the unfolding of lived experience from the implicate order. This unfolding from the implicate order Bohm considered to occur through the operation of the same mechanism as a hologram is activated. In other words our reality manifests as an inter-ference pattern of wavefunctions interacting with each other in the same way as images are 'unfolded' from holograms. For Bohm, then, the nature of pre-experienced reality is considered to be an incredibly complex holographic wavefunction which encodes the potential experiences of a material world, and, of course, much more.

The idea that holographic coding, or enfoldment, is a fundamental feature of the process of reality also figures in the work of Karl Pribram. He has suggested that the brain operates according to a holographic principle in which predispositions for modes of experience unfold the potentialities of the 'objective' wavefunction of reality in a similar manner to a hologram:

> For Pribram, ... the objective world does not exist, at least not in the way we are accustomed to believing. What is 'out there' is a vast ocean of waves and frequencies, and reality looks concrete to us only because our brains are able to take this holographic blur and convert it into the sticks and stones and other familiar objects that make up our world. [361].

As we shall see shortly, the notion that the holomovement contains the 'enfolded' latencies which are the result of previous activities by sentient beings maps seamlessly to the Yogachara view that the traces which are imprinted into the ground consciousness by actions are subsequently activated to produce an experience of similar kinds. This is precisely the mechanism that underlies the karmic process which operates at the quantum level; a process that drives the appearance of material reality; a mechanism that corresponds to David Bohm's process of 'enfolding' into, and 'unfolding' out of the implicate order, which is the domain of the wavefunction. We shall also find a precise correspondence with Stapp's account of this mechanism of this process at the quantum level. And in order to emphasis the fact that the universal law of action and feedback, cause and effect, is fundamental at the quantum level of reality we shall refer to this mechanism as *quantum karma*.

The fact that the process of karma is responsible for the appearance of the material world is little known or understood in the West even amongst Buddhists. But this understanding of the process of reality is clearly stated within the Buddhist worldview:

> ...the mind is the principle creator of everything because sentient beings accumulate predisposing potencies through their actions, and these actions are directed by mental motivation. These potencies are what create not only their own lives but also the physical world around them. All environments are formed by *karma*, that is actions and the potencies they establish. The wind, sun, earth, trees, what is enjoyed, used, and suffered-all are produced from actions.[362]

And it is this mechanism of karma that we can find clearly indicated within the quantum realm. When we juxtapose the previous characterisation of karma with the following observation from Wheeler, which we have already come across, the parallel is unmistakable:

> Directly opposite to the concept of universe as machine built on law is the vision of *a world self-synthesized.* On this view, the notes struck out on a piano by the observer participants of all times and all places, bits though they are in and by themselves, constitute the great wide world of space and time and things.[363]

It is this viewpoint which Wheeler graphically represented by his 'self-perceiving universe graphic image (fig 7.2).

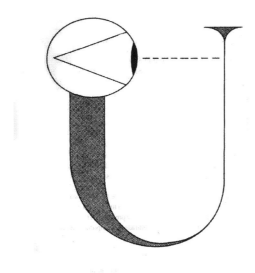

Fig 7.2

The Yogachara-Vijnanavada school of Buddhist philosophy asserts that all actions, and as we shall see simple perceptions constitute such karmically potent actions, leave potencies within the mind-streams of sentient beings. And, because sentient beings are illusory centers of temporarily coherent streams of experience which emerge from an even deeper, nondual ground of potential experience, such potencies are effective also on a deeper collective level. When these potencies are activated through being combined with potencies within the mind-streams of others an intersubjective creation of a shared material environment comes into being.

This description of the process of reality, including the production of the intersubjective illusion of the material world, involves the mechanism of karma, the carrying forward and subsequent inter-subjective activation of potencies within a collective mind-stream; when the subjective potencies resonate together in a reinforcing manner due their overall similarity the collective experiential solidity of the apparently material world emerges. From this perspective the 'objective' wavefunction of reality which underlies experiences of the material world is an inter-subjective creation.

Wheeler was aware of the fact that the experiential domain of material reality apparently emerged from the realm of the wavefunction through the process of wavefunction 'collapse' as a result of perception. However, he thought that the idea that the material world could be created through the perceptual activities of any one being was simply absurd and therefore he toyed with the idea that the material world was created by some kind of collapse of the wavefunction involving 'inter-subjective agreement'[364]. However he was never able to fully comprehend a mechanism through which this could occur. The mechanism becomes understandable, however, when it becomes clear that the objective wavefunction of reality and the subjective wavefunctions of perception, which constitute the minds which 'collapse' the objective wavefunction, originate from the same deep level, the ground consciousness, or Bohm's implicate order. Because we shall be mainly exploring the Yogachara perspective, from henceforth I shall refer to this nondual level of reality simply as the ground consciousness (*alayavijnana*).

The mechanism which underlies this karmic mechanism I shall call, for reasons which will become abundantly clear, *karmic quantum resonance*. This perspective arises quite naturally from the work of Stapp, Wheeler and Bohm. According to Stapp a 'choice' within consciousness establishes a record which tends to make the activation of the chosen record more likely in future. And it is clear that he conceives of this process as operating at a fundamental level of the universe over long time periods:

> Then, over the course of time, *choices are made* that inject into the universe the particularness that we observe.[365]

Stapp's perspective requires that the quantum choices made within the process of consciousness in the past build up the particular blend of possibilities contained within presently presented wavefunctions. Chosen forms are forms which are more likely to be activated by the process of consciousness in the future:

> …the forms that actually are chosen are forms of an exceeding special kind: they are forms that sustain themselves…[366]

As we shall see shortly this insight is also suggested in the remarkable insights of a new proposal called 'quantum Darwinism', an appellation that might be easily replaced by the term 'quantum karma'.

According to the Yogachara viewpoint reality is driven at its deepest level by the *alayavijnana*, the all-ground, or store, consciousness:

> To those of superior understanding,
> The Buddha taught the 'ground consciousness.'
> It was also named the 'foundation consciousness.'
> The 'location consciousness' and the 'acquiring consciousness.'
> All the other actions created by the other seven consciousnesses
> Are accumulated, distinctly and impartially within it,
> Like rain and rivers flowing into the ocean.
> Therefore it is also named the 'ripening consciousness.'[367]

The term *vijnana*, translated here as consciousness, actually indicates a cut, or division in a nondual undivided awareness or wisdom. Nondual awareness is *jnana*, which corresponds to the basic quality and function of awareness within the stream of embodiment and its quality embraces the entire structure of the experiential world of perception and awareness, both manifest and non-manifest, including what is in the West termed the 'unconscious'. But when *jnana*, the nondual undivided wisdom-awareness divides into the dualistic realm of *vi-jnana*, it becomes confused as to its own nature, it looses direct cognizance of its own vast potentiality:

> That very mind, being ignorant of itself,
> Is stirred by formational mentation.
> Due to being stirred like waves on water. [368]

It is this stirring of 'formational mentation', which is produced by the internal intentionality towards perception which lies within the fundamental wisdom, or nondual awareness, that triggers the extraordinary quantum cascade into manifestation of the dualistic world.

These movements within the quantum field of consciousness can be thought of as 'collapses' of wavefunctions, which are interactions which produce ever more dualistic realms of phenomena. Each such interaction is a flicker of dualistic 'divided' wisdom, wisdom corresponding to the ground state of the quantum field of awareness-consciousness. This presentation corresponds with quantum physicist Max Tegmark's understanding of the nature of dualistic consciousness:

> I believe that consciousness is the way information feels being
> processed. Since matter can be arranged to process information
> in numerous ways of varying complexity, this implies a rich
> variety of levels and types of consciousness.[369]

Dualistic consciousness, then, arises as a result of processing of 'information', a term often used by physicists when they wish to hide from the fact that the 'stuff' being processed must itself have the nature of consciousness. And at its deepest level it is a nondual ground of awareness, *jnana*; a pure knowingness which becomes the multitude of 'knowings' within the dualistic world of manifestation.

The alayavijnana is the way in which the process of reality 'seems' to function when sentient beings engage with reality from the mistaken attitude, which functions as a deep aspect of psychophysical embodiment, of clinging to existence from the point of view of 'me' and 'mine', not realizing that they are simply part of a universal flow of illusion-like appearance from the deeper nondual ground. It is this constant grasping for existence and individuated sense experience that produces the adventitious 'stains', which are identical to the potentialities within the wavefunction of reality.

The clinging involved within this mode of engagement with the flux of reality constantly 'collapses' the wavefunction of reality into an appearance of solidity. And the more this process occurs the more resilient becomes the illusion of the solidity of the seemingly external realm of materiality. This happens because the 'seeds' for future actualisation within the wavefunction of reality become amplified the more they are activated; in this way the essentially 'pure' nondual nature of the fundamental ground of awareness becomes 'stained' with the 'adventitious' potentialities for future dualistic experience:

> What is naturally pure and consists of permanent dharmas
> Is not seen because it is obscured by a beginningless cocoon, ...
> The dhatu of time without beginning
> Is the matrix of all phenomena.
> Because it exists, all beings
> And also nirvana are obtained. ...
> Sentient beings are buddhas indeed.
> However, they are obscured by adventitious stains.[370]

The designation 'buddha' indicates a fully awake, fully aware, and thereby completely enlightened sentient being. The path of transformation towards buddhahood requires that a sentient being 'purifies' his or her own quantum wavefunction structure to remove the 'defilements', the deep clinging structures of mentality, which are themselves quantum structures of consciousness.

The alayavijnana is described by Walpola Rahula as:

> The deepest, finest and subtlest aspect layer of ... consciousness.
> It contains all the traces and impressions of past actions and all ...
> future potentialities.[371]

Buddhist philosopher William Waldron refers to the alayavijnana as '*The Buddhist Unconscious*'[372] thus equating it with the ideas of Freud and Jung; however the fact that the alayavijnana clearly stores all perceptual movements of consciousness, including emotionally neutral perceptions of the appearance of the material world, suggests that it operates at a much deeper level than the personal unconscious, the racial unconscious, or even species unconsciousness. All these 'implicate' spheres of potentiality will themselves be enfolded into the overarching structure of consciousness of the objective wavefunction of reality, which can be identified as the alaya-vijnana, which itself emerges from jnana, together with the structures and processes of consciousness which emerge out of it, or, from another point of view, take place within it.

The Yogachara perspective describes the world of psychophysical embodiment as being comprised of seven consciousnesses, which are driven by, and emerge from, the eighth consciousness, which is the alayavijnana itself. The seven consciousnesses which are other than the ground consciousness, which is the eighth consciousness, comprise firstly the five basic sense consciousnesses which are associated with the faculties of sight, hearing, touch, smell, taste. As the Yogachara metaphysical analysis considers that 'consciousness', or 'mind,' is the fundamental category of reality[373] all the senses, as well as their objects, are not other than fundamental consciousness functioning on the level of gross cognition:

Both faculties and objects arise from the mind.
The manifestation of sensory objects and faculties
Is dependent upon an element that has been present
Throughout beginningless time.[374]

Fig 7.3 shows the perceptual 'cycle of existence' due to the functioning of the sense field consciousnesses, mental consciousness and the alaya consciousness. According to the third Karmapa's *Treatise on the Distinction between Consciousness and Wisdom*:

The dominant conditions are the six sense faculties,
Which possess form and are translucent.[375]

Although commentators such as Jamgon Kongtrul Lodro Taye state that these faculties possess 'physical' form consisting of 'minute particles', this must be understood as referring to subtle quantum structures of consciousness which possess a degree of continuous integrity of form. The fundamental Yogachara viewpoint is that any apparently material object is a matter of cognition:

What these objects are,
They are not established as external such as particles
That is other than cognizing consciousness.[376]

'Physical form', therefore, must be understood as referring to a level of quantum structuring of consciousness which is experienced as material by an individuated consciousness. The sense faculties are 'manifestations of invisible subtle matter' that is 'somewhat closer to the nature of consciousness.'[377] This presentation completely accords with the view that the sense faculties are quantum structures of consciousness, they therefore have a nature which is said to be 'translucent'.

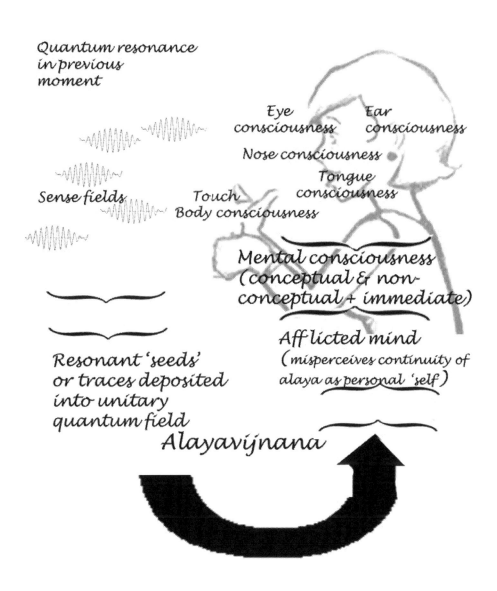

Quantum resonance in previous moment

Eye consciousness

Ear consciousness

Nose consciousness

Tongue consciousness

Sense fields

Touch

Body consciousness

Mental consciousness (conceptual & non-conceptual + immediate)

Afflicted mind (misperceives continuity of alaya as personal 'self')

Resonant 'seeds' or traces deposited into unitary quantum field

Alayavijnana

Fig 7.3

This is Jamgon Kongtrul's explanation of the term 'translucent' in the context of the functioning of the sense faculties:

> 'Translucent' means that, just like a clear reflection in a mirror, the sense faculties are clear vivid objects, due to their own particular locations being occupied by other particles, while at the same time appearing as something that is connected to consciousness. This connection is explained as one of being connected by virtue of internal mental seeds or potentials.'[378]

It is quite clear that the translucency or vividness of the sense faculty indicates that it has the fundamental nature of awareness. Furthermore the actual nature of the awareness generated by the functioning of a sense faculty depends on the connection between faculty and the subtle particles (which are of the nature of consciousness) which are being sampled by the faculty. The particles occupy space within the faculty in question and then an interaction involving some kind of 'potentiality' produces the resultant sense consciousness.

When we compare the foregoing account with the following account of recent research, which suggests that the experience of smell is a result of quantum resonance, the dovetailing is remarkable:

> The possibility that LCN physicists Jennifer Brookes, Filio Hartoutsiou, Andrew Horsfield and Marshall Stoneham have looked into is that electrons in the receptors can be triggered to tunnel between energy states, provided the odorant molecule's vibration frequency matches the energy difference of these states. The LCN group tested the physical viability of this mechanism, first suggested in 1996 by a scientist named Luca Turin, and found that a general model of this electron tunnelling is consistent with physics laws as well as with known features of smell.[379]

In the case of smell the evidence now suggests that it is the quantum wave nature of the electrons within the odorant's molecules which interacts with the quantum potentials within the receptor; this produces a quantum 'tunnelling' effect which in essence is a resonance effect. The direct effect of this resonance is the immediate awareness of smell. A similar case can easily be made for other sense faculties. It would seem that the actual direct production of the immediacy of sense experience is a result of quantum resonance. Furthermore this account exactly matches the Yogachara account, indicating that the correlation between the Yogachara perspective and the Quantum Mind-Only model of the functioning of reality is valid to a remarkable extent.

The direct experiences of the five sense consciousnesses are gathered into a perceptual unity by the functioning of the sixth consciousness, the non-conceptual and then the conceptual mental spheres:

Even though the sensory consciousnesses perceive external sense objects they are not recognised or perceived as a solid external objects until this perceptual process reaches the mental consciousness and the object is identified.[380]

The sixth consciousness, then, embraces both non-conceptual and conceptual aspects, which operate in that order, the non-conceptual aspects can be thought of as conveying the sense-consciousnesses to the conceptual aspect.

The seventh consciousness supplies the immediate awareness of continuity which acts as a condition for the functioning of the previous consciousnesses. This is called the 'immediate mind consciousness' and it functions as a gateway between the previous consciousnesses and the ground consciousness:

The immediate mentality is the condition for all appearances to arise from any of the consciousnesses and to settle into the ground consciousness.[381]

The seventh consciousness also has an aspect which is termed the 'afflicted mind consciousness.' The afflicted consciousness arises because of the function of the seventh consciousness as the supplier of continuity to the previous elements of consciousness which are all momentary, rapidly arising then ceasing. Because of this characteristic of continuity the seventh consciousness also causes an illusory experience of selfhood to arise:

It is called the afflicted-mentality because
It believes the mind as self, possesses pride,
Has attachment to the self, and has ignorance...[382]

Within all Buddhist schools the notion that there is a fixed, enduring 'self' is repudiated. Because attachment to the innate feeling of 'self' is, according to the Buddhist worldview, the source of all suffering, this aspect of the seventh consciousness is described as 'afflicted.'

This aspect of the seventh consciousness is also the source of all afflictions because it is responsible for the generation of the karmic mechanism; it acts as the gateway for 'seeds' to be deposited into the store consciousness:

Every action we take creates a latent karmic imprint and these tendencies automatically flow into the ground consciousness where they are stored. These karmic imprints do not, however, remain stored because they manifest sooner or later.[383]

These karmic impressions are evocatively called *vasanas* or 'perfumings'. The Britannica Online Encyclopedia offers the following dramatic description:

The universe consists of an infinite number of possible ideas that lie inactive in storage. That latent consciousness projects an uninterrupted sequence of thoughts, while it itself is in restless flux until the karma, or accumulated consequences of past deeds, is destroyed. That storage consciousness contains all the impressions of previous experiences (*vasanas*, 'perfumings'), which form the germs (*bija*) of future karmic action, an illusive force that creates categories that are in fact only fictions of the spirit.[384]

Although this process is said to be illusory and fictional it is important to hold in mind that this is asserted only from the ultimate point of view. From a conventional point of view, which is the everyday point of view for all except a few enlightened beings, the process of reality must be taken very seriously indeed. As Aldus Huxley is said to have said:

The world is an illusion, but it is an illusion which we must take seriously, because it is real as far as it goes...[385]

The suffering endured by unenlightened sentient beings is certainly 'real as far as it goes' and it is a vital aim of Buddhist practitioners to eradicate suffering from the mind-streams of all sentient beings.

The mechanism of karma produces the appearance of material reality as well as the living beings within it:

The sutra speaks of 'mind-alone' because the mind is chief within the world. ..
This vast array of sentient life,
The varied universe containing it, is formed by mind.
The Buddha said that wandering beings are from karma born.
Dispense with mind and karma is no more." [386]

The commentary by Jamgon Mipham to this stanza from Chandrakirti's *Introduction to the Middle Way* tells us that:

The minds of beings accumulate individual karmas, and these account for the variety of animate life. The mind is thus the principle factor. In addition, there is the common karma that individual minds share and that brings forth different inanimate environments...[387]

It is the collective karma, actions, or reinforced perceptions, which produces a shared world of experience which is embodied in potential form in the alayavijnana, which clearly has a resemblance to the 'objective' wave-function.

In his commentary *Transcending Ego: Distinguishing Consciousness from Wisdom* Khenchen Thrangu Rinpoche explains the fundamental karmic operation of consciousness as follows:

The ground consciousness is the foundation and location for mind because all karmic latencies are stored in the ground consciousness. A momentary visual consciousness instantly ceases (when the next instant appears). Similarly, a mental consciousness is created and ceases instantly; sometimes a mental consciousness does not appear at all. However, the latencies for the arising of these consciousnesses are contained within the ground consciousness. Thus we can remember a visual perception that occurred in the past; and remembering it, strengthens the latency.[388]

According to the Yogachara view a fundamental feature of consciousness is that even the tiniest movement of energy within the structure of consciousness leaves a trace within the ground consciousness *which increases the probability that the same movement of energy will occur at a later point in time.* This reinforcing process takes place at all levels of consciousness, including those deep structures of psychophysical embodiment not available to direct awareness. This mechanism, described by Yogachara Buddhist philosophy, is exactly the quantum mechanism which produces the probability distribution within wavefunctions; the repeated quantum activity of perception, a mechanism which is clearly indicated by the collapse of the wavefunction, a mechanism through which meaning is 'injected' into the universe, is the fundamental mechanism of the self-creation of the universe. The actual mechanism which is responsible for the unfolding of potentialities within the quantum ground consciousness would have to be some form of quantum resonance. This is the most appropriate mechanism by which karmic cause and effect operates to unfold the enfolded karmic 'seeds'. The universe, then, is not only a 'self-excited' phenomenon is also a self-resonating universe.

The accomplished scholar and Buddhist monk Nyanaponika Thera offers the following insight:

> Like any physical event, the mental process constituting a karmic action never exists in isolation but in a field, and thus its efficacy in producing a result depends not only on its own potential, but also on the variable factors of its field, which can modify it in numerous ways. [389]

Karmic traces, or seeds, are stored in the store consciousness, the alayavijnana, and consciousness could not be conceived of in any other manner than a field effect. Once we have seen that consciousness must be treated as a category in its own right which operates according to a resonance of meaning within the field, indeed the experience of meaning is nothing else than a resonance, it becomes natural to see the world as a production and play of resonating meanings within the field of consciousness.

The idea that the mechanism of resonance is primary at the quantum level was suggested by Schrödinger in a 1952 paper *Are There Quantum Jumps*. In this paper Schrödinger addresses the issue of the nature of the quantum jumps which are supposed to take place between allowed quantum states; when a photon, for instance, is absorbed by an atom, causing an electron to jump to an orbit in a higher energy level, it is generally assumed that the jump is instantaneous and discrete. A mechanism for the way in which electrons might be kicked into higher energy orbits, or fall into lower energy orbits was not established at that time, it just 'happened'; it was accepted that this was the way that electrons behaved. The process was fundamental to the notion that the unit of exchange at the quantum level was a quantum 'packet'. Schrödinger, however, was adamant that this phenomenon must be a result of some form of resonance:

> ...the great and genuine success of the idea of energy parcels has made it an ingrained habit to regard the product of Plank's constant h and a frequency as a bundle of energy, lost by one system and gained by another. How else should one understand the exact dove-tailing in the great 'double-entry' book-keeping in nature? I maintain that it can in all cases be understood as a resonance phenomenon.[390]

This observation by Schrödinger is remarkably deep. The formula which links together the energy of a wave and its frequency is

$$E = h f$$

where E is energy, f is frequency and h is Planck's constant. What Schrödinger is so cogently pointing out is that by focusing our attention on the energy packet, or particle, as the fundamental unit we lose the significance of the frequency. Schrödinger is clearly indicating that there is a deeper mechanism which underlies the seemingly particulate nature of energy exchange. This is a crucial insight; according to this perspective it is the phenomenon of resonance which accounts for the appearance of the world of the discrete from the world of the continuous wavefunction:

> The one thing which one has to accept and which is the inalienable consequence of the wave-equation as it is used in every problem, under the most various forms, is this: that the interaction between two microscopic physical systems is controlled by a peculiar law of resonance.[391]

Quantum physicists tend to talk of photons being 'absorbed' by a hydrogen atom, for example. When is occurs it is supposed that one electron in the hydrogen atom will instantaneously jump up to a higher energy level orbit. This only happens however if the photon has the correct frequency. It therefore makes equal sense, if not more sense, to talk of 'resonance' rather than 'absorption'. To speak of absorption gives no indication of the mechanism involved. According to Schrödinger the law:

...requires that the difference of two proper frequencies of the one system should be equal to the difference of two proper frequencies of the other.[392]

In other words the 'fabric' of reality is constructed by an astonishing resonant interchange of energy at the quantum level. Furthermore, each such interchange will leave a resonating trace of potentiality at a deep level of reality which the consciousness/cognition-only (*vijnanavada*) perspective refers to as the ground-consciousness, Bohm called the implicate order and is generally described within quantum theory as the universal wavefunction of reality.

According to quantum physicist Erich Joos the following three issues are *the* outstanding quantum conundrums of deep significance:

1. The meaning of the wavefunction
2. The exact nature of the mechanism of the collapse
3. The connection between the quantum and classical realm. [393]

These issues are given a comprehensive and coherent elucidation by the Quantum-Mind-Only perspective. The potentialities within wavefunctions which have the greater probabilities are precisely those which have been reinforced more often by perceptual movements within the individual consciousnesses of all sentient beings who inhabit or have inhabited the universe. These perceptual movements of consciousness have then left reinforcing traces in the ground consciousness, which is the domain of the wavefunction.

This viewpoint clearly resonates with Stapp's description of the fundamental nature of the appearance of 'physical' reality:

> According to the revised notion, physical reality behaves more like *spatially encoded information that governs tendencies for experiential events to occur* than like anything resembling material substance.[394]

Every perception that is made by any sentient being leaves a trace which strengthens the probability of the same perception manifesting at a later point. This karmic mechanism within the fundamental ground consciousness, then, provides a coherent explanation of the nature of the wavefunction. In 1990 Wheeler wrote:

> It from bit. Otherwise put, every 'it'—every particle, every field of force, even the space-time continuum itself—derives its function, its meaning, its very existence entirely ... from the ... answers to yes-or-no questions, binary choices, bits. 'It from bit' symbolizes the idea that every item of the physical world has at bottom—a very deep bottom, in most instances—an immaterial source and explanation...[395]

A wavefunction contains the probabilities of perceptual possibilities built up over an extraordinary period of time by vast numbers of sentient beings; the most likely 'collapse' will be in the direction of the most reinforced perception. This process has been going on for eons, involving countless sentient beings. And so, bit by bit, it provides the groundwork for the appearance of 'It' from bit, and the appearance of an external 'material' reality manifests. The entire edifice of material reality is the result of continuous perceptual karmic reinforcement within the ground consciousness.

The process of reality is of the nature of consciousness. The fundamental field of awareness-consciousness, which creates the appearance of a material world, contains encoded, or enfolded, to use Bohm's terminology, tendencies, or potentialities, for matter-like experiences to occur. It is these potentialities, when manifested, which build up the illusion of an external material reality. This is precisely the view proposed as early as 1944 by the historical founder of quantum theory Max Planck, who said in a lecture that:

> All matter originates and exists only by virtue of a force... We must assume behind this force the existence of a conscious and intelligent Mind. This Mind is the matrix of all matter.[396]

This is an observation which is worth contemplating alongside the following distillation from the fourteenth century Tibetan Buddhist masterpiece *The Mountain Doctrine: Ocean of Definitive Meaning: Final Unique Quintessential Instructions* by Dolpopa Sherab Gyaltsen:

> I am called the matrix of attributes....
> I am called the pure matrix....
> The essence of ... of cyclic existence
> Is only I, self-arisen.
> Phenomena in which cyclic existence exists
> Do not exist-even particles-
> Because of being unreal ideation.[397]

This exposition is devoted to a lengthy and comprehensive elucidation of the nature of the 'matrix of phenomena', a fundamental Buddhist concept which is clearly analogous to the quantum wavefunction.

When the above fragment is unraveled and explicated from within its own context, it turns out to be saying basically the same thing as Planck. 'Unreal ideation' is a Mind-Only term for the functioning of the fundamental mind-nature of reality. The term 'phenomena of cyclic existence' refers to the appearances of the apparent entities of the dualistic world, including the 'material' world; in the next chapter, *Many Worlds of Illusion*, we shall examine the actual process of cycling through the illusory worlds of embodiment. The 'matrix of attributes', or 'matrix of phenomena' corresponds to what quantum physicists call the 'wavefunction' of potentiality which underlies the manifestation of the appearance of the many worlds of cyclic existence, including the appearance of materiality.

Dolpopa is suggesting is that there is a fundamental 'matrix', which is essentially of the nature of mind, which gives rise to the appearance of the phenomena of the apparently material world. Planck's use of the term 'matrix of mind' actually refers to the quantum wavefunction, and it would appear that Planck's notion of 'matrix of mind' and Dolpopa's use of the term 'matrix of attributes' are very closely related. 'Cyclic-existence', for the moment, can be taken to be the repeated phenomena of dualistic perception; and, for good measure, it is worth mentioning that the term 'self-arisen' anticipated Wheeler's proposal that the universe creates itself through a quantum process of self-synthesis or self-perception.

Planck's notion of the 'matrix of mind' maps onto the Yogachara explanation of the basic mechanism of karma within the base consciousness, a mechanism which underpins the stability of cognition. Furthermore, the Yogachara analysis indicates the origin of the probabilities within wavefunctions. It also tells us why reality is composed of wavefunctions, and it also indicates the nature of the mechanism which underlies the appearance of the 'collapse' of wavefunctions. The apparent collapse is actually the point of emergence of the illusory dualistic experiential realm from the nondual domain of the wavefunction, which is also the domain of the ground consciousness.

The conceptual model of the process of reality indicated here is one within which a subjective and an objective aspect of experience arise together from the ground consciousness on the basis of previous moments of similar experiences, perceptions and actions:

> A seed or predisposition is activated and simultaneously produces both an object and a cognizing subject, much as in a dream.[398]

The result of each moment of perceptive experience, each intention, and each action is a strengthening of the latency within the ground consciousness for that event to occur again, and, when there is an activating resonance within the ground-consciousness, an interdependent subjective-objective dualistic experiential field arises into conscious awareness. Upon the basis of this mechanism a coherent perceptual world emerges. The cognition-only perspective indicates that the appearance of the inherent, or independent, existence of the realms of subjectivity and objectivity is an illusion. The cognition-only discourse emphasizes this by asserting the unity of apprehender and apprehended, perceiver and perceived:

> The nature of consciousness is real,
> But aspects of perceiver and perceived are delusive and mistaken.[399]

Stapp makes a similar point is with his approval of William James' assertion that 'the thought itself is the thinker'.[400]

The Yogachara account of how latencies are laid down through repetition bears an uncanny resemblance to a recent proposal as to how the potentialities of wavefunctions may be viewed. Quantum physicist Wojciech H. Zurek has proposed a new understanding of the way in which the appearance of the classical world emerges from the fundamental quantum basis. This view, which he has given the designation 'quantum Darwinism', provides a further correlation between quantum physics and the Quantum Mind-Only worldview:

> Thus, Darwinian analogy focuses on the fact that proliferation of certain information throughout the environment makes its further proliferation more likely.[401]

This formulation clearly accords very well with the 'quantum karma' viewpoint. According to Zurek's perspective the more often a quantum event becomes manifest the more likely it is to proliferate throughout the environment. This is a fresh approach to the understanding of the quantum phenomenon of decoherence, which is the assumed process by which the world of classical objects are supposed to impose themselves upon the realm of quantum probabilities. The usual notion of decoherence involves the idea that the sheer massiveness and gross classical weight of the world of everyday objects overcomes the fragile delicacy of the 'uncollapsed' probability state of quantum reality. The new perspective introduced by Zurek is that:

> ... the appearance of the classical reality can be viewed as the result of the emergence of the preferred states from within the quantum substrate through the Darwinian paradigm, once the survival of the fittest quantum states and selective proliferation of the information about them throughout the universe are properly taken into account.[402]

This view has been named 'quantum Darwinism' but 'quantum karma' is perhaps an equally appropriate appellation.

The insight that Zurek has given is that 'states that exist are the states that persist' and this is a persistence within a quantum realm which consists of, as Zurek puts it, 'the dream stuff which reality is made of'[403]; and the mechanism that underlies this persistence is 'an objective consequence of the relationship between the state of the observer and the rest of the universe'[404]. Zurek describes his view as follows:

> The main idea of quantum Darwinism is that we almost never do any direct measurement on anything ... the environment acts as a witness, or as a communication channel. ... It is like a big

advertising billboard, which floats multiple copies of the information about our universe all over the place.[405]

In this billboard advertising metaphor the image is that the more the observing punters buy into the advertisement and thereby make the product, which is in this case the solidified appearance of the apparently material world, more popular, the greater the number of billboards which spring up and, as a consequence, the more punters are enticed to join in the product craze. Thus the process of the multitudinous perceptional creation of the material world takes off in a self-reinforcing, or self-resonating, manner.

This is the metaphor which Zurek is extending to the generation of the classical, macroscopic, material world; the more often a perception of the appearance of materiality is made, the more potent becomes the advertising billboard campaign, or the environmental template, or matrix, for that perception of material reality to occur again at some future point. Stapp made a similar point in the following way:

> Each subjective experience injects one bit of information into this objective store of information which then specifies … the relative probabilities for various possible future subjective experiences to occur.[406]

Here Stapp reiterates Wheeler's 'It from bit' scenario.

Remarkably, this process is very similar to the process which the archmaterialist Richard Dawkins considers to underlie the propagation of cultural meanings, which he calls 'memes'. According to Dawkins' 'meme' proposal 'memes' are to be thought of as 'physical' meaning-patterns which are located in some manner within the brain. These patterns become externalised into the material world and are then able to 'replicate' themselves within other brains. Dawkins refers to this process as the 'phenotypic effect':

> The phenotypic effect of a meme may be in the form of words, music, visual images, styles of cloths, … They are outward and visible … manifestations of memes within the brain … They may so imprint themselves on the brains of the receiving individuals … The new copy of the meme is then in a position to broadcast its phenotypic effects, with the result that further copies of itself may be made in yet other brains.[407]

The imagery of Zurek's quantum Darwinism, within which the environment acts a 'communication channel', facilitating the proliferation of quantum 'advertising billboards' concerning the nature of experienced material reality, and Dawkins' phenotypic effect, within which cultural meanings are 'broadcast' into the material world and then copy themselves into yet more brains, thus increasing their 'broadcasting' power, is striking. In the case of the phenotypic effect, the greater the number of brains 'infected' with a particular meme, the greater the broadcasting power; this means that the externalisation into the material world becomes more effective. If we employ Zurek's billboard metaphor it is clear that the greater the number of brains infected by the meme then the more 'advertising billboards' for the cultural meme in question get put up in the material world! Dawkins' version, however, is a purely materialist account within which the nature of the actual meanings of the 'memes' is left unelucidated; it is simply assumed that they are fundamentally 'physical' in essence, but how the meaningless 'physical' realm of matter comes to have 'meaning' is left to the reader's imagination..

The enormous difference between the two perspectives is that Dawkins conceives this process as a completely materialist matter, fundamentally driven by material bits and pieces which somehow leave purely 'physical' etchings inside purely 'physical' brains, with no intervening meaning substance, as it were. The problem for this brazen materialist proposal, however, is that, as Stapp forcefully points out:

> ...no such brain exists; no brain, body, or anything else in the real world is composed of those tiny bits of matter that Newton imagined the universe to be made of.[408]

By this dramatic assertion Stapp is emphasizing the fact that the quantum realm is primary; there is no 'Newtonian' type matter in existence. And a consequence of this is that the Dawkins' type of notion of fully material memes is out of the question.

The quantum Darwinism, or Quantum Mind-Only perspective, on the other hand, requires that we view the situation from the correct quantum perspective within which the quantum 'dream stuff' is the meaning-matter of consciousness within which meaningful billboards as to how to experience the apparent matter of the material world can be meaningfully erected. According to Zurek:

> ...quantum states, by their very nature share an epistemological and ontological role – are simultaneously a description of the state, and the 'dream stuff is made of.' One might say that they are *epiontic*. These two aspects may seem contradictory, but at least in the quantum setting, there is a union of these two functions.[409]

In other words the quantum 'dream stuff' of reality is capable of producing the seeming solidity of the material world from out of the process of perception! Although Dawkins would hate the idea, the quantum evidence points towards the fact that the appearance of the material world is a matter of deeply etched quantum 'epiontic' memes! Furthermore, these quantum memes are not material but essentially comprised of experiential probabilities encoded into wavefunctions of consciousness!

According to the Mind-Only analysis the process of unenlightened perception overlays this other-powered quantum field of potentiality for experience with an illusory appearance of inherent existence; and, as previously outlined, this imputational process is called, unsurprisingly, the 'imputational nature'. This appellation corresponds closely with the appearance of classical reality from the quantum field of 'other-powered' potentiality (see discussion of the Mind-Only 'three natures' analysis in the chapter *Illusion or Reality?*). Understanding the 'empty' nature of conventional phenomena, therefore, requires the comprehension of the 'thoroughly established nature' which is defined as the realisation that the 'other powered nature' is 'empty' of the 'imputational nature'. This is the understanding of emptiness according to the 'three natures' analysis of the Mind-Only presentation of the process of reality; the imputational-nature of classical inherent reality is actually non-existent as an independent reality within the other-powered quantum nature.

The view of the imputational-nature, then, is the way that the conventional, macroscopic world is experienced by unenlightened sentient beings. Enlightened beings are said to experience the mere conventional reality, or mere relative, which is the other-powered nature devoid of any imputational natures. For unenlightened beings, however, conventional reality is experienced through a projected network of inherent existence which is superimposed on top of, or into, the field of the other-powered natures. This superimposition into the 'dream stuff' of the quantum 'other-powered-nature' is driven in large part by a karmically created inter-subjective template, or 'matrix', of the material world (fig 7.4).

What Zurek and his associates have not explicitly acknowledged is that it is the conscious perceptions made by countless observers, over vast stretches of time, which create and maintain the preferred states, or the matrix, of the universe. The persistence of the classical world that we all experience in everyday life arises from the quantum 'dream stuff' because of repeated perceptions which make future similar perceptions more probable. All the perceptions of every living being are encoded into the wavefunction of reality, and they are unfolded from it through the resonant process of perception.

The physicist and philosopher David Peat has come to a very similar conclusion. According to him physical objects can be considered to be 'habits of nature'[410], which is to say they are the forms that the underlying process of reality have adopted and which then continue through habituation. This is precisely the Yogachara understanding:

> …all of the external phenomena-mountains, houses, roads and their perceptions – originated from the mind. They all arose out of the ground consciousness. How is this possible? The answer lies in the fact that since beginningless time we have been perceiving sights, sounds, smells, tastes and bodily sensations and these perceptions have been creating imprints or latencies in the ground consciousness. Habituation of having

experienced a certain visual form will create a latency for that very form. Eventually, that latency will manifest from the ground consciousness as a visual form again, but it will be perceived as external to ourselves.[411]

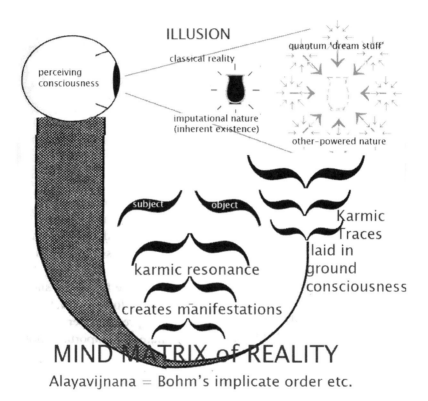

Fig 7.4

The idea that the physical laws of the universe are actually 'habits' goes back to the nineteenth century psychologist William James who, ahead of his time, suggested that to some degree all phenomena are produced by habituation. More recently the controversial biologist Rupert Sheldrake has proposed that all biological inheritance and development is driven by 'morphic resonance' within a 'morphic field':

> The idea is that there is a kind of memory in nature. Each kind of
> thing has a collective memory. ... And how that influence moves
> across time ... is given by the process I call morphic resonance. It's
> a theory of collective memory throughout nature. What the memory
> is expressed through is the morphic fields, the fields within and
> around each organism. The memory processes are due to morphic
> resonance.[412]

The notion of a morphic field clearly maps directly on to the Yogachara
notion of a fundamental field of consciousness, the alayavijnana, which lies
beneath the process of reality. The basic function of this field is to act as a
memory which facilitates further perception and manifestation. What Sheldrake calls 'morphic resonance', then, the Yogachara viewpoint calls karma,
or perhaps the term 'karmic resonance' is appropriate within the context of
the quantum perspective we are developing.

Actions are accumulated and 'stored' until surrounding conditions trigger
the necessary effect from the karmic seeds. Karma is triggered through a
mechanism of 'karmic resonance'. Karmic seeds, then, might be thought of
as being like vibrating potentialities which become actualised when there is a
karmic resonance. The resonance produces both the objective and subjective
aspects of experience and these two aspects are experienced as if they are
independent of the deeper level. Resonances within the ground field of consciousness are experienced as perceptions, intentions and so on, and this
resonance also leaves a further resonance trace in the ground-consciousness.
This constant process of resonant perception of an experienced reality, which
then conditions karmic traces that subsequently become the basis for further
perceptual resonance, constitutes the process which Wheeler describes as the
participatory 'self-excited' universe.

A question which naturally arises is exactly why this resonant field of
self-perceptive activity comes about. This question amounts to the question
which the philosopher Heidegger considered to be the most important
question for philosophy; 'Why is there something rather than nothing?'
Wheeler indicated that the solution to the question 'Why the quantum?'
might contain the solution to the question of existence itself:

> ...eventually we will have an answer to the question 'How come
> the quantum?' And to the companion question, 'How come
> existence?'[413]

The first point that a Madhyamika philosopher would make, concerning
the question concerning something and nothing, is that there are no inherently existent 'somethings' and therefore there can not be an inherently existent 'nothing'. As we have seen previously, at the quantum level existence
itself hovers between existence and non-existence according to the requirement of Heisenberg's Uncertainty Principle. This is the ground level of

reality that the Madhyamaka calls 'emptiness', which, as we have seen, is not 'nothingness' but a realm of interdependent potentiality; the often asserted notion of a 'big bang' creation from 'nothing' is a nonsense. The Madhyamaka is correct upon this point that the ground level of existence cannot be an absolute vacuity but, rather, must be an interdependent realm of potentiality. But if the ultimate question addresses the issue of why the illusory phantasmagoria of the appearances within seeming reality appears from the ground of potentiality then there is an answer. It turns out that there is a very simple answer to the riddle of existence! There actually is a simple answer to Stephen Hawking's question as to what 'breaths fire into the equations?'[414] And this answer also supplies the solution as to what supplies the motive force behind evolution.

In their recent book *Quantum Enigma* Bruce Rosenblum and Fred Kuttner remark that when physicists discovered the phenomenon of wave-particle duality they had stumbled upon a confrontation with consciousness and yet they did not realize it. A much more extraordinary situation, however, is that in the phenomenon of the 'collapse of the wavefunction', a phenomenon which has made, and continues to make, the great majority of physicists very uncomfortable, physics had actually discovered the most significant clue as to the ultimate nature of reality! In fact John Wheeler did know the answer, intellectually speaking of course – directly realizing the answer is an entirely different matter, but he did not entirely comprehend that he knew the answer!

In the Guardian obituary for John Wheeler we can read that:

> In 2002, he wrote: 'How come the universe? How come us? How come anything?' Although Einstein had once asked him whether, if no one looked at it, the moon continued to exist, Wheeler's answer to his 'how come?' questions was 'that's us'.[415]

So Wheeler was well aware that acts of perception were the creative force behind the manifestation of the universe, this was clearly embodied in his self-perceiving universe graphic. It only remained for the final step, the extraordinary knowledge known and realised by the great mystics of 'all times and all places', *the fundamental nature of reality is Universal self-perception.*

The phenomenon of the 'collapse of the wavefunction' is a direct indication of the fundamental self-perceiving process of the universe. In other words *the universe uses the perceiving process within the dualistic world of experience in order to explore and also perfect its own nature.* Human beings occupy a central place in this process because they are the universe's agents in the process of universal self-exploration, self-perfection and self-transcendence.

This insight derives from the fundamental perceptive nature of awareness-consciousness. The fundamental Buddhist definition of consciousness is 'clarity that cognizes.' This primordial nature is an essentially unified field of clarity, or emptiness, which has the core function of perception or cognition. Because of this fundamental nature there is an inner tension at the heart of reality. The fundamental nature of awareness-consciousness is undivided (*jnana*) but its function is cognition, and cognition is a process which involves duality. This is why nondual awareness-wisdom (*jnana*) spontaneously divides itself into dualistic appearances in the illusory divided realm of dualistic consciousness (*vijnana*). The prefix 'vi' indicates a cut or division; cognition cannot take place without a rift, a division, in the basic nature of the fundamental awareness (*jnana*). Within this paradoxical nature of the self-perceiving ground of reality lies the solution to the riddle of existence. And within the mechanism of 'quantum karma' lies the understanding of the process of experiential dualistic seeming reality which really is just a cycle of endless perception, giving rise to manifestation, driven by the universe's 'craving' to perceive its own nature!

There is within the very nature of the deepest level of awareness-consciousness a function and necessity of perception. Because the inner nature of reality is awareness, or inner luminosity, perception is a necessary activity for the fundamental ground of reality. And because of this, the illusory experience of subject and object must arise, and this process eventually gives rise to the level of 'obscured mentation' which is called the 'klesha mind' or the 'afflicted mind' which manufactures an illusory sense of a separate self, a center of seemingly independent and self-enclosed perception. This level lies beneath the individuated consciousness but is the first movement towards individuation. It is the beginning of the objectification process, which is to say it is the beginning of the tendency to grasp at phenomena as if they exist in their own right as completely independent, self-enclosed entities.

Primary amongst the productions within the klesha mind is the notion that the perceiving activity itself is an independent entity which exists separately from what is perceived:

> The first of these appears in the form of the thought 'I': this is exactly what the klesha mind is.[416]

This is the beginning of grasping onto a 'self in persons' and a 'self in phenomena', which are the two aspects of clinging to the view of the reality of the inherent existence of independent selves. It is this 'grasping' onto the reality of independent 'selfhood' within the interdependent field of the process of reality that activates the karmic process. An enlightened being, however, does not activate the karmic process:

> An Arahant, though he acts, does not accumulate karma, because he is free from the false idea of self, free from the 'thirst' for continuity and becoming...[417]

In other words enlightened beings do not collapse wavefunctions!

According to the Madhyamaka the embodied mind of human beings can be trained to directly perceive the ultimate nature of reality. Such a mind is the mind of a buddha, a fully awakened being; and the mind of a buddha is omniscient, knowing the nature of all objects, and the potentialities for all manifestation. The *Ornament of Sutras* says:

> Buddhahood is all phenomena,
> But it is no phenomenon whatsoever.[418]

In other words the mind of a buddha, or fully enlightened being, does not collapse the wavefunction of the process of reality. Buddhahood contains an awareness of all possibilities; therefore it embraces 'all phenomena.' However to produce a phenomenon the wavefunction must collapse into a definite manifestation; it therefore follows that buddhahood is 'no phenomenon whatsoever'. As the sutra says:

> With regard to the stainless expanse of dharmas,
> The explanation of the profound characteristics
> The state and the activity of the Buddhas
> Is nothing but sketching a colorful painting onto the sky.[419]

This conclusion, that a buddha's perception does not collapse the wavefunction, although startling, is clearly indicated by the discussion so far.

Unenlightened beings, however, instinctively, automatically and continuously collapse wavefunctions at an incomprehensible rate. This rate is indicated by the term 'subtle impermanence' within the Buddhist perspective, and is perhaps related to Planck's constant and the smallest unit of time which is hypothesised by physics. Because the inner quality within the ground consciousness is awareness, a quality which contains the necessity of perception, a world begins to manifest on the basis of the habituation of perception. The way that consciousness operates is according to a law of repetition and habituation. Already established movements of consciousness are more likely to arise at a later point; and it is through a vast cascade of tiny movements within the overall energy field of consciousness that the universe arises and develops or evolves.

According to the Buddhist philosopher-Yogin Manjusrimitra:

> Once that intelligence becomes the site of unbounded activity, imprints proliferate endlessly .... With the ripening of these vestigial imprints, further conditions for their production multiply profusely. The ripening of imprints are the cooperating conditions from whence the concatenation of effects resulting in the emergence of organic beings occurs.[420]

The term vestigial is used here because the direction of the self-development is not completely unguided, there are 'vestigial imprints' which remain from previous manifested universes which act like hidden 'seeds'.

In his book *Life Without Genes* Adrian Woolfson presents us with a poetic version of the sort of field of potentiality that he imagines must have 'existed' before the dawn of life within the universe:

> In the beginning there was mathematical possibility. At the very inception of the universe fifteen billion years ago, a deep infinite-dimensional sea emerged from nothingness. Its colourless waters, green and turquoise blue, glistened in the non-existent light of the non-existent sun ... A strange sea though, this information sea. Strange because it was devoid of location ...[421]

Woolfson's, strangely haunting, suggestion is that there must have been some kind of field of potentiality even at the inception of the universe. Although there was not a fully manifested and experienced reality there was, according to his picture, what he calls a mathematical possibility. This field, of course, can only be the wavefunction of the universe, a universal wavefunction which contains:

> ...all possible histories ... through which the universe could have evolved to its present state...[422]

In the beginning, of course, the wavefunction of the universe would contain all the future evolutionary possibilities.

Woolfson's significant insight, then, is that at the 'beginning' of the universe there was a field of potentiality which can only be conceived of in terms of quantum theory:

> The information sea is thus a quantum mechanical sea, composed from infinite repertoires of entangled quantum descriptions.[423]

And within this all encompassing wavefunction all possibilities for evolutionary manifestation are encoded. From out of the vast entangled web of infinite possibilities for manifestation only certain privileged members will actually make it into reality, so to speak:

> An information space of this sort would furnish a complete description of all potentially living and unrealizable creatures...[424]

It therefore follows that there is a sort of design woven into the potentialities for evolution; it is a vast complex design of all possible manifestations written into the wavefunction of the universe. We can only ask where this universal wavefunction of possible realities, standing on the brink of manifested time, can have come from. According to the *Ornament of Stainless Light*:

> When a world undergoes destruction, there follows a time of emptiness....During this time of emptiness the subtle particles of these five elements exist as isolated fragments and are not in any conventional sense objects of the sensory powers of the eye and so forth. They are known as empty particles and remain isolated in empty space. When the potential of the collective karma is ripened, the subtle air particles come together to form air whose nature is light and moving.[425]

The wavefunction for the current universe is a quantum karmic echo from the destruction of a previous universe.

It is an intriguing fact that according to the theory of the wavefunction of the universe, developed by Wheeler and DeWitt, time is frozen. The wavefunction of the universe contains all the possibilities which are potential within the universe but time is not an aspect of this description. So how does the illusion of time, which creates the appearance of evolution, come about? The answer should come as no surprise:

> Thus we see that without introducing an observer, we have a dead universe, which does not evolve in time. This example demonstrates an unusually important role played by the concept of an observer in quantum cosmology. John Wheeler underscored the complexity of the situation, replacing the word *observer* by the word *participant*, and introducing such terms as a 'self-observing universe'[426]

According to this viewpoint time and evolution are created within the scope of the frozen universal wavefunction when the universe divides into two aspects: an observer and the rest of the universe which is observed. Andrei Linde describes the situation as follows:

> ... one should first divide the universe into two main pieces: (i) an observer with his clock and other measuring devices and (ii) the rest of the universe. Then it can be shown that the rest of the universe does depend on the state of the clock of the observer, i.e. on his 'time.'[427]

This explanation of how a timeless universal wavefunction is propelled into the illusion of time and evolutionary activity through the autonomous creation of the processes of the observer and observed, a perceiving self and the seemingly self-enclosed, external, entities of a seemingly material world bears an uncanny resemblance to the Buddhist Mind-Only metaphysics which describes the generation of the illusion of duality from the nondual ground of reality.

In the foregoing manner the spectacular manifestation of a vast universe of experience is self generated within a fundamentally unitary field which divides itself up in order to perform its essential function of 'self'-perception. Wheeler described this spectacular vision of the universe's quest for its own nature as follows:

> The coming explosion of life opens the door to an all encompassing role for observer-participancy: to build, in time to come, no minor part of what we call *its* past – *our* past, present and future – but this whole vast world.[428]

The metaphor of resonance is a powerful means of picturing the operation of karma within this universal process. This is because each tiny act of perception within the field of consciousness leaves an echo-ripple which will interact with other perceptual echo-ripples. The effects of karmic actions are always related to the causes through some form of similarity. It makes eminent sense then to conceive of karmic causes and supporting conditions manifesting an effect through the resonance of similar frequencies which either amplify or dampen each other. The effects of an action for instance will depend not only on the vibration frequency but also the internal karmic status of the field of consciousness. Once something is vibrating at its resonant frequency it takes small inputs to keep it vibrating, and, in a similar fashion, the karmic implications of an action will not just depend on that action but whether a karmic frequency finds already vibrating karmic centers to resonate with and amplify.

The incorporation of the notion of karmic resonance into the quantum-karmic, or Quantum-Mind-Only, theory of reality offers us a means to understand just how the physical world can be a manifestation patterned by a karmic matrix built up by countless repeated perceptions which have solidified over vast stretches of time and space. As Sheldrake says:

> …morphic fields are fields of habit, and they have been set up through habits of thought, through habits of activity and through habits of speech.[429]

The mechanism that underlies the operation of these fields, says Sheldrake, is 'morphic resonance.'[430] Sheldrake's perspective, as expressed in the above quote, relates directly to the Buddhist description of 'evolutionary' actions as being those of body, speech and mind. These three types of actions are termed evolutionary because they create the 'morphic', or 'karmic', fields that drive the evolutionary process. These 'morphic' fields, which are non-local in nature, must be located at the quantum level and at present we would not be able to directly detect them. However this should not stop us taking these suggestions seriously given the amount of consistent and unifying considerations, both philosophical and empirical, that surround the development of this quantum-karmic viewpoint with its central notion of 'karmic resonance'. There is overwhelming evidence, both scientific and philosophical, that our experiences of reality unfold from the karmic patterns within an underlying field of awareness-consciousness.

Sheldrake's viewpoint almost seems like a modern reworking of the Yogachara paradigm within the context of biology; indeed in his discussion with Bohm, *Morphic Fields and the Implicate Order,* which is included in his recent updated and republished work *A New Science of Life* he refers to the alayavijnana, noting that it is similar to a 'cosmic memory.'[431] The laws of nature, Sheldrake supposes, like Wheeler and Paul Davies, are not fixed and immutable, operating in a rigidly fixed manner remorselessly over all time but are developed and strengthened through a memory of what went before:

> ...the laws of nature are more like habits; perhaps the laws of nature are habits of the universe, and the universe has an in-built memory.[432]

When Sheldrake originally proposed this viewpoint he was ridiculed by many within the 'mainstream' scientific community. However the accumulating evidence from the quantum domain is now making this kind of view much more attractive. In his recent work *The Goldilocks Enigma* the physicist Paul Davies, with reference to Wheeler's perspective, refers to the possibility of 'flexi-laws' which can be modified through the process of evolution. This is in line with Wheeler's pronouncement:

> Law without law. It is difficult to see what else than that can be the plan of physics. It is preposterous to think of the laws of physics as installed by Swiss watchmaker to endure from everlasting to everlasting when we know that the universe began with a big bang. The laws must have come into being. Therefore they could not have been always a hundred percent accurate. That means that they are derivative, not primary ... Events beyond law. Events so numerous and so uncoordinated that, flaunting their freedom from formula, they yet formulate firm form ... The universe is a self excited circuit. As it expands, cools and develops, it gives rise to observer-participancy. Observer-participancy in turn gives what we call tangible reality to the universe ... Of all the strange features of the universe, none are stranger than these: time is transcended, laws are mutable, and observer participancy matters.[433]

The laws of physics, therefore, might evolve of time; in a lawful fashion of course!

Sheldrake's viewpoint maps directly onto the Mind-Only view that:

> Emotions and evolutionary actions create superficial reality;
> Actions are instigated by the mind.

Mind is the sum of all instincts.[434]

The word 'superficial' refers to the 'seeming', 'conventional' realm of dualistic experience. Here mind, as the sum of all instincts, corresponds to the collection of habits which constitute the morphic, or karmic, patterns of reality. If we meld together Stapp's, Sheldrake's, Wheeler's view and the Mind-Only karmic perspective we can draw an enhanced version of Wheeler's picture of the self-referring, self-resonating universe shown in fig 7.5. The 'notes struck out on a piano by the observer participants of all times and all places' that Wheeler refers to as adding up to the production of the 'great wide world of space and time and things' corresponds within the Mind-Only quantum karmic view to the uncountable small acts of perception and intention which, over eons, have built up the appearance of the material world.

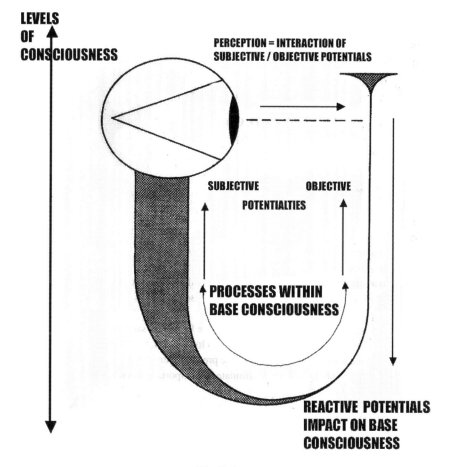

Fig 7.5

Wheeler's notion of a participatory universe is certainly a kind of anthropic perspective, a viewpoint that suggests that the genesis and development of the universe is, to some degree, a result of, and directed by, an inner necessity to create conscious beings. At the time Wheeler was developing his viewpoint such anthropic notions were ridiculed by many scientists as being 'quasi-religious mumbo jumbo'[435]. The scientific writer Martin Gardner, for instance, referred to the most emphatic version of the principle as CRAP – the Completely Ridiculous Anthropic Principle. This unsupported and prejudiced attitude, of course, was in line with the generalised intellectual denigration of viewpoints that treated the concept, and indeed the phenomenon, of consciousness seriously.

Today, however, the intellectual climate within physics and philosophy is gradually changing, largely because of the unmistakable experimental evidence which we have surveyed in earlier chapters. The fact that if the physical constants of the universe had only been marginally different then life, and therefore consciousness, would have been impossible, now forms an important insight for more recent views of the nature of the evolution of the universe. The explanation that is now increasingly gaining ground suggests that life and consciousness are intrinsic aspects of the universe; as a consequence of this the universe necessarily evolves in the direction of life:

> As long as the laws of physics are fixed ... their enigmatic bio-friendliness is left out of this explanatory loop. But with flexi-laws of the sort advocated by Wheeler, the way lies open to a self-consistent explanation. The fuzzy primordial laws focus in on precisely the form needed to give rise to the living organisms that eventually observe them.[436]

The idea of a 'flexi-law' derives from the inescapable fact that, as Wheeler indicates, the laws of physics themselves must come from somewhere, and the only place they can come from is the observer-participants who cooperate in the creation of the universe. According to Wheeler it is the observer-participants who somehow create and change laws over time.

The Buddhist view of cosmological evolution shares a lot in common with Wheeler's perspective. The idea that something simply comes into being without cause is not accepted, but neither is an external cause accepted. The naturalistic viewpoint that there is nothing significant about life beyond material appearances, and the ultra-Darwinian view that the spectacular order of life in the universe appears from an essential randomness are rejected. Such views are considered to be nihilistic:

> Nihilists claim that all worlds and beings have arisen naturally, without depending on causes. This is expressed in such words as these:
> Good lady, what learned people say

Is misleading like the tracks of a wolf.
Who created the pollen-bed of a lotus?
Who designed the patterns on the peacock's feathers?
Who sharpened the tip of a thorn?
Everything arose naturally, without causes.[437]

This corresponds to the current absurd 'scientific' view that an essentially 'material' reality springs into existence from 'nothing' at the moment of the 'Big Bang'. Victor Stenger for instance asserts that:

> If the laws of physics are the same laws as the laws of the empty void, the transition from nothing to something may not have been as difficult as people have assumed. Our Universe may be no more than rearranged, restructured nothingness.[438]

However, if the term 'nothingness' is taken to mean what it generally denotes, which is a complete absence – including the absence of the potentiality to become any kind of 'something,' this assertion is nothing more than philosophical absurdity, for nothing could ever emerge from this kind of complete vacant 'nothingness'; but if 'nothingness' were to be replaced with the notion of 'emptiness', a quantum field of potential awareness or intelligent energy , then Stenger's view would have more going for it.

According to the Madhyamaka:

> If things arise in total absence of a cause,
> It follows that at all times, everything can come from anything
> And if that were so, then worldly people would not gather seeds,
> In all the myriad ways, to cultivate their crops
> If wanderers were not themselves the cause, then like the scent and color
> Of the lotus in the sky, there would be no perception of the universe,
> And yet this world appears in all its brilliance.
> Conclude therefore that, like the mind, the world derives from causes.[439]

The term 'wanderers' actually refers to what Wheeler calls 'observer-participants', you, me and all sentient beings trapped within the cyclic web of repeated lives within cyclic existence.

The doctrine of the 'Charvakas', the nihilistic materialists who think that this life is all there is, which is that everything arises uncaused through the natural existence of a random spontaneity (although how there can be a 'random' anything within 'nothingness' is difficult to comprehend), is essentially the view of the ultra-Darwinians. It might be objected that ultra-Darwinians do not posit a 'total absence of a cause'; they do, however, assert an ultimate lack of causality. Dawkins, for instance speaks of the way in which the appearance of non-randomness manifests from the essential randomness of the process of existence[440], and this really amounts to an abandonment of the notion that the universe is essentially causal, in which case in essence 'everything can come from anything'; a position which the Madhyamaka repudiates.

This repudiation of lack of causality must apply to so-called 'objective randomness' at the quantum level which is accepted by the majority of quantum physicists today. This view of 'objective randomness' is rightly repudiated by Stapp:

> Yet it is an absurdity to believe that quantum choices can appear simply randomly 'out of the blue', on the basis of absolutely nothing at all. Something must select which of the possible events actually occur.[441]

The laws which science posits at the classical level are laws of cause and effect. This happens because that happens. Furthermore most such laws indicate that given certain conditions, a certain cause must invariably lead to its effect. This, of course, is why the term 'law' is used. To abandon causality at the quantum level is to abandon the view that the Universe is essentially coherent and comprehensible. But, of course, the kind of cause which drives the quantum level is very probably not a 'classical' type of cause, but that is no reason to abandon the notion of causality completely. As we have seen the type of cause operating is likely to be of the nature of 'quantum karmic resonance.'

This issue has been examined in the previous chapter *Interconnected Lightness of Being*. The patterns which emerge at the quantum level appear to be properties of quantum 'particles' considered as being one undivided system; they are not the result of any 'hidden' bits of information carried by each particle. It is as if the patterns generated by the quantum 'particles' are actually spread over the entirety of the quantum field in a similar fashion to a hologram. The patterns unfold when certain configurations of quantum interactions are imposed on the quantum field through the choice of various experimental setups. The 'hologram' of the universe must unfold out of a deep entanglement that is, indeed, hidden from us; and it is a hologram that each living being is a part of and, according to Wheeler, Bohm, Stapp, amongst many other quantum physicists and the Mind-Only perspective, helps to create.

According to the Buddhist view causality operates at all levels of the process of reality, even though there are aspects which are deeply hidden. The operation of karma operates on many levels of mind and it is the collective level of mind which creates the physical environment which is inhabited by the countless beings whose collective karma created it. The Mind-Only perspective is quite clear that what we experience as the physical world is in fact built up through the operation of the collective karma within the fundamental consciousness which is the ground of reality:

> The entire world was created through latent karmic imprints. When these imprints developed and increased, they formed the earth, the stones, the mountains, and the seas. Everything was created through the development or propagation of these latent karmic potentials.' … 'How can all these external forms arise out of latent karmic imprints? All these mountains, oceans, the sun and moon are so solid and so vivid. How can they arise out of latent karmic imprints in the mind.' … 'These things arise through the power and propagation of thought.'[442]

Karma is the non-local interconnection within consciousness which is the basis for all manifestation. Karma must be non-local because it forms the pattern for the development of the very structure of matter as it appears within consciousness. Evolutionary actions which take place in one place and time will reinforce the templates, or habits, of reality in all places and times.

Evolutionary actions and perceptions, actions of body, speech and mind which have karmic, and hence evolutionary, consequences, leave very fine vibration traces within the ground consciousness which have the potential to interact constructively with other karmic traces. This provides an explanation of how a common material world emerges and is kept manifest through karmic resonance within the ground consciousness at the quantum level. It is not the power of the subjective mind of one person, or a few people that produces the illusion of the external material world. It is the karmic resonance of unimaginably countless perceptions by incomprehensibly countless sentient beings over staggeringly vast stretches of time.

The Buddhist philosopher William Waldron describes this fundamental aspect of the Yogachara account of the functioning of reality as being driven by 'self-grasping' which is the deep instinctual habit within all sentient beings to crave individuated experience. Waldron describes this as a linguistically recursive process; however the linguistic levels operative within the Yogachara account of the process of reality operate deep within the psychophysical structure of embodiment, directly structuring and determining the potentialities for manifestation of future experience at deep psychophysical levels:

> …this linguistic recursivity, which colours so much of our perceptual experience, including our innate forms of self-grasping, now operates unconsciously … and … these processes are karmically productive at a collective level as well as individual level – that is they create a common 'world'.[443]

This constitutes an unconscious 'intersubjective feedback system' and therefore:

...it is the unconscious habits of body speech and mind to which we are habituated that give rise, in the long term and in the aggregate, to the habitats we inhabit, the 'common receptacle world' we experience all around us.[444]

The basic function of the evolutionary mind, then, is to habituate perceptions:

> The beginningless nature of the mind is empty, clear and
>   unobstructed,
> But its nature is not recognised.
> The fundamental consciousness, stirred by mental creations
>   produces dualistic appearances and the consciousnesses.
> Feeling develops from acceptance and rejection;
>   discernment from objectification habit.
> Discernment leads to mental formations which are
>   mental factors; habitual adherence creates form.
> With attachment and grasping as a link the wheel of existence
> turns.[445]

Within this quote resides the pith of the entire process of creation by the fundamental consciousness, depending on the deluded activities, which is to say actions which are prompted by ignorance of the real nature of phenomena, by sentient beings.

The fundamental base consciousness is beginningless and has the nature of being 'empty', in the sense that it is the ground of phenomenon but no particular phenomenon, 'clear' because it has the clarity to cognize, and 'unobstructed', in the sense that it is formless and has the capacity to reflect all forms that appear to it without changing their nature. This base consciousness produces the world of duality because its true nature is not recognised. It now manifests on the conventional level within which the mode of perception through habituation is dominant. So for the conventional mind 'habitual adherence creates form'. The tracks of habitual modes of perception, however, are not laid down in a single lifetime. The habitual patterns of collective perception which create the 'physical world' are developed over vast stretches of time, countless lifetimes for countless sentient beings lay down the web of collective perception which makes up the collective dream of the material world.

Jeffrey Hopkins, in the introduction to his *Emptiness in the Mind-Only School of Buddhism*, emphasizes the role that assenting to the false appearance of inherent existence plays in conditioning future experiences:

> By assenting to this false appearance (of inherent existence), beings are drawn into a series of detrimental mental states, exaggerating the status of phenomena, such that counterproductive emotions are generated. These lead to actions that in turn deposit predisposing poten-

cies in the mind in latent form, which, when activated, perpetuate further the round of powerless suffering. ....[446]

All mental acts have karmic repercussions because they leave karmic traces and, as the fundamental functioning of consciousness is to habituate perceptions, it becomes clear that the karmic consequence of affirming inherent existence must be to strengthen the tendency to perceive objects as inherently existent in the future. The implications of this process are dramatic. According to the Quantum Mind-Only view, the objects around us are created by the collective karma operating at the quantum fundamental level. In other words the 'physical' world is actually the manifestation of the quantum karmic matrix built up over eons by countless acts of 'afflicted' perception. What is 'afflicted' perception? It is perception that assents to the inherent existence of the perception itself. It follows, then, *that perceptions which assent to the inherent existence of the physical world must strengthen the tendency of the physical world to manifest in the form that it currently does.*

So we now see the mechanism that underpins the observation that 'habitual adherence creates form'. When we fully grasp this vital aspect of the Yogachara-Chittamatra understanding of the 'real nature of phenomena' it becomes clear that what is being implied is that *habitual perceptual adherence to the appearance that things exist inherently from their own side reinforces the quantum ground structure which maintains the material world that we inhabit.* Such an adherence, collectively maintained over eons of time by vast infinities of inhabitants of world-systems maintains the illusion of the solid material world and the laws it obeys. An unenlightened mind cannot see through the collective illusion which is written into the quantum ground. When Buddhist philosophers, agreeing with Wheeler, tell us that our minds create our reality they really mean it; over eons of time we have intersubjectively created the universe.

This may seem to be a quite preposterous idea. This perspective, however, fits quite happily with current quantum theory. Wheeler, together with others such as Stapp and Bohm, has proposed a view which fits quite harmoniously with the Quantum Mind-Only view of how the physical world is manifested from the patterning of the quantum ground, a patterning which is created by the perceptive activities of the consciousnesses of countless sentient beings over unimaginable stretches of time. Indeed, there are quantum physicists who, apparently without any mystical axe to grind, propose a fully Mind-Only view of reality which is completely in agreement with the karmic-quantum model:

> They will tell you that even an object as large as the Moon, full of atoms held together by gravity and jiggling about with the random thermal motion appropriate to its temperature, does not exist when nobody is looking at it. ... The Moon doesn't simply

disappear when nobody is looking at it … The probability waves spread out very slowly, from the states they were in when they were last observed; the whole moon begins to dissolve away into a quantum ghost. But because the Moon is so big the process is very slow. It doesn't take a few nanoseconds but millions (perhaps billions) of years for the Moon to dissolve away into quantum uncertainty.[447]

Because the moon has taken vast stretches of time to materialise through the operation of the resonant karmic perceptual activities of a countless number of sentient beings, it would take an equally vast period of time to quantumly melt away into emptiness.

Many Worlds of Illusion

..the only way to insist that (the universal wavefunction) holds for all processes, including measurement, would be to pass to a 'many-worlds' type of view in which two detector responses do actually coexist, but in what are referred to as different worlds.[448]

-Roger Penrose

(The many-worlds interpretation) has been regarded as both the most outlandish and extravagant interpretation of quantum mechanics and yet the most straightforward depending on which side you are on. In fact I tend to oscillate between these two extremes myself, one day wondering how any one could be so silly to give it the time of day, another wondering how anyone could possibly consider any alternative.[449]

-Jim Al-Khalili

Some realms are richly embellished
With the millions of realm-adornments.
These diversified ornaments of various styles
Appear as myriad optical illusions.[450]

-Jamgon Kontrul.

....one has to assume that 'our' (quantum correlated) minds are located in a component of the universal wavefunction...[451]

-H. Dieter Zeh.

Hugh Everett III

In 1935 Einstein wrote a letter to Schrödinger in which he discussed the quantum phenomenon of superposition as it would appear if it manifested on the everyday macroscopic level. He referred to a situation wherein there were two boxes, one of them containing a ball. On a quantum level this situation would require that we say that the situation was comprised of a superposed wavefunction of two possibilities, one of which contained a ½ probability that the ball was in the first box and the other a ½ probability it was in the second. Furthermore this quantum probability distribution means that the ball is actually quantumly spread out over the two boxes, hovering between existence and non-existence; before a box has been opened quantum theory requires, as we have seen, that the ball is not in the first box, not in the second, not in both, nor in neither box. Einstein, however, rejected the view that 'Before I open them, the ball is by no means in *one* of the boxes' and that 'being in a definite box only comes about when I lift the covers' as being absurd.[452] Einstein could not accept the quantum idea that reality is not independent of the consciousnesses of observers.

However, as we have seen, this is the view that quantum theory requires. Until an observation is made quantum reality is in a superposed state of many possibilities. The central problem for the interpretation, and comprehension, of quantum physics as it is currently formulated lies in the severe discontinuity between the behaviour of the unobserved wavefunction which develops smoothly over time according to a continuous equation and the sudden 'jumping' to a definite and particular state that apparently occurs whenever a 'measurement' is said to occur. Prior to the measurement the wavefunction contains many, perhaps an infinite number, of possibilities which are in a state of superposition but when a measurement is performed this superposed state of possibilities collapses into singularity; the rest, apparently, simply disappearing. The crucial issue at the heart of the interpretation of quantum theory is the question of how the state of many possibilities collapses down to just one.

Schrödinger posed his famous dead and alive cat paradox in order to highlight the apparent absurdity of this quantum requirement. He outlined his thought experiment in his reply to Einstein's letter (ψ denotes the wavefunction):

> Confined in a steel chamber is a Geiger counter prepared with a tiny amount of uranium, so small that in the next hour it is just as probable to expect one atomic decay as none. An amplified relay provides that the first atomic decay shatters a small bottle of prussic acid. This and – cruelly – a cat is also trapped in the steel chamber. According to the ψ-function for the total system, after an hour ... the living and dead cat are smeared out in equal measures.[453]

Just as the ball in Einstein's quantum thought experiment must hover between existence and non-existence in the two boxes, 'Schrödinger's cat' must be hover between the state of life and the after-life at the same time.

The cat's existential crisis from the point of view of its wavefunction seems to involve it hovering between life and death, the overall wavefunction (ψ) can be expressed:

$$\psi = \sqrt{\tfrac{1}{2}} \ (\psi_{dead} + \psi_{alive})^{454}$$

Which basically implies that the cat is half-dead and half-alive at the same time! The main point that Schrödinger is emphasizing, however, is that in the case of his thought experiment the strange 'smeared out' probability distribution that is the hallmark of the unobserved quantum world is brought into the realm of the everyday macroscopic world. He was trying to highlight the fact that the appearance of the determinate everyday world is a quantum paradox. As Penrose says with reference to the cat's quantum existential crisis:

> A great many (and probably most) physicists would maintain that … there is now so much experimental evidence in favour … – and none at all against it – that we have no right whatever to abandon that type of evolution, even at the scale of a cat[455]

From the perspective of the evolution of the wavefunction, then, reality is comprised of many possible actualities waiting to be 'really' actualised by an observation. When a measurement is performed one of the possible actualities becomes the actual actuality, and the rest appear to disappear. Which possible actuality actualizes cannot be predicted with certainly, the wavefunction can only supply the probability for each possibility. Once a measurement is performed, however, the ontological status of reality apparently becomes discontinuously and radically changed.

The notion that insentient objects, let alone conscious beings, can be in two different states at the same time is obviously difficult to comprehend from a classical, and everyday, perspective; but such superposed states have been demonstrated in quantum experiments. But what about conscious beings; if the cat is alive it must know that it is; how can it only half-know that it is half alive, so to speak? The situation of half-death doesn't bear thinking about. The quantum predicament of Schrödinger's cat brings the issue of consciousness into the focus of a quantum paradox.

It was this kind of existential quantum paradox that prompted Eugene Wigner to conclude that consciousness must be responsible for the transition from the realm of the wavefunction to a manifested reality. Wigner considered the situation in which he leaves a friend to observe a Schrödinger-cat type quantum system. Before the friend observes the outcome the system must be in a state of superposition; it is in both states at the same time but not completely in either so to speak. When the friend observes the outcome the wavefunction collapses into a definite result for the friend. Now according to quantum theory the state of the system and the friend taken as a whole must be:

$$\Psi \text{ cat-friend system} = (\Psi_{\text{cat dead}} \times \Psi \text{ sees cat dead}) + (\Psi_{\text{cat alive}} \times \Psi \text{ sees cat alive})$$

(Take '×' to signify combination, '+' indicates superposition)

So when Wigner returns he must regard his friend as being in a superposition of both, having seen a living cat and having seen a dead cat, each being the same cat of course. Wigner wrote that this situation 'appears absurd because it implies that my friend was in a state of suspended animation ...'[456]. We would expect, of course, that the friend to himself would be perfectly 'collapsed', in the sense of knowing the fate of the cat.

However, in the case of a purely physical system this situation of superposed states is correct; Wigner therefore concluded that his friend's consciousness must collapse the wavefunction. According to Wigner 'the wavefunction collapses when it interacts with the *first* conscious mind it encounters'.[457] In this case the above equation is disentangled so that the situation after the observation by Wigner's friend is either:

$$\Psi \text{ cat-friend system} = (\Psi_{\text{cat dead}} \times \Psi \text{ sees cat dead})$$

or

$$\Psi \text{ cat-friend system} = (\Psi_{\text{cat alive}} \times \Psi \text{ sees cat alive})$$

In his 1957 Ph. D. thesis Hugh Everett III, the instigator of the many-worlds interpretation, indicated further paradoxical features of the situation. He pointed out that if the situation involving an observer observing a Wigner-style friend who as witnessed the results of a quantum 'collapse' is problematic, it is even more problematic to consider the collapse of a wavefunction for a series of observers sequentially observing each other.

As Barrow and Tippler[458] point out there are five possible implications of this analysis:

1. Solipsism – which was ruled out by Wigner.
2. Any being with consciousness can collapse the wavefunction (including the cat)
3. A group of living beings with consciousness can collapse the wavefunction collectively.
4. There is an Ultimate Observer responsible for the collapses of all wavefunctions (this corresponds to Bishop Berkeley's Idealist position that God is responsible for the appearance of the material world).
5. Wavefunctions do not really collapse.

The first account is not really worth consideration. Whilst it can form the basis for pointless philosophical speculation, if it were true it really would render the speculation pointless because there would be no-one else to convince! The second account is held to be correct by Wigner, von Neumann and London and Bauer. According to London and Bauer it is the 'faculty of introspection' that is significant in the ability of conscious observers to actualize, and thus collapse, the wavefunction. As we shall see later this point of view has been given a new twist by the Russian physicist Michael Mensky, who suggests that for a conscious being to 'be in two minds' indicates a superposed wavefunction of consciousness and that a decision constitutes an internal collapse of the corresponding wavefunction of consciousness.

The idea that an individual consciousness might be capable of causing a collapse of an 'external' wavefunction, a wavefunction not intrinsic and internal to the mind of the observer so to speak, has serious drawbacks apart from its high degree of implausibility. As Abner Shimony has pointed out it is impossible to account for the coherence between multiple observers. In the case of just two observers, for instance, an agreement concerning wavefunction collapse would be coincidence unless the first observer collapses the wavefunction before the second. But such a sequentially coordinated manifestation of a coherent material reality for countless beings is simply incomprehensible.[459] As Barrow and Tipler conclude:

> It would seem that one could justify this coincidence of wavefunction reduction to the same state by two different observers only by reference to something like Leibniz's idea of 'pre-established harmony'.[460]

This observation is highly prescient; for if we replace the requirement for a 'pre-established harmony' by a pre-established mechanism by which a coordinated, or 'orchestrated', collapse of the wavefunction, or wavefunctions on multiple levels, can take place then we arrive at the mechanism of karmic resonance which has been previously outlined. This perspective also encompasses possibility number three, wavefunction collapse by a group, and this viewpoint provides the basis for the understanding of the karmic resonance mechanism discussed in the previous chapter. This is a direction of speculation that interested Wheeler and it led him to the notion of the participatory universe:

> John Wheeler has been intrigued by the notion of collapse by inter-subjective agreement, but he confesses that he does not see any way to make this idea mathematically precise. What really interests him about possibility three is that it would be a mechanism of bringing the entire Universe into existence![461]

The fourth suggestion, the idea that an ultimate observer, i.e. God, is ultimately responsible for collapsing the wavefunction has been grasped at by Christian apologists eager to co-opt quantum physics for their own cause of proving the necessity of a creator external to the created universe. The problem for this viewpoint, however, is that whilst the evidence does indicate that something akin to intelligence *internal* to the universe must be implicated, it in no way proves, or even indicates, the necessity for a God such as is defined within the Christian theology. This issue will be expanded upon in the last chapter.

Possibility five, the idea that the wavefunction does not collapse, leads to the so called many-worlds interpretation. This interpretation, which is based on the interpretation of quantum mechanics proposed by Hugh Everett in his 1957 Ph.D. thesis, and subsequently given impetus by Bryce DeWitt, sometimes referred to as the theory of the universal wavefunction, was quite consciously formulated to provide a viewpoint which defused the significance, or eliminated entirely, the implied mechanism of the 'collapse' of the wavefunction. The actual title of Everett's thesis was *'Relative State' Formulation of Quantum Mechanics'*; the 'many worlds' version of Everett's interpretation was due to the later reinterpretation by DeWitt and others.

There is no better way to begin to plumb the depths of the murky waters of the 'many worlds' phenomenon than by analyzing Everett's thesis. It is a masterpiece of conceptual confusion parading itself as clarity; but it did the job, he got a Ph.D.! This is not to say that the idea was not brilliant, it was, and is; however, like so much materialist thinking, and in its original form Everett's proposal was couched in a completely inappropriate materialist idiom, its essential insights are undermined by the incoherence of the underlying materialist perspective. The following characterisation of Everett's proposal clearly indicates the problem:

> Everett's proposal was to drop the collapse postulate from the standard formulation of quantum mechanics then deduce the empirical predictions of the standard theory as the subjective experiences of observers who are themselves treated as physical systems described by his theory.[462]

The problematic issue resides in ambiguity of the term 'physical', a term which generally indicates a materialist perspective. The essence of the Everett's proposal resides in his treatment of the 'subjective experiences of observers' as not actually being 'experiences' but merely 'physical' records, thus avoiding the necessity to articulate the relationship between the realms, of the 'physical' and the subjective. Everett's extraordinary blending of quantum wavefunction and physical mechanism has never been *explicitly* updated, although on a great many occasions commentators and reinterpreters have been forced to *implicitly* introduce a necessary background perspective of consciousness as a significant feature in order to make sense of the proposal. It is seldom, if ever, pointed out by adherents of the many-worlds scenario that it requires the ultimate nature of the 'physical' reality to be, in reality, consciousness. This must be the case because 'subjective experiences' are nothing if not a 'matter' of consciousness, so to speak! But if you look in the index of a book like *Parallel Worlds*, Michio Kaku's popular exposition of the wonders of the multiple universe scenario, you will find no entry of the term 'consciousness'; a matter worth being conscious of.

The first step in Everett's development of his thesis is the observation that the usual presentation of the quantum situation is from the perspective of an 'external observation.'[463] In this formulation there is an objective wavefunction of probabilities and an external observer who interacts with it. There are two ways that the wavefunction can change:

- **Process 1** – the discontinuous change when one probability is actualised by an observation.
- **Process 2** – the continuous and deterministic evolution of the wavefunction when not observed.

The step of brilliance proposed by Everett is to put a theoretical observer inside the objective wavefunction:

> Consider for example an isolated system consisting of an observer or measuring apparatus, plus an object system. Can the change with time of the state of the total system be described by Process 2? If so, then it would appear that no discontinuous probabilistic process like Process 1 can take place. If not, we are forced to admit that systems which contain observers are not subject to the same kind of quantum mechanical description as we admit for all other physical systems.[464]

Process 1 and process 2 are graphically represented in fig 8.1. Everett wants a way of saying that we can just consider the continuous wave equation of 'Process 2' to describe the functioning of quantum reality. He wants to banish 'Process 1', which is responsible for the inconvenient apparent 'collapses' that supposedly produce experienced reality. Everett's proposal is that, because 'Process 1' results from the perspective of external observers, if we move the observing process inside the 'Process 2', the smooth continuous functioning of the 'objective' wavefunction, then the task of theoretically getting rid of the collapsing of the wavefunction will be achieved. If we are unable to satisfactorily perform this theoretical conjuring trick, however, then we will be 'forced to admit that 'systems which contain observers' do not act like purely 'physical systems'; which is basically saying that sentient beings are significantly different from houses, chairs and tables and so on.

In order to fully appreciate the kind of amazing conjuring trick that is in store for us presently it is vital to be aware of the use of the term 'physical'.

This is a term which is of immense benefit for scientists and philosophers who wish to appear to accommodate the phenomenon of consciousness into their worldview at the same time as surreptitiously demoting it to existence in some kind of ontological wasteland. In order see this clearly let us first agree to amplify the term 'observers' by replacing it with the phrase 'observing consciousnesses.' In doing this we are only requiring that those of Everett's persuasion agree that 'subjective' observers are endowed with consciousness. Furthermore let us require that the term 'physical' be replaced with the term 'material' because, after all, this is generally what it is taken to mean. With these replacements the last sentence in the above quote from Everett reads that if we cannot coherently theoretically embed our observers inside the wavefunction then we will be:

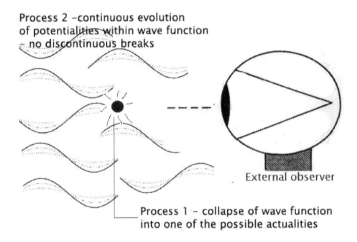

Process 2 –continuous evolution of potentialities within wave function – no discontinuous breaks

External observer

Process 1 – collapse of wave function into one of the possible actualities

Fig 8.1

> ...forced to admit that systems which contain observing-consciousnesses are not subject to the same kind of quantum mechanical description as we admit for all other material systems.

In other words, systems which contain consciousness cannot be described in purely materialist terms, which is something which is hardly surprising.

Now the other side of this characterisation of the situation requires that if we can embed the theoretical observers into the objective wavefunction then we will be able to treat 'systems that contain observers' in the same way as 'we admit for all other physical' systems. The fact that Everett will succeed in his relocation of his observers is a foregone conclusion because he adopts as a presupposition at the outset of his thesis, in the first sentence of the above quote, that an 'observer' and a 'measuring apparatus' are identical in nature. In other words Everett assumes at the outset that there is nothing beyond the materialist physicality of a 'measuring apparatus' which accounts for subjectivity. So Everett assumes at the outset that consciousness is nothing more than glorified materiality. Furthermore the 'physical' nature of the wavefunction, in terms of materiality or consciousness, is not elucidated, or even addressed as a significant issue.

At the same time as Everett places his theoretical observer inside an overall wavefunction, which encompasses the subjective-objective dichotomy of perception, he begins a process of dehumanising, or 'robotizing', his observer. Thus the familiar materialist sanitisation of the conceptual terrain, which requires the removal of implications of the necessity for consciousness to be effectively involved in the process of reality, is built into the Everett's theoretical perspective. But, as we shall see, the terrain of Everett's development of thought is so replete with implications of subjectivity that the framework of ontological physicality threatens to burst at the seams. The question as to the ontological nature of the wavefunction, matter or mind, screams for attention but is ignored and covered over by the use of the term 'physical.'

The 'conventional', pre-Everett, perspective of the 'collapse' of the wavefunction is shown schematically in fig 8.1; an 'external' observer 'observes' a wavefunction and thereby collapses it. Everett proposes that because observers are, after all, part of reality so they should also be 'inside' wavefunctions, so to speak. This, according to Max Tegmark, is simply moving from a 'birds eye' view to a 'frog view', the frog being inside the process of the wavefunction (fig 8.2). This situation is also portrayed in fig 8.3 where Wheeler's universally useful 'eye' takes the part of the frog inside an encompassing wavefunction which therefore now contains both aspects, subjective and objective, of the process of perception which is taking place within the universal wavefunction.

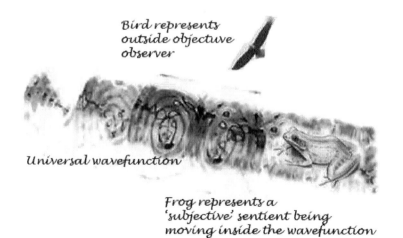

Bird represents outside objective observer

Universal wavefunction

Frog represents a 'subjective' sentient being moving inside the wavefunction

Fig 8.2

Fig 8.3

When the process of observation gets moved inside an all encompassing universal wavefunction in this way it becomes itself a part of a probabilistic field of potentiality, which is shown, somewhat clumsily, by the slight uncertainty of line in the diagram. Both the subjective and objective aspects of the process must have the nature of wavefunctions, which is to say they must both consist of probability distributions. So the next step which is required in order to maintain a semblance of conceptual coherence is that the observer must also become represented as a wavefunction. To have a 'collapsed' fully paid up member of the completely materialised, and apparently robotic, world masquerading as a wavefunction participating as part of an overall superposition is not just conceptually inept, it is misleading. The next stage in Everett's progression, therefore, should be as shown in fig 8.4. In this diagram there is an objective wavefunction and a subjective wavefunction which are superposed within an overall wavefunction which encompasses both aspects of the perceptual process.

Everett, however, does not do this. Instead he replaces the observer with a fully depersonalised robotic recording machine (fig 8.5):

> As models for our observers we can, if we wish, consider automatically functioning machines, possessing sensory apparatus coupled to recording devices capable of registering past memory data and machine configurations. We can further suppose that the machine is so constructed that its present actions shall be determined not only by its present sensory data, but by the contents of its memory as well.[465]

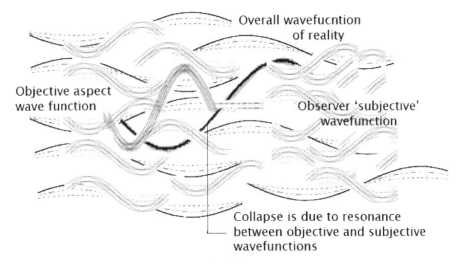

Overall wavefucntion
of reality

Objective aspect
wave function

Observer 'subjective'
wavefunction

Collapse is due to resonance
between objective and subjective
wavefunctions

Fig 8.4

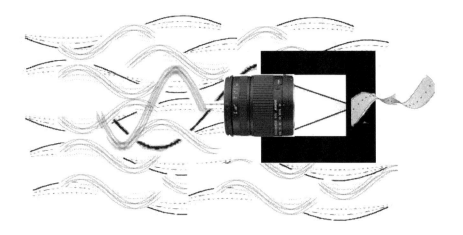

Fig 8.5

And, in a breathtaking leap of science fantasy (the Everett interpretation certainly started in the way it was destined to continue), not to mention a significant degree of deception, he also observes that:

> For such machines we are justified in using such phrases as 'the machine has perceived A' or 'the machine is aware of A' if the occurrence of A is represented in the memory, since the future of the machine will be based on the occurrence of A. In fact all of

the customary language of subjective experience is quite applicable to such machines, and forms the most natural and useful mode of expression when dealing with their behavior, as is well known to individuals who work with complex automata.[466]

Everett tells us that the output from this machine can be recorded by:

photoelectric cells, photographic plates and similar devices where a mechanistic attitude can hardly be contested.[467]

Elsewhere Everett contends that the record of events which constitute the observations:

…can be regarded as punches in paper tape, impressions on a magnetic reel, configurations of a relay switching circuit, or even configurations of brain cells.[468]

This, of course, is completely in accord with the behaviourist attitudes of Everett's day. For those too squeamish for such macho materialism Everett advises:

For the following one can *limit himself to this class of problems*, if he is unwilling to consider observers in the more or less familiar sense on the same mechanistic level of analysis.[469]

In other words Everett is suggesting that, if the reader of his thesis is queasy with his assumptions regarding the nature of subjectivity, he or she should just think about the 'class of problems' concerning robots rather than sentient beings! This was the age of behaviourism; nonetheless the claims concerning subjectivity are completely fallacious and absurd. The 'customary language of subjective experience' when employed for such robotic recording devices is not equivalent to the same discourse when employed for living beings, which are 'recording devices' endowed with consciousness as their primary recording mechanism. And, we shall see the problem is not solved by limiting ones thought to robots because the thesis directly concerns the functioning of subjectivity.

Everett's ambiguity regarding his understanding of the nature of subjectivity leads to a severe incoherence in his perspective which derives from the fact that he assumes fully 'collapsed', fully materially solidified items of recording apparatus can be coherently placed, even if only theoretically, within a wavefunction. However such fully materialised items are not the kind of entities which can be located coherently into the realm of the wavefunction. This is the kind of conceptual picture which conflates together two levels, or aspects, of ontology that cannot, as matter of conceptual coherence, coexist in the manner that they are required to for the proper functioning of the theoretical picture as a coherent conceptual model of reality.

This kind of conceptual confusion had been highlighted in 1949 by the philosopher Gilbert Ryle, in his book *The Concept of Mind*. The conflation of the concepts belonging to the material realm and those of the mental, Ryle said, was a 'category mistake' which occurs when philosophers talk about mind and matter as if they were "... terms of the same logical type". The difference in logical type is quite clear. Wavefunctions are types of entities which 'wf-exist', or 'semi-exist', prior to their 'collapse'. Recording machines, on the other hand, lie on the other side of the quantum existential divide. Ryle referred to the misconception of minds residing, as if they were material entities, in bodies, as the category mistake of the 'ghost in the machine'; in the case of Everett's proposal we are presented with the category mistake of the 'machine in the ghost!'

Everett is very confused about exactly what he considers to be 'physical'. It must be bourn in mind that prior to Everett's analysis, and indeed his analysis did not actually change attitudes much in this respect, the physical world was generally considered to be represented by the familiar realm of people and houses (fig 8.6) whilst the realm of the wavefunction was considered to occupy a ghostly semi-existence. Its 'physical' reality was somewhat ambiguous. Everett, however, blithely asserts that:

> The wavefunction is taken as the basic physical entity with no *a priori interpretation*. Interpretation only comes *after* an investigation of the logical structure of the theory.[470]

This is indeed a bold, and exciting, step; but Everett does not adhere to his own admonishments. In the very next paragraph we read that:

> For any interpretation it is necessary to put the mathematical model of the theory into correspondence with experience. For this purpose it is necessary to formulate abstract models for observers that can be treated as physical systems ... [471]

The notion of the nature of the 'physical' hovers and embraces two realms whereas logically speaking it should, in the absence of further elucidation, be allocated to one of the realms as shown in fig 8.6. If it is to be allocated to both then an explanation is required as to the nature of the two realms and their interaction. All this detail, however, is ignored.

The kind of 'physical' systems that Everett introduces into his theoretical model are not wavefunctions, which are actually conceptually required by his new allocation of the concept of 'physical', but they are fully fledged and paid up members of the realm of people and houses. If we are to take this conceptual arrangement seriously then Everett has already solved the problem of the collapse of the wavefunction because in his model there is no difference either side of the quantum divide, the quantum divide has been bridged by a conceptual sleight of mind; he has produced the illusion of a solution through the judicious misallocation of conceptual boundaries.

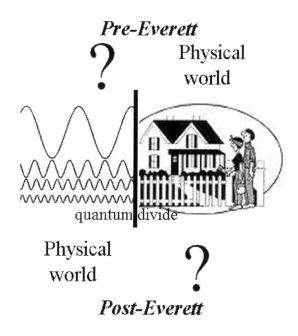

Pre-Everett

Post-Everett

Fig 8.6

At this point it should be quite clear that the conceptual surroundings of Everett's work are seriously compromised by a complete disregard for logical boundaries. The problem arises simply because of a desire to impose a solution onto a mathematical description of the functioning of reality without overdue, if any, regard for conceptual coherence. This is a weakness which seems endemic within the quantum physics community, they allow themselves latitude of conceptual fantasy they would never entertain, or perhaps could not entertain, when actually doing mathematics. Trying to devise a convincing and coherent interpretation of abstruse mathematical equations in the midst of conceptual confusion certainly leaves the coast clear for the concocting of entertaining vistas of science fantasy.

The only way of visualising Everett's proposal which maintains consistency and coherency is to conceive of the overall wavefunction, which Everett proposes to treat as the sole 'physical reality', as itself containing component subjective wavefunctions superposed within it. In particular it contains an overall objective aspect and a multitude of subjective wavefunctions which interact with the objective aspect to produce a profusion of experiential continuums; and experiential continuums, of course, can only have a coherent location within a field of consciousness.

According to Tegmark's presentation what the frog, which is moving inside the wavefunction of reality, sees as 'particles' moving and interacting in space and time the external soaring bird, which is not confined within the internal process of the wavefunction, sees as various forms of continuous 'spaghetti':

> If the frog sees a particle moving with constant velocity, the bird sees a straight strand of uncooked spaghetti. If the frog sees a pair of orbiting particles, the bird sees two spaghetti strands intertwined like a double helix.[472]

This way of viewing the situation relates to Bohm's example of the 'particle' which unfolds from the glycerin cylinders as the paddle is turned (see last chapter). Using Tegmark's image the frog represents a subjective centre of experience which is moving inside the wavefunction and, through the interaction produced by the movement, 'unfolds' the illusion of material particles from out of the stuff of the wavefunction. The bird, on the other hand, is outside the process and so sees just the movement taking place within the wavefunction without experiencing the results of the internal interaction. Tegmark then goes on to tell us that:

> The frog itself is merely a thick bundle of pasta, whose highly complex intertwining corresponds to a cluster of particles that store and process information.[473]

This means that a sentient being, and there are a vast number of them, is trapped, like the frog, inside the wavefunction, and can be thought of as a wavefunction substructure which, from the frog perspective, moves through the overall wavefunction and in so doing unfolds into experiential reality the potentialities within the wavefunction. It took the genius of Everett, Tegmark tells us:

> ... to realise that a single deterministically evolving wavefunction ... contains within it a vast number of frog perspectives where certain events appear to occur randomly.[474]

To be more precise, however, we must say that there are a vast number of frog perspectives, dog perspectives, cat perspectives, bird perspectives, fish perspectives, human perspectives and so on within the universal wavefunction. In fact each sentient being is a 'subjective' substructure moving, in fact cycling, through the universal wavefunction, or the matrix of reality.

The universal wavefunction is timeless:

> The Wheeler-DeWitt equation therefore appears to be telling us that ... the universe as a whole is frozen in time![475]

Furthermore:

> From a God's-eye view, we can suppose, there is just a timeless universal state, which consists of a vast entangled superposition ... of states of subsystems of the universe. In these entangled super-

positions, however, observables of certain subsystems of the universe are correlated with observables of other systems.[476]

It is these 'subsystems of the universe' which are sentient beings, the agents through which the universe perceives its own potentialities and creates the flow of time within the dualistic realms of existence. In other words all sentient beings are agents through which the potentialities of the universal wavefunction of reality are unfolded. This is what Buddhist philosophy refers to as *samsara*, the endless cycle of conditioned and interdependent existence, which is driven by the causal resonance mechanism of karma-vipaka, intentional actions or movements of consciousness and the subsequent effects (fig 8.7).

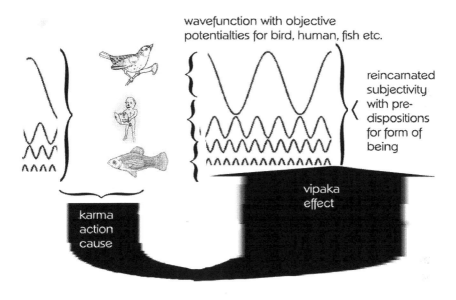

Fig 8.7

Henry Stapp indicates a similar overall perspective (although by no means sharing my interpretation[477]):

>...the quantum universe tends to create meaning: the quantum law of evolution continuously creates a vast ensemble of forms that can act as carriers of meaning; it generates a profusion of forms that have the capacity to sustain and refine themselves.[478]

David Bohm also drew a similar conclusion from his understanding of quantum theory:

...each entity is continually being formed from the infinite background and falls back into the background; to be generated again and again ... Thus each thing has its roots in the totality and falls back into the totality. Yet it still remains a thing having a certain degree of independent being. And this is possible because each thing contains in itself, its own special image of the totality (cosmos) out of which it formed itself and into which it is always dissolving (and reforming).[479]

What Bohm refers to as an 'own special image of the totality', which each entity appears to possess, Buddhism calls the illusion of a personal self and the illusion of the phenomenal self. The illusion of the personal self applies to the deep seated feeling of personal self-sufficient and independent existence that all sentient beings experience, and the illusion of the phenomenal self applies to the appearance that the entities that appear to be external and independent of our own beings also have there own self-enclosed inherent separateness. These are both 'illusions' precisely because there is no phenomenon in reality which 'inherently exists' as its own independent entity separate from the totality. All phenomena are 'empty' of inherent existence; the sense of selfhood is, rather, a reflection of the unified nature of the totality out of which all phenomena emerge, which is from the quantum perspective the universal wavefunction.

The following discussion, which goes a little deeper into the details of Everett's analysis, is based on Everett's thesis but the maths is defused and simplified as much as humanly possible by presenting it in a somewhat cavalier graphical format, whilst hopefully still conveying a flavour of Everett's presentation.

Each experiential continuum is made up of a sequence of 'observations'. Each observation, Everett states in his thesis:

...consists of an interaction which ... transforms each (total) state

$$y^{S+O} = f_I \, y^O[...]$$

into a new state

$$y^{S+O'} = f_I \, y^O[..a_i]$$

where a_i characterizes the state f_I . ... That is, we require the system state ... shall be unchanged, and that the observer state shall change so as to describe an observer that is 'aware' ..., some property is recorded in the memory of the observer which characterizes f_I, ...[480]

The first equation is the initial situation before any actual observations of the system takes place. The 'system', which is indicated by the superscript 'S', is made up of an objective wavefunction which contains a superposed set of possibilities; these are represented by f_I, where the subscript $\mathbf{i}=1,2,3, \ldots$, counts up to the number of possibilities in the wavefunction. The 'observer', which is indicated by the superscript '^{O}' has an empty memory which is represented by [...]. Figure 8.9 (overleaf) shows this diagrammatically. The situation after an interaction between the 'system' and the 'observer is shown in figure 8.10 in which the observers memory contains a trace of the experiences of the observation. The observers 'memory', therefore now contains traces of the experience $[..a_i]$. This process should be further elucidated by looking at fig 8.8:

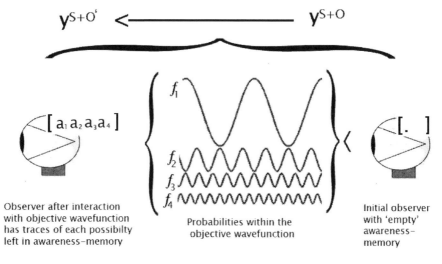

Fig 8.8

The first $\mathbf{y}^{S+O}$ represents the combined state of the observed system and the observer prior to the observation being made. The observer then does the observing, which means that we can imagine the observer's consciousness moving through the possible experiences $f_1, f_2, f_3, f_4, \ldots$ which are contained within the system wavefunction. $\mathbf{Y}^O$ is the observer and [...] simply represents the observer's awareness and memory, which at the outset is empty. The second equation represents the situation after the observation has been performed. According to Everett's presentation the system state is not changed but the observer's awareness-memory state is changed by the traces left by the interaction with the potentialities within the objective system, so a dash is added to the superscript $\mathbf{O}$ to represent this - $\mathbf{y}^{S+O'}$, and on the other side of the equals sign the observers 'memory' now has a memory, so it is now represented by $[..a_i]$, where $\mathbf{a_i}$ represents the traces left in the observer's memory.

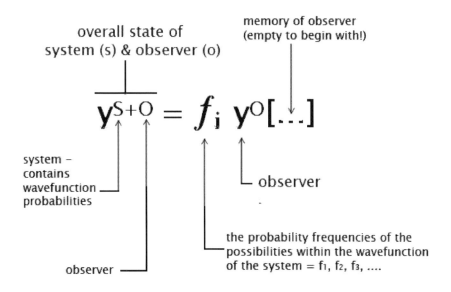

Fig 8.9 – before observation

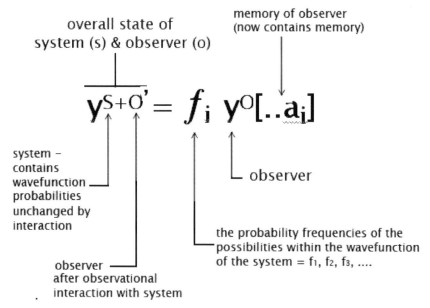

Fig 8.10 – after observation

The essential point to be gleaned here is that the interaction of the observed objective system wavefunction, which is assumed as being not changed by the interaction, and the subjective observing wavefunction, which is changed by the interaction, leaves a trace, or memory, a_i, which 'characterises' the objective state f_I that is contained within the possibility states within the system wavefunction. Thus we have the picture of a 'subjective' centre of experiencing, which is itself a wavefunction, which 'moves' within the overall 'objective' wavefunction, and in so doing produces a continuum of experience. Everett uses the term 'trajectory' for the path of experience which is trodden, so to speak:

> The 'trajectory' of the memory configuration of an observer performing a sequence of measurements is thus not a linear sequence of memory configurations but a branching tree, with all possible outcomes existing simultaneously in the final superposition...[481]

So according to Everett a subjective *experiencing* wavefunction of consciousness divides into a superposition and 'branches' between the various paths supplied by the field of possible experience (f_i) contained within the system wavefunction (fig 8.11). As a result the subjective wavefunction emerges (on the left of the diagram) as a composite wavefunction which has components corresponding to the various 'paths' travelled. For each path, each of which corresponds with a different f_I, the memory of the component contains a trace a_i that 'characterizes the state f_I' is left in memory.

In this version, which is Everett's original formulation, the many branches within the 'memory' of a single observer comprise a complex subjective superposed wavefunction. This was how Everett left his analysis in his thesis and, as a consequence of its lack of complete elucidation it was an 'interpretation' which still awaited a thorough interpretation; the full-blown 'many-worlds' flavour was proposed by Bryce DeWitt in 1971.

The theoretical picture of an interaction of subjective and objective wavefunctions within an overall universal wavefunction provides the basic framework for the Everettian analysis. It is a fundamental perspective that H. Dieter Zeh has lyrically characterised by quoting the Greek philosopher Anaxagoras:

> The things that are in a single world are not parted from one another, not cut away with an axe, neither the warm from the cold nor the cold from the warm. When Mind began to set things in motion, separation took place from each thing that was being moved, and all that Mind moved was separated.[482]

In other words it is the movement of the subjective wavefunctions of 'Mind' within the overall wavefunction of realty that produces the many possible

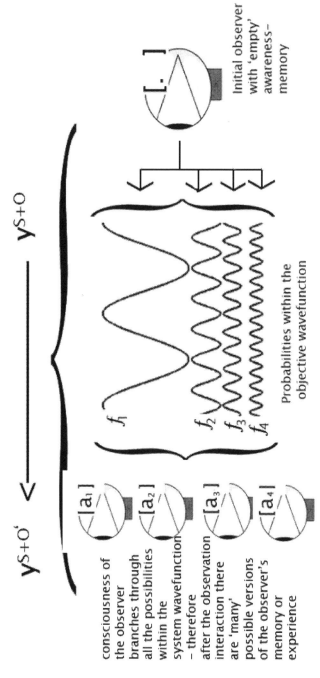

Fig 8.11

experiential continuums that it contains. For Everett, DeWitt, Dieter Zeh, Wojciech Zurek and others the wavefunction and its internal processes must be considered as fundamental for our understanding of reality. As Zeh says:

However you turn it: *In the beginning was the wavefunction.*[483]

And, of course, this can only mean that: in the beginning was Mind, or awareness-consciousness, a viewpoint that is completely in accord with the Buddhist Mind-Only perspective:

> Those nonexistent phenomena do appear,
> But neither from matter, nor from something other,
> Nor from non-existence, …
> Therefore they have the very identity of consciousness.
>
> It is taught that consciousness arises
> As something that is the opposite of the nature of matter.
> What is immaterial in nature
> Is asserted here to be suitable as the very identity of phenomena.
>
> Space, earth, wind, sun,
> The oceanside, and waterfalls
> Are aspects of the true, internal consciousness
> That appear as if being something external.
>
> Since both subjects and objects appear as having the nature of lucidity,
> Their connection is not something hidden.
> Since that which is aware is connected
> To the objects to be aware of, it is aware of them….
>
> Since clear appearances and mind have a connection
> Of identity, the former are mere referents.
> The nature of consciousness is real,
> But the aspects of perceiver and perceived are delusive and mistaken.[484]

These stanzas begin with a reference to the argument that demonstrates the impossibility of the existence of externally separate and independent 'material' entities. It follows that, despite their illusory appearance as external and independent entities, they can only be of a nature that is the opposite of matter, i.e. consciousness. It is important to be aware here that the term 'matter' refers to the apparent appearance of solidly which seems external to experience. The awareness-consciousness underlying the appearance of the experiential polarity of perceiver and perceived, or subject and object, is the fundamental unitary ground of lucidity that provides the ground for the possibility of such appearances; and the appearance of subject and object within its field is 'delusive and mistaken.' This is to say that the appearance of these two aspects as cut off and separate is mistaken, they are essentially the same entity. This illusion arises, of course, from movements within the wavefunction of reality.

The view that the process of reality is cogently represented by the image of the movements of subjectivities within an encompassing wavefunction of reality, movements which produces manifold worlds of experience, is fundamental to the Quantum Mind-Only worldview. Hopkins provides the following characterisation of the Mind-Only perspective:

> Although objects are not established by way of their own character as the referents of terms or of conceptual consciousnesses and although subject and object are not different entities, they appear even in raw sensation to be so established. Due to assenting to this seeming status, beings are drawn into afflictive emotions - misconceiving themselves and others to be substantially established in the sense of being self-sufficient and then, as a consequence of this, generating desire, hatred, confusion, enmity, jealousy, and so forth. These afflictive emotions, in turn, result in actions, which establish potencies in the mind that keep beings bound to cyclic existence.[485]

Here we see that the mistaken sense of being a separate 'self' embedded within a seemingly real realm of duality generates the very conditions which keep the cycle of manifestation active. This is a crucial feature of the Buddhist version of the Many-Worlds scenario.

The observation that objects are not established by way of their own characters, which means that they do not exist separately, independently or inherently, together with the assertion that subject and object are not different entities, correlates to a observation that Everett makes in his thesis:

> The mathematics leads one to recognize the concept of the *relativity of states*, in the following sense: a constituent subsystem cannot be said to be in any single well defined state, independently of the remainder of the composite system. To any arbitrary chosen state for one subsystem there will correspond a unique *relative state* for the remainder of the composite system. ... Thus the state of one system does not have an independent existence...[486]

The relative state analysis of reality, conceived of as a process of interacting subjective and objective wavefunctions taking place within the context of an overarching wavefunction of reality, clearly recapitulates core insights from the Buddhist Mind Only analysis of the functioning of reality:

> [The mind's] oneness appears as duality
> Due to its in every respect very ingenious
> Split between perceiver and perceived.

Since the perceived aspect is indifferent,
It looks as if it were outside,
But since the perceiving aspect throbs vehemently,
It seems as if it were inside.[487]

This can be compared to the part of Everett's analysis which indicates that the objective aspect of the apparent division within the wavefunction is relatively stable when compared to the experience of the subjective aspect:

> The requirement that the eigenstates for the system be unchanged is necessary if the observation is to be significant (repeatable), and the requirement that the observer change in a manner which is different for each eigenfunction is necessary if we are to be able to call the interaction an observation at all. [488]

The terms 'eigenstates' and 'eigenfunction' are mathematical terms which need not be elucidated, the terms 'states' and 'observation' can be adequately substituted to get the required meaning. The fact that Atisha's metaphoric characterisation, as when he refers to the perceiving aspect which 'throbs vehemently' for instance, is a little less clinical than Everett's should not blind us to the significance. The contents of the subjective awareness are constantly changing, thus leading to the characterisation that subjective awareness 'throbs vehemently', whilst the 'objective' aspect of the perceptual process remains relatively stable.

Furthermore, as Hopkins indicates, the subjective aspect of this process, which is an individuated mind, does not just throb passively within its subjectivity, it actively seeks experiences of a dualistic nature through the generation of 'desire, hatred, confusion, enmity, jealousy, and so forth' and thereafter performs actions which leave traces within the overall process; it is these traces which are responsible for the continuation of the entire mechanism of 'cyclic existence.' This additional aspect of the situation provides an avenue for understanding the process as a self-creating and self-sustaining mechanism suggested by Wheeler.

The visionary physicist Jack Sarfatti considered that a self-referring and self-structuring mechanism lies at the heart of the process of reality:

> …only when such a *strange loop of Gödel self-reference* is operating, is there an experience of one actual world. This is a Bohmian ontological model that derives from Wigner's and von-Neumann's epistemological idea that 'consciousness collapses the wavefunction'. The strange loop means that the mind-brain complex adaptive system is constantly measuring itself. Only then, is there the inner 'felt' experience of 'qualia'. This is the quantum dynamo generating our streams of consciousness.[489]

The reference to the 'strange loop of Gödel self-reference' indicates a similarity of the self reference situation to a famous mathematical demonstration by which the logician Kurt Gödel showed, by constructing a mathematical 'sentence' which referred to itself, that mathematics was not as conceptually watertight as had previously been supposed. The essential point in this observation is that 'the experience of one actual world' requires a 'strange loop' within consciousness which allows consciousness to measure, modify or solidify its own experiential field of awareness.[490]

David Bohm proposed the view that there is an implicate order which 'enfolds' the patterns of reality. When these patterns 'unfold' into the realm of experience, through a quantum process, the explicate order of experienced reality manifests. Sarfatti's perspective extends the idea of the implicate order proposed by Bohm; he adds into the picture of the interaction the notion of 'back-action' which he says is a 'peculiar property of consciousness'.[491] According to the specific model proposed by Sarfatti the fundamental process of reality involves an interaction between a 'field of thought patterns', denoted by the symbol $\mathbf{I(x,t)}$, the (x,t) indicates that the actual nature of the pattern depends on position and time, and an external field of 'external environmental forces', denoted by $\mathbf{F_e}$. Sarfatti considers that the environmental field $\mathbf{F_e}$, operates as if classical in nature and he goes so far as to identify it with 'Darwinian natural selection pressures of the environment'. The patterns of the thought field $\mathbf{I(x,t)}$ exert a quantum force field, denoted by $\mathbf{F_q}$ which interacts with the environmental force field $\mathbf{F_e}$ to produce a further field of possible experience $\mathbf{C}$. Sarfatti's theoretical thought model of the process of reality, then, requires 'subjective' and 'objective' fields of possibility to interact in order to produce a further field of possibility for experience $\mathbf{C}$.

According to Sarfatti when the quantum field of the brain $\mathbf{B}$ 'moves' through a path inside $\mathbf{C}$ 'felt' experiences arise and there is also a 'back-action' which acts to modify $\mathbf{I(x,t)}$. In one exposition of his viewpoint Sarfatti tells us that back-action is 'matter acting back on the wavefunction'. This means that the experiential resonance which gives rise to the appearance of the material world acts back and thereby leaves a trace, or modifies $\mathbf{I(x,t)}$. *$I(x,t)$, therefore, corresponds exactly to the Mind-Only alayavijnana.* Sarfatti describes this process as:

> Therefore, $\mathbf{F_q}$ $\mathbf{F_e}$ from $\mathbf{I(x,t)}$ to $\mathbf{B}$, together with back-action $\mathbf{b}$ from $\mathbf{B}$ to $\mathbf{I(x,t)}$, is a self-organising cybernetic feedback-control creative strange loop that creates the conscious experience and allows the $\mathbf{I\text{-}B}$ system to make free-willed choices...[492]

The schematic diagram fig. 8.12 adds the Sarfatti's strange loop into the presentation of Everett's perspective which has been outlined so far. The process of what Sarfatti calls back-action, the strange loop which enables the creative process within consciousness to turn back, and modify itself, he considers to be fundamental in the process of reality:

> Back-action is the universal physical mechanism for life. What happens is that the self-measuring system self-organises its wave-function so that it splits into non overlapping wave packets. That is the system creates its own measuring observable ... in a self consistent way and then chooses which channel to occupy. This is free will. Only conscious systems can do this trick. Without back-action beyond orthodox quantum theory there is never an effective collapse into one actual world.[493]

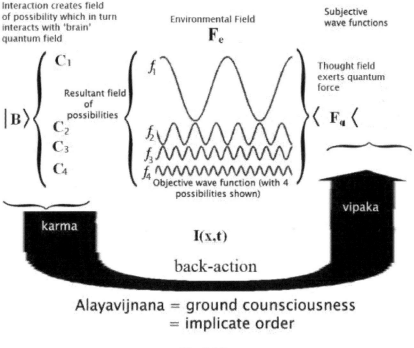

Fig 8.12

According to Sarfatti, therefore, consciousness is able to *choose* 'one actual world' from the many possibilities by an act of 'free will.'

Sarfatti's characterisation of the fundamental mechanism of life is extremely significant; according to Sarfatti's insight the self-measuring capability within consciousness is able to separate itself out into viable 'possible worlds' before 'collapsing', through the exercise of 'free will', into one of them. Given the fact that there will be a multitude of subjective wavefunctions waiting to collapse into possible worlds, this mechanism indicates a route towards a coherent theory of how a choice of the many worlds of manifestation, from amongst the many worlds of possibility, comes about. The extent to which this is a matter of 'free will', however, will be restricted as most of this process will take place at level deep beneath individual levels of awareness.

Sarfatti's viewpoint requires that the environmental field $\mathbf{F_e}$ is relatively unchanging; it is the environmental constraint which imposes limits upon the possibilities which can be occupied by the potentialities within subjective thought fields. However, we must allow the back action to impinge upon both these aspects. The back-action envisaged by Sarfatti must apply to both the 'subjective' and 'objective' aspects as shown in fig 8.13. The impact upon the environment field, which is a collective wavefunction built up by countless consciousnesses, however, will not be as great as that upon the species and individual aspect which is embodied in $\mathbf{F_q}$.

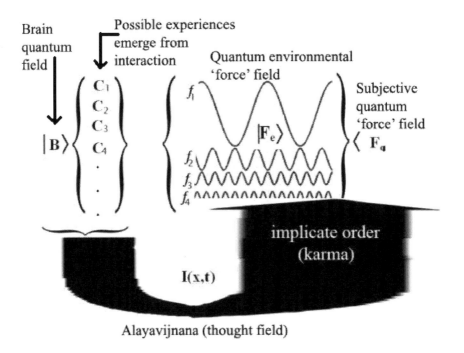

Fig 8.13

The realm of 'matter', which is actually 'solidified' mind, which 'acts back' is the manifested world of the everyday life of apparent, but illusory, material solidity interacting with the perceptions and actions of embodied sentient beings within it. It is the activities, actions and processes within this embodied realm that must provide the impetus for Sarfatti's back-action. In other words the actions that sentient beings perform within this material realm will affect the unmanifested wavefunction, which is Bohm's implicate order. It is in this way that the potentialities for future manifestation are 'enfolded' into the implicate order.

We can see, then, that Sarfatti's back-action is an action, due to perceptions and actions within the manifested world, of the manifested world 'back' upon the domain of the wavefunction from which it manifested. This back action, however, is not necessarily backward in time. Sarfatti says that his model is:

> ...globally self consistent in time of circular co-evolving cause and effect...[494]

And this, of course, is nothing else but the universal cause and effect mechanism of karma and dependent origination. Fig 8.14 shows how Sarfatti's 'back-action' actually operates as a forward patterning in time which lays down the potentialities for future experience. Viewed from this more natural perspective within time, the self-referring strange loop that drives the process of reality can be seen to be driven by a process in which latent tendencies laid down within the wavefunction at one point in time are later activated. This Wheeler-Bohm-Stapp-Everett-Sarfatti perspective[495] completely harmonises with and harmoniously completes the Quantum-Mind-Only metaphysical model of the process of the 'strange loop' of self-reference and self creation which lies at the heart of reality.

There is another way of deducing this metaphysical perspective of the functioning of reality which starts from DeWitt's exposition of the Everett Many-Worlds interpretation in his essay *The Everett interpretation of quantum mechanics*[496]. In the following derivation, which subjects DeWitt's formulation of the fundamental Schrödinger equation to some mathematical indignities with its graphical approach, we will derive the Buddhist wheel of samsara and quantum Darwinian evolution!

The overall quantum system is to be considered as being composed of a measured part of the system and a measuring apparatus, which should actually be a subjective awareness, which are 'coupled' together. For the moment we will allow DeWitt to treat the 'measuring apparatuses' as robotic recording devices with memories. In the following equation Ψ is the overall wavefunction, s represents individual states of the system and φ represents the states of the (subjective) measuring apparatus relative to the measured state of the system. DeWitt's version of the Schrödinger equation which leads to his assertion of the many-worlds hypothesis is:

$$|\Psi\rangle = \Sigma_s \, C_s \, |s\rangle \, |\varphi[s]\rangle$$

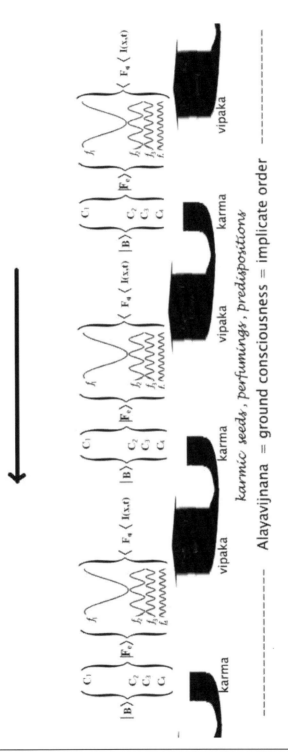

Fig 7.14

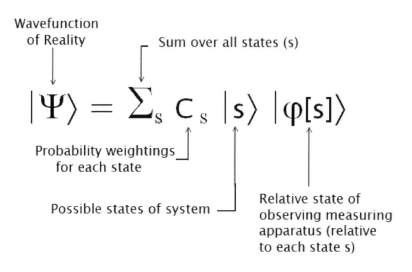

Fig 7.15

The elements of this equation may be read as follows: $|\Psi\rangle$ is the overall wavefunction which is a superposition of a set of component states $|s\rangle$, each of which is 'coupled' to a 'relative state' of an 'observing' measuring apparatus $|\varphi[s]\rangle$. Each of the individual states contained in $|s\rangle$ represents a possible state of the 'objective' wavefunction of the system and each of these possible states has an associated probability C_s. Each of the individual wavefunctions $|\varphi[s]\rangle$ represents the state of the measuring apparatus relative to the measured state of the system. The symbol Σ_s is an instruction to take the sum, or add up, all the individual components. DeWitt explains that this equation:

> ...shows that relative to each system state $|s\rangle$ the apparatus, as a result of the coupling, 'goes into' a corresponding state $|\varphi[s]\rangle$.[497]

The vital point here is that it is the measuring apparatus, the subjective awareness, which 'goes into' a state relative to the measured state of the system (fig 8.15). The implications actually contained within the equation can be illustrated as shown in fig 8.16. The description offered by DeWitt includes:

> ...it is useful to speak of the apparatus as having a *memory*; represented by the bracket [s] in the symbol $|\varphi[s]\rangle$ in which the measurement is stored.[498]

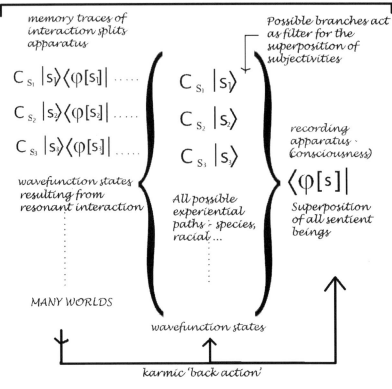

$$|\Psi\rangle$$

memory traces of
interaction splits
apparatus

Possible branches act
as filter for the
superposition of
subjectivities

$$C_{S_1}\,|s_1\rangle\langle\varphi[s_1]|\,\cdots\cdots$$

$$C_{S_2}\,|s_2\rangle\langle\varphi[s_2]|\,\cdots\cdots$$

$$C_{S_3}\,|s_3\rangle\langle\varphi[s_3]|\,\cdots\cdots$$

$$C_{S_1}\,|s_1\rangle$$

$$C_{S_2}\,|s_2\rangle$$

$$C_{S_3}\,|s_3\rangle$$

wavefunction states
resulting from
resonant interaction

recording
apparatus ·
(consciousness)

$$\langle\varphi[s]|$$

All possible
experiential
paths - species,
racial ...

Superposition
of all sentient
beings

MANY WORLDS

wavefunction states

karmic 'back action'

Fig 8.16

Of course, as our previous analysis of the desperate conceptual confusion contained in Everett's original thesis has taught us, the 'measuring apparatus' actually represents subjective awareness and, following Tegmark's correct presentation of the situation, there is actually a vast, in fact countless, number of such subjectivities, as many as there are sentient beings. If we are considering the wavefunction of reality then, as we clearly are, the symbol $|\varphi[s]\rangle$ (which is reversed for graphic convenience; the reversal does not indicate, as it should normally, complex conjugation) can only consist of a superposition of the subjective wavefunctions of all sentient beings. It would seem to be reasonable therefore to hazard a guess, then, that one of the filtering levels that the 'branches' contained within the 'objective' aspect of the overall wavefunction organise, by 'sorting' the incoming subjective superposition of sentient beings, is into the appropriate species branch. This would mean that the objective wavefunction performs its filtering function on multiple levels: species, racial, then higher collective levels (levels of Jung's archetypal collective unconscious for instance) and finally individual, this final level being the level on which some degree of 'free will' is operative. And a further implication is that at this higher individual level free will can have effect upon the resonant filtering process, which means that 'free will' will have an effect, albeit unimaginably tiny, on the entire process of the resonant cycle of the functioning of the wavefunction of reality.

We now imagine that the subjective superposition of sentient beings moves to engage the set of possible states within the 'objective' portion of the wavefunction, enclosed within {} brackets. As the subjective 'apparatus' moves through the body of the objective wavefunction it 'splits' into experiential continuums, on the left hand side, according to the paths, which are dictated by the states within the wavefunction. The states within the wavefunction act as a kind of filter, although in this provisional depiction of the Everett view nothing is filtered out. This filter is constituted by the possible branches of the objective wavefunction which divides the subjective aspect of the global wavefunction of reality into the various paths according to the internal states of the wavefunction. The resulting 'worlds' are actually subjective experiential continuums.

The most pervasively known presentation of the many-worlds 'interpretation' of quantum theory is the version in which it is asserted that all sentient beings are continuously splitting into new 'copies' of themselves, each of which are supposed to inhabit new 'parallel universes.' This is the science-fiction inspired 'hardcore' vision of the implications of quantum theory. One of the issues that the hardcore multiple-worlds scenario is incapable of accounting for, however, is the appearance and significance of the probabilities within the wavefunction. In the announcement details of a recent conference (2007) held in order to discuss such points of contention within the Everettian fold the following issue was singled out as being significantly problematic for the many-worlds viewpoint:

> A deeper question still is what it means, or could possibly mean, to ascribe a probability to experimental outcomes in an interpretation in which – in some sense – every possible outcome is realised.[499]

If each possible world manifests once then it would make sense for the probability associated with each world to be the same. As this is not the case it appears that some worlds are more real than others, so to speak. In fact such an 'interpretation' has been suggested:

> Although all the worlds are of the same physical size ... and in every world sentient beings feel as 'real' as in any other world, in some sense some worlds are larger than others. I describe this property as the measure of existence of a world.[500]

In other words in order to fix this philosophical problem it is suggested that it makes sense to make up out of the blue a completely fictitious, and completely unmeasurable, property. On the other hand, it is possible, but highly unlikely, that worlds with greater probability are duplicated more often than others. If this were the case then not only would there be other universes in which you decided to do something different, there would be some in which you were doing exactly the same thing. It is when the details are fully explored that the orthodox Many-Worlds fantasy begins to look decidedly unlikely, in any possible world.

There is, however, another way of interpreting the situation which begins to include the probabilities as a natural part of the situation in accordance with the 'quantum karma' perspective developed in the previous chapter. This perspective, schematically indicated in figure 8.17, leads to some extremely fertile insights. In this scenario the states of the objective wavefunction perform a function of both reduction and amplification. Subjective components which interact weakly with objective states will be reduced in size and will eventually filter out of the subjective wavefunction superposition. Subjective components which interact strongly will be amplified.

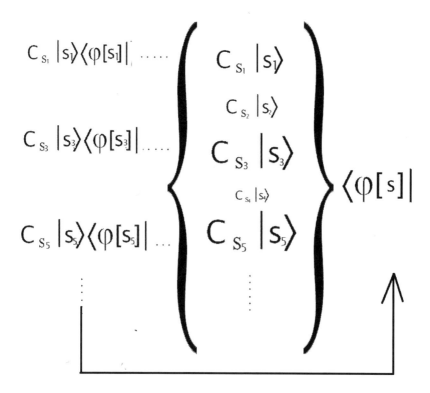

Fig 8.17

The size of the state representations within the {} are shown as being proportional to their probabilities (represented by the C_s terms – the letters and symbols have been adopted following DeWitt[501]). For components of the subjective wavefunction which are allowed through the filtering process they will be amplified according to the probability of the corresponding state within the objective wavefunction. The use of the mathematical symbolism in these schematic representations of the process is slightly cavalier. However this view of the process is actually in keeping with what should be actually occurring within the mathematical equation:

$$|\Psi\rangle = \Sigma_s \, \mathbf{C}_s \, |\mathbf{s}\rangle \, |\varphi[\mathbf{s}]\rangle$$

This is because the probability terms should obviously contribute to the way that the resultant wavefunction $|\Psi\rangle$ is constructed. If this were not the case there would be no point in the $\mathbf{C}_s$ terms, representing the probabilities, being in the equation.

We can now see that the subjective entity on the right ($\langle\varphi[\mathbf{S}]|$) can be viewed as a subjective wavefunction which is a superposition of all the $\langle\varphi[\mathbf{S}_i]|$ terms emerging from the left of the {}:

$$\langle\varphi[\mathbf{S}]| = \langle\varphi[\mathbf{S}_1]| \, \mathbf{x} \, \langle\varphi[\mathbf{S}_2]| \, \mathbf{x} \, \langle\varphi[\mathbf{S}_3]| \, \mathbf{x} \, \ldots..$$

So fig 8.17 shows one link in a continuous chain which is shown in fig 8.18 (moving from right to left):

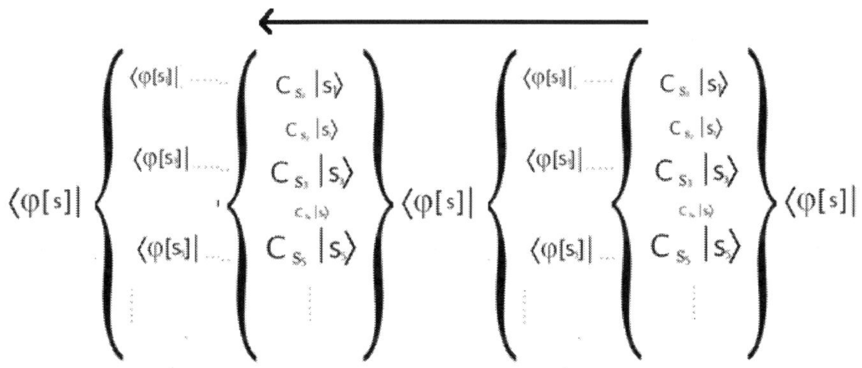

Fig 8.18

Every interaction between the measuring subjective entity and the environmental system wavefunction will perform a filtering or amplifying function. Thus through successive filtering cycles, causing reductions and amplifications, certain aspects of the wavefunctions, both subjective and objective, are either reinforced or annihilated; it's a bit like evolution really. In fact *it is evolution at the quantum level.*

Furthermore the fact that there is a reduction and amplification process in the continuous interaction implies a self-referring resonant system as shown in fig 8.19. The new superposition of the various subjective continuums is formed from the wavefunction addition of all the components that emerge from the previous cycle. And similarly the probabilities within the objective wavefunction, which forms the 'filter' for the subjective aspect of the process, are altered by the interactive process. This is the mechanism which underlies this self-referring and self-regulating process of the many-worlds system of reality which is clearly analogous with the earlier model which was developed from the insights of Everett, Bohm, Wheeler, Stapp and Sarfatti.

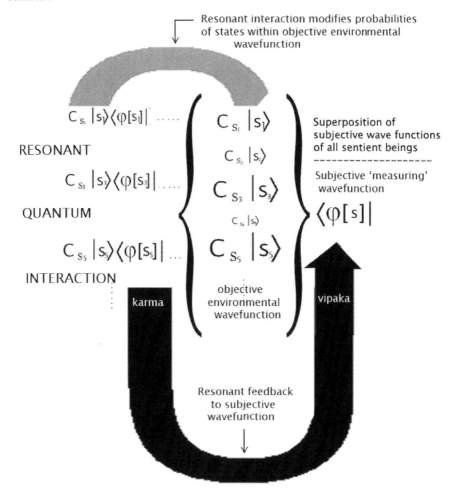

Fig 8.19

A crucial feature of this new perspective upon the many-worlds scenario is that it brings the proposal back from the extreme speculative and totally unsubstantiated realms of wild science fantasy, which has absolutely no explanatory relevance for the world that we actually do inhabit, back into exactly that, the world that we do inhabit. There are indeed many worlds, in fact many levels of many worlds, actually within our very own world. A very obvious example is the various different species of living beings. Although the many worlds perspective has not figured exactly very highly in the discussion of the evolutionary contribution of the quantum realm this is hardly surprising as the study of quantum evolutionary theory is in its infancy. But the fact that this kind of evolutionary process takes place at the quantum level is clearly suggested by a brief discussion in Barrow and Tippler's exposition of the many-worlds perspective:

> However, it is essential for the sensory apparatus of a living organism to record appropriate eigenstates correctly if the organism is to survive. ... Ultimately it is natural selection that determines that the senses will record that an object is in an eigenstate only if in fact it is. Natural selection even determines what eigenstates are the appropriate ones to measure ...[502]

Thus we see how an appreciation of the structure of the fundamental quantum equation contains the idea that the evolutionary process lays down the tracks at the quantum level for the development of the experiential continuums of the various species in interaction with the co-interdependent development of the objective environmental wavefunction. This is Darwinian evolution at the quantum level. The 'eigenstates' are the states that persist; they are templates for the structuring of the quantum level, structures which manifest as the diversity of the evolutionary process at the classical level. These templates clearly correspond to Sheldrake's *morphogenetic fields*, which Sheldrake identifies as quantum 'probability structures'[503].

This view of the implications of Everett's thesis, in which each sentient being is considered to occupy one of the many possible worlds which have their locus within a common universe, contrasts dramatically which the usual popular view of the many worlds perspective within which all sentient beings find themselves in the bizarre existential crisis of continuously 'splitting' into a vast number of copies of 'themselves'. University of Pennsylvania physicist Max Tegmark presents the following characterisation of Everett's viewpoint:

> In his 1957 Ph.D. thesis, Princeton student Hugh Everett III showed that this controversial collapse postulate was unnecessary. Quantum theory predicted that one classical reality would gradually split into superpositions of many. He showed that observers would subjectively experience this splitting merely as a slight

randomness, and indeed with probabilities in exact agreement with those from the old collapse postulate. ... This superposition of classical worlds is the ... multiverse.[504]

In order to illustrate the concept of the 'multiverse' as seemingly classical worlds or universes splitting into many other independent classical worlds or universes Tegmark supplies a picture of a cartoon strip which splits into two further strips along one of the frames (Fig 8.20).

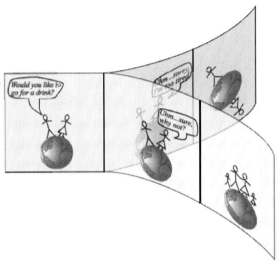

Fig 8.20

It is appropriate that Tegmark presents his extreme, yet widely prominent, view of the many-worlds version of the Everett proposal, in which all sentient beings divide into copies of themselves at every moment in time, as a cartoon. The acuity of conceptual analysis and philosophical perspicacity which is exhibited by those who assent to the caricature presentation of the many-worlds thesis is just about worthy of cartoon characters. The fascination and the frisson that accompanies a general reader's comprehension of most presentations of the many-worlds perspective derives from the use of astonishingly imprecise, loose and impressionistic, and thereby misleading, techniques of elucidation. This tendency certainly pervades all popular science writing but also, as is illustrated in the case of Tegmark's description, which occurs in a supposedly scholarly article, clearly extends to less popularist works.

An example of such dubious methods of exposition is supplied by Tegmark's assertion that Everett 'showed that observers would subjectively experience this splitting merely as a slight randomness'; a claim that stretches credulity towards impossible worlds. Most of the Western academic world, even today, is convinced that consciousness is a desperate mystery beyond the ken of human intellect; so how Everett, in 1957, used a few mathematical turns of equation to demonstrate a 'subjective experience' of 'slight randomness' is hard to comprehend.

Leaving aside the issue of what an experience of 'slight randomness' looks like on the page when written into a mathematical equation, there is the equally intriguing issue of exactly what an experience of 'slight randomness' actually feels like to experience? Given the fact that quantum events must be occurring at an astonishingly fast pace, if we take the Planck time, which is 10^{-43} sec, as an indicator, then in one second a living being experiences a 'slight randomness' more times than there are seconds since the birth of the universe. The experience of all living beings, then, should be suffused with a continuous 'slight randomness'. It might be true or it might not; it is doubtful whether the issue could be decided in any meaningful way. And this is a pity because if we actually knew what an experience of 'slight randomness', as opposed to 'no randomness', or perhaps even 'extreme randomness', actually was, then we could look at our subjective experience for evidence that the much admired science-fiction version of the many-worlds interpretation, including the splitting of observers into different copies of themselves in different worlds at an astonishing rate, with the concomitant continuous experience of slight randomness, was correct!

In fact it might be the case that Tegmark is mistaken about this issue of the 'subjective experience' of 'slight randomness' which he thinks that Everett discovered from his examination of the fundamental quantum Schrödinger equation. According to Bryce DeWitt, writing in the same volume as Tegmark:

> A greater worry is the following: the idea that the world may 'split' … into many worlds, is hard to reconcile with the testimony of our senses, namely that we do not split. Those who object to the many-worlds view for this reason Everett (1957) likens to the anti-Copernicans in the time of Galileo who did not feel the Earth move. To the extent to which we may be regarded as automata, on a par with ordinary measuring apparatus, it is not hard to show that *the laws of quantum mechanics do not allow us to feel ourselves split…*[505]

There does not seem to be unanimity between leading proponents of the many-worlds viewpoint regarding the experiential implications of quantum mathematical equations. Unless, that is, an experience of 'slight randomness' is meant to be the same as not being allowed to 'feel ourselves split.' With regard to Everett's appeal to the seventeenth century controversy concerning the movement of the Earth around the Sun, it should be noted that there was a weight of fairly clear evidence not requiring subtle interpretation for the natural view of the orbit of the Earth around the Sun. In the many-worlds scenario however, the interpretive element is foremost; there is mostly a fanciful and, as we shall see, philosophically dubious, interpretation of highly ambiguous evidence. The many-worlds view, however, is by no means as 'natural' as the notion that the Earth orbits the Sun.

As we have previously seen Everett was cavalier in his conceptual usage. But, when correctly understood, his original analysis views the universal perceptual process as the interaction between the objective wavefunction and observing subjectivities; a 'system' which contains multiple possibilities for experience and a multitude of 'observers' interacting with, or measuring the system. The many-worlds theory was originally called the relative-state hypothesis because it indicated that the appearance of the objective system within an experiential continuum was relative to the configuration of the observer. At the cosmological scale the objective system would have to be the entire universe, minus the observer. According to Barrow and Tipler:

> We have said in our interpretation … that the universe is split by the measurement. This is the standard terminology in the technical literature, but it is important to note this split is to be associated more with the measuring apparatus than with the system being measured.[506]

And, furthermore:

> Everett himself realised that it is more appropriate to think of the measuring apparatus rather than the Universe as splitting. In reply to a criticism by Einstein against quantum mechanics, to the effect that he [Einstein] '…could not believe … a mouse could bring about drastic changes in the Universe simply by looking at it', Everett said, ' … it is not so much the system that is affected by an observation as the observer … The mouse does not affect the Universe-only the mouse is affected.[507]

It turns out, then, that the popular images of the many-worlds perspective, which involve entire universes being wrenched asunder to pursue wildly differing trajectories within the multiverse is a more than a slight over-statement. We are left, however, wondering about the fate of the measuring apparatuses, be they Everettian robots, humans or even mice.

In a 1970 paper Bryce DeWitt wrote:

> I still recall vividly the shock I experienced on first encountering this multiworld concept. The idea of 10^{100+} slightly imperfect copies of oneself all constantly splitting into further copies, which ultimately become unrecognizable, is not easy to reconcile with common sense.[508]

Yes, indeed. No wonder John Bell declared that:

if such a theory were taken seriously it would hardly be possible to take anything else seriously.[509]

The number of supposedly separate worlds, occupied by 'imperfect' copies of multiple selves, at every moment in time, according to this extreme many-worlds perspective, must constantly increase by a vast amount; and the fact that each copy is, however slightly, 'imperfect' directs us towards one of the serious points of incoherence within this view of the theory. The crucial issue is just how logical is the notion of a 'self' that constantly splits into other 'selves' whilst supposedly still maintaining an identity. DeWitt referred to this idea as 'schizophrenia with a vengeance'.[510]

The many worlds that are implied by the Everett insight, when shorn of its exuberant taste for imaginative indulgence, are manifested exactly within the extraordinary diverse experiential worlds, each of which is a different revelation of reality, of the multitude of different forms of sentient life within our own universe. This leads to what Buddhist philosopher B. Alan Wallace calls 'the many worlds of ontological relativity'[511] which is based on an extension of the many-worlds hypothesis suggested by Michael Mensky. According to Mensky's *Extended Everett Concept* there is a mechanism within the interaction of the objective and subjective wavefunctions of reality which allows a selection of which possibility, amongst those with a sufficiently high probability, is actualised by the interaction. The subjective aspect of this process may be individual or it may be comprised of various levels of group structures of consciousness. It is important to be aware that such structures of consciousness need not be conscious in the sense of being instantly accessible to a living being's immediate consciousness; the quantum morphogenetic field of a species, for instance, will lie deeply buried beneath surface levels of awareness.

The patterns of experience, then, that are formed by the subtle interactions of objective and subjective wavefunctions within the process of the formation of the many experiential realms, or worlds, within the experiential domain of our universe must be fundamentally quantum in nature but experiential in manifestation:

> …every conscious being perceives the quantum world, with its characteristic non-locality, relative to its own cognitive frame of reference. Each of these individual classical projections is 'locally predictable,' and in each one, a conscious being realizes a world of lived experience. And each such classical world exists only relative to such a being or community of beings….
> It is important to note that in any one of Everett's worlds, because of the internal principles of quantum mechanical evolution, all valid observers within the same cognitive frame of reference see the same thing, so their observations are consistent.[512]

Thus the many worlds implied by the extended version of the interpretation of the Everett equation are those of the multi-layered multi-specied, multi-individuated and multi-faceted multi-world that exists within this universe. Other parallel universes may exist; indeed Buddhism asserts that they do, including hell-realms! However, there is absolutely no reason to claim that sentient beings are continuously being multitudinously rent asunder to inhabit a proliferating infinitude of newly spawned universes.

The counter intuitive notion that individual beings split into multiple copies of 'themselves', whatever that could possibly mean, each occupying a mysterious parallel or alternative reality, has no basis in experimental evidence. Neither does it have any conclusive theoretical demonstration or philosophical necessity. But for an adherent of the hardcore many-worlds interpretation observers are supposed to 'split', in some mystical fashion, into separate observers of newly spawned slightly different universes:

> In one of these worlds, an observer measures and records that the photon was detected in a state of vertical polarisation. In the other, the same observer measures and records that the photon was detected in a state of horizontal polarisation. The observer now exists in two distinct states in the two worlds.[513]

But this formulation glaringly displays the severe incoherence of this viewpoint. The notion of '*the same*' observer existing in *two* different worlds is quite clearly logically incoherent; we are confronted with a decision to ignore obvious conceptual nonsense in pursuit of science fantasy. Such assertions regarding the many-worlds theory can only make some sort of sense if our standards of what constitutes identity and difference are allowed to melt into a logical miasma. But philosophical rigor is not on the agenda of the many-worlds perspective; science fiction frisson seems to be the order of the day.

A question which naturally arises when confronted with a presentation of hardcore many-worlds faith is 'Why do I end up in the particular universe which I seem to inhabit?' The answers given to such questions often display an appalling conceptual and logical naiveté; according to Michael Clive Price for instance:

> There is no reason 'why' you ended up in this world – you end up in all quantum worlds. It is a subjectively random choice, an artefact of your brain and consciousness being split, along with the rest of the world that makes our experiences seem random.[514]

What does it mean to say that 'you end up in all quantum worlds?' At what point does an increasingly slightly different version of 'me' cease to be 'me'; a nanosecond, a millisecond, second, day, year or millennium?

A Madhyamaka style analysis of this view might require the following elucidation of such a claim. Does the 'you' in the split universes refer to an appearance which merely looks like the first 'you' but with a different consciousness? Does a split consciousness still have a connection to the stream of consciousness that went before, or is it irrevocably split away? If the former, then is this former consciousness spread over all the many universes that its descendent consciousnesses now individually inhabit? If so, how can it, at the same time as being single, be multiple, each part observing different branches? If the consciousness is irrevocably split away then how can it have access to the memories from before the split? And, also, if the consciousness is split away and so becomes different distinct consciousnesses in different quantum realms, what sense is there in the use of the term 'you' in the sense that 'you' are in all universes? The concept of 'you' is clearly singular and denotes a unitary phenomenon.

It is not possible to make sense of any of these alternatives, one of which must be the case if consciousness is taken to be indicative of a 'self'. The notion that a 'you' splits into alternative multiple, or parallel, worlds, then, is nothing but unsupported incoherent speculation. As Penrose points out, in order to have an acceptable account of the 'many-worlds' viewpoint:

> ...we would need a theory to explain that aspect of conscious perceptions which allows only individual detector responses to be consciously perceived, whereas superpositions of responses with non-responses are never consciously perceived![515]

In other words we need a theory of consciousness!

Michael Clive Price also suggests that our experiences, which are generated by the branching process in the many-worlds scenario, are a matter of 'subjective random choice', whatever that may be. But the truth of the matter is, of course, that contrary to the implications of the many-worlds theory most people's experiences are remarkably coherent. Michio Kaku for instance tells us that:

> I sometimes ask our Ph.D. students at the university simple questions such as, calculate the probability that they will suddenly dissolve and rematerialise on the other side of a brick wall. According to quantum theory there is a small but calculable probability that this could happen. Or, for that matter, that we will dissolve in our living room and wind up on Mars.[516]

The probabilities of such events are contained within the appropriate wavefunctions but their size is so small they should be, to all intents and purposes, impossible. But according to hardcore many-worlders they are not impossible, there must be at least one world where such events occur; this means, of course, that at least one copy of you has already been transported to Mars in some world. Such is the absurdity which follows in the wake of the hardcore many-worlds perspective. It is impossible, in this possible world, not to repeat John Bell's remark that:

if such a theory were taken seriously it would hardly be possible to take anything else seriously.[517]

Did you read that before in this world or another?

The hardcore version of the many-worlds perspective also requires that the great majority of such worlds would be so incoherent that the appellation 'world' would surely be far-fetched. As Schrödinger pointed out:

> The idea that they be not alternatives but *all* really happen simultaneously seems lunatic to him, just *impossible*. He thinks that if the laws of nature took *this* form for, let me say, a quarter of an hour, we should find our surroundings rapidly turning into a quagmire, or sort of featureless jelly or plasma, all contours becoming blurred, we ourselves probably becoming jellyfish.[518]

What is quite obviously required to rescue this picture is some kind of structuring mechanism. As Stapp points out:

> The Everett universe at the observable level probably does not separate into well defined discrete branches. The various 'branches' appear to blend continuously into each other ... in Everett's quantum world the human observers and their devices tend to become an amorphous distribution of properties. Consequently, no sharp separation of the observation aspects of nature into discrete well defined branches has yet been demonstrated. This leaves the technical viability of Everett's proposal open to serious doubt.[519]

So without some kind of mechanism involving the probabilities, a mechanism that operates to create a meaningful division of the fluid probability distribution into discrete branches of experience, the canonical view of the Everett proposal leads to an extremely vague notion of how the actual worlds manifest. It is only by keeping a vague and imprecise mental image of how the process of the many worlds scenario might function that the hardcore version can be seriously entertained. It is no wonder that Jim Al Khalili, on alternate days, and perhaps in alternate universes, finds himself 'wondering how any one could be so silly to give it the time of day'[520].

When the details of the unmodified hardcore many-worlds viewpoint are subjected to rigorous analysis the picture falls apart simply because of the ad-hoc and vague terminology employed. However, astonishingly, in a poll of physicists carried out a few years ago, 58% favoured the orthodox many-worlds view.[521] A notable dissenter is Roger Penrose who succinctly points out that the many-worlds interpretation does not solve the measurement problem:

> This quantum measurement problem is to understand how the procedure **R** can arise-or effectively arise-as a property of large scale

behaviour in **U** evolving quantum systems. The problem is not solved by merely indicating a possible way in which **R**-like behaviour might conceivably be accommodated. One must have a theory that provides some understanding of the circumstances under which (the illusion of?) **R** comes about.[522]

Penrose, who uses '**R**' to indicate wavefunction collapse and '**U**' for the continuous unitary development of the wavefunction, is incisive in his observation. The hardcore many-worlds interpretation is an accommodation because it lacks any precision. It is an impressionistic and loose metaphor which has no explanatory depth whatsoever. It is a science fiction fantasy employing vague terminology; a mind-boggling and attention capturing piece of pseudo scientific mythology. And if we were to accept such a viewpoint we are certainly projected into a completely illusory multi-existence:

> … according to this many-worlds type of viewpoint, the total state of the universe would indeed comprise many different 'worlds' and there would be many different instances of any human observer. Each instance would perceive a world which is consistent with that observer's own perceptions … (the manifest world) would, according to this view, be an *illusion* apparently arising as a consequence of how a macroscopic observer would perceive a quantum entangled world.[523]

And this is precisely true; any many-worlds theory, regardless of flavour, implies that the entities and events within any one of the observer's worlds would be exactly that, illusions. As the philosopher of science Michael Lockwood says regarding the many-worlds perspective:

> If, however, we stick with the equation and accept this smooth evolution, we are obliged to conclude that measurement, instead of collapsing the wavefunction, merely *entangles* the state of the measured system with the states of the measurement apparatus and the observer, who will have the *illusion* of wave-function collapse…[524]

Appearances to the many observers within the many-worlds scenario could not be indicative of independently existing entities and events in a real and external structure of reality because they could only be perceptions within the consciousness of the observer's 'branch' of the wavefunction. The appearance of a reality to any one observer, travelling any of the numerous possible paths of consciousness within the branches of the wavefunction, could be described:

> The root of the phenomena …
> Is your own mind.
> Whatever memories and thoughts appear to the mind,

Like haze in the sky,
They are not grounded in any substance.
They have no color and no shape,
And even the eyes of primordial wisdom of the Buddha
Do not see them as even a particle of matter.[525]

And, as we know, the aspect of reality which is at the 'root of phenomena' that is not 'grounded in any substance,' has 'no color and no shape,' and does not contain 'even a particle of matter' is the wavefunction.

One of the more technical problems of the many-worlds viewpoint is the 'preferred basis' problem. This problem arises because there is an infinite number of different ways in which any quantum state can be expressed as a superposition. Determining a way to make all the possible 'possible worlds' inhabitable for our 'split' selves is not an easy matter; and how it occurs naturally is not easy to explain. There are many distinct ways that the many worlds could be produced; and there is no obvious mechanism within the many-worlds proposal which accounts for which basis is chosen as a base for the decomposition into the many worlds out of which just one is seemingly manifested.

A solution proposed by the philosopher Michael Lockwood to this problem is:

> ... to accept that there is no *objectively* preferred basis, but to insist that there is a *subjectively* preferred basis, which is a projection onto the world at large of what I call the *consciousness basis* of the mind.[526]

According to Lockwood's insight each individuated consciousness, which is associated with the brain as a 'subsystem', has its own quantum structure and this:

> ...enables us to equate the consciousness basis of the mind with that basis that-amongst other states, such as occur, for example, in dreamless sleep-includes all the conscious states that we are capable of experiencing. Finally, then, the subjectively preferred basis of the world in general will be that which includes, as basis states, all such states of subsystems of the universe as sense perception, with or without the aid of instruments, is capable of detecting and that in so doing becomes entangled with the subsystems in general.[527]

According to Lockwood's picture the mind is said to be a subsystem of the brain which is 'self-revealing'[528] which certainly implies that the brain must have the capacity for self awareness, which means, of course, that its fundamental nature must be awareness-consciousness.

What Lockwood is suggesting here is that there must be a subjective structure of pre-experiential consciousness which interacts with the global objecttive environmental wavefunction of reality which operates in order to perform an initial delineation of a set of suitable alternative experiential possibilities for manifestation before one is selected for experiential manifestation. This is essentially the same observation which Sarfatti made:

> ...the self-measuring system self-organises its wavefunction so that it splits into non overlapping wave packets. That is the system creates its own measuring observable ... in a self consistent way and then chooses which channel to occupy. This is free will.[529]

Lockwood's 'consciousness basis of mind' is the structure which does the sorting before the exercise of 'free will' makes the final decision, so to speak. The degree of free will involved constitutes the central issue for the next chapter. Prior to the assumed exercise of 'free will', however, it is clear that Lockwood's solution conforms exactly to the perspective developed within this chapter.

A further feature of Lockwood's notion of a 'consciousness basis of mind' is that each species of sentient being clearly will have its own basis. In fact there will certainly be a hierarchy of such bases corresponding to various levels of embodiment. Any exercise of free-will will float on top of an extraordinary complex pre-experiential patterning of experiential reality which begins at a deep instinctual level of awareness-consciousness and reverberates up into the higher reaches of consciousness. All sentient beings are virtually completely unaware of the way that consciousness structures experience of reality through a resonant interaction of subjective and objecttive aspects of the wavefunction of reality at the quantum level.

The notion of the 'consciousness basis of mind' clearly fits naturally into the Mind-Only perspective of the alayavijnana, the consciousness basis of all. In fact the alayavijnana denotes the individual aspect of a deeper level of base consciousness called simply the *alaya*. These two were conflated in the discussions of the last chapter for convenience. However, we must be aware that such distinctions are conveniences; as we have previously noted there must be a complex hierarchy of such structures which interpenetrate each other. The individual structure of the alayavijnana must also contain the karmically created consciousness basis structure for the species, race and so on.

From this perspective the mind, which we may think of as an individuated structure of consciousness that is associated with the manifestation of the appearance of a material brain, has its own structure, comprised of a complicated superposed wavefunction; the elements of which are all the 'conscious states we are capable of experiencing'. In other words the total superposed wavefunction of the mind will contain all possibilities, with associated probabilities of course, for experience by the mind. This mind-wavefunction, which is comprised of a wavefunction of superposed possible experience within consciousness, may be considered to be a relatively stable centre of possible states of experience which interacts with a surrounding, global, shared and inter-subjectively created wave-function realm of possible 'objective' experiences.

The physicist Amit Goswami, after considering the many-worlds model, suggests a very similar view of the interaction of mind and an environmental wavefunction:

> Suppose that the parallel universes of the many-worlds theory are not material but archetypal in content. Suppose they are universes of the mind. Then, instead of saying that each observation splits off a branch of the material universe, we can say that *each observation makes a causal pathway in the fabric of possibilities in the transcendent domain of reality.* Once the choice is made, all except one of the pathways are excluded from the word of manifestation.[530]

In this version the many-worlds are conceived of as possibilities which are etched, as it were, into the fabric of the objective wavefunction or the 'transcendent domain of reality'. Only one of these possibilities can be actalised for any one sentient being; and Goswami considers that the one world which is actually materialised out of the possibilities is a matter of 'choice' rather than complete necessity, a perspective which clearly resonates with the views of Stapp.

Stapp is quite open about the fact that this presentation is partly his interpretation of Heisenberg's picture of the process of reality. Heisenberg's actual worlds can be found in his book *Physics and Philosophy*:

> The observation itself changes the probability function discontinuously; it selects of all possible events the actual one that has taken place .... Therefore, the transition from the 'possible' to the 'actual' takes place during an act of observation. If we want to describe what happens in an atomic event, we have to realize that the word 'happens' can apply only to the observation, not to the state of affairs between two observations. ... In classical physics science started from the belief – or should one say the illusion? – that we could describe the world without any reference to ourselves.[531]

Heisenberg, like Bohr and many quantum physicists today, tried to evade the issue of the actual nature of the wavefunction which contained the propensities for reality because there was no precedent for its understanding within the classical perspective. Stapp, however, is adamant that:

> The actual events in quantum theory are likewise idea like; each such happening is a *choice* that selects as the 'actual', in a way not

controlled by any known or purported mechanical law, one of the potentialities generated by the quantum-mechanical law of evolution.[532]

The vast majority of such 'choices', however, are not high-level intentional conscious acts but, rather, automatic, instinctive interactions which take place at a deep unconscious level of embodiment at the quantum level.

John Wheeler speculated about the possibility of developing a perspective capable of explaining a 'mechanism of bringing the entire Universe into existence', a mechanism which required some kind of 'intersubjective collapse of the wavefunction'. Wheeler drew the diagram which is now famous in quantum physics and cosmology circles as the Wheeler **U** which illustrates Wheeler's idea that the universe could be a 'self-excited circuit' which somehow creates itself through acts of participatory self-perception. In fig 8.21 we can see that the foregoing analysis of the quantum structuring of the many-worlds of illusion easily fit into Wheeler's schema, the **U** has been flipped horizontally to accommodate the direction of the equation. The reverberations from the interactive processes which create the many worlds of illusory experience cycle around to provide the objective and subjective aspects for further interactive processes which drive the experiential illusory web of reality. This is known within Buddhism as cyclic existence.

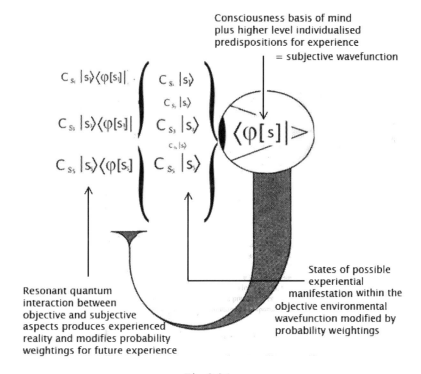

Fig 8.21

The process depicted in fig 8.21 can be overlaid on to the 'quantum karma' schematic image (fig 6.4) to show how the two perspectives perfectly interlock with each other, they are aspects of the same overall resonant quantum karmic process which creates the illusion-like dance of reality; this is shown in fig 8.22.

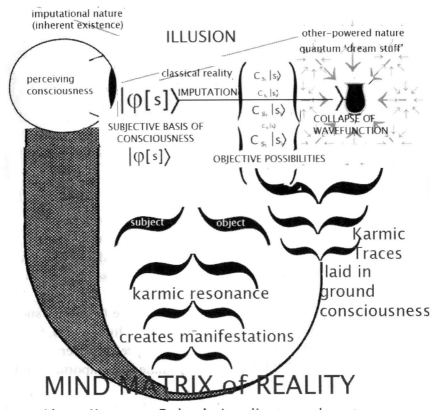

Fig 8.22

When the subjective basis of consciousness is imputed, at the quantum level, onto the objective possibilities, all of which have emerged from the fundamental ground consciousness through a process of karmic resonance, there is another resonant interaction which results in an amplification that produces an experienced world of illusion. This in turn leaves further traces in the ground consciousness and thereby the cycle of the 'self-excited' manifestation of the infinite multiplicity of the worlds of reality is kept cycling around a hub of emptiness. As Donald D. Hoffman, Professor of Cognitive Science, University of California, says:

> The world of our daily experience – the world of tables, chairs, stars and people, with their attendant shapes, smells, feels and sounds – is a species specific user interface between ourselves and a realm far more complex, whose essential character is conscious.[533]

The totality of all the different experiential continuums, which exist on many levels, species, race and individual are obvious examples of levels of manifestation for instance, make up the many-worlds of illusion:

> One commonly used Tibetan word for 'world' (*srid pa*)) has the connotation of 'possibility' and 'the process of becoming'' another closely related word (*snang srid*) refers to 'all phenomena that can possibly appear'. .... the act of meditation, or measurement, divides up the seamless fabric of reality, giving form to manifold worlds of illusory, dreamlike appearances.[534]

The reinforcing cycle of existence is shown again in figure 8.23 (overleaf). This is cyclic existence created by the cycling of subjectivities through the universal wavefunction, taking on many diverse life forms according to dispositions, driven by intentional actions and the resultant karma-vipaka, the universal law of cause and effect. And it is this mechanism which is discarded by bodhisattvas and buddhas who are described as:

> Cutter(s) of the noose of cyclic existence,[535]

According to the Buddhist worldview all sentient beings are quite literally trapped in the 'ocean of samsara', an obvious metaphor for the universal wavefunction, which is itself a metaphor. The uncontrolled perceptions and actions of countless numbers of sentient beings, over vast stretches of time, have built up the universal wavefunction, the ocean of samsara, into its present form. Furthermore our own past actions in previous lifetimes, for reincarnation of the mental continuums of sentient beings is a natural con-comitant of the view of the process of reality presented in this and previous chapters, have determined our own personal karmic environment for our current embodiment. Thus the 'noose of cyclic existence' has actually been constructed, both individually and collectively, by our own past perceptions and actions.

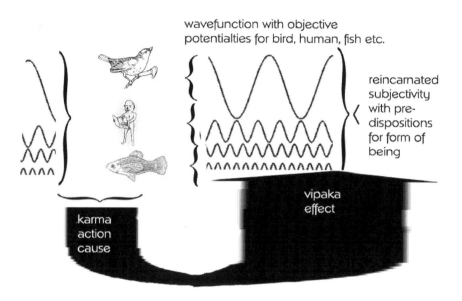

wavefunction with objective potentialties for bird, human, fish etc.

reincarnated subjectivity with pre-dispositions for form of being

vipaka effect

karma action cause

Fig 8.23

Choosing Reality

… choices are not fixed by quantum laws; nonetheless each choice is *intrinsically meaningful* : each quantum choice injects meaning, in the form of enduring structure into the physical universe. [536]

-Henry Stapp

…the person who recognizes himself to be an integral component of a universal process that selectively weaves waiting potentialities into dynamic new forms that create potentialities for still newer integrations should be inspired to engage actively and energetically in the common endeavour to enhance the creative potentialities in all of us.[537]

-Henry Stapp

…a theory that would describe not only the set of alternative results of measurement and the associated probability distribution, but also the mechanism of the selection of one particular result, ought to include the mind (consciousness) of the observer.[538]

-Michael B. Mensky

…the consciousness as a whole splits between the alternatives but the individual consciousness subjectively chooses (selects) one alternative.[539]

-Michael B. Mensky

It is very important to understand clearly that although karma conditions our experiences and actions, we still enjoy a certain measure of freedom – what would be called free will in the West – which is always present in us in varying proportions.[540]

-Kalu Rinpoche

Paul Dirac

As we have seen the process of the universe, or the process of reality, results from the operation of a fundamental cognitive feedback mechanism which is internal to the ground nature of consciousness. This feedback loop of universal consciousness is the driving force of reality and all sentient beings are the agents of the universal cognitive driving force. Thus quantum physics has to a certain extent validated the metaphysical perspective presented by the philosopher Arthur Schopenhauer who described the universe as being driven at its deepest level by a cosmic will, a kind of ceaseless striving for existence. The intentional activities of all sentient beings, therefore, are derived from a deep universal desire for existence, and it is this desire which produces the multitude of sentient beings with their own desires. Within this trap of embodiment imposed upon sentient beings by the Universal Will, however, quantum physics indicates that there is a degree of free will. As Stapp says:

> The basic building blocks of quantum theory are, then, a set of intentional actions by agents...[541]

Stapp has patiently and tenaciously, with great clarity and rigor, presented the inescapable conclusions regarding the natural function of human intentionality within the quantum context. In a recent paper he writes that:

> The only objections I know to applying the basic orthodox principles of physics to brain dynamics are, first, the forcefully expressed opinions of some non-physicists that the classical approximation provides an entirely adequate foundation for understanding brain dynamics, in spite of the physics calculations that indicate the opposite; and, second, the opinions of some physicists that the hugely successful orthodox quantum theory, which is intrinsically dualistic, should, for philosophical reasons, be replaced by some theory that re-converts human consciousness into a causally inert witness to the mindless dance of atoms. Neither of these opinions has any rational scientific basis.[542]

The first opinion indicated by Stapp is exemplified by recent works by the philosophers Jaegwon Kim[543] and John Searle[544] but also extends to the works of materialist 'philosophers' such as Daniel Dennett who proclaims a crude 'atomic' materialism without any rational argument for ignoring the evidence of quantum theory.[545] The second opinion is exemplified by physicists who still misrepresent the 'particles' of the Standard Model as being 'ultimate' constituents as if they were self-sufficient and independent entities. A more subtle form of the second position could be attributed to the view advocated by Roger Penrose, who wishes to replace quantum theory, which he considers to be incomplete, with something which demotes the phenomenon of consciousness to the ontological margins. Although Penrose recognises that all the evidence points towards the ontological primacy of consciousness, he simply refuses to believe it and concludes, without evidence, that the quantum evidence must be wrong; reality must be 'physical.'

With respect to the first position, which is an intellectual framework which seems to be held by the majority of the adherents of the latest academic craze for 'consciousness studies,' Stapp, although employing moderate language, is actually scathing:

> Philosophers of mind appear to have arrived, today, at less-than-satisfactory solutions to the mind-brain and free will problems, and the difficulties seem, at least prima facie, very closely connected with their acceptance of a known-to-be-false understanding of the nature of the physical world, and of the causal role of our conscious thoughts within it.[546]

The crucial phrase here is, of course, *'known-to-be-false'*. The astonishing fact is that, for some incomprehensible reason, the academic community has decided to allow some of its members, usually philosophers or purveyors of 'consciousness studies', to flagrantly misrepresent the truth of contemporary physics in order to defend obviously incorrect, 'classical' positions which are redolent of the worldview of the late nineteenth century. As Stapp points out:

> ...the re-bonding [between mind and matter] achieved by physicists during the first half of the twentieth century must be seen as a momentous development: a lifting of the veil. Ignoring this huge and enormously pertinent development in basic science, and proclaiming the validity of materialism on the basis of an inapplicable-in-this-context nineteenth century science is an irrational act.[547]

Indeed!

In order to explain the nature of the 're-bonding' between mind and matter Stapp employs an interpretation of von Neumann's presentation of the process of the 'collapse of the wavefunction', which is the quantum process through which an actual experienced reality appears to emerge from the potentialities that are contained within the quantum wavefunction of possible experiential 'reality' He outlines his version of von Neumann's analysis as the following three stages of the quantum experimental process:

Process 1: The 'free choice' of the experimental setup, Heisenberg called this phase 'a choice on the part of the 'observer' constructing the measuring instruments and reading their recording'. This choice is 'not controlled by any known physical process, statistical or otherwise, but appears to be influenced by understandings and conscious intentions.'[548] Whilst this process was originally delineated as a phase within the experimental setting, Stapp indicates that such 'free choice' of 'probing actions' is a part of the general human condition:

Probing actions of this kind are performed not only by scientists. Every healthy and alert infant is engaged in making willful efforts that produce experiential feedbacks ... Thus both empirical science and normal human life are based on paired realities of this action-response kind...[549]

The hugely significant point in this 'process 1' 'free choice' is that it poses a question to which 'reality' can feedback a 'yes' or a 'no', and the fact that the choice of the question is free means that the 'free choice' actually determines the nature of the possible feedbacks. Thus the 'free choices' determine the nature of experienced reality:

...the process is active: it injects into the physical state of the system being acted upon properties that depend upon the intentional chosen action of the observing agent.[550]

Stapp calls this process 1 'a dynamical psychophysical bridge.'[551]

Process 2: The deterministic quantum evolution of the potentialities within the Schrödinger wavefunction, this is the mathematical description of the development of the probabilities associated the potentialities within the quantum realm.

Process 3: This is what Paul Dirac called a 'choice on the part of nature.' It is the yes or no feedback from the experimental setup – yes, reality is this way or no, reality is not this way; Stapp indicates that complex questions can be reduced to yes-no choices.

This delineation of the experimental process, which starts in the classical realm, then evolves within the quantum realm, and finally gives its answer within the classical level again, is forced upon us because we are limited to perceptions and language within the classical realm. This, of course, is a fundamental aspect of our embodied existential situation which was often commented upon by the early quantum physicists; Bohr for instance:

...it is imperative to realize that in every account of physical experience one must describe both experimental conditions and observations by the same means of communication as the one used in classical physics.[552]

In other words we can only ask questions and receive answers in the experiential classical domain whilst the processes which determine the nature of the answer take place in the 'ultimate' quantum domain. The situation is graphically portrayed in fig 9.1.

In this schema the 'dynamical gap'[553], which is a natural opening for causal input from the 'consciously experienced intentions'[554] of those involved in the experiment occur at the Process-1 stage. And at the Process-3 stage they are involved in registering the answer given by nature. These two interconnected processes act as a filter which determines which of the 'objective' tendencies or potentialities which are contained within the Process-2 wavefunction become actualised within the experience of a stream, or streams, of consciousness. So the fact that the combination of Process 1 and Process 3 events filters the Process-2 wavefunction in this manner means that this intervention also determines the potentialities which are available for being activated at a later point in time. The Process 1&3 filter therefore determines what is experienced in the present and what can be experienced in the future.

This feature of quantum theory naturally accommodates the phenomenon of consciousness as a causally effective aspect of reality:

> ...the founders of quantum mechanics instituted a profound break with one of the basic principles of classical physics: they inserted the conscious experiences of human beings into the dynamical workings of the theory. Human beings were allowed, and indeed required, to act both as causally efficacious agents, and also as causally efficacious observers. ... Both of the two actions, the query and the feedback, are causally efficacious; they alter in different non trivial ways the physically described state of the universe.[555]

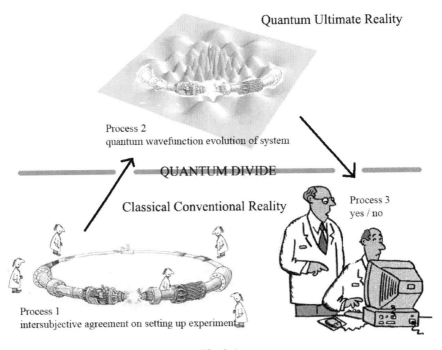

Fig 9.1

In this way Stapp demonstrates that current quantum theory is not 'incomplete' as Penrose suggests, on the contrary, it is actually completely complete in a way that the classical worldview could never be. In the classical perspective there is no 'natural' place for consciousness, considered as an ontologically significant aspect of reality; and as a consequence human choices and actions can have no significant ontological role. In quantum theory, however, consciousness, and therefore conscious choices, fit naturally and seamlessly into the 'physical' details of the functioning of reality:

> Within orthodox quantum mechanics our causally efficacious conscious intentional efforts remain 'free' of any specified physical coercion. Yet the conscious efforts do have, according to quantum mechanics, important physically describable effects.[556]

And in this revised quantum picture our conception of 'objective' reality has to replace the notion of a pre-existing structure of an independent realm of materiality with the notion of:

> ...'*potentialities for future psychophysical events*': i.e. as a representation of *objective tendencies*, created by past psychophysical events, for the occurrence of future psychophysical events.[557]

In fact in the work of Stapp the concept of 'physical' becomes in essence equivalent to 'psychophysical;' and the nature of the objective world is the 'objective wavefunction' which is characterised as a pool of potentiality for future experience. Actual experiential 'events' or 'occasions of experience,' which occur when potentialities are activated within the flow of experience, have both a physical and a psychological aspect, both of which, Stapp maintains, are equally 'real'. This is a form of process ontology which is derived from the work of the philosopher Alfred North Whitehead.

Buddhist philosophy, however, disagrees with Stapp's attribution of reality to all the entities, the potentialities and the psychophysical aspects of experience, within this process. This is because Buddhism requires that 'real' entities are considered to be necessarily permanent and enduring. How can an 'actual event', which is a fleeting, evanescent, nebulous occurrence, hardly isolatable, except theoretically, because of its lack of precise delineation (a Buddhist philosopher would say lack of solid independent inherent existence), be considered to be 'real'. From the point of view of Buddhist conceptual analysis there are serious problems with this deployment of the concept of 'real'. Briefly stated Buddhist philosophy requires that a 'real' entity is an independent self-enclosed entity having its own inherent existence independent of all other phenomena.

In his far ranging quest for uncovering reality Jim Baggott, in his excellent work *A Beginners Guide to Reality* concludes that:

> We must now come to terms with the fact that there is no hard
> evidence for this common sense reality to be gained from the
> entire history of human thought. There is simply nothing we can
> point to, hang our hats on and say *this is real*.[558]

It is quite clear from the context of his book that Baggott is using the term 'real' in the manner that a Buddhist philosopher would, which is to say that an entity or aspect of reality is considered to be 'real' if it is objectively established as an independent existent which has an objective, self-enclosed and self-sufficient ontological status which is completely independent of any observing consciousness. This is referred to in Buddhist terminology as being 'inherently existent' or 'established from its own side'. This usage corresponds very well to the online dictionary definition of the philosophical meaning of the term 'real': 'Existing objectively in the world regardless of subjectivity or conventions of thought or language.'

So it seems that the root meaning of the notion of 'real' both within basic Western philosophical parlance and Buddhist terminology carries a fundamental implication that the entities to which reality is ascribed should exist independently of the human sense faculties and mind in order warrant the attribution of being 'real'. Using this understanding of the meaning of the term 'real', then, means that experiential appearances cannot be considered 'real' in this ultimate sense precisely because they do not indicate independently existing entities which exist in an external reality which is completely separate from the human, or any other, sentient mind. For this reason a modern Buddhist exponent says:

> We come to understand the importance of knowing the difference
> between apparent reality and genuine reality, between the way
> things appear and the way they really are.[559]

And a clear definition of what a 'real' entity consists of is given:

> We need to understand what it is to say that something truly exists.
> What characteristics would something need to have in order to be
> truly existent? It would have to exist independently, with its own
> inherent nature; it would have to exist without depending on
> anything else and be impervious to causes and conditions acting
> upon it. If it were like that, then we could say that it was real.[560]

The point is that in our classical reality this is exactly how the entities of the experiential world *appear* to us, as self-enclosed independent entities. Thus the notion of what a 'real' entity is *is* essentially a 'classical' concept; it derives from our experience of the classical world of mostly solid objects which were always, mistakenly, taken within classical Newtonian based physics to be exactly what they appeared to be – independent self-existing entities. Such a view obviously involves the idea that 'real' independent entities have some kind of substantial (usually material) basis. The following characterisation by Bohm of the classical worldview presents precisely this point of view:

> ...the world is regarded as constituted of entities which are *outside of each other*, in the sense that they exist independently in different regions of time and space (and time) and interact through forces that do not bring about changes in their essential nature.[561]

This is the, *ultimately* mistaken, classical, conventional worldview of a world made up of 'real' entities.

The Buddhist analysis always remains cognizant of the fact that concepts are experientially grounded in our embodiment as sentient beings in a 'classical', 'conventional' reality. This is exactly an awareness that the early quantum pioneers highlighted in their many discussions as to how 'classical' notions could be extended into the quantum domain. The term 'matter' for instance, although it now has a precise location within a mathematical formulism, does not loose its origin in our intuition of the amount of 'stuff' which an object contains. In the quantum world the notion of classical type 'matter' has become invalid; but this does not stop physicists and philosophers often using the term in a manner which inappropriately carries over the classical associations. In the quantum context the term 'the appearance of matter' is far more appropriate, unless a new definition of matter is given which clearly refutes the Cartesian form.

From the Buddhist perspective the Cartesian-Newtonian 'classical' worldview describes 'conventional' reality (or 'seeming' reality) whilst quantum theory is closer to the ultimate view. The problem with the Cartesian delineation derives from the belief, endemic within the corridors of classical science and philosophy prior to the twentieth century, that this delineation into mutually exclusive 'substances' was correct as an ultimate description of the ontological structure of reality. Consequently when the appearances of the classical realm were shown to be 'deceptive' in terms of the 'ultimate' quantum nature (and according to Buddhist philosophy conventional appearances are also said, from an ultimate point of view, to be 'deceptive' because ultimately all phenomena are 'empty' of inherent, independent solidity) the 'real' nature of phenomena became a point of confusion.

However, adopting the Buddhist notion of the two truths, which is entirely appropriate to the metaphysical-ontological structure of reality revealed by quantum physics, solves this problem quite naturally. The essential issue which must be first determined, however, is what element in the current quantum arena exemplifies properties which are those which correspond to the classical properties which indicted classical 'reality'. The two most important properties are those of independence from other entities, including perceiving minds, and having some kind of substantial basis. We might say that these two constitute a minimal requirement for objectivity.

And, as Penrose points out, the only quantum entity which comes close to providing these requirements is the Schrödinger equation:

> If we are to believe that any one thing in the quantum formulism is 'actually' real, for a quantum system, then I think that it has to be the wavefunction ...[562]

And, as we have seen, this 'thing' must be considered to be of the nature of mind or awareness-consciousness. This view clearly corresponds with Stapp's viewpoint:

> But even deeper than the actual event is the **basic process**: the process that takes the potentialities, which are what the physically described aspect, the quantum mechanical state of the universe, embodies, and the psychologically described reality, which is all we know, and brings them together to form a newly created "actual event", which is both a new act of knowing and an associated "collapse" of the prior quantum state to a new quantum state that is compatible with the new state of knowledge.[563]

Thus the apparently separate 'physical' and 'psychological' aspects must emerge out of a background 'psychophysical' aspect of the process of reality which is described by 'the quantum analogue of the classical word, namely the Schrödinger wave equation'. Furthermore, Stapp writes concerning the primal 'stuff' of reality:

> If mathematics is deemed to belong to the category of 'mind', then the primal quantum stuff could simply be called *mind*, but only in a sense that allows mind to include not only human conscious experience but also the mathematical aspects of the way this primal stuff evolves.[564]

This constitutes the fundamental unitary 'substantial' ground from which all events emerge; each event having a subjective and objective aspect. This ground is called in Yogachara Buddhism the *alayavijnana*, the ground consciousness.

This perspective fits easily into the Buddhist metaphysical-ontological structure of the two levels of reality (fig 9.2). The only aspect of reality which can be accorded an independent 'ultimate', 'objective' reality is the nondual quantum ground that is implied by the Schrödinger equation, within which the physical and psychological aspects have their origin and locus. Dualistic experience derives from the nondual ground according to its 'enfolded' contents which are 'unfolded' into manifestation. The dualistic realm of experience, therefore, has a dependent reality derived from the more fundamental reality of the nondual ground; the experiential world is, then, a 'relative', 'seeming', 'conventional' or 'classical' reality derived from the deeper quantum reality. This is in line with the assertion by quantum physicist Erich Joos that the distinction between the quantum realm and the classical realm is a 'delusion.'[565]

It is essential to understand the Buddhist notion of an ultimate, or thorough, analysis. Such an analysis examines the phenomena of the experiential world in search of their 'real' nature, using the definition of 'real', or 'true' or 'inherent' given above. Consider the Cartesian epistemological-ontological determination of the lineaments of reality into the categories of 'matter' and 'mind'. In terms of our first-order, direct, experiential awareness this delineation, treated as a description of appearances without a thorough analysis, is 'correct'. Within my own experiential continuum the most significant and basic delineation I can make is between my direct awareness of the apparent immediacy of perception, thought, intention and so on and the entities which seem to stand in opposition as 'obstructive contact' (a Buddhist term) which appear to make up an external realm of 'materiality' which also appears to have a completely different 'substance' to the inner realm of 'thinking substance'.

Fig 9.2

In terms of the 'conventional', 'seeming' level there seems nothing wrong with this delineation, it provides a provisional starting point for analysis. And it was a starting point which provided considerable value, as indicated by the dramatic advances of classical physics, which is based on treating the Cartesian delineation as 'real', with the concomitant manipulation of the material world. In other words the validity of the Cartesian delineation, as a provisional and effective division of the realm of the 'conventional', 'classical' realm of experience is indicated by its sheer effectiveness. Thus within Buddhist philosophy it is said that it is futile to question the appearances of the functioning of the 'seeming' reality of the conventional world because it is quite clear to any sensible person that, on the level of no-analysis, phenomena do function according to conventional laws, even though a thorough, ultimate analysis shows that the phenomena of the 'seeming' reality cannot possibly function the way they appear to.

Thus conventional phenomena are, from an ultimate point of view, unreal (fig 9.3). This metaphysical-ontological structure of the process of reality results from the operation of a feedback loop wherein the dualistic realm emerges from the deeper implicate realm and the results of the interactions of the dualistic realm feed into the potentialities within the implicate order. The present intentional activities of all sentient beings, conscious and unconscious, determine the possibilities for future experience through the filtering of the potentialities within the wavefunction.

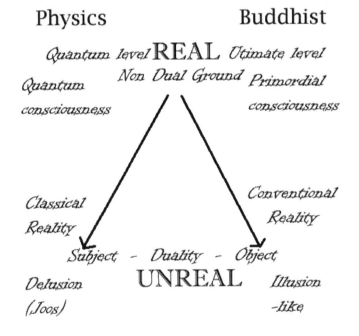

Fig 9.3

John Wheeler concocted an intriguing illustration of the way in which the functioning of a participatory Universe would allow the process of participation to determine the nature of the future of the Universe on the basis of a kind of intersubjective party game of 'Twenty Questions' involving 'yes' or 'no' responses to 'probing' questions. The usual way the game is played is that one of a group of people leaves a room whilst the rest of the group agree on an object or concept. The other person now returns and tries to discover the chosen object or concept by asking questions to which the rest of the group may only reply 'yes' or 'no' Apparently the answer is often found quite quickly. Wheeler's version is that instead of the group inside the room agreeing on a definite object or concept they agree to allow any 'yes' or 'no' response which is consistent with what has gone before. Anton Zeilinger says that 'this is a beautiful example of how we construct reality out of nothing.'[566]

The fact that quantum experiments indicate that at the quantum level the 'stuff' of the world is not a completely self-sufficient structure of materiality which is independent of the observing mind was apparent to Bohr who observed that:

> ...the new situation in physics has so forcibly reminded us of the old truth that we are both onlookers and actors in the great drama of existence.[567]

And Heisenberg concurred with this viewpoint:

> Our scientific work in physics consists in asking questions about nature in the language we possess and trying to get an answer from experiment by the means that are at our disposal. In this way quantum theory reminds us, as Bohr has put it, of the old wisdom that when searching for harmony in life one must never forget that we are ourselves both players and spectators.[568]

More recently, the quantum physicist Wojciech H. Zurek describes the quantum realm in the following terms:

> ...quantum states, by their very nature share an epistemological and ontological role – are simultaneously a description of the state, and the 'dream stuff is made of.' One might say that they are *epiontic*. These two aspects may seem contradictory, but at least in the quantum setting, there is a union of these two functions.[569]

There can hardly be a more precise delineation of the fact that, in the quantum realm, our experience, which is a result of the epistemological function, the way in which we interrogate reality and thereby gain knowledge, determines ontology, which is the appearance of reality within experience. Thus the image that recent quantum physicists such as Zurek, H. Dieter Zeh and Erich Joos propose as being appropriate for our understanding of the emergence of the classical from the quantum aspect of reality is that of the production of an illusion of the 'classical' realm of materiality which is somehow generated from the fundamental 'dream stuff' of the quantum basis of reality; Erich Joos clearly implies this when he says that:

> The disturbing dichotomy between quantum and classical notions was only a delusion.[570]

Thus the intentional actions of sentient beings unfold experiences from the quantum 'epiontic dream stuff' of reality and thereby fashion, in some fashion, a 'delusory' 'classical' reality!

With regard to this issue the following observation by Stapp is pertinent:

> The evolving quantum state, although controlled in part by mathematical laws that are direct analogs of the laws that in classical physics govern the motion of 'matter', no longer represents anything substantive. Instead, the evolving quantum state would represent the 'potentialities' and 'probabilities' for actual events. Thus the 'primal stuff' represented by the evolving quantum state would be idealike in character rather than matterlike … quantum theory provides a detailed and explicit example of how an idealike primal stuff can be controlled in part by mathematical rules based in spacetime.[571]

For, of course, only idea-like 'stuff' could possibly be fashioned by ideas!

Stapp examines the actual nature of the wavefunction and asks the question: what does it most closely resemble in nature, matter or consciousness? As Stapp points out the way in which the wavefunction is known within the experiential realm is as a mathematical entity, and since the time of Plato mathematics has been associated with the notion of an ideal realm of pure meaning. Indeed the mathematical physicist Roger Penrose comes close to counting himself amongst mathematical Platonists who believe in the existence of such an ideal realm, but he sees the invalidity of ascribing the 'substance' of reality to the Platonic mathematical realm:

> My own position on the matter is that we should certainly take Plato's world as providing a kind of 'reality' to mathematical notions …, but I might baulk at actually attempting to actually *identify* physical reality with the abstract reality of Plato's world. I think that [Fig 9.4] best expresses my opinion on this question, where each of the three worlds … has its own kind of reality, and where each is (deeply and mysteriously) in the one that precedes it (the worlds being taken cyclically). I like to think that, in a sense, the Platonic world may be the most primitive of the three, since mathematics is a kind of necessity, virtually conjuring its very self into existence through logic alone.[572]

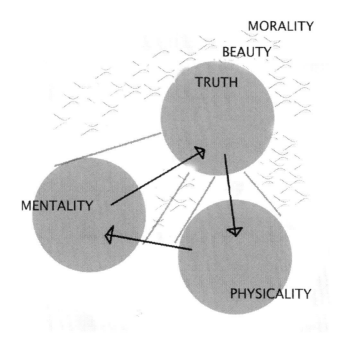

Fig 9.4 – Penrose's three realms

Penrose considers that 'mathematics is a kind of necessity, virtually conjuring its very self into existence through logic alone.' In which case it is also a necessity to ask, to slightly alter an important observation made by Penrose's associate Stephen Hawking, 'what breaths fire into the logic'[573] such that it is enabled to perform such a remarkable feat?

In the light of the massive weight of evidence that we have previously surveyed, evidence that must be completely available and known to Penrose; and the fact that Penrose himself, in the pages of his massive and impressive tome *The Road to Reality*, following the above quote, makes the following observations:

> …almost all the 'conventional' interpretations of quantum mechanics ultimately depend upon the presence of a 'perceiving being'…[574]

And:

> The issue of environmental decoherence … provides us with a merely stopgap position … 'lost in the environment' does not literally mean that it is *actually* lost, in an objective sense. But for the loss to be subjective, we are again thrown back on the issue 'subjectively perceived – by whom?' which returns us to the consciousness-observer question.[575]

And:

> ...the behaviour of the seemingly objective world that is actually perceived depends on how one's consciousness threads its way through the myriads of quantum-superposed alternatives. In the absence of an adequate theory of conscious observers, the many-worlds interpretation must necessarily remain incomplete.[576]

And:

> As far as I can make out, the only interpretations that do *not* necessarily depend upon some notion of 'conscious observer' ... require some fundamental change in the rules of quantum mechanics...[577]

The only thing that can possibly keep Penrose from coming to the most obvious conclusion that it is a Universal Mind, or awareness-consciousness which supplies the cognitive teleological 'fire' of internal perception, not an insubstantial and inert Platonic realm, that provides the ground of the process of the universe, and therefore stands at the end of his road to reality, is nothing more than his personal distaste for the conclusion.

The wavefunction cannot be said to occupy space in the same way as matter was thought to exactly because of its ideal nature; any number of wavefunctions can exist together within an overall superposition. Furthermore the fact that it requires an interaction with consciousness to produce 'matterlike' experiences indicates that the wavefunction and consciousness must share a common nature. It therefore seems quite natural to conclude, with Stapp amongst others, that the wavefunction must be 'idealike' and therefore of the same nature as awareness-consciousness.

However, the illusion of the ineluctable materiality of the material world undermines many physicists' understanding of their own ideas. Physicist John Gribben, for instance, presents a remarkable example of this. In 2003 he co-authored, with Paul Davies, a book entitled *The Matter Myth*. In this book, unsurprisingly in view of the title, the authors confidently pronounced that 'materialism is dead':

> ...the reality exposed by modern physics is fundamentally alien to the human mind and defies all power of direct visualisation.[578]

This observation quite clearly derives from observations made by Bohr in the 1920s, that in matters of the quantum realm we must 'be prepared to meet with a renunciation as to visualisation in the ordinary sense.'[579] And, in point of fact, Gribben and Davies' claim regarding the continued incapacity of the human mind to comprehend quantum reality, which is made within the perspective of 2003, is, to say the least, overstated; the picture that can be constructed from the insights of Bohm, Stapp and Wheeler and the Yogachara metaphysics, for example, does not exemplify a 'fundamentally alien' nature; the Quantum Mind-Only picture only defies visualisation for those who are desperate to visualize nothing but inherently existent 'matter'.

In a later (2006) book, *The Universe: a biography*, Gribben says that:

> Just as bosons can be thought of as field quanta, so fermions are regarded as quanta associated with 'matter fields' that fill all space...[580]

Fermions are particles associated with the qualities of matter such as electrons, protons and neutrons, which are thought of as being the constituents of the 'material' world; bosons are force carrying particles such as photons, which are bosons that mediate the electromagnetic force.

The interesting point here is the use of the term 'matter field', a neologism which seems to creep into use to cover over the conceptual gap left by the rapidly disintegrating notion of the type of 'real' solid matter associated with classical physics. According to the Cartesian account of matter, which has not been explicitly updated by any new definition, a wavefunction type field is precisely something that 'matter' cannot be a part of; 'matter' is located in space and generally thought to be solid and obstructive and so on. A material particle should have a definite location and occupy a definite space and not be spread out in a probabilistic field of potentiality like a wavefunction.

What Gribben calls a 'matter' field is actually a field of potentiality for the experience of matter-like events; and in order for such material events to materialise it is necessary for the so called 'matter' field to interact with a field of consciousness. And in order to interact in this fashion it must have a nature akin to consciousness, which means that to call it a 'matter field' is being disingenuous, to say the least. Matter-like events are experienced when objective and subjective fields of consciousness interact and resonate in a way that produces a matter-like experience, which are in essence a matter of 'congealed' consciousness.

It might be argued that the foregoing analysis, and the rejection of the 'matter-wave' perspective, is nothing more than quibbling over words. To a degree this might be true, but, on the other hand, such uses of terms like 'matter' conceal the actual true nature of the reality of the process of reality, which primarily consists of awareness-consciousness and not matter. As Stapp indicates the nature of the wavefunction is idea-like, not matter-like. The words we use have a dramatic effect upon our attitudes and therefore the nature of our engagement with reality. Both Bohm and Stapp emphasize the importance of this point:

> The change in our world indicates a change in our perception. By changing our perception of the kind of world we live in we change our perception of the possibilities.[581]

Furthermore, according to the Quantum-Mind-Only account any intentional action, including perception, leaves a trace in the ground of possibility for future perceptions. No matter how small the effect of an individual perception has on the possibilities for experience which are projected into the future for other beings to participate in, it nevertheless has such an effect. It is exactly through such a 'bit by bit' continuous sequence of perceptual activity that the 'matrix' of future possible experience is built up. *The way we perceive reality has a determining effect upon the way reality will be perceived and this process operates a deep quantum level of reality.*

There is a deeply held conviction that consciousness is so ineffable, mysterious and beyond comprehension that to consider it as having a role in creating illusions of the material world cannot be entertained. And this really boils down to the fact that consciousness cannot be directly, and Western style objectively, measured. But then, how could the ground of measurement directly measure itself? The answer to this is that the universe, through the agency of consciousness, measures itself by creating the objective and subjective aspects of the process of reality, and the process of measurement, which is the interaction of these two aspects, creates the realms of experience through which the universe of awareness-consciousness explores its own nature.

But, although all the evidence points to the fundamental role that consciousness plays in the process of reality, when faced with the practical facts of what we experience as an external material world the idea that such an independent autonomous structure of materiality does not exist in the manner that it appears to seems ridiculous. Surely, it is thought by materialist thought, 'consciousness', whatever it may be, simply is not, and cannot be, solid and dependable enough for the job. Thus the materialist 'philosopher' Daniel Dennett simplistically describes the dualist conundrum with the homely allusion to the cartoon character Casper the Friendly Ghost:

> How can Casper both glide through walls and grab a falling towel? How can mind stuff both elude all physical measurement and control the body A ghost in the machine is of no help in our theories unless it is a ghost which can move things around … but anything which can move a physical thing around is itself a physical thing.[582]

Dennett, of course, uses the term 'physical' as interchangeable with 'material' and with this invalid attribution he thinks that he can easily show consciousness is not up to the job of interacting with what he has decided is the real stuff of reality – matter. Consciousness is far too insubstantial for the job. But he ignores all the quantum evidence which clearly shows that the kind of 'matter' he conceives of 'does not exist,' as Stapp emphatically describes the matter of the insubstantiality of matter.

To disabuse oneself of Dennett's form of recalcitrant materialist prejudice it is useful to consider the effect of the gentle substance water, the stuff we wash with every day, when travelling at considerable speed in its form as a tidal wave or tsunami. A liquid substance which slips through our fingers and can gently sooth the dirt away from our bodies can also turn into a solid wall of destruction. Similarly the effect of air when it is whirled into a hurricane is similarly devastating. Apparently innocuous substances may become otherwise when energised and solidified by conditions.

The substance we take to be 'matter' itself can exist in various states; solid, liquid and gas. The more energetic it becomes, the more distant the molecules become from each other due their increased kinetic energy. As this happens, of course, the less solid matter becomes. We move quite freely through air as if it did not exist, but air is as much matter as concrete; concrete, however, is much more 'congealed', so to speak. But this does not alter the fact that all matter is actually 99.999999999999 percent empty space. It is not solid, extended, continuous and impenetrable 'stuff' that makes matter have the appearance and qualities of solid materiality, it is, rather, the nuclear and electromagnetic forces which 'hold' it together. In this respect the appearances which are presented within our experiential world are, as is repeatedly emphasised by the Madhyamaka, *completely* misleading and deceptive as to their *ultimate* nature. This fact became dramatically revealed to the Western world at the beginning of the twentieth century with the advent of quantum physics. But, as we have seen, it has been known to Buddhist philosophy for at least two and a half thousand years.

If you are close to an intense electromagnetic field the feel of it is quite palpable, the stronger it becomes the more pronounced the electric feel of the surrounding space becomes. The quantum biologist Johnjoe McFadden has suggested that consciousness is a manifestation of a field, similar to an electromagnetic field, which is associated with the brain:

> The brain with its action potentials still represents the bottom layer but above this is the conscious mental field (CMF) that generates 'a unified or unitary subjective experience'. This CMF would have a 'causal ability to affect or alter neuronal function' and thereby provides the veto or reinforcing role on unconsciously initiated actions ...[583]

McFadden, however, is still a materialist; he believes that the material brain, an entity which actually does not exist *ultimately* as an independent and autonomous entity, is the fundamental causal entity in his description. But the kind of picture he presents indicates the fact that once the necessity for treating consciousness seriously as a significant ontological aspect of reality is accepted then it becomes also necessary to view it as some sort of field of potentiality; potentiality for what? Consciousness is the field of potentiality for dualistic awareness and cognition. And, given that according to Zurek and others the ultimate stuff of reality is 'epiontic dream stuff', it follows that the cognitions of consciousness will have a role in creating and maintaining the appearance of a material reality in accord with the cognitions performed by consciousness.

McFadden's fundamentally materialist stance needs to be inverted. It is the field of awareness-consciousness that is the ontological ground of reality. The Madhyamaka definition of consciousness is 'that which is clear and knowing'; it has the natural function of cognition. And it is because of this inner nature of perception that the universe is able to turn back upon itself, so to speak, in order to examine its own nature, or many possible natures, and thus give rise to the Wheeler image of universal self-referential self-perception. Because of this inner capacity for self-cognition, which is built into the self-aware substance of reality, the universe appears to be an essentially unified epiontic perceptual field which divides against itself, as it were, in order to explore the multiple possibilities for manifestation that it contains. And it is the role of sentient beings to 'choose' avenues of experience from out of the multiple possibilities:

> Then, over the course of time, *choices are made* that inject into the universe the particularness that we observe. Each choice in the present era is taken to be a choice from among the observable possible branches that are generated by the deterministic laws of quantum evolution. Under the condition that prior choices have been made, this process can be conceived to generate ... a statistical mixture of reasonably distinct branches, some *one* of which will be selected.[584]

Embodied existence in the realm of the interaction of subjective and objective wavefunctions contains within it a reflective awareness of fundamental unity of the deeper level of reality, and this awareness of the source creates a longing or thirst for ever deeper experiences of the unity of source. But this longing is mistakenly projected into the dualistic world of experience. It is this dualistic and conditioned thirst, called *tanha*, or craving, that is enshrined as the second noble truth of basic Buddhism, the cause of suffering, which is exactly this attached thirst for dualistic experience. When this thirst is misplaced it becomes the basis for the insatiable thirst of materialism, the craving for substantial matter and the material things of the world, which are thought both to *be,* inherently, made of matter and also *to,* inherently, matter!.

In order to explore all the possible avenues of experiential manifestation the subjective aspects of the universal process of reality would theoretically need only to passively experience the various pathways within the many worlds of appearance. This viewpoint, which corresponds to the generally accepted version of the many worlds interpretation, however, does not encompass the direct experienced awareness of intentionality. The inclusion of the aspect of intentionality produces a much more comprehensive and cohesive understanding to the process, a comprehension which corresponds to our experience. The mechanism for producing a material environment within which living beings operate involves a set of 'choices', which are determined by a patterning of intersubjective agreement built up over vast numbers of lifetimes, which would take place at a deep, unconscious level.

This process has been already thoroughly discussed; it is the mechanism of karmic quantum resonance within fundamental awareness-consciousness which underpins the Heisenberg ontology of the process of reality. The Cartesian division is replaced by a two stage interconnected process. Firstly, the Heisenberg state, this is the superposition of the 'objective tendencies' contained within the wavefunction. The probabilities for these tendencies are a result of the frequency with which the individual tendencies have been previously activated. Secondly, the discontinuous change in which one of the objective tendencies is actualised whilst the others seemingly disappear. This occurs because of a resonant interaction of a subjective wavefunction with the objective tendencies within the objective wavefunction which generates the illusion of the collapse of the wavefunction.

The discontinuous change from multiple potentialities to an apparent single actuality is the result of a resonant interaction of the global objective tendencies and the subjective potentialities for experience, which are encapsulated within an embodied consciousness. This, however, is not the full story; there is a further ingredient in this mechanism. Recent work by Mikhail B. Menskii[585] (Mensky) suggests that the resonant interaction produces a subjective superposition state within which the intentionality of the individual can function as a determining factor in deciding which of a set of possibilities, those which exists within a certain range of high probabilities, is actually 'chosen'.

The crucial insight which is implied by Mensky's Extended Everett Concept (EEC) is that the 'chosen' path of reality results from a resonant interaction of the objective and pre-established subjective probabilities, together with a small, but nonetheless significant, element of conscious determination, or 'free will'. This perspective clearly relates to that proposed by McFadden that individual consciousness has a 'causal ability to affect or alter neuronal function' and thereby provides the veto or reinforcing role on unconsciously initiated actions ...[586]. It also completely accords with Stapp's views.

Before exploring Mensky's perspective it will be useful to quickly review, as a contrasting viewpoint, the Orchestrated Objective Reduction (Orch-OR) model which has been proposed by Roger Penrose and Stuart Hameroff. In this proposal for the explanation of the collapse of the wavefunction, or state-reduction, the possibilities within the overall wavefunction are assumed to develop separately, each one becoming more separated over time, until the 'strain' in space-time geometry, which is associated with Penrose's notion of quantum gravity, causes an 'objective reduction'(OR), as opposed to a consciousness induced subjective reduction, into one actuality. Hameroff describes this view:

> ...an OR transition from quantum, pre-conscious processing, to classical, non-conscious processing may be closely identified with consciousness itself. But what is consciousness? According to the principles of OR (Penrose, 1994), superposed states each have their own space-time geometries. When the degree of coherent mass-energy difference leads to sufficient separation of space-time geometry, the system must choose and decay (reduce, collapse) to a single universe state, thus preventing "multiple universes".... In this way, a transient superposition of slightly differing space-time geometries persists until an abrupt quantum classical reduction occurs and one or the other is chosen. Thus consciousness may involve self-perturbations of space-time geometry. [587]

In other words the many quantum possibilities have their own space-time configurations, or gravitational fields, and when the overall configuration of the combined space-time field becomes too unstable it must 'collapse' into the most stable state, thus eliminating competitors (fig 9.4).

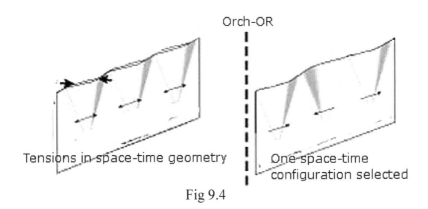

Fig 9.4

The Orch-Or view, therefore, unexpectedly and somewhat hazily connects together the concepts of consciousness and gravity; the implication seems to be that consciousness, in some unspecified manner, is an emergent phenomenon based upon the 'physical' operation of a quantum gravitational effect, a view for which Penrose has attracted significant criticism. In his book *Shadows of the Mind* Penrose, using the symbol '**R**' to stand for the 'state reduction', or collapse, of the wavefunction writes that:

> ...the modification of quantum theory that will be needed, if some form of **R** is to be is to made into a *real* physical process, must involve the effects of *gravity* in a serious way.[588]

The italics in this quote are in the original; it is impossible when reading Penrose not to notice the serious discomfort that he clearly feels when he contemplates the fact that the evidence of quantum theory clearly suggests that 'reality' might not be as *real* as he would like it to be! Hence his obvious desire to *make* the state reduction 'into a *real* physical process'. One has the sense that if he could do so through an effort of conscious will he would do so.

In a sense the first three quarters of *Shadows of the Mind* is an extensive and detailed examination of why reality cannot be *real* in the sense that the term 'real' is usually employed; meaning by 'real', of course, an autonomous structure of materiality which is independent of mind. The final part seems to be a desperate attempt to rescue some kind of reality. In conformity with Penrose's obvious intellectual acuity the discussions are detailed, logical, cogent and precise. Until, that is, he comes to consider the possibility which he seems to dread – *Is it consciousness that reduces the state vector?*[589] Penrose writes:

> No doubt some readers might expect that, since I am searching for a link between the quantum measurement problem and the problem of consciousness, I might find myself attracted by ideas of this general nature. I should make myself clear that this is *not* the case. It is probable after all that consciousness is a rather rare phenomenon throughout the universe. ... It would be a very strange picture of a 'real' physical universe in which physical objects evolve in totally different ways depending upon whether or not they are within sight or sound or touch of one of its conscious inhabitants. ... Can we really believe that the weather patterns on some distant planet remain in complex number superpositions of innumerable distinct possibilities ... until some conscious being actually become aware of it...[590]

The problem for Penrose, however, is that this is precisely what current quantum physics does indicate. It is precisely for this reason that Penrose believes that quantum theory must be incomplete and requires a modification which will encompass the phenomenon of gravity. This, he thinks, would solve the problem of the incompatibility of Einstein's relativity theory and quantum theory, as well as getting rid of the disturbing spectre of the ontological primacy of consciousness. However, if the foregoing mapping between the quantum-classical divide and the Buddhist two truths analysis is correct, it would follow that a completely watertight melding of quantum theory and relativity is impossible because they belong to radically different levels of the process of reality.

In order to try and fulfil his desire for an essentially classical type of reality, however, Penrose is forced into thought experiments within which the notion of space-time, an essentially classical concept, becomes central. The quantum suppositions are envisaged as being stresses or wrinkles perhaps within the geometric fabric of space-time which are ironed out by the force of quantum gravity acting at the Planck scale (fig 9.4):

> We might attempt to imagine that these two geometries are trying to be forced into coincidence, but when the measure of the difference becomes too large, on this kind of scale, reduction to **R** takes place ... Nature must choose one geometry or the other. [591]

The salient question is, however, how does nature choose? What causal mechanism is in place to decide on which geometry should prevail; the most probable one? Then where do the probabilities come from? And what exactly is the ultimate nature of space-time, matter or consciousness, or a bit of both?

Penrose tells us that his approach is a matter of 'taking $|\Psi>$ seriously'[592], but in reality it is a matter of not taking consciousness seriously! The fact that Penrose considers that consciousness is nothing but an epiphenomenon of the 'physical' world, by which he can only mean a *material* world (he offers no other alternative), is quite clear:

> ...the measurement problem must be solved in entirely *physical* terms. Once we are in possession of a satisfactory solution, then we may be in a better position to move towards some kind of answer to the question of consciousness.[593]

It is quite clear, then, that Penrose must have already decided that consciousness cannot be considered to be the ultimate nature of reality otherwise he would not say that 'consciousness is a rather rare phenomenon throughout the universe.' What he actuality means, however, although he does not seem to realise the distinction, is that manifested individuated consciousness is a rather rare phenomenon throughout the universe. This may be true, but it does not alter the fact that, according to quantum physics, any part of the universe, when unobserved, is in a state of superposition of possibilities and is therefore not a fully 'real' phenomena; potential phenomena become experientially real when they interact with consciousness. It is for this reason that physicist Nick Herbert completely disagrees with Penrose:

> ...mind is not a rare phenomenon associated with certain complex biological systems but is everywhere, universal in nature, a fundamental quantum effect...[594]

Dr. Stuart Hameroff, co-instigator of the Orch-OR model of the quantum functioning of collapse of the wavefunction, has elucidated the implications of the Orch-OR model for our understanding of 'free will':

> Free will may be seen as a combination of deterministic pre-conscious processes acted on by a non-computable influence.[595]

Hameroff's type of 'free will', however, turns out to be not the kind of free will that really free willed sentient beings would expect. This is because the Hameroffian 'free will' derives from the ubiquitous 'Platonic influences' which seems to a fundamental feature of the Penrose-Hameroff Orch-OR account. It is these hidden influences which are supposed to determine the actual direction of wavefunction collapse. Where these influences are derived from, however, is not explained.

The non-free nature of Hameroff's 'free will' is clearly indicated by the analogy that Hameroff offers us:

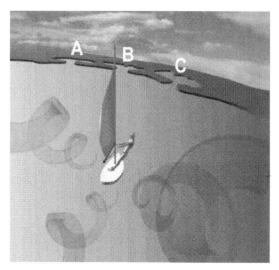

Fig 9.5 - Hameroff's non-free free will – *Free will may be seen as the result of deterministic processes (behavior of trained robot windsurfer) acted on repeatedly by non-computable influences, here represented as a seemingly capricious wind.*

Consider a sailboard analogy for free will. A sailor sets the sail in a certain way; the direction the board sails is determined by the action of the wind on the sail. Let's pretend the sailor is a non-conscious robot zombie run by a quantum computer which is trained and programmed to sail. Setting and adjusting of the sail, sensing the wind and position, jibing and tacking (turning the board) are algorithmic and deterministic, and may be analogous to the pre-conscious, quantum computing phase of Orch OR. The direction and intensity of the wind (seemingly capricious, or unpredictable) may be considered analogous to Planck scale hidden non-local variables (e.g. "Platonic" quantum-mathematical logic inherent in space-time geometry). The choice, or outcome (the direction the boat sails, the point on shore it lands) depends on the deterministic sail settings acted on repeatedly by the apparently unpredictable wind. Our "free will" actions could be the net result of deterministic processes acted on by hidden quantum logic at each Orch OR event. This can explain why we generally do things in an orderly, deterministic fashion, but occasionally our actions or thoughts are surprising, even to ourselves.[596]

In this analogy it is quite clear that the aspect which represents the 'free-willed' bit of the process, the 'seemingly capricious' wind, is accounted for within the actual Orch-OR model by the 'hidden', 'Planck-scale', 'Platonic', 'quantum-mathematical logic'. In other words it can by no means be considered to be a really free will, which should be a real conscious decision of the part of a sentient agent to act in one particular way rather than another. Hameroff's 'free will' is actually an illusory free will. However, it must be said that this model is actually extremely close to the really free 'free-will' which will be presented shortly.

In his discussion of the nature of free will in his book 'Mindful Universe' Stapp suggests that a correct understanding of the nature of free will is:

> ...that a person has both a mind (his stream of conscious thoughts, ideas and feelings) and a brain (made of neurons ... etc), and that his decisions (his conscious moral choices) are free (not determined by any known law), and that, moreover, the rules that govern his brain *determine* the activity of his brain *jointly* from the physically described properties of the brain combined with those conscious decisions.[597]

In other words a free-willed choice is exactly that, a choice which is made independently of the associated deterministic physical phenomena, and such a choice is also an 'injection of meaning' into the universe[598].

Michael B. Mensky's Extended Everett Concept (EEC) supplies exactly such an understanding of free will which is based on quantum physics. In this model of conscious, free-willed, decision making it is assumed that in some circumstances an individual mind can be in 'two minds'. This situation arises when the individual quantum state of consciousness is in a superposition of possibilities with equal probability weightings. In this situation it is natural to suppose that an individuated consciousness could have a direct, but constrained, effect upon the alternative possibilities for action:

> If I wish to go to the right and actually go to the right, how (does) this happen? In fact there is no explanation of this simple ability of consciousness. In the framework of EEC, if the modification of probabilities is assumed, free will is explained quite naturally. There are two alternatives: in one (of) Everett's world(s) I go to the right, in the other I go to the left. Both alternatives have non-zero probabilities. My consciousness modifies the probabilities, increasing the probability of the first alternative. As a result, with a high probability I go to the right. This is my free will.[599]

Suppose someone is approaching a fork in the road and either alternative will do as well to reach the intended destination. At this point the traveller has not decided which fork to take; we may consider them to be 'in two minds' about which way to go. This view of the situation actually corresponds to Albert and Loewer's 1988 many-minds interpretation of the wavefunction[600] according to which our traveller will actually have two minds which are superposed within the overall wavefunction of the situation. When the traveller actually makes a decision as to which route to take this process may be considered to be an imposition of an intention, which is a further, consciously produced, structure of consciousness, an internal amplification, or internal 'collapse' of the superposed wavefunction which alters the probabilities, or 'collapses' in favour of the route decided upon.

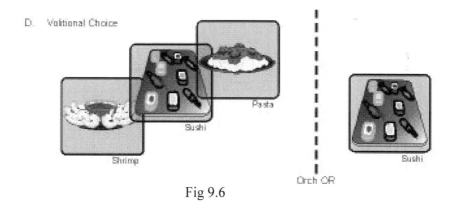

Fig 9.6

Hameroff describes the quantum functioning of the Orch-OR model of 'volitional choice' as follows (fig 9.6):

> In a volitional act possible choices may be superposed. Suppose for example you are selecting dinner from a menu. During pre-

conscious processing, shrimp, sushi and pasta are superposed in a quantum computation. As threshold for objective reduction is reached, the quantum state reduces to a single classical state. A choice is made. You'll have sushi![601]

Hameroff's depiction, however, is manifestly not that of a volitional choice, it is an account of the illusion of a volitional act. Furthermore, it is an account which requires one to believe that the 'influence' to prompt you to decide for 'sushi' is somehow pre-encoded into a 'Platonic' realm; surely an implausible notion. Mensky's account is depicted in fig 9.7; the decision is truly a free willed volitional act.

Real free will, however, operates within a narrow band of possibility. As the Tibetan Buddhist master Kalu Rinpoche said:

It is very important to understand clearly that although karma conditions our experiences and actions, we still enjoy a certain measure of freedom – what would be called free will in the West – which is always present in us in varying proportions.[602]

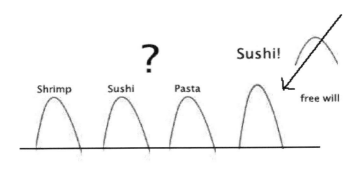

Fig 9.7

This view of the way in which consciousness can affect the overall situation through the addition of intentionality as an amplification of a branch within the overall wavefunction produces a completely natural and seamless understanding of the way in which consciousness functions to make a choice between pre-determined alternatives.

In Mensky's Extended Everett Concept an observer's mind, when encountering a superposition of possibilities will, for a brief moment, become itself a superposition of possibilities. Normally however, this superposition will collapse into one actuality virtually instantaneously because of the deeply etched predispositions to experience in a manner laid down by the evolutionary process. Evolution has, as we have previously seen, produced a template for the experience of the material world which is effective in all sentient beings, according to their species. Mensky describes the emergence of a preferred 'classical' reality from the many potentialities of the wavefunction as follows:

> All alternatives are realised, and the observer's consciousness splits between all the alternatives. At the same time, the individual consciousness of the observer subjectively perceives what is going on in such a way as if there exists only one alternative, the one she exists in. In other words, the consciousness as a whole splits between the alternatives but the individual consciousness subjectively chooses (selects) one alternative.[603]

In other words the subjective mind, an individual structure of consciousness, determines, or chooses, usually unconsciously, which potentiality becomes experienced as being the 'real' experienced world. This is not to say that the individual concerned consciously examines the possibilities as he or she might select an article from a catalogue; it is not a conscious choice in this sense. In the above quote Mensky does not offer a mechanism and the description seems to imply an almost self-conscious choice. However, this is not the case; in fact he or she will be unaware at the self-aware levels of consciousness that this choice between alternatives is going on.

It is useful to recall the model of this process which developed naturally from our investigation of Lockwood's discussion of the problem of the preferred basis; according to this view there is a subjective preferred basis which is a structure within individual consciousnesses that produces a definite separation of the many possible worlds. The crucial aspect that the EEC adds to this is the implication that there is a natural process through which one of the alternatives is chosen as the single experience of a definite reality. This mechanism is facilitated at a deep level of consciousness which is not usually available for conscious observation from the point of view of more self-aware levels of consciousness. Mensky indicates that the level of consciousness involved:

> ...the most primitive, or the most deep, level of consciousness, differing perceiving from not perceiving.[604]

Such deep levels of consciousness contain shared structures of possible experience. These aspects of the structures of consciousness are coterminous with those that the analytic psychologist C.G. Jung called archetypes. Although Jung's archetypes are primarily concerned with deep emotional determinations of aspects of reality, his work led him to suggest, like Bohm, that there is a deep level of connection between the physical world and the realm of the subjective.[605] This view of the deep inner and hidden connection between the manifest realms of the objective world and the subjective experiential world was also shared by physicist Wolfgang Pauli who corresponded for a time with Jung on the subject.

The experiential templates for the material world, which can be thought of as archetypal templates which interact with the established features of the objective wavefunction that provides the potential for a material world, must be shared, at least in part, by all conscious beings. Mensky's account of how such deep structures of consciousness, which select the experiences conforming to a stable material world from the wealth of quantum possibility, arise in the first place provides a fertile starting point for the development of the view of evolution as an essentially quantum process. This is a topic which will be explored in the later chapter *Self-Perceiving Universe*.

According to Mensky's account 'consciousness is nothing else than the separation of the alternatives'[606]. This view conforms to the view that consciousness can be thought of as being the actual qualitative 'feel' of the dualistic functioning of the global wavefunction as suggested also by Tegmark. To say it is 'nothing else', however, is incorrect because as we have seen the entire process of the wavefunction is the objectified process of fundamental awareness manifesting as dualistic consciousness, *jnana* manifesting as individuated self-aware *vijnana*.

Mensky commends his definition of consciousness:

> In this assumption, two unclear concepts, one from quantum mechanics and the other from psychology, are identified and thus 'explain each other'.[607]

A claim which some might think walks into the path of Dennett's attempt at a scathing dismissal of such attempts to connect the phenomena of consciousness and the quantum realm:

> ... by wedding two bits of magic together you are going to say its not magic. By letting consciousness be a mysterious and magical property, in saying that quantum enlargement in effect depends on consciousness you nicely tie together two themes and I think its just magical thinking. There is no reason to believe either side of it.[608]

But, in fact, the truth of the issue is that Dennett is actually hovering on the verge of philosophical obfuscation and fraudulence when he claims that there is 'no reason to believe either side of it.' For as Rosenblum and Kuttner have vigorously concluded:

> Consciousness and the quantum enigma are not just two mysteries; they are *the* two mysteries; first, our physical demonstration of the quantum enigma, faces us with the fundamental mystery of the objective world 'out there;' the second, conscious awareness, faces us with the fundamental mystery of the subjective, mental world 'in here.' Quantum mechanics seems to connect the two.[609]

The 'reason to believe' the connection is precisely the quantum evidence which indicates that consciousness is clearly implicated within the quantum realm.

Consciousness is an interior aspect or quality of the wavefunction which reflexively operates upon the potentialities for experiential existence. For consciousness itself to become manifest, from fundamental awareness, as an explicit experiential aspect of reality it must bring an experienced world into being; and such a world is manifested through the actualisation of the potentialities within the wavefunction and the subsequent selection of a primary experiential pathway. According to Mensky a crucial question which requires explication is why the alternatives which naturally arise (the preferred basis) are classical, or at least close to classical, in demeanour. Mensky gives the following account:

> If the picture of the world as it appears in consciousness were far from classical, then, due to quantum non-locality, this would be a picture of a world with 'locally unpredictable' behaviour. The future of a restricted region in such a world could depend on events even in very distant regions. No strategy of surviving could be elaborated in such a world for a localised living being. Life (of the form we know) would be impossible. On the contrary, a (close to) classical state of the world is 'locally predictable'. The evolution of a restricted region of such a world essentially depends only on the events in this region or not too far from it. Influence of distant regions is negligible. Strategy of surviving can be elaborated in such a world for a localised living being.[610]

Recall that entangled quantum phenomena can instantaneously affect each other over vast cosmic distances. In fact distance does not seem to be an issue for this kind of entangled mutual determination. It follows, therefore, that in a non-classical scenario there would be no environments wherein environmental behaviour was determined purely by local events. Such environments would not be locally coherent and predictable and consequently they could not support coherent life. If Mensky's argument is correct then the classical lineaments of a life-supporting manifested reality is fashioned by consciousness itself for its own manifestation! The objective tendencies towards, and the subjective propensities for, experience of a seemingly stable material world, then, naturally emerge as essential for the manifestation of life and dualistic consciousness.

With the mechanism of a holographic resonance of wavefunctions providing the background for our understanding of how a coherent experience of a single reality, including the appearance of a material world, is generated from the many alternative possibilities, Mensky's proposal provides a fertile model of the relationship between the experiences of embodied consciousness and the many alternatives within the wavefunction.

From the perspective of Mensky's EEC it is natural to suppose that an individuated consciousness could have a direct, but constrained, effect upon the alternative realities:

> There is only one universal probability distribution in quantum mechanics…, but the probabilities may in principle be different from the point of view of the consciousness of a living being: various observers may elaborate different probability distributions for what alternatives they are going to see.[611]

As we have previously noted Mensky does not explicitly propose a mechanism through which such an alteration in probability might be achieved by an individuated consciousness; he simply assumes that probabilities of more favourable outcomes may be increased whilst the others are decreased. Our own perspective, however, includes the idea that such a reinforcing or decreasing of probabilities is a resonance phenomenon.

The possibility for consciousness to directly affect the probability distribution leads to Mensky's suggestion that 'probabilistic miracles' become understandable[612]. One kind of such 'probabilistic miracle' that was considered by Bohm is psychokinesis that, according to Bohm:

> …could arise if the mental processes of one or more people were focused on meanings that were in harmony with those guiding the basic processes of the material systems in which this psychokinesis was to be brought about.[613]

Such an effect, if it exists, would be, as Michael Talbot points out, the result of a 'resonance of meanings'[614] And such a resonance would be an interaction between the 'environmental' wavefunction and the subjective dimension of wavefunction probabilities.

Jung's notion of 'synchronicity', or 'meaningful coincidence', is another aspect of such a 'probabilistic miracle'. In his autobiography Jung recounts the following incident. One day he was listening to a patient recounting a dream involving a golden scarab beetle. Whilst the patient was describing the dream an insect continuously flew against the window seemingly trying to get into the room. When Jung opened the window and caught the insect it turned out to be a golden green beetle resembling a scarab, an insect not common to the area. Jung handed it to the patient as a synchronistic demonstration of a phenomenon beyond the explanation of the rational mind.[615] It was this aspect of Jung's perspective, what Jung termed the *Unus Mundus* (One World), which impressed Wolfgang Pauli as being indicative of a common ground behind the appearance of the realms of subjectivity and objectivity.

According to Mensky's account of the Everett Extended Concept the many worlds within the superposed wavefunction of reality become more accessible in their variety 'at the edge of consciousness.'[616] In the full light of completely focused consciousness only one reality is experienced. However when consciousness is 'almost turned off', the state of sleep or in a trance for instance, it can access information from the 'other' worlds. This, Mensky suggests, accounts for the some of the 'unusual' capacities of consciousness such as predictive capabilities.

An important aspect of this view of the process of actualizing experienced reality through both conscious and unconscious intentionality is the fact that the wavefunction of the intention and the overall wavefunction of the situation must resonate sufficiently to produce the actuality. One might intend with great fervour to dematerialise and appear on Mars, a possibility which Michio Kaku tells us is contained within any person's wavefunction. The probability of this possibility within the 'objective' wavefunction, however, is simply too vanishingly small to even murmur out of improbability. The possibility for actualisation through the intentionality of consciousness, which may be conscious but usually is unconscious to immediate awareness, therefore, is restricted to those possibilities that have significantly high values of probability.

According to Stapp:

> ...every structural and functional aspect of each conscious thought is completely represented within the physicist's representation of the host brain. Even the special 'feel' of a conscious thought, the feel that the thought is somehow *bringing itself into being*, is captured by the actualizing quality of Heisenberg's quantum transition.[617]

In other words thoughts and decisions, manifested within their internal feeling tones, are collapsed wavefunctions, the quality of having a thought, or making a decision, is the experience of a collapsing wavefunction inside an individuated consciousness, this is the inner experience of 'meaning'. These choices on the part of individuated consciousnesses can be very significant beyond the immediacy of the act itself because not only do they determine an individual thought or action, they also act upon, and leave a trace upon the universe. As Stapp says:

> ...each choice is *intrinsically meaningful*: each quantum choice injects meaning, in the form of enduring structure, into the physical universe.[618]

It is these choices that collapse the wavefunction of reality in certain directions and thereby leave traces, or reinforce paths of possible experience, within both the subjective wavefunction of the consciousness of the individual and the objective wavefunction which contains the possibilities for future experiences. This means that every perception and every choice we make determines, to a vanishingly small degree, the future possibilities encoded into the universal wavefunction. So, as Henry Stapp points out:

Causally efficacious mind is a prerequisite of ethical theory, and quantum theory allows it to be supplied by science...[619]

Self-Perceiving Universe

Directly opposite to the concept of universe as machine built on law is the vision of *a world self-synthesized.* On this view, the notes struck out on a piano by the observer participants of all times and all places, bits though they are in and by themselves, constitute the great wide world of space and time and things.[620]

- John Wheeler

In the beginning there were only probabilities. The universe could only come into existence if someone observed it. ... The universe exists because we are aware of it.[621]

- Martin Rees

...only self-consistent loops capable of understanding themselves can create themselves, so that only universes with (at least the potential for) life and mind really exist.[622]

- Paul Davies

Thus we see that without introducing an observer, we have a dead universe, which does not evolve in time. This example demonstrates an unusually important role played by the concept of an observer in quantum cosmology. John Wheeler underscored the complexity of the situation, replacing the word observer by the word participant, and introducing such terms as a 'self-observing universe.'[623]

- Andrei Linde

According to a Hindu mythic depiction of the process of reality the universe hides itself in its own productions in order to explore its own possibilities. From this perspective the process of reality is the result of the universe's questioning of its own nature. Using, again, Wheeler's Universal U we can illustrate this as in figure 10.1. This ancient perspective upon the inner nature of reality has now been revived in the work of physicist Paul Davies, for one example, who proposes the possibility that the universe comes into existence as a *self-explaining universe*. Such a universe would necessarily contain organisms that embody the capacity for cognition, which is to say consciousness, precisely because the purpose of self-explanation, to use Davies' perspective, or self-cognition, to use the perspective contained within the Quantum-Mind-Only perspective, is fundamental to the universe. According to Davies:

> ...a good case can be made that life and mind *are* fundamental physical phenomena, and so must be incorporated into the overall cosmic scheme. One possible line of evidence for the central role of mind comes from the way in which an act of observation enters into quantum mechanics. It turns out that the observation process conceals a subtle form of teleology.[624]

Here Davies is reworking Wheeler's subtle notion that the process of the universe's unfolding into multiplicity suggests a minimalist teleology, which Davies calls 'teleology without teleology.'[625] By this phrase Davies indicates that the Universe contains the minimalist 'purpose' to manifest intelligent life in some form or other. As we shall see, the mechanism of this unfolding is the collapse of the wavefunction, a mechanism which requires perception. This leads to the notion of a universe Self-created through its inner tendency for Self-cognition, or Self-perception.

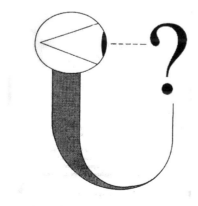

Fig 10.1

Because cognition is a fundamental function of the ground of manifestation, which is nondual awareness-consciousness, the universe of manifestation necessarily comes into existence. As we have seen it is through this process that the universe becomes a multiverse of illusory worlds. Thus the realm of dualistic experience is said by Hindu philosophy to be *maya*, a term which literally means 'illusion.'

In his book *Hidden Dimensions* Wallace has pointed out that the Sanskrit root of the term *maya*:

> ...has the dual meaning of 'to measure' and 'to create illusions.' Like quantum physicists, Indian contemplatives connected the act of measurement to the manifestation of illusory appearances. ... the act of ... measurement, divides up the seamless fabric of reality, giving form to manifold worlds of illusory dreamlike appearances.[626]

The early Yogachara Mind-Only 'contemplatives' conceived of the epistemogical-metaphysical process of reality as fundamentally consisting of an exquisitely sensitive and responsive experiential field within which all sentient beings were immersed and had their being. This field, which was conceived of as being of the fundamental nature of cognitive-awareness, is the 'stuff' from which all sentient beings are constructed, and this 'stuff' is experiential in nature and responds with great sensitivity to all intentional activity carried out by all sentient beings. Such actions can be performed by body, speech or mind but it is the intentionality behind any such action which is paramount in the mechanism by which all such activities leave traces within the fundamental cognitive-experiential field of reality, traces which will be activated at later moments when surrounding conditions within the field are resonantly conducive for the potentiality of the 'seed' to emerge into full experiential reality.

The Yogachara cognitive 'stuff' which is conceived of as forming the fabric of reality bears an uncanny resemblance to the quantum 'dream stuff' of reality as portrayed by Zurek:

> ...quantum states, by their very nature share an epistemological and ontological role – are simultaneously a description of the state, and the 'dream stuff is made of.' One might say that they are *epiontic*. These two aspects may seem contradictory, but at least in the quantum setting, there is a union of these two functions.[627]

Here Zurek characterizes the quantum 'dream stuff' as being exactly the kind of cognitive medium capable of creating the appearance of a 'solidified' classical world through its own infinite web of internal acts of cognition, acts which may be considered equivalent to 'collapses' of wavefunctions.

Zurek, then, refers to the inner process of quantum realm as consisting of the 'union' of the two functions of epistemology, the process of perception and knowing, and ontology, the actuality of being; the quantum epiontic principle, then, indicates that perception creates being. This is precisely adumbrated within Buddhist philosophy which posits the ultimate nature of reality as being a fundamental ground comprised of 'emptiness and cognition inseparable', or 'empty cognizance'.[628] The field consists of 'empty' potentiality for manifested experience, a field of possibility which neither exists nor not exists, and thus hovers indeterminately and interdependently between existence and non-existence in a fashion redolent of the Heisenberg Uncertainty Principle. And it is the inner function of cognizance, a function which is internal to the ground of reality, which activates the potentialities within the ground field. Thus Zurek's 'epiontic' 'dream stuff' corresponds precisely with a characterisation of the fundamental ground of the process of reality according to the Buddhist philosophy of the Yogachara-Vijnanavada, the Cognition-Only epistemological-metaphysical view of the process of reality.

According to the Yogachara perspective the dualistic world of experienced phenomena is driven by a deeply entrenched 'grasping' for the manifested experiences of the dualistic world. This primordial desire for experienced existence is intrinsic to the fundamental ground of reality. There is, then, a minimalist intentionality, a 'teleology without teleology' which lies deep within the heart of the process of reality, and this drives the multitudinous manifestation of the appearances of the dualistic experiential realm of the process of reality, which is termed within Buddhist thought *samsara*, or cyclic existence.

Latent within the heart of reality there is a 'thirst' (*tanha*) for individuated experience and it is this fundamental drive towards existence that builds up, through repeated momentary perceptual or cognitive movements within the fundamental layers of awareness-consciousness a complex web of predispositions for experience for each sentient being entering once again the cyclic dualistic realm:

> ...the mind which has all the seeds ... matures, congeals, grows, develops and increases based upon the twofold appropriation... that is
>
> 1. the appropriation of the material sense faculties...
> 2. and the appropriation which consists of the predispositions towards profuse imaginings in terms of conventional usage of images, names, and concepts...[629]

The term 'conventional' here does not merely mean 'by common agreement', it indicates the very deep structures of intentionality which can actually create the appearance of the materiality which physics calls the 'classical' level of reality, Buddhist thought refers to this as 'conventional' reality. The 'material sense faculties' are actually considered to be gross structures of the 'epiontic' cognitive stuff of reality, which has the ultimate nature of consciousness, and the 'predispositions' are subtler structures which provide potential experiential templates for experiencing 'objective' aspects of the cognitive stuff of reality according to pre-established patterns which have been built up through repetition or habituation:

> Buddhists and biologists ... largely concur that the very forms and structures of human life result from the accumulative actions of innumerable beings over countless generations. Like all species, we too have been formed and conditioned by an immensely long and complex series of transformations ... we are ... assemblages of dynamic yet wholly conditioned structures (*samskara*) forged through the crucible of past actions and experience.[630]

The subjective structures of intentionality, which are termed *samskara* – conditioned structural intentional processes produced by previous intentional activities, are embodied within the various types of sentient beings and operate upon an intersubjectively created 'objective' field of potentiality fashioned from the 'epiontic' stuff of reality, which is the *alayavijnana*, the ground consciousness, the layer of consciousness which 'collects' all the traces from intentional activities performed by sentient beings:

> 'The common characteristic of the alayavijnana is the seed of the receptacle-world' means that it is the cause of perceptions which appear as the receptacle world. It is common because these perceptions appear similarly to all who experience them through the force of maturation that is in accordance with their own similar karma.[631]

As we have seen, karma simply means 'action', and it refers to any action of body, speech and mind which leaves a trace within the alayavijnana, the ground consciousness of potentiality. These resonant traces, or seeds, will later 'mature', or be activated into experiential reality. *Karma-vipaka* is the universal law of action and maturation, cause and effect, which operates at all levels of reality, including the creation of the potentialities, or seeds, within the ground consciousness which mature or manifest as experiences of a supposedly external 'material' reality:

> Space, earth, wind, sun,
> The oceanside, and waterfalls
> Are aspects of the true, internal consciousness
> That appear as if being something external.[632]

According to the Yogachara account of the process of reality the vast experiential web of reality is a resonant interactive field of the primordial epiontic dream stuff which is fundamentally of the nature of awareness-consciousness.

This account of the functioning of reality involves the interaction of a multitude of subjective experiencing structures of 'epiontic' stuff, which is of the nature of consciousness, that interacts with and triggers into manifestation, a field of objectified 'epiontic' stuff. This is a view which agrees remarkably with the emerging quantum understanding of the process of reality. As Stapp says:

> The basic structure of orthodox (Heisenberg, von Neumann) quantum mechanics is very simple. The primary reality is a sequence of psychophysical events. Each such event has a psychological aspect and an associated physiological aspect. The connective support that links these events together is a *field of potentialities* that determines the *objective tendencies* (expressed in terms of probabilities) for specified psychophysical events to occur.[633]

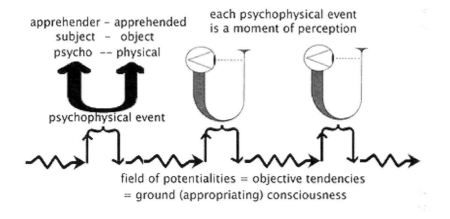

Fig 10.2

This process is schematically pictured in fig 10.2 in which John Wheeler's famous self-observing universal 'U' is employed to depict momentary pulses of individuated consciousness, each corresponding to a 'wavefunction collapse'. It is through an extraordinary complex hierarchical structure of such quantum processes of consciousness that the rich dualistic world of all sentient beings is built up by the unfolding process of reality through what David Bohm called the implicate orders from which the explicate world unfolds. This picture of the development of levels of consciousness towards greater individuation is implied by Max Tegmark's understanding of the nature of dualistic consciousness:

> I believe that consciousness is the way information feels being processed. Since matter can be arranged to process information in numerous ways of varying complexity, this implies a rich variety of levels and types of consciousness.[634]

This emerging quantum picture of the process of reality as being an emergent experiential realm from a more fundamental field of potentiality was anticipated by the Yogachara account according to which a subjective and an objective aspect of experience arise together from the ground consciousness on the basis of previous moments of similar experiences, perceptions and actions:

> A seed or predisposition is activated and simultaneously produces both an object and a cognizing subject, much as in a dream.[635]

The result of each moment of perceptive experience, each intention, and each action is a strengthening of the latency within the ground consciousness for that event to occur again, and, when there is an activating resonance within the ground-consciousness, an interdependent subjective-objective dualistic experiential field arises into conscious awareness. And, because according to the Yogachara perspective this resonant process is amplificatory, each momentary perception reinforces, to a miniscule degree, the probability of the same perception occurring at a future moment, and upon the basis of this mechanism a coherent perceptual world emerges (fig 10.3). This describes the mechanism which underpins John Wheeler's assertion that:

> Directly opposite to the concept of universe as machine built on law is the vision of *a world self-synthesized.* On this view, the notes struck out on a piano by the observer participants of all times and all places, bits though they are in and by themselves, constitute the great wide world of space and time and things.[636]

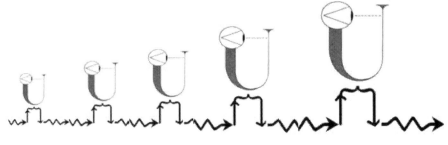

Fig 10.3

According to the Yogachara perspective it is the amplificatory mechanism of the universal karmic cause and effect process within the fundamental epiontic stuff of reality that creates the appearances of the dualistic world. In this characterisation of the quantum process the appearance of the 'classical' world is generated through a continuous web of rapidly repeated perceptions on the part of countless numbers of sentient beings over vast timescales.

The Buddhist philosopher William Waldron describes this fundamental aspect of the Yogachara account of the functioning of reality as being driven by 'self-grasping' which is the deep instinctual habit within all sentient beings to crave individuated experience. Waldron describes this as a linguistically recursive process; however the linguistic levels operative within the Yogachara account of the process of reality operate deep within the psychophysical structure of embodiment, directly structuring and determining the potentialities for manifestation of future experience at deep psychophysical levels:

> ...this linguistic recursivity, which colours so much of our perceptual experience, including our innate forms of self-grasping, now operates unconsciously ... and ... these processes are karmically productive at a collective level as well as individual level – that is they create a common 'world'.[637]

This constitutes an unconscious 'intersubjective feedback system' and therefore:

> ...it is the unconscious habits of body speech and mind to which we are habituated that give rise, in the long term and in the aggregate, to the habitats we inhabit, the 'common receptacle world' we experience all around us.[638]

Although this formulation attributes the creation of the 'common receptacle world' to the unconscious habits that 'we' have become habituated to (over countless lifetimes) it is important to understand that this is an intersubjective process that begins at a deep non-individuated quantum level of the universal process of manifestation into the dualistic experiential world. The universal process of the unfolding of the 'empty' (i.e. an interdependent realm of non-manifested possibility – empty of manifestation) potentialities within the ground of reality arises because the function of cognition, which unfolds the potentialities, is itself an innate function of the 'epiontic' stuff of reality. Thus sentient beings are necessary agents of the universal process of manifestation of experiential realms of duality and they therefore become entrapped within the samsaric cyclic process of reality (fig 10.4).

Wheeler was well aware that acts of perception were the creative force behind the manifestation of the universe; this was clearly embodied in his self-perceiving universe graphic. It only remained for the final step, the extraordinary knowledge known and realised by the great mystics of 'all times and all places', *the fundamental nature of reality is Universal Self-perception. The process of the Universe is an extraordinary manifestation of all possible expressions of Self-perception. Through this process the Universe explores all of its own perceptual potentialities. This explains why the universal wavefunction contains an infinite pool of potentialities; it is the infinite pool of Universal potential Self-expression. Furthermore all the sentient beings, Wheeler's observer-participators, are the Universe's agents of Self-perception. And the phenomenon of the 'collapse of the wavefunction' is a direct indication of the fundamental Self-perceiving process of the Universe.*

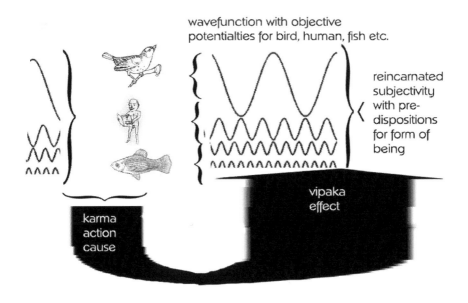

Fig 10.4

This process of Universal Self-perception creates the multitudes of intentional cycles of embodiment as described by the twelve links of dependent origination, which is a central Buddhist teaching (fig 10.5). In its quest for its own Self-nature the Universal process generates an endless profusion of illusory 'selves' (fig 10.6), these are the sentient beings acting as the Universe's agents of Self-perception through their imagined process of 'self' perceptions. Unfortunately for all sentient beings, dualistic embodiment is a matter of suffering (*dukkha*). The Buddhist vision of the cyclic process of suffering is represented by the well known 'Wheel of Life' image which graphically portrays the links shown in fig 10.5.

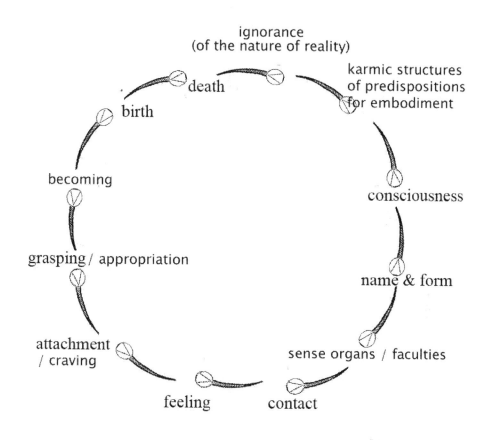

Fig 10.5

Briefly the twelve links may be understood as follows. Because of the operation of the first link in the chain of dependent origination, which is **ignorance** *(avidya)* as to the nature of reality, the following links are activated and subsequently the operation of the cycle of the twelve links traps sentient beings ever more deeply into the suffering round of existence. This link is ignorance of the fact that the experience of selfhood, the seemingly innate experience of being or having an independent 'self', is illusory *(anatta-* no fixed permanent self) and, furthermore, there is no permanent condition of satisfaction to be had within the cycle of dualistic samsara because all phenomena are impermanent *(anicca)*.

Because of ignorance sentient beings perform *formative actions* *(samskarakarma)* which have karmic consequences. These consequences

Buddhist Wheel of Life

generate a future continuum of **dualistic consciousness** (*vijnana*), there are six kinds of consciousness: eye, ear, nose, tongue, body and mind. These consciousnesses generate the psychophysical continuum of a sentient being; this structural complex is termed **name and form** (*namarupa*). In this designation 'name' (*nama*) designates mind and the sense-consciousnesses (*psycho*) whilst 'form' (*rupa*) covers eye, ear, nose, tongue, and body (*physical*). On the basis of *name and form* the **six sense sources** (*ayatana*) operate and on the basis of these there arises **contact** (*sparsha)* between the sources and their objects. And contact gives rise to *feeling* (*vedana*), feeling is pleasant, unpleasant or neutral. Feeling gives rise to **craving** (*trshna*) then **grasping** (*upadana*) which activates the 'becoming' of future **existence** (*bhava*). As a result all unenlightened sentient beings repeatedly experience **birth** (*jati*) and subsequent **ageing and death** (*jaramarana*).

This can be understood from the quantum perspective; dualistic consciousness (*vijnana*) is generated through a multitude of levels through the operation of the minimalist universal requirement for the process of perception, which takes place through the quantum mechanism of the collapse of the wavefunction. When this takes place it follows that 'name and form', which are the necessary mental and physical factors for embodiment, must develop. And the continuity of the process of embodiment within the dualistic world depends upon the fact that embodiment entails 'attachment' or 'craving' and 'grasping' for sensuous 'contact', which are links within the chain of cyclic existence.

This spontaneous momentary cycle of 'becoming' echoes and cascades at a inconceivable speed of relentless manifestation, and its operation is revealed through the 'collapse of the wavefunction ' and Zurek's 'quantum Darwinism', both of which indicate the minimalist, yet infinitely fecund and productive, intentionality for perceptual experience which lies at the heart of reality. This is what Schopenhauer called the universal 'Will' for existence. This momentary quantum mechanism cascades into manifestation at more explicate and long term levels thus driving the higher level cycles of the 'classical' world. The second link, for instance, which produces the karmic structures of predispositions for experiential embodiment, is a manifestation of the operation of the mechanism of 'quantum Darwinism' across lifetimes. This is the intentionality of the universe operating to produce the multitude of perceiving sentient beings and their illusory 'receptacle world' from the quantum epiontic dream stuff of the fundamental ground of the process of reality.

For unenlightened sentient beings this process is beyond their comprehension, they believe the process is real in the sense that the products of the deeper ground actually exist in their own right independently of that ground. They also believe that they exist in their own right; they do not realize that they are actually merely pawns in the universe's quest for continuous experiential activity. Furthermore, although the overwhelming prevalence of suffering within dualistic samsaric existence is clearly obvious, the great majority of sentient beings assume that it is possible to obtain substantive and lasting happiness through chasing after the products and experiences of the dualistic realm. It is this completely deluded belief that all Buddhist traditions refute unconditionally.

As a result of the process of manifestation into the experiential realm of duality, which is driven by the minimalist intentionality towards dualistic perception which lies within the fundamental nondual quantum ground, a countless multitude of quasi-stable experiencing 'centers' of individuated awareness are manifested (fig 10.6). These quantum structures of subjectivity are 'created' through the process of quantum Darwinism and they are actually interconnected agents of the process of Universal Self-perception. But each of these centers experience a seemingly solid illusion of separateness, a sense of 'self', or 'I-ness'. The sense of independent, individuated self-sufficiency is a reflection of the unity of the nondual source and is built into the psychophysical structure of all sentient beings at a very deep level; it is the sense of independent existence which drives the process of continuous embodiment lifetime after lifetime. It is an immensely powerful illusion which Buddhist thought refers to as the illusion of the personal self, which is the deep seated feeling that each sentient being has that it 'exists' as an completely independent entity within the process of reality.

Fig 10.6

Figure 10.7 shows an image that quantum evolutionist Johnjoe McFadden, Professor of Microbiology at the University of Surrey, uses to illustrate the process of quantum self-observation which he suggests is the driving force for evolution:

> ...we are now on the brink of a new adventure which will bring about the synthesis of physical and biological sciences through quantum mechanics. On the one hand, electronic engineers are constructing nanotechnology devices – electronics on the scale of living cells – manipulating single atoms and single electrons, on a level where they invariably confront the quantum nature of their raw materials. Biologists are coming to appreciate the fact that living cells have been performing nanotechnology for billions of years...[639]

There is now evidence that the processes of life may be 'evolved' through a quantum process through which nature tests out various possible 'paths' of development at the quantum level, before 'collapsing' into the most appropriate one. If this is the case then it would seem that evolution might, to a certain degree, to be able to 'look', or perceive ahead to see where it is going, so to speak.

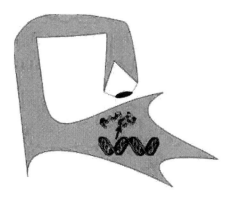

Fig 10.7

In 2007 a study carried out by researchers at the U.S Department of Energy's Berkeley Lab and the University of California discovered that the answer for the high efficiency of photosynthesis, a vital and fundamental mechanism of life, lies in the quantum mechanics of the process. A quantum wavelike electronic coherence plays an important role:

> The wavelike characteristic can explain the extreme efficiency of the energy transfer because it enables the system to simultaneously

sample all the potential energy pathways and choose the most efficient one.[640]

This is an extraordinary discovery of how the quantum superposed wavefunction is used by a natural mechanism in order to try out all the possibilities before the most efficient one is selected. In this mechanism we find that reality actually functions by directly utilising the possibilities within the wavefunction before 'choosing' the most appropriate pathway. According to the researchers the classical explanation, which requires the transfer of electrons, is simply 'inadequate and inaccurate'. What has been discovered, then, is that the essential process is one of a sustained coherent superposed state of resonant interaction within a quantum wavefunction superposition which results in a collapse into the most efficient possibility.

McFadden has suggested that a similar mechanism underlies the mutations of DNA, the molecular string which contains genetic coding. Such mutations, which were previously thought to be purely due to chance, are more likely to be quantum mechanical in origin:

> Quantum mechanics tells us that the protons in DNA that form the basis of DNA coding are not specifically in localised positions but must be smeared out along the double helix. ... At the quantum mechanical level, DNA must exist in a superposition of mutational states.
> If these particles can enter quantum states then DNA may be able to slip into the quantum multiverse and sample multiple mutations simultaneously.[641]

Such a quantum mechanism would supply the means for the subtle teleology towards the evolution of perceiving organisms to operate. We would expect that the various possible mutations are coded into the DNA quantum wavefunction, or superposition, with various different probabilities; probabilities which are determined to a large extent, of course, by the frequency of previous activation, although presumably there must be possibilities for completely new mutations. Which mutation actualizes will depend on a probabilistic interaction of the DNA wavefunction with its environment, an interaction which selects the most efficient outcome. Such a mechanism means that, in a certain sense, DNA molecules 'know' which mutations will be beneficial. It seems that the self-perceiving mechanism of manifestation could be a fundamental aspect of the evolutionary process of reality from the quantum level upwards.

As we have previously seen the nature of the wavefunction is such that when it is unobserved it will spread out, its probability distribution becoming increasingly smeared out over larger and larger areas. It is only when observed that it collapses back into a momentary fixed position and, as soon as the observation ceases, the wavefunction will once more begin to smear out, becoming more and more spread out from the position it was observed at. Rapid observations, or measurements, at the quantum level therefore can pin a quantum phenomenon into a relative stability; this is called the quantum Zeno effect (fig 10.10).

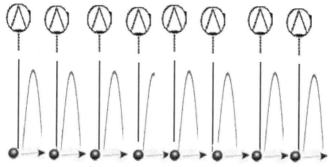

Fig 10.10 – quantum zeno effect

This mechanism of fixing quantum reality through habitual rapid perception is not speculation; it has been demonstrated in quantum experiments. John Gribben describes an experiment carried out at the U.S. National Institute of Standards and Technology which employed the Zeno effect 'to make the pot beryllium ions boil, and to watch it while it was boiling – which stopped it boiling.'[642] The experiment involved getting beryllium ions to jump between quantum states in a given period of time, the time being the time required for 100% of the ions to move from one state to another. The experimenter then stopped this quantum jumping by constantly observing, using a laser, and thereby fixing the ions into the first state:

> The act of looking at the ion has forced it to choose a quantum state, so that it is now once again purely in level 1. The quantum probability wave starts to spread out again, but after another 4 milliseconds another peek forces it to collapse back into the state corresponding to level 1. The wave never gets a chance to spread far before another peek forces it to collapse back into level 1 … [643]

This is an example of the quantum Zeno effect being consciously employed to manipulate quantum reality through rapid perception.

The inverse Zeno effect is a subtle development of this by which a manifested particle is coerced along one particular path, rather than other possible paths within its quantum possibilities, by making a sequence of measurements. Once a 'particle' has been fixed by measurement at a particular location its probability of being located a moment later, by a further measurement, in an adjacent location is large. So a rapid sequence of measurements can manifest and guide a particle along a chosen path. This is the mechanism which McFadden believes is able to drive the development of a manifest world from the possibilities within the quantum ground:

> The special relationship between quantum objects and quantum measuring devices draws out classical reality from the quantum world ... Can living cells draw out their own reality or do they need an audience.[644]

He continues by considering the catalytic role of enzymes in speeding up molecular transformations:

> "Enzymes are *catalysts* that speed the rate of chemical reactions by *directing the motion of electrons and protons along specific paths.*"[645]

Enzymes achieve this because their particular molecular make up interacts with the other molecules that are involved in the reaction in a way that makes the pathways that the particles must move along more probable; in this way the reaction is speeded up. With this image in mind McFadden proceeds to outline a method by which cells can manipulate particles at the quantum level by the inverse Zeno effect (fig 10.11).

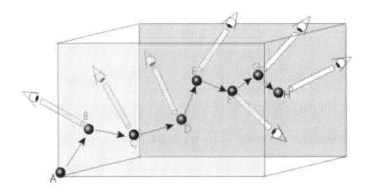

Fig 10.11 – inverse quantum zeno effect

The picture that McFadden presents is that if proto-enzymes in the 'primordial soup' develop the mechanism of producing copies of themselves by the utilizing the self-referential quantum measurement effect of the inverse Zeno effect, then we would have an example of a classical level structure which could bring other instances of itself into the 'classical' realm from the pool of quantum possibility by manipulating its own internal quantum states through a mechanism of self-perception:

in the proto-cell it was the emergence of the self-replicator that nailed the system to the classical world. Emergence of the self-replicator was at the end of the line for the inverse quantum Zeno effect. Quantum measurements by proto-enzymes along the route to the self-replicator laid down a series of stepping stones that led to the emergence of life.[646]

If, as it seems to be the case, life is coiled into the quantum level then, given what we know about the relationship between the quantum and classical dimensions, which involves the collapse of a wavefunction, by the agency of awareness-consciousness, then some kind of mechanism as that suggested by McFadden is quite clearly a serious possibility. McFadden's molecular mechanism turns inward to manipulate its own quantum states by unfolding its own enfolded potentialities:

> the living cell is turned in upon itself to perform measurements on its own particles and thereby perform internal quantum measurement.[647]

This is the proposal put forward by Jim Al-Khalili and Johnjoe McFadden in their paper *Quantum Coherence and the Search for the First Replicator*:

> They suggest that a quantum superposition of possible combinations between molecules in the primordial soup could be built up before decoherence intervened, and that this would be an efficient way of searching for the right combination of a replicator. Quantum systems can check out an array of possibilities simultaneously.[648]

As Al-Khalili and McFadden say, 'a quantum system can 'feel out' a vast array of alternatives simultaneously.'[649]

This proposal is clearly coherent with the view that the most natural conception of the starting point for the evolution of not only life but also the universe must be a ground of quantum potentiality, the quantum universal wavefunction. Furthermore, such a proposal requires that a minimal degree of cognitive functionality is internal to the quantum mechanisms driving the evolutionary process. This cognitive drive, which supplies Davies' 'teleology without teleology', produces a cognitive self-referential feedback loop either within the quantum level or at the boundary between the classical and the quantum level.

The following is taken from Amit Goswami's excellent book *Creative Evolution*:

> Life itself, in the form of the first living cell, is the first observer. … If we ascribe to a living system the capacity for observership by virtue of … hierarchical quantum measurement, the biologists' consternation about defining life and at the same time distinguishing it from nonlife is over.

The biologist Humbero Maturana came close to this position by characterising life as the capacity for cognition. Cognition requires a cognizer, thinking requires a thinker, perception requires a perceiver…

Behold the causal circularity of the role of the observer in quantum measurement … This circular logic of dependent co-arising of the subject and object(s) is called *tangled hierarchy*. … how does self-reference arise in the living cell? The answer: via tangled-hierarchical quantum measurement in its creation. And through this feat, accomplished in the first living cell, the universe became self-referent.[650]

It is interesting to note Goswami's use of the phrase 'dependent co-arising' in the context of the interdependent manifestation of the fields of subjectivities and objectivity, sentient beings and their environment. This manner of description accords precisely with the Buddhist view of emptiness as the interdependent arising of the fields of perceiver and perceived through the operation of the primordial cognitive function of the fundamental awareness-consciousness.

Darwin himself was not unfamiliar with the notion of a co-dependent aspect within the process of evolution for at the beginning of his chapter *The Struggle for Existence* in his *The Origin of Species* we can read:

How have all those exquisite adaptations on the part of one organisation to another part, and to the conditions of life, of one distinct organic being to another being been perfected? We see these beautiful *co-adaptations* most pleasantly in the woodpecker and mistletoe…[651]

This quote clearly shows us that Darwin, however, was undermined by his belief in inherent, or as he describes it 'distinct', existence! According to the Madhyamaka, as we know, any 'thing' that takes part in a process such as evolution cannot be inherently and absolutely distinct; because, if it was, it could not take part in the process!

The naturalistic quantum Mind-Only view, a view which completely accords with the facts of quantum theory contrasts with the dogmatic and clearly incorrect ultra-materialist Darwinism valiantly and faithfully defended by Richard Dawkins. According to Dawkins, living biological organisms are characterised by a complexity of organisation that appears to be goal-oriented towards 'working' to stay alive and 'propagate genes,' although the appearance of the gaol is an illusion generated by the operation of 'chance.' But he is very ambiguous about his use of the idea of 'chance' in this process. He is at great pains to refute the idea that the kind of chance involved in Darwinism is 'blind' or 'random', even though the title of his first hit book, of course, was *The Blind Watchmaker*:

The great majority of people that attack Darwinism leap with almost unseemly eagerness to the mistaken idea that there is nothing other than random chance in it[652]

We have seen that living things are too improbable and too 'beautifully designed' to have come into existence by chance.[653]

...people, ... Often expert in their own field ... seem sincerely to believe that Darwinism explains living organisation in terms of chance – 'single step selection' – alone. This belief, that Darwinian evolution is 'random', is not merely false. It is the exact opposite of the truth. Chance is a minor ingredient in the Darwinian recipe, but the most important ingredient is cumulative selection which is quintessentially *non-random*.[654]

Whereas Davies suggests that there must be a subtle teleology at work within the evolution of the universe and the life within it, Dawkins seems to derive teleology from the complete lack of teleology. According to Dawkins, certain people, who are 'often expert in their own field', which implies, of course, that they are completely incompetent at evaluating the veracity of ultra-Darwinian theory, miss the crucial distinction between 'single step selection' and 'cumulative selection'. Single step selection is, according to Dawkins, 'random chance' whereas cumulative selection is a kind of accumulation of chance events which, believe it or not, is 'quintessentially *non-random'*. You did read that correctly! According to Dawkins, Darwinian evolution is a process of non-random chance. This process is one of:

gradual step by step transformations from simple beginnings, from primordial entities sufficiently simple to have come into existence by chance. Each successive change in the gradual evolutionary process was simple enough, *relative to its predecessor*, to have arisen by chance. But the whole sequence of cumulative steps constitutes anything but a chance process when you consider the complexity of the final end product relative to its starting point.[655]

According to Dawkins each little step of the process is a chance event. However because the end result is a complex organisation, which has been directed by 'non-random survival', whatever that may be, 'cumulative selection' is 'a fundamentally non-random process'; in other words an accumulation of chance 'single selections' add up to a non-random 'cumulative selection' if the end result is sufficiently complex. Presumably if the end result just looks random then it still is random. Going a step further, it must be the case that a process made up of a sequence of steps is to be considered random or not on the basis of the end result, not on the basis the nature of the steps themselves. We can conclude that a couple of chance events will probably add up to a chance process but a large number of chance events can miraculously produce a completely non-random result. Magic!

Dawkins offers a few examples to try and gee us into his mode of paradoxical thinking. The simplest example is that of a hole which is able to sort balls into those bigger than it and those smaller. This analogy is meant to illustrate a system generating non-randomness by a non-intentional 'random' natural mechanism. This thinking leads Dawkins to his notion of a natural sieve. Dawkins thinks of 'natural selection' as a kind of sieve through which the single step chance events of evolution are sequentially fed through:

> the result of one sieving process are fed into a subsequent sieving, which is fed into ..., and so on.[656]

The random jiggling of the sea of endless possibility, thrown up by the chance workings of completely non-conscious, non-intentional molecular interactions endlessly ordered, in small gradual steps, by the taming influence of the natural sieve (fig 10.2).

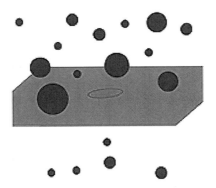

Fig 10.12 Dawkins' Balls

This picture, however, has one small, but vastly significant mistake. Where does the sieve come from? In the example of the balls and the hole, for instance, the hole is external to the random system of balls waiting to be ordered. The theory of evolution, if it is to claim an ultimate significance, should be self-contained, that is to say it should apply to the universe as a whole, *without recourse to external agencies*. This is, after all, exactly the kind of metaphysical requirement that Dawkins appeals to in his refutation of the notion of a creator God. And the fact that Dawkins does consider his vision to have ultimate metaphysical relevance is clearly apparent; he tells us, for instance, that:

Darwinism is true, not just on this planet but all over the universe wherever life may be found.[657]

The sieve, therefore, must be internal to, a part of, the evolutionary process. The only other alternative is that the sieve is already in place, expectantly waiting for emergent life to make a bid for survival so to speak.

The only other metaphysically viable possibility is that the sieve is generated by the very process which Dawkins is trying to explain by means of the sieve; which means that the sieve must be itself generated by its own process of sieving! This might seem like a tall order. Until, that is, it is realised that this mechanism is exactly provided by the Quantum-Mind-Only perspective which has been developed over the course of the previous chapters. In the chapters *Quantum Karma* and *Many Worlds of Illusion* we developed a self-resonating model of the evolutionary universe on the basis of a natural analysis of the implied functioning of DeWitt's formulation of the Schrödinger equation. This model of the functioning of reality involves the self-resonating feedback interaction between an objective environmental filtering wavefunction and the myriads of subjective individuated wave-functions that make up the structures of consciousnesses of all sentient beings of all species (fig 10.13). It is the objective wavefunction, of course, that naturally provides the sieve. The objective wavefunction, being an intersubjective creation, changes far more slowly than the more malleable subjective sentient beings cycling through it lifetime after lifetime, it would therefore appear as if it were the cycling sentient beings that were doing all the adapting so to speak.

The idea that the development of the structures of the vast variety of life within the universe can take place within hidden quantum dimensions, an idea intimated by Schrödinger in his 1944 essay *What is Life*, fits into the emerging evolutionary development (evo-devo) paradigm. For instance one of the early discoveries in the field was that the same 'master' genes were responsible for directing the layout of fundamental aspects of the body, such as the senses and limbs, in widely differing species. One example of this is that the genes in the Pax6 family direct the development of eyes in animals as different as flies and humans. It might look according to the usual Darwinian viewpoint, therefore, that flies and humans should have a fully materialised common ancestor, but it is surely unlikely that a fully physically manifested animal, or proto-animal, or even proto-cell, which was the ancestor of flies and humans, roamed the earth millions years ago, so to speak. The Quantum Mind-Only perspective replaces this patently absurd viewpoint with a much more plausible account, an account which is fully coherent with the emerging evolutionary-development paradigm.

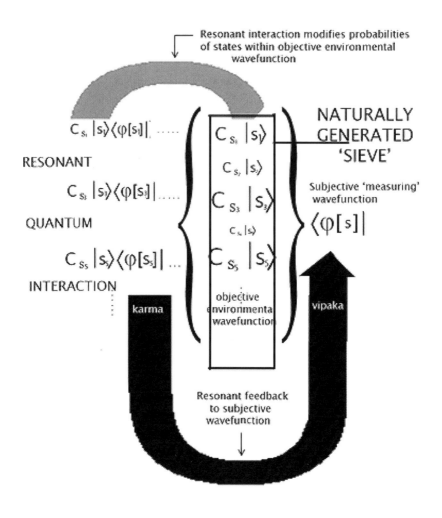

Fig 10.13 Quantum-Mind-Only natural evolutionary 'sieve'.

We can usefully begin with a brief overview of object oriented programming, which is a method of computer programming within which abstract 'objects' become increasingly more detailed by a process of 'inheritance' through a series of levels. This will serve as an illustration of how it maybe the case that quantum morphogenetic 'probability-structures' may develop through quantum 'implicate' levels of increasingly more 'explicate' degrees before fully manifesting within the 'material' world. The operation of such a quantum evolution within implicate quantum morphogenetic orders would explain evolutionary anomalies such as the Cambrian explosion.[658]

Figure 10.14 shows a much simplified example of an object diagram for an object oriented bank account system. The following discussion uses very loose terminology, the term 'class' refers to a template for an object, an object is usually thought of as an instance of the class. At the top of the hierarchy there is the class of the abstract object, this is a template which supplies the fundamental structural shape of the objects below. The general object template has properties and methods. Properties are attributes which each object may have; an account holder class for instance would have name, address, date of birth etc. Methods are operations which may be performed with the properties; a simple operation, for instance, would be sending the name of any particular account holder to an object below. Such a sending of details would be performed when an object below sends a message up the hierarchy asking for the details. Another 'method' within the class would be that of calculating the actual interest accrued by an account. Thus 'messages' are passed up and down the hierarchy of objects.

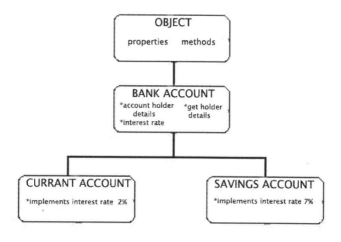

Fig 10.14

Objects below can 'inherit', 'override' or 'implement' properties and methods within the preceding object. If the object below inherits a property or method from one above, it simply takes the property over as it is, if it overrides a property or method it replaces the property or method within the object above with its own version. The term 'implements' is used when the object above has an abstract property or method; this is a property or method which is prefigured but not implemented within the object. Such an abstract property or method must be implemented somewhere below in order for the system to function correctly.

Through this concept of 'inheritance' through levels of implementation programmers are able to build more complex objects out of simpler ones or to take an object that would almost serve the intended purpose and easily modify it. Inheritance makes this much easier. New objects can extend existing ones. These new objects thereby inherit all of the properties and methods of the base object, but can modify or completely replace those that it needs to. In this way incredibly complex and useful objects can be easily created by building them from simpler objects.

For example, if a programmer wants to create a new type of object called 'horse,' this is most easily achieved by extending an already existing 'mammal' object. In this way the horse object inherits all the features and functionality of the basic mammal and the programmer only needs to modify or add those features that would differentiate it from a generic mammal. Likewise, the mammal object will be derived from some other simpler object, which was derived from an even simpler one and so on.

Figure 10.15 applies this perspective to the way in which an infinitely fecund nondual 'epiontic' ground of potential perceiving awareness-consciousness, the origin of the manifested universe, which, because of its limitless potentiality, innately functions to produce as many types of perceiving centres of awareness as possible, and also as many individuated instances of each type as possible, might proceed through a sequence of templates, starting from the most general and abstract, or implicate, becoming ever more manifested and explicate, might proceed in order to realize its dream, so to speak.

Thus the process of evolution is driven by a minimalist quantum intentional-perceptual cascade down through ever more 'explicate' orders from out of the deeper implicate orders of quantum awareness-consciousness. Bohm indicates that there must be a 'continuum of ordering principles':

> The super-implicate order, which is a so called higher field (the implicate order would be a wavefunction) would be a function of the wavefunction, a higher order, a super-wavefunction. The super-implicate order makes the implicate order non-linear and organises it into relatively stable forms with complex structures.[659]

Goswami likens the cascade of quantum templates to Sheldrake's notion of 'morphogenetic fields':

> The self-organisational dynamics of the 'possibility stuff' of the living form plays out, producing many macroscopic possibility forms (e.g., organs) … When quantum consciousness sees a match (i.e., a resonance) of movements between a morphogenetic blue-

print and a gestalt of many possibility patterns of form for an organ, it collapses actuality.[660]

The very first glimmer of perception, deep within the quantum ground, would simply be a movement of consciousness which gathers into a centre an intentional disposition for perception towards an aspect of the ground of reality which is interdependently posited as being that which is perceived. The first quantum implicate templates, therefore, would simply be that of perceiver-perceived, or grasper and grasped as the Buddhist Mind-Only philosophy terms the division. At this point there is only the intention, so to speak, as yet there is no actual perceiving going on as it were, there is the mere potentiality for a division into perceiving entities and perceived entities. The next requirement would be to divide the perceiving aspect into actual varieties of perception: sight, hearing, smelling, touching, tasting. This step will be accompanied by the kind of objects which can be perceived according to which sense faculty and so on. Again, however, such a 'virtual' formation of the possibility for manifestation would be 'implicate' not 'explicate', which is to say it would be a deep level quantum template for perceptual manifestation. This process will cascade down, through many quantum implicate levels, or 'orders', to ever more explicate 'gross' levels of manifestation, until, of course, an actual teaming experiential dualistic interconnected manifold of perceiving creatures and concomitant perceived worlds is 'created.'

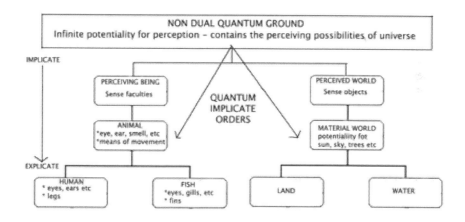

Fig 10.15

From this perspective genes are not the fundamental units of evolution which are desperate to survive on their own account, although they are obviously significant, they are, rather, the manifested gateways through which quantum morphogenetic patterns are expressed. This view of the process of the unfolding of the multifarious possibilities within the quantum ground of reality through a resonant interactive development of subjective and objective aspects of the innate universal unfolding of perceiving organisms can be immediately applied to some iconic Darwinian scenarios. We shall consider, briefly, Darwin's finches and the African cichlids.

The crucial Darwinian point concerning the Galapagos finches is that the beaks were supposed to have evolved by natural selection to fit the environmental surroundings, in this case the kind of nuts available being the evolutionary environmental factor (fig 10.16). This process is generally considered to have taken place gradually over a long time span due to random mutation. But the evidence gathered by researchers trying to support Darwin's gradualist account actually undermines it:

> He describes the evidence they gathered demonstrating the correlation of beak size with food supply ... and follows that with a good summary of the observations that the Grants made of beak size on the Island of Daphne Major after a drought. As the available supply of edible seed dwindled, only tough hard-to-open seeds were left, and only birds with larger, deeper beaks could eat them. Subsequent generations showed a dramatic increase in overall beak size in the population.[661]

This, however, does not indicate a mechanism which hangs around for a random mutation to ride to the rescue of the starving finches; it indicates an exquisitely tuned responsive interaction between the population about to inhabit an environment and the conditions of the environment immediately prior to the habitation by the subsequent generations. It is as if the experiences of the finches inhabiting the environment during the drought had left a trace within a deep level of the quantum field which then determined the form of the subsequent generations of finches. This corresponds exactly to Rupert Sheldrake's notion of a 'morphogenetic field', a kind of memory within nature, and the Buddhist alayavijnana and Bohm's 'implicate order'. All of these, of course, map onto the notion of the universal quantum field of reality.

The way that such a mechanism could function is easily comprehended when one recalls that according to quantum theory it must be the case that all possibilities for manifestation are contained within the universal quantum wavefunction. This is the basis for the Everett-DeWitt Many-Worlds theory of the functioning of reality, which says that all the possibilities within the universal wavefunction do actually happen in different experiential worlds. The Quantum Mind-Only vision of the functioning of reality, on the other hand, asserts that whilst all the possibilities for the type of finch beak are contained within the universal wavefunction, which one is expressed depends upon the environmental conditions that the finches are about to be expressed into. There is a 'morphic resonance' between the implicate finch template about to manifest and the possibilities for manifestation such that the most appropriate manifestation for the environmental conditions occurs. This quantum mechanism clearly has echoes of that expressed within the process of photosynthesis; the process of quantum manifestation into the classical realm quantumly tests out the environment before determining which potentiality of finch beak to actually implement.

Fig 10.16

Work on the actual mechanism underlying the phenomenon of the morphing finch beak has been carried out by Dr. Cliff Tabin and a team of developmental biologists at Harvard Medical School. The key to the process was found to lie within the operation of the BMP4 (bone morphogenetic protein number 4) gene which signals for the production of the BMP4 protein. This gene turns out to be remarkably multitalented as it also coordinates the development of the embryo. In order to verify the significance of the BMP4 gene in the morphology of beaks the researchers artificially increased the production of BMP4 in chicken embryos and the beaks of the chicks became wider and more robust. Researchers also found that a different gene was responsible for the expression of another protein, calmodulin, which resulted in long probing beaks. So the operation of just two genes, which coordinate the expression to the amounts of two different proteins, appear to control the morphology of beaks.

It appears as if there is an overall template for a finch, for instance, which could be conceived of as being of the form of a Sheldrakian 'morphogenetic field', which is then tweaked in its expression by the detailed operation of the genes underlying the template. Viewed from the perspective of Zurek's quantum Darwinism, it becomes clear that both the morphogenetic template field of the finch and the information which determines the actual expression of the details of the template, the exact form of the beak for instance, must reside in a quantum information field. This, again, is clearly homologous to Bohm's notion of the implicate order. This is a dramatic insight bringing together crucial insights from cutting edge quantum theory and evolutionary biology, and we can only expect exciting developments are close at hand within this field.

What is quite clear from the evidence so far, however, is that the materialistic notion of gradual step by step random mutations which is promulgated with pugilistic fervour by Richard Dawkins and others turns out not to be the full story. The only reasonable picture that can be drawn in the light of all the evidence available clearly points to the 'emergence' of the subjective perceiving aspect of the overall quantum process, together with the objective environmental container (the terms 'container' and 'contained' are used within Buddhist philosophy), in co-dependence on the overall interconnected field conditions. Such a co-ordinated co-arising through levels of quantum resonance is completely consonant with quantum non-locality. I hope that John Wheeler would have approved of my appropriation of his famous graphic image in figure 10.16 which illustrates this viewpoint.

It has been suggested by some evo-devo enthusiasts that the emerging perspective clearly shows that some form of subtle teleology is clearly indicated within the process of reality. The form of this teleology, however, has yet to be explicated. The Quantum Mind-Only perspective, with its assertion of the minimalist teleology of a self-perceiving function within the quantum ground of reality, as is clearly indicated by the phenomenon of the collapse of the wavefunction, provides exactly the form of teleology that is required to explain both basic quantum phenomena and developmental evolution at all levels, even that of the cosmos itself. Also, quite clearly this perspective completely elucidates the nature of the 'goldilocks enigma' of the anthropic fine-tuning of the universe.

Another 'iconic' Darwinian phenomenon is that of the African fish called cichlids which have evolved into such a huge diversity of species that they have become one of the best known evolutionary radiations. The cichlids have evolved into a dramatic diversity of different shapes and sizes, with a variety of jaw types which are adapted for different kinds of foods. Research has shown that exactly the same process operates in this case as in the case of Darwin's finches. All of the different types of cichlid have the same gene profile but the astonishing diversity is produced by the expression of the basic gene profile into different forms according to the environmental opportunities.

Subjective Perceiver

'Objective' Environment

Dependent Co-origination

Quantum non-local Interdependence

Quantum morphogenetic beak templates

Alayavijnana Matrix of Mind Implicate Order Quantum Information Ground

NON DUAL GROUND OF REALITY = EMPTINESS

Fig 10.16

It seems, then, that the same template will be expressed in any form which will fit into an environmental niche. This is exactly what one would expect of a creative self-perceiving universe which operates in order to maximize the number of perceiving organisms, of all possible types, according to the possibilities offered by the surrounding environments. This process, however, is not one in which the environment is fixed and given but, as we have seen previously, it is a process of interdependent co-origination between perceiving organisms and their environment. As we have also seen previously in the discussion of the Many-Worlds derivation of the process of evolution from an analysis of the structure of the Schrödinger equation, the environment is relatively stable in relation to the flexibility of perceiving organisms; this is indicated by figure 10.17.

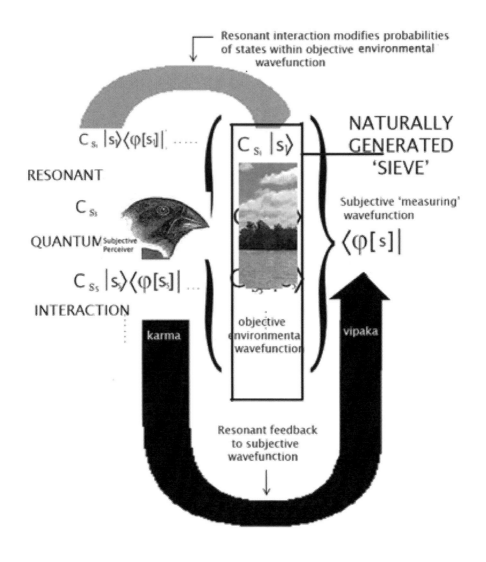

Resonant interaction modifies probabilities of states within objective environmental wavefunction

NATURALLY GENERATED 'SIEVE'

$C_{S_i} |s\rangle\langle\varphi[s_i]|$ .....

RESONANT

C_{S_i}

QUANTUM Subjective Perceiver

$C_{S_s} |s\rangle\langle\varphi[s_s]|$ ....

INTERACTION

$C_{S_i} |s\rangle$

Subjective 'measuring' wavefunction

$\langle\varphi[s]|$

karma

objective environmental wavefunction

vipaka

Resonant feedback to subjective wavefunction

Fig 10.17

In this way the subtle teleology within the process of the evo-devo universe is demonstrated by examining the structure of the fundamental quantum equation of reality.

This view of a quantum interdependent evolutionary manifestation driven by a minimalist universal 'intention' to generate the function of dualistic perception from a ground of awareness-consciousness is now becoming embodied within the quantum-informational approach to the functioning of the universe. Goswami agrees with Paul Davies' suggestion, in respect of the quantum process of evolution, that the form of consciousness at some point in time can have ontological impact even backwards in time. Davies refers to the necessity of:

> abandoning a rigid Platonic view of the nature of physical laws and replacing it with an information-theory picture in which the inbuilt laws of physics come with an inbuilt level of looseness or flexibility – a level which is miniscule today, but significantly higher in the universe's very early moments when its life friendly laws and parameters were being established.[662]

But there is no reason to limit the assumed flexibility of the ontological flexibility of manifestation just to 'physical laws' and the first few moments after the big bang. In fact such a view is clearly forced, it makes far more sense for the solidity of the ontological form of the manifestation of the universe to gradually become more ossified as consciousness itself becomes more individualised. The material environment and the inhabitants are intersubjectively created temporary illusions which emerge from the *quantum* 'primeval soup' through a hierarchy of interdependent organising perceptual movements within the overall universal quantum field of awareness through a process essentially described by the Quantum Mind-Only perspective described above.

As we have seen previously, John Wheeler, a quantum physicist and cosmologist who by consensus within the worldwide community of physicists is one of the most significant scientists of the later part of the twentieth century, tells us that the universe is self-created through the agency of all the conscious beings who ever existed over vast stretches of time. This act of universal self-creation takes place through the mechanism of continuous perception by the inhabitants of the universe. The entire fabric of the Universe is, according to Wheeler, created, or gradually built up, through 'small acts of perception' which are made by 'the observer participants in all times and all places'. This must, then, quite literally, mean that the perceptions of living beings create the fabric of the world of experience, including the appearance of the material world. .

Anton Zeilinger, the physicist who has been primarily responsible for extending the delicacy of quantum split beam experimentation to greater degrees of accuracy, emphasizes the significance of Wheeler's perspective by highlighting the far-reaching importance of the quantum implication of the non-existence of a reality which is independent of observation:

> The outstanding feature of Professor Wheeler's viewpoint is his realisation that the implications of quantum mechanics are so far-reaching that they require a completely novel approach in our view of reality and the way we see our role in the universe. This distinguishes him from many others who in one way or another

tried to save pre-quantum viewpoints, particularly the obviously wrong notion of a reality independent of us.[663]

According to Wheeler the role that all sentient beings must fulfil, to greater or lesser extent, in the quantum universe is that of participatory creator, participating in the creation of the experienced universe and the laws that it follows. The following is Wheeler's further explanation of his insight:

> Law without law. It is difficult to see what else than that can be the plan of physics. It is preposterous to think of the laws of physics as installed by a Swiss watchmaker to endure from everlasting to everlasting when we know that the universe began with a big bang. The laws must have come into being. Therefore they could not have been always a hundred percent accurate. That means that they are derivative, not primary ... Events beyond law. Events so numerous and so uncoordinated that, flaunting their freedom from formula, they yet formulate firm form ... The universe is a self excited circuit. As it expands, cools and develops, it gives rise to observer-participancy. Observer-participancy in turn gives what we call tangible reality to the universe ... Of all the strange features of the universe, none are stranger than these: time is transcended, laws are mutable, and observer participancy matters.[664]

For Wheeler the suggestion that the 'physical' laws which underpin the functioning of reality spring into manifestation from nothingness fully formed is simply unintelligible.

The 'laws' of quantum physics allow the nature of reality to be determined by consciousness even backwards in time. This introduces an extraordinary self-referential circularity in which the laws of quantum physics can allow for their own self modification backwards in time. This possibility was intimated by Wheeler in an imaginary experiment he proposed in which a split beam experiment is conducted on a cosmic scale. In this experiment a beam of light which originates in a distant quasar is bent around the two sides of an intervening galaxy on its way to earth, when it reaches earth the split beam is used in a conventional split beam experiment (fig 10.18). The new feature that this imaginary cosmic scale setup incorporates is a 'delayed-choice', as to the measurement of particle or wave aspect, which appears to act backward in time. The decision as to whether to measure the light as particle or wave is made on earth but the light might have been travelling across the universe for millions or billions of years. So the question that this cosmic scale 'delayed choice' experiment poses is what state, particle or wave, the photons have prior to their observation on Earth. The experiment has been interpreted as suggesting that the light must be influenced in some manner backwards in time across 'billions of years.'[665]

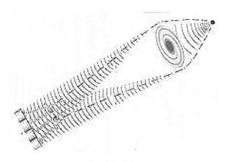

Fig 10.18

A version of this experiment has now been carried out by Zeilinger and his team at the University of Vienna, albeit not on a cosmic scale[666], and Wheeler's ideas have been verified, it therefore seems likely that the process of the universe constitutes a closed self-manifesting loop:

> Physics gives rise to observer-participancy; observer-participancy gives rise to information; information gives rise to physics.[667]

The physicist Freeman J. Dyson indicates the remarkable and radical nature of this viewpoint:

> Wheeler would make all physical law dependent on the participation of observers. He has us creating physical laws by our existence.[668]

According to Wheeler's participatory viewpoint the existence of the participating observers, which means all creatures endowed with consciousness, creates both the physical laws and also the appearance of the material world to which the laws apply. It is a direct consequence of the equations of quantum physics that it must be the case that processes of the physical world are the result of, or created by, the perceptions made by conscious beings that inhabit, or have inhabited, the universe.

The crucial notion in Wheeler's view lies in the assertion that 'the universe is a self-excited circuit'. Wheeler is quite clearly claiming that the universe has a natural tendency to observe, and at the same time create, itself through acts of observer participation, or perception. These participatory acts of perception constitute the actual mechanism through which 'the tangible reality of our universe' is generated. Furthermore this tendency for self-perception is an innate and fundamental aspect of reality. Perception is directly involved in the structuring of the physical world and its laws. So as Wheeler suggests quantum physics has vindicated Bishop Berkeley's view, who proposed two centuries ago that 'to be is to be perceived,'[669] on a universal scale. Wheeler was not precise concerning the exact nature of the mechanism involved, but 'observer-participancy' is a central feature of Wheeler's quantum universe.

As we have previously noted, Wheeler presented his vision in the graphic form of the 'Wheeler U', reproduced in fig 10.19, which illustrates his conclusion that a thorough consideration of the evidence of quantum theory, especially that of the delayed choice quantum experiments, indicates that the universe was brought into existence by the perceptual activities of the observer-participants, 'of all times and all places', who inhabit, or who have inhabited, it. Without its community of observer-participants the Universe would not exist.

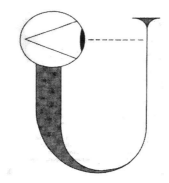

Fig 10.19 – The Wheeler U

It is interesting to note that the implications of such ideas are so dramatic that quite often the very physicists involved in their promulgation demonstrate a tendency to tone them down. Paul Davies, for instance, attempts to defuse the radical nature of Wheeler's perspective in this explanation of the significance of the Wheeler U:

> In this symbol Wheeler seeks to integrate mind and cosmos via quantum physics in a dramatic and provocative manner. He is not claiming that the physical universe doesn't exist unless it is observed, only that past states are less than real (if by real one means possessing a full set of physical attributes, such as all particles having a definite position, motion, etc.), and that present observers have a hand in determining the actuality of the past, even the remote past.[670]

This presentation attempts to say and not say something at the same time in order to lessen the radical nature of the claim. It is quite obvious that the idea that the participants within the universal process have a role in bringing it into full reality must require an integration of 'mind and cosmos'. This clearly means that mind must be incorporated into what was once thought to be a purely material, or 'physical', domain. It follows that Stapp's view that mind and matter must in some sense be 'two sides of the same coin' is unavoidable. It also follows that consciousness and the physical must be of the same nature and consciousness must determine the nature of the appearance of the 'physical.' All of which would suggest that consciousness was a primary, if not the primary, aspect of reality. Davies' description, however, constantly tends towards emphasizing the fact that a 'physical' realm exists independently of consciousness, even though without con-sciousness it is 'less than real'.

Wheeler's viewpoint clearly requires that consciousness must be firmly situated in the centre of quantum affairs. This is indicated by another of Davies' depictions of Wheeler's point of view:

> A true observation of the physical world, he maintained, even of something as simple as the decay of an atom, must not only produce an indelible record, it must somehow impart meaningful information. Measurement implies a transition from the realm of mindless material stuff to the realm of knowledge. So it was not enough for Wheeler that a measurement should record a bit of information; that lowly bit had to mean something.[671]

Once again, a significant point in this characterisation by Davies is its hasty imprecision in that it implies that there could be an independent realm of 'mindless material stuff'. Whether Davies really thinks this is Wheeler's viewpoint is not at all clear; however, it is certainly the case that Wheeler's perspective requires no realm of 'mindless material stuff' which could which make a transition into anything! Such a presentation is more in line with the views of the intellectually pugilistic arch-materialist Dan Dennett who op-ines to the tune that:

> An impersonal, unreflective, robotic, mindless little scrap of molecular machinery is the ultimate basis of all the agency, and hence meaning, and hence consciousness, in the universe.[672]

Amongst other such mindless characterisations of the process of reality.

In Wheeler's presentation of the role of information in the process of reality the interconnected nature of the experience of the *appearance of a material world* and the realm of 'meaning', which is, of course, the realm of consciousness is clear. A key slogan with which Wheeler delineated his viewpoint was 'it from bit' by which he meant that the physical 'it-ness' of reality is derived, in the last analysis, from 'bits' of information or meaning. So for Wheeler:

> ... the universe is fundamentally an information-processing system from which the appearance of matter emerges at a higher level of reality.[673]

It is intriguing, in the light of our previous analysis of the concept of 'matter', a concept that turns out to be an 'appearance' rather than a ground level fundamental aspect of reality, that Wheeler suggests that the 'appearance of matter' emerges as a by-product of a more fundamental system of information interchange. And a further implication of this perspective is that the concept of 'meaning' must have an important role in our understanding of this process; information is, of course, essentially a matter of meaning.

The picture that Wheeler proposed involved his notion of a 'meaning circuit' which is presented by Davies as the chain of the observer created material world:

observers -> information (meaning) -> matter

This is contrasted with the, now discredited, classical view:

matter -> information -> observers

Wheeler's new perspective, which corresponds closely with the perspective developed by Stapp, places the creation of 'meaning' through the process of observation, or perception, at the heart of the process of reality. According to Wheeler this process is actually a 'strange loop' which is able to self-refer and act upon itself through the agency of the 'observer participants', which are the sentient beings 'of all times and all places.' And, furthermore:

> ...the making of observations is a continuing process. Moreover, it is extraordinarily difficult to state sharply and clearly (1) where the community of observer-participators begins and where it ends, and (2) what the degree of amplification must be to define an observation...[674]

Wheeler's metaphysical perspective requires, then, that the elements of the physical world, the 'its' of reality, are creations of the inner tendency of the Universal process of reality to observe itself through a process of 'amplification', of many degrees of it-ness, so to speak, it-ness itself being an aspect of the process of reality which is implied rather clearly defined. Within the 'continuing process' of Universal 'amplification' of its own nature it conjures the 'bits' of meaning out of a deeper level of reality which are experiences as the 'its' of dualistic reality. The ontological driving force behind this cycle of self-perception on the part of the universe is consciousness of meaning, not matter; *as a matter of fact the universe is a meaning–machine*. As Stapp points out:

> ...the quantum universe tends to create meaning: the quantum law of evolution continuously creates a vast ensemble of forms that can act as carriers of meaning; it generates a profusion of forms that have the capacity to sustain and refine themselves.[675]

Here Stapp, like Bohm and Wheeler, locates the core quality of 'meaning' as central, it is 'the capacity of sustain'. Meanings are produced when perceptions become repeatable and therefore sustainable. This aspect of the concept of 'meaning' is also highlighted in Bohm's discussion of the notion of 'relevant':

> The word 'relevant' derives from a verb 'to relevate' ... whose meaning is 'to lift' ... In essence, 'to relevate' means 'to lift into attention', so that the content thus lifted stands out 'in relief'.[676]

In this characterisation Bohm is bringing attention to the fact that the aspects of experience which emerge into significance are those which are 'relevated' as meaningful through perception. This process corresponds to the 'amplificatory' meaning function within consciousness.

Wheeler, Bohm and Stapp consider that the qualitative experience of 'meaning' is a crucial, and central, aspect of quantum functioning and the creation of an experienced realm of reality. In Stapp's Heisenbergian model of the interaction of the objective and subjective aspects of the wavefunction he identifies the collapse of the objective wavefunction with a choice within subjective consciousness, not necessarily a fully conscious one; it might be instinctual, at the quantum level, which creates experienced meaning:

> ...each such choice is *intrinsically meaningful*: each quantum choice injects meaning ...[677]

This view clearly harmonizes with Wheeler's idea of a meaning circuit (fig 10.20) that connects mind and the appearance of matter. It also correlates very closely with ideas that Bohm presented in his 1985 essay *Soma-Significance and the Activity of Meaning*. In this essay Bohm presents meaning as the central stuff of reality. The three interrelated aspects of reality which Bohm isolates as fundamental for understanding experience are energy, matter, and meaning. Each of these three enfolds and implies the others and this mutual enfoldment provides the unity exemplified within experience (fig 10.21).

But a crucial extra dimension that Stapp adds in his description is the fact that each meaningful choice 'injects' further meaning into the quantum ground. In other worlds each choice must leave a meaning-trace in the quantum ground. The process of the meaning circuit, which operates at the quantum level, is self-reinforcing; each meaningful choice adds 'solidity' to the meaning value of the choice. This is the mechanism that underlies the self-creation through self-perception of the Universe. This metaphysical model, of course, is exactly that which has been presented in the chapter *Quantum Karma*.

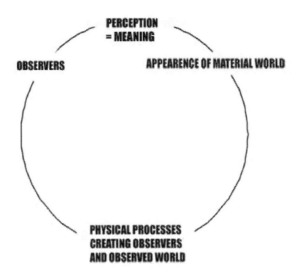

Fig 10.20

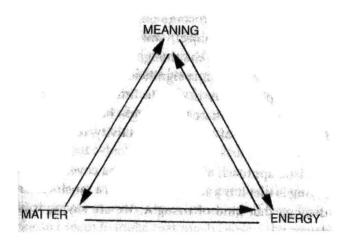

Fig 10.21

According to Bohm 'meaning' can be considered to be the most fundamental aspect of reality because it enfolds the others and it can also enfold itself, which is to say that it is possible to have multiple levels of meanings; higher level meanings can relate together meanings on levels beneath it, and so enfold them into a unity. So because the qualitative aspect of 'meaning' enfolds all three aspects, including itself, it is the fundamental aspect of experience:

> ... meaning refers to itself directly and this is in fact the basis of the possibility of that intelligence which can comprehend the whole, including itself. On the other hand, matter and energy obtain their self-reference only indirectly, first through meaning.[678]

Wheeler, Stapp and Bohm, then, clearly agree on the view that the aspect of meaning within the field of experience is fundamental. Meaning makes all comprehension and understanding possible. And it also underlies the creation of the appearance of the material world. The quality of 'meaning', which results from the functioning of consciousness, is able to refer to itself and thus can act as a basis for a self-referring or self-perceiving universe. Bohm indicates that meaning is a self-referring function that is intrinsic to reality; it is the inner quality of the universe:

> Rather than ask what is the meaning of the universe, we would have to say that the universe *is* its meaning. ... And of course, we are referring not just to the meaning of the universe for us, but its meaning 'for itself', or the meaning of the whole for itself.[679]

Without this inner quality of meaning being intrinsic to the universe from the start the universe could never mean anything, to itself or to anything within it. The function of meaning, then, can be looked at as the central source of the experiential polar aspects of mind and matter. Matter is an appearance of objective meaning to mind, and individuated consciousness, or awareness, is the ground of subjectively experienced meaning.

The idea that the manifestation of reality depends upon a deeper level of some kind of self-referential information-processing realm is rapidly becoming a popular paradigm. This idea has a more recent incarnation within the vision of a self-computing universe. In his recent book *Programming the Universe* Seth Lloyd, a professor of quantum mechanical engineering at M. I. T, agrees that the process of the creation of the universe is self-referential. The universe, he says, 'computes itself.'[680] According to Lloyd:

> ...the complex world we see around us is the manifestation of the universe's underlying quantum computation.[681]

The computing metaphor, however, is taken to a mechanistic extreme in Lloyd's perspective and he takes Wheeler's 'it from bit' metaphor a bit too far. The concept of 'meaning', he tells us, is too imprecise and unclear to be of relevance. In order to solve this problem he suggests that the concept of 'information', a concept which Lloyd assumes can have significance without recourse to the arena of the meaningfulness of consciousness, is, according to him, a much more precise notion. Information, he claims, is simply a matter of 'bits' as they are employed in computers; bits can be either a '0' or '1', on or off.

It follows, therefore, that from Lloyd's point of view it can only be concluded that, to parody the foregoing quote from him, the complex world we see around us is the manifestation of the universe's underlying manipulation of zeros and ones. And as the universe in question, according to the Lloyd scenario, is itself nothing but a matter of information exchange, being therefore just a matter of '0's and '1's manipulating other '0's and '1's, then it follows that the universe is nothing but a load of '0's and '1's manipulating themselves. Very illuminating! Lloyd's attempt to defuse the relevance of the direct realm of meaning, which is the realm of consciousness, by ignoring it, leads directly to absurdity; the intrinsically meaningful metaphysical circle shown in fig 10.14 is reduced meaningless binary juggling, within which there is no 'degree of amplification'. This is shown in fig 10.22.

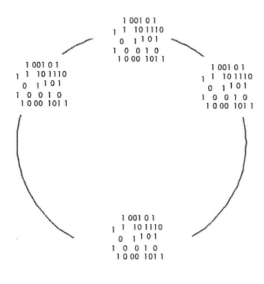

Fig 10.22

This absurdity disappears when the sphere of consciousness and meaning is restored into its proper place, the place where quantum physics clearly indicates that it ontologically occupies, as the creative force which is able to perform acts of 'amplification':

> Such a projection can be described as creative, rather than mechanistic, for by creativity one means just the inception of new content, which unfolds into a sequence of moments that is not completely derivable from what came earlier....[682]

The idea of the universe being comprised, in some fashion, of '1's and '0's, or 'Yes's and 'No's, is still contained in Stapp's picture. But Stapp's version is not a pointless juggling and jumbling of units of unawareness, in his picture the putative units of information spring into meaning, which actually transforms them into real 'bits' of information, so to speak, because they are given 'meaning' by appearing within a field of consciousness for which they have meaning.

In his important book *Wholeness and the Implicate Order* Bohm gives an overview of his perspective as follows:

> Our overall approach has thus brought together questions of the nature of the cosmos, of matter in general, of life, and of consciousness. All of these have been considered to be projections of a common ground. This we may call the ground of all that is, at least in so far as this may be sensed and known by us, in our present phase of unfoldment of consciousness. Although we may have no detailed perception or knowledge of this ground it is still in a certain sense enfolded in our consciousness...[683]

In this version, which incorporates the necessary cognitive function of consciousness as fundamental, it becomes clear that sentient beings are the 'agents' through which the universe acquires both meaning and structure. The universe, therefore, programs itself only through the intermediate programming agents – the sentient beings of all times and places. The Bohm, Wheeler, Stapp metaphysical perspective places the phenomenon of consciousness into the scenario in a completely natural manner whereas as Lloyd's notion of a purely impersonal, mechanistic juggling of '0's and '1's leads to absurdity; the kind of absurdity that results when an attempt is made to portray the process of reality in a way that minimizes the ontological significance of consciousness.

This kind of mechanistic madness reaches extraordinary degrees of absurdity in some extreme materialist 'emergent' accounts of how consciousness might develop from a self-referential loop, a strange loop, a loop which turns back upon itself in order to alter its own functioning in a purely mechanical manner – the computer programming model of consciousness is only a more sophisticated mechanistic perspective. Douglas Hofstadter, in his recent book *I Am a Strange Loop*, describes his own 'strange' materialist version. Hofstadter considers that when non-conscious and non-aware units of matter, beer-cans for instance, get organised together in a sufficiently complex manner then a completely new category of reality, the capacity for 'knowing', comes into being.

Hofstadter's strange loop version is indeed very strange and it pushes the limits of materialist credibility, not to mention philosophical credulity, to breaking point; for in his discussion of his disagreements with the philosopher John Searle he seems to seriously suggest that a sufficiently complex machine comprised of beer cans would become, to some degree, conscious:

> When one seriously tries to think of how a beer-can model of thinking or sensation might be implemented, the 'thinking' and the 'feeling', no matter how superficial they might be, would not be localised phenomena associated with a single beer can. They would be vast processes involving millions or billions or trillions of beer cans, and the state of 'experiencing thirst' would ... reside ... in a very intricate pattern involving huge numbers of beer cans.[684]

Hofstadter's beer-can model could also, apparently, develop a rudimentary awareness of a 'self' which, Hofstadter tells us, is:

> ...that 'special kind of pattern' that I have come to believe underlies, or gives rise to, what I have been calling a 'soul' or an 'I'. I could just as well have spoken of 'having a light on inside', 'possessing interiority', or that old standby, 'being conscious'.[685]

A very sobering thought!

This is an extreme example of the kind of absurdity which devolves from a determination to view the process of reality as a purely material phenomenon from which a strange emergent ontological illusion called consciousness 'emerges' as an apparently different, but essentially the same, medium as its material base. To choose beer-cans as the chosen elements of the description invites parody and ridicule, but the assertion that consciousness arises simply because of the self-referential interactions of completely *non-conscious* zeros and ones is in essence no less absurd.

In contrast to Hofstadter's inebriated version of the beer-can I–creating strange loop, Wheeler's Universe–creating strange-loop version which is embodied in his graphic image of the Wheeler U has an interesting feature which has not been heretofore noticed. It also indicates an I–creating function within the Universe–creating strange loop. The image consists of a 'U' which obviously represents the universe with an 'eye' on the left branch of the 'U' which looks back at its 'tail'. Wheeler's U is clearly reminiscent of the ancient Uroboros symbol which represents self-reflexivity or cyclicality, indicating the Universe constantly re-creating itself (fig 10.23). The branch of the tail which the 'eye' looks back at is actually an 'I' (fig 10.24). This tells us that in order for the universe to Understand its own nature It needs to create an embodied sense of Independent **I**-ness, and it does this continuously by creating the embodied sense of **I**-ness in a countless multitude of '**I**'s in a restless quest for its own meaning (fig 10.25).

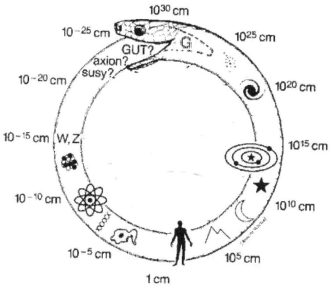

Fig 10.23

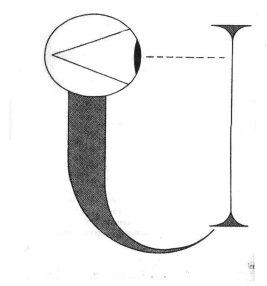

Fig 10.24

Fig 10.25

The image now is one in which the universe projects the illusion of many seemingly independent centres of experience, each of them a seemingly independent 'I' occupying one of the many illusory many realities of experience. This can be compared to the schema presented in the *Many Worlds of Illusion* chapter.

The experience of each individual 'I', therefore, is an illusion generated by the necessity for the universe to explore, and discover its own nature. It is precisely for this reason that Buddhism tells us that in order to know reality as it really is it is necessary to deconstruct, at a deep level, the illusion of the 'I'. The illusion of the conditioned 'I' within the realms of subjectivity and objectivity has its source in the unconditioned unity of the Universal process of reality. Because of this fact each individuated 'I' experiences the dis–ease generated by a 'thirst for the real', a deep seated thirst for the unconditioned that is an aspect of conditioned embodied experience. This 'thirst', which is called '*tanha*' within the Buddhist worldview, becomes a craving for existence which drives the wheel of *samsara*.

It is the reflection of the unconditioned unity of the source, Bohm's 'common ground', within the realm of the conditioned that gives embodied sentient beings the sense of being a unity, their I-ness, within the conditioned world of manifestation:

> The course of personal life is a continuous organic system of events. But still, what gives it its unique character of being personal is the sense of 'I', the fundamental fact of subjectivity, the experiencing of the inner life as 'I' and 'mine' … But the point

about this principle is that it is not any unconditioned, substantial entity. It is essentially a process, a function of determining and experiencing from within itself the course of events which it gives rise to as its self expressions in response to the basic urge in it, the thirst for the real, …its function is conditioned at root by the sense of the unconditioned which is its basic insight. The fundamental fact about man is his thirst for the real.[686]

The experiential dualistic field of consciousness-reality results from the division of a fundamentally unified field of meaning-consciousness (*jnana*) that splits into a multitude of experiences and meanings within the manifested world of phenomena. Subsequently all of the manifested experiences and meanings within the world of the dualistic field of seeming reality carry the mark of their origin in the unified source because they present themselves as inherently existent and self-enclosed entities. The experiential illusion of 'inherent existence', the deeply embedded sense of selfhood is the Universe's way of saying '**I** am'.

The Wheeler **U** presents a stylised image of the universe 'looking at itself' or even 'creating itself'; and in the previous discussions we have viewed the universe as a process which is in search of itself; an endless task of self-perception in search of the certainty of an inherent self, of *being* some-*thing*. And, paradoxically, in order to find itself it has to hide itself, so to speak, in a continuous process of dualistic experience. This much is apparent, but can we give an answer to the ultimate question regarding the reason, or the genesis of this universal search?

There is an answer to this universal question, the question that Leibniz and Heidegger considered to be *the* essential philosophical problem; and the question Wheeler posed in the form 'Why the quantum?' All manifestations from the ultimate into the conventional realm derive from an undivided field which lies at the heart of reality. Although fundamentally undivided, the undivided nature paradoxically divides itself; and when an essentially undivided field divides against itself there arises a craving, or thirst, for wholeness. This is *tanha*, craving; the fundamental thirst for experience of a 'self,' which lies at the heart of the process of samsaric, or unenlightened, reality.

If we ask where this craving arises from then we must understand that the process of reality is an essentially impersonal process of manifestation which results from the fact that there is a fundamental and incongruous tension which resides at the heart of reality. This apparent contradiction arises from the fact that it is the fundamental inner nature of reality to perceive precisely because awareness is a fundamental intrinsic aspect of the process of reality. Primordial awareness-consciousness, which is the fundamental ground of reality, has an inner necessity for perception. But from an ultimate point of view *there is nothing to perceive except itself;* herein lies the necessity to create experiences of selfhood in a dualistic world of perception.

Such experiences, however, are ultimately illusory:

> And thus there is no self existing separate from the aggregates;
> Divided from the aggregates there is no self to grasp.
> The common man does not ascribe his sense of 'I' to such a source.
> He does not know of such a self, and yet he thinks 'I am'
> And we may see that beings born as beasts for many ages
> Never apprehend a self unborn and permanent.
> And yet they clearly have a sense of 'I'.
> Thus, separate from the aggregates, there is no self.[687]

The fundamental nature of reality, therefore, necessarily forces a manifestation within the realm of the conditioned. An 'empty' nature, the mere potentiality for experience, which actually is neither existent, nor non-existent, but hovers between the two, so to speak, must create the illusion of actual 'existence' within a realm of duality, which necessarily contains illusory experiences of selfhood, in order to fulfill the fundamental requirement of perception. It is because of this inner conflict that, what Wheeler describes as, the 'self-excited circuit' of reality comes into being. The self-excitation is caused by the inner tendency for perception within the ground of the process of reality.

This inner tendency or inner necessity for the manifestation of perception, together with the fact that the perceptive activity, which is manifested within all sentient beings, operates upon the fundamental ground of emptiness, is clearly indicated in quantum theory. The fact that the 'ground' is 'emptiness', which as we saw in the chapter *Quantum Emptiness*, can be characterised as the state of hovering between existence and non-existence, is precisely indicated by the nature of the ground of quantum reality, also called the quantum void. In the following quote the reader must be aware that Paul Davies is using the term 'emptiness' as he understands it from a Western philosophical point of view, which does not correspond to the notion of emptiness employed within the Madhyamaka. The following use of the term 'emptiness' equates to 'nothingness':

> So the intuitive notion of emptiness, one in which all fields have and maintain the value zero, is incompatible with quantum mechanics. A field's value can jitter around the value zero but it can't be uniformly zero throughout a region for more than a brief moment. In technical language, physicists say that fields undergo vacuum fluctuations.[688]

This describes the state of the 'zero point vacuum', the quantum ground state prior to any kind of manifestation. But because Davies is using the term *emptiness* to mean 'nothingness', it is clearly 'incompatible with quantum physics.'

The 'zero point vacuum', which is due to Heisenberg's Uncertainty Principle, can be seen to be completely consistent with the state of *shunyata-emptiness*, the state of 'neither existence nor non-existence', as the term is used within Buddhist philosophy. The root of the term *shunyata*, which is translated as *emptiness*, is *sunya*, the zero point, the cosmic seed of emptiness which is 'swollen' with potentiality. One meaning of *sunya,* which is the Indian origin of the concept of zero, is 'the swollen', in the sense of an egg of potentiality which is about to burst into manifestation.

If we replace Davies' use of the 'emptiness' with *shunyata-emptiness*, with the correct Madhyamaka meaning of 'hovering between existence and non-existence', taking existence to indicate the zero-point field's positive value and non-existence to indicate a field's negative value, then we can slightly amend the Davies' portrayal as follows:

> So the intuitive notion of *shunyata-emptiness*, one in which all fields do not maintain the value zero, *is required by quantum mechanics*. A field's value can jitter around the value zero but it can't be uniformly zero throughout a region for more than a brief moment. In technical language, physicists say that fields undergo vacuum fluctuations.

Indeed, David Bohm did make exactly this attribution:

> It would be the holomovement, you see, the flowing movement. But it goes beyond that. We could say that even at this level of thought there is a way of looking at it in which emptiness is the plenum...[689]

This is, on a physical level, exactly the Madhyamaka concept of emptiness. The *Kalacakra Tantra* describes this state as it exists between the destruction of one universe and the karmic arising of the next as follows:

> During this time of emptiness the subtle particles of these five elements exist as isolated fragments and are not in any conventional sense objects of the sensory powers of the eye and so forth. They are known as *empty particles*....[690]

There follows a cascade of an infinitude of acts of quantum self-perception that stabilizes a subject-object duality and thereby brings potentiality into experienced reality.

The Buddhist Mind-Only metaphysical perspective presents the process of reality within which there is a unified 'common ground' of Mind which gives rise to the illusion of the perceptual 'poles' of subject and object, perceiver and perceived, or apprehender and apprehended:

Because of its appearance as dualistic being
And because of its being one due to being mere delusion,
The nature called 'other-dependent'
Is thought of as having the character of duality and unity.[691]

With the foregoing in mind, the following observations by Bohm, contained in a letter to a friend, are truly remarkable:

> I suggest that consciousness is a distorting mirror, which is able, in effect, to give two apparently different but related and interacting reflections of one process. In reality there is neither 'I' nor 'me', but the individual in his totality (individual=undivided). The ego process with the 'I-me' division could be called the 'dividual'. In the individual perception is going on without the need for a 'perceiver' to do the job. Our language forces us to say that a subject is acting on an object. Thus we say 'It is raining''. But where is the 'it' that is doing the raining. Similarly we say 'I am observing.'[692]

This is exactly the description of the manner in which an undivided ground of awareness-wisdom (*jnana*) divides into dualistic consciousness (*vijnana*) as described by the Buddhist Mind/Cognition-Only analysis of the process of reality. The result of the operation of the 'self-excited circuit' of the Universal process of manifestation is the production of the illusions of two types of 'self' within the conditioned world of dualistic phenomena. These are called within the Madhyamaka the illusion of 'personal self' and the illusion of the 'self of phenomena' (fig 10.26). It is these two illusions of selfhood which need to be penetrated in order for a sentient being to see into the real nature of reality – Emptiness. As Tsongkhapa explains:

> To grasp the world as existent is the ignorance of grasping true existence. Of these two, confused ignorance about the self of phenomena is, having objectified such phenomena as the eye, nose, etc, grasping them *qua* existing in virtue of their own characteristic. The confused ignorance about the self of the person is, having objectified the person, grasping it *qua* existing in virtue of its own characteristic.[693]

In other words it is the very nature of psychophysical embodiment to create the illusion of duality, an illusion that is so powerful that an innate grasping at existence as being real, rather than illusory, produces a deeply held belief that there is an inherently real internal psychological centre of operation, which is the personal self, and also the corresponding illusion that there is an external field of inherently material phenomena, including the phenomena which makes up the appearance of one's own body:

The self is that which is the essence or nature of things, and is their independence of others. The non-existence of this is selflessness. On the basis of the distinction between person and phenomena two selflessnesses are conceived: the selflessness of the person and the selflessness of phenomena.[694]

This is why the Buddhist doctrine of *anatta*, or no permanent 'self', is crucial, it is precisely the illusion of fixed and permanent 'selves' and essences that keeps sentient beings bound within the suffering wheel of samsara. The two types of 'self', inward and outward, the 'self' of persons and the 'self-natures' of phenomena, are illusions; whereas the realisation of the two selflessnesses constitute entrances to enlightenment, and it is by employing the deconstructive techniques of Buddhist deconstructive philosophy, together with meditational insight, that it is possible to 'burst the bubble of the universe' by penetrating this powerful delusion of the two illusory 'selves'.

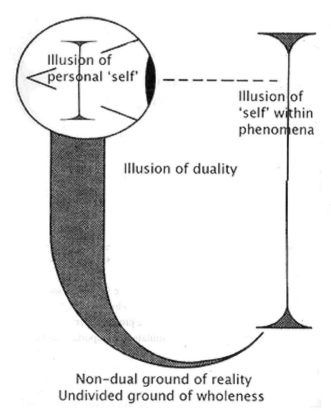

Fig 10.26

Burstng the Bubble of the Universe

[The Buddha] sat under the Bodhi tree at Gaya, wrapped in deep
meditation. It was then that His mind burst the bubble of the
universe and realised the true nature of all life and all things. At
the age 35 years, He was transformed from an earnest truth
seeker into the Buddha, the Enlightened one.[695]

The Buddhist analyses of the nature of reality, upon which the teachings concerning the methods of transformation of psychophysical embodiment towards the attainment of enlightenment are based, are presented in three main phases; or three turnings of the wheel of *dharma*, a term which indicates the truth of the Buddhist teaching. The three phases are: the fundamental vehicle (*Hinayana*), the Mind-Only presentation (*Yogachara-Chittamatra*) and the Middle Way presentation (*Madhyamaka*). The place in the sequence of the latter two is a matter of debate. Furthermore, the Madhyamaka itself has a twofold division into *Svatantrika*, the Autonomy School which employs arguments involving the provisional attribution of substantiality, and the *Prasangika,* which is the Consequence School employing reductio-ad-absurdum arguments, thus avoiding any attribution of substantiality. On the basis of these there are further refinements which are formed by melding together perspectives from different points of view. An example of this is provided by the important 8th century contemplative-scholar Shantarakshita, one of the early Buddhist teachers in Tibet, who integrated the Yogachara and Madhyamaka and taught the system of the *Yogachara-Svatantrika-Madhyamaka*, which is the primary perspective of this book. This system, as well as the others mentioned above, will be described in this chapter.

The basic ideas of these various presentations will be elucidated within this overview. It is essential to hold in mind that the fundamental perspective adopted within Buddhist philosophy of the nature of the process of reality is such that there is a hierarchy of perspectives, each perspective incorporating important aspects concerning the truth of the ultimate. Furthermore each perspective depends upon the level and mode of comprehension of the practitioner or student. This is the reason why there are a variety of perspectives within the Buddhist philosophical tradition. This is a mode of what is called within Western philosophy '*relativism*,' which is the idea that the truth concerning the ultimate nature depends upon the mind of the observer-participator, a view which has an interesting echo within quantum theory. For many Western philosophers relativism often seems to be understood as a kind of ungrounded free-for-all within which any super-ficially coherent account of reality is treated as viable. Within Buddhist thought, however, it is asserted that there is an ultimately inexpressible and experiential ultimate truth which manifests in a variety of perspectives each of which is coherent with its essential nature.

Over-arching this threefold division and the various subdivisions there is the basic division into the *Hinayana*, often translated as the 'Lesser Vehicle' but more appropriately called by the Dalai Lama the 'fundamental vehicle,' and the *Mahayana*, or the 'Great Vehicle.' The basis of this twofold division is the fact that the Hinayana presents the fundamental teaching and practices which form the essential basis for the practice of any of the techniques and methods of the Buddhist path to enlightenment; the Mahayana contains more extensive teachings which are based upon the insights contained in the fundamental teachings. There were originally eighteen schools of Hinayana but the only remaining version is the *Theravada,* the teachings of the Elders. The basic flavours of the Mahayana are the Yogachara-Chittamatra, Yogic Practitioners of the Mind-Only School, and the Madhyamaka, the Middle Way School.

It is sometimes thought that the division into the Hinayana and Mahayana is far more significant and rigid than it actually is. One such idea, for instance, is that the Theravada teachings are purely practical and contain no metaphysical implications. This is mistaken and the truth is that, whilst there is a difference in emphasis on the scope of teachings employed, the fundamental Buddhist psycho-metaphysical vision of the functioning of reality, which comes into full flower within the Mahayana, is contained within the earlier teachings.

For instance, in his biography of Ajahn Mun, the inspirational re-invigorator of the Thai Forest Tradition, which is a Theravada tradition, Acariya Maha Boowa Nanasampanno writes about Ajhan Mun that:

Ajahn Mun

Occasionally obliged to give instruction to lay supporters, he was always very frugal with his words. The little he did say could be summed up like this:

> You should renounce evil and cultivate goodness. Being fort-unate enough to be born human, don't waste this good opport-unity now. Our status as human beings is a very noble one; so, avoid all animal-like behavior. Otherwise, you'll sink below the animals, and be much more wretched as well. When you even-tually fall into hell, your tortuous existence there will be far more grievous than that of any animal.[696]

This teaching resonates strongly with the presentation of the first phase of Buddhist practice, which is that of lesser scope, which appears within the *Lamrim – The Stages of the Path to Enlightenment*, which is one of the central presentations of Mahayana Buddhism. The meditations of the lesser scope of the Lamrim include the fortunate status of human rebirth, the inevitability of death, the sufferings of the lower (animal and hell) realms, karma or cause and effect. These are quite clearly the issues covered by Ajahn Mun's pithy discourse. In fact it is quite clearly stated in the biography that Ajahn Mun had in a previous life taken the Mahayana bodhisattva vow, the vow to keep cycling through samsara in order to save all sentient beings, but he subsequently thought better of it:

> Acariya Mun renounced his vow to be a Buddha ... for he then realised that its fulfillment would take far too long. It required eons of traversing the round of samsara: being born, growing old, becoming ill, and dying over and over again, enduring misery and pain indefinitely.[697]

Thus we see that the basic framework of understanding the process of reality as a process of continuous transmigration of sentient beings through the various realms of samsara and the possibility of achieving a merely personal liberation from the cyclic realm or the universal achievement of buddha-hood seems to be fundamental to both Hinayana and Mahayana.

The primary focus of the fundamental level of study and practice is a thoroughgoing gritty examination of the suffering nature of conditioned dualistic experience and the adoption of some basic modes of behaviour which are capable of offering the beginnings of a way out. This fundamental perspective is embodied in the first turning of the wheel of dharma that Buddha began outlining in his first discourse, the *Dhammacakkappavattana Sutta* which was given at the Deer Park at Sarnath shortly after his enlighten-ment. The foundation of the fundamental ground for Buddhist practice is the **Four Noble Truths**:

1. The truth of suffering (Sanskrit: *duhkha*; Pali: *dukkha*): *Duhkha* is usually translated as 'suffering' but actually has a broad range of application including aspects such as general dissatisfaction, in the sense that there is nothing within the experiential realm of samsara that can bring lasting satisfaction. Generally speaking human beings have an extraordinary capacity for self-deception and are able to maintain an 'all things bright and beautiful' attitude in the face of all the evidence to the contrary. In fact it seems that they are 'hard-wired' to ignore the facts of existence as long as it is possible to grasp at some form of temporary relief from the basic ground of suffering that constitutes the basic feature of samsaric life.

This aspect of the foundational Buddhist analysis of the nature of reality is emphasised in the story of the Buddha's explorations of the world outside of his palaces when he was the unenlightened Prince Siddhartha. His father, King Shuddhodana, had hoped to protect him from seeing the grimmer aspects of reality outside of the pleasures arranged for the Prince within the confines of the three palaces that had been built for him, but the Prince persuaded his father to let him explore outside of the palaces.

Although King Shuddhodana attempted to make sure that Prince Siddhartha did not encounter any disturbing sights, this attempt was in vain as the future Buddha came across sights of sickness, old-age and death. To make things worse Siddhartha's charioteer explained that these unpleasant events would befall all sentient beings. When Siddhartha subsequently came across a homeless ascetic seeker after the deeper truth concerning the nature of reality, he realised that the pleasures that were available to him would only be temporary and in order to find a solution to the dissatisfactoriness of existence he would have to renounce such temporary pleasures in order to seek a deeper truth.

Siddhartha gave up all trappings of royalty and became an ascetic, practicing under the instructions of two renowned spiritual teachers. Under their guidance he quickly mastered the meditation techniques which enabled focused awareness called the four *jnanas,* or concentrations, and the subsequent absorptions: infinite space, infinite consciousness, the sphere of nothingness, and the final sphere of neither perception nor non-perception. These are advanced states of focused consciousness which can be attained through concerted, rigorous meditation practice; however, in order to so this it is generally necessary to remove oneself from everyday life.

The future Buddha also practiced extreme asceticism until he came to the conclusion that a middle path between the extremes of mortification and indulgence was preferable. He then finally sat in meditation posture under the Bodhi tree in Bodh Gaya, determined to use his laser-like meditative concentration to penetrate the inner secret of the functioning of reality. The following description from the excellent introductory work *Buddhism for Dummies* is probably difficult to better:

It was the night of the full moon in the fourth Indian month (which falls in May or June of our Calendar). As the moon rose higher and higher in the sky Siddhartha's meditative concentration deepened. The fire of his growing wisdom burnt away whatever layers of unknowing still obscured his mind. He directly and unmistakably perceived the stream of his past lives and understood exactly how past action lead to present results. He saw how attachment, the source of suffering, is rooted in ignorance. As his wisdom got rid of subtler and subtler levels of this ignorance, his mind grew increasingly luminous. Finally, as the moon was setting and the sun of the next day was rising, Siddhartha attained the ultimate goal – full and complete enlightenment.[698]

With this 'bursting of the bubble of the universe' the Buddha directly penetrated, with one-pointed focused wisdom, the mechanisms which created and maintained the dualistic suffering realms of samsara within which all unenlightened sentient beings were trapped.

2. The truth of the cause of suffering: As the above quote indicates, the essential point that the Buddha was able to distil from his deep insight was that the source of the pervasive suffering which is the condition of all sentient beings was rooted in the desirous attachment that itself was rooted in ignorance of the true nature of reality. It is often thought that this is a simple teaching, and in a sense it is, just give up wanting things and wanting things to be a particular way, stop trying to change conditions in order to bend them to one's desires, and the suffering which derives from such attachment will clearly be removed; if, that is, one truly does remove the desire.

The surface simplicity of this teaching belies its depth. On the surface level we might think of the way in which many people resort to shopping in order to give themselves a lift, which means, of course, to 'lift' their mood, usually a mood of mild to severe depression. Where does this depression come from? Often it comes exactly from the pervasive dissatisfaction which most sentient beings experience as the ground of the experience of embodiment. In order to cover over this seemingly innate perception of the dissatisfactory nature of embodied existence it is often the case that the attention turns towards the possibility of acquiring external material items to bolster ones hope of finding satisfaction. This psychological mechanism is well known to senior members of retail corporations. In a recent radio interview a CEO of a major retail chain of stores quite openly stated that most people who visited his stores did not need the cloths they were buying. What they needed, he said, was the 'experience.' The secret of his success, by his own admission, was in his orchestration of the maximisation of the shopping 'experience,' even though most of the time the goods (even the term 'goods' gives the game away!) bought were unnecessary. We are so used to this kind of manipulation of pathology in modern Western life; the interviewer did not give any indication that anything might be amiss!

This kind of desire for acquisitive experience, however, is only the tip of the iceberg of craving. Whilst 'ignorance' of the ultimately self-defeating consequences of this kind of addiction to acquisition clearly contributes to the continuous disappointment which accrues from the fact that the temporary highs which result from the experience of material acquisition are short-lived, the Buddha was indicating a much deeper ignorance; the ignorance of the fact that there is ultimately no 'self' which acquires anything and, perhaps even worse, there is nothing which can be permanently acquired.

The entire process of craving driven by ignorance is founded upon a complete illusion regarding the nature of the process of reality. For at the deepest level of the operation of the cycle of suffering existence it is the deeply rooted innate craving for dualistic experience, a mode of experience which creates the illusion of there being a separate and independent 'self' within the continuum of a sentient being, that endlessly maintains the transmigration of sentient beings from lifetime to lifetime, possibly with differing forms of embodiment, within the dualistic cycle of samsara.

3. The truth of the cessation of suffering: the third truth simply asserts that it is possible to break out of the cycle of suffering though the spiritual practice outlined in the fourth truth.

4. The truth of the path which leads to the cessation of suffering: the final 'noble' truth outlines the stages of a 'path' through which it is possible to transcend, or liberate oneself from, the cycle of suffering. But whilst this truth presents a 'path,' it is important to be aware that the term 'path' is used metaphorically, for it is also asserted that at the end of the path it is realised that in actuality there never was a 'path' to embark on precisely because there never was any 'self' to engage in such a 'path' in the first place. However, for deluded beings it is necessary to present an illusory spiritual path in order for them to overcome ignorance and delusion regarding the nature of the process of reality.

In the first turning of the wheel of dharma the Buddha taught the noble eightfold 'path':

- **Correct view:** initially it is necessary to form a correct understanding of the functioning of the process of reality. This includes clearly seeing the overwhelming suffering which is innate within the cycle of existence and the operation of karma or cause and effect across lifetimes. As practice deepens the most significant view which it is essential to realise directly and continuously is the truth of the lack of a 'self' in all phenomena.

- **Correct intention:** the intention to act on the basis of correct view. This requires the intention to abandon selfish attitudes which cause suffering to oneself and others
- **Correct speech:** avoiding harmfulness with speech. Harsh speech and lying, for instance, not only harms others, such actions also tend to rebound harmfully upon one's own mental continuum.
- **Correct action:** avoiding harmful actions such as stealing and violence. Also a Buddhist practitioner should positively seek to perform beneficial actions on behalf of all sentient beings.
- **Correct livelihood:** avoiding occupations which can harm oneself and others. Examples of harmful livelihood include butchering animals, drug dealing; any occupation which involves deception.
- **Correct effort:** the maintenance of joyful and enthusiastic effort which furthers spiritual practice.
- **Correct mindfulness:** Mindfulness is cultivated within meditation but must be extended to all aspects of life. The serious practitioner is constantly mindfully aware of the consequences of all actions, such mindfulness is essential for the practice of the previous stages of the path. Within meditation the practitioner seeks to deepen focused peaceful non-distracted awareness of the nature of mind.
- **Correct concentration:** on the basis of the previous stages the practitioner must cultivate a focused penetrating meditative concentration through which the final insight into the ultimate nature of reality – emptiness – can be realised.

The four noble truths are called 'noble' because they are only directly realised and thoroughly known by Noble ones (*Aryans*) or enlightened beings. Furthermore, the practice of the teachings of the four noble truths is ennobling because it leads towards the goal of becoming such a Noble one.

The Buddha's second discourse, the *Anattalakkhana Sutta: The Discourse on the Not-Self Characteristic*, introduced the three marks of existence: *dukkha* (suffering and unsatisfactoriness), *anicca* (impermanence) and *anatta* (lack of a permanent self). The Sutta begins:

> The body, monks, is not self. If the body were the self, this body would not lend itself to dis-ease. It would be possible (to say) with regard to the body, 'Let my body be thus. Let my body not be thus.' But precisely because the body is not self, the body lends itself to dis-ease. And it is not possible (to say) with regard to the body, 'Let my body be thus. Let my body not be thus.'[699]

This observation is then repeated for each of the other *skandhas (Pali: khandhas)*. The term 'skandha' is usually translated as 'aggregate' but a more appropriate characterisation is 'constituent process of psychophysical embodiment.' The primary focus of this deconstructive analysis is to highlight the changing and evanescent nature of the experiential processes within a continuum of awareness that forms the basis for the mistaken attribution of a permanent 'self'. These five process-aggregates are:

1. **'Form' or 'matter'** (Skt., Pāli *rupa*): external and internal matter. Externally, *rupa* is the experienced physical world. Internally, *rupa* includes the body and the physical sense organs.

2. **'Feeling'** (Skt., Pāli *vedana*): the reaction to an experience as either pleasant or unpleasant or neutral.

3. **'Perception' or 'discrimination'** (Skt. *samjñā*, Pāli, *sañña*): registers whether an object is recognised or not.

4. **'Mental formations,' 'volitional impulses,' or 'compositional factors'** (Skt. *samskāra*, Pāli, *sankhara*): mental predispositions and habits, conceptions, opinions, prejudices, compulsions.

5. **'Consciousness'** (Skt. *vijñāna*, Pāli *viññāna*): is the cognitive capacity of awareness that forms the basis for the operation of mind and the sense faculties.

According to the first set of teachings of the Buddha these constituent processes make up the entire process of the psychophysical continuum of a sentient being. A crucial point of this analysis is that the interconnected process of the five skandhas is conceived as giving rise to a continuum of momentary flickering pulses of awareness and, because of the speed and interconnection of the process, the illusion of a permanent 'self' within the midst of the continuum is generated.

It is this illusion of personal 'selfhood' that the Buddha sets out to deconstruct in his second discourse. One essential feature of the illusion of selfhood is that it appears in some sense to be in charge of its constituents. In the formulation exemplified in the above quote the Buddha asks with reference to each of the skandhas: if the skandha in question were to be the 'self' how is it that the skandhas are of the nature of suffering, because a self that was in charge would be able to change the nature of the skandhas.

In the next section the following exchange, again for each of the skandhas, between the Buddha and the monks takes place:

-How do you construe thus, monks -- Is the body permanent or impermanent?

-Impermanent, lord.

-And is that which is impermanent satisfactory or unsatisfactory?

-Unsatisfactory, lord.

-And is it fitting to regard what is impermanent, unsatisfactory, subject to change as: 'This is mine. This is my self. This is what I am'?

-No, lord.[700]

Thus we see the basic teaching of the fundamental presentation of the Buddhist psycho-metaphysical worldview is intensely empirical and practical. In this regard it appears to share little in common with other religious traditions; it begins with a simple and devastating analysis of the reality of the process of reality.

The psychophysical process which underlies the continuums of sentient beings generates a deeply rooted craving for permanence, stability and desire for satisfactory experience. Furthermore, the depth of this craving impels human beings to project desperate illusions onto the fleeting and evanescent flickering illusory appearances of experience. However, the projection of permanence where there is none is precisely the mechanism which digs the projectors of illusion into deeper suffering. And the only way to escape this entrapment in the suffering illusion of selfhood is to reverse the process and deconstruct the illusion, by directly seeing with focused penetration the interplay of *anicca, anatta* and *dukkha*. First we need to deeply comprehend the truth of the impermanence of all phenomena, the subsequent truth of the lack of selfhood in phenomena, including our own psychophysical continuums, then becomes apparent, it will then become clear that clinging to a permanent self where there is none can only produce suffering.

The result of the effective deconstruction of inherent selfhood is called *nirvana* (Pali: *nibbana*) – the complete liberation from suffering, or enlightenment. But what exactly is enlightenment? The term *nirvana* literally indicates the 'extinguishing' of a flame, in this case the flame is generated by the fire of desire and craving for self-gratifying experience, a desire which derives from a powerful and innate clinging to the illusion that there is a 'self' which is separate and cut off from the rest of the universe. Nirvana, then, can be thought of, although it is vital not to remain satisfied with only the thought, as the extinction of the contracted and mistaken state of being which constantly grasps at a separate self-enclosed identity which must operate at the expense of others. It is a radically transformed state of awareness within which there is simply no trace of the contracted sense of being a separate entity from the universe. It is precisely because of the disappearance, at the deepest level of being, of the sense of I-ness that this state was called by the Buddha the 'deathless,' there is nobody to die! This state is also said to be accompanied by unimaginable bliss.

It is important be aware that, although the focus in the first presentation of the Buddha's teachings is on the necessity of relinquishing the deep grasping at an directly experienced innately solidified sense of inherent 'selfhood,' this by no means that the Buddha suggested that the terms 'I', 'me' and so on had no use. To adopt a later Wittgenstienian perspective wherein the meanings of terms are to be located purely within their 'use' in a 'language game', the Buddha was not proposing that such personal denoting terms had no meaning in this sense. But, rather, he did mean that such terms did not have meaning if we adopt the 'picture theory' of language that Wittgenstein presented in his earlier philosophy of the *Tractatus Logico Philosophicus*, wherein he suggested, somewhat akin to Einstein's approach to physical theory, that terms must indicate elements and structure of reality. Furthermore it is vital to comprehend that grasping this fact on a purely intellectual and philosophical level, as one would to pass an exam, will not bring about enlightenment.

Enlightenment requires a profound realisation, a transformation at a deep level of psychophysical embodiment. Such a profound psychological turning around of ontological perception can appear to occur almost spontaneously, preceded by the appropriate preparation, when prompted by a catalyzing insightful observation or instruction. In large measure this is the approach of Zen Buddhism. An example from the early suttas is contained in the *Udana* when 'Bahiya of the Black-Garment,' a non-Buddhist ascetic, requested instructions from the Buddha. The Buddha offered the following cryptic instruction:

> When in the seen will be only what is seen, in the heard only what is heard, in the sensed only what is sensed, in the known only what is known, you will not be by that, you will not be therein; when you are not therein, you will be neither here, nor there, nor in between. This is the end of *dukkha*.[701]

In this beautiful forerunner of the Madhyamaka analysis the message clear, when there is only the continuum of the cognitive process without any trace of ownership of the cognitions then there is liberation and enlightenment. Bahiya was duly enlightened.

Although the emphasis within the first presentation of the Buddha's vision was upon the lack of self in the personal mental continuum, the later Mahayana spectacular insight into the universal lack of selfhood, or inherent existence, in all phenomena is contained within the early suttas. The following formula, which is from the *Phena Sutta*, contains the seeds of later Mahayana metaphysical exuberance:

Form is like a glob of foam; feeling, a bubble; perception, a mirage; [mental formations], a banana tree; consciousness, a magic trick …. However you observe them, appropriately examine them, they're empty, void to whoever sees them appropriately. Beginning with the body as taught by the One with profound discernment: when abandoned by three things — life, warmth, & consciousness — form is rejected, cast aside. When bereft of these it lies thrown away, senseless, a meal for others. That's the way it goes: it's a magic trick, an idiot's babbling. … No substance here is found.[702]

In this sutta the Buddha does not hold back any metaphorical punches as he presses home the point that all the skandhas are 'empty, void, without substance':

Monks, suppose that a large glob of foam were floating down this Ganges River, and a man with good eyesight were to see it, observe it, & appropriately examine it. To him — seeing it, observing it, & appropriately examining it — it would appear empty, void, without substance: for what substance would there be in a glob of foam?

And as 'form' is the aggregate which encompasses 'material form' it is quite clear that even in the earliest teachings the Buddha indicated that 'matter' was 'empty' of inherent substantiality, an insight which, as we have seen, is completely vindicated by modern quantum physics (see *What's the Matter with Matter?*). And this observation is repeated for the other skandhas, employing appropriate metaphors:

Feelings:

Now suppose that in the autumn — when it's raining in fat, heavy drops — a water bubble were to appear & disappear on the water, and a man with good eyesight were to see it, observe it, & appropriately examine it. To him — seeing it, observing it, & appropriately examining it — it would appear empty, void, without substance: for what substance would there be in a water bubble?

Perception and discriminations:

Now suppose that in the last month of the hot season a mirage were shimmering, … — it would appear empty, void, without substance: for what substance would there be in a mirage?

Mental formations (fabrications):

Now suppose that a man desiring heartwood, in quest of heartwood, seeking heartwood, were to go into a forest carrying a sharp ax. There he would see a large banana tree: straight, young, of enormous height. He would cut it at the root and, having cut it at the root, would chop off the top. Having chopped off the top, he would peel away the outer skin. Peeling away the outer skin, he wouldn't even find sapwood, to say nothing of heartwood. ... — it would appear empty, void, without substance: for what substance would there be in a banana tree?

And consciousness:

Now suppose that a magician or magician's apprentice were to display a magic trick at a major intersection, ... — it would appear empty, void, without substance: for what substance would there be in a magic trick?

The attribution of emptiness or lack of substantiality to the skandhas, and therefore all phenomena, is relentless, paving the way for the later spectacular formulations of emptiness within the Mahayana.

The teachings of the Buddha were not written down until the early first century BCE when monks of the Theravada school in Sri Lanka gathered together, at their Fourth Buddhist Council (29 BCE), in order to create a written record which is now called *The Pali Cannon*. Up until this time the teachings were preserved by memory, the enlightened monks gathering together from time to time in order to recite the teachings. According to one version of Buddhist history three of the liberated-enlightened monks (*arhats*) would recite the teachings and the rest, at that time about five hundred in number, would confirm the accuracy of the teachings. The teachings were divided into three 'baskets' (Skt. *Tripitaka*):

- *Vinaya* – ethical discipline.

- *Sutra* – teachings on meditation techniques, absorption, concentration and insight

- *Abhidharma* – psycho-metaphysical 'wisdom' teachings.

At the Second Buddhist Council or shortly thereafter, sometime between 386 and 350 BCE, the first split in the monastic community occurred. The point of contention concerned the scope of a liberated being, in particular whether a distinction could be made between the liberation from suffering achieved by an arhat and the omniscient wisdom of a buddha. This metaphysical disagreement produced the division into the *Theravada*, the tradition of the elders, and the *Mahasangikas*, the 'great' or 'majority' community. The Mahasangika school of thought made a clear distinction between the liberation of an arhat and the omniscient scope of buddhahood. Thus the Mahasangika perspective became the forerunner of the Mahayana.

At the Third Buddhist Council, in mid third century BCE, another philosophical split occurred which gave rise to the *Sarvastivada* school of thought, which asserted that the momentary-functioning atomic constituents of reality, or *dharmas*, were fully 'real' and eternal and therefore past, present and future happenings can be said to exist. From the Savastivada perspective the apparent movement from past to present to future occurs because of the way in which the ultimate constituents function interdependently to create the experiential world.

The fundamental Sarvastivada philosophical position is that unless the ultimate constituents of existence that make up interdependent arisings are real, then nothing else could be real. According to the Sarvastivada the ultimate existents (*dharmas*), out of which ordinary things are constructed, are self-existent (*svabhava*) and are not dependent on anything else for their existence. Furthermore they have their own essence (*svalaksana*), which means that each ultimate thing has its own inherent and unique defining characteristic. Thus for the Sarvastivadin perspective the ultimate constituents of existence have their own separate and independent existence, and it is this Realist position that became the target for the Madhyamaka anti-Realist critique.

There are two variations of the Hinayana Sarvastivada perspective, *Vaihbashika* and *Sautrantika*, which are studied within Tibetan Buddhism as part of what Alexander Berzin[703] describes as a graded system of meditation:

> Regardless of the interpretation of the features of each tenet system, the Tibetan masters have taught the Indian systems as graded steps in meditation, which are then to be applied to daily life. ... it is important not to see the refutations of non-Prasangika systems ... as directed primarily at winning debates against proponents of other systems. They are intended to help us go deeper in our own understanding. ... The methodology is to narrow in on the most sophisticated explanation, as when first learning Newtonian physics, then refining it with Einstein's theory of relativity, and then refining that with superstring theory. Each theory is relatively true and functional; they differ merely in accuracy.[704]

This is an important point. We have seen that there seems to be an ingrained tendency within Western thought to look for the final and completely correct theory, the theory which shows all others to be false. But, as Berzin points out, the fact that relativity theory shows the inaccuracies in Newtonian mechanics does not render Newtonian mechanics completely and absolutely false, it remains true on its own level of analysis. This is the approach that has always been crucial to graded levels of analysis which became central to the Tibetan systemisation of Indian Buddhist philosophy. Contemporary Buddhist philosopher Sara L. McClintock refers to this philosophical approach as a 'sliding scale of analysis':

> The tool … permits these authors to move among apparently contradictory ontological and epistemological schemes, even within the purview of a single philosophical treatise.[705]

As we shall see in the next chapter this is an approach which has a significant role in harmonizing the interpretations of quantum theory.

Ruins of Nalanda University - The library of Nalanda University had three great buildings called the Sea of Jewels, Ocean of Jewels, and the Delight of Jewels. This was a great repository of Buddhist knowledge, which was set ablaze by Muslim invaders.

Monks studying at the first Indian Mahayana Buddhist monastic University, Nalanda, one of the world's earliest residential universities which was established in the fifth century CE and by the seventh had a faculty and student population of over 10,000, were taught, and meditated on, four systems of Buddhist philosophy. These four make up the *Gelugpa*[706] 'ascending scale of analysis'[707]. The first two in the scale are subdivisions of the Sarvastivada – *Vaibashika* and *Sautantrika,* and the final two are the fundamental schools of the Mahayana – *Chittamatra* and *Madhyamaka.*

Although this sequence of stages can be thought of as an 'ascending' sequence in the context of the subtlety of understanding, it can also be considered as a 'descending' deconstruction of the illusion of the substantiality of the material and psychological world:

> With this approach, we ... narrow in on an increasingly more sophisticated understanding of the illusion-like aspects of phenomena through the refutation and nullification of increasingly more refined impossible modes of existence.[708]

It is worthwhile keeping in mind the outline of the development of quantum theory as described in the previous chapter *What's the Matter with Matter?* when pondering the descent through the following levels of Mahayana dismantling of the illusion of an independent material reality.

The Buddhist adept primarily responsible for the presentation of the **Vaibashika** system was **Vasubandhu** (400-480 CE) in his *Abhidharma-kosha* (Treasury of Abhidharma– Treasury of Special Topics of Knowledge). The following is Vasubandhu's presentation of the two truths – the 'seeming' or 'relative', and the 'absolute' or 'ultimate':

> Things which, when destroyed or mentally dissected,
> Can no longer be identified by the mind,
> Such as pots or water, are relative;
> All else besides is ultimately existent.[709]

This view clearly roughly corresponds to an atomic presentation of the two truths. The seemingly solid entities that sentient beings experience as the 'truth' or mode of apprehension of the everyday world can be broken down into increasingly small particles. When we recall that at the end of the nineteenth century many physicists did not consider atoms to be 'real' entities and that matter was actually continuously solid, the reasoning by which Buddhist philosophers argued for this conclusion is remarkable, although completely obvious and perspicacious when comprehended:

> The change that these conditioned phenomena undergo over time is reasonable only if they are subject to a form of disintegration in which they arise and pass away with each moment; this phenomena is not reasonable if entities remained in an unchanging state.[710]

In other words, if material entities were solidly continuous – with no internal structure – they simply could not deteriorate over time in the manner that the actually do. For instance the laptop I am typing this on has been my mainstay for the last eight years during which I have written with it most days. As a consequence one of the corners, where my right hand constantly strokes over the surface, is clearly being worn away. We know also that water constantly dripping on to a surface will, over time, gradually wear it away and create a groove. Such deteriorations would not be possible without some kind of internal momentary internal structure. One can only wonder why such a reasoning process did not occur to late nineteenth century physicists!

From the Vaibhashika perspective, then, any composite entity which can be physically smashed to pieces or dissected into parts by the mind, so that the mind which apprehended that apparent entity no longer identifies it as such, belongs to the 'relative' or 'seeming' 'truth' or 'reality'. Any such seemingly solid material thing or state of consciousness can be broken down into its ultimate constituents, which are individual particles or moments. Therefore the partless particles, which are the ultimate constituents of composite entities, and the indivisible moments of consciousness, which are the ultimate constituents of mental phenomena, are said to be 'absolute' or 'ultimate' 'truth' or 'reality'.

This constitutes the first level of the descent into the illusion-like nature of the process of reality. The realm of the apparently solid world of independent material reality has been shown to be an illusion to the extent that the appearance of solid continuous materiality has been shown to be an illusion. It must consist, from the basis of the Vaibhashika analysis, of a finer structure of 'partless particles' of matter and consciousness. This corresponds to the atomic level of the deconstructive analysis by Western physics, although physics, of course, did not bother itself to worry about consciousness.

The *Sautrantika* view extended the Vaibhashika fundamentally Realist position with respect to the ultimate constituents of reality by adding the analysis of 'valid cognition' which was presented in the works of **Dignaga** (6th century) and **Dharmakirti** (7th century). These two rejected the Vaibhashika account of how an external world was directly connected with mental objects, the mind supposedly being able to 'nakedly' grasp the forms of external objects. Instead the Sautrantika posited that the mental domain does not connect directly with the external world but only perceives an aspect created by the sense organs and the sense consciousnesses. The sense consciousnesses, therefore, assume the form of the aspect of the external object and what is perceived by the mind is actually the sense consciousness which has taken on the form of the external object.

This approach is an attempt to solve the problem of how material entities, which are of an antithetical nature to consciousness, can connect through to the mental world. However, whilst being more sophisticated than the Vaibhashika view, it only moves the issue of the nature of the connection between the realm of the material and that of the mental to the sense consciousnesses. But the significant feature that the Sautrantika adds is the insight that the way that the process of reality is experienced must of necessity involves a large degree of projection from the side of the experiencer. Like Kant, Dignaga and Dharmakirti suggested that all perception involves a degree of conceptual construction and, also like Kant, they held the view that the 'thing in itself,' or what they call the pure particular (*svalakshana*), is the basis of all perception, even though it is never directly perceived. The issue of the manner of the connection between the pure particulars and the mental aspects, however, still remains mysterious.

The **Chittamatra (*Yogachara*)**, Mind-Only, school, which is primarily associated with **Asanga** (300–370 CE) has been covered in great detail in previous chapters. In this stage of the decent into the illusion-like nature of the process of reality the notion of independently existent 'partless particles' or 'pure particulars' is removed from the picture. Berzin describes this phase:

> Chittamatra emphasizes the fact that the cognitive appearances that we see and the sense consciousness that sees them both come from the same natal source, namely from the same seed of karmic potential on our mental continuums. In fact all that we see are cognitive appearances, and they are like an illusion, in that they appear to arise from actual objectively existing objects out there ... However they do not exist in that impossible way.[711]

As we have seen this level of the Buddhist analysis takes us into the realm of the quantum wavefunction; it is the level which 'bursts the bubble' of the pre-quantum viewpoint which adopted what physicist Anton Zeilinger calls 'the obviously wrong notion of a reality independent of us.'[712]

According to the Tibetan Gelugpa systemisation of Buddhist philosophy the **Madhyamaka**, or Middle Way doctrine, represents the pinnacle and culmination of Buddhist philosophical thought and doctrine. Deriving from the remarkable deconstructive metaphysical analyses carried out by the second century Buddhist philosopher-practitioner **Nagarjuna** (150-250 CE) in works such as the *Mulamadhyamakakarika* (*Fundamental Verses on the Middle Way*), the Madhyamaka philosophical corpus developed in the form of commentaries to his works. These commentaries developed subtly differing approaches to the understanding of Nagarjuna's paradoxical conceptual juggling and, furthermore, also established differing views concerning the philosophical procedures that were appropriate in the task of transmitting the central meaning of the Middle Way philosophy, a meaning which it must always be born in mind is primarily transformative in nature.

Because of this central concern, which is the liberation of all sentient beings from the realms of suffering in the cycle of samsara, some modern Western academic attempts to force Nagarjuna's razor sharp poetic-metaphysical dismemberment of notions of inherently existent entities and processes surely miss the mark. In a recent academic work, *Nagarjuna's Madhyamaka*, by Jan Westerhoff, for instance, we read that:

The idea is to present a systematic overview of Nagarjuna's arguments concerning different philosophical problems in order to present an account of the whole of his philosophy, showing how its individual parts fit together as elements in a single philosophical project.[713]

Such an approach, however, seems to ignore the central import of Nagarjuna's 'philosophical project.' Opponents of Nagarjuna's presentation of the notion that all phenomena are 'empty' of inherent substantiality, or 'without nature,' attempted to refute his assertions as follows:

> Arguments are not established,
> Because they are without nature, so where is your argument?
> Once the absence of a reason is established,
> Your point cannot be proven.[714]

In other words, if all phenomena are 'without nature' then it follows that the arguments that Nagarjuna employs are also without a nature and are therefore not established; and if the arguments are not established then the thesis of emptiness cannot be established. It seems as if Nagarjuna's own assertion of emptiness undermines that very assertion!

Nagarjuna, however, counters with some conceptual aikido:[715]

> My words are without nature.
> Therefore, my thesis is not ruined.
> Since there is no inconsistency,
> I do not have to state an argument for a distinction.[716]

This move is simply brilliant. Nagarjuna accepts the opponent's observation that his own arguments, like all phenomena, lack nature. And precisely because his arguments do lack nature the point is proved! The fact that his words 'lack nature' is not a problem for Nagarjuna precisely because it is not his 'philosophical project' to establish a systematic philosophy. As Karl Brunnhölzl, author of the magnificent book on Kagyü Madhyamaka *The Center of the Sunlit Sky,* comments (in the following the term 'Centrist' refers to the Madhyamaka):

> Usually, logic and reasoning are employed to establish and defend certain positions or reference points to which a certain reality is ascribed. However, Centrist reasonings are not refutations in the sense of rejecting an opponent's view and promoting one's own view instead. The Centrists' whole point is to dissolve our already existent reference points and the clinging to them. They definitely do not try to provide new views or reference points to which to cling. This is precisely what they are very careful to avoid.[717]

In stanza 65 of his *Seventy Stanzas on Emptiness (Shunyatasaptatikarika)* Nagarjuna makes the following point:

> *Understanding* the non-inherent existence of things means *seeing* the *reality* [i.e. *emptiness*] which *eliminates ignorance* about the reality of things. *This* brings about the *cessation* of *ignorantly* grasping at an apparently true existence.[718]

There can hardly be a more explicit indication that the aim of Nagarjuna's work is to aid the practitioner towards a direct insight into the empty nature of reality. As Geshe Sonam Rinchen comments on this stanza 'Seeing reality is the path.'[719] Nagarjuna's Madhyamaka, therefore, is a path towards the transformation of consciousness into a direct insight of the empty nature of the process of reality, not a path towards a Western academic style 'single philosophical project.'

What is it about reality that needs to be clearly, directly and continuously seen in order to prepare for enlightenment? It is the dramatic and shocking insight that the world cannot possibly function in the manner that we conventionally assume that it does. This is a vital point which must be grasped in order to comprehend the fact that Buddhism, and especially the Madhyamaka, really does 'burst the bubble of the universe,' it really does uncover the illusion-like, dream-like nature of reality. In the 69th stanza of his *Seventy Stanzas* Nagarjuna says:

> Ultimate reality is contained within the limit of the non-inherent existence of a thing.[720]

And Geshe Sonam Rinchen comments:

> Reality is not beyond the limit of what is known by a valid direct perceiver. This limit must also subsume conventional reality. Within this limit the Buddha makes two kinds of comparisons. One is to examine the various things of conventional reality, to determine whether the names used to designate these objects are actually suitable for the purpose. In the second case, he compares the different aspects of an object to each other and to their names. These comparisons require that the Buddha utilize the different conventional terms used by the people of the world in order to examine the objects which they believe to exist. This process will eventually lead to a mental image of emptiness whose actual limit corresponds to that of reality.[721]

The method employed by Nagarjuna's Madhyamaka is, as Geshe Sonam Rinchen indicates, to examine with razor sharp precision the actual way in which our concepts force us to comprehend the process of reality in order to 'see' whether they hang together coherently as an inherently existent reality. And the way in which the Madhyamaka performs this analysis is to rigorously compare 'different aspects' of a conceptual situation to look scrupulously into the conceptual coherence of the interconnections of the imputed objects and processes within that conceptual picture.

For example consider Nagarjuna's 'Examination of Prior Entity,' which is Chapter 9 of the *Fundamental Verses on the Middle Way*; here are the first four verses:

> Since such things as seeing, hearing and feeling exist,
> Some say that it follows that
> Someone who has them must exist prior to their occurrence.
>
> If there were no prior existent thing
> How could such things as seeing occur?
> Therefore prior to the seeing
> There must be an enduring thing.
>
> If something existed prior to
> Such things as
> Seeing, hearing and feeling,
> How could it be designated?
>
> If the prior entity can endure
> Without such things as seeing,
> Then, without a doubt, the 'seeing' also
> Can exist without it.[722]

The experiential situation of the process of perception naturally gives rise to the idea that the seer, seeing and seen, hearer, hearing and heard and so on are all distinct entities. This is graphically illustrated in figure 11.1, note that

Interconnected process of 'seeing'

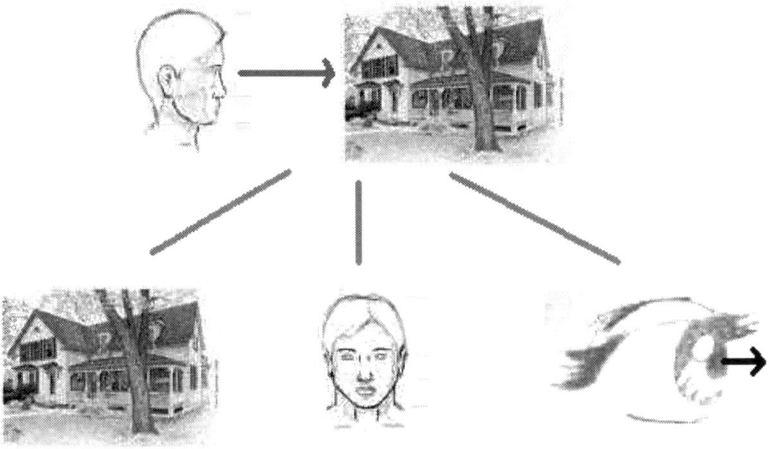

The 'seen'   The 'seer'   The 'seeing'

Fig 11.1

the elements of the 'seen', 'seer' and 'seeing' are arranged in order to emphasize the fact that the conceptual imputation of inherent existence reifies, or objectively 'solidifies' these aspects into apparently independent entities. As Geshe Sonam Rinchen says: 'conventional expressions make things seem permanent, and 'such permanence would imply a true existence for things'[723]. When analyzing processes from the point of view of inherent existence we must always employ a rigor of demarcation regarding the designations involved, a rigor which seems on first meeting to be somewhat contrived. However, the reason for this is that we are engaged in the task of examining 'the various things of conventional reality, to determine whether the names used to designate these objects are actually suitable for the purpose' and comparing 'different aspects of an object to each other and to their names,' as Geshe Sonam Rinchen describes the process.

Now the question arises: prior to the actual act of seeing, how are we to designate, in the context of this act of seeing, the seer? Prior to this act of seeing he or she is not a 'seer' precisely because the act of seeing in question is not happening at that prior time. If the person in question really were inherently and distinctly a 'seer' then they would always be seeing exactly the 'seen' thing within the process we are considering. As Khenpo Tsultrum Gyamtso says:

> The one who sees form cannot exist before – that is, inde-
> pendent of – the experience of seeing form, for if she did, it
> would absurdly follow that she would always see that form.
> The reason for this is that if an individual is called a 'seer of
> form,' it is actually because she sees some form, and thus if the
> seer of form existed independently of the experience of seeing
> it, the self which was called a seer of form would always see
> the form in order to earn that name.[724]

So Nagarjuna now asks:

> By what is someone disclosed?
> By whom is something disclosed?
> Without something, how can someone exist?
> Without someone, how can something exist?[725]

The designation of the actor or perceiver cannot be given without the action or perception. It follows quite clearly that there cannot be an unchanging enduring 'entity' which is inherently and distinctly defined at a prior moment by an action it is currently engaged in. And the same applies to the situation after, and even during, the 'seeing' event. What if someone happened to be 'seeing', 'hearing' and 'feeling' at the same time:

> If the seer itself is the hearer itself,
> And the feeler, then

For it to exist prior to each of these
Would make no sense.

If the seer is distinct,
The hearer is distinct, and the feeler is distinct,
Then when there is a seer there would also be a hearer,
And there would have to be many persons.[726]

Many Western philosophers would probably be irritated by such conceptual gymnastics because the illusion of the apparent entities and processes of material world conforms so closely to the kind of picture which is contained within our conceptual categories. In the West most mainstream academic philosophers have become accustomed to letting conceptual categories slip and slide for convenience; the convenience of maintaining the illusion that the conventional seeming world is not an illusion!

Recall the Western 'philosopher' of science we met in the chapter *Illusion or Reality?* who, when questioning a physicist about an experiment on the edge of the quantum realm was told that certain particles were sprayed with positrons, exclaimed:

> From that day forth I've been a scientific realist. *So far as I am concerned, if you can spray them then they are real.*[727]

Such a lax philosophical attitude derives from a deeply seated, and mistaken, conviction that the entities of seeming reality *must* be real!

The philosophical work of the physicist David Bohm, which is based primarily on his interpretive reflections upon the implications of quantum theory, is remarkable in its Madhyamaka flavour. In *Wholeness and the Implicate Order* he spends a significant amount of time on a consideration of the role of language in our experience of reality:

> ...consider the sentence 'It is raining.' Where is the 'It' that would be 'the rainer that is doing the raining'? Clearly, it is more appropriate to say: 'Rain is going on.' Similarly, we customarily say, 'One elementary particle acts on another', but ... each particle is only an abstraction from a relatively invariant form of movement in the whole field of the universe. ... the same sort of description holds also on the larger scale level. Thus instead of saying, 'An observer looks at an object', we can more appropriately say, 'Observation is going on, in an undivided movement involving these abstractions customarily called 'the human being' and 'the object he is looking at'.[728]

For Bohm, then, Nagarjuna's Madhyamaka deconstructive analysis is completely validated by quantum physics. And, when the deconstructive analysis is followed with concentrated and insightful attention, the entities, categories and processes of the conventional world dissolve into the same kind of emptiness as the 'It' in 'It is raining.'

The claim by Nagarjuna that the arguments employed to demonstrate the Madhyamaka understanding of emptiness are themselves empty of inherent nature leads us into the territory of the subtle distinction between the two styles of Madhyamaka: the *Svatantrika*, or Autonomy school of thought and the *Prasangika,* the Consequentialist school. This distinction in approach is a Tibetan systemisation of a debate concerning correct philosophical procedure within the Indian development of Buddhism. This debate began when *Bhavaviveka* (500-570 CE), who according to the later Tibetan doxological analysis was the instigator of the Svatantrika style of Madhyamaka, questioned the manner in which the Madhyamika philosopher *Buddhapalita* (c.500 CE), who is considered, together with *Chandrakirti* (600-c.650 CE), to be the founder of the Prasangika, presented the ideas of Nagarjuna primarily contained in the *Fundamental Verses*.

The actual details need not detain us in great detail. The crux of the issue was that Buddhapalita, when explaining Nagarjuna's viewpoint, did not present it with the full logical formulaic rigor that had been propounded as necessary by the Buddhist logician Dignaga. He only drew out the absurd consequences which were entailed by affirming any of the limbs of the tetralemma of existence. Thus his procedure was later identified within the Tibetan tradition as being Prasangika, or Consequentialist. Bhavaviveka, on the other hand, suggested that such a procedure was not logically watertight and more rigorous, autonomous, or *svatantra*, logical arguments were required.

A *svatantra* argument stands on its own because it makes a positive statement, whereas a *prasanga* procedure requires a statement by the philosophical opponent which is then subjected to a reductio-ad-absurdum analysis in order to show the absurd consequences. For example consider the following opening verse (after the homage) of Nagarjuna's *Fundamental Verses*:

> Neither from itself nor from another
> Nor from both,
> Nor without a cause
> Does anything anywhere, ever arise.[729]

Consider the first limb of the tetralemma, the assertion that 'things arise from themselves,' which is a statement of the Samkhya position that effects are latent within their causes. A prasanga refutation of this position would merely state that 'there is no point in the arising of already existing things.' A svatantra refutation, as offered by Bhavaviveka, would be:

> Thesis – Inner sense fields (*ayatanas*) do not ultimately arise from themselves.

Reason – Because they already exist
Example – Consciousness.

A svatantra argument has a fully stated thesis, reason and example.

The rise of the Prasangika can be attributed to **Tsongkhapa** (1357-1419), the founder of the *Gelug* sect, according to whom the distinction between the two styles of Madhyamaka involves not only issues of logical presentation, it also has implications for the two school's ontological understanding of emptiness (*shunyata*). According to the *Sakya* sect of Tibetan Buddhism, however, the distinction is pedagogical in nature, not ontological.

The issue is admittedly a subtle one; but it can be significantly elucidated by returning to Nagarjuna's assertion that:

My words are without nature.
Therefore, my thesis is not ruined.
Since there is no inconsistency,
I do not have to state an argument for a distinction.[730]

The Prasangika point is that because the ultimate understanding of emptiness is beyond words and conceptual systems and, furthermore, the words and conceptual systems which are employed to move a practitioners mind in the right direction are themselves 'without nature,' then to use a mode of discourse which seems to imply even a subtle form of substantiality, so to speak, will undermine a correct understanding. In other words, *to employ words and conceptual systems as if they were not empty undermines the elucidation of emptiness!*

The final presentation of Mahayana philosophy we need to cover is the composite system of the renowned 8th century Indian Buddhist practitioner-scholar and abbot of Nalanda University **Shantarakshita**, who founded the philosophical school known as the *Yogachara-Svatantrika-Madhyamaka* which united the Madhyamaka tradition of Nagarjuna and the Yogachara tradition of Asanga with the logical and epistemological thought of Dharmakirti. The primary work by Shantarakshita presenting this system is the *Madhyamakalankara - The Ornament of the Middle Way*, in the 93rd stanza of which he writes:

Therefore, due to holding the reigns of logic as one rides the chariots of the two systems [Yogachara and Madhyamaka], one attains the path of the actual Mahayanist.[731]

According to this presentation the attainment of the correct 'Mahayanist' understanding of emptiness, the ultimate nature, can be accomplished in two phases. The first, Yogachara, phase requires the understanding and realisa-tion that the conventionally experienced aspect of emptiness is mind or consciousness. And then, from that basis, the final movement of understanding penetrates to the ultimate aspect that Mind itself is empty of

Shantarakshita

any inherent essence. James Blumenthal, author of the excellent work on Shantarakshita *The Ornament of the Middle Way* summarises the Yogachara-Svatantrika-Madhyamaka system presented by Shantarakshita as follows:

> Because he rejects the existence of any ultimate nature or essence in phenomena while accepting some form of conventional existence of those phenomena, he is a Madhyamika. Because conventional truths are described as not being utterly distinct entities from the mind perceiving them and because he

accepts self-cognizing cognition conventionally, ... he is seen as accepting a Yogachara position conventionally. Because he advocates the use of autonomous inferences, he is representative of a certain type of Madhyamaka view known by the appellation coined in Tibet at least two centuries after his death as 'Svatantrika-Madhyamaka.'[732]

This dual aspect presentation has an intriguing echo within quantum theory. It should be apparent from the preceding chapters that the primary perspective of this current work is Yogachara-Svatantrika-Madhyamaka. The identification of the wavefunction with the Mind-Only alayavijnana, or ground-consciousness, corresponds to the Yogachara phase of Shantarakshita's analaysis. The further Madhyamaka phase, wherein Mind itself is shown to be devoid of inherent existence and substantiality, is represented by the sections of this work wherein the ultimately empty nature of the process is indicated by the analysis of the Heisenberg Uncertainty Principle which maps it onto the Madhayamaka tetralemma of existence.

This indicates a mapping of Yogachara perspective onto Schrödinger's quantum viewpoint whilst the Madhaymaka has greater affinity with Heisenberg's point of view. This polarisation of viewpoint actually did exist between Schrödinger and Heisenberg:

> Heisenberg understood that Einstein and Schrödinger wanted 'to return to the reality concept of classcal physics or, to use a more general philosophic term, to the ontology of materialism.' The belief in 'an objective real world whose smallest parts exist objectively in the same sense as stones and trees exist, independently of whether or not we observe them', was for Heisenberg a throw-back to 'simplistic materialist views that prevailed in the natural sciences of the nineteenth century'.[733]

Although Schrödinger's viewpoint was not quite as crudely rooted in materialism as Heisenberg presents it, he did want to think of his equation as representing something 'physically' and independently existent, suggesting that it might be 'intimately connected to the cloud like distribution of electric charge as it travelled through space'.[734] In the light of the later revelations of the interconnection of the quantum realm and consciousness, it is clear that the identification of Schrödinger's perspective with the notion of the mind-based subtle substantiality of the alayavijana is appropriate. Heisenberg, on the other hand, emphasised the:

> ...subjective element in atomic events, since the measuring device has been constructed by the observer, and we have to remember that what we observe is not nature in itself, but nature exposed to our method of questioning.[735]

Heisenberg's 'matrix mechanics,' therefore brings to the fore a kind of discontinuous spontaneity within the interdependent matrix of observer and observed which did not entail the necessity for a deeper substantiality.

But, whereas Buddhist philosophy finds no problem with an ultimately inexpressible reality that gives rise to interdependent yet seemingly contradictory perspectives, both Schrödinger and Heisenberg were thoroughly convinced of the inherent existence of the truth of their respective positions. Because of the 'lack of visualisation' in matrix mechanics Schrödinger felt 'repelled' by Heisenberg's view. Heisenberg, on the other hand told Wolfgang Pauli:

> What Schrödinger writes about the visualizability of his theory
> is probably not quite right,' in other words it's crap.[736]

How remarkable, then, that Schrödinger demonstrated that these two ways of conceiving the quantum realm are mathematically equivalent, or are different mathematical formulations of the 'same' underlying process of reality!

Empty Metaphors of Emptiness

What is dependent origination
Is explained as emptiness.
It is a dependent designation
And in itself the middle path.[737]

Whatever is dependently arisen
Does not arise, does not cease,
Is not permanent, is not extinct,
Does not come, does not go
And is neither one thing nor different things.[738]

Once you have realised the actuality of the empty
    nature of phenomena,
The sign or result of that is as follows:
Externally, the objects of the five sense gates-
All forms, sounds, smells, tastes and tangible objects-
Are utterly lucid as emptiness.[739]

Even emptiness is empty of being empty.[740]

Buddha Manjushri wields the sword of wisdom which cuts through the illusions of the seeming appearances of the conventional world.

The notion of *svabhava*, 'inherent existence', occupies a crucial place in the philosophical analysis of the Madhyamaka, even though it actually denotes something that is completely nonexistent! It is the theoretical entity that all phenomena are 'empty' of. Emptiness, or *shunyata,* is the central Madhyamaka concept which indicates the fact that all phenomena lack *svabhava*. There is no phenomenon that has its own inner core of independent, self-enclosed own-nature which marks it off and separates it absolutely from all other phenomena. But, as has been indicated previously, it is vital that 'emptiness' is not thought to be synonymous with 'nothingness', this would be seriously misleading. 'Nothingness' is the assertion of total non-existence, without a trace of appearance or experience, and this is definitely not the meaning of the 'emptiness' which is indicated by the Madhyamaka:

> What has the character of appearance
> Is definitely not negated.
> It is not appropriate to negate
> That which is experienced.[741]

The fact that there is an interdependent web of experience which appears within the mental continuums of sentient beings is not by any means denied by the Madhyamaka analysis. What is refuted, or negated, is the notion, a notion that is deeply buried within the psyches of all sentient beings, that the experiential web of appearance has any ultimate inner stable independent nature anywhere within it. This is the ultimate nature of reality: emptiness; a nature which, paradoxically, indicates the ultimate lack of independent nature of all phenomena.

There are various way of presenting the concept of emptiness; two of the most fundamental from the perspective of the Madhyamaka are, firstly, the lack of 'inherent existence', which is sometimes also referred to as 'true existence', 'own nature' and other synonyms, and, secondly, dependent origination, which highlights the fact that there is nothing which does not depend upon something else for its apparent existence. The Chittamatra Mind-Only school presents emptiness from the viewpoint of the three natures: the imputational nature, the other-powered nature and the thoroughly established nature. Within this analysis, emptiness is the thoroughly established nature, which is defined as the absence of the imputational nature within the other-powered nature. These three presentations: the lack of inherent existence, dependent origination and the thoroughly established nature, are quite clearly all variations on a theme, and understanding the way in which they connect and relate to each other deepens our understanding of the idea of emptiness.

It should be fairly apparent that the Mind-Only formulation that emptiness can be understood as the absence of the imputational nature from the other-powered nature corresponds, although from a different point of view, with the formulation that emptiness is to be understood as the lack of inherent existence within all phenomena; what is intriguing is the shift of perspective between viewpoints. A more esoteric, and probably more difficult to comprehend, perspective is the Mind-Only view that emptiness is the lack of ultimate reality within the experiential duality of apprehender and apprehended; the subject–object duality of everyday unenlightened experience. It is the relationships and mutual illuminations between these subtly differing presentations that provide the focus of this chapter. Emptiness is a subtle and centrally important topic within Buddhism, a fact that is hardly surprising because it is the ultimate nature of reality. For this reason, then, illuminating its characteristics from as many perspectives as possible is of great benefit.

The historical founder of the Madhyamaka, Nagarjuna, wrote a concise summary of the concept of emptiness within the opening verses of the mind-stretching and inherent-reality-deconstructing *Fundamental Verses on the Middle Way (MulaMadhyamakakarika)*:

> Whatever is dependently arisen
> Does not arise, does not cease,
> Is not permanent, is not extinct,
> Does not come, does not go
> And is neither one thing nor different things.[742]

Within this short set of observations there is contained an entire program for the deconstruction of the illusion of the world of inherent-existence, the illusion-like appearance of independent objects and processes which appear to manifest to all unenlightened sentient beings.

A comprehensive explanation of this verse was given in the chapter *Why the Quantum?,* so only a brief summery will be given here. Something which appears to 'arise' on the basis of other entities cannot be given credence as being an *ultimately* 'real', 'inherently existent' 'thing' because it has arisen in dependence on other things, so it is not self-powered, it depends on other entities. It follows that this illusory 'thing' that we might think has come into being has not actually arisen because it's not actually there as an inherently existent entity! It cannot, inherently, cease because there is no inherently-existent-thing to cease. It cannot be permanent because it appeared to arise in the first place and because of this it cannot become extinct because there was never anything to become extinct! Furthermore something which does not exist can not come or go! It cannot be one thing for the reasons already given. It cannot be different things because the analysis would apply to each of those things in turn.

It is always of great importance to constantly be aware that, captivatingly fascinating as the Buddhist philosophical analysis of the Madhyamaka is, especially when sharing the same stage as modern quantum theory, it was not developed as an entertaining armchair intellectual diversion. It was, rather, a response to the life-transforming and mind-turning observation of the completely pointless and unacceptable nature of a trivial and worldly life in the face of the some very significant facts of existence. And foremost amongst these facts are those of the inevitable suffering of ageing, illness and disease, and death, facts which are quite obviously unavoidable in the current life. When it becomes apparent, however, that all sentient beings are trapped within an unremitting cyclic process of birth and death, with the attendant sufferings of samsara, the desperate nature of the unenlightened perspective becomes apparent.

One way of viewing the perilous situation of unenlightened sentient existence is that all sentient beings are trapped in a dualistic web of materialised metaphor, an illusion-like prison of dependently-conditioned suffering which has been constructed by their own perceptions and actions. It is a dream-like, and therefore ultimately unreal, karmic construction within the field of fundamental awareness-consciousness. All sentient beings are dreaming within the dream, and the nature of their dreaming determines the future course of the dream. Because of this it is vital to find a way to control one's own waking dreaming, as well as our sleep induced dreams:

> All of this is the mind. I have realised the nature of mind. Now even if one's faults are exposed, it is the mind. Even if one is praised, it is the mind. Whether happy or sad, it is the mind. Given that all these are equal in being the mind, whatever defects arise in your mental continuum wherein self is perceived wherein there is no self, crush them and let them go. There is no point concealing such unestablished defects within a cave that is itself not established. ... There is no need for these to sever the life of liberation.... Although dreams are unreal, it serves no purpose to dream of suffering. [743]

And a vital method of taking control is to become aware of the dream-like nature of, and the lack of 'self' within, all phenomena at a deep level of one's psychophysical embodiment. The only way to escape the prison of samsara is to use the liberating metaphors of the Madhyamaka, or another spiritual path of liberation, to disentangle the limited mind of entrapment into the limitless realm of liberation and enlightenment.

The first significant requirement of the Buddhist path is the decision to abandon worldly engagement with cyclic existence, this is renunciation. In particular a resolution has to be made to engage upon the spiritual path for the benefit of oneself and all other sentient beings in countless future lifetimes. Concern with issues of advancement purely within the current lifetime, then, should drop away as the need to practice the Buddhist spiritual path during all future lifetimes becomes a central concern. And an essential requirement of the Mahayana perspective is the explicitly articulated determination to practice the path to enlightenment with the intention of liberating all other sentient beings from their suffering within the cyclic realm. This is called 'the altruistic intention', which is sometimes described as the determination to practice relentlessly until samsara is 'emptied.'

The important fourteenth century scholar-practitioner Tsongkhapa indicated the importance of developing the correct view of emptiness as follows:

> If you do not have the wisdom realising the way things are,
> Even though you have developed the thought definitely to leave cyclic existence
> And the altruistic intention, the root of cyclic existence cannot be cut.
> Therefore work at the means of realising dependent-arising.

> Whoever, seeing the cause and effect of all phenomena
> Of cyclic existence and nirvana infallible,
> Thoroughly destroys the mode of misapprehension of those objects [as inherently existent]
> Has entered on a path that is pleasing to Buddha.

> As long as the two, realisation of appearances - the infallibility of dependent-arising - and the realisation of emptiness -
> The non-assertion [of inherent existence] -
> Seem to be separate, there is still no realisation
> Of the thought of Shakyamuni Buddha.

> When [the two realisations exist] simultaneously without alternation
> And when from only seeing dependent-arising as infallible,
> Definite knowledge entirely destroys the mode of apprehension
> [of the conception of inherent existence],
> then the analysis of the view [of reality] is complete.

> Further, the extreme of [inherent] existence is excluded
> [by knowledge of the nature] of appearances
> [existing only as nominal designations],
> And the extreme of [total] non-existence is excluded
> [by knowledge of the nature] of emptiness
> [as the complete absence of inherent existence and not the absence of nominal existence].

> If within emptiness the appearance of cause and effect is known
> You will not be captivated by extreme views.[744]

This presentation of the path to enlightenment, which is the achievement of the peace of nirvana, the extinction of suffering, indicates the three principal aspects of the path, which are:

1. disillusionment with samsara (cyclic existence) and the generation of the thought to leave cyclic existence through renunciation of its possible pleasures;

2. the cultivation of an altruistic intention to also save all sentient beings from the fate of continuous suffering the results of cyclic existence;

3. the correct view of emptiness.

And the emphasis on the third, the correct view of emptiness, which is the wisdom realizing the way things are, is unmistakable.

The following are the crucial points concerning the correct view of emptiness which are presented by Tsongkhapa's verses. Emptiness is identified as 'dependent-arising' which is the 'cause and effect' nature of all phenomena, including phenomena viewed from the perspectives of 'cyclic existence and nirvana'. This indicates that cyclic existence and nirvana, or enlightenment, are not separate domains of reality; and, furthermore, emptiness is the fundamental nature of both. A realisation of the emptiness of all phenomena 'thoroughly destroys the mode of misapprehension of those objects as inherently existent.' The correct view of emptiness also requires a direct awareness of the inseparability of the infallibility of dependent-arising appearances and their necessary emptiness of inherent existence. This aspect is indicated in the Heart Sutra by the adage 'form is emptiness and emptiness is form.' These two realisations, the dependence of appearance upon the empty nature and the empty nature of appearances, must be maintained simultaneously 'without alternation.' In this way an accomplished prac-titioner will comprehend the functioning of the process of reality at the same time as being directly aware of its illusion-like 'empty' nature.

The last aspect of emptiness mentioned by Tsongkhapa is the fact that appearances are 'nominal designations' and are thus dependent upon mind, because of this they cannot have an independent nature of their own, but neither are such appearances asserted to be 'totally non-existent.' In these verses then, Tsongkhapa covers most of the possible perspectives upon the ultimate nature of reality: emptiness. Such a comprehensive understanding of the nature of emptiness, he tells us, will prevent one falling into 'extreme views', which are, on the one hand the view of permanence, and on the other, the view of nihilism, or the assertion of absolute nothingness and complete pointlessness.

A crucial aspect of Tsongkhapa's view is that it is essential to have a correct understanding of the relationship between the appearances of conventional reality and the nature of the ultimate experiential sphere of reality. The Madhyamaka tradition contains within it an immortalisation of an unfortunate Chinese monk, 'Hvashang', whose viewpoint that the ultimate nature, and the realised meditative state, was a kind of vacuity was refuted by Kamalashila in a public debate during the early spread of the teachings. Hvashang's name subsequently became mud because of his misunder-standing of emptiness and the nature of meditation. According to Tsongkhapa the idea that the experience of emptiness could be achieved by simply 'emptying' the mind of concepts engendered a deficient understanding worthy only of the disreputable Hvashang. It encouraged a lazy, unfocused meditation style which could never penetrate into the true nature of reality.

Tsongkhapa's technique required that the non-conceptual direct experience of emptiness was to be approached through the employment of a conceptual facsimile of emptiness which was focused upon in one-pointed meditation practice. He proposed that the formula 'neither existent nor non-existent' should be interpreted as meaning:

> Not truly existent ultimately but not non-existent conventionally.[745]

And he illustrated his proposal with the adage 'a vase is not empty of vase but of the true existence of vase.'[746] The point of this emphasis on a kind of provisional 'existence' of the conventional aspect of reality was to counteract the tendency towards a vacuous nihilism which simply could not grasp the full import of the notion of emptiness which requires an 'infallibility of appearances.' Emptiness could not, and should not, be conceived of as simply a complete nihilism; but, rather, the 'infallible' functioning of the interdependent-arisings of the conventional world take place within the illusion-like potency of emptiness. For Tsongkhapa, therefore, it was essential to be aware that removing 'inherent existence' did not, conceptually, leave absolutely 'nothing' behind, so to speak. Experientially, however, Tsongkhapa insisted that emptiness was to be understood as a purely 'non-implicative' negation of inherent existence, a view which is not shared by all schools of Tibetan Buddhism.

The following list indicates significant features that an inherently real or existent object, if such an entity were existent, would have to exhibit:

- An inherently existent entity exists in splendid isolation without the need to reference any other entity. It is completely defined by its own nature.

- An inherently existent entity is uncaused.

- It is indestructible, eternal and unchanging.

- It has no constituent parts.

- It could not be observed or viewed in any way because this would require a physical interaction which involves some kind of change.

- It could not take part in a causal process that involved change in its inherent nature; it could not therefore take part in any known physical process of causality.

Although such an entity cannot possibly exist, this is the kind of view that unenlightened sentient beings innately adopt concerning the world of 'objects' that apparently surround them. This instinctive reification of fluid experience arises because of an innate mode of apprehension of what appears to be an independent external reality. It is a superimposition which is projected onto the fluid world of experience.

The appearance of inherent existence operates at a very deep level of psychophysical embodiment; and, because of this the practice of maintaining a correct view of emptiness requires a constant awareness of the lack of the features, which are mistakenly imputed onto or into reality, listed above. It is, therefore, necessary to transform one's mode of perception into a process which is a continuous awareness of the 'empty', fluid and interdependent, nature of reality. However, in the face of the appearance of the immutable wall of gross materiality presented by the everyday world it is extremely difficult to cultivate and maintain awareness of emptiness as a continuous mode of perception. The developmental process of the correct view of emptiness, therefore, is one of continuous training in familiarity with the experience of emptiness through repeated meditation; and between meditation sessions the Madhyamika practitioner attempts to maintain a state of 'illusion-like subsequent attainment'; a subsequent state of a sustained awareness of the fundamental illusion-like nature of reality.

In order to maintain a familiarity and a certainty regarding the illusory and empty nature of reality the Madhyamika practitioner in previous times would review the various logical deconstructions such as the 'diamond slivers' and the 'neither one nor many' analyses. Such remarkable logical deconstructions of the nature of reality reveal the quantum nature of the conventional world; as we have seen quantum physics now clearly indicates that the essential nature of all reality is thoroughly quantum and the 'macroscopic' or 'conventional' world is an illusion produced by the interaction of our sense faculties with quantum reality. The deconstructive reasonings employed within the Madhyamaka bring this quantum nature of the everyday world into plain view in a remarkable manner.

However, the sheer solid immutable presence of conventional reality is overwhelming, so overwhelming that the idea that it is an illusion seems almost insane. Madhyamikas today, however, are actually extremely lucky because not only do they have the time tested Madhyamaka logical methods of deconstructing the appearance of the conventional world to reveal the 'empty' nature of the underlying reality, they also have the testimony of quantum physics which shows, from a scientific basis, the precise cogency of the Madhyamaka analysis. This fortunate situation for the modern day Madhyamika has been covered in great detail in previous chapters.

An important distinction which must be born in mind whilst engaged in the task of intellectually comprehending the various aspects of emptiness as presented within the phases of the Madhyamaka is between the 'conceptual ultimate' and the 'non-conceptual ultimate'. The former is a conceptual facsimile of the ultimate direct experiential emptiness; an intellectual fabrication which functions within the conventional realm of analysis. This facsimile, sometimes called a 'generic image', indicates the nature, and direction, of the experience of actual emptiness, which is the 'non-conceptual ultimate', an experience which is nondualistic and is therefore beyond words, concepts and expression.

To have an intellectual understanding of emptiness in its conceptual form is in no way equivalent to having experienced it. But such an intellectual understanding is vital because it points in the right direction and it gives an indication of what the experience might be like:

> The destination, ultimate reality, is pointed out or pictured in the view. The ultimate, however, is what has always been the case, regardless of how it is variously conceived in evanescent thoughts. Ultimate reality is not the finger that points to the moon, but the moon itself. The ultimate is not known through imagination, but through the cessation of imagination in direct perception.[747]

The conceptual facsimile of emptiness is used as a tool which enables the mind to acclimatize to, and familiarize itself with, through analysis and meditation, the target experience of actual emptiness. Through continual focused meditation upon a mental image of emptiness, generated through a resolute inner investigation and analysis of its nature, the image becomes increasingly subtle; the conceptual generic image thereby supplies a basis for the actual direct experience to naturally manifest.

According to the Madhyamaka 'emptiness' indicates the true nature of reality at its ultimate core. So, if we take the Madhyamaka seriously as indicating an ultimate fact about the nature of the apparently material world, then the notion of emptiness must apply to the quantum nature of phenomena. At the quantum level the interdependence of external appearance and perceiving consciousness is indicated quite clearly by the fact that 'particles' only 'collapse' into definite existence at the moment they are observed, after which the wavefunction spreads out into indefiniteness until another observation is made. Conventionally speaking, a macroscopic 'object', however, is made up of a mind boggling number of quantum 'particles'. The question arises therefore as to how such a macroscopic object, a pot for instance, a favorite example used by Madhyamika philosophers, maintains its form when not observed.

The most up to date answer given by quantum physics is that, once the macroscopic world gets under way, it gathers momentum in the sense that it establishes a matrix or pattern which imposes itself upon the quantum domain. This corresponds to what Max Planck called the 'matrix of mind' which he considered to be the fundamental field of energy from which the appearance of matter emerges. This process is either called 'decoherence', or 'quantum Darwinism'. The term 'Darwinism' is used because of the view that large-scale states which establish themselves as preferred at the macroscopic level then proliferate and therefore persist at the quantum level. This process maintains the appearance of an independent, inherently existent reality of materiality. As quantum physicist Erich Joos indicates:

> The properties of the 'ordinary' objects of our experience – precisely those we call macroscopic –are now seen not to be inherent in these objects. Instead they emerge from, or are *created* by, irreversible interactions with their environment.[748]

Here again we find a physicist indicating that phenomena, even the 'ordinary' objects of the everyday world, do not possess their properties in an inherent fashion. And, as we have previously seen on many occasions, the notion that the objects of the conventional reality of the everyday world do not exist inherently and independently, in such a manner that they inherently possess their properties, is exactly the central doctrine of the Mind-Only and Middle-Way analyses of reality. The point is made by Madhyamika master Äryadeva as follows:

> Those which have a dependent arising
> Are not under their own power.
> All these are not under their own power;
> Therefore, they do not have self [that is to say, establishment
>   by way of their own nature].[749]

If objects did own their properties inherently, of course, then the objects themselves would have to exist inherently, and, because they do not, they quite clearly are not under their 'own-power.'

According to the Mind-Only viewpoint this illusory appearance is due to the superimposition of the imputational nature into the other-powered nature. In Joos' description of the 'emergence' of the classical world from the foundational quantum substratum the 'dependent arising' results through an interaction of the quantum realm and an 'environmental' template which gives the quantum 'dream stuff' an apparent macroscopic form.

A crucial question, of course, concerns the manner in which the macro-scopic environmental template arises in the first place. This problem, however, is not directly addressed by modern quantum theory; the actual detail of the mechanism underlying the process once it gets under way is enough of an enigma for the time being! However Joos, like many others, is quite clear that:

> …the last and final evidence comes in the form of perceptions made by some observer.[750]

Professor Roger Penrose makes the similar point:

> …at the large end of things, the place where 'the buck stops' is provided by our *conscious perceptions*. …[751]

So it seems that the epistemological nature of the quantum situation shares a great deal of similarity with the Mind-Only 'three-natures' analysis, as shown in figure 12.1. In this epistemological viewpoint the appearance of the independent pot which is experienced as having its own internal self-nature, results from the projection from the perceiving consciousness into the realm of potentiality of the 'other-powered' nature. This view can be viewed as analogous to the 'collapse' of the wavefunction which appears to be a result of an interaction of a deep level of perceiving consciousness and the realm of potentiality of the other-powered wavefunction.

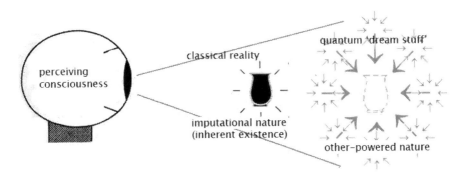

Fig 12.1

The notion that the nebulous entity referred to as the 'environment' acts as a 'measuring device' which imprints itself on the quantum realm to produce the illusion of the macroscopic everyday reality does not sound too revolutionary. But the idea that the collective observations on the part of a vast number of sentient beings is responsible for the maintenance of the environment template itself makes the process of the everyday world look like too much of an illusion for many tastes. But this is exactly the conclusion which must be drawn, as John Wheeler indicated:

> ..the notes struck out on a piano by the observer participants of all times and all places, bits though they are in and by themselves, constitute the great wide world of space and time and things.[752]

The realm of the material world, then, is an intersubjective illusion-like creation at the intersection of the innumerable observations made by countless individuated consciousnesses.

The originator of the perspective of quantum Darwinism, Wojciech Zurek, describes his view:

> The main idea of quantum Darwinism is that we almost never do any direct measurement on anything … the environment acts as a

witness, or as a communication channel. ... It is like a big advertising billboard, which floats multiple copies of the information about our universe all over the place.[753]

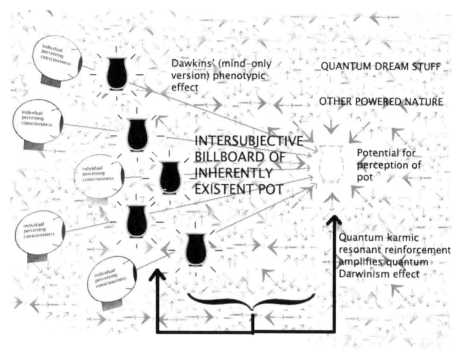

Fig 12.2

From this perspective it becomes apparent that the 'information' about the dualistic appearance of the universe 'floats' within the fundamental 'epiontic' quantum ground, which is the awareness 'stuff' of the process of reality, as shown in fig 12.2. The subjective intentional predispositions of sentient beings, which have been built up through habituation over vast tracts of time of continuous re-embodiment of mental continuums, activate and thereby reinforce these latent modes of perception.

In the following passage, taken from the commentary to the *Diamond Sutra* by the contemporary Chinese Buddhist teacher Hsing Yun, this 'floating' information is compared to 'dust' floating within 'clarity of perfect awareness,' the term '*lakshana*' indicates activated 'characteristics' or 'signs,' which we may interpret as activated 'bits' of quantum information:

> Dust clouds the metaphorical pool of enlightened awareness. ...
> Lakshana rush into the mind and appear before it like clouds of
> dust-like lakshana; impure intentions are based on deluded visions

of dust. Dust clouds the mind on all levels; matter is dust, illusion is dust, and thoughts and perception also are dust. Only the Tathagata sees the 'vast realm of emptiness' in which all of this floats in the clarity of perfect awareness.[754]

And in the directly following paragraph Master Hsing Yun relates this mechanism to the Mind-Only three natures:

...the metaphor of dust is used to reveal three levels of truth: 1) the false level of ordinary reality which is nothing but dust, 2) the level of emptiness in which that dust has no fundamental reality, and 3) the level of ultimate truth that merges and transcends these two levels. All Buddhas dwell on this third level, simultaneously in both ordinary and ultimate awareness.[755]

In other words buddhas see through the illusion-like informational 'dust' of the dualistic conventional seeming realm which 'floats' within the epiontic 'clarity of perfect awareness.'

The understanding of the process by which the 'dust' of the material world is created and maintained has been developed in the chapter *Quantum Karma*. The continuous intersubjective 'collapsing' of the wavefunction of the process of reality into the 'billboard' of the material world maintains the quantum Darwinian advertising campaign of the material world as a going concern. From the viewpoint of an individual consciousness the situation is shown in fig 12.1. From this perspective the illusory field of potential phenomena consists of an interpenetrating and mutually dependent matrix of 'other-powered' illusion-like, or dream-like, phenomena. The 'imputational nature' produces the illusion of solidity within the other-powered dream-stuff.

According to the Mind-Only analysis the process of unenlightened perception overlays the other-powered quantum field of illusion-like potentiality for experience with a completely illusory appearance of 'inherent existence;' this is created by the 'imputational nature'. This process clearly corresponds with the appearance of classical reality from the quantum field of other-powered potentiality. Understanding the 'empty' nature of conventional phenomena, therefore, requires the comprehension of the 'thoroughly established nature' which is defined as the realisation that the 'other-powered-nature' is 'empty' of the 'imputational nature'. This is the understanding of emptiness according to the 'three natures' analysis of the Mind-Only presentation of the process of reality; the imputational-nature of classical inherent reality is non-existent within the other-powered quantum nature.

The view of the imputational-nature, then, is the way that the conventional, macroscopic world is experienced by unenlightened sentient beings. Enlightened beings are said to experience the mere conventional reality, or mere relative, which is the other-powered nature devoid of any imputational natures. For unenlightened beings, however, conventional reality is experienced through a projected network of inherent existence which is superimposed on top of, or into, the field of the other-powered natures. Fig 12.3 illustrates the process of the projection, or superimposition, of the imputational nature on top of the other-powered nature. This is Fig 12.1 turned around so we are looking from the point of view of the perceiving consciousness; so it represents an other-powered pot being mistakenly perceived as an inherently existent pot, the inherent existence is represented by the solid fill.

Fig 12.3

The practice of the meditation on emptiness is used to deconstruct, and ultimately see through, the illusion of the conventional appearance of inherent existence within the perception of reality. Tsongkhapa developed a graphic form of meditation on the empty nature of phenomena which, according to the nineteenth century Madhyamika scholar Ju Mipham, is appropriate for beginners because of its graphic nature.

If we take a pot or vase as an example of a generic object for meditation on emptiness, for instance, then the following analysis is employed as the analytic phase of a meditation on emptiness. The analytic meditation phase is actually a discursive analysis which is carried out, prior to the focused placement meditation, in order to generate a mental image for the meditation. We first comprehend that, as we usually perceive the vase, the entity we think that we are correctly perceiving is actually an amalgam of what is actually there, which is an interdependent matrix of illusion-like causes and conditions, plus the projection of inherent existence that we add in, or superimpose, subjectively. Tsongkhapa likens this to an audience being beguiled by a magician's illusion:

> When external and internal phenomena appear as truly existent, sentient beings, like the audience of magic … apprehend that there is mode of subsistence of those phenomena not posited through the force of an awareness. This apprehension is the innate apprehension of true existence which has operated beginninglessly.[756]

In other words the apprehension of inherent, or 'true', existence is not actually within the untainted awareness of reality but it is a mistaken innate mode of apprehension which has become a mistaken habituated aspect of perception.

Fig 12.4 schematically shows the vase perceived in this amalgam state of being composed of the vase as it actually is (shown as the grey outline), which is to say an impermanent, temporary confluence of causes and conditions that give rise to a conventional functioning object, together with the imputed aspect of inherent existence (indicated by the solid black fill). The imputed aspect of inherent existence gives the vase the appearance of a completely separate, independent and self-enclosed object.

Fig 12.4

In fig 12.5 the aspect of inherent existence is imaginatively removed from the amalgam. This gives the two aspects separately comprehended by the imagination; the mistaken attribution of the inherent existence of the pot and the other-powered conglomeration of causes and conditions which make up the temporary 'functioning entity' which is the actual nature of the perceived pot. Tsongkhapa explained this by saying that:

> The pot is not empty of pot; it is empty of the inherent existence of pot.[757]

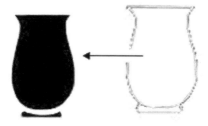

Fig 12.5

In the next stage we imaginatively perform what is termed a 'non-implicative negation'. This is a negation of the inherent aspect of the pot which does not put anything in its place (Fig 12.6).

Fig 12.6

At the end of this imaginative process we are left with the non-inherently existent pot which is a conventional functioning entity comprised of inter-secting causes and conditions (Fig 12.7). This is a simple outline of the main features of a basic meditation designed to undermine and defuse the innate tendency to automatically perceive all phenomena as existing separately and inherently in their own right, or 'from their own side'.

Tsongkhapa's analytic procedure, however, has not found universal acc-eptance amongst Buddhist scholar-practitioners. The twentieth century Tib-etan scholar Gendün Chöpel (1903-1951), for instance, wrote in his *Orna-ment to Nagarjuna's Thought:*

Fig 12.7

No matter how much one distinguishes the objects that are to be negated by reasoning, the truth is that, as far as refutation is concerned, you need to refute the vase; you need to refute the pillar; you need to refute existence; you need to refute non-existence. What use is there in positing the vase and then refuting a 'truly existent vase' off to the side? ... Leaving alone all vivid appearances, they look for something with horns to refute. ... There are those who fear that if vases, pillars and so on were refuted through reasoning, everyone would come to espouse nihilistic views of non-existence. Their worries are pointless. For in the case of ordinary everyday beings who are looking at a vase presently in front of them, how is it possible that a nihilistic view regarding the vase to be utterly non-existent could arise?[758]

According to Gendün Chöpel, then, Tsongkhapa's strategy of visualizing a conventional pot as being comprised of an other-powered-pot, or dependently originated pot, which contains an imputation of an inherently-existent-pot which must be imaginatively removed, is over contrived and unnecessary. The quip about looking for 'something with horns to refute' derives from the tradition within Tibetan Buddhism of using examples such as 'rabbits with horns' to indicate imaginative entities which have no possibility of having instantiation within the real world. In this case the criticism is that the idea of an inherently-existent-pot, on top of the actual pot so to speak, is equivalent to that of a 'rabbit with horns'; not only is it something which does not exist, neither is it something which an 'ordinary everyday being' would even conceive of as existing!

Tsongkhapa's reason for adopting this mode of reasoning is that he is worried that if an 'ordinary everyday being' practices conceiving of phenomena as being non-existent then they really might think that pots and pillars and so on, really did not exist at all. This, Gendun Chopel suggests, is ridiculous.

When considering the concept of emptiness it is useful to keep in mind the distinction between the conventional ultimate, or the conceptual ultimate, and the 'ultimate ultimate', or the non-conceptual ultimate. The final goal of the Madhyamaka path is the continuous, stable experiential direct awareness of emptiness. This is an irreversible uninterrupted and spontaneous awareness of the dependent-arising empty nature of all phenomena that pervades every moment and every atom of a practitioner's psychophysical being. This ultimate experiential emptiness is a direct awareness which cannot be completely and definitive captured within words and conceptual systems. This is beautifully captured in the verses previously discussed in the first chapter, but worth revisiting:

> It's just as if the sun's eclipse is taking place,
> You see reflections of its changing shapes. To say the sun and its reflection
> Touch or do not touch would indeed would be absurd.
> Such things arise dependently and on the level of convention.
> Reflections are not real, but using them we smarten our appearance.
> In just the same way we should understand that arguments
> That have the power to cleanse the face of wisdom.[759]

The conceptual ultimate can be thought of as a conceptual reflection of the nature of emptiness within the conventional, seeming experiential realm of dualistic appearances. And just as, in the absence of a completely perfect mirror, different types of mirror give different reflections of the target reality, all conceptual formulations are considered to be merely conventional pointers, from different perspectives, to an ultimate reality beyond concepts.

Western thought often dogmatically asserts a sharp dividing line between concept and reality and is then surprised when it is plunged into rapids of paradox at the quantum level. The Buddhist viewpoint, on the other hand, acknowledges the relative distinction between the two, but at the same time recognises that both arise from a deeper undivided source, what Bohm called the implicate order. Because of this commonality of source, correct conceptual analyses employed with conceptual rigor and precision can produce veridical 'reflections' of the nature of reality which are capable of pointing beyond themselves. Different reflections, from different perspectives, however, may have different strengths and weaknesses.

Tsongkhapa

The idea of a 'conceptual system' within Madhyamaka philosophy, is not that of a final completely precise structure of independent word and sentence meaning-units which map directly, unambiguously and with logical razor sharp precision on to an independent, external, unambiguous frame of objective reality, a view which is now shown to be inappropriate for quantum understanding. A conceptual system within the practice of the Madhyamaka is a system of increasingly subtle analysis and perspectives upon the interaction of thought and reality which can lead the awareness of an individual mind in the direction of greater understanding. The conceptual tools of the Madhyamaka do not leave crude inerasable 'physical' 'memes' scratched into the (ultimately non-existent) neuron jelly of the material brain; they transform the subtlety and flexibility of the potentialities for under-standing within the awareness-consciousness of the practitioners in the dir-ection of enlightened understanding and activity.

It is because conceptual systems are conceived of as being tools for the transformation of consciousness towards greater comprehension, under-standing and enlightened engagement with reality that they are sometimes referred to as 'vehicles' and 'chariots'. Thus the eighth Karmapa, Mikÿo Dorje, entitled his wonderful commentary on Chandrakirti's commentary on Nagarjuna the *Feast for the Fortunate: A Commentary on the Entrance to the Middle Way That Easily Pulls Along The Chariot of the Takpo Kagyü Siddhas*:

> A chariot that blissfully leads one down the vast and profound path
> of excellent non-abiding-
> The Middle Way – the peak of all vehicles.[760]

And one aspect of the 'excellent non-abiding' of 'The Middle Way' is the skillful practice of being able to employ all possible views upon the ultimate nature of reality to the extent of their applicability within any context. All limited views, when grasped and reified as ultimate to the exclusion of all others, can become nothing more than obscuring misunderstandings. Only by understanding that all views are limited viewpoints upon the ultimate non-fixed-view can such views be correctly applied:

> Attachment to one's view and
> Aversion to the views of others are nothing more than conception.
> Therefore if you first overcome attachment and aggression
> And *then* analyse, you will be liberated.[761]

Only by appreciating the terrain from all viewpoints can its full nature be fully comprehended.

The final, dramatic, phase of the Madhyamaka movement of thought is when it deconstructs itself in order to leave only the direct 'empty' experience of reality:

What is dependent origination
Is explained as emptiness.
It is a dependent designation
And in itself the middle path.[762]

Here emptiness is identified as a dependent designation; which clearly indicates that the conventional description of the ultimate nature of realty is itself 'empty' of independent reality but also, furthermore the ultimate itself must be empty of emptiness otherwise it would not be empty! In the chapter *The Self Perceiving Universe* we saw that the process of reality may be graphically depicted as a snake eating its own tail. In order to disentangle this self-consuming process we require a conceptual system with a sting in its tail so to speak. Emptiness itself is a conventional dependent designation, so emptiness itself is empty. In other words the Madhyamaka deconstructs itself in the last phase of its own understanding; this is necessary because only a self deconstructing system can deconstruct the illusion of reality in order to reveal the true nature of the 'empty' reality beyond concepts.

The nineteenth century Madhyamika scholar Jamgon Mipham, in his commentary to Shantarakshita's *Madhyamakalankara (The Adornment of the Middle Way)*, observed that:

> ... even though there is an infinite variety of beliefs; none of them ever gets beyond the assumption of true existence.[763]

The Madhyamaka analysis indicates that any conceptual system which is based on the assumption that there are truly existent entities that form the foundation of a view of the totality of reality will be internally inconsistent. And such internally inconsistent systems will automatically generate alternative viewpoints which derive from the inconsistencies or conceptual weaknesses in the original system. Any view that begins with the assertion of the reality of the inherent existence of its favored set of entity or entities, therefore, will lead to a proliferation of alternative, equally unstable views.

This has certainly been the case within the realm of the interpretation of the meaning of quantum physics. As we saw in the first chapter Nick Herbert, in his book *Quantum Reality,* identified eight different interpretations, or views, concerning what quantum theory really means. And, as we have seen, there is no complete resolution to this day. There has not only been a proliferation of views, there has also been a deluge of works by quantum physicists and philosophers which explore the puzzling terrain of the quantum world and none of them has been able to demonstrate any clear ascendancy for any of the views through reasoning alone, although some, like the overworked Many-Worlds interpretation, are gaining the upper hand.

These views are not generally held as different perspectives upon a multifaceted, fluid dimension of reality; they are usually thought to be mutually exclusive. This situation seems to vindicate the Madhyamaka assertion that whenever a conceptual framework starts from a belief in inherent existence then a proliferation of views will follow. In quantum physics we certainly find a proliferation of views which all operate from the basis of a belief in a definite inherently existent reality to some degree, it is generally thought there must be a definitely final description of the nature of quantum reality we can grasp hold of as an ultimate reality.

If, however, we relinquish our desperate craving for clinging to a single formulation of reality as being the complete, absolute, unimpeachable, inherently and exclusively correct description of a fixed ultimate reality, a craving which derives, as we saw in the chapter on *The Self Perceiving Universe*, from the 'ontological insecurity' of the universe itself, then perhaps it is quite reasonable to accept that each formulation captures an aspect of reality which is dependent upon context and level of analysis. If we apply this principle to the views concerning quantum reality outlined by Herbert, for instance, we can understand the truth of each in the following manner:

1. **Copenhagen interpretation part 1 – there is no deep quantum reality, it's all a fiction.** If the notion of a 'deep quantum reality' involves the attribution of independently and inherently existing entities then this view is correct. The assertion that it is 'all a fiction' might be a step to far, the phrase 'illusion-like' is a better description.

2. **Copenhagen interpretation part 2 – reality is created by observation.** This assertion is definitely indicated by many quantum experiments and is indicated by the 'collapse of the wavefunction' phenomenon.

3. **Reality is an undivided wholeness** – the phenomenon of entanglement, in which non-locally interconnected particles instantaneously affect one another across vast distances, indicate that this is, as held by Bohm, correct.

4. **Many worlds interpretation** – this is considered to be the most likely 'ultimate' interpretation by 48% of physicists. The extent to which this view is correct has been investigation in the *Many Worlds of Illusion* chapter. The version presented in that chapter requires the potential 'existence' of many illusion-like worlds, only some of which are activated during the course of cyclic existence.

5. **Quantum logic – the world is non logical or has a different logic to humans** – that the quantum realm does not conform to the kind of either-or logic which is generally adopted by Western philosophers is certainly appropriate.

6. **Neo realism – the world must be real, quantum physics is wrong** – is the only one in the list which is clearly wrong, it may perhaps be correct if deployed against a dogmatic view that quantum physics indicates that reality does not exist at all.

7. **Consciousness creates reality** – the fact that consciousness manifests experienced reality from the potential realm of the wavefunction is clearly indicated by the phenomenon of the 'collapse of the wavefunction.'

8. **The world consists of potentials and actualities** – is a description of the two stage process of reality as outlined by Stapp and others. Unobserved reality is constituted by the 'objective' propensities for experience within the wavefunction which are brought into manifestation through interaction with consciousness.

Thus all of these positions, then, can be viewed as containing, to some degree (number 6 is admittedly forcing this claim a bit), a partial truth and be considered to have be correct within an appropriate context.

It is so easy to fall into the trap of expecting a fixed inherently existent reality and therefore think that a particular way of viewing reality represents *the* definite and absolute truth excluding all other possibilities, but it is salutary to be aware that, as the physicist John Gribben reminds us:

> …all our models of fundamental particles and their interactions are no more than artificial aids to help us get a picture of what is going on in terms that seem familiar, or at least recognizable, from everyday life. … even our best models are no more than aids to the imagination…[764]

Or as the psychologist Alfred Korzybsky succinctly expressed this important caveat: 'the map is not the territory'[765].

According to the eleventh century Madhyamaka master Atisha a great deal of enmity and confusion is caused by dogmatic and aggressively clinging to extreme views concerning ultimately existing entities:

> If you accept entities,
> Desire and hatred well up in inexhaustible ways,
> You cling firmly to horrible views,
> And quarrels are nurtured by this source.
> For those who entertained notions with reference points,
> There is no attainment and no clear realisation.[766]

It is important to be clear that Madhyamaka warnings such as this relate to the holding, or clinging, onto extreme views which are asserted to be correct on an ultimate level. Such views are proposed as *the* final theory regarding the ultimate constituents of reality.

Eighth Karmapa: Mikyo Dorje

With respect to the idea that the ultimate nature of reality is emptiness Tsongkhapa says:

> ...to hold emptiness as a *view* means to be fixated on emptiness as an *entity* – that is, to grasp emptiness as truly existent or as existing inherently.[767]

In other words to assert emptiness as a view is to assert the ultimate inherent existence of emptiness, which is incorrect. Tsongkhapa reiterates this point in various variations:

> Similarly, when it is demonstrated that entities do not exist inherently, it is not that one should not take them to be truly empty, but that one should not take the entities' emptiness of true existence to be truly existent.[768]

And this observation on the part of Tsongkhapa suggests that the ninth Karmapa, Wangchuk Dorje, misrepresents Tsongkhapa's position when he says:

> There was also Shar Tsongkhapa, who maintained that emptiness exists and that therefore so does the natures of things, the supports for emptiness.[769]

However it must be recalled that Tsongkhapa did propose the adage:

> Not truly existent ultimately but not non-existent conventionally.[770]

Which might be taken as suggesting that the conventional 'natures of things, the supports for emptiness' are 'not non-existent conventionally'. But here the issue becomes whether 'not non-existent' means the same as 'inherently existent', or even merely 'existent.' This is why the philosophical practice of the Madhyamaka is exhilarating, and can even be intoxicating; for to engage in a true Madhyamaka philosophical analysis requires the analytic balancing on a razor edge of conceptual precision. But it is not a gratuitous balancing act; the wavefunction, for instance, is not non-existent, but it is not fully existent. The razor sharp, conceptual tight-walking precision of the Madhyamaka is, truly, a precision appropriate to quantum reality.

The fact that even emptiness must not be conceived of as ultimately existent is indicated in the following extraordinary and powerful verse from Nagarjuna's *Fundamental Verses*:

> If there were even the slightest bit nonempty,
> Emptiness itself would be the slightest bit existent.
> But when there is not even the slightest nonempty thing,
> How could emptiness exist?[771]

This verse demonstrates the razor edge precision to perfection. If there were something, anything, somewhere, anywhere in the universe of reality, or multiverse of realities, that was actually just slightly nonempty then there would be at least one tiny aspect of reality which would be inherently existent. If this were to be the case then emptiness itself would be projected into inherent existence because all the empty phenomena would have to 'exist' within the same domain of existential possibility as the nonempty phenomena. And this domain is that of inherent existence and inherent non-existence. Therefore the lack of inherent existence would become an inherent lack, which is the inherent existence of a lack. But when there is nothing 'the slightest bit nonempty', emptiness itself remains empty!

All of this might seem to be going around in circles chasing one's own tail, just like the process of reality itself, until that is, it is realised that all this relentless hair-splitting analysis is not for the purpose of establishing a view, they are conceptual tools with the purpose of projecting the awareness-mind of the practitioner of the Madhyamaka beyond all views into direct experience of reality; the experiential reality of reality, which is the emptiness of reality, rather than a conceptual view about reality. As Dennis Genpo Merzel says regarding Zen Koans:

> Koans are like can openers for the mind. Our minds are stuck in duality, and koans pry them open to a new way of seeing the world.[772]

It is quite easy to see the origin of the practice of the art of the Zen koan in the Madhyamaka. And in some respects the cutting edge of the original opener is sharper than its' descendent.

Nagarjuna supplied the core analysis for the development of the philosophical analysis of the process of reality within the perspective of the Madhyamaka. The primary source is undoubtedly his extraordinary present-ation of the view of emptiness within his seminal work *Mulamadhya-makakarika*, the *Fundamental Verses on the Middle Way*. In this astonishing work Nagarjuna relentlessly deconstructs the 'things' and 'processes' of the everyday conventional reality in order to reveal their illusion-like empty nature. Nagarjuna's seemingly paradoxical philosophical analysis lays bare the quantum face of the everyday world. Here is his superb demolition of the notion of inherently different things:

> A different thing depends upon a different thing for its difference.
> Without a different thing, a different thing wouldn't be different.
> It is not tenable for that which depends upon something else
> To be different from it.
>
> If a different thing were different from a different thing,
> Without a different thing, a different thing could exist.
> But without that different thing, that different thing does not exist.
> It follows that it doesn't exist.
>
> Difference is not in a different thing.
> Nor is it in a nondifferent thing.
> If difference does not exist,
> Neither different nor identical things exist.[773]

In order to appreciate the full significance of this demonstration it is necessary to appreciate that the effectiveness of a Madhyamaka analysis requires that the concepts involved are treated as if they are inherently existent in nature; this is the manner in which we unconsciously employ them whether we are aware of this fact or not. The illusion of the substantial reality of the conventional world of experience arises precisely because concepts are generally employed in a very imprecise and fluid manner whilst a background investment in their supposedly precise boundaries is implicitly maintained.

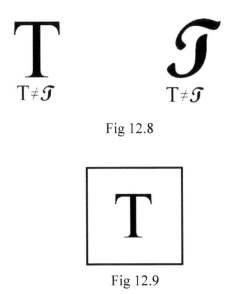

Fig 12.8

Fig 12.9

Nagarjuna's 'different thing' conundrum elegantly demonstrates this point. If a 'different thing' truly were an independent, completely, self-enclosed inherently 'different thing' then we should be able to place it in its own universe wherein it would maintain its identity as a 'different thing'. In fig 12.8 we see two things (represented by the letter 'T' In different fonts) which are different in comparison to each other; to indicate this situation the entities both appear with their difference represented by the non-equality relationship '$T \neq \mathcal{T}$' ('$\neq$' is the mathematical symbol for 'not equal to' , in this case it is used to mean 'is different from'). The 'difference' accompanies both entities when they are together in comparison as in fig 12.8. When one of the 'different things' is removed into its own universe (fig 12.9) it must lose its 'difference', '$T \neq \mathcal{T}$', because there is nothing for it to be different to; it is now clearly no longer a 'different thing', it's just a 'thing'; the difference, '$T \neq \mathcal{T}$', just vanishes. So we see it never was an inherently existent 'different thing.'

Nagarjuna

The point has been made but it is worth examining aspects of Nagarjuna's conceptual demolition if only to appreciate its elegance.

The last two lines of the first stanza are:

> It is not tenable for that which depends upon something else
> To be different from it.

The point here is that if something is truly different from something else then it must be completely different, which means it has absolutely no relationship or commonality to the thing it is supposed to be different from. But if this is the case then there should be no relationship between such 'different' things. However we have just seen that the fact of being 'different' actually requires a relationship; the concept of 'difference', viewed as an inherent aspect of 'things', then becomes problematically elusive.

The next stanza requires a resolute attribution of inherent existence in order to activate its full effect. It is necessary to treat the composite entity 'different thing' as a completely inseparable independent object in its own right. This is to say that the difference and the thing-ness are taken as inseparable, so that the difference within the 'different thing' cannot be removed from the 'different thing'. This way of conceiving of the situation follows from the first two lines of the stanza:

> If a different thing were different from a different thing,
> Without a different thing, a different thing could exist.

Here we are conceiving that the difference does not depend upon there being another 'different thing' to be different to or from. The difference is conceived of as inhering within the 'different thing' itself, with or without the existence of another independently 'different thing'. This is to say a 'different thing' can exist by itself, without a necessary relationship outside of itself, because of its inherent difference; and at this point we are now in full possession, so to speak, of a fully inherently existent 'different thing'. We can hold this 'different thing' up and say 'here is a fully independent different thing!' But we know that in reality a 'different thing' does depend on something outside itself for its difference; so the mirage of a fully independent 'different thing' vanishes into ...?

Nagarjuna's scrutiny demonstrates that 'difference' does not inherently exist; without 'different things' 'difference' is nowhere to be found; and without a 'difference' 'different things' are nowhere to be found! Furthermore, neither can we anywhere find identical things (for exactly the same reason)! In this way Nagarjuna's analysis of the phenomena of the conventional everyday world, the world that sentient beings generally take for granted as existing as an independent reality, is shown to be dependent upon the conceptual network which is imputed upon it by the mind; it is this ungraspability of the definitively 'inherent' aspects of the lineaments of reality that constitutes Nagarjuna's elucidation of 'emptiness'.

The fundamental interdependent relationship which is the hallmark of emptiness is further illustrated in the section *Examination of Fire and Fuel*:

If fuel were fire,
Agent and object would be one.
If fire were different from fuel,
Then it could arise without fuel.

It would be forever aflame;
Ignition could occur without a cause.
Effort regarding it would be pointless
…

Since it would not depend upon another,
Ignition would be without a cause.
If it were eternally in flames,
Effort regarding it would be pointless.

So, if one thought that
That which is burning is the fuel,
If it is just this,
By what is this fuel being burned?[774]

In order to fully appreciate this analysis it is necessary to hold in mind that the term 'fuel' refers to the actual wood that is currently in the process of being burned, not the wood which is awaiting ignition. From the rigorously precise standpoint of the Madhyamaka the wood waiting to be burnt is just wood, 'fuel' is the actual wood which is 'fuelling' the fire. The focus here is on the actual moment of the process of the burning.

In this analysis emptiness is demonstrated through the fact that the entities of fire and fuel can be neither identical nor different. If two putative entities exist inherently then they must either be the same entity or different entities, there is no third possibility. If neither of these two mutually exclusive alternatives applies within the situation then we are in the midst of 'emptiness'.

If fire and the fuel were the same entity, which is to say that the wood which is in the process of burning and the fire which at that moment was doing the burning were identical, then we would have to say that there is no difference between agent, the fire, and the object, the fuel. But this is equivalent to saying that a pot is identical to the potter who makes it, or a cut is identical to someone who makes the cut. Although the division in the process of burning is less clear, it is still necessary; for without this distinction the process itself disappears. So it is not appropriate to claim the identity of fire and fuel.

If, on the other hand, it is claimed that fire is inherently different from the fuel, then it must be able to stand alone, burning away happily all to itself without needing any fuel to fuel it, so to speak. In this case there would be no need to start fires, they would just be there, you might be able to hide them and reveal them but they would have to be burning eternally, independently of any fuel. You might ask why inherently existent fire would have to be 'eternally in flames'. If this were not the case then it would need a starting point, and a starting point requires a cause, and the cause would have to be fuel! In the last stanza the process of burning, which is the fire, is identified as being the fuel. This effectively eliminates fire from the picture because we identify it as fuel. But in this case we must ask what is consuming the fuel?

Nagarjuna's fire and fuel analysis can be applied to the concept of an electromagnetic wave. According to Maxwell's equations of electromagnetic wave propagation the electromagnetic wave consists of two aspects, or parts; there is an electric wave which oscillates in one direction and there is a magnetic wave which oscillates at right-angles to the electric wave. The quantum physicist Roger Penrose gives the following explanation of how an electromagnetic wave functions:

> One implication of Maxwell's equations was that electric and magnetic fields would indeed 'push' each other along through empty space. An oscillating magnetic field would give rise to an oscillating electric field ... and this oscillating electric field would, in turn, give rise to an oscillating magnetic field ... and this again would give rise to an electric field and so on.[775]

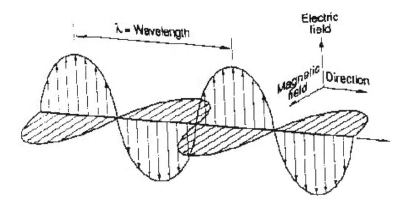

Fig 12.10 : electromagnetic wave

So the two aspects of the electromagnetic wave are supposed to be mutually dependent. Superficially this might seem innocuous. But when examined from the point of view that the electric and magnetic aspects are supposed to be inherently existent independent entities, which is how they are generally viewed by physicists and, indeed, as they must be in order to be causally effective, then the picture becomes incoherent. As Nagarjuna, pointed out in his *Mulamadhyamakakarika* :

> If that on which an entity depends
> Is established on the basis
> Of the entity depending on it,
> What is established in dependence on what?[776]

To clarify this observation Khenpo Tsultrum Gyamtso cites the illustration of two rocking boats given by the 19th century Tibetan scholar Ju Mipham:

> ... since neither boat is steady to begin with, it is impossible for either one to be the cause of steadying the other. Similarly, when one thing must depend upon another for its existence, but that other one must in turn depend on the first for its own existence, in genuine reality it is impossible for either one to be the support for the other's existence. Therefore, neither one of them truly exists – they are mere interdependent appearances.[777]

It might be thought that this analysis can be defused by claiming that the magnetic fluctuation causes the subsequent electric disturbance and so on. This will not do, however, for in this case we must enquire which came first, if neither comes first then there is an infinite regress of mutual dependency.

This analysis is not mere word play, it actually goes straight to the heart of the crucial issue of what physicists mean by 'real' and 'physical' phenomena. Physicists regularly use the term 'real' to refer to the existence of definitely established independent and self sufficient features of reality. Such features are certainly thought to be independent of the consciousness perceiving them. These features, or entities, are conceived of as being self powered, independent and inherent existences. As David Bohm has pointed out:

> They do use the ideas of fields and particles and so on, but when you press them they must agree that they have no image whatsoever what these things are and they have no content other than the results of what they can calculate with their equations. [778]

But appearance of inherent existence in the 'physical' phenomena postulated by physicists quickly falls apart when analysed.

But it is important to be clear that the Madhyamaka does not deny that there is a web of experience which creates the illusion of a seeming reality. To claim that there was absolutely nothing would be absurd; emptiness is not the same as nothingness. As Nagarjuna pointed out:

To say 'it is' is to grasp for permanence.
To say 'it is not' is to adopt the view of nihilism.
Therefore a wise person
Does not say 'exists' or 'does not exist'."[779]

Phenomena are said to be neither existent nor non-existent, a formulation which, as we have seen, acquires a greater depth when viewed from the perspective of quantum physics. What the Mind-Only analysis refers to as the realm of the other-powered nature corresponds to the realm of the quantum wavefunction, which is a field of potentiality that hovers between existence and non-existence. When consciousnesses interacts with the wavefunction realm with attachment for experience of inherent existence it imputes 'inherent existence' at a deep level of reality, and thereby 'collapses' the potentiality of the wavefunction into experienced reality. Ultimately, however, this process itself is 'empty' of all definite graspable existence:

Thus phenomena are of one taste,
Unhindered, and non-abiding.
Through the meditative concentration of reality as it is,
They are all luminosity.[780]

Here emptiness is described as 'non-abiding'; it is the true sub–stance; that which lies beneath and provides the possibility of reality; although it is clearly not a 'substance' as we usually conceive of this term. It is the support and essence of all phenomena but it abides in none of them; it is the condition for all dualistic conditioned phenomena but it is not conditioned by any of them. Like buddhahood, which is the attainment of the direct awareness of emptiness, and which is also sometimes described as embracing all phenomena but being no particular phenomenon[781]; emptiness itself may be described as being the condition, potentiality, support and essence of all phenomenon whilst not being limited within any of its manifestations.

Although emptiness is not limited or contained within any of the phenomena of the dualistic world, its essential nature may be experienced through the 'meditative concentration of reality as it is'. By this means of going behind the appearance of phenomena in order to experience their 'one taste' it is found that they are all of the nature of 'luminosity'. This quality of luminosity is the experiential manifestation of emptiness; and it is also the inner quality of the quantum realm of the wavefunction. It is a remarkable fact that the two possible avenues for the exploration of the nature of reality, meditation and scientific investigation have arrived at the same ground, expressed as different metaphors but clearly equivalent; and that ground is emptiness (fig 12.11).

MEDITATION   SCIENCE

← MIND   MATTER →

LUMINOSITY   MATHEMATICAL

WAVEFUNCTION

EMPTINESS

Fig 12.11

The primary scientific metaphor, of course, is the mathematical metaphor of the wavefunction, which as we have seen, is the mathematical equation of the potential experiential possibilities within various objective configurations of consciousness. The metaphors of emptiness which have been developed within the Mahayana philosophical discourse are those contained within the fundamental Chittamatra and Svatantrika/Prasangika metaphysical analyses of reality. And there can surely be no more dramatic demonstration of the validity and cogency of the meditative tradition of Buddhism than the fact that it was able to find an avenue to the direct experience of the nature of this ultimate reality, the same ultimate reality that has been discovered by the most subtle and precise experiments available to modern science.

It is always worth bearing in mind that this new quantum viewpoint was not a whim on the part of mystically crazed 'new age' physicists, which is how some of the materialist detractors would like to present the situation, but, rather, it was forced upon them by the evidence. As Professor Stapp points out:

> The founders of quantum theory certainly had no desire to bring down the grand structure of classical physics of which they were the inheritors, beneficiaries, and torch bearers. It was stubborn facts that forced their hand, and made them reluctantly abandon the two hundred year old classical ideal of a mechanical universe, and turn to what should have been seen from the start as a more reasonable endeavour: the creation of an understanding of nature that includes in a rationally coherent way the thoughts by which

we know and influence the world around us. The labours of scientists endeavouring merely to understand our inanimate environment produced, from its own internal logic, a rationally coherent framework into which we ourselves fit neatly.[782]

The way that the 'we ourselves fit neatly into' our current understanding of reality, which has 'forced the hand' of quantum physicists because of its 'own internal logic' corresponds exactly to the subtle presentation of the Madhyamaka by the eighth century Madhyamika master Shantarakshita.

In his work *Madyamakalankara (Ornament of the Middle Way)* Shantarakshita presents the *Yogachara-Svatantrika-Madhyamaka*, which is the style of presentation of the Madhyamaka that this current work has primarily adopted. This presentation is Yogachara because it begins from the understanding that the conventional nature of reality is mind, or consciousness. Chandrakirti expressed this insight by asserting that 'the mind is king within the world'[783]; a view which is now completely validated by quantum theory. The term 'Svatantrika' denotes a method of logical analysis which employs autonomous (*Svatantra*) logical arguments, that is arguments which stand on their own and make independent assertions concerning both the conventional and the ultimate nature of reality. This type of philosophical procedure is contrasted, within the Tibetan Madhyamaka, with the *Prasangika* mode of reasoning; which is considered by some to be the proper philosophical engagement of a practitioner of the Madhyamaka philosophy. The Prasangika exegetical logical practice is to only employ *prasanga* arguments, which are consequential, *reductio ad absurdum* demonstrations of the hidden contradictions within an opponent's position. This distinction was not made within Indian Buddhist philosophy, it is a later imputation made by Tibetan scholars who had a passion for systemisation of conceptual systems. The core of the distinction lies in the assertion that making any kind of conceptually substantive assertions about ultimate reality must undermine the emptiness of emptiness by imputing conceptual substantiality into it, so to speak.

Quantum theory, of course, does make definite assertions about reality at the conventional and the ultimate level; the essential nature of the quantum realm is 'epiontic'. This indicates it consists of the 'stuff' of potential experience, which can be activated through resonant interaction with subjectively embodied temporarily functioning centres of awareness, which is more or less Shantarakshita's view on the matter of Mind-Only. Starting from the conventional apprehension that consciousness is the primary constituent, however, Shantarakshita delved deeper into the nature of reality to discover that the mind itself is ultimately unfindable within dualistic experience.

Thus he indicates an aspect of the make up of reality which causes quantum physicists much difficulty and headache. Although they clearly have a mathematical trace of the movements of consciousness within the theoretical wavefunction, there is no substantial trace of the trace, so to speak. It seems that the tracks of wavefunction of emptiness can be likened to 'sketching a colourful painting onto the sky.'[784] This is why physicists such as Penrose and Tegmark, for instance, entertain the untenable possibility that mathematics *is* ultimate reality. As Sir James Jeans wrote in 1931:

> ...substantial matter [resolves] itself into a creation and manifestation of mind ... [which leads to] ... the tendency to think [of the universe] in the way which, for want of a better word, we describe as mathematical...[785]

However, the notion that mathematics *is* ultimate reality is clearly born of desperation to avoid the conclusion, which should be clear and incontrovertible, that, at the conventional level at least, reality is fundamentally of the nature of consciousness. Mathematics has no substantial nature of its own; it is a relational structure of meaning developed within the developmental activity of consciousness.

There is a serious problem for minds which are acclimatised to thinking in terms of their experiences of what appears to be an external world as actually being an independent external realm of materiality. Such habituation leads to an attitude that simply cannot accept that a truly immaterial 'substance' such as nondual awareness could be the ultimate support of reality; such a 'substance' seems to be too insubstantial! It might be countered that mathematics is also insubstantial so why would physicists prefer to grasp at mathematics as an ultimate substance. The answer is precisely that mathematics is dualistically 'graspable' as a definite pattern of dualistic experience whereas to posit nondual awareness as the ultimate nature of reality moves the answer out of the realm that physicists want to deal with. If one accepts the Buddhist answer to the riddle of existence then in order to actually 'know' the answer, directly and really, it is necessary to do something beyond reading books and manipulating mathematical equations. It is necessary to train in a completely different arena of experience, outside of the usual comfort zone of Western scientists and philosophers - the direct investigation of the immediate experience of one's own structure of awareness through disciplined meditation techniques.

For someone who has no direct experience through meditation of deeper levels of consciousness the idea that awareness-consciousness could underlie the remarkable appearances of the dualistic world might seem unlikely. For anyone who has a grasp of the power of the inner luminosity of mind, however, the plausibility factor increases dramatically.

The immaterial and ungraspable nature of consciousness, taken together with the fact that consciousness is generally held to be the conventional aspect of emptiness; whilst the ultimate nature of emptiness is held by

Buddhist philosophy to be beyond words and concepts, leads to some extremely subtle distinctions and gentle paradoxical disagreements within Madhyamaka viewpoints which require a great deal of gentle and subtle intellectual reflection and investigation to comprehend. But this is not a result of vague and incompetent philosophical reasoning capacities of pre-scientific intellects; it is precisely the conclusion arrived at by quantum physicists attempting to make conventional, classical sense of the results of their experiments. Heisenberg, for instance, made the following observation:

> It is not surprising that our language should be incapable of describing the processes occurring within the atoms, for, as has been remarked, it was invented to describe the experiences of daily life, and these consist only of processes involving exceedingly large numbers of atoms. Furthermore, it is very difficult to modify our language so that it will be able to describe these atomic processes, for words can only describe things of which we can form mental pictures, and this ability, too, is a result of daily experience.[786]

And it is exactly in order to undermine the misleading mental pictures of the 'everyday experience' of the conventional realm of reality that the deconstructive philosophical procedures of the Madhyamaka are employed.

Whilst the subtleties and nuances of thought may appear to be extremely delicate, so vanishingly fine perhaps that they approach the point of conceptual ungraspability, when the point of these distinctions is grasped it becomes clear that the very intellectual comprehension of the subtleties involved projects ones mind into a clarity and subtlety of thought which provides a more fertile ground for the understanding of the dramatically subtle nature of the concept, and ultimately the experience, of emptiness itself. Engaging with these intricate debates, together with an appropriate meditation practice, is a method of increasing the flexibility of one's metaphysical imagination.

The type of metaphysical 'imagination' involved, however, is not that of some modern physicists and philosophers who appeal to alien computer simulations, or infinities of infinite numbers of slightly differing version of the 'same' person being continuously generated, in order to explain the seemingly unexplainable in comic book terms. It is, rather, the rigorous and razor sharp delineation of the implications of the philosophical and experiential investigations of the conceptual limits of the process of reality.

The Madhyamika philosophers were aware that no conceptual system, treated as a final and exclusive formulation of *the* fixed and absolute nature of reality, is able to fully capture the reality of reality, only direct experience can accomplish that ultimate direct knowledge. It was because of this that it is understood by Madhyamika philosophers that concepts and elucidations employed by them are as empty as the emptiness that they attempt to elucidate:

> Thus, when one's son dies in a dream,
> The conception "He does not exist"
> Removes the thought that he does exist,
> But it is also delusive.[787]

It is a process by which:

> ... one magical creation may be annihilated by another magical creation.[788]

Or, as the Eighth Karmapa said:

> An illusionlike knowable object that lacks nature is known or realised by an illusionlike knowing that lacks nature...[789]

If you think carefully about this formulation, it is an extraordinarily potent description of the collapse of the wavefunction.

Quantum Luminous Heart of the Empty Wave of Reality

If quantum theory appears as a 'smokey dragon' ..., the dragon itself may now be recognised as the universal wavefunction, greatly veiled to us local beings by the 'smoke' represented by our own entanglement with the rest of the world.

However you turn it: *In the beginning was the wavefunction.*[790]

- H. Dieter Zeh

The clear light nature of the minds of all sentient beings, the matrix of the one-gone-thus, like the nature of space, ... does not change due to clouds, smoke and so forth...

- Maitreya

All matter originates and exists only by virtue of a force... We must assume behind this force the existence of a conscious and intelligent Mind. This Mind is the matrix of all matter.[791]

- Max Planck

The dhatu of beginningless time
Is the matrix of all phenomena.
Since it exists, all beings
And also nirvana are obtained.[792]

- Abhidharmasutra

The body of attributes of natural clear light, the uncontaminated basic element, is not made by causes and conditions,
And functions indivisibly as the nature of all sentient beings;
It is just spontaneously endowed from the start with all attributes...[793]

- Maitreya

Just that final Buddha, the matrix of the one-gone-thus, the ultimate clear light, element of attributes, self-arisen pristine wisdom, great bliss, and partless pervader of all is said to be the basis and source of all phenomenon, the void basis, and the basis pure of all defilements. It also is said to be endowed with the qualities of the body of attributes beyond the count of the sands of the Ganges River within an indivisible nature.[794]

- Dolpopa Sherab Gyaltsen

Dolpopa Sherab Gyaltsen

In the previous chapter we examined the view of intrinsic-emptiness, or self-emptiness, which is denoted by the Tibetan term *Rangtong*. This is the presentation of the notion of emptiness which is foundational for all forms of Buddhist philosophical-soteriological analysis. It is the fundamental understanding that all phenomena lack any intrinsic and inherent stable and persisting core of self-existence. There is, however, a further, more esoteric, presentation of emptiness called 'other-emptiness,' or 'extrinsic-emptiness' (*Shentong*). This presentation of the concept of emptiness takes us into the midst of the qualitative nature of the quantum wavefunction.

As we saw Tsongkhapa's presentation of intrinsic-emptiness focuses upon the notion of the 'non-implicative negation' of inherent existence, a procedure which deliberately restrains itself from making any conceptual picture or assertion regarding what remains after the negation is performed. The view of other-emptiness, on the other hand, focuses upon the experiential remainder which is the abode of the tathagatas, the sentient beings gone-to-thusness, the fully enlightened, fully awakened beings, or buddhas.

The Tibetan fourteenth century monumental work on other-emptiness, *Mountain Doctrine, Ocean of Definitive Meaning: Final Unique Quintessential Instructions* by Dolpopa Sherab Gyaltsen, who proposed the controversial view of ultimate other-emptiness, known as the Jonang doctrine after the monastery that Dolpopa became head of, is replete with descriptions of ultimate reality which resonate with the theoretical entity that modern physics calls the wavefunction. Some of the synonyms offered by Dolpopa, which are indicative of an appreciation of the fact that the underlying nature of the process of reality is a field, or matrix, to use Planck's terminology, of potentiality are:

- Body of attributes
- Element of attributes
- Buddha-element of attributes
- Source of attributes
- Abode of attributes
- Basic element that is the abode of attributes
- Source of all phenomena
- Basis that is empty of all phenomena
- Space element
- The essential constituent of space
- Partless pervader of all
- Emptiness endowed with all aspects
- Emptiness of the ultimate
- Emptiness of specific characteristics
- Emptiness of all attributes
- Emptiness of the indestructible

- Aspectless endowed with all aspects
- Signless basic element
- Uncontaminated Buddha-element of attributes
- Basic constituent of cyclic existence
- Basic element of selflessness
- Pure basis
- Basis empty of all phenomena
- Limit of reality
- Limit of cyclic existence
- Limit of emptiness
- Buddha Matrix
- Matrix of the one gone thus
- Matrix of the one gone to bliss
- Matrix of phenomena
- The uncompounded noumenon
- Noumenon of phenomena
- Abidingness of phenomena
- Character of phenomena
- Nature of non-entities
- Illusory like noumenon
- Noumenal thoroughly established nature
- Mode of subsistence
- Great emptiness
- Ultimate other-emptiness
- Uncontaminated basic element
- Self-cognizing and self-illuminating ultimate pristine wisdom
- Entity of fully aspected form
- Final entity
- Inconceivable sphere
- Sphere of nonduality
- Knowledge of all aspects
- Ultimate mind of enlightenment
- Natural spontaneity
- Variegated mental body
- A nature of dreams
- Containing all worlds

The characterisations 'body of attributes', 'element of attributes', 'source of attributes', 'matrix of phenomena', 'noumenon of phenomenon' and 'source of all phenomena' and so on adumbrate what physicists consider today to be a wavefunction, the realm of potentiality which exists prior to manifestation through observation. The epithet 'containing all worlds' indicates the close connection with the quantum many-worlds hypothesis, which we have explored in detail in *Many Worlds of Illusion*. We might also note that the nature of this fundamental element, or matrix, of reality is described as 'a nature of dreams,' a designation which resonates with Zurek's description of the quantum epiontic 'dream stuff' of reality.[795]

Dolpopa's elucidation of the 'element of attributes' states that, whilst it is fundamentally undifferentiable, at the same time all possible attributes which might be manifested are contained within it:

> It also is said to be endowed with the qualities of the body of attributes beyond the count of the sands of the Ganges River within an indivisible nature.[796]

And:

> Just as space is asserted as always pervading all,
> So the uncontaminated Buddha-element of attributes also is asserted as always pervasive,
> Just as space pervades all forms in the sense of opening a way for them,
> So it also pervades the groups of sentient beings.[797]

And:

> Just as space which has a non-conceptual and unobstructed nature
> Pervades undifferentiably all physical phenomena
> So the luminous nature of mind, the primordially undefiled element of attributes,
> Also entirely pervades without differentiation all states of persons.
> That naturally pure element of attributes is the general character or noumenon of all phenomena...[798]

And:

> Dwelling in the bodies of all
> In a dual and nondual manner
> The principle essence of effective things and non-effective things.
> Abiding pervading the stable and the moving,
> It is asserted as just having the form of illusion.[799]

And:

> Space is the element of attributes.
> The element is thought of as 'seed.'
> It exists inside all phenomena.
> It is the cause of all supreme states.
> Just as oil exists in sesame,
> Just as fire exists in wood,
> So it exists in all phenomena.

Though it exists in that way
In all phenomena, it is not seen.[800]

Many of the other synonyms which may not immediately leap off the page as indicating an appreciation of the wavefunction nature of the underlying reality are generally given descriptions that indicate an equivalent nature:

The thusness of what are called 'phenomena
Of apprehended-object and apprehending subject' are individually investigated.
Because of being indivisible from the element of attributes...[801]

Thusness, *tathata*, or the Buddha-matrix, is the eternal and immutable nondual empty ground and condition for the illusory play of subjective-objective experience, the field of illusory apprehender and apprehended:

The entity is the pristine wisdom of the one-gone-thus, knowing itself; it is apprehended by that entity and is devoid of the manifestations of the eighteen constituents of apprehended-object and apprehending-subject...[802]

The 'eighteen constituents' are the sense constituents that create the illusion of the samsaric world, three (sense faculty, consciousness, and object) for each sense (eye, ear, nose, tongue, body and mental sense). Dolpopa amplifies the above description as follows:

Thus the ultimate truth-knowing itself by itself, devoid of extremes of existence and non-existence has a nature that is beyond the phenomena of dependent-arising, does not deteriorate from its own entity, and is not empty of its own entity.[803]

In this description of the ultimate other-empty final matrix of reality, which is beyond existence and non-existence, Dolpopa asserts that the ultimate nondual nature is experiential in nature, having the quality of self-knowing luminosity. In this context the observation by physicist Nick Herbert that 'consciousness both in humans as well as in other sentient beings is identical to the inner experience of some quantum system'[804] is of immense significance. For quite clearly Dolpopa's characterisation of the experiential ultimate nature must apply to the quantum realm as it may be experienced in a nondual manner, which means that we may take Dolpopa to be speaking of the inner luminous direct experiential awareness which is a fundamental quality of the uncollapsed wavefunction.

This is the experiential sphere of the tathagatas, the ones who have gone to thusness or suchness (*tathata*), which is the ultimate experiential sphere of the nondual ground of the process of reality. Such thus-gone-ones are buddhas, awakened sentient beings. Furthermore all sentient beings are embryonic buddhas; this is the *tathagatagarba* doctrine, which is the doctrine that the minds of all sentient beings contain the potential to become the minds of buddhas:

> A Buddha dwells in ones own mind.
> There is no Buddha anywhere else.
> Those obscured by the darkness of unknowingness.
> Seek Buddha aside from their own bodies.
> The great pristine wisdom that has abandoned
> All conceptuality resides in the body.
> Pervading all things, it dwells in the body
> But is not produced from the body.[805]

The minds of all sentient beings actually contain the seed of the universal awareness-consciousness which lies at the heart of the process of reality. In the above quote the term 'buddha' actually indicates the direct awareness of the universal awakened awareness of buddhahood. This can only be discovered within the development and transformation of ones own mind, which is seemingly trapped within dualistic embodiment. Furthermore, buddhahood, the direct awareness of the nondual universal consciousness is overlaid and obscured within all sentient beings by the adventitious 'stains' and 'defilements' which have been injected into the essentially stainless nondual universal awareness over beginningless time by the dualistic activities by countless unenlightened sentient beings:

> Sentient beings are just Buddhas
> But they are obscured by adventitious defilements,
> When those are removed they are just Buddhas.[806]

It is intriguing to consider this view in juxtaposition to H. Dieter Zeh's observation that the universal wavefunction is:

> ...greatly veiled to us local beings by the 'smoke' represented by our own entanglement with the rest of the world. [807]

It is the dualistic 'classical' realm of the everyday world, which is created by the multitudinous collapses of wavefunctions which creates the 'smoke' which veils the essential nature of the 'uncollapsed' ultimate realm of the wavefunction. As we have seen previously the universal mind of a buddha does not of necessity collapse wavefunctions. And it is for this reason that, from an enlightened point of view, the ultimate experiential reality of the nondual realm is empty of 'other' dualistic and conditioned phenomena. So Dolpopa's exposition of other-emptiness or extrinsic emptiness, in contrast to Tsongkhapa's self-emptiness or intrinsic-emptiness which is the canonical view of the Svatantrikas and Prasangikas, describes emptiness from the experiential dimension of enlightenment.

From the perspective of Tsongkhapa's viewpoint, which asserts that phenomena are empty of their own inherent entity, Dolpopa's assertions seem like pure heresy; and, indeed, they were for a long time treated as such. Recall that, according to Tsongkhapa, a useful way of summarizing the import of the view that emptiness indicates a rejection of the extremes of existence and non-existence is with the adage:

> Not truly existent ultimately but not non-existent convention-ally.[808]

Dolpopa, however, proposes a seemingly inverse proposition regarding emptiness. The Buddhist translator and scholar Karl Brunnhölzl writes that:

> Dolpopa explicitly declares that nondual wisdom and ultimate reality withstand analysis. In other words, self-emptiness – phen-omena being empty of a nature of their own – pertains only to conventional reality, but not ultimate reality, which is not empty of itself. Consequently the views of the Svatantrikas and Prasangikas-who assert the opposite-are impure.[809]

And Dolpopa certainly seems to radically disagree with Tsongkhapa's view that reality is 'not truly existent ultimately':

> I say that the Buddha-nature has six qualities-permanence, reality, truth, purity, and perception.[810]

A similar positive view of the ultimate nature of the process of reality is shared by the profound teachings of the Third Karmapa, Rangjung Dorje, concerning the 'luminous mind' of the buddha-nature which is the 'stainless Heart of the victors.'[811] The following is from Nagarjuna's *In Praise of Dharmadhatu (Dharmadhatustava)* :

> …mind that is so luminous
> Is soiled by stains of craving and so forth.
> The afflictions burn in wisdoms fire,
> But its luminosity does not.[812]

Rangung Dorge comments:

> Through misconceiving the Buddha heart – naturally luminous mind – as subject and object, we think of it as 'me' and 'mine'. Through such mental formations, we conceive of something to be adopted and something to be rejected, which leads to craving for certain abodes and objects. The mind streams of those who entertain clinging due to this cause are ignorant.[813]

It is this 'naturally luminous' 'Buddha heart' which Dolpopa identifies as the 'matrix-of-one-gone-thus' which is the unchanging background, which is available for direct experience, against which the 'flaws' of dualistic sentient activity takes place:

Just as uncompounded space pervades all physical compounded phenomena
But due to being subtle ... is not affected by flaws of form such as impermanence and so forth...
So this luminous element of attributes, the matrix-of-one-gone-thus, dwelling pervasively in all sentient beings as the nature of their minds
Also is not ever affected by the flaws of sentient beings such as afflictive emotions and so forth, since it is naturally pure.[814]

Rangjung Dorje was a contemporary of Dolpopa and it is possible that they met and discussed their respective viewpoints on the qualities of the ultimate sphere of reality, viewpoints which do have a great deal in common, despite subtle differences in presentation and emphasis.

In his preface to his excellent translation of Rangjung Dorje's commentary to Nagarjuna's *In Praise of Dharmadhatu* Brunnhölzl writes that the dharmadhatu, or expanse of phenomena (which Dolpopa calls the 'element of attributes' etc.), should not be understood:

Third Karmapa: Rangjung Dorge

as some mere emptiness or abstract nature of all phenomena but as the true state of our mind, luminous nonconceptual wisdom, or the present moment of mind's fundamental awareness and vast openness being inseparable.[815]

The important point here is that the teachings regarding buddha-nature and luminous mind and so on should not be entertained as merely descriptive intellectual curiosities but are instructions and elucidations to be employed together with spiritual and meditative practice in order to actually transform the experiential process and quality of the practitioners' own minds towards enlightenment (*nirvana*), which is a mode of being for which all traces of dualistic clinging have been eradicated; thus transforming *vijnana*, which is divided dualistic consciousness, into *jnana*, nondual pristine wisdom-awareness:

> The essence of mind is natural luminosity. To put an end to this mind being ensnared by itself means the freedom from adventitious stains and the fundamental change of state.[816]

This transformative process is actually a quantum process, accomplished through the mind acting upon its own internal process, precisely because the functioning of the mind is itself a quantum process. The inner experience of awareness, the natural, directly experienced luminosity which is the fundamental nature of mind is, as physicist Nick Herbert has pointed out, the inner quality of the quantum system which is experienced as the psychophysical continuum of a sentient being. This transformative process, which is beautifully presented in Karl Brunnhölzl's translations of the teachings of the Third Karmapa, constitutes what Herbert refers to as an 'inner physics' which he mistakenly thinks is 'yet to be developed.'[817]

Before investigating the nature of this 'inner physics' of transformation it is necessary to outline the three fundamental aspects, or levels, of the functioning of the wavefunction which can be postulated on the basis of the mathematical structure and meaning of the Schrödinger equation and the method of its solution. In so doing it will be possible to answer Brunnhölzl's query:

> ...how does the concept of a universal wavefunction fully tally with mind/consciousness,... does that mean that the wavefunction is self-aware and is aware of wave collapse. ... I think for physicists it is hard to equate the wavefunction with consciousness and, for Buddhists, it is even harder to reduce mind to a wavefunction...[818]

We have clearly seen that it is, indeed, the case that 'for physicists it is hard to equate the wavefunction with consciousness.' However we have also seen that the evidence is now stacked up in favour of the conclusion that the ultimate qualitative nature of the 'substance' of the process of reality, described by the mathematical wavefunction, is nondual awareness, a deep level of 'epiontic' potentiality which divides up into a multitude of continuums of individuated subject-object experience. The nature of the self-awareness of the nondual ground (*jnana*) can only be directly known to enlightened beings, but its limited individuated form, which is in the form of consciousness (*vijnana*), which is divided awareness, is the feel of the cognitive-epiontic 'collapse of the wavefunction.' As physicist Max Tegmark says:

> …consciousness is the way that information feels when it is being processed.[819]

Primordial awareness (*jnana*), however, is the ground potentiality for any such 'information' which can get 'processed.' As so often we find that Western thinking is remarkably imprecise in its presentation. What exactly is 'information'; it is nothing other than 'meaning' in some form or another and is therefore based upon awareness, which is the ground of all meanings. But, as we have found on many occasions, there seems to be a tendency amongst a great majority of Western physicists and philosophers to grasp at any likely looking concept as long as it does not directly imply the fundamental substantive ontological nature of the process of reality as being awareness-consciousness.

The quantum Mind-Only metaphysical understanding of the process of reality, however, does not 'reduce mind to a wavefunction,' as Brunnhölzl fears. It suggests, rather, that the mathematical wavefunction is an 'objective' description of the underlying potentialities which are etched into the 'epiontic' substance of the quantum ground through the operation of Mind, or the manifested minds of all sentient beings. It is, therefore, the wavefunction that is reduced to 'Mind,' or awareness-consciousness. As we have previously seen, it is precisely because the undivided ground awareness has a fundamental function of cognition that the process of the manifestation of the illusory realms of duality takes place. Within this process the 'collapse of the wavefunction' is an objective indication of the cognitive, or 'epiontic,' operation of the nondual awareness 'dividing' itself up, through a multitude of levels of 'implicate' orders or levels, into increasingly more individuated levels of consciousness, or divided awareness (*vi-jnana*).

When we examine the mathematical structure of the Schrödinger equation we can clearly see three phases (fig 13.1). The Schrödinger equation, which is the fundamental equation of quantum physics, is a second order differential equation. This means that it is the equation from which the actual wavefunction of potentiality is derived. In order to get the wavefunction of potentiality for any particular set of circumstances it is necessary to plug into the basic equation, the equation which represents the potentiality for potentiality, the parameters for the set of circumstances, such

1

SCHRODINGER EQUATION = POTENTIALITY FOR POTENTIALITY

$$i\hbar\frac{\partial}{\partial t}\psi(\mathbf{r},t) = -\frac{\hbar^2}{2m}\nabla^2\psi(\mathbf{r},t) + V(\mathbf{r},t)\psi(\mathbf{r},t)$$

plus environmental parameters and mathematical computation

ACTUAL WAVEFUNCTION = POTENTIALITY FOR EXPERIENCED REALITY

2

plus interaction with consciousness

collapse of wave function

3

EXPERIENCED 'REALITY'

Fig 13.1

as the mass of particle and the surrounding potential configuration. The experienced 'reality' is unfolded from the wavefunction of potentiality through an interaction with consciousness. Thus there are three phases of the functioning of the wavefunction – potentiality for potentiality, the potentiality of the derived wavefunction, and the experienced discreteness of dualistic 'reality.'

In the opening verses of Nagarjuna's *In Praise of Dharmadhatu* we can detect the beginnings of an equivalent threefold division echoing the three level quantum process of the wavefunction of cyclic existence, the 'pure', 'pure and impure' and the completely 'impure'; the notion of purity involved here is not that of moral conduct, although that would be an aspect, the main issue is the degree of nonduality or duality, the 'pure' being completely nondual. The purely quantum nondual realm gives rise to the dualistic emergent 'classical' 'impure' realm which requires 'purification,' as has already been described in *Many Worlds of Illusion*.

The following is the translation offered within Dolpopa's *Mountain Doctrine*:

> Homage and obeisance to the sole jewel, the element of attributes
> Definitely dwelling pervasively in all sentient beings,
> Which if one does not thoroughly know with pristine wisdom,
> One wanders in the three existences.

> From having purified by means of the path the defilements of just that element of attributes
> Which serves as the cause of cyclic existence due to being together with adventitious defilements,
> That very element of attributes purified of defilement is nirvana.
> The element of attributes is also just that.[820]

In this depiction it is clear that the metaphysical structure of reality is conceived of as a two tier process, with an intermediate realm, which makes up the overall functioning of the dharmadhatu. This is graphically portrayed in fig 13.2. The 'element of attributes,' in its nondual aspect, makes up the upper 'real' tier, the ultimate nondual expanse which is the fundamental nature of all phenomena. However, mistaken dualistic perceptions, which are deeply etched over beginningless time, produce the 'adventitious defilements' which produce the realm of suffering: *samsara*. These are the seeds or potentialities that give rise to the dualistic functioning of the alayavijnana, which produces the cycle of existence within which sentient beings cycle endlessly through the 'three existences' of the lower, the human and the godlike (form and formless) realms. This creates the illusory 'lower' tier of the process of reality, which is driven by craving for dualistic experience. The intermediate realm, which gives us the threefold division, is the realm within which the 'adventitious stains' reside before they are activated. When these adventitious stains are purified then the experience of the functioning of reality is radically transformed into *nirvana*, which is the nondual functioning of state of enlightenment. Brunnhölzl describes this:

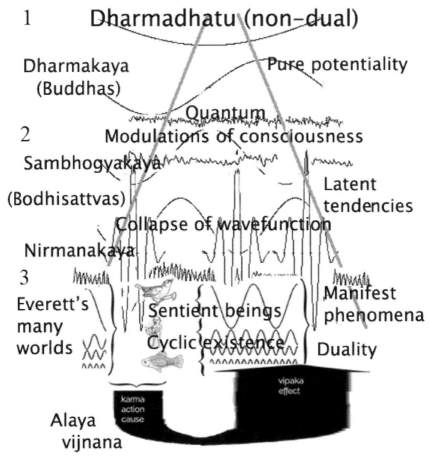

Fig 13.2

Thus, when the aspect of the twofold purity of the 'enlightened' expanse of dharmas – its primordial purity and its purity in the sense that all adventitious stains have been relinquished – is emphasised, it is called the Essence Body. When one refers to this expanse of dharmas in terms of the aspect of wisdom or realisation, it is usually called Dharma Body. Another way of expressing the meaning of 'Buddha' refers to the awakening from the dull sleep of ignorance into the bright daylight of the expanse of omniscient wisdom.[821]

There seems to be a subtle ambiguity in the treatment of the notion of the dharmadhatu, the expanse of dharmas or the element of attributes. This ambiguity arises because, although the dharmadhatu is clearly the basis for the appearance of the samsaric wandering of unenlightened sentient beings, it is also said that only by purifying it of the dualistic defilements can nirvana, which is the experiential attainment of the unobstructed nature of the dharmadhatu, be activated. In other words from one point of view it has both a 'pure' and 'impure' mode, and yet from an enlightened perspective it is thoroughly pure:

> The stainless Heart of the victors
> Being impure, impure and pure,
> And utterly pure, in due order,
> Is expressed as sentient beings, those who dwell in the path,
> And Tatagathas, respectively.
> Therefore, the actuality of this is to be realised.[822]

Rangjung Dorje elucidates this as follows:

> …the indestructible Buddha heart is the basis from which all of samsara and nirvana never move away … Since the matrix is not tainted by any stains at all, it is stainless. Because it is of the nature of Buddhahood it is called 'Buddha heart.' It has three phases – the phase of the sentient being with impurity; the phase of the Bodhisattvas on the path, which is by virtue of them being endowed with certain degrees of both purity and impurity; and the phase of the utterly pure Tatagathas. These three aspects … are expressed by earlier scholars … as many synonymous conventional terms such as ground, path and fruition…[823]

The previous chapter *The Self-Perceiving Universe* explored the image of a universe constantly exploring its own nature through the agency of all the sentient beings which it gives rise to from its own fundamental awareness-nature. In the above passage we have a description of the three phases of the process through which the Universe manifests the power of its internal awareness within the dualistic world. Buddhahood, the universal, unconditioned and nondual awareness, which embodies the omniscience of the universal awareness, is the 'fruition' of the universal process of reality. Sentient beings, who are unceremoniously projected into the suffering realms of dualistic experience in order to begin the journey towards universal awareness, make up the 'ground.' However, in their bewildered and 'impure' mode they are completely baffled and ignorant of the true nature and purpose of the process of reality and, as a consequence, perform karmic actions which constantly muddy the waters of the wavefunction of the process of reality, thereby producing further suffering for themselves and others.

But when a glimmer of a spiritual spark of understanding concerning the fact that the Universe is simply an awareness-machine which is constantly seeking to project awareness to ever greater levels of intensity, dawns, a sentient being may then begin the journey towards buddhahood by engaging the 'path' of a bodhisattva. And through this path of transformation the nature of the functioning of the process of reality is radically transformed. According to the *Suvarnaprabhasottamasutra*:

> Through relinquishing the alaya-consciousness, the dharmakaya is displayed. Through mentation, which rests in it, having become pure, the sambhogakaya is displayed. Through the consciousnesses that engage entities having become pure, the nirmanakaya is displayed.[824]

This is the dramatic 'change of state' of the psychophysical functioning of the eight consciousnesses (described in the *Quantum Karma* chapter) of a bodhisattva which results in buddhahood; the perfect awakening of the universal awareness-consciousness of reality which embraces all sentient beings through spontaneous compassionate activity.

The dharmakaya, 'dharma-body' or 'body of attributes,' which is the direct experiential realisation of the dharmadhatu or the expanse of phenomena, is described as being the achievement of the direct welfare of the practitioner. The following description refers to the metaphor of enlightenment as being the result of 'consuming' the 'reification,' or the imputation of inherent existence, of the 'firewood' of all knowable objects:

> When wisdom has consumed all that is to be consumed, it just naturally settles within the primordial expanse. In this way, the expanse of dharmas is revealed in its primordial uncontrived state. This is what is called 'attaining the Dharma Body' and 'the perfection of one's own welfare.' This very Dharma body then appears to various disciples as the manifold manifestations of the two Form Bodies: the Body of Complete Enjoyment and the Emanation Body. Through such appearances, it teaches the dharma and helps the disciples realize true reality, or the Dharma Body. In this way, the Form Bodies constitute 'the perfection of the welfare of others.'[825]

The sambhogakaya, the body of enjoyment, can be thought of as an expanse of potentiality for compassionate activity directed at helping all sentient beings who remain trapped in the suffering realms of mistaken dualistic perceptions of reality. Nirmanakayas are manifested bodies, of all kinds of form dependent on the requirements of the sentient beings they manifest to help, which embody and actualize the compassionate potentialities within the sambhogakaya.

The attainment of the dharmakaya is the direct and irreversible passing beyond conditioned dualistic modes of experience. Sentient beings who enter this universal achievement are called Tathagatas or 'thus gone ones', a term which is used because to actually precisely say how and where such experiential continuums have 'gone' is not possible because it is beyond words and concepts. The following description from the *Mahayanasutralankara*, however, is indicative of the way that the nature of the state of buddhahood may be described:

> Buddhahood is endowed with all dharmas, or devoid of all dharmas...
> Just as space is held to be always omnipresent,
> Also this Buddhahood is held to be always omnipresent
> Just as space is omnipresent in what has form,
> Also this Buddhahood is omnipresent in the host of beings....
> Though without difference between before and after,
> It is immaculateness in terms of all obscurations,
> Being neither pure nor impure,
> Suchness is held to be Buddhahood...
> Therefore, Buddhahood is said to be
> Neither existent nor nonexistent.[826]

As buddhahood can be understood as the direct experiential nondual awareness which is the fundamental nature of the dharmadhatu, the expanse of phenomena, we can certainly take this characterisation to also apply to the dharmadhatu. Thus we may say that a cogent description of the 'expanse of phenomena' is that it is an omnipresent background and foundation, which is 'neither existent nor nonexistent', within which all forms emerge. Another presentation of the 'expanse of phenomena' or 'element of attributes' is:

> ...the luminous nature of mind, the primordially undefiled element of attributes,
> Also entirely pervades without differentiation all states of persons.
> That naturally pure element of attributes is the general character or noumenon of all phenomena...[827]

Elsewhere in the same sutra we find that:

> Buddhahood is all dharmas,
> But itself is no dharma whatsoever.[828]

According to the Tibetan master Pawo Tsugla Trengwa:

> ...perfect Buddhahood is beyond all phenomena, or does not move away from all phenomena, or is present as the nature of all phenomena. But since it is not observable as anything whatsoever, perfect Buddhahood is also said to be single and not divisible into anything, because any of its divisions depends upon the minds of individual beings, while Buddhahood itself is not an object of anybody's mind.[829]

And, of course, it is the 'minds of individual beings' which, collectively, collapse wavefunctions.

The significant parallel between the depictions of both the dharmadhatu the nature of the first level of the quantum wavefunction is remarkable, and an extraordinary implication is that buddhas do not collapse wavefunctions! This corresponds with the notion that it is 'grasping' at existence, or grasping at an inherent 'selfhood' within the flux of phenomena, which operates at a deep level of psychophysical embodiment that is responsible for the collapsing of wavefunctions. Furthermore it is the task of the path to enlightenment to dismantle the quantum mechanisms of deep intentionality which are responsible for the continuation of samsara. By employing the 'remedies' of the path, practitioners can become 'discarders of the mechanism of cyclic existence.'[830] And the mechanism which drives the process of cyclic existence is, as we have seen, the 'epiontic' 'collapse of the wavefunction.'[831]

The internal quality of the quantum wavefunction, which must be of the nature of awareness-consciousness, can be identified with the 'luminous nature of mind, the primordially undefiled element of attributes' which is the 'noumenon of all phenomena'. The term 'noumenon' is actually derived from the present participle of νοέω, "I think, I mean," and denotes the objects or events of reality as they are independent of the senses. The Western philosopher Immanuel Kant, of course, defined the noumenon as the 'thing in itself.'

From the point of view of modern quantum physics Dolpopa's perspective is an astonishingly prescient description of the functioning of reality. The vistas which open to view from Dolpopa's perspective actually prefigure, in broad metaphysical outline, the discoveries of quantum physics. In fact in a sense our modern knowledge of the quantum wavefunction indicates how the viewpoints of Tsongkhapa and Dolpopa can meld together in a particle-wave manner. Thus Tsongkhapa's analysis applies to the task of removing the illusion that 'particles' have inherent existence, thus demolishing the illusion of an independent self-sufficient external material world. Dolpopa's metaphysical perspective, however, is much closer to the quantum understanding that the nature of reality prior to the collapse of the wavefunction is a realm of potentiality hovering between existence and nonexistence.

The entity that Dolpopa is referring to cannot be a conventional entity because it is the entity which is attained by bodhisattvas when they finally attain buddhahood; thus it is called the 'pristine wisdom of the one-gone-thus'. The wisdom attained by a buddha is 'pristine' because it is unsullied by the adventitious defilements which are the result of an unreal and illusory dualistic mode of perception, a mode of perception which gives rise to the appearance of apprehender and apprehended, a mode which involves the collapse of the wavefunction. Thus a buddha's mode of perception does not involve collapsing wavefunctions.

The ultimate entity, not being subject to dependent-arising – which is dependent on the apparent collapse of the wavefunction, is not self-empty; it does not 'deteriorate from its own entity' and is not 'empty of its own entity'. But it is empty of the 'eighteen constituents of apprehended-object and apprehending-subject', which are the six sets of three sense constituents. The ultimate entity is said to be devoid of any of these:

> The basic constituent, the matrix-of-the-one-gone-thus, is empty of adventitious defilements, compounded conventional phenomena suitable to be abandoned.[832]

This is 'other-emptiness', or 'extrinsic emptiness'; the eternal and immutable ultimate entity that is empty of the defilements of dualistic perception.

The relationship between the ultimate nondual entity and the adventitious defilements, which are the dualistic illusory perceptions and experiences of unenlightened beings, is both subtle and in some ways paradoxical, as when it is asserted for instance that the:

> …partless pervader of all is said to be the basis of all phenomena and also is said to be the basis that is empty of all phenomena…[833]

The crucial point, however, is that within the Mind-Only and Jonang perspectives dualistic experiences are considered to be unreal:

> Concerning this, the character of phenomena
> Is unreal ideation in which there is
> Appearance of duality and concordance with verbalisation;
> Because the non-existent appears, it is *unreal*.
> Since all those are non-factual
> And mere conceptualisation, it is *ideation*.[834]

What is being asserted here is truly astounding and almost unbelievable; whilst the existence of a noumenal entity which contains the ground of all possible attributes is posited by the Jonang doctrine as having a metaphysical and experiential nondual 'existence', it is further asserted that all experience of duality, experiences of chairs, tables, cars, roads, houses, people and sentient beings in general and so on, are completely unreal and are actually produced by unreal ideation:

> Whether ones-gone-thus arise or whether ones-gone-thus do not arise, the thusness, unerring thusness, non-other thusness, noumenon, element of attributes, source itself of attributes, limit of reality, and inconceivable basic element of those phenomena remain thus. If in those there is no self, sentient being, living being, transmigrator, nourisher, creature, person, personage, ruler, doer, feeler, knower and seer, then how could there be form among those![835]

It is for this reason that the Jonang analysis can assert that:

> There are no phenomena
> Except for the element of attributes.[836]

Whilst the element of attributes may be said to exist in its own mode of existence, or 'subsistence', to use the term employed by Dolpopa, it is empty of any other phenomena, it is other-empty or extrinsically empty.

In the previous chapter we investigated the fundamental insight, codified by Tsongkhapa, that all phenomena were characterised by self-emptiness or intrinsic-emptiness, the fact that when phenomena are rigorously examined as to their apparent claim to be self-possessed and self-powered aspects of reality they are found to fail dismally. The analysis of phenomena carried out by Tsongkhapa starts from the basis that for any entity to claim a status of really existing it must have an inner core of immutable existence. This, both Tsongkhapa and quantum physics clearly indicate, is not the case; as has been amply demonstrated previously, all phenomenon turn out to be empty of inherent self-existence.

In the other-empty presentation of emptiness, however, Tsongkhapa's view that emptiness is arrived at through the employment of a non-affirming negation is supplemented with the idea that it is possible to arrive at a complementary, to employ Bohr's term for the quantum particle-wave paradox, view of other-emptiness by employing an affirming negation of conventional phenomena, such an affirmation going beyond the level of conventional phenomena:

> ...because all do not abide as non-existent and non-established, and so on, and there exists an affirming negative as the basis of non-affirming negatives... because an inclusionary elimination abides as the basis of an exclusionary elimination[837]

The important point is that the affirmation is not an affirmation on the same level as the negation. All manifest, conventional entities are devoid of their own self, they are self-empty in the sense that they are not inherently full of themselves so to speak; so to employ Tsongkhapa's negation of the apparent individual selves of phenomenon does not in any way affirm as fully existent some other individual inherent entity on the same level as the negated inherent selfhood:

> The thoroughly established character, thusness, which is empty of imputational and imputed forms and called 'reality's form' –is not an entity of form because of being isolated in all ways from the aspects of form.[838]

The point that the Jonang perspective emphasizes is that a purely and thoroughly non-affirming negation must amount to nihilism; if there is nothing left over then there is exactly nothing left at the end of metaphysical analysis.

According to the Jonang view, however, there is a remainder on a deeper level of reality which is other-empty. This is the presentation of emptiness that Dolpopa takes as the basis for his view that the remainder left after the elimination of all the illusory entities of the phenomenal world is the noumenon which contains the ground for all illusory appearances. And the basic nature of this ground is that it is other-empty, it is empty of the illusions of the phenomenal world. This is other-emptiness or extrinsic emptiness:

> About that, what is other-entity emptiness? Whether ones-gone-thus arise or whether ones-gone-thus do not arise, the source itself of attributes, noumenon, element of attributes, flawlessness of attributes, thusness, unerring thusness, non-other thusness, and limit of reality remain thus. In this way that which is their emptiness of other entities is called 'other-entity emptiness.'[839]

The remarkable correspondence between the dharmadhatu, the element of attributes, and the quantum wavefunction becomes even more surprising when we come upon the following observation offered by Dolpopa:

> Because the entity of the element of attributes is empty, Bodhisattvas do not apprehend a prior limit. Because thusness, the limit of reality, and the inconceivable basic element are empty, Bodhisattvas do not apprehend a prior limit.[840]

This can only mean that because bodhisattvas, trainee buddhas, are practicing (on the path of seeing and onwards) direct insight into the ultimate nature of reality, which is emptiness, they do not collapse the wavefunction. A limit which is 'prior' to the 'limit of reality' can only refer to a potentiality which is etched into the basic empty nature of the wavefunction. In its fundamental state of complete voidness the essential nature of the wavefunction is void in the sense of having no potentialities stored, in this state it consists of the potentiality to contain potentialities, hence its description as the:

> Aspectless endowed with all aspects[841]

In its fundamental ground state it must be completely 'aspectless' and thus it is the ultimate 'limit of reality'. It is through the operation of karma that potentialities, or 'prior limits' are etched on top of the ultimate limit. These prior limits therefore correspond to the potentialities which quantum physics tells us reside in the wavefunction and is able to describe with the wave equation.

The path to enlightenment, which is direct insight into the nature of the ultimate 'limit of reality,' is divided in to five path sections:

- Path of accumulation
- Path of preparation
- Path of seeing
- Path of meditation
- Path of no more learning

Hopkins describes the transition from the path of preparation to the path of seeing as follows:

> The fourth stage of meditation on emptiness occurs in direct realisation of emptiness. During the period of supreme mundane qualities at the end of the path of preparation, one can no longer ascertain the factors of an object meditated and a subject meditating; however subtle forms of both still appear. Subsequently, through continuous meditation, all appearance of subject and object are extinguished in suchness-emptiness - and subject and object become like water poured into water, undifferentiable.[842]

It is at the end of the path of preparation and the beginning of the path of seeing, then, that the illusion of the subject-object divide begins to dissolve and merge into one. This is described as being like 'water poured into water' which means that the nature of both become of the same essence. This is because both aspects have dissolved into their fundamental nondual nature in the 'illusory like noumenon' of the wavefunction. The nondual experience of bliss which accompanies this meditative absorption is the inner nondual experiential quality of the wavefunction in its fundamental uncollapsed state. And in this meditative absorption a bodhisattva does not 'apprehend a prior limit', which is to say does not collapse the wavefunction.

By not collapsing the wavefunction a bodhisattva begins a career as a 'discarder of the mechanism of cyclic existence', which has been explored in great depth in the chapter on the *Many Worlds of Illusion*. In the diagram presented towards the end of that chapter it was suggested that the correct interpretation of the many-worlds hypothesis was that the universal, objective wavefunction contains, amongst other levels, the potentialities for all the possible species of sentient being that can possibly exist. The potentiality for each species has been etched into the wavefunction by the evolutionary process of reinforcing resonance over vast stretches of time.

When a subjectivity, a continuum of consciousness, is reincarnated into the samsaric world of cyclic existence it comes into the world with its karmic predispositions to take a particular form. The subsequent interaction between the subjective predispositions and the objective potentialities will usually pick out the same general form, unless, that is, some dramatic transformation within the continuum of consciousness occurred in some previous lifetime, a transformation which activates in this lifetime to change the form of reincarnation. Dolpopa makes the point that in general the form of embodiment is hard to change without a radical transformation of consciousness by quoting the following from the *Angulimala Sutra*:

> Those sentient beings who, when earlier they were cattle, fought against their own mothers and were crazed, still when they sleep, they tap and grind their teeth and do not believe the matrix-of-the-one-gone-thus, suchness. In the future also, those sentient beings who whistle through their teeth and do not believe the matrix-of-the-one-gone-thus will not be otherwise; venerable Purna, they, being cattle, do not know the noumenon.[843]

In other words, one of the main obstructions to starting out on the task of transformation is the fact that the vast majority of sentient beings 'do not believe the matrix-of-the-one-gone-thus, suchness.' Of course, according to the Buddhist worldview it is only human beings who have a chance to come to a belief in the reality of such a deep matrix of awareness underlying the astonishing illusion of the dualistic world. However, the illusion of the dualistic seemingly material world is so dramatically convincing that, even in the face of the overwhelming evidence of quantum physics, many Western scientists and philosophers prefer to ignore the evidence.

As we have seen the mechanism which underlies the reinforcing cycle of existence produces the illusion of cyclic existence or the cycle of suffering, the cycling of subjectivities through the universal wavefunction. It is this mechanism which is discarded by bodhisattvas and buddhas. And, remarkably, when the attachment to and entrapment within the mechanism of cyclic existence, is severed, the mind of the one-gone-thus both transcends and encompasses the transcended mechanism:

> Cutter of the noose of cyclic existence,
> I am the great ocean of cyclic existence.[844]

The question which immediately arises is that of where exactly do the minds of bodhisattvas and buddhas go? In fact it is made quite clear that they do not go anywhere, they realize the natural nondual state that was always their true nature. Buddhas are described as 'ones-gone-thus' and the implication is that such beings have achieved an identity with the Buddha-matrix. Is it actually possible to locate this assertion into the context of quantum theory? Dolpopa offers the following clue:

> The leader thoroughly proclaimed, 'Discrimination is on this side.
> Destroying and abandoning discrimination is to go beyond.[845]

It is the mental activity of discrimination taking place at a deep instinctual level of the psyche that collapses the wavefunction. The minds of buddhas and bodhisattvas, therefore, can be thought of as being located on the other side of the collapse of the wavefunction. The relationship between the minds of unenlightened sentient beings, bodhisattvas and buddhas and the three spheres of the wavefunction – pure potentiality, potentiality with encoded latent tendencies, collapsed wavefunction – is schematically portrayed in figure 13.3. The fact that the minds of unenlightened beings, bodhisattvas and buddhas occupy different areas of the continuum of awareness-consciousness, which is the continuum of the spheres of the wavefunction, is clearly indicated:

> Furthermore, thusness has three states – an impure state, a pure and impure state, and a very pure state. Concerning those, the impure state is all common beings. Since they do not have the state of enlightenment and are limited to the state of a sentient being, that thusness is called with the name 'sentient being'.

> The pure and impure state is superiors. Since they have both- the state of enlightenment and the state of sentient being-that pure and impure thusness is called with the name 'Bodhisattva'.

> The state of thorough purity is limited just to the state of enlightenment. Hence, that thusness is called with the name 'one-gone-thus'. As it is said, "Subhuti, 'one-gone-thus' is a synonym for thusness."[846]

In other words buddhas have achieved a completely pure state beyond duality, bodhisattvas have penetrated the outer levels of the illusory deception of the solidity of the world of duality and thereby see into an intermediate sphere which is a mixture of pure and impure, whereas 'common beings' are limited to the impure state of complete illusory duality.

The three spheres of the wavefunction are enumerated as follows. Firstly the fundamental, completely void, a completely empty emptiness, a state of potentiality for storing potentialities; this corresponds to the thoroughly established nature which is the abode of buddhas:

> The body of a one-gone-thus is a non-body body, unproduced, unceasing.[847]

And:

> When the consciousness that is the support of all cyclic existence and nirvana is transformed,
> Excellent wealth is attained
> With regard to the nirvana that does not abide in the extremes of cyclic existence and nirvana
> In the undefiled Buddha abode.[848]

And:

> Dustless, free of defect,
> Free from dust, conquering sin,
> Having a nature without waves,

Final bliss, knowing bliss
Supreme secrecy…[849]

And:

…the thusness of the one-gone-thus is unchanging, immutable and non-conceptual, non-conceptualised, and indestructible in any way…[850]

And:

Having bowed to that which, though isolated from all phenomena, is the body of uncontaminated, innumerable attributes,
Though devoid of a self of phenomena and persons, is thusness, self, and pure self,
Though beyond the extremes of existence and non-existence, permanence and annihilation, resides as just permanent, stable and everlasting,
Though without the nature of things, is the natural clear light,
That which is to be known like a great treasure under ones own home…[851]

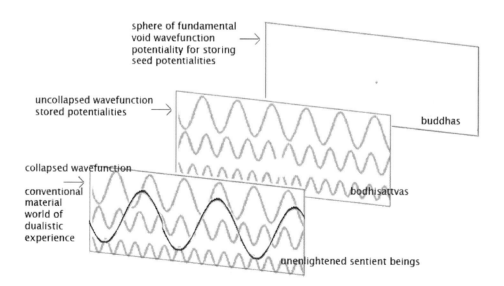

Fig 13.3

The second sphere of the wavefunction, moving away from the source into manifestation, is the realm within which the karmic potentialities are stored but none of the potentialities have been collapsed into full dualistic actuality through the activity of deluded conceptuality. This is the realm of bodhisattvas:

> Those endowed with intelligence, that is Bodhisattvas, from knowing nonduality on the occasion of the supreme mundane qualities of the path of preparation abandon the distractions of an apprehending subject, and through the force of this
> They immediately dwell in the element of attributes which does not have the appearance of duality.[852]

And:

> Bodhisattvas in meditative equipoise,
> Perceive a mental image, and hence
> Upon reversing the discrimination of objects,
> Definitely apprehend a discrimination of the mind itself.
> In that way they abide within internal mind
> And realise the absence of an apprehended-object.
> After that, they know the absence of an apprehender
> And then they know the unapprehendable.[853]

The third and last sphere of the wavefunction is the realm of the collapse of the wavefunction which is the realm of unenlightened sentient beings:

> Childish common beings, due to being obstructed from seeing reality
> Perceive in all ways the unreal.[854]

And:

> How atrocious is this aspect of the world's awful obscuration
> Such that even though in the worlds of transmigrating beings
> nothing other than that noumenon exists,
> Even the entirety of transmigrators with a mind thoroughly
> obscured about it
> Abandon in all ways the existent noumenon and manifestly
> adhere to the non-existent![855]

It is because of the dreadful situation that unenlightened sentient beings are in, wandering ceaselessly and pointlessly in a completely illusory and dissatisfactory realm of suffering, the realm of samsara, that buddhas, in line with their compassionate nature, throw out lifelines, as it were, as they pass beyond the realm of duality. These lifelines, the buddhas' 'hooks of compassion', form bodies or communication bodies, are prepared, or 'grown' as bodhisattvas practice and work their path towards enlightenment:

And having made homage to form bodies, endowed with resultant
 qualities of fruition,
Born from collections of merit from a conquerors good seed,
I will write in accordance with the scriptures also about how
sage's bodies of communication
Are grown like growing a great tree with overflowing supreme
fruits.[856]

The exposition of Dolpopa's *Mountain Doctrine* contains a dramatic description of the way in which the mechanism of the path to enlightenment leaves
behind, like echoes within the wavefunction of reality, channels of communication that can be activated by sentient beings in order to find help in
their own efforts towards enlightenment:

> This body of attributes as the fulfillment of others welfare
> becomes the complete enjoyment body, agent of the welfare of
> multitudes of sentient beings like an echo
> Again this complete enjoyment body becomes emanation bodies
> of Buddhas for the sake of ripening sentient beings.[857]

There is a threefold classification of the ontological results of the achievement of buddhahood. This delineation describes the structure of buddhahood
as it relates to the three spheres of the wavefunction which have been previously described; this is called the doctrine of the 'trikaya', the three bodies
of a Buddha:

- Dharmakaya   – ultimate body of attributes
- Sambhogakaya – complete enjoyment body
- Nirmanakaya   – emanation body

The dharmakaya is a nondual ultimate body which can be thought of as
residing within the sphere of the fundamental nondual awareness of the
empty wavefunction. The sambhogakaya is an archetypal body of potentiality which operates within the middle wavefunction sphere of potentiality.
Nirmanakayas, or emanation bodies, arise on the basis of the sambhogakaya;
they are brought into manifestation through the interaction of the archetypal
sambhogakaya and the predispositions of sentient beings:

> That which is a composite of Buddha-qualities … and is nondual
> with and non-different from the perfection of wisdom is the body
> of attributes. That which arises from its blessings and depends on
> that foundation is the complete enjoyment body. Those which
> arise from its blessings and arise in accordance with the interests
> of trainees are emanation bodies.[858]

The term 'blessings' has a precise meaning; a 'blessing' denotes positive
mental energy for transformation, an empowerment to transform conscious-

ness in a positive direction. Thus the sphere of buddhahood automatically sends out waves of blessings, waves of potentiality for positive transformation are radiated from the dharmakaya into the form realms. These radiated waves of wisdom and compassion are given form by bodhisattvas working their way towards enlightenment. The sphere of the wavefunction of potentiality receives these radiated energies in the form of the archetypal sambhogakayas and it is the resonant interaction of a sambhogakaya with the 'interests' or predispositions of 'trainees' which determines the many manifestations of nirmanakayas within the realm of duality (fig 13.4).

According to Dolpopa the ultimate matrix, the body of attributes, has two aspects, an 'actual' and an 'imputed'. Whilst the actual nature is 'undefiled' and 'naturally luminous'; it is also 'the object of activity of buddhas' pristine wisdom'. The character of this activity is to provide a mechanism by which deluded sentient beings can be taught about the ultimate nature of reality. Such teachings have to be in accord with the predispositions of each sentient being, or 'trainee':

> The body of attributes of teaching also has two aspects-in terms of ultimate truth, suchness, teaching the modes of the profound …
> and in terms of the obscurational truths in accordance with the thoughts of various sentient beings…[859]

Thus the nirmanakayas are communication bodies which appear to sentient beings in a way that they can comprehend and, although from an ultimate point of view the communicated truths are 'obscurational truths', they function to lead the minds of deluded sentient beings in the right direction.

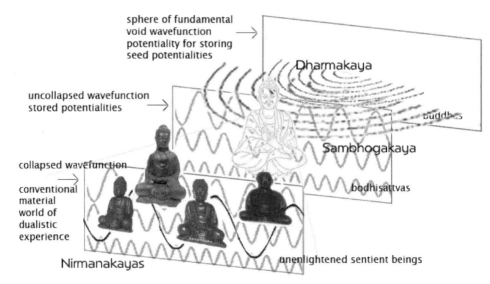

Fig 13.4

Although the sambhogakayas have their ultimate source within the clear light dharmakaya, within which all enlightened qualities are contained within an undifferentiated nature, the actual form of the sambhogakaya is a result of the aspirations and activities of bodhisattvas during their practice of the path to enlightenment. According to Khenchen Thrangu Rinphoche:

> All the yidams and deities used in meditation have the same fundamental nature and are utterly pure. Nevertheless they have different appearances, which reflect the different activities that they embody and engage in. These different activities are primarily determined by the individual aspirations they made at their initial generation of bodhichitta.[860]

Bodhichitta, the awakening mind, awakening heart or spirit of enlightenment is the driving force towards complete enlightenment. It is the internal energy of compassion used by bodhisattvas to 'grow' the sambhogakayas which then act as communication channels for sentient beings within the wave-function of reality.

Within Mahayana Buddhism all practices begin with the generation of bodhichitta which is the intention to perform the practice in order to bring all sentient beings to enlightenment. In the visualisation practices of the vajrayana the generation of bodhichitta is followed by the visualisation of oneself as the particular chosen deity, yidam[861] or buddha. The significance and effectiveness of these practices become apparent when viewed from the perspective of the functioning of the wavefunction of reality. Becoming a buddha requires that one's mental continuum becomes identical to the ground of the wavefunction itself, so there cannot be a trace of any kind of limited self, or ego, left. One becomes universal, embracing all beings within the sphere of compassionate activity; one's mind becomes the awareness and wavefunction of the universe.

The generation of bodhichitta, therefore is an essential aspect of extending the wavefunction of the limited self, which exists as a mini-wave-function which is functioning for itself so to speak, in a more expansive direction. The generation of bodhichitta, then, is a foundational practice of dissolving the limited wave of egotism and embracing the suffering of all creation, all the limited split-off and deluded waves with the overall universal wavefunction, with compassion. There are other practices which support this aim such as the meditations of viewing all beings as one's mother, exchanging self and others, wishing love and so on.

All of these practices extend one's compassionate range within the wavefunction of reality. For most of us the degree of the extension will be tiny. But as we have seen the potentialities within the wavefunction of reality have been built up, bit by bit, in tiny amounts over eons of time. Smoothing out the wavefunction of reality through the generation of bodhichitta and compassion, then, is an equally time consuming task, which is why bodhisattvas work tirelessly over eons of time to achieve the welfare of all sentient beings.

A further vital aspect of such practices is the fact that through the individual generation of, and thereby connection with, the waveforms within the wavefunction of reality left by bodisattvas on the way to buddhahood we keep the resonant echoes of transcendence open for the future. Every time we invoke and visualize a deity or buddha we are amplifying, to a degree dependent on the power of our mental continuum and motivation, the resonant trace of a path to enlightenment which has been trail blazed by a supreme spiritual being who has both gone before and also gone-thus.

The description of the attributes of the trikaya, the three bodies of buddhahood provides us with a map of the spiritual structure of the wavefunction of reality. The dharmakaya is the ultimate sphere and according to Dolpopa it has the following characteristics:

(1) being without beginning [production], middle [abiding], and end [cessation], that is not having the character of being compounded,

(2) indivisibility [since the uncontaminated element of attributes and complete pristine wisdom are mixed into one],

(3) not having fallen into the extremes of superimposition and deprecation since it is free from existence and non-existence

(4) being devoid of three obstructions-afflictive obstructions, obstructions to objects of knowledge, and obstructions to meditative stabilisation

(5) clear light, seen directly by yogis who are ones-gone-thus always dwelling in meditative equipoise realizing the naturally pure element of attributes, undefiled by afflictive emotions and not an object of the activity of conceptuality. [862]

This ultimate body is not a form body, it is the ultimate nondual inseparability of pristine wisdom and the body of attributes. It is the basis for the manifestation of the two conventional form bodies. These conventional form bodies are, in a sense, left behind by a buddha's transcendence, they are echoes of transcendence:

Their display of varieties of eloquence through their secrecy of speech by way of their occurrence being difficult to find in that way is like echoes which are difficult to find due to not being truly established outside or inside ... echoes arise adventitiously in reliance on conditions ... [863]

The first echo, the sambhogakaya or enjoyment body has the following five features:

(1) Continuous speech through spreading the illumination of light rays of excellent doctrine…

(2) Continuous display of various appearances by way of bodies endowed with limitless light rays of excellent doctrine...

(3) Continuous activities of making effort at achieving the aim of release for many ... transmigrators who are trainees,

(4) Spontaneity not being composed by conceptualisation, and exertion in ... fulfilling hopes and desires,

(5) Displaying various phenomena such as color, size and so forth due to the thoughts of trainees but not truly having the nature of those.[864]

As a result of the last feature of the enjoyment body, by which the subjecttivities of sentient beings interact with it in order to produce manifestations accessible to ordinary sentient beings, the final form body of buddhahood is produced, the nirmanakaya:

An emanation body has three attributes: the emanation bodies appearing in various ways due to the needs of trainees-

(1) that cause ordinary worldly beings who have not entered the path to enter the path of quiescence [nirvana, generating discontent with the three existences,

(2) that cause those who have entered the path of liberation to be ripened...

(3) that prophesy the release of those ripened by the great vehicle, setting them by degrees on the grounds of purification...[865]

And all of this extraordinary illusory activity on the part of the enjoyment and emanation bodies takes place within the emptiness of the wavefunction of reality. For as Dolpopa points out the activities of sambhogakayas and nirmanakayas:

...always dwell uninterruptedly as long as cyclic existence lasts in this immutable basic element, the body of attributes, ...

Just as the uninterrupted continuum of production and disintegration of compounded form constituents continuously dwells in the uncompounded space constituent.[866]

As quantum physicist H. Dieter Zeh has said:

In the beginning was the wavefunction.[867]

Anthropic Self-Transcending Universe

This pure Mind, the source of everything, shines forever and on all with the brilliance of its own perfection. But the people of the world do not awake to it, regarding only that which sees, hears, feels and knows as mind. Blinded by their own sight, hearing, feel-ing and knowing, they do not perceive the spiritual brilliance of the source substance. If they would only eliminate all conceptual thought in a flash, that source substance would manifest itself like the sun ascending through the void and illuminating the whole universe without hindrance or bounds.[868]

- Hung Po

Buddha nature has lost track of itself and created samsara, but it is also Buddha nature, recognising itself...[869]

-Tulku Urgyen Rinpoche

I see no way for contemporary science to disprove, or even render highly unlikely, this religious extension of quantum theory, or to provide any strong evidence in support of an alternative picture of the nature of these "free choices." These choices *seem to be* rooted in reasons that are rooted in feelings pertaining to value or worth. Thus it can be argued that quantum theory provides a rational opening for an idea of nature and of our role within it that are in general accord with certain religious concepts...[870]

- Henry Stapp

When he speaks of 'reality' the layman usually means some-thing obvious and well-known, whereas it seems to me that precisely the most important and extremely difficult task of our time is to work on elaborating a new idea of reality. This is also what I mean when I always emphasize that science and religion *must* be related in some way.[871]

- Wolfgang Pauli

God!

Quantum physics has provided a new opportunity for revisiting the problem of the existence of 'God' in a remarkable new setting. Although the existence of an independent creator God which is required by mainstream, non-mystical Christianity certainly cannot be rescued by a quantum expedition, the philosophical dimension of quantum theory has a radically revelatory impact for our understanding of the authentic nature of spirituality; a fresh approach which finds a significant and powerful context within what might be described as a Quantum Mind-Only Anthropic 'mystical' metaphysics of the process of reality.

The enquiry concerning the possibility, or not, of harmonizing and interconnecting the realms of science and religion occupies an important and significant place in modern scholarly debate. This situation is due in large part to the devastating intellectual assaults upon the rational status of religion in general and theistic theology in particular by modern philosophical and scientific pundits such as the philosopher Daniel Dennett and the evolutionary biologist Richard Dawkins, both of whom are widely known as ferocious proponents of an uncompromising materialist atheism. Dawkins was voted author of the year for 2007 in the Galaxy British Book Awards and his most recent assault upon theistic belief, *The God Delusion*, an unremittingly acerbic assault upon dogmatic notions of an independent creator God, quickly went into the bestseller list and has been accorded highly recommendatory reviews on the part of a large section of modern nontheistic thinkers. Dennett's stridently materialist-monist work *Darwin's Dangerous Idea* was a finalist in America's 1995 National Book Awards for nonfiction; in this work Dennett suggests that the religious impulse is indicative of intellectual, and perhaps emotional, immaturity.

As we shall see, in response to such vituperative claims for the complete vacuity of theistic claims various Christian thinkers have marshaled their intellectual forces by attempting to assemble new defenses involving the discoveries of modern physics, quantum physics being primary in this respect. For instance the theologian and physicist John Polkinghorne has recently produced a slim volume entitled *Theology and Quantum Physics: an Unexpected Kinship* in which he claims that there are significant parallels between quantum physics and Christian theology. In works such as this Christian theologians have attempted to turn tables on the Dawkins' type of appropriation of the scientific paradigm by claiming that the modern findings of quantum physics open up a foundation of indeterminism beneath the apparent ground of the everyday world of experience, a shaky foundation that is theologically thought to be shored up by the determining 'mind of God.'[872]

It is important to be clear that the crucial issue around which the current debate revolves concerns the extent to which religious claims can be considered to be as ontologically significant, or 'real,' as those which depend upon the scientific method for their validity. This is the ground for instance upon which Dawkins launches his attempted rout of theistic claims in his *God Delusion*. This point is extremely important because there is another, far less plausible and resilient, approach to the attempt to rescue a role for God in the modern scientific world. An example of this somewhat disingenuous maneuver was recently offered by Victor Stock, Dean of Guildford Cathedral, in discussion with physicist Brian Cox and comedian Robin Ince during a episode of BBC Radio Four's bizarre 'popular science' program *The Infinite Monkey Cage*, when he claimed that 'religion' does not claim to have all the answers and neither does science.[873]

In this sweeping statement, however, the Dean is clearly incorrect, mainstream Christianity prior to its perception of the necessity to continuously reinvent itself in order to appear more in keeping with modern more sophisticated modes of thought, and, of course, science, did make a claim to have a final and complete answer. Furthermore, it does appear that the great majority of Christians, Muslims and Jews do believe that they have a final answer to the question of existence. As we shall see shortly, there are several Christian theologians with scientific credentials who seem to fallaciously argue for the existence of an external, independent God on the basis of the evidence of quantum physics.

It should be apparent that the idea that 'religion,' if we mean by this term the search for a way of life which accords with the ultimate metaphysical nature of reality rather than the paying of devoted lip-service to the totem of a particular social grouping, *must* offer something approaching an ultimate answer to the mystery of existence if it is fulfill its role. In other words it must make significant ontological claims. Furthermore such ontological claims must also have moral implications. Because of this necessity, the idea that religious claims are completely independent and cut-off from scientific evidence, the 'non overlapping magisteria'[874] claim, must be rejected.

As previous chapters should have thoroughly indicated the notion that the realm of the mind and spirituality is separate from the process of the material functioning of reality is completely foreign to philosophical schools of Buddhism such as the Yogachara-Chittamatra and Madhyamaka. And the overall thrust of the arguments of this book lead precisely to the inescapable conclusion that a comprehensive and metaphysical picture of the process of reality, and the place of humanity within it, is provided, within what Buddhist philosophy calls the conventional level, by the Quantum Mind-Only philosophy developed herein. This constitutes what physicists call a 'Theory of Everything', or TOE. But it is not the kind of TOE which physicists are likely to run with precisely because it goes beyond what they are comfortable with as constituting the 'physical.' As we have seen the idea that the ontological foundation of reality is mind or awareness is a conclusion that Western academic thought seems to be congenitally uncomfortable with.

Fig 14.1 shows a formulation of the master equation for the standard model, the fundamental theory of the functioning of elementary 'particles.'

$$\mathcal{L}_{GWS} = \sum_f (\bar{\Psi}_f(i\gamma^\mu\partial\mu - m_f)\Psi_f - eQ_f\bar{\Psi}_f\gamma^\mu\Psi_f A_\mu)+$$

$$+\frac{g}{\sqrt{2}}\sum_i(\bar{a}_L^i\gamma^\mu b_L^i W_\mu^+ + \bar{b}_L^i\gamma^\mu a_L^i W_\mu^-)+\frac{g}{2c_w}\sum_f\bar{\Psi}_f\gamma^\mu(I_f^3-2s_w^2Q_f-I_f^3\gamma_5)\Psi_f Z_\mu+$$

$$-\frac{1}{4}|\partial_\mu A_\nu - \partial_\nu A_\mu - ie(W_\mu^-W_\nu^+ - W_\mu^+W_\nu^-)|^2 - \frac{1}{2}|\partial_\mu W_\nu^+ - \partial_\nu W_\mu^+ +$$

$$-ie(W_\mu^+ A_\nu - W_\nu^+ A_\mu) + ig'c_w(W_\mu^+ Z_\nu - W_\nu^+ Z_\mu|^2+$$

$$-\frac{1}{4}|\partial_\mu Z_\nu - \partial_\nu Z_\mu + ig'c_w(W_\mu^- W_\nu^+ - W_\mu^+ W_\nu^-)|^2+$$

$$-\frac{1}{2}M_\eta^2\eta^2 - \frac{gM_\eta^2}{8M_W}\eta^3 - \frac{g'^2M_\eta^2}{32M_W}\eta^4 + |M_W W_\mu^+ + \frac{g}{2}\eta W_\mu^+|^2+$$

$$+\frac{1}{2}|\partial_\mu\eta + iM_Z Z_\mu + \frac{ig}{2c_w}\eta Z_\mu|^2 - \sum_f\frac{g}{2}\frac{m_f}{M_W}\bar{\Psi}_f\Psi_f\eta$$

Fig 14.1

The details of this equation need not concern us, the point is that this equation is said to be a 'theory of almost everything' (which is the title of a book on the subject by Robert Oerter). However, suppose the small bit which is apparently missing, the Higg's mechanism, were to be discovered and validated, would we then actually have the complete TOE? Would understanding this equation reveal the mystery of existence, including the reason and substance of the process of reality? Of course not! As Michio Kaku points out we still need to know 'what is doing the waving.'[875]

Until the so-called 'linguistic turn,' which took place at the beginning of the twentieth century, modern Western philosophy was actually concerned with discovering the ultimate nature of reality. In particular the core issue was located in the constant analysis, with increasingly subtle nuances, of the possibility that a final allocation could be made to one of the principle apparent constituents of reality: the material or the ideal, matter or cons- ciousness. The fundamental philosophical question at the basis of all others was always addressed to the discovery of which of these was ultimately real and which illusory. This issue, which seemed to be not fully decidable on purely logical grounds, a least within the Western tradition, has now, as we have seen, been completely resolved by physics rather than philosophy. As physicist Victor Mansfield has pointed out:

> We can now demonstrate that 'quantum moons' do not exist when unobserved. Such 'experimental metaphysics' has an extraordinary resonance with the Middle Way Buddhist principle of emptiness...[876]

So quantum physics now constitutes the doorway to true metaphysics; if we are asked to decide between the provisional principles of consciousness or matter as the essential constituent of reality we must choose consciousness, which can be considered to be the 'conventional' manifestation of the ultimate ground of emptiness – the interdependent field of potentiality which underlies the process of reality. Equations such as that shown in fig 14.1 actually describe in mathematical terminology the dance of the manifestation into conventional, dualistic, 'seeming' reality of the interdependent nondual ground of emptiness, which is the infinite potentiality of dependent origination. To actually 'know' the nature of this ground on a deeper level, however, it is necessary to use some method of directly experiencing it, a point which seems generally lost on the majority of physicists and philosophers who seem to think that knowing an equation is the same as knowing reality.

The Quantum Mind Only metaphysical model of the functioning of the universe is truly a comprehensive metaphysics which is based both upon the experimental and theoretical developments of modern physics, and also the experiential and theoretical knowledge of Buddhist investigations of inner reality through techniques of meditation. One definition of metaphysics, for instance, is 'the philosophical study of being and knowing'[877]. With this definition of metaphysics in mind the following observation by Wojciech H. Zurek is hugely significant:

> ...quantum states, by their very nature share an epistemological and ontological role - are simultaneously a description of the state, and the 'dream stuff is made of.' One might say that they are *epiontic*. These two aspects may seem contradictory, but at least in the quantum setting, there is a union of these two functions.[878]

This cogent insight makes clear that, at the quantum level, being and knowing, perception and reality, epistemology and ontology are inextricably entangled. As we have seen, at the fundamental quantum level Bishop Berkeley's dictum that 'being is perception' becomes completely realised. However, as we have also seen, the details of the mechanism involved are far more subtle than any Western philosopher has ever managed to fathom. Furthermore the fact that the quantum level *is* the fundamental level is now inescapable. Although the appearance of matter appears to be impressively ineluctable, solid and immovable; the essential nature of the material world is congealed perception within the quantum ground, as we saw in the chapter *Quantum Karma*.

This is a truly remarkable situation. Up until the quantum age metaphysics had always been in large measure speculative. These speculative attempts were based on conceptual and logical analysis of the scientific and experimental evidence, together with previous philosophical analysis, available at the time. However, there was never any direct evidence which could decide finally between the fundamental aspects of reality: mind or matter. Despite this, however, it is worth noting that there is a consensus amongst many significant Western philosophers on the side, in some form, of consciousness, rather than the view of a completely independent and separate realm of materiality. Professor Keith Ward has pointed out that:

> Plato, Aristotle, Anselm, Aquinas, Descartes, Leibniz, Spinoza, Locke, Berkeley, Kant, Hegel – they all argued that the ultimate reality, often hidden under the appearances of the material world of time and space, is mind or Spirit.
>
> Even the great philosophical dissenters ... were not materialists. Hume and Ayer thought that the ultimate realities were what they called 'impressions' or 'sense data', respectively.[879]

So, if we accept that 'impressions' and 'sense data' are of the nature of mind, for they are certainly not independent and externally located 'matter', then it seems that most   significant Western philosophers were essentially of a Mind-Only persuasion. And with the advent of the quantum era this, heretofore purely philosophical, conclusion has been experimentally verified. It is indeed amazing that anyone considering themselves a serious philosopher today could, with integrity, embrace a thoroughgoing materialist viewpoint. Remarkably, however, there are many Western philosophers and scientists who resist the rising tide of evidence washing away the flimsy wisps of the materialist worldview.

Perhaps chief amongst them is Daniel Dennett who engages in a surprising form of philosophical practice which involves simply waving away inconvenient evidence. According to Dennett the view that consciousness is a quantum phenomenon is indicative of a 'bandwagon,' a 'loose confederation of reactionaries' who:

> ...speculate that the solution [to the problem of consciousness] will not come from biology or cognitive science but – of all things – physics.[880]

When Dennett is on dubious ground he relies not on rigorous argument but implied ridicule and brazen disregard of the facts. Today it is becoming clearly apparent that all of the significant processes of life have a quantum basis. Biology clearly depends upon the processes of chemistry and the molecular interactions of chemistry are incontrovertibly determined by quantum processes. Why consciousness, a fundamental aspect of life, should be immune from this natural downward progression Dennett never explains. It is true, however, that it is generally accepted that physics is the foundational science.

In comparison with the subtlety and precision of the Buddhist philosophical analyses of the nature of reality much Western philosophy actually seems almost childish. For instance one of Dennett's favorite analogies when considering the issue of the allocation of the nature of reality to mind or matter is that of 'skyhooks' verses 'cranes'; a 'skyhook' according to Dennett's exposition descends invitingly from nothingness, offering no solid grounding for reality; this is Dennett's view regarding the idea that consciousness is primary in the process of reality. A sturdy industrial strength 'crane' on the other hand is, according to Dennett, able to ground its chain and hook in the, supposedly, solid material ground (fig 14.2). Dennett's simplistic perspective, however, only works as long as we do not include what modern physics now knows about the ultimate nature of the quantum realm (Fig 14.3).

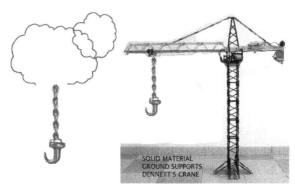

Fig 14.2

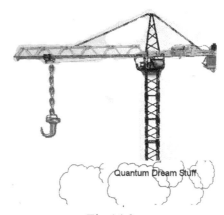

Fig 14.3

Dennett is always scathing at the proposal that quantum physics indicates that consciousness may be ontologically significant at any level of reality and he targets for his ridicule what he refers to as the 'quantum-physics-to-the-rescue squad.'[881] But he never offers any arguments in support of his position. In a radio discussion, for instance, he dismisses the suggestion that consciousness and quantum phenomena are connected simply by applying the attribution that such ideas are 'magical thinking':

> … by wedding two bits of magic together you are going to say its not magic. By letting consciousness be a mysterious and magical property, in saying that quantum enlargement in effect depends on consciousness you nicely tie together two themes and I think its just magical thinking. There is no reason to believe either side of it.[882]

But that's the extent of his lack of philosophical analysis; it's simply his unsupported opinion based on a 'known to be false', to quote Professor Stapp, prejudice in favor of a materialist worldview. As we have seen the actual evidence stacks up with Rosenblum and Kuttner's conclusion that:

> Consciousness and the quantum enigma are not just two mysteries; they are *the* two mysteries; … Quantum mechanics seems to connect the two.[883]

If we take into account the discoveries of modern quantum physics, something which both Dennett and Dawkins resolutely refuse to do, Dennett's crane-hook turns out to be nothing more than a quantum hook which is ultimately supported on the phenomena of the quantum ground which, according to quantum physicist Zurek, is comprised of the 'dream stuff is made of' (fig 14.3)[884]. The dynamic duo would no doubt scoff at such claims in the same way that Dr. Johnson abused his foot in exasperation when confronted with the watertight reasoning for the Mind-basis of reality presented by Bishop Berkeley but, as we have seen, the only way to cling to a materialism which is grounded in the classical age of physics is simply to remain intellectually within the classical age of physics and ignore the evidence of modern quantum physics. And this, in essence, is the intellectual standpoint of both Dennett and Dawkins.

Dawkins has inexplicably managed to carve himself a reputation as being a ferociously penetrating intellect on the basis of clearly indicating limitations which force him to operate on a simplistic and unsophisticated level, a level which is incapable of dealing with quantum issues, issues which it must be held in mind are *the ultimate issues*. When it comes to quantum theory he tells us that:

> …this is where I must make my excuses and leave. Sometimes I imagine I have some appreciation of the poetry of quantum theory,

but I have yet to achieve an understanding deep enough to explain it to others. Actually it may be that no-one understands quantum theory, possibly because natural selection shaped our brains to survive in a world of large slow things, where quantum effects are smoothed out.[885]

This lack of sufficient understanding of the fundamental theory which underpins the physical world, however, he considers to be no great problem for his task of accounting for the mechanisms driving evolution. Biologists, we are told 'can explain elephants, provided they are allowed to take certain facts of physics for granted'. According to Dawkins it is not the job of the biologist to justify these 'facts of the world of simplicity'. This is the job for a physicist; and, according to Dawkins 'this he (i.e. the physicist) succeeds in doing'[886]. By employing this piece of intellectual subterfuge Dawkins seems to feel happy that he has gained the right to adopt the technique of 'reductionism' at a level of reduction that he feels most appropriate for 'explaining elephants.' And the appropriate level, according to Dawkins, is that which is 'suitable for everyday purposes'[887]. So it would seem that, by his own admission, Dawkins' lack of capability in understanding the most significant quantum issues concerning the ultimate nature of reality leaves him no option but to analyze the facts of the world from a simplistic perspective only relevant for everyday purposes.

In the opposite corner of the dogmatic contest there seems to be not a little smoke and mirrors employed within the arena of modern theology to try and extend quantum insights beyond their natural implications. For instance Keith Ward's slim volume *Why There Almost Certainly Is a God* is, in all respects except its final attempted demonstration that the undeniable existence of a universal mind *must* constitute the 'Mind of God,' an exceedingly cogent and well argued demolition of the simplistic, and unfounded, philosophical procedures of the materialist viewpoints of Dennett, Dawkins and others. However, when he addresses the issue of who, or what, is responsible for the collapse of the wavefunction he throws logical coherence overboard in his pursuit of a predetermined dogmatic theistic position; in this respect his methodology is as flawed as that of the materialist viewpoint.

Using the term 'turtle' to mean 'universe'[888] Ward frames his unfounded argument as follows:

> God can ... think of all possible turtles, can discern that many of them are interesting and beautiful, can decide to make some of them exist precisely because of that discernment, and then can just enjoy them for what they are. This provides an excellent reason for the existence of turtles – God enjoys them.[889]

In other words God thinks up possible universes to fill in his spare time, and he has a lot of it on his hands which is presumably why there are an infinite number of possible universes; and he subsequently actualizes his preferred ones to add a further frisson of entertainment provided by the sight of 'real', rather than possible, sentient beings wandering around completely bewildered as to why they exist!

Such a bizarre view is as lacking in scientific evidence or philosophical cogency, and is remarkably similar in structural lack of essence, as the quantum physicist's adolescent thought experiments involving alien civilisations producing computer simulations of 'fake' universes! If, however, we stick to the quantum evidence, it is quite clear that sentient beings are collectively responsible for the state of the universe at a very deep quantum level; there is no evidence of an outside agency at work.

The post-Kantian Idealist philosopher Ernst Cassirer, amongst the last serious philosophers of the Western tradition, brilliantly describes the extraordinary see-saw historical development of philosophical depictions of possible configurations of reality, swinging between forms of realism and idealism, in his life's work *The Philosophy of Symbolic Forms*. In this work Cassirer presents the development of Western philosophical thought as a restless intellectual quest on the part of a universal Mind, or spirit (*geist*) which is in search of its own nature. As Cassirer points out, this activity of self-comprehension on the part of the universal process of reality can only take place by a direct internal metaphysical analysis of the nature of experience, a quest which itself is located within the domain of experience, or duality:

> ...in each case a certain aspect of experience has been posited as absolute and then taken in isolation, whereupon this absolute positing is declared to be primordial, being in itself. ... Now it is being, now becoming, now unity, now plurality, now it is nature, now God, now the soul (mind), now matter, that are posited in this way as 'absolute', as fundamentally original.[890]

Such a metaphysical project, then, seems to require the attribution of 'inherent existence' to an aspect of experience which is then 'posited as absolute and then taken in isolation'. The quantum era, however, has clearly set the scene for a new metaphysical determination, one in which the full quantum nature of Mind, which emerges from the ultimate realm of emptiness, may be comprehended.

Enough has been said in previous chapters concerning that fact that what physicists often claim as being ultimate physical particles cannot, in fact, be such, simply because they are clearly, on the basis of physical theory itself, phenomena which are dependent on an observing consciousness or consciousnesses for their manifested existence. This discovery has perhaps provided leeway for some indulgence in over optimistic wish-fulfilling speculative metaphysics; a situation which has provided died in the wool materialists such as Richard Dawkins targets for his exuberant and vituperative parodying talents. Here's Dawkins in fine form:

Similar mileage is got out of Heisenberg's Uncertainty Principle ('Aren't we all, in a very real sense, uncertain?), Fuzzy Logic ('Yes, it's OK for you to be fuzzy too'), Chaos and Complexity Theory (the butterfly effect, the platonic, hidden beauty of the Mandelbrot Set – you name it, somebody has mysticised it and turned it into dollars).[891]

Very amusing and, of course, Dawkins is correct that someone has almost always packaged and marketed some popularisation of all kinds of extremely unlikely 'spiritual' remedies for the ever present difficulties of living in the difficult world of *samsara*, the cyclic existence of the conditioned world.

But, on the other hand, perhaps it would be possible to make a case for the view that Dawkins, who until recently held a weighty position as being responsible for the public understanding of science, was actually engaged in materialising current scientific knowledge, on the basis of his lack of understanding of quantum physics, and thereby misleading the public, and turning the result into intellectual notoriety; there is certainly a market for the materialist worldview, despite its vacuity. The hugely significant fact remains, however, that there is now incontrovertible evidence for the assertion that consciousness and the quantum level of reality are intertwined, whilst there is absolutely no evidence, other than the misleading common sense appearances of the everyday world, for the materialist claim that consciousness is a material conjuring trick.

From the perspective of quantum theory it is an extraordinary interconnected activity of a universal Mind, or primordial awareness, which autonomously orchestrates the infinitely complex and intricate field of 'collapsing' wavefunctions within the overall universal wavefunction of the Mind of reality, and, in so doing, produces the appearance of 'classical' reality. This discovery validates the Buddhist metaphysical perspective that the essential nature of all conventional phenomena is mind, or awareness-consciousness, and at the deepest level this is primordial nondual awareness (*jnana*), which is the epiontic 'dream-stuff' of the process of reality.

But what kind of 'stuff' is *jnana*, the primordial mind, or awareness-consciousness? The first thing to be said about this issue is that Western academic thought in the area of 'consciousness studies' is hopelessly confused. In her book *Consciousness an Introduction* Susan Blackmore says that the problem of consciousness is perplexing, 'mind-boggling' and 'brain-hurting,'[892] and in a more recent collection of interviews with various philosophers and neuroscientists conducted at a conference concerning the nature of consciousness, *Conversations on Consciousness*, she observes in the introduction that:

> … I came more and more to appreciate why the conference can only be called *Towards* a Science of Consciousness. There is so little agreement.[893]

And reading the views of the assembled 'experts' does not engender confidence in their abilities to solve the problem; the interviews mostly present a morass of personal opinions with little serious support. Furthermore very few of the interviewees consider quantum physics to be relevant; the general worldview is thoroughly 'classical'.

According to Susan Greenfield, one of the heavyweights in the field of consciousness studies:

> The fact is that [mind is] a subjective phenomenon that we can't really define properly. Everyone knows what it is, but we can't use the normal operational definitions for defining it; and therefore it's very hard to know how to even frame the question as to how a subjective inner state is associated with something physical.[894]

Here we are presented with the obvious source of the Western academic incapacity to comprehend the phenomenon of consciousness. Firstly the approach is that of trying to reduce a first order immediately known phenomenon to an objectified external phenomenon, an obviously self-defeating attitude. Secondly there is a generally obvious materialist bias – the physical, by which most exponents of consciousness studies seem to imply 'material', *must produce mind.*

This unexamined and deeply held belief, which promotes an extraordinary lack of coherency and cogency within the academic field of consciousness studies, is poignantly illustrated by an exchange between Blackmore and Greenfield. Greenfield remarks that:

> I think that you and I would probably both go along with the assumption: we're not pan-psychics, or I'm not and I don't think you are. So lets assume that consciousness is generated by the brain.[895]

Blackmore then presses Greenfield as to whether she would say that 'neuronal networks generate consciousness.'[896] Greenfield then retreats and claims that actually she is only talking about correlations rather than direct causal links, Greenfield now repudiates her use of the term 'generates':

> No, only correlate, because … if you'd said to me you'd found out how the brain generates consciousness, I don't know what answer I would expect. Would it be a formula, would it be an experiment, would it be a subjective experience, - what kind of thing would it be that would satisfy someone that you had discovered how the brain generated consciousness?[897]

One would have thought that at this point in the interview Greenfield might have regretted her cavalier and simplistic statement concerning brains 'generating' consciousness, and yet eight pages on, at the very end of the interview, when Blackmore asks Greenfield 'what is the really big question for you?', Greenfield replies:

> Well, how the brain generates consciousness.[898]

It seems that an awareness of maintaining consciousness of conceptual coherence and consistency is not is always at the forefront of the thought processes of exponents of consciousness studies!

According to some of Blackmore's interviewees:

> 'Minds are simply what brains do' (Minsky, 1986, 287); 'Mind is designer language for the functions that the brain carries out' (Claxton,1994, 37); Mind is 'the personalisation of the physical brain' (Greenfield, 2000,14).[899]

All these definitions attempt to reduce the notion of 'mind' to the material level of the brain in some manner of verbal ingenuity. But can any of these proposals remove the 'mystery' from the concept of 'mind' simply by making it some kind of nebulous smokescreen for the mechanistic operations of the brain? Blackmore, however, defends these bizarre formulations:

> Such descriptions make it possible to talk about mental activities and mental abilities without supposing that there is a separate mind. This is probably how most psychologists and neuroscientists think of 'mind' today ...[900]

And it has to be said that Blackmore is correct in this observation that the materialist perspective is uppermost in the academic slot called 'consciousness studies' and beyond. In a recent work the neuropsychologist Paul Broks writes that:

> Neurons are the basic functional units of the brain and that is their task: to fire or not to fire. It's all they do. Whichever region of the cortex you plunge into, the scene is the same. Where is the mind in this tangled wood of neurons and nerve fibres? It isn't anywhere. And the self? What did you expect? A genie in a bottle?[901]

The apparent dramatic qualitative gap between the material operations of the brain and the direct awareness of consciousness defies explanation because it is based on an incorrect assumption that the material world is independent of consciousness. As a consequence exponents of consciousness studies tend to proffer 'definitions' that attempt to cover over the fact that it is an utter impossibility for a non-conscious by definition, non-existent as shown by quantum physics, assumed aspect of reality such as 'matter' to generate the world of awareness. The pseudo definitions offered by exponents of consciousness studies are no more than advertising slogans for an unexamined preference for a materialist worldview.

Max Velmans, Professor of Psychology at Goldsmith's College, University of London, characterises the current Western academic attitude to the 'problem' of consciousness as follows:

> Consciousness is something ineffable and mysterious – we can't fit it into a natural science view of the world, so we have to demonstrate in one way or another, by hook or by crook, that this ineffable conscious entity is nothing more than a state or function of the brain.[902]

In other words the reason why consciousness is considered to be 'ineffable and mysterious' is because it is not taken seriously as a fundamental aspect of reality on its own terms and it is therefore thought that it *must* be reducible to matter. But it resists all attempts to reduce it to an 'objective' third party description. It is impossible to demonstrate how 'physical' arrangements 'physically' become, so to speak, the actual first hand inner awareness of experience. Such a demonstration is simply impossible because consciousness is, by its original Cartesian definition and also by direct introspection, not 'physical,' in the usual sense of the term. Western thought, therefore, assumes that it must be an illusion generated by 'matter' doing amazing and incomprehensible things.

Within Buddhist philosophy the emphasis is emphatically upon direct awareness of the nature of mind through the immediacy of meditation experience. This of course leads to raised eyebrows in Western academic circles but it is surely only by looking at the mind with a direct technique that we can possibly know the nature of this firsthand internal phenomenon. The Buddhist philosopher B. Alan Wallace, in his essay *A Science of Consciousness: Buddhism(1), The Modern West(0)*, writes that the Modern West has failed to produce an adequate science of consciousness, but Buddhism, on the other hand:

> …has made major strides in developing such a science, and … the contemplative refinement of attention and the subsequent utilisation of such attention in exploring the mind firsthand plays a crucial role in such an endeavour. Such training of the mind is vital for investigation the nature of consciousness…[903]

From a Buddhist perspective the idea that consciousness can be better understood by examining the material world, rather than examining consciousness itself with a properly focused and non-conceptual mind, which provides a direct and immediate experience of the inner qualities of mind or consciousness, is bizarre simply because consciousness provides the ground for any experience. This is true whether consciousness were to be an (illusory) 'internal' mental experience generated by an assumed external purely material process (Dennett's position) or the direct experience of the 'higher', or more manifest, levels of the fundamental awareness 'stuff' of the process of reality.

When the epistemological situation of perception is clearly examined it cannot be denied that the only aspect of experience that we have direct access to is the direct experience of consciousness itself, not something which is imputed beyond the experience. As the Dalai Lama has pointed out:

> Whatever our philosophical views about the nature of consciousness, whether it is ultimately material or not, through a rigorous first-person method we can learn to observe the phenomena, including their characteristics and causal dynamics.[904]

The fundamental basis for this knowledge is located no where else but in direct first order experience. The Dalai Lama here is actually, in accord with his compassionate nature, being kind to the materialist viewpoint, for, as we have seen, there is no chance of consciousness being reduced to a purely material substrate, unless, of course, the definition of matter is altered to include consciousness.

The reason that the special techniques of meditation are required to gain this insight into the nature of mind is simply that the mind by its very nature is directed outward into the world and this outward engagement obscures its own nature. This tendency of mind to flow outwards results from the fact that cognition is an innate function of mind and therefore it spontaneously grasps towards dualistic experience, even though its essential nature is non-dual. Therefore it is only by reducing the natural tendency of the dualistic mind to constantly grasp at dualistic experiences, through appropriate meditational mind training techniques, that the fundamental features of awareness-consciousness can be uncovered.

The effectiveness of meditation techniques in changing brain functioning is now scientifically validated through experimental investigation. Foremost in this area research is the work of Richard Davidson, director of the Waisman Laboratory for Brain Imaging and Behavior at the University of Wisconsin. In June 2002, Davidson's associate Antoine Lutz positioned 128 electrodes on the head of Mattieu Ricard, a monk from the Shechen Monastery in Katmandu who had more than 10,000 hours of meditation experience. Lutz asked Ricard to perform focused meditation on 'unconditional loving-kindness and compassion.' In this session Lutz immediately noticed powerful gamma activity - brain waves oscillating at roughly 40 cycles per second -indicating intensely focused thought, Gamma waves are usually weak and difficult to see. But those emanating from Ricard were easily visible; and oscillations from various parts of the cortex were synchronised.

The researchers had never seen anything like it and in order to extend their research pool they brought in more monks, as well as a control group of college students inexperienced in meditation. The monks produced gamma waves that were 30 times as strong as the students'. In addition, larger areas of the meditators' brains were active, particularly in the left prefrontal cortex, the part of the brain responsible for positive emotions.

Davidson realised that the results had important implications for ongoing research into the ability to change brain function through mind training. In the traditional view, the brain becomes frozen with the onset of adulthood, after which few new connections form. In the past 20 years, though, scientists have discovered that intensive training can make a difference to brain structure. For instance, the portion of the brain that corresponds to a string musician's fingering hand grows larger than the part that governs the bow hand - even in musicians who start playing as adults. Davidson's work suggested this potential might extend to emotional centres.

Research work such as this shows that the focused meditation techniques such as those employed in *Lamrim* - stages of the path to enlightenment - meditation, in which the mind is focused powerfully upon an internal awareness or quality of mind, will have significant effects on brain function and structure. Until recently the idea that the focused mind could take control of the functioning of individual consciousness and effect dramatic changes in brain structure was completely, arrogantly and erroneously discounted by Western 'experts' who asserted that the adult brain was immutable. We now know, however, that neuroplasticity is a fact, it has been shown that controlling and manipulating the functioning of consciousness has a significant physical effect upon brain structure, it can mould brain structure. Furthermore, as the work of Henry Stapp in collaboration with the neuropsychiatrist Jeffrey M. Schwartz indicates, the mechanism involved is quantum in nature: the quantum zeno effect. This is, of course, what one would expect as the brain itself is nothing else than a classical manifestation of the more fundamental 'epiontic' quantum realm.

The evidence for the reality of neuroplasticity is now conclusive; as is demonstrated by Schwartz's excellent book *The Mind and the Brain*. However some of the far–reaching implications are probably not fully comprehended by all who read it. Schwartz clearly draws the conclusion that the brain is moulded by the mind:

> Mind, we now see, has the power to alter biological matter significantly; that three pound lump of gelatinous ooze within our skull is truly the mind's brain.[905]

This means that if we are asked to decide which category of reality is ultimate we must, in line with the Yogachara-Chittamatra and other Buddhist viewpoints, assert that it is the mind, or perhaps a universal Mind, which provides the ontological ground for the process of reality. As the opening verse of the *Dhammapada*, an early Buddhist sutta, says:

All states of being are determined by mind.
It is the mind that leads the way.[906]

The discovery of neuroplasticity clearly lends macroscopic support to the incontrovertible evidence of quantum theory that the ultimate stuff of reality is 'epiontic.'

However, despite the growing dramatic evidence of the epiontic power of meditation, the image of meditation held by many Western scientists and philosophers amounts to little more than a parody. For instance Dennett, answering a question about the validity of meditative introspection, observes that:

> Every experimenter should, of course, put herself in the apparatus, to see what its like from the inside. You should certainly treat yourself informally as a subject and see if you've overlooked something, for instance. But having done that then you do the experiment. You use naïve subjects, and you figure out someway to get what you've discovered from the first person point of view to manifest itself for neutral observers from the third person point of view. And if you can't do that, then you have to be suspicious of the insights that you thought you had.[907]

This view of the nature of meditation reveals a complete lack of understanding. It is not possible to demonstrate the nature of consciousness experimentally using naïve subjects, in the sense that Dennett means naïve, because in order to get the results of meditation it is necessary to learn to meditate in order to experience the nature of consciousness as it can be experienced in increasingly refined states.

Meditation *is* the experiment and once 'naïve' subjects have learned to do it they are no longer 'naïve' in the sense the Dennett conceives of. As their meditation skills progress the quality of their experience of consciousness will alter. This alteration, which will conform to the expectations indicated by those who have previously practiced and refined meditation abilities, can be thought of as the results of the experiment. Dennett's proposal is as absurd as to suggest that 'naïve subjects' could be high-jacked off the street to perform experiments in quantum physics.

The meditation based investigation of the nature of consciousness that is employed within Buddhist practice, however, is not generally accepted as valid in the West. The current Western academic attitude towards consciousness corresponds to the crude notions that late nineteenth century physics had about the nature of the material world. It also hangs onto late nineteenth century speculative misinformation regarding the capabilities of consciousness. For instance Alan Wallace points out that:

> ...more than a century ago, William James, founder of the first psychology laboratory in the United States, concluded on the

basis of the best scientific research that voluntary attention cannot be sustained for more than a few seconds at a time.[908]

Wallace then reminds us that this is more or less the accepted view today. No doubt James employed just the kind of 'naïve' subjects who had never undergone any training in controlling their minds, the kind of untrained subjects that Dennett suggests is appropriate for understanding the nature of consciousness.

From the point of view of Buddhist philosophy and practice, however, the idea that subjects, or researchers even, who are incapable of bringing their own minds under control might have something significant to say about the actual nature of consciousness is absurd. Advanced Buddhist meditation practitioners, on the other hand, can maintain unswerving focused mental one pointed attention, without distraction, for hours at a time. The Buddhist methods of meditation training are based on centuries of careful meditative experience and analysis, and precise knowledge of the levels of the focused mind have been distilled. Included within this mind training there are precise techniques for exploring the levels of consciousness called the *jnanas*, which are states of focused one pointed concentration, each of which have specific qualities. The first step required to cultivate such direct experiential explorations of the nature of consciousness is to be able to control the mind in a way that produces the beginnings of non-conceptual awareness, the direct experience of the mind resting in its own nature before thoughts and concepts disrupt the mind's essential 'clarity'.

It does not take a great deal of effort to discover that generally the mind is, as Buddhism describes it, like an 'unruly elephant.' This image comes from the necessity for Indian villagers to keep their elephants under control by tethering them to a post. Meditation here is likened to the process of tethering the mind to the non-conceptual experience of awareness without the disturbance of thought processes. Beginners in this 'clarity of mind' meditation find, to their immense frustration, that the mind functions independently of their will, they are not in control. Try and clear the mind of thought and you will find that the mind starts making a shopping list, or worrying about something or other, or constructing fantasies. In fact the mind will do anything except remain calm, peaceful and focused on its own nature. What hope of understanding the mind when you cannot begin to examine its qualities?

Practitioners who persevere under guidance from someone skilled in teaching the techniques of meditation will find, however, that the mind can rest focused within its own nature beyond interference by gross conceptual thought processes. This is not an experience of blankness; it is, rather, an experience of inner luminosity and clarity:

> ...if you examine the mind also when it remains without
> fluctuation, you will see an unobscured, clear and vivid

vacuity, without any difference between former and latter states. Among meditators that is acclaimed and called "the fusion of stillness and dispersion.[909]

When the task of seriously examining the nature of consciousness through using the precise techniques of meditation developed within the Buddhist meditative tradition is undertaken the descriptions within the literature become vivid and precise. They provide another kind of 'measure' to that employed within the external 'physical' sciences; they are measures of the internal states of consciousness.

The early twentieth century philosopher Edmund Husserl proposed a method of phenomenology by which he hoped to uncover the essential nature of mind. According to Husserl it is possible to introspectively retrace the constructive activities of the mind in order to reveal the source and structure of our mental 'contents'. This activity, he believed could lead to a purified and direct knowledge of the ideal, essential structures of consciousness. Husserl, however, believed that all he had to do was turn his attention inward and report back, so to speak, on what he observed. It did not occur to him that he would need to prepare the nature of his own mind, in the same way that a quantum physicist must prepare his theoretical and physical tools, in order for his results to have validity.

According to the Buddhist meditative tradition such a phenomenological investigation is impossible without the necessary preparation which allows the mind to observe itself. As Wallace points out:

> In general, a pivotal element in the emergence of a new science is the development and refinement of instruments to precisely observe and possibly experiment with the phenomena under investigation. ... The only instrument humanity has ever had for directly observing the mind is the mind itself, so that must be the instrument to be refined.[910]

A distracted and confused mind will simply observe its lack of clarity. However by refining the introspective capabilities of the mind through the practice of meditation the Buddhist meditative techniques offer a true phenomenology of mind. It does this by employing the remarkable techniques developed within the tradition for producing objective states of mind which are not tainted by adventitious subjectivity of the practitioner. These states can be verified because all practitioners are able to identify the inner qualities that are precisely described within the meditation mind maps which have been developed within the tradition.

Such mind-maps obviously employ, like physics and science in general, metaphors from the familiar world of everyday life in order to convey the experiential qualities of the meditation states described. Thus the meditation master Lozang Chokyi Gyaltsen describes how it is possible to take "the fusion of stillness and dispersion", described previously, as a meditation object in order to focus on stillness:

> Whatever sort of ideation arises, without suppressing it, recognise where it is dispersing and where it is dispersing to; and focus while observing the nature of that ideation. By doing so, eventually the dispersion ceases and there is stillness. ... This is like the example of the flight over the ocean of an uncaged bird that has long been kept onboard a ship at sea. Practice in accord with the description ... Like a raven that flies from a ship, circles around in all directions, and alights there again.[911]

Unless one has practiced diligently enough to be able to go beyond conceptual thought in meditation, to the point that you have had a direct experience of the mind actually being able to non-conceptually explore itself in all directions and then settle onto a central point of focus, 'like a raven that flies from a ship, circles around in all directions, and alights there again', it will not be possible to understand the significance of this mind map description. Once the genuine experience within meditation becomes realised, however, the precision of the mind map to the actual experiences within meditation becomes apparent.

Although introspection is generally denigrated in Western intellectual disciplines the hardcore materialist exponent of consciousness studies Paul M. Churchland has speculated about the possible uses of introspection in the investigation of consciousness. In his book *Matter and Consciousness* he writes:

> How then might we improve or enhance this introspective access? Surgical and genetic modification of our innate introspective mechanisms is one possibility, but not a realistic one in the short term. Short of this, perhaps we can learn to make more refined and penetrating use of the discriminatory mechanisms we already possess.[912]

Examples of the kind of development of discriminatory skill which he gives include: the difference between a child's apprehensions of music compared with that of a conductor of a symphony orchestra, the acute taste discrimination of a wine taster and the visual acuity of an astronomer observing the night sky:

> In each of these cases, what is finally mastered is a conceptual framework-whether musical, chemical or astronomical - a framework that embodies far more wisdom about the relevant sensory domain than is immediately apparent to untutored discrimination. Such frameworks are usually a cultural heritage, pieced together over many generations, and their mastery

supplies a richness and penetration to our sensory lives that would be impossible in their absence.[913]

In other words Churchland is suggesting the necessity of a technique of sharpening our inner faculties of introspection. In fact Churchland, being a unmitigated and intransigent materialist, suggests that we might develop the precision of our introspective faculties to the point that we will be able to detect introspectively an event within consciousness corresponding to individual physical events or processes:

> Glucose consumption in the forebrain, dopamine levels in the thalamus, the coding vectors in specific neural pathways, resonances in the nth layer of the peristriatal cortex, and countless other neurophysiological and neurofunctional niceties could be moved into the objective focus of our introspective discrimination and conceptual recognition...[914]

So Churchland is proposing that the brain might be able to train itself to observe its own material processes, by 'generating,' of course, the material trick of mentality - a truly amazing and surely highly unlikely proposal.

Churchland, in line with his belief that the fabric of inner awareness is actually made up of nothing more than the firing of individual neurons, each individual firing, as it were, giving a single pulse of consciousness, or something similar, seems to be suggesting that it should be possible to refine introspection to the point at which it is possible to locate an inner flicker of consciousness and then be able to map it, within consciousness, perhaps even to the firing of a specific neuron, of at least a group of neurons! In which case, of course, we must entertain the mind-boggling situation of a group of neurons happily firing away in such a manner that they become conscious, whatever that means in this context, of themselves firing away! Do they appear, within the introspective field of consciousness, to be material or mental? Is Churchland really suggesting that we could actually introspectively see the material neurons materially sparking at full pelt within the mentality that the sparking produces?

Leaving aside the massively improbable nature of such an image, we might ask what kind of introspective attention this level of inward awareness would require. The kind of attention required by the sort of project Churchland envisages would have to be able to maintain clear awareness of the background fabric of consciousness for more than James' few seconds. The mind would surely have to be steadily focused, without distraction, for a reasonable period of time. An introspecting subject undertaking this task is hardly likely to notice the tiny pulse of consciousness generated by a few neurons firing whilst engaged in formulating the next days shopping list or worrying about the car insurance!

In fact the kind of introspection required for Churchland's proposal is exactly the rigorous control and exploration of the inwardness of consciousness which already exists in the Buddhist tradition of meditative investigation, a framework which is 'a cultural heritage, pieced together over many generations' which supplies a mastery over inward states of consciousness. And it is only this kind of precise mastery, which constitutes Nick Herbert's requirement for an 'inner physics' of quantum consciousness, which can provide a deep understanding of the nature of consciousness because it is the only method of exploring consciousness in its intrinsic nature. But the notion that such an introspective activity will produce a direct apprehension of various groups of neurons firing, or any other 'neuro-physiological and neurofunctional niceties', is ridiculous. What happens when you focus the mind on consciousness is that you experience exactly that: the direct awareness of consciousness.

The 'phenomenological' methods of Buddhist meditation techniques have been developed in order to probe the nature of the mind beyond thoughts and conceptuality. It is possible quite early on in serious meditation practice to experience the background mind out of which thoughts arise, and when this experience becomes familiar the various descriptions of the nature of mind, luminous clarity, cognizant luminosity, emptiness and cognition inseparable, and so on become quite obviously cogent. In the variety of Tibetan Buddhism called Dzogchen, or the 'Great Perfection' the basic 'pure' ground consciousness is called *rigpa,* or pure primordial awareness which underpins all phenomena of apparent matter and dualistic mind.

The general reason that awareness, consciousness or mind is thought by many Western philosophers to be incapable of being responsible for the production of what appears to be a material reality is simply that it is so immaterial! Even if we accept, it is thought, that the 'material' world cannot be completely independent of consciousness the idea that the nature of reality is, at root, a matter of mind just seems too bizarre, whatever the quantum evidence, how could something so immaterial possibly do it?

However, the fact that matter is actually congealed energy is now incontrovertible, Einstein's famous equation, and the atomic bomb, guarantees this. Furthermore the amount of energy released by the annihilation of the matter is extraordinary as indicated by the energy released in atomic explosions. When Robert Oppenheimer saw the first atomic test he quoted the Hindu Bhagavad Gita:

> If the radiance of a thousand suns were to burst into the sky, that would be like the splendour of the Mighty One and I am become Death, the destroyer of worlds.

The amount of matter required to release a vast amount of energy is tiny. Therefore if, as the quantum evidence indicates, a deeper realm of awareness-consciousness lies beneath the manifestations of matter and energy, as well as individuated mind, then it would seem likely that the nature of the power locked into this self-aware ground of reality might be dramatic beyond comprehension.

The extraordinary Thai meditation master Ajahn Chah, in one of his extemporary inspirational Dharma talks that he was famous for, spoke of the necessity for developing the direct understanding of the processes of consciousness; to actually be able to watch, and then directly experience them within direct focused meditation practice in order to become aware of the fact that they take place within a deeper level of fundamental awareness:

> Whatever we experience, it all arises within this knowing. If this mind did not exist, the knowing would not exist either. All this is phenomena of the mind. ... the mind is merely the mind. It's not a being, a person, a self, or yourself. Its neither us nor them. ...The natural process is not oneself. It does not belong to us or to anyone else. It's not any thing.[915]

And:

> This mind is free, brilliantly radiant, and unentangled with any problems or issues... In the beginning what was there? There is truly nothing there. It doesn't arise with conditioned things, and it doesn't die with them.[916]

The basic field of the nondual mind is the vibrant, empty capacity for the fundamental act of knowing; and it provides the ground from which all the phenomena of the experiential dualistic world emerge. It is just this fundamental mind, the ground of knowingness, so to speak, that provides the basis of both the coordinated appearances of the apparently external material world and the apparently 'internal' conceptual structures of 'knowingness' by which the functioning of appearances are comprehended.

The entire vast array of appearances, experiences, reflective conceptual systems, and so on arise from a primordial flickering, knowing movement of consciousness that disturbs its quintessential unity:

> Please clearly understand that when the mind is still it's in its natural, unadulterated state. As soon as the mind moves, it becomes conditioned. ... The desire to move here and there arises from conditioning. If our awareness doesn't keep pace with these mental proliferations as they occur, the mind will chase after them and be conditioned by them. Whenever the mind moves, at that moment, it becomes a conventional reality.[917]

The ground which Ajahn Chah refers to as 'mere unconditioned mind' the physicist David Bohm described in the following terms:

So we see that the ground of intelligence must be in the undetermined and unknown flux, that is also the ground of all definable forms of matter. Intelligence is thus not deducible or explainable on any basis of knowledge (e.g. physics or biology). Its origin is deeper and more inward than any knowable order that could describe it.[918]

Ajahn Chah

Ajhan Chah gives some idea of the dramatic nature of a direct experience of the nondual nature of the ground of reality:

...just before my head hit the pillow, the mind's awareness began flowing inward; I didn't know where it was headed, but it kept flowing deeper and deeper within. It was like a current of electricity flowing down a cable to a switch. When it hit the switch my body exploded with a deafening bang. The knowing at that time was extremely lucid and subtle. Once past that point the mind was released to penetrate deeply inside. It went inside to the point where there wasn't anything at all. Absolutely nothing from the outside world could come into that place. Nothing could reach it.[919]

This is a description of an experience of the nondual mind; and it gives an indication that, in the deeper reaches of mind beneath the dualistic overlay there lies an extraordinary quality of deep powerful awareness which resides within the ground of reality. It is this quality of the nondual ground which is the wisdom-awareness that is the target of the various paths of transformation described by Buddhism:

Without a centre, without an edge,
The luminous expanse of awareness that encompasses all-
This vivid, vast brightness:
Natural, primordial presence.

Without an inside, without an outside,
Awareness arisen of itself, as wide as the sky,
Beyond size, beyond direction, beyond limits-
This utter complete openness:
Space, inseparable from awareness.

Within that birthless wide-open expense of space,
Phenomena appear-like rainbows, utterly transparent.
Pure and impure realms, Buddhas and sentient beings
Are seen brilliant and distinct.

As far as the sky pervades, so does awareness.
As far as awareness extends, so does absolute space.

Sky, awareness, absolute space,
Indistinguishably intermixed:
Immense, infinitely vast-
The ground of samsara,
The ground of nirvana.
To remain, day and night, in this state-
To enter this state easily-this is joy.[920]

A crucial question which is raised by this quite astonishing revelation that awareness-consciousness is the fundamental category of reality concerns the spiritual implications which follow from it.

Before proceeding into this area of analysis, however, it will be useful to set the scene by briefly considering recent philosophical-theological approaches to the central theological issue concerning the existence of God. The vitally significant point here lies in the general theological characterisation of an 'independent' and 'external' creator God. This is generally the core Christian conception of an ultimate creator God, who stands apart from the universe, perhaps meddling from time to time. For instance the theologian William Lane Craig draws the conclusion that the mind-like nature of the universe must indicate the existence of an independent 'personal' mind of God:

> Therefore, it follows that the explanation of the existence of the universe is an external, transcendent, personal cause-which is one meaning of 'God'.

In his recent work *Why There Almost Certainly Is a God*, Professor Keith Ward, former Regius Professor of Divinity at the University of Oxford, makes a similar progression from the primacy of mind within the universe in general to what he asserts, without any proof or logical demonstration, *must be* the 'Mind of God':

> The final explanation of our universe is the eternal and necessary mind of God. ... if there *is* a final explanation – and many scientists think there should or must be – then God is it.[921]

This leap of faith, shall we say, is also shared by Christian physicist-theologians such as John Polkinghorne and Michael Heller.

However, the fact of the matter, or perhaps lack of matter is more appropriate in this context, is that the fact that the nature of all phenomena turns out to be awareness-consciousness means just that the universe is fundamentally the nature of awareness-consciousness. Whether one might want to call this the Mind of Buddha, the Mind of Allah, the Mind of God, or, to take a leaf out of the work of the popular philosopher Anthony Grayling, the Mind of a Garden Gnome[922], depends upon context and the conceptual surroundings and implications of the chosen designation (which really rules out the Garden Gnome, which obviously has no religious or mystical context). It is not *inherently* the mind of anything; as the Madhyamika philosopher Shantarakshita concluded after his deconstructive path though the Mind-Only and ultimate Madhyamaka analyses:

> By relying on the Mind-Only system know that external objects do not exist. And by relying on this Madhyamaka system, know that no self at all exists, even in that mind.[923]

In other words, once the illusion of the material world has been penetrated, rather than construct another illusion of an independent and permanent entity, penetrate into the empty nature of mind itself in order to become liberated from all extreme, restricting views! The point is to cultivate a direct experience of the ultimate, not to merely cling to a limited conceptual image of it.

It is because of the fact that within the Buddhist perspective the ultimate nature of reality is asserted to be only known through direct nondual experience, unmediated by conceptual frameworks, that the notion of an ultimate creative being, viewed as independent and external, is considered to obstructive to direct knowledge of reality. Thus Nagarjuna is severe in his appraisal of the usefulness of notions of God, or gods:

> The gods are all eternal scoundrels
> Incapable of dissolving the suffering of impermanence.
> Those who serve them and venerate them
> May even in this world sink into a sea of sorrow.
> We know the gods are false and have no concrete being;
> Therefore the wise man believes them not
> The fate of the world depends on causes and conditions
> Therefore the wise man may not rely on gods.[924]

The eighth century Madhyamika contemplative and philosopher Shantideva wrote a succinct refutation of the theist account of a permanent creator God, in his *Guide to the Bodhisattva's Way of Life*. In Shantideva's time the corresponding concept to a Christian creator God was the concept of Ishvara which was held by certain non-Buddhist schools of thought as being a permanent creator. When a proponent of Ishvara is asked to identify the nature of Ishvara with reference to the phenomena of the experienced world the answer can only be either that he is a separate and independent entity, or that he is actually identical and of the same nature as the phenomena of the world of experience. Both these theological moves, of course, can be found within modern radical theology, often mixed together.

According to the Madhyamaka analysis, however, the former cannot be the case because if Ishvara is completely independent of the supposed creation he can have no connection with it; completely independent entities can have no interconnection because there is nothing to establish a connection. The second possibility, that Ishvara is identical to the 'earth and the other great elements,' is also incoherent:

> ...since earth and the other great elements are multiple, imperm-
> anent, without conscious movement, not divine, something
> trodden upon and unclean...[925]

In others words the qualities of the permanent creator entity Ishvara and the impermanent elements of the process of reality are clearly opposite and therefore not identical. Ishvara has been defined as being opposite in nature to the realm of phenomena, but just as two entities with absolutely different natures cannot connect with each other they certainly cannot be identical! Furthermore, the world of phenomena appears to function quite happily without the extra imputed ingredient, Ishvara, so why is it necessary:

> Indeed these elements are the cause of whatever is formed from
> them, but why tire yourselves out over the mere name 'Ishvara'
> that you [add] to them.[926]

The addition of a name has no ontological significance, and for the reasons indicated previously the addition is logically indefensible.

Shantideva

There have been quite a few recent Christian theological attempts to give God a quantum leg-up rather than leap. For instance Nancy Murphy and George F. R. Ellis, in their work *On the Moral Nature of the Universe*, claim that 'God's noncoercive dealings with human creatures finds a nonmoral analogue at the quantum level'[927] In their preface they outline their fundamental thesis:

> The (apparent) fine tuning of the cosmological constants to produce a life-bearing universe (the anthropic issue) seems to call for explanation. A *theistic* explanation allows for a more coherent account of reality-as we know it from the perspective of both natural and human sciences, and from other spheres of experience such as the moral sphere – than does a non-theistic account.[928]

This notion, however, that a theistic account of the metaphysical structure and functioning of reality provides a 'more coherent' explanation than any non-theistic version is an extraordinarily over-inflated, and easily refuted, claim. The 'fine-tuning' of the universe is easily and much more naturally accounted for from the perspective of the self-perceiving universe which arises from a nondual ground which has an internal nature of cognition, for this is exactly implied by the idea that the quantum realm is 'epiontic'. And Buddhism provided the groundwork of such an account at least two thousand years ago; furthermore the Buddhist fundamental philosophical analysis did not change, whereas Christian Theology now seems to have adopted the peculiar conceit that the fact that it is constantly reinventing itself is an indication of its relevance and correctness!

It must be said that the nature of ethical perspective and principles derived from Murphy and Ellis' work can only be said to be unimpeachable and inspirational:

> This account of the character of divine action as refusal to do violence to creation, whatever the cost to God, has direct implications for human morality; it implies a 'kenotic' or self-renunciatory ethic, according to which one must renounce self interest for the sake of the other, *no matter what the cost to oneself.*[929]

The derived 'kenotic' ethic is clearly familiar to serious practitioners of any authentic spiritual path; here is a similar, equally uncompromising, formulation from Shantideva's *Guide to the Bodhisattva's Way of Life:*

> All the joy the world contains
> Has come from wishing happiness for others.
> All the misery the world contains
> Has come from wanting pleasure for oneself.

> Is there need for lengthy explanation?
> Childish beings look out for themselves.
> Buddhas labor for the good of others:
> See the difference that divides them![930]

However in the presentation of the Christian 'kenotic' (self-emptying) principle that a practitioner of the spiritual path must attempt to seek the welfare of other beings, whatever the cost to his or her self, Murphy and Ellis point to a modern highly recondite theological doctrine concerning the supposed nature of God, a doctrine which is far from clearly obvious or even acceptable to many Christians. Christian theology is constantly reinterpreting itself in the light of new discoveries whereas Buddhist insights regarding the illusion-like nature of seeming reality have not changed for two thousand years and can be directly traced back to the early teaching of the historical Buddha.

Certainly Dawkins for instance, would find the account of the 'character of divine action as refusal to do violence to creation, whatever the cost to God' more than slightly dubious:

> The God of the Old Testament is arguably the most unpleasant character in all fiction: jealous and proud of it; a petty, unjust, unforgiving control freak; vindictive, bloodthirsty ethnic cleanser; a misogynistic, homophobic, racist, infanticidal, genocidal, fili-cidal, pestilential, meglomaniacal, sado-masochistic, capriciously malevolent bully.[931]

And it is true that a literal and unbiased reading of the Old Testament clearly gives this impression of a meglomaniacal and psychotic God rather than that of an ultimate benevolent being resolutely refusing to do 'violence to the universe.' And the simple facts of the everyday world clearly suggest a divine nature more in the direction of Dawkins' view rather than Murphy and Ellis' non-violent creator. Both the facts of the world and the contents of the Bible certainly seem to undermine Murphy and Ellis' view of a *benevolent* 'kenotic' God.

The Buddhist emphasis on the essential practice of self-renunciation, on the other hand, derives, in part, from the direct perception that the nature of all phenomena is emptiness, which is interdependent co-origination. It follows therefore that reality is a field of interdependent continuums of experience, and consequently it further follows that one's own experience is not ultimately separate from the entire field. In his recent work *Tibetan Buddhism and Modern Physics* the Buddhist professor of physics Victor Mansfield, writes that:

> The Middle Way rests on the two great pillars of emptiness and compassion. A realisation of emptiness, of our profound interdependence with each other and the world surrounding us, decreases egotism and increases the genuine concern for all life.'[932]

The Buddhist ethic derives from a direct realisation of the way reality actually functions at its deepest levels. And as Mansfield points out the Buddhist viewpoint accords precisely with modern physics: the quantum realm is empty of inherent and independent existence because it is a field of potentiality and non-local interdependency.

In the face of considerations such as the above, and indeed also taking into account the astonishingly deep interconnections and mutual elucidations between modern physics and Buddhist philosophy which are described in this book, it is difficult to see how it is possible to hold that a Christian theistic account of reality is the most comprehensive and coherent metaphysical perspective upon reality as revealed by modern science. But this claim is reiterated by Murphy and Ellis in several places. In fact Murphy and Ellis seem to go as far as to suggest that given their claim that their new theology has determined that God has 'decided' to 'respect' the 'rights' of created creatures to 'be themselves', and yet 'manipulate' them 'within strict limits'[933] then theology could have predicted the indeterminacy of the quantum level:

> Thus, from a theological point of view, we can say that something like this indeterminacy could have been predicted on the basis of a theory of noncoercive divine action in the subhuman world.[934]

Unfortunately for the scientific status of theology, however, no such dramatic predictions were made by any of its practitioners. But, on the other hand, as we have seen, Buddhist Chittamatra and Madhyamika philosophers consistently made spectacular assertions concerning the nature of reality during the two thousand years before those assertions were validated by quantum discoveries.

Murphy and Ellis point to the significance of the fine-tuning of the Universe that is now accepted to be necessary for the development of sentient beings. If certain fundamental physical constants of nature had been different to a tiny degree there could have been no development of life and consciousness. This is the 'Anthropic Principle,' the notion that life and consciousness are fundamental aspects of the process of reality and not some kind of cosmic accident. Physicist-theologian John Polkinghorne has written on this subject that:

> For many scientists, cosmic fine-tuning came as an unwelcome shock. Their natural inclination is to believe that our universe is just a fairly typical specimen of what a cosmos might be like. The Anthropic Principle showed that this is not so, but that our universe is special, one in a trillion, so to speak. Recognising this seemed like an anti-Copernican revolution. Of course, human beings do not live at the centre of the cosmos, but the intrinsic physical structure of that world has to be constrained within narrow limits if the evolution of carbon-based life is to be feasible. Some also feared that they detected here an unwelcome threat of theism. If the universe is endowed with fine-tuned potentiality, this might indicate that there is a divine Fine-Tuner.[935]

This leads us into the astonishing unintelligence of the 'intelligent design' controversy, a controversy deeply flawed with dogmatic illogicality on both sides: the Dennett-Dawkins materialist random-chance dogma verses the equally dogmatic theistic 'if there is mind there must be a God' non-quantum leap of faith.

. The controversy between proponents and detractors of 'intelligent design' is in full swing and the battle lines seem hard and fast. Dawkins' first book *The Blind Watchmaker* took its title from the argument advanced by William Paley's book *Natural Theology*. If an intelligent being, unfamiliar with the construction of timepieces, finds a watch and examines the watch mechanism they could only conclude that there must have been a designer. The functioning of the universe as revealed by science quite clearly requires a great many extraordinary, and delicately balanced, mechanisms within its scope, so according to Paley's argument from design the universe also must have a designer. This viewpoint is vigorously and aggressively resisted by the materialist ultra-Darwinists. Dawkins' recent book *The God Delusion*, for instance, is a no hold barred attack upon every variety of theism. Furthermore both Dawkins and Dennett are resilient in their stringent materialism which allows no truck with views leaning in the direction of the primary significance of consciousness at the quantum level.

Richard Dawkins asserts that evolution is the result of an essential nonrandom random process. However the fact of the remarkable appearance of some sort of intelligence being behind it all is undeniable. In his book *The Quantum Brain* Jeffrey Santinover describes his continued amazement at the phenomenon of cell division:

> But watching cell division, especially the 'mitotic spindles' – the symmetrical starbursts – and the orchestration that followed their appearance, I had the overwhelming impression that I was watching an extraordinary order and power- an intelligence - at *a level beneath and within* that of the simplest single celled creature.[936]

He tells us that this basic mechanism of life always suggests to him that there must be something more than mechanism, something mysterious, at the heart of reality. However, the kind of intelligence required in no way requires a external independent entity, this appearance of intelligence is quite easily comprehended from the point of view that there is a fundamental mechanism of interdependent origination within a field of primordial awareness operating at a level beneath and within all phenomena. When Santinover says that he thinks that there must be more than mechanism involved he means, of course, more than mindless mechanism. And, as we have seen from various points of view, this is precisely correct. The mechanism cannot be mindless because it is fundamentally of the nature of mind, or awareness-consciousness.

When Dawkins entitled his book *The Blind Watchmaker* he meant to imply that the process of evolution was in no way driven by intelligence. This is in line with his campaign against the claims of creationists and proponents of crude theistic intelligent design, which involve the claim that the appearance of intelligence within the process of the development of life demands the intrusion of some entity extraneous to the creative process, usually the God of traditional Christianity. In order to stand firm against these absurdities Dawkins and others of his persuasion believe that it is essential to maintain a staunch materialism of the Dennett flavour; the process of reality must be driven by 'mindless scrapes of molecular machinery.' But, as should be quite clear by now, this position is as absurd as the viewpoint it is deploying itself against. If 'matter' is completely devoid of any kind of quality of awareness then awareness would never emerge as a new quality of reality.

The actual fatal flaw in the Intelligent Design argument is simply the assumption that the appearance of intelligence demands an 'external' designer; there is no validity in this viewpoint whatsoever. The kind of explanation which is required in order to produce a coherent account of the nature of the Universe, which Wheeler described as a 'self excited circuit,' must be internal to the process of the Universe itself. Importing an extraneous creator or sustaining God is simply without internal justification. As Paul Davies says

> The central objection to invoking such a being to account for the ingenious form of the universe is the completely ad hoc nature of the explanation.[937]

Wheeler correctly diagnosed the universe as being 'self excited' not 'other excited,' so we need an explanation which accounts for the self-excited nature of the universe. Paul Davies describes this requirement as 'teleology without teleology'.[938]

The Quantum Mind-Only account of the process of reality provides exactly this requirement because it is a metaphysical account which involves no external agencies. The manifestation of the experiential field of the universe arises because of the necessity of the fundamental ground of awareness-consciousness to explore its own nature by giving rise to manifested fields of perception. As a result the operation of the mechanism of karmic resonance produces the appearance of intelligent design, but there is no designer other than mind, or awareness-consciousness, itself. Furthermore, the manifestation of the experiential field of reality is not designed by a fully fledged intentionally so to speak, it is more akin to a reflex mechanism. Paradoxically it appears as if the fundamental awareness-consciousness creates its multitudinous field of experience 'unconsciously.' To a large extent the operation of the fundamental ground of awareness-consciousness is completely oblivious to the safety and requirements of its individuated creatures within the dualistic experiential fields of consciousness and seeming materiality.

In fact the sentient beings, which are the agents of the Universe's self-exploration, are from their own point of view trapped within a pitiless cycle of suffering: *samsara*. As we have seen the Chittamatra and Madhyamaka perspectives in no way questions the existence of the appearance of a *seemingly* external world that is *seemingly* constituted by a multitude of various types of material substance; in fact they emphasise that the appearance of duality cannot be ignored because it constitutes part of the experiential ground from which true knowledge of reality can be gained. The notion that this *seemingly* independent material world is an illusion does not prompt practitioners to adopt some kind of mystical vagueness. On the contrary, the illusory nature of the apparently material world requires great seriousness because from the perspective of unenlightenment it is a trap within which unenlightened sentient beings endlessly cycle and suffer.

According to the Chittamatra and Madhyamaka viewpoints, therefore, one of the primary aims of the spiritual path is to deconstruct the overwhelmingly convincing appearance of the material world as an independent external phenomenon. In order to do this they supply cogent methods of reasoning:

> To withdraw from appearances, it is necessary to come to disbelieve in their veracity, this being why Tibetan colleges put great emphasis on multiple approaches for reasoned understanding of the thoroughly established nature, emptiness. The underpinnings of habitual assent to the deceptive allure of the consciousness of objects' being established by way of their own character...are challenged through argumentation internalised in meditation such that the reasonings themselves rise above mere verbiage with shattering import.[939]

And the illusion that is shattered is the deeply held idea that the objects of the material and psychological world, including other persons, are self-enclosed, independent, and separate entities. The fact that Buddhist philosophy came to its conclusion that the appearance of the external world was an amazing illusion created by a deep level of mind along with the detailed outline of how the illusion is created, without the supporting evidence of quantum physics, is extraordinary.

According to Roger Penrose, writing in his massive tome *The Road to Reality*:

> If we are to believe that any one thing in the quantum formulism is 'actually' real, for a quantum system, then I think that it has to be the wavefunction ...[940]

Quantum physicist H. Dieter Zeh has also pronounced that 'in the beginning was the wavefunction', obviously echoing the beginning of John's Gospel which states that: 'In the beginning was the Word, and the Word was with God, and the Word was God.' To what extent the wavefunction is with God, or perhaps is God, however, is an issue for interpretation. Quantum physics clearly indicates that our experience of the dualistic sphere of reality emerges from a deeper level, a level which Bohm called the implicate order and which is the domain of the wavefunction.

Quantum physicist Nick Herbert tells us that the evidence of quantum theory leads him to:

> assume that every quantum system has both an 'inside' and an 'outside', and that consciousness both in humans as well as in other sentient beings is identical to the inner experience of some quantum system. A quantum system's outside behaviour is described by quantum theory, it's inside experience is the subject matter of a new 'inner physics' yet to be developed.[941]

From this perspective, then, a wavefunction has two aspects, an 'objective' aspect which is manifested as 'objective' measurements within quantum experiments, and a subjective aspect which is our direct experience which manifests within our sphere of consciousness. Karl Pribram referred to the deep quantum wavefunction level or aspect of reality as the 'frequency realm.' And a crucial feature of this fundamental realm of reality is that its nature must be of the 'order', to use Bohm's terminology, of consciousness, and this means that reality has an inner fundamental quality of meaning, or potential cognition. This would clearly indicate that a deep experience of nondual awareness would be an experience of the ultimate meaning nature of the wavefunction, and this must also be an experience of the ultimate meaning nature of reality. Buddhist psycho-metaphysics calls this 'ultimate' experience the direct realisation of the 'clear light' nature of mind, which is the most subtle level of mind. At this level of experience the subjective clear light mind and objective clear light object conditions merge into one and dissolve onto nondual direct cognition of emptiness.

As Nick Herbert suggests the only way that the phenomenon of consciousness can be explored must be through a direct 'inner physics'. But he is mistaken in his assumption that such a discipline is 'yet to be developed,' such a discipline has existed for at least two and a half thousand years within the practice of Buddhism. He refers to the 'inner physics' that he envisages as a way of directly exploring the 'inner' nature of reality as 'Quantum Tantra.' However, he seems to be intent on developing his own idiosyncratic version rather than give serious consideration to the body of established Tantric practices within the Buddhist spiritual tradition. But if we examine the nature of Tantric meditation and visualisation techniques which are the central practices of the Buddhist *Vajrayana*, or Diamond Way Vehicle, methods which are employed in order to directly manipulate the minds of practitioners through increasingly subtle levels towards the nondual ground, we find that they make complete sense from a Quantum Mind-Only point of view.

According to Buddhist Tantric methodology the gross psychophysical continuum of a sentient being is supported by subtle levels of functioning of 'winds' and 'channels', which themselves have levels of subtlety. The 'winds' can be thought of as subtle energy flows, which would have to be quantum in nature, that flow within the structure of 'channels' which make up the 'subtle body' of the sentient being. The techniques of Tantra are used in order to take control of the winds, through focused meditation and visualisation techniques, in order to deconstruct, or dissolve, the winds into a central focused point on order to directly cognize the ultimate nature of reality:

> ...the aim is ... to draw [the winds] into the body and then into the central channel by the power of meditation. When the winds are caused to enter the central channel, they are held there, moved around, and drawn into various places where they dissolve (cease). The dissolution or cessation concomitantly causes the cessation of the minds that rely upon them. Thus, as the courser winds cease, so do the courser types of minds, leaving only subtle winds and minds. The remaining subtle mind (mounted on the remaining subtle wind) is then used to cognize emptiness.[942]

This process, which is the direct meditative manipulation of the subtle mind-energies of the psychophysical continuum, must also constitute a direct manipulation of the structure of quantum functioning within the subtle levels of embodiment. It is the direct deconstruction of the layers of 'implicate orders' through which the psychophysical functioning of a sentient being manifests.

According to Buddhist philosophy and practice the embodied mind of sentient beings can be trained to directly perceive the ultimate nature of reality. Such a mind is the mind of a buddha, a fully awakened being; and the mind of a buddha is omniscient, knowing the nature of all objects, and the potentialities for all manifestation. The *Ornament of Sutras* says:

> Buddhahood is all phenomena,
> But it is no phenomenon whatsoever.[943]

In other words the mind of a buddha, or fully enlightened being, does not collapse the wavefunction. Buddhahood contains an awareness of all possibilities; therefore it embraces 'all phenomena'. However to produce a phenomenon the wavefunction must collapse into a definite manifestation; it therefore follows that buddhahood is 'no phenomenon whatsoever'. As the sutra says:

> The state and the activity of the Buddhas
> Is nothing but sketching a colourful painting onto the sky.[944]

This conclusion, that a buddha's perception does not collapse the wave-function, although startling, is reached through a precise and painstaking analysis of quantum physics and Buddhist metaphysical philosophy.

In ordinary life the mind is trapped in duality, a trap that is etched into the core of embodiment over countless lifetimes. The function of perception which is innate within awareness-consciousness necessarily splits into the experiential continuum of subject and object. This clearly suggests, therefore, that it is this nondual quality of the ground of reality which must be the source and target of authentic religious sensibility and practice. In Buddhism the quality of the ground of reality is indicated as being a nondual, non-conceptual awareness which has the experiential quality of bliss, in the Hindu tradition the nondual state is called 'sat-chit-ananda' or 'being-awareness-bliss', and perhaps in Christianity such a nondual state might be implied by the phrase a 'peace which passes all understanding'.

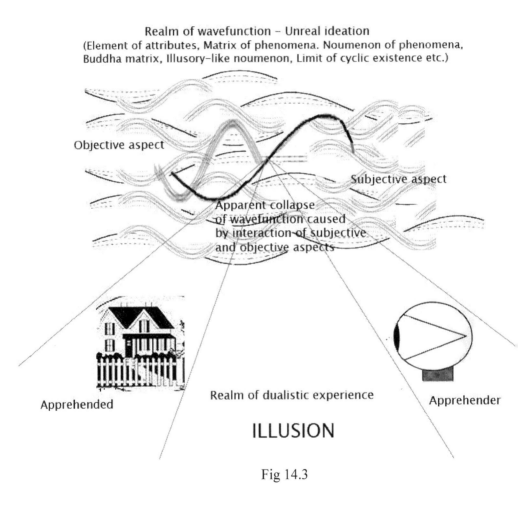

Realm of wavefunction – Unreal ideation
(Element of attributes, Matrix of phenomena. Noumenon of phenomena, Buddha matrix, Illusory–like noumenon, Limit of cyclic existence etc.)

Objective aspect

Subjective aspect

Apparent collapse of wavefunction caused by interaction of subjective and objective aspects

Apprehended

Realm of dualistic experience

Apprehender

ILLUSION

Fig 14.3

A way of visualizing the metaphysical structure of the functioning of reality in which the experiential continuum of duality is an illusion generated by a fundamentally nondual domain, which is derived from the Buddhist Mind-Only metaphysical analysis, is shown in fig 14.3. In this diagram there is an objective wavefunction and a subjective wavefunction which are contained within an overall universal wavefunction which encompasses both aspects of the perceptual process. The generation of the illusion of the dualistic world of experience is also shown in this diagram. It is important to bear in mind that the process of the experiential continuum of reality illustrated in fig 14.3 is partly illusory; it is a schematic diagram of the generation of the illusion of the dualistic world within a unitary process of the fundamental field, or expanse, of phenomena – the dharmadhatu, which is the Buddhist equivalent of the universal wavefunction:

Apart from the basic field of phenomena
There are no phenomena.[945]

According to Mind-Only Buddhist philosophy the appearance of the separation of apprehender and apprehended; perceiver and perceived, is a projection upon the fundamental 'field of phenomena' – the dharmadhatu - which is the realm of the fundamental wavefunction:

Because of the dual nature of the imaginary referent
And because of its being one because of the non-existence of that duality
The nature imagined by childish beings
Is thought of as having the character of duality and unity.[946]

The illusion of separation of subject and object as 'distant and cut off' is overwhelming and seems insurmountable; it appears as if we are forever cut off from knowledge of reality.

According to the Buddhist worldview the 'religious' task consists in overcoming the apparent division between subject and object by achieving a nondual awareness within which the nondual inner nature of reality is directly, and non-conceptually, experienced. In the *Udana* the Buddha expressed the realm of the unconditioned, the nondual ground from within which the illusion of duality arises, in inspirational language:

There is that dimension where there is neither earth, nor water, nor fire, nor wind; neither dimension of the infinitude of space, nor dimension of the infinitude of consciousness, nor dimension of nothingness, nor dimension of neither perception nor non-perception; neither this world, nor the next world, nor sun, nor moon. And there, I say, there is neither coming, nor going, nor staying; neither passing away nor arising: unestablished, unevolving, without support. This, just this, is the end of stress.[947]

And:

> There is, monks, an unborn, an unbecome, an unmade, unfabricated. If there were not that unborn, unbecome, unmade, unfabricated, there would not be the case that emancipation from the born, become, made, fabricated would be discerned. But precisely because there is an unborn, unbecome, unmade, unfabricated, emancipation from the born, become, made, fabricated is discerned.[948]

An intimation of the experiential nature of this realm can only be achieved to various degrees through the development of meditation techniques which enable the mind to break through the surface conceptual levels in order to focus on its own fundamental nature. This deep quality of mind is called the clear light nature of mind and, because it is the base from which both the objective and subjective aspects of experience arise, it is also the fundamental nature of reality, it is direct experience of Bohm's implicate order. The fundamental religious issue, therefore, is not a matter of existence or non existence of God or gods; it is a matter of how to achieve a direct experience of the ultimate ground of the process of reality. For the Buddhist experiential-metaphysical analysis the preoccupation with external entities of this sort are nothing but distracting blocks to realizing the ultimate nature within ones own mental continuum. The essential issue concerns the metaphysical correctness and psychological feasibility of the gathering together of the fragmented world of dualistic experience into a direct nondual experience of unity, which is the hallmark of all authentic religious, often referred to as 'mystical,' activity.

The notion that the fundamental concern of the religious perspective is that of the piercing of the illusion of multiplicity in order to experience an awareness of a deeper unity is powerfully depicted in some early esoteric Christian mystical writings. This is from the *Gospel of Truth*:

> So from that moment on the form is not apparent, but it will vanish in the fusion of unity. ... It is within Unity that each one will attain himself; within knowledge he will purify himself from multiplicity into Unity...[949]

And this theme of the interaction and interdependence of unity and multiplicity is clearly central to Sufism, the esoteric or 'mystical' core of Islam:

> Sufi's compare the Universe to a combination of mirrors in which the infinite Essence contemplates itself in a multiplicity of forms, or which reflect in different degrees the irradiation of the One Being. These mirrors symbolise the possibilities of the Essence to determine Itself, possibilities it contains by virtue of its infinity.[950]

Titus Burckhardt characterizes the fundamental perspective of the Sufi doctrine as that ultimate reality can be described as a process of 'the manifestation of God to himself.'[951] Clearly this viewpoint has deep echoes with the idea that the universe is produced by a process through which the universal potentiality within the wavefunction of the universe divides into subjective and objective aspects which then interact to manifest a realm of illusion from its infinite possibilities. This universal process has been immortalised, so to speak, in the graphic image of the Wheeler **U**. Extending this manner of representation we can model the Sufi **G** (fig 14.4) in which the term '**G**od' simply indicates the process of the **U**niverse observing, or 'contemplating' itself.

Fig 14.4

As we have seen previously there is significant evidence that some kind of minimalist self-observing process could be operating at the molecular quantum level in order to drive the unfolding of evolution. It seems that there is a subtle teleology, a directional tendency to greater levels of aware-ness, a 'teleology without teleology' which operates within the evolutionary process. A crucial advantage of this viewpoint is that it overcomes the awkward and unacceptable notion that a creator God stands outside and inde-pendent of the creation. Instead of this 'classical', or pre-quantum, view of the Christian God we can now move to a process orientated understanding of God in which sentient beings, amongst which human beings have the most developed consciousness and are therefore the most potent, are essential as Instruments of the creative process, they are the '**I**'s of God, so to speak.

This perspective clearly approaches the kind of view that modern Christian radical theology is grasping for. However the tendency on the part of Christian theologians to want to maintain the notion of the sublime self-enclosed omnipotence of their God leads them to undermine the crucial aspect that sentient beings are essential ingredients in the universal creative process. Keith Ward, for instance, clearly moves in the direction of identifying God with the mind behind the wavefunction :

> ...the most adequate ultimate explanation will be in terms of an actual being, an ultimate mind, that necessarily contains within itself all possible worlds and states and actualises some of them ... for the distinctive forms of goodness they exhibit...[952]

However, the view that God is an isolated absolute being who does the collapsing into actuality of the possibilities he takes a fancy to, because of their goodness quotient, is an absurd theological fantasy. It is, rather, the sentient beings extant within the universe who do the actualizing and, furthermore, in so doing they determine future possibilities within the universal wavefunction. The inspirational mystic-psychologist Carl Jung described the insight that humanity completes the universal creative process as follows:

> ...man is indispensable for the completion of creation, ... in fact he himself is the second creator of the world, who alone has given to the world its objective existence ... (without consciousness) it would have gone on in the profoundest night of non-being down to its unknown end. Human consciousness created objective existence and meaning...[953]

Jung was fascinated with Gnostic philosophy and the Western Alchemical tradition and it was within these traditions that he found this message, later to be deduced by John Wheeler from the evidence of quantum physics, that sentient beings are the agents of the universal process of creation, a process that occurs at every moment, at every point of reality from a beginningless past into an endless future.

In fact from the ultimate point of view the appearance of time itself appears to be an illusion created by the movement of the subjective awareness of consciousness, a view which is shared both by Gnostic philosophy and quantum cosmology. Bryce DeWitt, the physicist primarily responsible for the Many-Worlds version of Everett's proposal, indicated in 1967 that the wavefunction of the universe itself is a static phenomenon because there is no external observer. As we have seen, the many-world illusions of dualistic experience arise from the movement of subjective consciousness and therefore the experiential continuum of time only arises because of a split internal to the overall universal wavefunction into subjective and objective components, an observer and the rest of the universe. As quantum cosmologist Andrei Linde points out:

> Thus we see that without introducing an observer, we have a dead universe, which does not evolve in time. This example demonstrates an unusually important role played by the concept of an observer in quantum cosmology. John Wheeler underscored the complexity of the situation, replacing the word observer by the

word participant, and introducing such terms as a 'self-observing universe.'[954]

It is a remarkable fact, then, that the motif of a ground of unity that divides into the multiplicity of a manifested realm of duality underlies all the major esoteric traditions and is also implicated as being fundamental to the metaphysical picture of reality necessitated by quantum physics.

The Quantum Mind Only metaphysical perspective indicates that it makes perfect sense to conceive of the fundamental nondual ground of reality to be the source of all experience of meaningfulness within the dualistic world of experience. As we have seen, the notion that a completely meaningless, completely non-conscious material base of reality produces the vivid realm of meaning and significance is simply incoherent. As many significant quantum physicists, including Wheeler, Stapp, Bohm, Penrose, Linde etc., have indicated, the evidence from the quantum realm is tending to suggest that at its fundamental level the universe is pure undifferentiated meaningfulness, meaning beyond duality. It is from the pure meaning of Bohm's implicate order that the manifested meanings, including the appearance of the material world, of the explicate order emerge. It is from this perspective that Andrei Linde suggests that:

> Will it not turn out, with the further development of science, that the study of the universe and the study of consciousness are inseparably linked, and the ultimate progress in the one will be impossible without the other?[955]

And, as we have seen, this conclusion is inescapable; furthermore a deeper necessary conclusion from all the evidence is that only through direct, nondual experiential knowledge of consciousness will a 'thoroughly established' understanding of consciousness become possible. And it is upon such a basis that mutual understanding and appreciation between science and religion can become a possibility. The beginnings of such a discourse is exemplified in the establishment of the *Mind and Life Institute*, which is a forum for 'fostering dialogue and research at the highest possible level between modern science and the great living contemplative traditions, especially Buddhism.'[956]

The viewpoint developed within this work is, of course, primarily from a Buddhist perspective; a perspective from which the universe is not only self-observing or self-perceiving, it is also a self-transcending universe. In other words the final movement of the development of the conscious awareness of 'self' or 'I-ness' within the realm of duality is the direct realisation of the illusory nature of the embodied selves, or '**I's**', which the universe manifests in order to real-**Ize Its**-self.

The figure 14.6 is a reproduction of the graphic image offered by the 'Strong AI' writer Douglas Hofstadter in his book *I am a Strange Loop*[957] to illustrate his view of the hierarchical development of **I**-ness into ever higher, more solidified forms of manifestation. According to Hofstadter this manifestation occurs from a material level of complete and absolute no I-ness, tin cans for example! A relevant issue, however, is where the tin cans[958] come from in the first place!

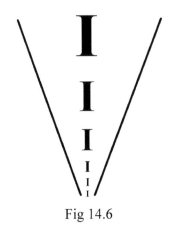

Fig 14.6

The notion that a 'material' world might spring into existence from absolutely nowhere is, almost, endorsed by Dennett:

> What does need its origin explained is the concrete universe itself, and as Hume's Philo long ago asked: Why not stop at the material world? It … does perform a version of the ultimate bootstrapping trick; it creates itself *ex nihilo*. Or at any rate out of something that is well-nigh indistinguishable from nothing at all.[959]

But this formulation clearly fudges the issue. 'Something that is well-nigh indistinguishable from nothing at all', is nothing like nothing, precisely because it is something. This is typical Dennett obfuscation, and he resorts to it probably because he is uncomfortably aware that the idea of something magically arising out of absolutely nothing is both logically and experientially incoherent. However, the Universe 'performing the ultimate bootstrapping trick' from a fundamental ground of 'emptiness and cognition inseparable' is another matter, so to speak.

We have noted this point previously. The fact that Dennett, and even the physicist Paul Davies, resort to the notion that a seemingly material world can spontaneously arise from absolute nothingness via Heisenberg's Uncertainty principle just indicates the appalling lack of clarity and the imprecision that this area of metaphysical discourse is riddled with within Western thought. Here is Jim Al-Khalili's thoughts on the matter:

...here there is a definite and beautifully simple consequence: that of particles being created out of nothing.[960]

And Frank Wilczek joins the celebration of the void of nothingness:

The answer to the ancient question 'Why is there something rather that nothing?' would be that 'nothing' is unstable.[961]

As well as Victor Stenger:

The laws of physics are simply the laws of nothing.[962]

It seems nothingness is all the rage! But this is not uncertainty, Heisenberg's or anyone else's, it is philosophical imprecision which is being used for media effect (Jim Al-Khalili is a well known media physicist). In the chapter *Self-Perceiving Universe* we saw quite clearly that the Heisenberg uncertainty principle indicates that the ground of reality is not a ground of nothingness, a formulation which is meaningless anyway for nothingness can hardly be said to be a 'ground'; it is, rather, a ground of emptiness which hovers between existence and non-existence, and furthermore this fundamental ground has a function of cognition internal to its own nature. The fact that the zero-point vacuum is actually not at all a vacuum but is a field of potential manifestation indicates that the term 'nothing' or 'nothingness' is simply incorrect.

Hofstadter, however, has no time for such niceties; Hofstadter's I-ness comes from nowhere and in a sense goes nowhere except into ever more solidified forms of Itself. This view of the manifestation of consciousness locates its base in a mindless conglomeration of material entities, as we have seen Hofstadter does seem to impute a possible consciousness to an interactive system of tin cans, and the resulting sense of I-ness seems purposeless beyond keeping the self-aware bunch of tin cans in the evolutionary race to nowhere.

Hofstadter considers that for a purely materialist sense of self to get off the ground requires a self-referring 'strange loop', but is it a loop which is strange in that it is supposed to start off in complete darkness which then subsequently claws itself into the light of mindfulness through the operation of mindlessness. Although evolutionary materialists deny the fact, this assertion of an evolutionary adaptive utilitarian type of material mind actually undermines the claim that such a mind can comprehend its own ultimate basis. As the theologian John F. Haught, says in his work *God and the New Atheism*:

Since our minds are said to have evolved gradually from a mindless state of nature, why should we trust these same minds to put us in touch with reality. Where and how did they acquire such an exquisite competence, especially given the lowliness of their origins in nature?[963]

Such material minds, whilst useful for keeping a mindless bunch of molecules in the tooth and claw business of evolution, have no credentials for direct perception of ultimate reality!

The Quantum Mind-Only interpretation of quantum theory, however, indicates that meaningful perception is an intrinsic quality of the ultimate nondual ground of reality which necessarily manifests into the realm of duality through an inner process of breaking its own unity. This process is reflected in the process of symmetry breaking which is posited by physics as the way that the universe devolves into the distinct fundamental forces from an ultimate unified force. The reason why *emptiness* is 'unstable' and therefore manifests into dualistic experience is that its inner nature is cognitive.

A more coherent metaphysical image of the development of **I**-ness, based on the Sufi esoteric perspective, is shown in figure 14.7a. In this figure we see the Universal God-process of Self-perception manifesting the sense of **I** in the dualistic realm in order to apprehend its own presence: '**I** am that **I** am', a formulation that contains the implication of a strange loop of self-perception within itself – I perceive in order to be! However, the actual mechanism which drives this universal process of the manifestation of perceiving centres of awareness, the sentient beings or 'observer participants of all times and all places,' is an internal cognitive self-referential, 'self-synthesizing' process operating from the quantum level through the atomic-molecular, then through the cellular and upwards into the realm of biological organisms, as described by Johnjoe McFadden's quantum evolutionary perspective (fig 14.7b).

A crucial aspect of this process is that the multitude of **I**'s which spew out of this process of Universal Instantiation (fig 14.8) are completely unaware of their own source in the fundamental process of reality; they do not know their own nature which is essentially that of being the Universe's Instruments of self knowledge. It follows, therefore, that they have a further step to accomplish which is to transcend their limited self-awareness in order to achieve a truly universal awareness. It is this goal which is embodied in the paths of esoteric religious traditions.

A Sufi hadith, or saying, expresses this situation of the unknown universal awareness-consciousness of reality as follows:

> I was a hidden treasure and I longed to be known,
> So I created both worlds, the visible and the invisible,
> In order that My hidden treasure ... would be known.[964]

Buddhist philosopher Dolpopa quotes the *Mahaparinirvana sutra* in a similar vein:

> ...the matrix-of-one-gone-thus exists in all sentient beings, but they just cannot see it ... Just as a poor woman has a great treasure

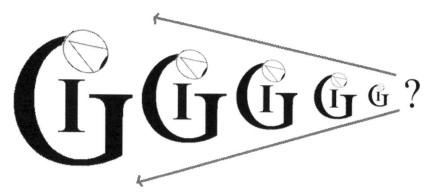

Fig 14.7a

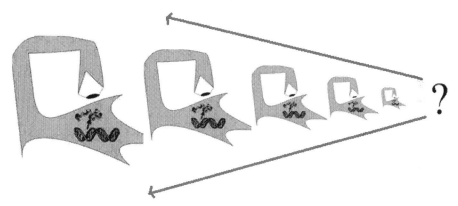

Fig 14.7b

Fig 14.8

but does not know it, so all sentient beings have the matrix-of-one-gone-thus…[965]

The matrix-of-one-gone-thus can be viewed as analogous to the wave-function, although the notion of a 'wavefunction' is a paltry description of the treasure of the Dharmadhatu, in its pure state when it is emptied of the 'adventitious stains of the afflictions,' the stains which bind sentient beings to the realm of cyclic existence as a result of their deep adherence to the view of the inherent existence of the appearance of the two kinds of illusory self; the self of persons and a self within all phenomena. The 'treasure' referred to in both quotes, of course, is the direct experiential awareness of the nondual universal background of reality of which each individual is a representative of. This is also the import of notions such as 'Man is created in God's image.' In Buddhism this principle is articulated with the idea that the buddha-nature, which is the potentiality to become co-extensive with the mind of the universe, is potential within each sentient being:

> I bow to you the dharmadhatu,
> Who resides in every being,
> But if they aren't aware of you
> They circle through this triple being.[966]

And some of the synonyms applied to this treasure are cited by Dolpopa from the *Glorious Vajra Garland Sutra* are:

> Consciousness, element of attributes,
> The ultimate, great bliss,
> Release from apprehended-object and apprehending-subject,
> Undefiled mind of enlightenment,
> Vajrasattva, great peace,
> Amazing nondual reality.[967]

According to the contemporary Sufi writer Kabir Helminski:

> …we must understand that this word *God* has the following synonyms: reality, the Source of Life, the Most Subtle state of Everything.[968]

In his seminal work *The Hero with a Thousand Faces* the comparative mythologist Joseph Campbell, summarising his exhaustive investigation of the myths of probably all accessible cultures, tells us that:

> The standard path of the mythological adventure of the hero is a magnification of the formula in the rights of passage separation-initiation-return.[969]

In order to graphically represent this cyclic process Campbell uses, of course, a circle (fig 14.9). At the bottom of the circle lies the point of separation, or duality; the left hand arm of the circle is representative of the inner psychological ascent, usually through some form of initiation, to a magical realm within which some kind of transformative knowledge, or power, is conferred upon the mythical hero; the hero then descends back into the dualistic realm to share this knowledge and power with others.

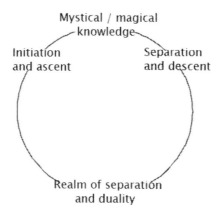

Fig 14.9

The structural similarity between this circular depiction of the manner in which a cultural hero acquires a deeper knowledge of reality which he or she then conveys, and therefore in some manner 'saves' or 'rescues' his or her compatriots, is clearly analogous to other circular diagrams we have encountered during previous chapters. The mystical realm which confers deeper knowledge corresponds to an ultimate unified realm of pure experiential perception into the nondual nature of the ground of reality, a realm which Jung, following the Gnostics, called the Unus Mundus, Buddhism calls the dharmadhatu and Sufism calls al-Haqq, the Real, or Haqîqa, the interior nondual reality of all manifested entities. The right hand arm of the circle represents the descent into the realm of the duality of material entrapment of individuated consciousnesses, each of which is transfixed by the illusion that the limited 'self' which is experienced by the gross material entrapment as an inherently real phenomenon. The left hand arm, consequently, represents the religious quest for the rediscovery of the unity of all phenomenon within the source of all phenomena; a source which is, in reality, the sole reality (fig 14.10). This metaphysical structure is found as a central image within Sufism and is implied in other metaphysical-mystical traditions:

> According to Sufi metaphysics, and in fact other metaphysical traditions in general, all that exists comes from that reality which is at once Beyond-Being and Being, and ultimately all things return to

that Source. In the language of Islamic thought, including both philosophy and Sufism, the first part of this journey of all beings from the Source is called the 'arc of decent' and the second part back to the Source is called the 'arc of ascent.'[970]

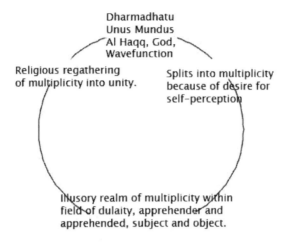

Fig 14.10

Just as the fundamental circular structure of mythology is found as underlying all mythologies, so too the fundamental structure of the metaphysical circle involving a descent from unity into the multiplicity of a dualistic realm of perception, and the subsequent religious task of the experiential unification of consciousness forms the structural basis for all esoteric religious traditions, and also, therefore, forms the basis for the authentic exoteric formulations, when they are properly comprehended. The striking similarity between this circular metaphysical and religious configuration and the Wheeler-Bohm circle which was explained previously and is shown again in fig 14.11 is unmistakable. This vision of the process of reality, now also suggested by quantum physics, reveals aspects of a deep and vitally important ultimate truth concerning reality. The dramatic and unavoidable conclusion can only be that duality is, from an ultimate perspective, an overwhelming illusion taking place within a fundamental unitary reality.

In the following passages it is vital to bear in mind the previous stipulations concerning the concept of God. In employing this term it must be released from its stultifying and reified implication of indicating a supernatural being standing apart from its creation. The term should be understood as indicating the deeply interior metaphysical essence, of the nature of nondual consciousness-awareness, of the entire process of reality. The spiritual nature of this extraordinary metaphysical essence, however, may manifest within the dualistic universe in multiple ways, giving rise to differing religious expressions.

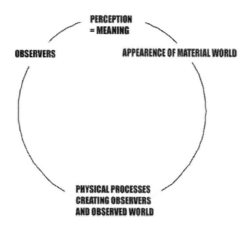

Fig 14.11

The following extraordinary exposition of the Sufi metaphysical world-view maps us dramatically into the realm of the wavefunction, which, as we have seen previously, has both objective and subjective aspects:

> ...multiplicity is objective as well as subjective-the cause of the diversifying contingency being in each of the two poles of perception-and that multiplicity or diversity is in reality a subdivision, not of the divine Principle of course, but of its manifesting projection, which is existential and universal Sub-stance. Diversity or plurality is therefore not opposed to Unity; it is within it not along side it. Multiplicity as such is the outward aspect of the world; but it is necessary to look at phenomena according to their inward reality, hence as a diversified and diversifying projection of the One. The metacosmic cause of the phenomenon of multiplicity is All-Possibility, which coincides by definition with the Infinite, the latter being an intrinsic characteristic of the Absolute. The divine Principle, being the Sovereign Good, tends by this very fact to radiate, hence to communicate itself-to project or make explicit all the 'possibilities of the Possible'.[971]

Here it becomes clear that the notion of the 'Sovereign Good' is used to indicate an ultimate principle that naturally contains within itself the necessity of the 'radiation' of the manifestation of the dualistic world of multiplicity. Within the Buddhist metaphysics, as we have seen, this requirement is taken care of by the indication that the fundamental ground contains the innate function of cognition. Within the Sufi proposal the ultimate ground also contains an inner necessity of radiation into multiplicity, which is indicated in the formulation:

> The metacosmic cause of the phenomenon of multiplicity is All-Possibility, which coincides by definition with the Infinite, the latter being an intrinsic characteristic of the Absolute.[972]

The 'Infinite' by definition must contain all possibilities and therefore *must* by necessity contain the possibility its own manifestation. In other words the wavefunction must 'collapse', or at least appear to 'collapse', somewhere! Here we find that by pure transcendental logic the Sufi doctrine of the quality of the Ultimate Nature contains the seeds of the Many-Worlds perspective upon reality.

The following description of the manifestation of multiplicity from the Ultimate Unity of God, according to the Jewish Mysticism of the Kabbalah, is remarkably consistent with the Sufi perspective:

> According to the Kabbalah, the emergence of the universe into existence, and its development leading to the emergence of an autonomously willed being, was a process involving increasing differentiation, fragmentation of the initial unity, and loss of the original harmony and symmetry of the cosmos. When the universe does not exist, there was only God. When the universe exists, there exists other than God - the universe. Thus, in order to create a universe, God must seemingly fragment somewhat the Divine unity and unique existentiality - a fragmentation which is however real only from the perspective of the beings inhabiting this physical universe rather from the perspective of the divine unity.[973]

And the following passage from the thirteenth-century German scholar and mystic Meister Eckhart resonantly echoes the preceding formulations:

> Though creatures here are manifold they are but one single idea in God. God in himself is just the *one alone*. When creature goes back to her first cause she knows God simply as one in form and essence and threefold in operation. What intellect knows is knowledge and knowledge stops at what is known, with what is known becoming one. Into the simple idea no knowledge ever entered, for this impartible exemplar after which God created all creatures towers God-high above creatures. Creature in pursuing God to his eternal heights must mount above all creatures, nay beyond her very self, her own wont and uses, and follow agnosia

(knowlegelessness) into the desolate Godhead. St Dionysius says, 'God's desert is God's simple nature.' A creature's desert is her simple nature. In the desert of herself she is robbed of her own form and in God's desert, leading out of hers, she is bereft of name; there she is no more called soul, she is called God with God.[974]

Here, again, we find an emphasis that God, or the Ultimate Unity, is the sole reality. The multiplicity of the perceptual realm of duality is actually an illusion created by a 'threefold operation' through which the dualistic realm comes into being. In order to achieve direct nondual knowledge of the Ultimate, therefore, it is necessary to go 'beyond her very self' ('her' being indicative of the individuated 'soul') into a realm of nondual consciousness which is 'bereft' of, or beyond, names or concepts. And such a state would clearly be also bereft of the concepts of both 'self' and 'God'; hence it is described as a desert; a conceptual desert which can be a disconcerting and frightening place.

Vedanta is the central mystical formulation of Hinduism. This tradition asserts that the apparently individuated selves of sentient beings, called the Atman, are actually manifestations of the Universal Self, or Brahman, and are in essence identical to Brahman. A pithy summary of the Vedanta doctrine is contained in the formula 'Tat tvam asi', which translates as 'Thou art that'; the Atman is actually identical to Brahman. When an Indian teacher of Vedanta was shown writings by Meister Eckhart he refused to believe that Eckhart had not been tutored in Vedanta, and it is easy to see why.

According to Meister Eckhart the achievement of a nondual knowledge of the Ultimate Reality of God requires going beyond the self. And according to all forms of Buddhism the deconstruction of the notion of an independent 'self' is also required in order to move towards a direct understanding of the ultimate nature of reality. Here is the exact same requirement articulated within the mystical path of Sufism:

> You name His name; go, seek the reality named by it!
> Look for the moon in the sky, not in the water!
> If you desire to rise above mere names and letters,
> Make yourself free from self at one stroke.
> Become pure from all attributes of self,
> That you may see your own bright essence,
> Yea, see in your own heart the knowledge of the Prophet…[975]

And a similar message that the dualistic realm of the limited self is an illusory dream from which it is possible to wake up in order to perceive pure nondual reality is also central to the Gnostic tradition ($4^{th} - 5^{th}$ century CE). The following is from the Nag-Hammadi Gospel of Truth:

They were ignorant of the Father, he being the one whom they did not see ... there were many illusions at work ... and they were empty fictions, as if they were sunk in sleep and found themselves in disturbing dreams. ... When those who are going through all these in the midst of all these things wake up, they see nothing, they who are in the midst of all these disturbances, for they are nothing. Such is the way of those who have cast ignorance aside from them like sleep, not esteeming it as anything, nor do they esteem its works as solid things either, but they leave them behind like a dream in the night. The knowledge of the Father they value as the dawn. This is the way each one has acted, as though asleep at the time he was ignorant. And this is the way he has come to gnosis, as if he had awakened.[976]

In this formulation the unity of ultimate reality is referred to as the 'Father', a term which clearly symbolic and metaphorical.

The 'structuralist' cultural philosopher Claude Levi-Strauss suggested that all 'mythological' cultural productions could be analyzed in order to reveal a deep structure. A similar situation certainly holds in the formulations of religious esoteric traditions which exemplify exactly such a unified deep structure, in more than one sense. The nondual experience of the unity of ultimate reality, which is of the nature of nondual awareness-consciousness, can only be achieved by breaking through the illusion of the world of multiplicity. This dualistic realm is portrayed as a kind of con-trick that a unified field of awareness plays on itself in order to know itself. In reality, however, the duality of subject and object, apprehender and apprehended, is illusory.

The Buddhist Dzogchen, or Great Perfection, teachings take the radical point of view that the illusory and 'miraculous field of play' is complete and 'perfect' in itself when seen from the ultimate vision of nonduality:

The nature of multiplicity is nondual
And things in themselves are pure and simple;
being here and now is construct free
and it shines out in all forms, always all good;
it is already perfect, so exertion is redundant
and spontaneity is ever-immanent.
All and everything emanates from me,
so all and everything, whatever appears,
is revealed as transmission,
revelation of the timelessly pure reality-field.
All outer and inner is the timeless field of reality
and in such a miraculous field of play
Buddha and sentient beings are not distinct-
so why try to change anything? [977]

This amazing con-trick that Universal Mind plays on itself is exactly the production an illusory dualistic realm of perception which is kept in business by a deep and seemingly innate belief, on the part of each unenlightened sentient being, in the reality of the individual limited self which is often identified by the term 'ego'; although as Buddhism indicates, the deep illusion of selfhood which underpins the illusion of the dualistic world actually goes deeper than a Freudian-type ego. When the illusion of this innate sense of 'self' is penetrated and deconstructed, however, a transcendent experiential unity beyond the limited experiences of duality can be comprehended and even, with determined effort, experientially achieved. And, as we have seen, there is compelling evidence that such unitary experience is a direct awareness of the qualitative dimension of the quantum realm of the wavefunction, the matrix-of-one-gone-thus.

The teachings of the esoteric core of religion are so radical as to appear outlandish and unacceptable to limited and unprepared minds. The teaching that the appearances of the dualistic world of experience, including the appearances associated with what we think of as the realm of external materiality, are, actually, in reality and ultimately, completely illusory, is simply beyond the comprehension of most minds. It appears that even many apparently very clever intellects are incapable of grasping this irrefutable truth concerning the nature of reality, even though it is thoroughly vindicated by modern quantum physics. Both Richard Dawkins and Daniel Dennett, for instance, both appear on 'The Edge' website, which is putatively restricted to the most incisive and brilliant minds currently extant. And yet both these thinkers prefer to stand against the tide of the quantum wavefunction rather than grasp the fact that modern physics has shown that the classical view of an independent world of materiality has disappeared for ever. If such elevated intellects are incapable of comprehending this astonishing quantum fact, what is the hope for lesser minds to understand the situation correctly?

Such metaphysical perspectives are difficult to fully comprehend; the 'noose' of the everyday world, however illusory, that most people are caught up in, is far too convincing. It is because of this fact that the metaphorical and provisional formulations of the teachings of the various religions are generally taken as ultimate. This is because they are taken as being as real as the illusory world of dualistic experience is mistakenly thought to be. It is not generally comprehended that the fact that the *direct experiential realm* that such conceptual formulations are designed to convey *is ultimate* does not mean that the formulation itself is also ultimate. Indeed, if someone truly understands what is communicated concerning the ultimate nature of reality through any religious perspective then they should understand all religious perspectives:

> I have meditated on the different religions, endeavouring to understand them, and I have found that they stem from a single

principle with numerous ramifications. Do not therefore ask a man to adopt a particular religion (rather than another), for this would separate him from the fundamental principle; it is this principle itself which must come to seek him; in it are all the heights and all the meanings elucidated; then he will understand them.[978]

This is why the division of experiential reality into the realms of the conventional and the ultimate is crucial in Buddhist philosophy. The ultimate realm is the inner heart of all esoteric traditions, which Buddhism calls 'emptiness' the nondual ground of pure meaningful potentiality for perception. Bohm actually identified this hidden sphere of 'emptiness' with what he termed the 'holomovement':

It would be the holomovement you see, the flowing movement. But it goes beyond that. We could say that even at this level of thought there is a way of looking at it in which emptiness is the plenum, right? I'm saying that what we call real things are actually tiny little ripples which have their place, but they have been usurping the whole, the place of the whole.[979]

Here Bohm identifies emptiness as the realm of the quantum void which is the deep foundational level of reality within which virtual, or evanescent semi-existent, particles hover between existence and non-existence in conformity with Heisenberg's Uncertainty Principle.

Although the experiential ultimate nature of reality is beyond concepts it can, nevertheless, be indicated by appropriate conceptual systems. If this were not the case this book could not have been written! We must use conceptual systems in order to articulate the nature of our reality and it is vital that the metaphysical conceptual systems that we employ are coherent with the best knowledge that we have concerning reality in all significant areas. This is because metaphysics should supply a universal context within which our complete understanding of reality in all its aspects finds a coherent and interconnected 'wholeness', to use the term used by Bohm.

For most of the recorded history of human thought such overarching conceptual systems were also religious in nature, embracing all aspects of human existence including issues of ultimate significance and morality. In the seventeenth century in the West, however, a new mode of thought took hold which increasingly left issues of the meaning and significance of existence, the nature of morality and humanity's role in the process of reality to one side, eventually becoming embarrassingly out of place in a universe which was conceived of as a matter of mechanism, or matter and mechanism.

The quantum revolution, however, changes matters in a spectacular way because physics turns out to be the 'royal road'[980] to metaphysics and also, via the self-perceiving Wheeler **U**, to 'mysticism.' However, we must now be careful in employing the term 'mysticism.' When Bohm was asked by Professor of Philosophy Renée Weber whether his conclusions concerning the nature of reality, based on quantum physics, might be virtually the same as 'what the great mystics have said,' he replied:

> I don't know that there's necessarily any difference. What is mysticism? The word 'mysticism' is based on the word 'mystery,' implying something hidden. Perhaps the ordinary mode of consciousness which,' elaborately obscures its mode of functioning from itself and engages in self-deception is 'mysticism.' Or we could call it 'obscurantism,' and say there's an opposite mode that we could call 'transparentism'...

Weber: A transparence with respect to the whole.

Bohm: Yes, as opposed to obscuring the whole.

Weber: Kierkegaard had a wonderful phrase for that. He said true religion is 'to be grounded transparently in the power that constitutes one.'

Bohm: Yes, that's exactly what it would mean.[981]

Here Bohm, in 1986, makes the bold claim that the discoveries of quantum physics makes the insights which were once considered to be 'mystical' now 'transparent', which is also to say 'obvious.'

Perhaps the most dramatic of these 'obvious' facts concerning the nature of reality which have been clearly demonstrated during the course of our investigation is that every act, every thought, every intention, every perception that anyone performs or has, has an immediate impact, however infinitesimally and unimaginably tiny, upon the quantum ground of reality. The fact that every quantum 'particle' has been shown to be implicated in the existence of every other quantum phenomenon, which ultimately means every other phenomenon, in the universe means that our acts at every moment have an impact, albeit generally tiny beyond comprehension, upon the universe in the current moment.

Furthermore the fact that all our actions, including thoughts, intentions, perceptions and so on, are karmically potent at the quantum level for the future possibilities within the wavefunction of the universe means that everyone in existence is responsible for the future state of the universe! To use the phrase used by Wheeler 'the notes struck out by the participators' within the universe at every moment in time have implications for the current and future state of the universe at all levels! This is human responsibility on a cosmic, or universal, scale. The deep implications of quantum theory suggest that the nature of the relationship between all sentient beings is that of a universal interconnection at a deep, quantum, universal and implicate level of reality; this is shown in fig 14.12, another appropriation of the universally useful Wheeler **U**.

This image is beautifully amplified by the culmination of the Sufi parable written by Fariduddin Attar called *The Conference of the Birds*. A large group of birds are persuaded by a hoopoe[982] to go in search a mysterious king called the Simurgh. The 'mystical' journey is long and arduous with many difficulties; and it requires passing through seven valleys:

> **The Valley of the Quest:** within which the birds must renounce the world and all their possessions.
>
> **The Valley of Love:** within which they practice the development of love of the sought after divine unity.
>
> **The Valley of Understanding:** each bird experiences this valley different according to their nature. The essential aspect of this valley is the transcendence of the sense of selfhood and the consequent understanding of the nature of the ultimate divine unity.
>
> **The Valley of Detachment:** here all striving and desire cease – 'An icy wind blows through the soul, laying everything to waste...'
>
> **The Valley of Unity:** the unity of all phenomena is directly perceived.
>
> **The Valley of Astonishment:** the perception of unity is lost, leaving pain and sadness.
>
> **The Valley of Poverty and Annihilation:** the ultimate experience of unity beyond concepts.

Illusion of separation in realm of duality

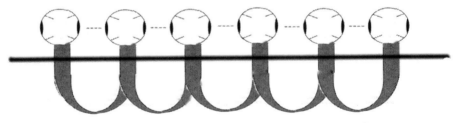

Truth of quantum and universal interconnection and unity

Fig 14.12

Thirty birds complete the journey and the punch-line of the story resides in the fact that the Arabic word 'Simurgh' means 'thirty birds':

And in the Centre of the Glory there
Beheld the Figure of – *Themselves* as 't were
Transfigured – looking to Themselves...
Until their Eyes themselves and *That* between
Did hesitate which *Seer* was, which *Seen*;
They That; That They: Another, yet the Same;
Dividual, yet One...
All who reflecting as reflected see
Themselves in Me and Me in Them; not Me,
But all of Me that a contracted Eye
Is comprehensive of Infinity...[983]

It is extraordinary that this remarkable twelfth century Sufi image of the multiple self-perceiving and self-reflecting strange loop of reality should find a echo, eight centuries later, in Wheeler's quantum 'Universal Eye' which might also be said to be 'comprehensive of Infinity'. In fact this Sufi tale is remarkably reminiscent of Wheeler's 'mystical' formulation that we met in the first chapter:

The Question is what is the Question?
Is it all a Magic Show?
Is Reality an Illusion?
What is the framework of the Machine?
Darwin's Puzzle: Natural Selection?
Where does Space-Time come from?
Is there any answer except that it comes from consciousness?
What is Out There?
T'is Ourselves?
Or, is IT all just a Magic Show?[984]

It seems that the fundamental universal religious mystical quest must be to understand the ultimate nature of the universe through the development of each person's embodied awareness to its fullest. Within Mahayana Buddhism the ultimate goal, usually achieved across countless lifetimes, is buddhahood, the universal nondual omniscient awareness. Chandrakirti's magnificent sixth century manual for bodhisattvas, or trainee buddhas, *Entrance to the Middle Way (Madhyamakavatara)*, maps out the Madhyamaka path to enlightenment in a series of ten stages, each of which is associated with a particular perfection (*paramita*); the stage beyond the tenth is, of course, buddhahood:

Supreme Joy - Perfection of Giving or Generosity: Bodhisattvas on the first level have a direct insight into the lack of self in all phenomena. This produces great joy and the ability to practice sublime and transcendent generosity in order to help all beings towards a similar realisation of 'emptiness'.

The Stainless – Perfection of Discipline or Ethics: The delight in the insight and experience of emptiness generates the ability to practice ethical conduct to perfection. This acts as an essential basis for the deepening of insight.

The Luminous – Perfection of Patience: Because of the supreme insight of the bodhisattvas they generate extraordinary compassion for sentient beings who lack such insight and therefore behave in destructive ways. This compassion manifests as the perfection of patience.

The Radiant – Perfection of Diligence or Effort: Bodhisattvas are diligent in practice and delight in overcoming obstacles because of the ever deepening levels of insight into the empty, yet luminous and radiant, nature of reality which manifests within their practice.

Difficult to Overcome – Perfection of Concentration: On this ground the power of the bodhisattva's meditative concentration becomes intense and stable. The stable concentration power of the focused mind on this ground is unswerving.

The Manifest – Perfection of Wisdom: On this ground the insight into the empty nature of all phenomena becomes unwavering and the awareness of the illusion-like nature of all phenomena is continuous.

Gone Far Beyond – Perfection of Methods or Skillful Means: On this ground bodhisattvas are able to move in and out of meditative absorption at will at every instant of time. Despite this, however, they do not turn away from the task of benefiting samsaric beings; they develop skillful means and methods in order to teach, cultivate and benefit all sentient beings.

The Immovable – Perfection of Aspiration: At this point the omniscience of buddhahood is assured. On the previous grounds bodhisattvas need to make effort but once this ground is attained progression towards the goal becomes automatic. On this ground all defilements are eliminated and samsaric existence is transcended. However, bodhisattvas are able to manifest within samsara in order to benefit sentient beings.

Excellent Intelligence – Perfection of Strength: On this level the ten strengths – of thought, proficiency, mastery, fearless ability, aspiration, paramitas, love, compassion, ultimate reality, being blessed by buddhas – become completely perfected. On this level also the knowledge of the nature, meaning, expression and insight regarding all phenomena becomes complete.

Cloud of Dharma – Perfection of Primordial Wisdom: When the final ground is achieved the bodhisattva is on the edge of buddhahood and can abide ceaselessly within the nondual awareness of the ultimate expanse, *the dharmadhatu*. Ultimate reality and its relative and conventional manifestations are experienced seamlessly; they are of 'one taste' and dualistic appearances subside. From this transcendent realm on the verge of buddhahood the bodhisattva, can rain down 'blessings', which are energies for positive transformation, for the benefit of all sentient beings:

> ...from the great Bodhisattvas residing on the tenth ground, there falls a spontaneous effortless shower of the rain of sacred Dharma, so that the excellent harvest of virtue might grow in the hearts of beings, bringing forth the fruit of their happiness.[985]

Buddhahood When bodhisattvas pass into the non-conceptual realm of complete elimination of duality they become coextensive with the universe, fully awakened ones. In a certain sense they can be said to become identical with the Mind, or wavefunction, of reality. However the extraordinary energy and power of accomplishment also alters the quality of the wavefunction, they alter its spiritual potentialities. By passing beyond into the liberation and omniscience of buddhahood the bodhisattva leaves an indestructible echo within the realm of the relative which can be activated by aspiring sentient beings according to their needs:

> The Buddhas, who, while dwelling in a body of form, actualize the dharmakaya and who, by virtue of hundreds of accumulations of merit, assume a sambhogakaya, all expound the profound and ultimate reality.[986]

When bodhisattvas finally attain full buddhahood they become 'transcendent conquerors' who are indeed 'comprehensive of infinity'. In fact they become co-extensive with the universe, merging with the universe. In this fashion they fulfill the only function that the universe has, which is to perceive itself in its full nature which is, of course, limitless. Furthermore, through the nature of the spiritual path itself, the continuous training in, aspiration towards and the intention to work tirelessly for the alleviation of suffering and the leading of all sentient beings towards enlightenment, buddhas acquire dramatic faculties to guide others along the path to enlightenment:

> These pure ones, by simply directing their intention,
> Can display worlds to the reaches of space in the area
> of one atom,
> And make an atom pervade the space of limitless
> worlds,

But without enlarging the atoms or shrinking the worlds

…

Buddhas remember all of the births they took in cyclic existence due to ignorance;
They also know the births of others-all sentient beings-
And the bases and locations of these births.

…

Buddhas know the deaths and births of each sentient being
In all world realms as limitless as space.
They know these in all their variety in a single instant,
In an unattached, completely pure, and limitless way …

Through the power of their omniscient knowledge, the victorious ones rapidly
Cognize the dissolutions of mental afflictions and habitual tendencies.
They also know how the intelligence of their students causes
the cessation of mental afflictions.[987]

Compassionately, [they] lead all worldly deceptive beings, who are bound in the nooses of [cyclic existence],
To the ground of nirvana

…

Since worldly beings are afflicted by the pollutants that give rise to the shortcomings
They do not enter the deep sphere of the experience of the Buddhas.
Nevertheless, you, the sugatas, do not give up on them…
…because, before, you made the promise 'I will liberate sentient beings.'

For Mahayana Buddhism the salvation of the manifested Universe is not dependent upon some external entity. Such an independent, external entity does not exist. It is the responsibility of each and every sentient being, at some point in the seemingly unending sequence of rebirths in samsara, to make the effort and become a buddha. Buddhahood is the fulfillment of the capacity to transcend the limitations of the manifested universe, and thereby engage in the universal compassionate activity of helping all unenlightened sentient beings to reach the same state.

This is the achievement of the final and only worth-while goal of existence and the universe. This new perspective upon the Quantum Mind-Only Universe has dramatic consequences. As Henry Stapp puts it:

Ones weighting of the welfare of the whole, and one's sensitivity to the feelings of others will surely be enhanced when the individual sees that his or her own judgments and efforts as causally effective – hence important – inputs into a cooperative effort to develop the vast yet-to-be-fixed potentialities of a quantum universe that, as Bohr emphasised, can be properly conceived only as an intricately interconnected whole.[988]

The Buddhist perspective, in common with all esoteric religious perspectives, is quite clear about the kind of potentiality that it is essential to develop. As Master Hsing Yun says:

> A buddha is a human being who has realised that he is a buddha; a human being is a buddha who has not yet realised that he is one.[989]

When a human being realizes the full potential of the universal awareness that resides at the heart of the process of reality he or she becomes co-extensive with that universal awareness and thereby becomes a buddha; a fully awakened being. It is the universal spiritual task of all human beings to awaken to the task, and then to completely realise that task of becoming fully awakened to the universal awareness-consciousness. And an essential component of that task is to encourage and help all other sentient beings along the path to full awakening or enlightenment; the embodiment of the ultimately empty yet effulgent luminosity of the universal awareness-consciousness within the midst of samsara. As the great Buddhist yogi Milarepa said:

> Regard this life as a dream and illusion,
> And cultivate compassion for those who do not realize this.[990]

Sources and Notes

[1] Mu Soeng (2010) p40

[2] Mu Soeng (2010) p37

[3] Carroll, Sean (2010) p 230

[4] Carroll, Sean (2010) p402

[5] Vedral, Vlatko (2010) p200

[6] Vedral, Vlatko (2010) p211

[7] Personal email communication.

[8] Thupten Jinpa (2008)

[9] Thupten Jinpa (2008)

[10] Wilczeck, Frank (2008) page xiii

[11] Science and Ultimate Reality p201

[12] Barrow, John D., Davies, Paul C. W., Harper, Charles L. (eds) (2004) p577 – Wheeler, J A (1999) 'Information, physics, quantum: the search for links.' In *Feynman and Computation: Exploring the Limits of Computers*, ed A. J. G. Hey, p309 (314). Cambridge, MA: Perseus Books.

[13] Herbert, Nick (1985) p16

[14] Zukav, Gary (1979)

[15] Dalai Lama, H. H. (2008)

[16] d'Espagnat, Bernard, 'The Quantum Theory and Reality' Scientific American, Nov. 197

[17] N. Bohr, Speech on quantum theory at *Celebrazionne del Secondo Centenario della Nascita di Luigi Galvani*, Bologna, Italy, October 1937.

[18] Smolin, Lee (2002) p36

[19] Al-Khalili, Jim (2003) p85

[20] Penrose, Roger (1999) p295

[21] Penrose, Roger (1995).p237

[22] Discover September 2009

[23] Baggott, Jim (2004) p105

[24] Kaku, Michio (1995).

[25] Zukav, Gary (1979) p121

[26] Herbert, Nick (1985) p15

[27] Herbert, Nick (1985) p15

[28] Rosenblum, Bruce and Kuttner, Fred (2006) p87

[29] Smolin, Lee (2002) p34

[30] Smolin, Lee (2002) p34

[31] Smolin, Lee (2002)

[32] Aharanov, Yakir and Rohrlich, Daniel (2005) p1

[33] Aharanov, Yakir and Rohrlich, Daniel (2005) p1

[34] Baggott, Jim (2004) p98

[35] Wallace, B. Alan (2003) p87

[36] Penrose, Roger (1995) p309

[37] Oerter, Robert (2006) p49

[38] Barrow, John D., Davies, Paul C. W., Harper, Charles L. (eds) (2004) p221 – Steinberg, Aephraim M.: *Speakable and unspeakable, past and future.*

[39] Stenger, Victor (1996)

[40] WILCZEK, FRANK 'On the Origin of Mass' - MIT PHYSICS ANNUAL 2003

[41] Bryson, Bill 'Notes From a Large Hadron Collider' - Times 5 Nov 2009

[42] Dennett, Daniel (1991) p33

[43] Dyson, Freeman (2001) p251

[44] Dennett, Daniel (1995) p27

[45] Stapp, Henry (2004) p197

[46] Stapp, Henry (2004)

[47] Barrow, John D., Davies, Paul C. W., Harper, Charles L. (eds) (2004) p577 – Wheeler, J A (1999) 'Information, physics, quantum: the search for links.' In *Feynman and Computation: Exploring the Limits of Computers*, ed A. J. G. Hey, p309 (314). Cambridge, MA: Perseus Books.

[48] Stapp, Henry (2004) p199

[49] Rosenblum, Bruce and Kuttner, Fred (2006) p

[50] Stapp, Henry (2004) p223

[51] Schrödinger, E. (1944) p121.

[52] Das Wesen der Materie" (The Nature of Matter), speech at Florence, Italy, 1944 (from Archiv zur Geschichte der Max-Planck-Gesellschaft, Abt. Va, Rep. 11 Planck, Nr. 1797)

[53] Michael Brooks: 'The Second Quantum Revolution,' New Scientist 23rd June 2007

[54] Vlatko Vedral quoted in New Scientist 23rd June 2007

[55] New Scientist 23rd June 2007

[56] Oerter, Robert (2006) p130

[57] Feynman, Richard (1988) p7

[58] Yogachara literally means 'practitioners of Yoga' because of their commitment to the practice of meditation, Vijnanavada, or 'way of cognition' describes the epistemological-metaphysical understanding of the process of reality as a process based upon the operation of consciousness. The Chittamatra perspective emphasises the Mind-Only aspect, often Yogachara and Chittamatra are conflated together. In this work they are treated as differing perspectives upon the same metaphysical viewpoint.

[59] Thrangu Rinpoche, Kenchen (2001)

[60] Science & Ultimate Reality p451

[61] Dawkins, R (2004) – 'The Great Convergence'

[62] Michael Shermer, *"Quantum Quackery"*, Scientific American, January 2005

[63] Bohm, D (2002)

[64] Bohm, D (2002) p219

[65] Interview with Amit Goswami

[66] Rosenblum, Bruce and Kuttner, Fred (2006) p67

[67] Dolling, L.M.; Gianelli, A. F. & Statile, G. N. (eds) (2003) p491 – John A. Wheeler (1978): 'The 'Past' and the 'Delayed Choice' Double-Slit Experiment.'

[68] Thrangu Rinpoche, Kenchen (2001) p16

[69] Kaufman, Marc: 'Shining a Light on a Dream' – FQ(x) (The Foundational Questions Institute) February 8th 2008.

[70] Dolling, L.M.; Gianelli, A. F. & Statile, G. N. (eds) (2003) p492 – John A. Wheeler (1978): 'The 'Past' and the 'Delayed Choice' Double-Slit Experiment.'

[71] Sarfatti , Jack 'Wheeler's World: It From Bit?' - Internet Science Education Project, San Francisco, CA.

[72] Brunnhölzl, Karl (2007) *Straight from the Heart: Buddhist Pith Instructions* p25

[73] Goswami, Amit (2008) p22

[74] Penrose, Roger (1995) p313

[75] Al-Khalili, Jim (2003) p294

[76] Al-Khalili, Jim (2003) p148

[77] Penrose, Roger (1995) p309

[78] Rosenblum, Bruce and Kuttner, Fred (2006) p139

[79] Capra, Fritjov (1975) p152

[80] Capra, Fritjov (1975)

[81] Internet document - Newsletter of the American Scientific Affiliation - Canadian Scientific & Christian Affiliation Volume 21 Number 6 December 1979/January 1980.

[82] Wilber, Ken (Editor) (1982) p219 'The Tao of Physics Revisited'

[83] Thupten Jinpa (2008) p98

[84] Kumar, M (2008) p198

[85] Wilczeck, Frank (2008)

[86] Dolling, L.M.; Gianelli, A. F. & Statile, G. N. (eds) (2003) p432 – Niels Bohr: 'Debate with Einstein' in *Philosophical Essays Vol2.*

[87] Piburn, Sidney(1990) p67

[88] Gould, Stephen Jay (2002)

[89] Wilber, Ken (Editor) (1982) p224

[90] Woit's blog - Not Even Wrong: www.math.columbia.edu/~woit/wordpress/?p=588

[91] Wallace, B. Alan (2007) page ix

[92] Stapp, Henry (2004)

[93] Oppenheimer, Robert (1954) p8-9

[94] Fritjof Capra, interviewed by Renee Weber in *The Holographic Paradigm* (page 217–218)

[95] Penrose, Roger (1999) p295

[96] Gribben, John (2009) p511-512

[97] Reviews of Modern Physics vol XXI p343

[98] Science fiction novel by John Wyndham

[99] Rosenblum, Bruce and Kuttner, Fred (2006) p201

[100] Shermer, Michael: 'Quantum Quackery' - January 2005 Scientific American Magazine

[101] Wolf, Fred Alan: Dr. Quantum Presents: A User's Guide to Your Universe. Audio CD. (www.learnoutloud.com/Sale-Section/Self-Development/Spirituality/Dr-Quantum-Presents-A-Users-Guide-to-Your-Universe/19730)

[102] Rosenblum, Bruce and Kuttner, Fred (2006) website (quantumenigma.com)

[103] Rosenblum, Bruce and Kuttner, Fred (2006) p154

[104] Rosenblum, Bruce and Kuttner, Fred (2006)

[105] Rosenblum, Bruce and Kuttner, Fred (2006) p152

[106] Rosenblum, Bruce and Kuttner, Fred (2006) p156

[107] d'Espagnat, Bernard (2006) p433

[108] d'Espagnat, Bernard (2006) p440

[109] Brunnhölzl, Karl (2004) p120

[110] Brunnhölzl, Karl (2004) p79

[111] Wilczeck, Frank (2008) p3

[112] Wilczek tells us that he rejected the term 'Matrix' because of its cinematic associations..

[113] Brunnhölzl, Karl (2004) p73

[114] Brunnhölzl, Karl (2004)

[115] Chandrakirti and Jamgon Mipham (2002)

[116] There has been some disagreement in Western scholarship on the use of the terms Madhyamaka and Madhyamika. Great Sanskritists such as T. R. V. Murti, a member of the Sanskrit Commission set up by the Indian government in 1959, advocated the use of "Madhyamika" on all occasions. Others use Madhyamaka for the system and the texts, and Madhyamika for its advocates. This is the use employed within this work.

[117] Brunnhölzl, Karl (2004) p114

[118] Wallace, B. Alan (2003) p16

[119] Shantarakshita (2005 - Padmakara Translation Group) p97

[120] Herbert, Nick (1985) p16

[121] Herbert, Nick (1985) p17

[122] Herbert, Nick (1985) p18 – quoting Bohm

[123] Herbert, Nick (1985) p19

[124] Herbert, Nick (1985) p20

[125] Herbert, Nick (1985) p24

[126] Herbert, Nick (1985) p26

[127] Ramanan, K. Venkata (1998) p38

[128] A realised being who correctly perceives the nature of reality.

[129] Chandrakirti and Jamgon Mipham (2002) p74

[130] Dolling, L.M.; Gianelli, A. F. & Statile, G. N. (eds) (2003) p393 – Niels Bohr: 'Complementarity and the New Quantum Theory' in Nature (1928).

[131] Brunnhölzl, Karl (2004) p73

[132] Khenpo Tsultrum Gyamtso (2003) p59

[133] Herbert, Nick (1985) p46

[134] Brunnhölzl, Karl (2004) p257

[135] See Kumar, M (2008) for full account of the interchange.

[136] Avatamsaka Sutra

[137] Chown, Marcus (2007). *Quantum Physics Cannot Hurt You*

[138] Bohm, David (2003) p156

[139] Chown, Marcus (2009) p3

[140] The title of Chown's first chapter.

[141] Lucretius - On the Nature of the Universe.

[142] Rosenblum, Bruce and Kuttner, Fred (2006) p60

[143] Rosenblum, Bruce and Kuttner, Fred (2006) p60

[144] Satinover, Jeffrey (2001) p141

[145] Chown, Marcus (2009) p15

[146] Chown, Marcus (2009) p16

[147] Chown, Marcus (2009) p33

[148] Stapp, Henry (2004) p41

[149] Brunnhölzl, Karl (2004) p507

[150] Chown, Marcus (2009) p30

[151] Chown, Marcus (2009) p16

[152] Zajonc, Arthur (2004) p19

[153] Bell's inequality is a mathematical expression which can be used to indicate whether related objects are carrying 'hidden' local information. See any introduction to quantum physics for details.

[154] Chown, Marcus (2007). *Quantum Physics Cannot Hurt You* p59

[155] Goswami, Amit (1995)

[156] Bohm, D (2002) p219

[157] Bohm, D (2002) p237

[158] Bohm, D (2002) p238

[159] A term used by Tibetan Buddhist philosophers to indicate something which is entirely impossible (other than as a concept of non-existence).

[160] Hopkins, Jeffrey (1996) p9

[161] Chown, Marcus (2003) p77

[162] Dolling, L.M.; Gianelli, A. F. & Statile, G. N. (eds) (2003) p490 – John A. Wheeler (1978): 'The 'Past' and the 'Delayed Choice' Double-Slit Experiment.'

[163] Penrose, Roger (1999) p292

[164] Garfield, Jay (1995) p2

[165] Internet: threeplusone.com/misc/quotes

[166] Barrow, John D., Davies, Paul C. W., Harper, Charles L. (eds) (2004) page xi

[167] Feynman, Richard (1988) p130

[168] Al-Khalili, Jim (2003)

[169] Rosenblum, Bruce and Kuttner, Fred (2006) p67

[170] Barrow, John D., Davies, Paul C. W., Harper, Charles L. (eds) (2004) p201 – Anton Zeilinger: 'Why the quantum? "It" from bit"? A participatory universe? Three far-reaching challenges from John Archibald Wheeler and their relation to experiment.'

[171] Thupten Jinpa (2008) p50

[172] A 'rabbits horn' and the 'son of a barren woman' are Madhyamaka indicators of impossible entities.

[173] Bohm, D (2002) p219

[174] Shantarakshita (2005 - Padmakara Translation Group) p295

[175] Shantarakshita (2005 - Padmakara Translation Group) p295

[176] Shantarakshita (2005 - Padmakara Translation Group) p295

[177] Smolin, Lee (2002)

[178] Allday, Jonathan (2009) p408

[179] Allday, Jonathan (2009) p4

[180] Rosenblum, Bruce and Kuttner, Fred (2006) p179

[181] 'Yogachara' means practitioner of Yoga (i.e. meditation) – in this work, however, it primarily indicates the Vijnanavada, or Cognition-Only, perspective.

[182] Brunnhölzl, Karl (2004) p228

[183] Chown, Marcus (2007) p93

[184] Geshe Sonam Rinchen (2006) p19

[185] Kaku, Michio (2006) p148

[186] Al-Khalili, Jim (2003) p77-78

[187] Herbert, Nick (1985) p124

[188] The following discussion and diagrams are based on www.chem1.com/acad/webtut/bonding/TunnelBond.html

[189] Khenpo Tsultrum Gyamtso (2003) p95

[190] Brunnhölzl, Karl (2004) p507

[191] Aczel, Amir D. (2002) p85

[192] Barrett, Jeffrey A. (2001)

[193] Ghirardi, Giancarlo (2005) p348

[194] Oppenheimer, Robert (1954) pp 8-9

[195] Ghirardi, Giancarlo (2005) p70

[196] Brunnhölzl, Karl (2004) p214

[197] Stapp, Henry (1995) – Why Classical Mechanics Cannot Naturally Accommodate Consciousness But Quantum Mechanics Can.

[198] Bohm, D (2002) p95

[199] Penrose, Roger (1995) p237

[200] Penrose, Roger (1995) p237

[201] Oerter, Robert (2006) p59

[202] Capra, Fritjov (1975)

[203] Bohm, D (2002) p219

[204] Interview with Amit Goswami

[205] Bohm, D (2002) p219

[206] Smolin, Lee (2006) p13

[207] Oerter, Robert (2006) p59

[208] Oerter, Robert (2006)

[209] Oerter, Robert (2006)

[210] Baggott, Jim (2004) p59

[211] Baggott, Jim (2004) p59

[212] Baggott, Jim (2004) p28

[213] Baggott, Jim (2004) p31

[214] Al-Khalili, Jim (2003) p66

[215] Rosenblum, Bruce and Kuttner, Fred (2006) p75

[216] Penrose, Roger (1999) p293

[217] Al-Khalili, Jim (2003) p67

[218] The many worlds interpretation supposedly avoids this model. But even with the many-worlds interpretation an individual inside one world would perceive the situation in these terms.

[219] Penrose, Roger (1995) p309

[220] Al-Khalili, Jim (2003) p85-86

[221] Al-Khalili, Jim (2003) p82

[222] Al-Khalili, Jim (2003) p85

[223] Al-Khalili, Jim (2003) p153

[224] Dolling, L.M.; Gianelli, A. F. & Statile, G. N. (eds) (2003) p432 – Niels Bohr: 'Debate with Einstein' in *Philosophical Essays Vol2*.

[225] Al-Khalili, Jim (2003) p86

[226] Hay, Tony & Walters, Patrick (2003) p157

[227] Hay, Tony & Walters, Patrick (2003) p 159.

[228] Penrose, Roger (1995) p308

[229] Baggott, Jim (2004) p97

[230] Dolling, L.M.; Gianelli, A. F. & Statile, G. N. (eds) (2003) p527 – John Stewart Bell (1971): 'Introduction to the Hidden Variable Question' in the *Proceedings of the International School of Physics*.

[231] Polkinghorne, John (2002).p56

[232] Greene, Brian (2004) p83

[233] Greene, Brian (2004) p81

[234] Penrose, Roger (1995) p300

[235] Aczel, Amir D. (2002) p203

[236] Thupten Jinpa (2008) p98

[237] Das Wesen der Materie" (The Nature of Matter), speech at Florence, Italy, 1944 (from Archiv zur Geschichte der Max-Planck-Gesellschaft, Abt. Va, Rep. 11 Planck, Nr. 1797)

[238] *The Observer* (January 25th, 1931)

[239] Albert, David Z. (1992) p11

[240] Brunnhölzl, Karl (2004) p84

[241] www.namgyal.org

[242] Heisenberg, W (1999)

[243] Albert, David Z. (1992) p33

[244] Albert, David Z. (1992) p11

[245] Albert, David Z. (1992) p11

[246] Albert, David Z. (1992) p15

[247] Albert, David Z. (1992) p15

[248] Brunnhölzl, Karl (2007) p34

[249] Brunnhölzl, Karl (2007) p142

[250] Garfield, Jay L. & Geshe Ngawang Samten (Translators) (2006) p154

[251] Penrose, Roger (1995) p313

[252] Westerhoff, Jan (2009) p40

[253] Baggott, Jim (2004) p105

[254] Dolling, L.M.; Gianelli, A. F. & Statile, G. N. (eds) (2003) p432 – Niels Bohr: 'Debate with Einstein' in *Philosophical Essays Vol2*.

[255] Dolling, L.M.; Gianelli, A. F. & Statile, G. N. (eds) (2003) p432 – Niels Bohr: 'Debate with Einstein' in *Philosophical Essays Vol2*.

[256] Rosenblum, Bruce and Kuttner, Fred (2006) p157

[257] Baggott, Jim (2004) p109

[258] Dolling, L.M.; Gianelli, A. F. & Statile, G. N. (eds) (2003) p432 – Niels Bohr: 'Debate with Einstein' in *Philosophical Essays Vol2*.

[259] Al-Khalili, Jim (2003) p235

[260] Garfield, Jay (1995) p250

[261] Kaufman, Marc February 8, 2008 – 'Shining a Light on a Dream' (www.fqxi.org).

[262] Joos, Erich (2006). 'The Emergence of Classicality from Quantum Theory' in *The Re-Emergence of Emergence: The Emergentist Hypothesis from Science to Religion* (Eds: Philip Clayton and Paul Davies). Oxford: Oxford University Press.

[263] Khenpo Tsultrum Gyamtso (2003) p52

[264] Khenpo Tsultrum Gyamtso (2003) p53

[265] Khenpo Tsultrum Gyamtso (2003) p35

[266] To be precise this is the fundamental procedure of the Madhyamaka Prasangika.

[267] The Buddha revealed his insights into the nature of reality in three levels, or turnings of the wheel of dharma. The analysis into the skandhas is a first turning teaching.

[268] According to Hopkins the term 'heap' derives from the fact that the Buddha used piles of rice in his exposition of the skandhas.

[269] Hopkins, Jeffrey (1996) p181

[270] Brunnhölzl, Karl (2004) p762

[271] Shantarakshita (2005 - Padmakara Translation Group) p53

[272] Shantarakshita (2005 - Padmakara Translation Group) p53

[273] Shantarakshita (2005 - Padmakara Translation Group) p53

[274] Brunnhölzl, Karl (2004) p236

[275] Bohm, David (2002) p220

[276] Smolin, Lee (2002)

[277] Garfield, Jay (1995) p3

[278] Chandrakirti and Jamgon Mipham (2002) p70

[279] BBC Focus Magazine Jan 2009

[280] Brunnhölzl, Karl (2007) *Straight from the Heart: Buddhist Pith Instructions*

[281] Smolin, Lee (2002) p53

[282] Brunnhölzl, Karl (2007) *Straight from the Heart: Buddhist Pith Instructions* p27

[283] Baggott, Jim (2005) p228

[284] Garfield, Jay (1995) (Translator) p250

[285] Rae, Alastair I. M. (2006)

[286] Brunnhölzl, Karl (2004) p78

[287] Stapp, Henry (2004) p41

[288] Penrose, Roger (1999) & Al-Khalili, Jim (2003)

[289] Gribben, John (1996) p 150

[290] Penrose, Roger (1995) p313

[291] Smolin, Lee (2002) p53

[292] Joos, Erich (2006). 'The Emergence of Classicality from Quantum Theory' in *The Re-Emergence of Emergence: The Emergentist Hypothesis from Science to Religion* (Eds: Philip Clayton and Paul Davies). Oxford: Oxford University Press.

[293] Brunnhölzl, Karl (2004) p73

[294] Brunnhölzl, Karl (2004) p75

[295] Brunnhölzl, Karl (2004) p79 (Yogins = realised beings)

[296] Hopkins, Jeffrey (1996) p405

[297] Someone adept in the practice of meditation techniques which reach non-dual levels of experience.

[298] Thrangu Rinpoche, Kenchen (2001) p106

[299] Hopkins, Jeffrey (1996) p405

[300] Geshe Yeshe Tobden (2005) p244

[301] Mahayana schools of Buddhism accept the reincarnation or transmigration of a subtle mind, this subtle mind carries the seeds of enlightenment.

[302] Brunnhölzl, Karl (2007) *Straight from the Heart: Buddhist Pith Instructions* p68

[303] Brunnhölzl, Karl (2007) *In Praise of Dharmadhatu* p119

[304] Brunnhölzl, Karl (2007) *Straight from the Heart: Buddhist Pith Instructions* p80

[305] The term 'consciousness' is used here in a general manner, in opposition to 'matter'; it is important to be aware that often the term vijnana (Sanskrit) trans as consciousness – refers to dualistic consciousness. It is necessary always to be aware of such subtleties.

[306] Brunnhölzl, Karl (2007) *Straight from the Heart: Buddhist Pith Instructions* p62

[307] Rigpa Wiki (www.rigpawiki.org)

[308] See Hopkins, Jeffrey (2003) - *Emptiness in the Mind Only School of Buddhism* etc.

[309] Rosenblum, Bruce and Kuttner, Fred (2006) p179

[310] Herbert, Nick: 'Holistic Physics -or- Introduction to Quantum Tantra' – Internet document (www.southerncrossreview.org/16/herbert.essay.htm)

[311] Rigpa Wiki (www.rigpawiki.org)

[312] Brunnhölzl, Karl (2007) *Straight from the Heart: Buddhist Pith Instructions* p49

[313] Stapp, Henry: 'The Effect of Mind upon Brain' p6

[314] Hopkins, Jeffrey (1996) p389

[315] d' Espagnat, B (2006) p348

[316] Greene, Brian (2004) p482-3

[317] Wheeler quoted in Barrow, John D., Davies, Paul C. W., Harper, Charles L. (eds) (2004) p73 – Freeman J. Dyson: 'Thought-experiments in honor of John Archibald Wheeler.'

[318] Becker, Kate: 'Down the Rabbit Hole.' www.fqxi.org - September 2009

[319] Scott Aaronson – cited in Becker, Kate: 'Down the Rabbit Hole.' www.fqxi.org - September 2009

[320] Becker, Kate: 'Down the Rabbit Hole.' www.fqxi.org - September 2009

[321] Cited in Baggott, Jim (2005) p239

[322] Bohm, David (2002) p220

[323] Hawking, Stephen (1998) p12

[324] Penrose, R. 2005. 'The Theory of Everything' Nature Magazine

[325] Barrow, John D., Davies, Paul C. W., Harper, Charles L. (eds) (2004) p451 – Andrei Linde: 'Inflation, quantum cosmology and the anthropic principle.'

[326] Brunnhölzl, Karl (2007) *Straight from the Heart: Buddhist Pith Instructions* p27.

[327] Barrow, John D., Davies, Paul C. W., Harper, Charles L. (eds) (2004) p136 – Wojciech H. Zurek: 'Quantum Darwinism and envariance.'

[328] Bohm, David (2002) and the Implicate Order p237

[329] Here consciousness is used in its western general sense – synonymous with 'mind', 'awareness'.

[330] Bohm, David (2003) p104-5

[331] d' Espagnat, B (2006) p417

[332] d' Espagnat, B (2006) p425

[333] Chandrakirti and Jamgon Mipham (2002) p82

[334] Bohm, David (2003) p104

[335] Shantarakshita (2005 - Padmakara Translation Group) p295 p54

[336] Stapp, Henry (2004) p128

[337] Jung, C. G. (1981) p48

[338] Wolfgang Pauli, letter to M. Fierz, August 12, 1948

[339] Brunnhölzl, Karl (2004) p606.

[340] Stapp, Henry (2004) p239

[341] Brunnhölzl, Karl (2004)

[342] Stapp, Henry (2004) p183

[343] Zajonc, Arthur (Editor) (2004)

[344] Thrangu Rinpoche, Kenchen (2001) p28

[345] Barrow, John D., Davies, Paul C. W., Harper, Charles L. (eds) (2004) p136 – Wojciech H. Zurek: 'Quantum Darwinism and envariance.'

[346] Rahula, Walpola (1974) p32

[347] Stapp, Henry (2007) p22-23

[348] Stapp, Henry (2007) p20

[349] Wheeler quoted in Barrow, John D., Davies, Paul C. W., Harper, Charles L. (eds) (2004) p73 – Freeman J. Dyson: 'Thought-experiments in honor of John Archibald Wheeler.'

[350] Thrangu Rinpoche, Kenchen (2001) p34-35

[351] Quoted in Stapp, Henry (2007) p162

[352] Bohm, David (2002) p250

[353] Bohm, David (2002) p227

[354] Bohm, David (2002) p250

[355] Stapp, Henry (2004) p222

[356] Stapp, Henry (2004) p223

[357] Stapp, Henry (2004) p197

[358] Stapp, Henry (2004) p120

[359] Bohm, David (2003) p131

[360] Interview with David Bohm, conducted by F. David Peat and John Briggs, was originally published in Omni, January 1987

[361] Talbot, Michael (1992) p54

[362] Hopkins, Jeffrey (1996) p375

[363] John D., Davies, Paul C. W., Harper, Charles L. (eds) (2004) p577 – Wheeler, J A (1999) 'Information, physics, quantum: the search for links.' In *Feynman and Computation: Exploring the Limits of Computers*, ed A. J. G. Hey, p309 (314). Cambridge, MA: Perseus Books.

[364] Barrow, D. John & Tipler, Frank J. (1986)

[365] Stapp, Henry (2004) p192

[366] Stapp, Henry (2004) p194

[367] Thrangu Rinpoche, Kenchen (2001) p41

[368] Brunnhölzl, Karl (2009) p140

[369] Piet Hut, Mark Alford, and Max Tegmark (2009): 'On Math, Matter and Mind' p6 (Foundations of Physics)

[370] Brunnhölzl, Karl (2009) p353

[371] Walpola, Rahula (1974)

[372] Waldron, William S. (2003)

[373] This identification is the step prior to the final Madhyamika analysis of the mind into emptiness.

[374] Thrangu Rinpoche, Kenchen (2001) p34

[375] Brunnhölzl, Karl (2009)

[376] Brunnhölzl, Karl (2009) p270

[377] Brunnhölzl, Karl (2009) p464

[378] Brunnhölzl, Karl (2009) p280

[379] Quantum mechanics may explain how humans smell (www.neuroquantology.com/repository/index.php?option=com_content&view=article&id=86: quantum-mechanics-may-explain-how-humans-smell&catid=296:quantum-biology&Itemid=50)

[380] Thrangu Rinpoche, Kenchen (2001) p36

[381] Thrangu Rinpoche, Kenchen (2001) p37

[382] Thrangu Rinpoche, Kenchen (2001) p38

[383] Thrangu Rinpoche, Kenchen (2001) p38

[384] Britannica Online Dictionary

[385] Spotted in advertisement in Hi-Fi magazine – source no longer known.

[386] Chandrakirti and Jamgon Mipham (2002) p 80

[387] Chandrakirti and Jamgon Mipham (2002) p256

[388] Thrangu Rinpoche, Kenchen (2001) p43

[389] Nyanaponika Thera: 'Karma and its Fruit' in Samuel Bercholz (Editor), Sherab Chodzin Kohn (Editor): *The Buddha and His Teachings* – Shambhala (2002) p123

[390] Dolling, L.M.; Gianelli, A. F. & Statile, G. N. (eds) (2003) p469 – Erwin Schrödinger (1952): 'Are There Quantum Jumps.'

[391] Dolling, L.M.; Gianelli, A. F. & Statile, G. N. (eds) (2003) p469 – Erwin Schrödinger (1952): 'Are There Quantum Jumps.'

[392] Dolling, L.M.; Gianelli, A. F. & Statile, G. N. (eds) (2003) p469 – Erwin Schrödinger (1952): 'Are There Quantum Jumps.'

[393] Joos, Erich (2006). 'The Emergence of Classicality from Quantum Theory' in *The Re-Emergence of Emergence: The Emergentist Hypothesis from Science to Religion* (Eds: Philip Clayton and Paul Davies). Oxford: Oxford University Press.

[394] Stapp, Henry (2004)

[395] Wheeler information, physics, quantum: The search for links" in W. Zurek (ed.) *Complexity, Entropy, and the Physics of Information.* Redwood City, CA: Addison-Wesley.

[396] Das Wesen der Materie" (The Nature of Matter), speech at Florence, Italy, 1944 (from Archiv zur Geschichte der Max-Planck-Gesellschaft, Abt. Va, Rep. 11 Planck, Nr. 1797)

[397] Hopkins, Jeffrey (2006) p138

[398] Hopkins, Jeffrey (1996) p368

[399] Brunnhölzl, Karl (2007) p77

[400] Stapp, Henry (2007) p133

[401] Barrow, John D., Davies, Paul C. W., Harper, Charles L. (eds) (2004) p129 – Wojciech H. Zurek: 'Quantum Darwinism and envariance.'

[402] Barrow, John D., Davies, Paul C. W., Harper, Charles L. (eds) (2004) p121 – Wojciech H. Zurek: 'Quantum Darwinism and envariance.'

[403] Barrow, John D., Davies, Paul C. W., Harper, Charles L. (eds) (2004) p136 – Wojciech H. Zurek: 'Quantum Darwinism and envariance.'

[404] Barrow, John D., Davies, Paul C. W., Harper, Charles L. (eds) (2004) – Wojciech H. Zurek: 'Quantum Darwinism and envariance.'

[405] 'The Evolution of Reality' – www.fqxi.org/community/articles/display/122 (The Foundational Questions Institute) November 10, 2009.

[406] Stapp, Henry (2004) p268

[407] Dawkins, Richard (1999) p109

[408] Stapp, Henry (2007) p139

[409] Barrow, John D., Davies, Paul C. W., Harper, Charles L. (eds) (2004) p136 – Wojciech H. Zurek: 'Quantum Darwinism and envariance.'

[410] Talbot, Michael (1992)

[411] Thrangu Rinpoche, Kenchen (2001)p35

[412] www.gaianxaos.com/notes/morphogenetic_fields.htm

[413] Barrow, John D., Davies, Paul C. W., Harper, Charles L. (eds) (2004) page xi

[414] Hawking, Stephen (1998)

[415] Guardian obituary – Michael Carlson

[416] Thrangu Rinpoche, Kenchen (2002) p32

[417] Walpola, Rahula (1974) p32 – Arahant = enlightened being.

[418] Brunnhölzl, Karl (2004)

[419] Brunnhölzl, Karl (2004) p332

[420] Dharma Fellowship (www.dharmafellowship.org/library/essays/yogacara-part2.htm).

[421] Woolfson, Adrian (2000) p74

[422] Barrow, D. John & Tipler, Frank J. (1986) p105

[423] Woolfson, Adrian (2000) p83

[424] Woolfson, Adrian (2000) p76

[425] Khendrup Norsang Gyatso (2004)

[426] Barrow, John D., Davies, Paul C. W., Harper, Charles L. (eds) (2004) p450 – Andrei Linde: 'Inflation, quantum cosmology and the anthropic principle.'

[427] Barrow, John D., Davies, Paul C. W., Harper, Charles L. (eds) (2004) p450 – Andrei Linde: 'Inflation, quantum cosmology and the anthropic principle.'

[428] IBM Journal of Research and Development (See - Davies, Paul (2007))

[429] Sheldrake, Rupert (2009)

[430] Sheldrake, Rupert (2009)

[431] Sheldrake, Rupert (2009) p311

[432] Sheldrake, Rupert:'Mind, Memory, and Archetype Morphic Resonance and the Collective Unconscious' (www.sheldrake.org/papers/Morphic/morphic1_paper.html)

[433] Wheeler quoted in Barrow, John D., Davies, Paul C. W., Harper, Charles L. (eds) (2004) p73 – Freeman J. Dyson: 'Thought-experiments in honor of John Archibald Wheeler.'

[434] Jamgon Kongtrul & Kalu Rinpoche Translation Group (1995) p197.

[435] Davies, Paul (2007) page x

[436] New Scientist 30th June 1970 p34

[437] Jamgon Kongtrul & Kalu Rinpoche Translation Group (1995) p172

[438] Chown, Marcus (2007) p144-145

[439] Chandrakirti and Jamgon Mipham (2002) p82

[440] Dawkins, Richard (2006). *The Blind Watchmaker*.

[441] Stapp, Henry (2004) p182

[442] Thrangu Rinpoche, Kenchen (2001) p28-29

[443] Waldron, William S. (2003) p168

[444] Waldron, William S. (2003) p169

[445] Jamgon Kongtrul & Kalu Rinpoche Translation Group (1995)

[446] Hopkins, Jeffrey (2003) p31-32

[447] Gribben, John (1996) p 150

[448] Penrose, Roger (2005) p532

[449] Al-Khalili, Jim (2003) p146

s[450] Jamgon Kongtrul & Kalu Rinpoche Translation Group (1995) p100

[451] Barrow, John D., Davies, Paul C. W., Harper, Charles L. (eds) (2004) p115 – H. Dieter Zeh: 'The wave function: it or bit?'

[452] Lockwood, Michael (2005) p303

[453] Lockwood, Michael (2005) p304

[454] Barrow, D. John & Tipler, Frank J. (1986) p465

[455] Penrose, Roger (1999) p377

[456] Baggott, Jim (2004). p245

[457] Baggott, Jim (2004). p245

[458] Barrow, D. John & Tipler, Frank J. (1986)

[459] Barrow, D. John & Tipler, Frank J. (1986) p469

[460] Barrow, D. John & Tipler, Frank J. (1986) p469

[461] Barrow, D. John & Tipler, Frank J. (1986) p469

[462] Barrett, J.(2008): 'Everett's Relative-State Formulation of Quantum Mechanics' (p2) Stanford Encyclopedia of Philosophy (http://plato.stanford.edu/entries/qm-everett/)

[463] Everett's thesis - Hugh Everett, II (1957). 'Relative State" Formulation of Quantum Mechanics' (Reviews of Modern Physics Volume 29.Number 3. July. 1957) p1

[464] Everett's thesis p2

[465] Everett's thesis p6

[466] Everett's thesis p6

[467] Everett's thesis p2

[468] Everett's thesis p6

[469] Everett's thesis p2

[470] Everett's thesis p3

[471] Everett's thesis p3

[472] Piet Hut, Mark Alford, and Max Tegmark (2009): 'On Math, Matter and Mind' p6 (Foundations of Physics) p6

[473] Piet Hut, Mark Alford, and Max Tegmark (2009): 'On Math, Matter and Mind' p6 (Foundations of Physics) p6

[474] Piet Hut, Mark Alford, and Max Tegmark (2009): 'On Math, Matter and Mind' p6 (Foundations of Physics) p6

[475] Lockwood, Michael (2005) p350

[476] Lockwood, Michael (2005) p353

[477] In personal correspondence with Professor Stapp he has vigorously resisted the details of my Buddhist conclusions, whilst commending some aspects of my work.

[478] Stapp, Henry (2004) p192

[479] Bohm, David (2003) p202

[480] Everett's thesis p7

[481] Everett's thesis p9

[482] Barrow, John D., Davies, Paul C. W., Harper, Charles L. (eds) (2004) p114 – H. Dieter Zeh: 'The wave function: it or bit?'

[483] Barrow, John D., Davies, Paul C. W., Harper, Charles L. (eds) (2004) p119 – H. Dieter Zeh: 'The wave function: it or bit?'

[484] Brunnhölzl, Karl (2007) p85

[485] Hopkins, Jeffrey (2003) p31

[486] Everett's thesis p3

[487] Brunnhölzl, Karl (2007) p86

[488] Everett's thesis p7

[489] Sarfatti, Jack (1996). 'The Field of Qualia' (www.qedcorp.com/pcr/pcr/histpcrg.html) p2

[490] It is this capacity which underlies the effectiveness of meditation!

[491] Sarfatti dialogue with Fred Wolf

[492] Sarfatti, Jack (1996). 'The Field of Qualia' (www.qedcorp.com/pcr/pcr/histpcrg.html)

[493] Sarfatti, Jack (1996). 'The Field of Qualia' (www.qedcorp.com/pcr/pcr/histpcrg.html)

[494] Sarfatti, Jack (1996). 'The Field of Qualia' (www.qedcorp.com/pcr/pcr/histpcrg.html)

[495] These four would not completely agree in the details, but the convergence of the overall perspective is clear.

[496] Barrow, John, D; Davies, P. C. W. & Harper, C. L. Jr. (eds)(2004) p167

[497] Barrow, John D., Davies, Paul C. W., Harper, Charles L. (eds) (2004) p175 – Bryce S. DeWitt: 'The Everett interpretation of quantum mechanics'

[498] Barrow, John D., Davies, Paul C. W., Harper, Charles L. (eds) (2004) p176 – Bryce S. DeWitt: 'The Everett interpretation of quantum mechanics'

[499] Perimeter Institute, September 21-24, 2007 'Many Worlds at 50' (www.perimeterinstitute.ca/manyworlds/)

[500] Vaidman, L. (2002): 'Many Worlds Interpretation of Quantum Physics.' Stanford Encyclopedia of Philosophy (http://plato.stanford.edu/entries/qm-manyworlds/)

[501] Barrow, John D., Davies, Paul C. W., Harper, Charles L. (eds) (2004) p167 – Bryce S. DeWitt: 'The Everett interpretation of quantum mechanics'

[502] Barrow, D. John & Tipler, Frank J. (1986) p478

[503] Sheldrake, Rupert (2009) p105

[504] Barrow, John D., Davies, Paul C. W., Harper, Charles L. (eds) (2004) p473 – Max Tegmark: 'Parallel Worlds'

[505] Barrow, John D., Davies, Paul C. W., Harper, Charles L. (eds) (2004) p176 – Bryce S. DeWitt: 'The Everett interpretation of quantum mechanics'

[506] Barrow, D. John & Tipler, Frank J. (1986) p475-476

[507] Barrow, D. John & Tipler, Frank J. (1986) p476-477

[508] Barbour, Julian (2001) p225 (Paperback)

[509] Hay, Tony & Walters, Patrick (2003) p176

[510] Barbour, Julian (2001) p225 (Paperback)

[511] Wallace, B. Alan (2007)

[512] Wallace, B. Alan (2007) p82

[513] Baggott, Jim (2004) p265

[514] Michael Clive Price – Many Worlds FAQ (www.hedweb.com/manworld.htm)

[515] Penrose, Roger (2005) p532

[516] Kaku, Michio (2006) p147

[517] Hay, Tony & Walters, Patrick (2003) p176

[518] Quoted in Lockwood, Michael (2005)

[519] Stapp, Henry (2004) p190

[520] Al-Khalili, Jim (2003) p146

[521] Michael Clive Price – Many Worlds FAQ (www.hedweb.com/manworld.htm)

[522] Penrose, Roger (1995) p312

[523] Penrose, Roger (1995) p312

[524] Lockwood, Michael (2005) p305

[525] Wallace, B. Alan (trans) & Karma Chagme (author) (2000) p126

[526] Lockwood, Michael (2005) p313

[527] Lockwood, Michael (2005) p313

[528] Lockwood, Michael (2005) p313

[529] Sarfatti, Jack (1996). 'The Field of Qualia' (www.qedcorp.com/pcr/pcr/histpcrg.html)-

[530] Goswami, Amit (1995) p140

[531] Dolling, L.M.; Gianelli, A. F. & Statile, G. N. (eds) (2003) p452 – Werner Heisenberg: from 'Physics and Philosophy.'

[532] Stapp, Henry (2004) p223

[533] www.davidsmuse.co.uk/hoffman.html

[534] Wallace, B. Alan (2007) p93

[535] Hopkins, Jeffrey (2006) p140

[536] Stapp, Henry (2004) p197

[537] Stapp, Henry (2004) p207

[538] Mensky, Michael (2005): 'Concept of Consciousness in the Context of Quantum Mechanics'

[539] Mensky, Michael (2005): 'Concept of Consciousness in the Context of Quantum Mechanics'

[540] Brunnhölzl, Karl (2009) p32

[541] Stapp, Henry (2004) p241

[542] Stapp, Henry: 'Quantum Interactive Dualism: An Alternative to Dualism' p18

[543] Kim, Jaegwon (2005)

[544] Searle, John (2006).

[545] See Dennett (2003,2004) – Freedom Evolves p27.

[546] Stapp, Henry: 'Philosophy of Mind and the Problem of Free Will in the Light of Quantum Mechanics' p19

[547] Stapp, Henry: 'Quantum Interactive Dualism' p18

[548] Stapp, Henry: 'The Effect of Mind upon Brain' p12

[549] Stapp, Henry (2004) p241

[550] Stapp, Henry (2004) p241

[551] Stapp, Henry (2004) p241

[552] Bohr, Neils: *Essays 1933 to 1957 on Atomic Physics and Human Knowledge*

[553] Stapp, Henry: 'The Effect of Mind upon Brain' p12

[554] Stapp, Henry: 'The Effect of Mind upon Brain' p12

[555] Stapp, Henry: 'The Effect of Mind upon Brain' p2-3

[556] Stapp, Henry: 'The Effect of Mind upon Brain' p3

[557] Stapp, Henry: 'The Effect of Mind upon Brain' p6

[558] Baggott, Jim (2005)

[559] Khenpo Tsultrum Gyamtso (2003)

[560] Khenpo Tsultrum Gyamtso (2003)

[561] Bohm, David (2002) p219

[562] Penrose, Roger (2005) p508

[563] Personal email communication

[564] Stapp, Henry (2004) (p284)

[565] Joos, Erich (2006). 'The Emergence of Classicality from Quantum Theory' in *The Re-Emergence of Emergence: The Emergentist Hypothesis from Science to Religion* (Eds: Philip Clayton and Paul Davies). Oxford: Oxford University Press.

[566] Barrow, John D., Davies, Paul C. W., Harper, Charles L. (eds) (2004) p218 – Anton Zeilinger: 'Three challenges from John Archibald Wheeler.'

[567] Bohr, Neils. Atomic Theory and the Description of Nature, Cambridge University Press 1934 p119

[568] Heisenberg, Werner. Physics and Beyond. New York: Harper and Rowe. 1958 p58

[569] Barrow, John D., Davies, Paul C. W., Harper, Charles L. (eds) (2004) p136 – Wojciech H. Zurek: 'Quantum Darwinism and envariance.'

[570] Joos, Erich (2006). 'The Emergence of Classicality from Quantum Theory' in *The Re-Emergence of Emergence: The Emergentist Hypothesis from Science to Religion* (Eds: Philip Clayton and Paul Davies). Oxford: Oxford University Press. p54

[571] Stapp, Henry (2004) p223

[572] Penrose, Roger (2005) p1029

[573] What breaths the fire into the equations?

[574] Penrose, Roger (2005) p1031

[575] Penrose, Roger (2005) p1031

[576] Penrose, Roger (2005) p1031

[577] Penrose, Roger (2005) p1032

[578] Davies, Paul & Gribben, John (2007)

[579] Dolling, L.M.; Gianelli, A. F. & Statile, G. N. (eds) (2003) p406 – Neils Bohr: 'in Nature (1928) 'Complementarity and the New Quantum Theory.'

[580] Gribben, John (2008)

[581] Stapp, Henry (2004) p223

[582] Dennett, Daniel (1991) p35 (Paperback)

[583] McFadden, Johnjoe (2002)

[584] Stapp, Henry (2004) p192-193

[585] Mikhail B Menskii 2005 *Phys.-Usp.* **48** 389-409

[586] McFadden, Johnjoe (2002

[587] Stuart Hameroff & Roger Penrose: Orchestrated Objective Reduction of Quantum Coherence in Brain Microtubules: The "Orch OR" Model for Consciousness. (www.quantumconsciousness.org/penrose-hameroff/orchOR.html)

[588] Penrose, Roger (1995) p335

[589] Penrose, Roger (1995) p329

[590] Penrose, Roger (1995) p330

[591] Penrose, Roger (1995) p337

[592] Penrose, Roger (1995) p331

[593] Penrose, Roger (1995) p331

[594] Herbert, Nick: 'Holistic Physics -or- Introduction to Quantum Tantra' – Internet document (www.southerncrossreview.org/16/herbert.essay.htm)

[595] Hameroff - www.quantumconsciousness.org/presentations/whatisconsciousness.html

[596] Hameroff - www.quantumconsciousness.org/presentations/whatisconsciousness.html

[597] Stapp, Henry (2007)

[598] Stapp, Henry (2004)

[599] Mensky, Michael: 'Reality in quantum mechanics, Extended Everett Concept, and Consciousness' p11

[600] Albert, David Z. (1992) p130-131

[601] Hameroff - www.quantumconsciousness.org/presentations/whatisconsciousness.html

[602] Brunnhölzl, Karl (2009) p32

[603] Mensky, Michael: 'Concept of Consciousness in the Context of Quantum Mechanics'

[604] Mensky, Michael: 'Reality in quantum mechanics, Extended Everett Concept, and Consciousness' p6

[605] Jung, C.G.(1977) p538

[606] Mensky, Michael : 'Reality in quantum mechanics, Extended Everett Concept, and Consciousness' p6

[607] Mensky, Michael: 'Reality in quantum mechanics, Extended Everett Concept, and Consciousness' p6

[608] http://meaningoflife.tv/transcript.php?speaker=dennett

[609] Rosenblum, Bruce and Kuttner, Fred (2006) p179

[610] Rosenblum, Bruce and Kuttner, Fred (2006) p179

[611] Mensky, Michael: 'Reality in quantum mechanics, Extended Everett Concept, and Consciousness' p9

[612] Mensky, Michael: 'Reality in quantum mechanics, Extended Everett Concept, and Consciousness' p10

[613] Bohm, David: 'A New Theory of the Relationship of Mind and Matter' - Philosophical Psychology, VOL. 3, NO. 2, 1990, pp. 271-286

[614] Talbot, Michael (1992) p 122

[615] Such synchronistic events seemed to be a matter of course for Jung. When he died his favourite tree was struck by lightening. When L. van de Post recounted this event during a tv program about Jung there was a dramatic clap of thunder which clearly nonplussed the narrator.

[616] Mensky, Michael: 'Reality in quantum mechanics, Extended Everett Concept, and Consciousness' p7

[617] Stapp, Henry (2004) p181-182

[618] Stapp, Henry (2004)

[619] Stapp, Henry (2007) p125

[620] Barrow, John D., Davies, Paul C. W., Harper, Charles L. (eds) (2004) p577 – Wheeler, J A (1999) 'Information, physics, quantum: the search for links.' In *Feynman and Computation: Exploring the Limits of Computers*, ed A. J. G. Hey, p309 (314). Cambridge, MA: Perseus Books.

[621] Rosenblum, Bruce and Kuttner, Fred (2006) p

[622] Davies, Paul (2007).p301

[623] Barrow, John D., Davies, Paul C. W., Harper, Charles L. (eds) (2004) p450 – Andrei Linde: 'Inflation, quantum cosmology and the anthropic principle.'

[624] Davies, Paul (2007) p275

[625] Davies, Paul: 'Teleology without Teleology: Purpose through Emergent Complexity'

[626] Wallace, B. Alan (2007)p93

[627] Barrow, John D., Davies, Paul C. W., Harper, Charles L. (eds) (2004) p136 – Wojciech H. Zurek: 'Quantum Darwinism and envariance.'

[628] Schmidt, Marcia Binder (Editor) (2002) p29

[629] Waldron, William S. (2003) p94-95 (Samdhinirmocana sutra)

[630] Wallace, B. Alan (2003) (Editor) p153 – Waldron, William: 'Common Ground, Common Cause: Buddhism and Science on the Afflictions of Identity'

[631] Waldron, William S. (2003) p165

[632] Brunnhölzl, Karl (2007) p85

[633] Henry Stapp – The Mind is NOT What the Brain Does (2009) p6

[634] Piet Hut, Mark Alford, and Max Tegmark (2009): 'On Math, Matter and Mind' p6 (Foundations of Physics) p6

[635] Hopkins, Jeffrey (1996) p368

[636] Barrow, John D., Davies, Paul C. W., Harper, Charles L. (eds) (2004) p577 – Wheeler, J A (1999) 'Information, physics, quantum: the search for links.' In *Feynman and Computation: Exploring the Limits of Computers*, ed A. J. G. Hey, p309 (314). Cambridge, MA: Perseus Books.

[637] Waldron, William S. (2003) p168

[638] Waldron, William S. (2003) p169

[639] McFadden, Johnjoe (2002) p265

[640] Nature 12 2007

[641] Quantum Evolution - http://www.surrey.ac.uk/qe/O4.htm

[642] Gribben, John (1996) p133

[643] Gribben, John (1996) p135

[644] McFadden, Johnjoe (2002)

[645] McFadden, Johnjoe (2002)

[646] McFadden, Johnjoe (2002)

[647] McFadden, Johnjoe (2002)

[648] Abbot, Derek, Davies Paul C. W., Pati, Arun K. (Editors) (2008) – Abstract announcing the collection of essays – *Quantum Aspects of Life*.

[649] Abbot, Derek, Davies Paul C. W., Pati, Arun K. (Editors) (2008) p42 – Jim Al-Khalili and Johnjoe McFadden: *Quantum Coherence and the Search for the First Replicator*.

[650] Goswami, Amit (2008) p120-121

[651] Darwin, Charles (1859)

[652] Dawkins, Richard (2006) *The Blind Watchmaker* pxv

[653] Dawkins, Richard (2006) *The Blind Watchmaker* p43

[654] Dawkins, Richard (2006) *The Blind Watchmaker* p49

[655] Dawkins, Richard (2006) *The Blind Watchmaker* p43

[656] Dawkins, Richard (2006) *The Blind Watchmaker* p45

[657] Dawkins, Richard (2006). *The Blind Watchmaker*

[658] The Cambrian explosion or Cambrian radiation was the relatively rapid appearance of most major groups of complex animals which took place around 530 million years ago. The Cambrian explosion has generated extensive scientific debate. The seemingly rapid appearance of fossils in the "Primordial Strata" was noted as early as the mid 19th century, and Darwin considered it as one of the main objections that could be made against his theory of evolution by natural selection..

[659] Bohm, David (2003) p140

[660] Goswami, Amit (2008) 215-216

[661] Jonathan Wells and Darwin's Finches - http://www.talkorigins.org/faqs/wells/finches.html

[662] Davies, Paul (2007) p281

[663] Barrow, John D., Davies, Paul C. W., Harper, Charles L. (eds) (2004) p201 – Anton Zeilinger: 'Why the quantum? "It" from bit"? A participatory universe? Three far-reaching challenges from John Archibald Wheeler and their relation to experiment.'

[664] Wheeler quoted in Barrow, John D., Davies, Paul C. W., Harper, Charles L. (eds) (2004) p73 – Freeman J. Dyson: 'Thought-experiments in honor of John Archibald Wheeler.'

[665] Davies, Paul (2007) p279

[666] Davies, Paul (2007) p280

[667] Davies, Paul (2007) p281

[668] Barrow, John D., Davies, Paul C. W., Harper, Charles L. (eds) (2004) p72 – Freeman J. Dyson: 'Thought-experiments in honor of John Archibald Wheeler.'

[669] Bishop Berkeley -

[670] Barrow, John D., Davies, Paul C. W., Harper, Charles L. (eds) (2004) p10 – Paul C. W. Davies: 'John Archibald Wheeler and the clash of ideas.'

[671] Barrow, John D., Davies, Paul C. W., Harper, Charles L. (eds) (2004) p8 – Paul C. W. Davies: 'John Archibald Wheeler and the clash of ideas.'

[672] Dennett, Daniel (1996) p27

[673] Barrow, John D., Davies, Paul C. W., Harper, Charles L. (eds) (2004) p10 – Paul C. W. Davies: 'John Archibald Wheeler and the clash of ideas.'

[674] Dolling, L.M.; Gianelli, A. F. & Statile, G. N. (eds) (2003) p492 – John A. Wheeler (1978): 'The 'Past' and the 'Delayed Choice' Double-Slit Experiment.'.

[675] Stapp, Henry (2004) p192

[676] Bohm, David (2002) p42

[677] Stapp, Henry (2004) p197

[678] Bohm, David (2002)

[679] Bohm, David (2003) p181

[680] Lloyd, Seth (2007) p3

[681] Lloyd, Seth (2007) p5

[682] Bohm, David (2003) p119

[683] Bohm, David (2003) p119

[684] Hofstadter Douglas (2007) p30

[685] Hofstadter Douglas (2007) p23

[686] Ramanan, K. Venkata (1998) p226

[687] Chandrakirti and Jamgon Mipham (2002) p85

[688] Greene, Brian (2004) p331

[689] Bohm, David (2003) p150

[690] Khendrup Norsang Gyatso (2004) p78

[691] Brunnhölzl, Karl (2007) p49

[692] Bohm, David (2003) p203

[693] Garfield, Jay L. & Geshe Ngawang Samten (Translators) - Tsongkhapa (2006) p35

[694] Tsongkhapa in Garfield, Jay L. & Geshe Ngawang Samten (Translators) (2006)

[695] Dhammananda, K. Shri - *What Buddhists Believe* p5 (The Corporate Body of the Buddha Educational Foundation) (www.budaedu.org).

[696] *Venerable Acariya Mun Bhuridatta Thera – A Spiritual Biography* by Acariya Maha Boowa Nanasampanno. p18 (Forest Dhamma Publication)

[697] *Venerable Acariya Mun Bhuridatta Thera – A Spiritual Biography* by Acariya Maha Boowa Nanasampanno. p18 (Forest Dhamma Publication)

[698] Landaw, Jonathan & Bodian, Stephan (2003) p55

[699] Anatta Lakkhana Sutta

[700] Anatta Lakkhana Sutta

[701] Udana

[702] Translated from the Pali by Thanissaro Bhikkhu

[703] Alexander Berzin, born in 1944 in Paterson, New Jersey, received his B.A. degree in 1965 from the Department of Oriental Studies, Rutgers University in conjunction with Princeton University; and his M.A. in 1967 and Ph.D. in 1972 from the Departments of Far Eastern Languages (Chinese) and Sanskrit and Indian Studies, Harvard University. From 1969 to 1998, he resided primarily in Dharamsala, India, initially as a Fulbright Scholar, studying and practicing with masters from all four Tibetan Buddhist traditions.
In 1998, Berzin moved back to the West to have conditions more conducive for writing. Travelling occasionally, he teaches at several Dharma centers, but devotes most of his time to preparing his unpublished materials for the Berzin Archives website. He currently lives in Berlin, Germany.
See www.berzinarchives.com/web/en/about/author/short_biography_alex_berzin.html

[704] The Four Indian Tenet Systems Regarding Illusion: A practical Approach – Berzin Archives p1

[705] Dreyfus B. J., & McClintock Sara L. (Editors) (2003) p139 – Sara L. McClintock: 'The Role of the 'Given' in the Classification of Santaraksita and Kamalasila as Svatantrika-Madhyamikas'.

[706] One of the four main divisions of Tibetan Buddhism – Gelug, Sakya, Kagyu and Nyingma.

[707] The term coined by Buddhologist Georges Dreyfus

[708] The Four Indian Tenet Systems Regarding Illusion: A practical Approach – Berzin Archives p1

[709] *Abhidharmakosha* - Treasury of Abhidharma, VI, 4

[710] Engle, Artemus B. (2009) p127

[711] The Four Indian Tenet Systems Regarding Illusion: A practical Approach – Berzin Archives p7

[712] Barrow, John D., Davies, Paul C. W., Harper, Charles L. (eds) (2004) p201 – Anton Zeilinger: 'Why the quantum? "It" from bit"? A participatory universe? Three far-reaching challenges from John Archibald Wheeler and their relation to experiment.'

[713] Westerhoff, Jan (2009) p3

[714] Brunnhölzl, Karl (2004) p201

[715] Aikido is the ultimate Japanese Martial Art which defeats an opponent only by using the force directed by the opponent.

[716] Brunnhölzl, Karl (2004) p202

[717] Brunnhölzl, Karl (2004) p202

[718] Komito, David Ross (1987) p176

[719] Komito, David Ross (1987) p176

[720] Komito, David Ross (1987) p178

[721] Komito, David Ross (1987) p178

[722] Garfield, Jay L. & Geshe Ngawang Samten (Translators) - Tsongkhapa (2006) - I have modified to enhance readability.

[723] Komito, David Ross (1987) p179

[724] Khenpo Tsultrum Gyamtso (2003) p60

[725] Garfield, Jay L. & Geshe Ngawang Samten (Translators) - Tsongkhapa (2006) p239

[726] Garfield, Jay L. & Geshe Ngawang Samten (Translators) - Tsongkhapa (2006) p241-242

[727] Cited in Baggott, Jim (2005) p239

[728] Bohm ref

[729] Garfield, Jay L. & Geshe Ngawang Samten (Translators) - Tsongkhapa (2006) p47

[730] Brunnhölzl, Karl (2004) p202

[731] Blumenthal, James (2004) p41

[732] Blumenthal, James (2004) p42

[733] Kumar, M (2008) p321

[734] Kumar, M (2008) p214

[735] Dolling, L.M.; Gianelli, A. F. & Statile, G. N. (eds) (2003) p469 – Werner Heisenberg: from 'Physics and Philosophy.'

[736] Kumar, M (2008) p212

[737] Brunnhölzl, Karl (2004) p257

[738] Garfield, Jay (1995) p2

[739] Brunnhölzl, Karl (2007) p69

[740] Brunnhölzl, Karl (2007) p28

[741] Brunnhölzl, Karl (2004) p194 (Jnanagarbha's Distinction between the two Realities)

[742] Garfield, Jay (1995) p2

[743] Thupten Jinpa (2008) p124-125

[744] www.trincoll.edu/depts/phil/philo/phils/khapa.html - extracted from *Kindness Clarity and Insight*, Dalai Lama XIV, 1981, Snow Lion, USA; translated by Jeffrey Hopkins, University of Virginia.]

[745] Petitt, John Whitney (1999) p 135

[746] Petitt, John Whitney (1999) p148→200

[747] Petitt, John Whitney (1999) p106

[748] Joos, Erich (2006). 'The Emergence of Classicality from Quantum Theory' in *The Re-Emergence of Emergence: The Emergentist Hypothesis from Science to Religion* (Eds: Philip Clayton and Paul Davies). Oxford: Oxford University Press. p71.

[749] Hopkins, Jeffrey (2008) p91

[750] Joos, Erich (2006). 'The Emergence of Classicality from Quantum Theory' in *The Re-Emergence of Emergence: The Emergentist Hypothesis from Science to Religion* (Eds: Philip Clayton and Paul Davies). Oxford: Oxford University Press. p72

[751] Penrose, Roger (1995) p309

[752] Barrow, John D., Davies, Paul C. W., Harper, Charles L. (eds) (2004) p577 – Wheeler, J A (1999) 'Information, physics, quantum: the search for links.' In *Feynman and Computation: Exploring the Limits of Computers*, ed A. J. G. Hey, p309 (314). Cambridge, MA: Perseus Books.

[753] 'The Evolution of Reality' – www.fqxi.org/community/articles/display/122 (The Foundational Questions Institute) November 10, 2009

[754] Hsing Yun, Master & Tom Graham (trans)(2010) p113

[755] Hsing Yun, Master & Tom Graham (trans)(2010) p113-114

[756] Hopkins, Jeffrey (2008) p197

[757] Petitt, John Whitney (1999)

[758] Dewer, Tyler (2008) p40-41

[759] Chandrakirti and Jamgon Mipham (2002)

[760] Dewer, Tyler (2008) p78

[761] Dewer, Tyler (2008)

[762] Brunnhölzl, Karl (2004) p114

[763] Shantarakshita (2005 - Padmakara Translation Group) p97

[764] Gribben, John (1999)

[765] Phrase coined by Alfred Habdank Skarbek Korzybski) (July 3, 1879 – March 1, 1950) Polish-American philosopher and scientist, most remembered for developing the theory of general semantics.

[766] Brunnhölzl, Karl (2007) p82

[767] Garfield, Jay L. & Geshe Ngawang Samten (Translators) - Tsongkhapa (2006) p299

[768] Garfield, Jay L. & Geshe Ngawang Samten (Translators) - Tsongkhapa (2006) p299

[769] Dewer, Tyler (2008) p146

[770] Petitt, John Whitney (1999) p 135

[771] Garfield, Jay L. & Geshe Ngawang Samten (Translators) - Tsongkhapa (2006) p 297

[772] Merzel, Dennis Genpo (2003) p97

[773] Garfield (1995) p38

[774] Garfield, Jay L. & Geshe Ngawang Samten (Translators) - Tsongkhapa (2006) p252-3

[775] Penrose, Roger (1999) p240

[776] Garfield (1995) p29

[777] Khenpo Tsultrum Gyamtso (2003) p67

[778] Wallace, B. Alan (2003) p87 (quoting Bohm)

[779] Garfield (1995) p224

[780] Brunnhölzl, Karl (2007) p170

[781] Brunnhölzl, Karl (2004)

[782] Stapp, Henry (2007) p145

[783] Chandrakirti and Jamgon Mipham (2002).

[784] Brunnhölzl, Karl (2004) p332

[785] Jeans, James (2007) - Originating from the Rede Lecture delivered at the University of Cambridge in November 1930

[786] Introductory" in *The Physical Principles of the Quantum Theory* (1930) as translated by Carl Eckhart and Frank C. Hoyt, p. 10 (1930)

[787] Brunnhölzl, Karl (2004) p204

[788] Brunnhölzl, Karl (2004) p203

[789] Brunnhölzl, Karl (2004) p325

[790] Barrow, John D., Davies, Paul C. W., Harper, Charles L. (eds) (2004) p119 – H. Dieter Zeh: 'The wave function: it or bit?'

[791] Das Wesen der Materie" (The Nature of Matter), speech at Florence, Italy, 1944 (from Archiv zur Geschichte der Max-Planck-Gesellschaft, Abt. Va, Rep. 11 Planck, Nr. 1797)

[792] Brunnhölzl, Karl (2009) p138

[793] Hopkins, Jeffrey (2006) p371

[794] Hopkins, Jeffrey (2006) p561

[795] Barrow, John D., Davies, Paul C. W., Harper, Charles L. (eds) (2004) p136 – Wojciech H. Zurek: 'Quantum Darwinism and envariance.'

[796] Hopkins, Jeffrey (2006) p561

[797] Hopkins, Jeffrey (2006) p84

[798] Hopkins, Jeffrey (2006) p84

[799] Hopkins, Jeffrey (2006) p124

[800] Hopkins, Jeffrey (2006) p147

[801] Hopkins, Jeffrey (2006) p138

[802] Hopkins, Jeffrey (2006) p332

[803] Hopkins, Jeffrey (2006) p332

[804] Herbert Herbert, Nick: 'Holistic Physics -or- Introduction to Quantum Tantra' – Internet document (www.southerncrossreview.org/16/herbert.essay.htm)

[805] Hopkins, Jeffrey (2006) p66

[806] Hopkins, Jeffrey (2006) p66

[807] Barrow, John D., Davies, Paul C. W., Harper, Charles L. (eds) (2004) p119 – H. Dieter Zeh: 'The wave function: it or bit?'

[808] Petitt, John Whitney (1999). p 135

[809] Brunnhölzl, Karl (2009) p115

[810] Hopkins, Jeffrey (2006) p64

[811] Brunnhölzl, Karl (2009) p129

[812] Brunnhölzl, Karl (2007) *In Praise of Dharmadhatu* p231

[813] Brunnhölzl, Karl (2007) *In Praise of Dharmadhatu* p231

[814] Hopkins, Jeffrey (2006) p85

[815] Brunnhölzl, Karl (2007) *In Praise of Dharmadhatu* p17

[816] Brunnhölzl, Karl (2007) *In Praise of Dharmadhatu* p78

[817] Herbert, Nick: 'Holistic Physics -or- Introduction to Quantum Tantra' – Internet document (www.southerncrossreview.org/16/herbert.essay.htm)

[818] Personal email communication

[819] Piet Hut, Mark Alford, and Max Tegmark (2009): 'On Math, Matter and Mind' (Foundations of Physics)

[820] Hopkins, Jeffrey (2006) p102

[821] Brunnhölzl, Karl (2004) p324

[822] Brunnhölzl, Karl (2009) p129

[823] Brunnhölzl, Karl. (2009) p129

[824] Brunnhölzl, Karl. (2009) p303

[825] Brunnhölzl, Karl (2004) p329

[826] Brunnhölzl, Karl (2009) p328

[827] Brunnhölzl, Karl (2009) p328

[828] Brunnhölzl, Karl (2009) p329

[829] Brunnhölzl, Karl (2009) p329

[830] Hopkins, Jeffrey (2006) p311

[831] In a recent conversation with Alan Wallace he observed that he did not really understand precisely what is meant by the collapse of the wavefunction. It must be stated then that the term is a metaphor which is derived from the mathematical graphical representation of the quantum to classical 'event' that occurs when an observation brings a classical experience 'out' of the pre-existing realm of potentiality described by the wavefunction; a spread out graphical representation 'collapses' to a 'point.'

[832] Hopkins, Jeffrey (2006) p225

[833] Hopkins, Jeffrey (2006) p561

[834] Hopkins, Jeffrey (2006) p530-531

[835] Hopkins, Jeffrey (2006) p365-366

[836] Hopkins, Jeffrey (2006) p425

[837] Hopkins, Jeffrey (2006) p206

[838] Hopkins, Jeffrey (2006) p223

[839] Hopkins, Jeffrey (2006) p366

[840] Hopkins, Jeffrey (2006)

[841] Hopkins, Jeffrey (2006)

[842] Hopkins, Jeffrey (1996) p96

[843] Hopkins, Jeffrey (2006) p156

[844] Hopkins, Jeffrey (2006) p140

[845] Hopkins, Jeffrey (2006) p200

[846] Hopkins, Jeffrey (2006) p87

[847] Hopkins, Jeffrey (2006) p473

[848] Hopkins, Jeffrey (2006) p479

[849] Hopkins, Jeffrey (2006) p274

[850] Hopkins, Jeffrey (2006) p356

[851] Hopkins, Jeffrey (2006) p555

[852] Hopkins, Jeffrey (2006) p243

[853] Hopkins, Jeffrey (2006) p245

[854] Hopkins, Jeffrey (2006) p529

[855] Hopkins, Jeffrey (2006) p529

[856] Hopkins, Jeffrey (2006) p556

[857] Hopkins, Jeffrey (2006) p432

[858] Hopkins, Jeffrey (2006) p428

[859] Hopkins, Jeffrey (2006) p477

[860] Thrangu Rinpoche, Kenchen (2002) p10

[861] Literally means 'mental commitment' – the deity that one has made a commitment to (see medicine buddha teachings p22)

[862] Hopkins, Jeffrey (2006) p423

[863] Hopkins, Jeffrey (2006) p508

[864] Hopkins, Jeffrey (2006) p424 (paraphrased)

[865] Hopkins, Jeffrey (2006) p424 (paraphrased)

[866] Hopkins, Jeffrey (2006) p424

[867] Barrow, John D., Davies, Paul C. W., Harper, Charles L. (eds) (2004) p119 – H. Dieter Zeh: 'The wave function: it or bit?'

[868] Addiss, Stephen; Lombardo, Stanley; Roitman, Judith (2008) p39

[869] Schmidt (2002)

[870] Stapp – Recent paper: 'Minds and Values in the Quantum Universe'

[871] Wolfgang Pauli, letter to M. Fierz, August 12, 1948

[872] John Polkinghorne, Keith Ward etc.

[873] Monday 21st December

[874] Gould, Stephen Jay (2002)

[875] Kaku, Michio (1995)

[876] www.namgyal.org

[877] Worldweb Dictionary

[878] Barrow, John D., Davies, Paul C. W., Harper, Charles L. (eds) (2004) p136 – Wojciech H. Zurek: 'Quantum Darwinism and envariance.'

[879] Ward, Keith (2008) p12

[880] Dennett, Daniel (2005)

[881] Review of Cairns-Smith, Evolving the Mind – and Consciousness Explained.

[882] http://meaningoflife.tv/transcript.php?speaker=dennett

[883] Rosenblum, Bruce and Kuttner, Fred (2006) p179

[884] Barrow, John D., Davies, Paul C. W., Harper, Charles L. (eds) (2004) p136 – Wojciech H. Zurek: 'Quantum Darwinism and envariance.'

[885] Dawkins, Richard (2006). *Unweaving the Rainbow* p50

[886] Dawkins, Richard (2006). *The Blind Watchmaker*

[887] Dawkins, Richard (2006). *The Blind Watchmaker*

[888] Alluding to the 'its turtles all the way down' joke.

[889] Ward, Keith (2008) p81

[890] Cassirer, Ernst (1998) p154

[891] Dawkins, R (2004) p175

[892] Blackmore, Susan (2003) p1

[893] Blackmore, Susan (2005) p1

[894] Blackmore, Susan (2005) p92

[895] Blackmore, Susan (2005) p95

[896] Blackmore, Susan (2005) p95

[897] Blackmore, Susan (2005) p95
[898] Blackmore, Susan (2005) p103
[899] Blackmore, Susan (2003).p7
[900] Blackmore, Susan (2003).p13
[901] Broks, Paul (2003) p48
[902] Blackmore, Susan (2005) p234
[903] The Pacific World: Journal of the Institute of Buddhist Studies, 3rd Series No. 4 Fall 2002
[904] Dalai Lama, H. H. the (2008) p169
[905] Schwartz, Jeffrey M. & Sharon Begley (2003) p369
[906] Dhammapada
[907] Blackmore, Susan (2005) p86
[908] Wallace, B. Alan (2005) p17
[909] Wallace, B. Alan (2005) p174
[910] Wallace, B. Alan: 'A Science of Consciousness' p2
[911] Wallace, B. Alan: 'A Science of Consciousness' p2
[912] Churchland, Paul M. (1988) p178
[913] Churchland, Paul M. (1988) p179
[914] Churchland, Paul M. (1988) p180
[915] Chah, Ajahn (2002) p181
[916] Chah, Ajahn (2002) p183
[917] Chah, Ajahn (2002) p179
[918] Bohm, David (2002) p67
[919] Chah, Ajahn (2002) p192
[920] Ricard, Mathieu (1996) p92
[921] Ward, Keith (2008) p81
[922] Grayling, A.C. (2007)
[923] Shantarakshita (2005 - Padmakara Translation Group)
[924] Mahaprajnaparamita shastra [Lamotte trans. I, p.141]
[925] *Guide to Bodhisattva's Way of Life* – Trans Steven Batchelor, Library of Tibetan Works p171
[926] *Guide to Bodhisattva's Way of Life* – Trans Steven Batchelor, Library of Tibetan Works p170
[927] Ellis, George & Murphy, Nancy (1996)p214
[928] Ellis, George & Murphy, Nancy (1996) pxv
[929] Ellis, George & Murphy, Nancy (1996) pxv
[930] Ricard, Mathieu (1996) p66
[931] Dawkins, Richard (2006)
[932] Mansfield, Vic (2008) p57
[933] Ellis, George & Murphy, Nancy (1996)
[934] Ellis, George & Murphy, Nancy (1996) p215
[935] Polkinghorne, John:'The Anthropic Principle and the Science and Religion Debate' p3 - Faraday Paper No. 4
[936] Satinover, Jeffrey (2001) p156
[937] Davies, Paul (2007) p226

[938] Davies, Paul (2007) p280

[939] Hopkins, Jeffrey (2002) p465

[940] Penrose, Roger (2005) p508

[941] Herbert, Nick: 'Holistic Physics -or- Introduction to Quantum Tantra' – Internet document (www.southerncrossreview.org/16/herbert.essay.htm)

[942] Cozort, Daniel (2005)

[943] Brunnhölzl, Karl (2004)

[944] Brunnhölzl, Karl (2004)

[945] Maitreya (with Commentaries by Khenpo Shenga and Ju Mipaham) (2006). p140

[946] Brunnhölzl, Karl (2007) p 49

[947] Udana Viii-1

[948] Udana Viii-3

[949] Ehrman, Bart D. (2005). P48

[950] Burckhardt, Titus (1997 p50-51.

[951] Burckhardt, Titus (1997 p50-51

[952] Ward, Keith (2006)

[953] Jung, C.G.(1989)

[954] Barrow, John D., Davies, Paul C. W., Harper, Charles L. (eds) (2004) p450 – Andrei Linde: 'Inflation, quantum cosmology and the anthropic principle.'

[955] Barrow, John D., Davies, Paul C. W., Harper, Charles L. (eds) (2004) p451 – Andrei Linde: 'Inflation, quantum cosmology and the anthropic principle.'

[956] Mind and Life Website - www.mindandlife.org

[957] Hofstadter Douglas (2007)

[958] This refers to Hofstadter's absurd image of consciousness arising from a complex organisation of beer cans. For 'tin cans' one can read 'material particles'.

[959] Dennett, Daniel (2007) p244

[960] Al-Khalili, Jim (2003) p169

[961] Chown, Marcus (2007) p164

[962] Chown, Marcus (2007) p144

[963] Haught, John F. (2007) p49

[964] Helminski, Kabir (1999)

[965] Hopkins, Jeffrey (2006) p54

[966] Brunnhölzl, Karl (2007) *In Praise of Dharmadhatu* p117 The 'triple being' refers to the three realms of samsara.

[967] Hopkins, Jeffrey (2006) p310

[968] Helminski, Kabir (1999) p4

[969] Cambell, Joseph (2008) p30

[970] Seyyed Hossein Nasr (2007)p6

[971] Fithjof Schuon: 'The Quintessential Esotericism of Islam' in *Sufism: Love and Wisdom* p258-259. edited by Jean-Louis Michon & Roger Gaetani (2006) World Wisdom Inc.

[972] Fithjof Schuon: 'The Quintessential Esotericism of Islam' in *Sufism: Love and Wisdom* p258-259. edited by Jean-Louis Michon & Roger Gaetani (2006) World Wisdom Inc.

[973] Cosmology and Kabbalah: (This is ch 11 of "The Retroactive Universe") Broken Symmetry and Shvirat Hakelim, Tzimtzum and Free Will - www.pages.nyu.edu/~air1/Cosmology%20and%20Kabbalah.htm.

[974] Cohen, J. M. (1995) p57-58

[975] Balldock, John (2004). p62

[976] Churton, Tobias (2005) p111

[977] Eye of the Storm – http://www.keithdowman.net/dzogchen/eyeofthestorm.htm

[978] Balldock, John (2004) p 117

[979] Bohm, David (2003)

[980] Freud called dreams the 'royal road' to the unconscious.

[981] Bohm, David (2003) p151-2

[982] A bird with a slender downward curved bill

[983] Balldock, John (2004) p154-5

[984] Sarfatti , Jack 'Wheeler's World: It From Bit?' - Internet Science Education Project, San Francisco, CA..

[985] Chandrakirti and Jamgon Mipham (2002) p 329-330

[986] Chandrakirti and Jamgon Mipham (2002) p337

[987] Dewer, Tyler (Translation & Introduction) (2008) p532 -

[988] Stapp, Henry (2007) p116-7

[989] Hsing Yun, (Master) & Tom Graham (trans)(2010) p120

[990] Brunnhölzl, Karl (2004) p323

Bibliography

Abbot, Derek, Davies Paul C. W., Pati, Arun K. (Editors) (2008). *Quantum Aspects of Life*. Imperial College Press.

Aczel, Amir D. (2002) *Entanglement: The Greatest Mystery in Physics*. Basic Books

Addiss, Stephen; Lombardo, Stanley; Roitman, Judith (2008). *Zen Source Book: Traditional Documents from China, Korea and Japan*. Hackett Publishing Company.

Aharanov, Yakir and Rohrlich, Daniel (2005). *Quantum Paradoxes: Quantum Theory for the Perplexed*. Wiley-VCH.

Albert, David Z. (1992) *Quantum Mechanics and Experience*. Harvard University Press.

Al-Khalili, Jim (2003): *Quantum: A Guide for the Perplexed*. Weidenfield and Nicolson, New York.

Baggott, Jim (2004). *beyond measure*. Oxford University Press, Oxford.

Baggott, Jim (2005). *A Beginner's Guide to Reality*. Penguin Books.

Balldock, John (2004). *Essence of Sufism*. Booksales.

Barbour, Julian (2001). *The End of Time: The Next Revolution in Physics*. Oxford University Press.

Barrett, Jeffrey A. (2001). *Quantum Mechanics of Minds and Worlds*. Oxford University Press.

Barrow, D. John & Tipler, Frank J. (1986). *The Anthropic Cosmological Principle*. Oxford University Press.

Barrow, John D., Davies, Paul C. W., Harper, Charles L. (eds) (2004). *Science and Ultimate Reality*. Cambridge University Press.

Blackmore, Susan (2003). *Consciousness-An Introduction*. Hodder & Stoughton.

Blackmore, Susan (2005). *Conversations on Consciousness*. Oxford University Press.

Blumenthal, James (2004). *The Ornament of the Middle Way: A Study of the Madhyamaka Thought of Śāntarakṣita*. Snow Lion.

Bohm, D (2002) *Wholeness and the Implicate Order* (First published: Routledge & Kegan Paul, 1980; Routledge Classics, 2002)

Bohm, David (2003). *The Essential David Bohm* ed Nichol, Lee (Routledge, London)

Broks, Paul (2003). *Into the Silent Land: Travels in Neuropsychology*. Atlantic Monthly Press

Brunnhölzl, Karl (2007). *Straight from the Heart: Buddhist Pith Instructions*. Ithaca: Snow Lion Publications.

Brunnhölzl, Karl (2007) *In Praise of Dharmadhatu*. Ithaca: Snow Lion Publications.

Brunnhölzl, Karl. (2009) *Luminous Heart: The Third Karmapa on Consciousness, Wisdom, and Buddha Nature.* Ithaca: Snow Lion Publications.

Brunnhölzl, Karl (2004) *Center of the Sunlit Sky: Madhyamaka in the Kargyu Tradition.* Ithaca: Snow Lion Publications.

Burckhardt, Titus (1997). *Introduction to Sufism.* Thorsons.

Cambell, Joseph (2008). *The Hero With a Thousand Faces.* New World Library-Third Edition.

Capra - IN - The Holographic Paradigm and Other Paradoxes. Shambhala Publications.

Capra, F (1975) *The Tao of Physics* Shambhala Publications.

Cassirer, Ernst (1998). *The Philosophy of Symbolic Forms: Volume 4: The Metaphysics of Symbolic Forms.* Yale University Press.

Chah, Ajahn (2002). *Food for the Heart: The Collected Teachings of Ajahan Chah.* Wisdom Publications.

Chandrakirti and Jamgon Mipham (2002). *Introduction to the Middle Way: Chandrakirti's* Madhyamakavatara *with Commentary by Jamgon Mipham.* Translated by the Padmakara Translation Group. Boston: Shambhala Publications.

Chown, Marcus (2003). *The Universe Next Door.* Faber and faber.

Chown, Marcus (2007). *Never-Ending Days of being Dead.* Faber and faber.

Chown, Marcus (2007). *Quantum Physics Cannot Hurt You.* Faber and faber.

Chown, Marcus (2009). *We Need to Talk About Kelvin.* Faber and faber.

Churchland, Paul M. (1988). *Matter and Consciousness: A Contemporary Introduction to the Philosophy of Mind.* The MIT Press.

Churton, Tobias (2005). *Gnostic Philosophy.* Inner Traditions.

Clayton, Philip & Davie, Paul (editors) (2006). *The Re-Emergence of Emergence: The Emergentist Hypothesis from Science to Religion.* Oxford University Press.

Cohen, J. M. (1995). *The Common Experience.* Quest.

Cozort, Daniel (2005). *Highest Yoga Tantra.* Snow Lion Publications.

d' Espagnat, B (2006) *On Physics and Philosophy* (Princeton University Press)

Dalai Lama, H. H. the (2008). *The Universe in a Single Atom: The Convergence of Science and Spirituality.* New York: Morgan Road, 2005. Abacus paperback: 2006, 2008.

Darwin, Charles (1859). *The Origin of the Species.*

Davies, Paul & Gribben, John (2007). *The Matter Myth: Discoveries that Challenge Our Understanding of Physical Reality.* Simon & Schuster.

Davies, Paul (2007). *The Goldilocks Enigma.* Penguin Books (First published 2006:Allen Lane)

Dawkins, R (2004) *A Devil's Chaplin: Selected Essays* (First published: Weidenfield & Nicolson, 2003; Phoenix paperback, 2004)

Dawkins, Richard (2006). *The Blind Watchmaker*. New Edition – Penguin (First published 1986)

Dawkins, Richard (2006). *Unweaving the Rainbow*. New Edition – Penguin (First published 1998).

Dawkins, Richard (1999). *The Extended Phenotype*. Oxford Paperbacks.

Dawkins, Richard (2006). *The God Delusion*. Black Swan.

Dennett, Daniel (1991)' *Consciousness Explained*, The Penguin Press, (UK Hardcover edition, 1992)

Dennett, Daniel (1996). *Darwin's Dangerous Idea*. Penguin Edition, 1996.

Dennett, Daniel (2005). *Sweet Dreams: Philosophical Obstacles to a Science of Consciousness (Jean Nicod Lectures)*. The MIT Press.

Dennett, Daniel (2007). *Breaking the Spell: Religion as a Natural Phenomenon*. Penguin.

d'Espagnat, Bernard (2006). *On Physics and Philosophy*. Princeton University Press.

Deutsch, David (1998). *The Fabric of Reality*. Penguin.

Dewer, Tyler (Translation & Introduction) (2008). *The Karmapa's Middle Way: Feast for the Fortunate by the Ninth Karmapa, Wangchuk Dorje*. Snow Lion, New York.

Dolling, L.M.; Gianelli, A. F. & Statile, G. N. (eds) (2003). *The Tests of Time: Readings in the Development of Physical Theory*. Princeton University Press.

Dreyfus B. J., & McClintock Sara L. (Editors) (2003). *The Svatantrika-Prasangika Distinction: what difference does a difference make?*. Wisdom Books.

Dyson, Freeman (2001). *Disturbing the Universe*. Basic Books.

Ehrman, Bart D. (2005). *Lost Scriptures: Books that Did Not Make It into the New Testament*. Oxford University Press.

Ellis, George & Murphy, Nancy (1996). *On the Moral Nature of the Universe: Theology, Cosmology and Ethics*. Fortress Press.

Engle, Artemus B. (2009). *The Inner Science of Buddhist Practice: Vasubhandhu's Summary of the Five Heaps with Commentary by Sthiramati*. Snow Lion, New York.

Ehrman, Bart D. (2003). *Lost Scriptures: Books that Did Not Make It into the New Testament*. Oxford University Press.

Feynman, Richard (1988). *QED: The Strange Theory of Light and Matter*. Princeton University Press.

Garfield, Jay (1995) (Translator). *The Fundamental Wisdom of the Middle Way (Nagarjuna's Mulamadhyamakakarika)*. Oxford University Press.

Garfield, Jay L. & Geshe Ngawang Samten (Translators) (2006). *Ocean of Reasoning: A Great Commentary on Nagarjuna's Mulamadhyamakakarika (by rJe Tsong Khapa)*. Oxford University Press.

Geshe Sonam Rinchen (2006) *How Karma Works* trans & ed. Ruth Sonam. Snow Lion Publications.

Geshe Yeshe Tobden (2005). *The Way of Awakening: A Commentary on Shantideva's* Bodhicharyavatara. Wisdom Publications.

Gould, Stephen Jay (2002).*Rocks of Ages: Science and Religion in the Fullness of Life*. Ballantine Books.

Goswami, Amit (1995) *The Self Aware Universe: How consciousness creates the material world.* Tarcher/Penguin, (First published 1993)

Goswami, Amit (2008). *Creative Evolution.* Quest Books

Grayling, A.C. (2007). *Against All Gods*. Oberon Books.

Greene, Brian (2004). *The Fabric of the Universe*. Allen Lane.

Gribben, John (1996). *Shrodinger's Kittens and the Search for Reality*. Phoenix.

Gribben, John (1999). *In Search of Superstrings*. Penguin (1998); Little, Brown & Co (1999)

Gribben, John (2008). *The Universe: A Biography*. Penguin Books.

Gribben, John (2009). *Science: A History*. Penguin Books.

Haught, John F. (2007). *God and the New Atheism: A Critical Response to Dawkins, Harris and Hitchens*.Westminster John Knox Press.

Hawking, Stephen (1998). *A Brief History of Time*. Bantum.

Hay, Tony & Walters, Patrick (2003). *The New Quantum Universe*. Cambridge University Press.

Heisenberg, W (1999). *Physics and Philosophy*. Prometheus Books.

Helminski, Kabir (1999). *The Knowing Heart: A Sufi Path of Transformation*. Shambhala.

Herbert, Nick (1985). *Quantum Reality: Beyond The New Physics.* Random House (Anchor Books), New York.

Hofstadter Douglas (2007). *I am a Strange Loop*. Basic Books.

Hopkins, Jeffrey (1996). *Meditation on Emptiness*. Wisdom Publications, U.S.A. (First published 1983).

Hopkins, Jeffrey (2003). *Emptiness in the Mind-Only School of Buddhism: Dynamic Responses to Dzong-ka-ba's The Essence of Eloquence Volume 1.* University of California Press. First edition 1999.

Hopkins, Jeffrey (2002). *Reflections on Reality-The Three Natures and Non-Natures in the Mind-Only School: Dynamic Responses to Dzong-ka-ba's The Essence of Eloquence Volume 2*. University of California Press.

Hopkins, Jeffrey (2005). *Absorption in No External World-170 Issues in Mind-Only Buddhism: Dynamic Responses to Dzong-ka-ba's The Essence of Eloquence Volume 3*. University of California Press.

Hopkins, Jeffrey (2006). *Mountain Doctrine: Tibet's Fundamental Treatise on Other-Emptiness and the Buddha Matrix by Dol-bo-ba Shay-rap-gyel-tsen*. Ithaca: Snow Lion Publications.

Hopkins, Jeffrey (2008). *Tsong-kha-pa's Final Exposition of Wisdom*. Snow Lion.

Hsing Yun, (Master) & Tom Graham (trans)(2010). *Describing the Indescribable*.Wisdom Publications.

Jamgon Kongtrul & Kalu Rinpoche Translation Group (1995). *The Treasury of Knowledge:Myriad Worlds*. Snow Lion.

Jeans, James (2007). *Mysterious Universe*. Kessinger Publishing.

Jung, C.G.(1989). *Memories, Dreams and Reflections*. Vintage.

Jung, C. G. (1981). *The Archetypes and the Collective Unconscious*. Princeton University Press.

Jung, C.G.(1977). *Mysterium Coniunctionis* (Collected Works of C.G. Jung Vol.14) (Paperback). Princeton University Press.

Kaku, Michio (1995). *Hyperspace: A Scientific Odyssey Through Parallel Universes, Time Warps and the 10th Dimension*. Anchor Books.

Kaku, Michio (2006). *Parallel Worlds: The Science of Alternative Universes and our Future in the Universe*. Penguin Books (First published by Doubleday 2005).

Kalu Rinpoche (1997). *Luminous Mind: The Way of the Buddha*. Wisdom Publications.

Khendrup Norsang Gyatso (2004). *Ornament of Stainless Light: An Exposition of the Kalacakra Tantra*. Library of Tibetan Classics; Wisdom Publications; Boston.

Khenpo Tsultrum Gyamtso (2003) *The Sun of Wisdom* (Shambhala Publications)

Kim, Jaegwon (2005). *Physicalism, or Something Near Enough*. Princeton University Press.10010

Komito, David Ross (1987). *Nagarjuna's "Seventy Stanzas"*. Snow Lion Publications.

Kumar, M (2008) *Quantum: Einstein, Bohr and the Great Debate about the Nature of Reality* (Icon Books)

Landaw, Jonathan & Bodian, Stephan (2003). *Buddhism for Dummies* Wiley Publishing Inc..

Lloyd, Seth (2007). *Programming the Universe: A Quantum Computer Scientist Takes On the Cosmos*. Vintage.

Lockwood, Michael (2005). *The Labyrinth of Time: Introducing the Universe*. Oxford University Press.

Lucretius - *On the Nature of the Universe*.

Maitreya (with Commentaries by Khenpo Shenga and Ju Mipham) (2006). *Middle Beyond Extremes (Madhyantavibhaga)*. Snow Lion (Dharmachakra Translation Committee)

Mansfield, Vic (2008). *Tibetan Buddhism & Modern Physics*. Templeton Foundation Press.

McFadden, Johnjoe (2002). *Quantum Evolution: How Physics Weirdest Theory Explains Life's Biggest Mystery*. Norton & Co.

Merzel, Dennis Genpo (2003). *The Path of a Human Being*. Shambhala

Mu Soeng (2010) *The Heart of the Universe*. Wisdom.

Murphy, Nancy and Ellis, George F. R. (1996) *On the Moral Nature of the Universe:Theology, Cosmology, and Ethics*. Augsburg Fortress.

Oerter, Robert (2006). *The Theory of Almost Everything*. Pi Press.

Oppenheimer, Robert (1954). *Science and the Common Understanding*. Oxford University Press.

Penrose, Roger (1995). *Shadows of the Mind*. Oxford University Press:1994, Random House-Vintage:1995

Penrose, Roger (1999). *Emperors New Mind*. Oxford University Press:1989, Oxford University Press paperback:1999

Penrose, Roger (2005). *The Road to Reality: A Complete Guide to the Laws of the Universe*. Vintage.

Petitt, John Whitney (1999). *Mipham's Beacon of Certainty: Illuminating the View of Dzogchen*. Wisdom Books.

Piburn, Sidney(1990). *The Dalai Lama: Policy of Kindness*. Snow Lion.

Polkinghorne, John (2002).*Quantum Theory: A Very Short Introduction*. Oxford University Press, USA

Rae, Alastair I. M. (2006). *Quantum Physics: A Beginner's Guide*. Oneworld Publications.

Ramanan, K. Venkata (1998) *Nagarjuna's Philosophy*. Delhi:Shri Jainendra Press.

Ricard, Mathieu (1996). *Journey to Enlightenment*, Aperture.

Rosenblum, Bruce and Kuttner, Fred (2006). *Quantum Enigma: Science Encounters Consciousness*. Oxford University Press, U.S.A.

Satinover, Jeffrey (2001). *The Quantum Brain* (John Wiley and Sons , Inc., New York)

Schmidt, Marcia Binder (Editor) (2002). *The Dzogchen Primer*. Shambhala

Schrödinger, E. (1944) *What is Life?* (Cambridge University Press, Cambridge)

Schwartz, Jeffrey M. & Sharon Begley (2003). *The Mind & The Brain: Neuroplasticity and the Power of Mental Force*. First Published: HarperCollins Publishers 2002; First Harper Perennial paperback edition 2003).

Searle, John (2006).*Freedom and Neurobiology: Reflections on Free Will, Language and Political Power*. Columbia University Press.

Seyyed Hossein Nasr (2007). *The Garden of Truth: The Vision and Promise of Sufism, Islam's Mystical Tradition*. Harper One.

Shantarakshita (2005 - Padmakara Translation Group) *The Adornment of the Middle Way* (Madhyamakalamkara). Shambhala Publications.

Sheldrake, Rupert (2009). *A New Science of Life* (Revised Edition). Icon Books.

Smolin, Lee (2002). *Three Roads to Quantum Gravity*. Perseus Book Group:2002 (first published 2000)

Smolin, Lee (2006). *The trouble with Physics: The Rise of String Theory, the Fall of a Science, and What Comes Next.* Houghton Mifflin Harcourt.

Stapp, Henry (2004). *Mind, Matter and Quantum Mechanics*. Springer-Verlag Berlin Heidelberg 1993, 2004.

Stapp, Henry (2007). *Mindful Universe*. Springer-Verlag Berlin Heidelberg.

Stenger, Victor (1996). *The Unconscious Quantum*. Prometheus Books.

Talbot, Michael (1992). *The Holographic Universe*. Harper Perennial.

Thrangu Rinpoche, Kenchen (2001). *Transcending Ego: Distinguishing Consciousness from Wisdom*. Namo Buddha Publication., Boulder, Colorado

Thrangu Rinpoche, Kenchen (2002). *Everyday Consciousness and Buddha-Awakening* (Tranlated and edited by Susanne Schefczyk). Snow Lion.

Thrangu Rinpoche, Kenchen (2002). *Medicine Buddha Teachings*. Snow Lion Publications.

Thupten Jinpa (translator) (2008) *The Book of Kadam*. Wisdom Publications: Library of Tibetan Classics.

Vedral, Vlatko (2010). *Decoding Reality*. Dutton.

Waldron, William S. (2003). *The Buddhist Unconscious*. Routledge-Curzon.

Wallace, B. Alan (trans) & Karma Chagme (author) (2000) *Naked Awareness: Practical Instructions on the Union of Mahamudra and Dzogchen*. Snow Lion Publications.

Wallace, B. Alan (2003) *Choosing Reality.* Snow Lion Publications.

Wallace, B. Alan (2003). *Buddhism and Science: Breaking new Ground.* Columbia University Press.

Wallace, B. Alan (2005). *Balancing the Mind: A Tibetan Buddhist Approach to Refining Attention*. Snow Lion Publications.

Wallace, B. Alan (2007). *Hidden Dimensions: The Unification of Science and Consciousness*. Columbia University Press.

Walpola, Rahula (1974). *What the Buddha Taught*. Grove Press.

Ward, Keith (2006). *Pascal's Fire: Scientific Faith and Religious Understanding*. Oneworld Publications.

Ward, Keith (2008). *Why There is Almost Certainly a God: Doubting Dawkins*. Lion Books.

Westerhoff, Jan (2009). *Nagarjuna's Madhyamaka: A Philosophical Introduction*. Oxford University Press.

Wilber, Ken (Editor) (1982). *The Holographic Paradigm and Other Paradoxes*. Shambhala.

Wilczeck, Frank (2008). *The Lightness of Being*. Penguin Books (2010)

Woolfson, Adrian (2000). *Life Without Genes*. Harper Collins.

Zajonc, Arthur (Editor) (2004). *The New Physics and Cosmology: Dialogues with the Dalai Lama*. Oxford University Press.

Zukav, Gary (1979). *The Dancing Wu Li Masters: An Overview of the New Physics* New York: William Morrow and Company: 1979. Bantam mass market paperback:1984.

Index

Note – because of the manner in which this index was generated by computer, based on paragraph position, in some instances the actual page where the word occurs is one page back – the paragraph is primarily located on the page indicated in the index.

't Hooft, Gerald   200

A

I

S

Printed in Great Britain
by Amazon